Analitikul Cogita

FROM THE MIND BEHIND DA GHETTO TYMZ MAGAZINE

ANALITIKUL
COGITATIONZ

by
M'Bwebe Aja Ishangi
fka Jehvon Buckner

FROM THE MIND BEHIND DA GHETTO TYMZ MAGAZINE

ANALITIKUL COGITATIONZ

by
M'Bwebe Aja Ishangi
fka
Jehvon Buckner

Published by
DGT NTR-Prizes, LLC
DGT Edutainment Group
P.O. Box 71
New York, NY 10159
email: *analitikul@daghettotymz.com*
website: *www.daghettotymz.com/analitikul/analitikul.html*
Da Ghetto Tymz magazine website: *www.daghettotymz.com*

Cover Illustration/Graphics/Photography: *M'Bwebe Aja Ishangi of Nebulution Studios*
Book Layout & Design: *M'Bwebe Aja Ishangi of Nebulution Studios*

Library of Congress Catalog Card Number:
ISBN# 978-0-6151-4651-5

1st Printing
May 2007
Paperback $32.00 USA
$37.00 CAN/INT'L

DEDICATION

I thank my life partner and luv of my life for her patience, encouragement, luv and inner-standing. I am forever grateful for you granting me the tyme and space to complete this book. Eternal luv...

I also dedicate this book to the spirit physically manifested as Michelle, none of this would be were it not for you. Eternal thanx for saving me…

And to those willing to go beyond the realm of question; that place where many have told you not to inquire about simply because they, themselves did not know.

ACKNOWLEDGEMENTS

I acknowledge the "Force(s)" or "Supreme Intellect(s)" as the foundation of everything — some may refer to you as "God", whereas my definition goes beyond the human characteristics most have reduced you to. I respectfully call you 'Energy' for it is energetic molecular compoundz that's microcozmically responsible for everything that exists. Whether knowingly or through ignorance, our western mindset makes us dissect you into many thingz instead of simply concluding that 'Energy' is sufficient enuff.

Many cannot fathom thc idca of "God" being pure energy with the ability to take on the shape of any and everything that exists both physically and non-physically or unseen to the naked eye.

Most fear they are lost if they do not have a human depiction of "God" to look at or bow down and pray to when in actuality you are any and everywhere at the same tyme! Just takin' in a breath of air is a relation with "Energy".

I was told once that life is a journey. Another name for journey is a 'quest' which is also found in the word 'questionz'. If it weren't for questionz, my quest to know myself would've ended when I finished college, or even high school for that matter. We all have someone (or several hedz) in our family who told you at one tyme or another to *"stop askin' questionz! You're not s'posed to know EVERYthing!!"* — as if it were criminal to want to know. And although I went through the same mental/ spiritual shutdown throughout my school yearz, it was questionz that brought me back to my essence and the person you will get to know reading this book.

Havin' the courage to continue to ask questionz is a journey seldom dare travel, but for those that do, the rewardz are a challenge to put into wordz.

LARGE UP!

I give luv, honor and respect to the following. Each having played a vital role in my life. I thank you for allowing me to be a part of yourz:

Energy (my name for 'God') which is the true spirit of truth and balance, the Ancestorz, past, present and future Freedom Fighterz, my Mother and Sisterz, Will, Chop, E.D. & Family, Shabaka & Family, JMatt & Jules Family, Ed & Sharon Family, Derrick & Sara Family, Shawn, Jahmed & Lyn.Z Family, the whole Kinsey Family, Mark & Cheryl Family, Faro-Z, Enensa, Malik & Adilliah Family, Harold & Beth Family, Chelsie & Musa Family, Bro. Shabazz, The Black Dot, Teferu Azr, 4Korners Crew, Bro. Rahle and A&B Bookstore (Brooklyn, NY), M-1 & Stic of Dead Prez, Tahir, KRS-One, Lumumba & Kamau of Malcolm X Grassroots Movement, Lelieth, Lisa, Keidi Obi Awadu, Abiodun Oyewole of the Last Poets, Ainsley Burrows, Joe Davis & Family and Marcus Kline of Frontline Magazine as well as each and every person who subscribed to Da Ghetto Tymz magazine or bought some of DGTs merchandise — past, present and future!

I also give honor and reespek to Author/Lecturerz: Anthony T. Browder, Wayne Chandler, Dr. Yosef Ben-Jochannan, Mwalimu K. Bomani Baruti, Alton Maddox, Dr. Bobby Wright, Llaila O. Afrika, Ashra & Meri Ra Kwesi, Neilly Fuller, Francess Cress-Welsing, Marimba Ani, KRS-One, Ayi Kwei Armah, Karl Evanzz, Jewel Pookram, Albert Taylor, Ph.D, Ivan Van Sertima, Na'im Akbar, Molefi Asante, Runoko Rashidi, Haki Madhubiti, Carol Barnes, The Schomburg Center, Deepak Chopra, Paulo Coehlo, Michael Joseph, Eric Schlosser, William Dufty.

Ancestorz: George GM James, Gerald Massey, Chancellor Williams, John G. Jackson, Dr. John Henrik Clarke, J.A. Rogers, Octavia Butler, Del Jones, Amos Wilson, Ishakamusa Barashango, Malcolm X, Marcus Garvey, Peter Tompkins. Ashe'.

AFFILIATES

DGT NTR-Prizes, LLC serves as the parental entity of Da Ghetto Tymz magazine, DaGhettoTymz.com, DGTv, Nebulution Studios, Heru Vision Films and 3D Voice.

DGT NTR-Prizes, LLC translates as a double-meaning; in the corporate-sense as an 'Enterprise' as well as our acknowledged lineage to our Ancestorz of the Nile Valley: 'NTR' (pronounced 'Neter') which meanz 'God'.

We at **DGT NTR-Prizes, LLC** work to bring 'God's prizes' into fruition for the entire poly-verse to know of past, present and future contributionz of Afrikan people.

DGT Edutainment Group — this group functionz as the umbrella for Da Ghetto Tymz magazine, DaGhettoTymz.com, DGTv, Heru Vision Films and our publishing. Est. 2006

DA GHETTO TYMZ
magazine

Da Ghetto Tymz magazine (DGT) — a publication that annihilates false perceptions of the Afrikan experience chauffeured by the western-eurocentric mindset.
Est. April 10, 1993

DaGhettoTymz.com — the website version of the magazine. January 2006 marked the 10th anniversary online. Est. January 1996 *(daghettotymz.com)*

DGTv: Conscious Webvision — one of the first conscious web/tv-based websites on the internet. Est. January 2006 *(daghettotymz.com/dgtv/dgtv.html)*

DGT720 — a sister-site to DaGhettoTymz.com where you get the wholistic truth or 720-degree view on issues pertaining to the Diaspora by watching and/or listening to Podcast's, Video blogz and inner-viewz. Est. April 2007
(daghettotymz.com/dgt720/main.html)

Nebulution Solutions — The graphic/web design and editing division responsible for every company in DGT NTR-Prizes, LLC visual, graphic and layout as well as offering a host of products and services to other clients. Est. 1997
(daghettotymz.com/dezine/dzine.html)

Heru Vision Films — The film and editing division responsible for DGTv's content as well as M'Bwebe Ishangi's DVD lectures. Est. 2003

3D Voice — Dubbed "Decisionz Determine Destiny", 3D Voice sets up M'Bwebe Ishangi's speaking engagements and appearances. In addition to his lectures, M'Bwebe conducts workshops on personal and spiritual development and time management enabling one to truly live out and do what they were born to do. Est. 1994
(www.daghettotymz.com/lecture/lecture.html)

QUOTES

"M'Bwebe Ishangi has written a coming of age story for readers in the age of Information. For more than a decade he has researched ancient and contemporary histories and published his findings in Da Ghetto Tymz magazine, which has been widely read by his peers within the Hip Hop community. With his "best of" compilation of essays, M'Bwebe is now poised to be introduced to a wider audience who I hope will use these essays as a blueprint for their mental and economic liberation. Brother M'Bwebe is to be congratulated for unselfishly doing what few souls have done — freed their minds and then helped others free theirs."

— **Anthony T. Browder** author, *From the Browder File*

"There are consequences for choosing to follow the Afrikan Way. You will be assaulted by alien minds in Afrikan garb. There will be a loss of friends and family who cannot understand without losing the fragile security they hold so dearly on to. There will be worse than these, the pull of a lifetime of eurocentric habit, a battle against the reason which has validated this reality that brought you thus far. But for those of us who follow the spirit of our Ancestors are no more than mere distractions that we, with time, come to ignore because we know the correctness of our righteous rage. They do not disappear as long as this reality is a dominant force on this planet.

This book is about the life and mind of an individual who has made such a choice. With the style and the truth of (Francess) Cress-Welsing, M'Bwebe Ishangi takes us through his transformation from one who only knew that something was very wrong with this reality to one who learned what it was and how to critique and confront it in and outside of himself. The process all of us experience who have discovered the wisdom of our traditions is explained here, in an up close and personal way, in the way that it effected and molded this Afrikan man into the frontline warrior that stands before us today.

The reawakening process of "thesis " (realization that something is wrong), followed by "antithesis " (search for and study of what is wrong and study and assimlation of what is right), followed by "synthesis " (discovery and break from any contradictions in newfound truths), are all evident, time and time again, in his journey back home. It is through telling us of this process that he teaches the reader how to go about the business of thinking better as an Afrikan — how to break through layer upon layer of ignorance and humbly embrace knowing. No Afrikan should be without the lessons and experience of this book."

— **Mwalimu K. Bomani Baruti** author,
Homosexuality and the Effeminization of Afrikan Males

ABOUT THE AUTHOR

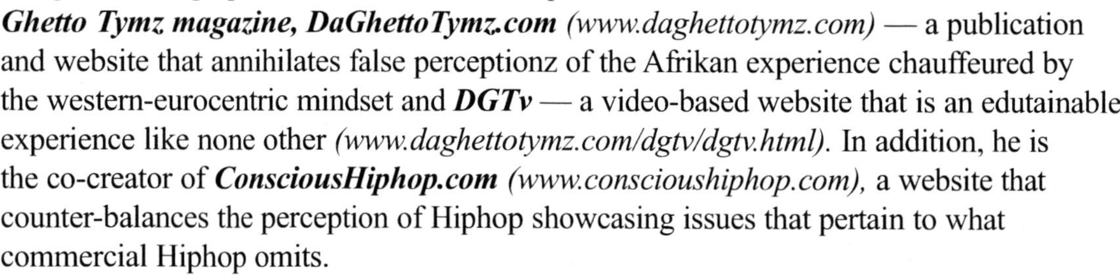

M'Bwebe Aja Ishangi

M'Bwebe Aja Ishangi *(formerly known as Jehvon Buckner)* is a humble student and follower of the Pan-Afrikan movement. He is a qualified, young and powerful speaker who has dedicated his life to working and speaking out forcefully for the rights and empowerment of the Afrikan Diaspora. His specialty is developing creative arts and educational projects that strengthen the mindz of Afrikan people in general, youth and students in particular. He does this with a simple and practical style that clearly explainz all areas of life including self, history, health, economics, spirituality, creativity and politics.

M'Bwebe is a writer, artist, graphic and web designer, videographer, lecturer, creator and publisher of ***Da Ghetto Tymz magazine, DaGhettoTymz.com*** *(www.daghettotymz.com)* — a publication and website that annihilates false perceptionz of the Afrikan experience chauffeured by the western-eurocentric mindset and ***DGTv*** — a video-based website that is an edutainable experience like none other *(www.daghettotymz.com/dgtv/dgtv.html).* In addition, he is the co-creator of ***ConsciousHiphop.com*** *(www.conscioushiphop.com),* a website that counter-balances the perception of Hiphop showcasing issues that pertain to what commercial Hiphop omits.

His educational background includes self-education starting in 1990, the University of Pittsburgh for undergraduate studies majoring in Black Studies/Education with psychology as a minor, and three yearz working with the National Aeronautics and Space Administration's (NASA) educational department.

M'Bwebe [**M**ind & **B**ody **W**orking **E**qually exudes **B**lessingz **E**ternal — meaning, if I allow my mind and body (including my spirit) to work equally, the blessingz will continue to come in abundance] started with learned information from renowned edutainer, KRS-One, an artist who bringzs a conscious element to Hiphop. After three yearz of underground study, M'Bwebe felt he was ready to express what he learned to the public. Starting out speaking to people in the streets, M'Bwebe felt he needed to create another outlet that would enable the message to reach an even larger audience.

M'Bwebe started putting his thoughts on paper and submitted them to several major national publicationz. The negative response he received from the editorz and publisherz inspired him to develop a newsletter, ***Ghetto Tymz*** in April 1993. After ten consecutive issues, M'Bwebe started publishing other writerz. July 1994 the newsletter flourished into a national publication, ***Da Ghetto Tymz magazine.*** January 1996 marked ***DaGhettoTymz.com***'s premiere on the internet. The spring of '98 also marked the birth of ***DGT NTR-Prizes,*** which is where all his projects including his lectures, ***Da Ghetto Tymz, DGTv,*** and ***Nebulution Studios*** fall under. April 2003, marked ***Da***

Ghetto Tymz magazine's 10th Year and its 100th published issue. January 2006 marked ***DaGhettoTymz.com***'s 10th year online and January 22nd ***DGTv*** was born.

M'Bwebe believes his greatest contribution to date is continuing the promotion of self-reliance through creative business development, developing his love for art, drawing, graphic design and speaking, and having the ability to construct his own enterprise addressing real problems and providing alternative solutions that raise self-esteem through knowledge of self.

TRANSITION 13

We knew not
We studied
We learned all there was to know
We taught others

Then we forgot what we had learned
And then we forgot that we had forgotten

Now we are taught
(By those who where once taught by us)
Knowledge
(That we already had)

So…
We study
We learn all there is to know
We teach others

Will we forget…AGAIN?

(Untitled poem from page insert of The Browder Files*, written by Anthony T. Browder. The first book I read cover-to-cover)*

ANALITIKUL COGITATIONZ

Analitikul [Analytical (an·a·lyt·i·cal) [ànna líttik'l] *adj.*]

1. Dividing into elemental parts or basic principles.
2. The separation of an intellectual or material whole into its constituent parts for individual study.
3. Logical, investigative, diagnostic, systematic, critical, methodical, questioning, reasoned, rational, analytic

Cogitationz [Cogitations (cog·i·ta·tion) [kòjji táyshun] *n.*]

1. **deep thought:** deep thought or consideration that somebody gives to a particular problem or subject
2. **act of deep thought:** an act of thinking deeply about something

GLOSSARY/PRONOUNCIATION/WRITING STYLE

While reading ***Analitikul Cogitationz***, I ask that you look over my preference of writing style. Over the yearz with my publication, Da Ghetto Tymz magazine (DGT), I've received numerous letterz and emailz about my use of *'z'*s instead of *''s'* in wordz, as well as my occasional fondness to use what has been academically classified as "Ebonics".

I humbly ask that you overlook this and choose not to get caught up in *how* I'm sayin' something, but *what* I am sayin'.

There are many who choose to think of tonz of reasonz Y someone will find a reason to believe writing like this dumbz-down the intellect of the reader. This is truly not my intent. I consider myself to be an artist and as an artist, I opt to feel free in my expression regardless of traditional european standardz some of our people so valiantly protect.

Most of the wordz I phonetically spell are pronounced by simply sounding them out. Some other keywordz you need to be familiar with:

YT — Simply say the two letterz faster. "Y…T…, Y-T, whitey!" It also serves as an acronym meaning, Yakubian Tribe if you're familiar with the story of Yakub (or Jacob) and his ability to graft (create) a race of people.

Y — I use 'Y' instead of the word 'why'.

MENTAL ADVISORY

DEEP PANAFRIKAN-CENTERED CONTENT.
INFO WILL CAUSE YOU TO WAKE UP.
WEAK-MINDED ENTER AT YOUR OWN RISK!

TABLE OF CONTENTS

You may have heard of me, maybe you haven't. You may have heard of Da Ghetto Tymz magazine (DGT), perhaps there's only a small percentage of you where DGT is totally foreign to you (I hope). Regardless, I feel there's a need for you to know who I am and how I became M'Bwebe so you can overstand how DGT, and the type of info that grace the pages, came to be.

It's been said you can't judge a book without knowin' the author. ***Déjà vu*** goes back to 1991 focusing on the first few yearz of my re-awakening process to 'Knowledge of Self.'

In ***Déjà vu,*** I will reveal never before written accounts of spiritual encounterz that at one tyme, I was too afraid to let hedz know I experienced — one in particular that could've cost my life! I hope you enjoy knowin' me for the first tyme.

CHAPTERS

V. ANALITIKUL COGITATIONZ: BY TOPICS

VI. TABLE OF CONTENTS BY SERIES: SPIRIT, BODY, MIND

SPIRIT

BODY

MIND

We use this grafik in each edition of DGT as a dedication to 'Energy' (God), our Ancestorz and the unknown elements that make us who we are. (designed by m'bwebe aja ishangi of Nebulution Studios)

Mentor vs. Jegna:
The story of Mentor and Telemachus

We must overstand that greek mythology is just that... a *myth!* These made-up stories are of people that never existed. Y YT created them? Probably to validate their existence... But we must understand many customz we've adopted have been done so through ignorance of this "*little* white lie". Case-in-point, the use of the word 'mentor' we so lovingly use for our Afrikan scholarz that have influenced us.

We forget the power we give to somethin' when you call on its name. Couple this with ignorance of the origin of these wordz, we actually disrespect somethin' we intend to respect.

The word 'Mentor' is defined as an *"adviser, guide, guru, counselor, consultant; confidant."* Look at the last word in the definition... 'confidant'.

Now let's look that definition up: *"a person with whom one shares a secret or private matter, trusting them not to repeat it to others."* Now let's look at the history of the word 'Mentor' again.

In Greek mythology, Mentor was the son of Alcumus and, in his old age, a friend of Odysseus aka Ulysses. When Odysseus left for the Trojan War he placed Mentor in charge of his son, Telemachus, and of his palace.

Preface

For nearly fifteen yearz (if you're familiar with my magazine, Da Ghetto Tymz, DGT for short), I've attempted 'shock therapy' on the mindz of Afrikan people by challenging us to dispute everything from history to politics, diet to religion, on down to historic African-American organizationz. Some dubbed me the *"Brutha who likes to destroy Black organizationz,"* and I've alwayz returned the alleged insult with a simple *"give thanks (thank you)"* quickly adding, *"I'm not tryin' to convert you. I'm only offering alternative thinking."*

My quest was and alwayz will be to challenge you; to dare you to face who taught you; to reveal that not everything you may believe now, you had the opportunity to thoroughly investigate. I test you as I test myself for I've come to believe that we *can* use more than 1/3rd of our brain as western medicine would dispute. We have the capability of literally flying to higher heights if one is able to rid themselves of the illusionary mental borderz placed on most of our mindz by YTs ('whitey' if you say it faster, or Yakubian Tribe — from the story of Yakub or Jacob in the Bible) propaganda (school, television, media). This challenge is, in retrospect, directed at myself for I could not challenge an individual if I were not willing to do the same myself.

You may not agree with the message I convey, but I hope you will use my arguments as inspiration to further confirm your own beliefs whatever they may be. Ask yourself, what is it that brought you to the decision you now follow? I use myself as an example. Instead of accepting what I knew — or actually was told or taught to believe – since I was a 'likkle yute,' I decided to challenge myself to investigate how I came to believe/follow my current philosophy.

What separates a master mind from a primitive one is one who has the will to begin the quest of <u>quest</u>ionz, with the final destination being 'knowing'. That's what thinkin' is all about.

To veggie-back (not piggie-back — *I'm not a meat eater*) on a brutha and someone I'd refer as a Jegna of mine, Anthony T. Browder. (I use the word 'Jegna' instead of 'mentor' thanx to what I heard from lecturer, Mwalimu K. Bomani Baruti, author of *"Homosexuality and the Effeminization of Afrikan Males,"* and other works as well as the site www.akobenhouse.com, in early 2007. Biggup Bro. Baruti!!)

Browder posed the question, *"What kind of thinker are you?"* He explained in his book, '*Survival Strategies'*, there are but three kinds: Literal, Influential and Evaluative.

The Literal thinker — One who is taught to take all information at face value. This level thinker is a trait well over 90% of the people of this planet possess.

The Influential thinker — One who learnz to read between the lines and isn't so quick to take thingz told to them.

And last, **the Evaluative thinker** — One who's able to make an informed decision based on comparison. In addition, this type is not afraid to challenge "authority" figures presenting information they're trying to persuade you with.

I consider myself to be an Evaluative thinker. Over the yearz, I've come to realize that I have my own mind and the ability to interpret individually yet still be concise with logic. Hence, the reason for this book, ***Analitikul Cogitationz***. Through the process of analysis, one is able to find the deeper meaning or the ability to *"think outside the box,"* a coined phrase you may have heard a tyme or two before.

Many are not aware that greece was a society where homosexuality was the norm. Men took great pride in feelin' the greatest luv could only be experienced between two men. Women were only used for procreative purposes.

This is the source of the modern use of the word mentor: a trusted friend, counselor or teacher, usually a more experienced person. Some professionz have "mentoring programs" in which newcomers are paired with more experienced people in order to obtain good examples and advice as they advance, and schoolz sometymz have mentoring programz for new students or students who are having difficulties.

According to legend, Mentor and Telemachus had a bond that included a sexual relationship. Now when we use this word, we are unknowingly honoring and condoning the acts of this imbalanced man and society.

The history of the hedz who created the english language have a completely different value systemz than us. That's Y it's important we get in the practice of using the right terminology.

Wade Nobles introduced a more suitable word when referring to those who've been an influence. The word is 'Jenga', which basdically meanz *'someone who demonstrates fearlessness; one who has the courage to protect their people, culture and way of life; one who produces a hight quality of work.'*

Yeah, that's more appropriate...

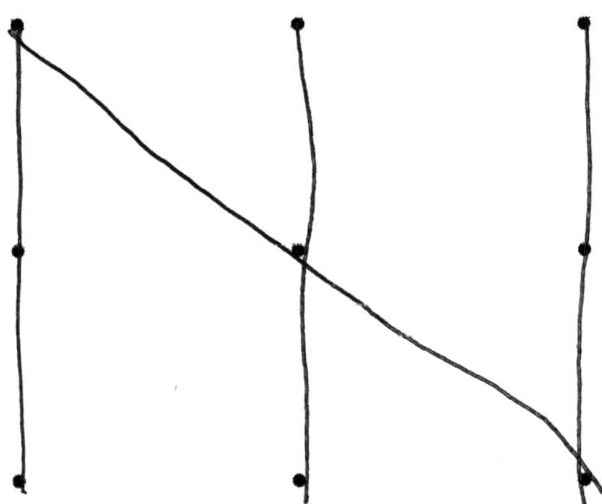

CONNECT ALL DOTS USING ONLY 4 LINES, OVERLAPPING ONE LINE ONLY ONCE WITHOUT LIFTING THE PENCIL OFF THE PAGE

Exercise 1

As an exercise, I'd like to share with you what I learned that helped me become an Evaluative thinker. Above you will notice a 3 x 3 dotted graph. Using a pen or pencil, draw just four (4) lines, connecting each of the dots, overlapping only one (1) of the lines without lifting the pencil off the page. If you don't connect each of the dots with just 4 lines, you fail to correctly complete the exercise. If you draw more than 4 lines, you also fail. If you lift the pencil off the page before connecting the lines, you fail. If your lines cross over another line more than once, well, you get the point by now.

This exercise is not to test your level of intellect; it is a merely a test on your mental conditioning. Take a moment and try this exercise. Truly take a few extra minutes and give yourself a chance to try this exercise. I advise you to use a pencil instead of a pen in case you mess up. Or even copy the diagram on a separate piece of paper. If you like challenges, this is pivotal and compliments the rest of what you'll read in this book.

I'd like to point out that you cannot become an Evaluative thinker without asking questionz; not even an Influential thinker for that matter. I've been told life is a quest and on this *'quest'* you ask *quest*ionz. Browder once told me, *"we are spiritual Beingz having a human experience that chose to come back for a purpose."* So what is *your* purpose, Afrikan? Just beginning to find an answer to a question like this promotes you from the lower level of thinkerz, the Literal thinker.

Have you thought how to connect each of the nine dots? If not, take a few more moments and once you've completed it, or can't figure it out, turn the page.

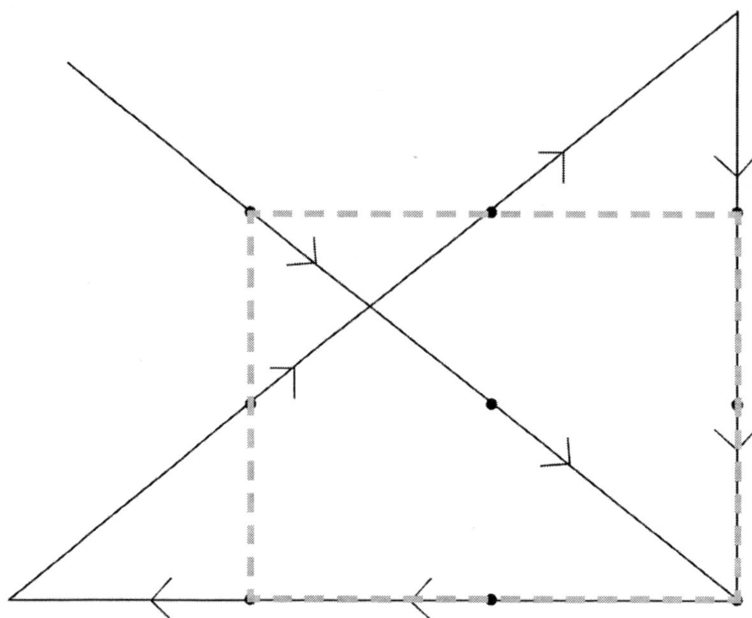

CONNECT ALL DOTS USING ONLY 4 LINES, OVERLAPPING ONE LINE ONLY ONCE WITHOUT LIFTING THE PENCIL OFF THE PAGE

Exercise 1 continued

Above you will see the answer to how all nine dots can be connected. Does it shock you how it was done? You will notice my first of four lines started outside the illusionary lines you probably saw enforced by the outer eight dots (see dotted square). Most of you may have had difficulty connecting all the dots with just 4 pen strokes. No matter how you sized it, it seemed impossible as you tried to ration how you could do this 'inside' this box.

That's the thing, Afrikanz, the Evaluative thinker, or Free Thinker as I call it, thinks *outside* the box! This eurocentric society has us thinkin' only of what happenz in our immediate environment — ie. Earth, not *outside* the illusionary boundaries. We've been 'trained' so well, our actionz are carried out automatically! YT ain't gotta be here to tell me to stay within the parameterz of intellect they want us to have; they don't have to tell us not to read or attain knowledge to free yourself, we make this choice on our own! Of course, this choice is biased, for one, many of us are not exposed to the fact that there *is* even a choice to know or not to know… Their school and religious systemz are systematically designed to be so wack with dumbed-down methodz of learning, we've become disinterested by the tyme we reach second grade!

Our Ancestorz, in particular, of the Nile Valley of Kemet (Egypt) applied the Hermetic — which should be called Djhuitic Principle of Correspondence: *'As Above, So Below, As Below, So Above'*. In other wordz, in order to study the unknown, study the known; the microcozm of the macrocozm, if you will. When you're able to think outside the box, you are free to explore true knowledge.

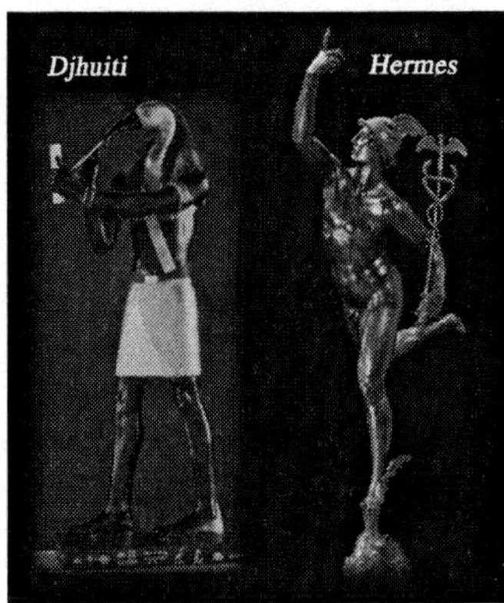

Hermetic? or Djhuitic Principles
One of the most respected principles followed by people who align themselves with consciousness is the Seven Hermetic Principles:

1) The Universe is Mental
2) Correspondence
3) Vybration
4) Polarity
5) Rhythm
6) Cause and Effect
7) Gender

We forget the greeks were one of the main pirates who went into the Nile Valley and plagiarized the true authorz of philosophy, arts and sciences.

Many, including myself have followed these principles never really questioning the root of the name 'Hermetic'.

Doin' a little research, you'll find these principles are named after the greek imposter Hermes. The true name is Djhuiti, the Netcher – or god – of science, writing, speech and medicine.

It is well past tyme that we, who choose to be the next generation of vanguardz remove the 'whiteout' that has covered our legacy for millenniumz!

I've alwayz said if you ever wanted to know who M'Bwebe is, just read my magazine, because that's who I am. I remember bein' told by a couple of my closest friendz when I first started writing, *"you think too dam much! You alwayz analyzin' this and analyzin' that!"* Truth is, I *am* analytical. I take information, dissect and re-view it through the lenses of both an individual and Pan-Afrikan perspective.

But I was not alwayz like this, at least in *this* lifeform. I'm convinced I am goin' through a *'Transition 13,'* right along with the rest of us. This journey has led me on a quest, a quest where many questionz have and will continue to be asked. And with the proper research, perseverance and humility, I will reach the *'summon bonum,'* or *'greatest good'* our Ancestorz taught during the era of the Nile Valley.

But don't think this is a cakewalk, Sun. It is a constant battle, as you will read in ***Déjà vu***. I know of numerous hedz that lost their lives in the physical AND mental. Each day I give thanks and ask for continued protection against the opposing forces that lay waiting for an opening.

Just over fifteen yearz ago, I was approached by these 'opposing forces,' and I am still frequented by them. Part of me feelz they may possibly have the power to take my physical as well as spiritual life, which is the reason I am writing this book. I felt if I didn't write ***Analitkul,*** these thoughts and experiences would die with me and to me, that would be criminal, 'cause there's a chance perhaps even a spoonful of what you'll read in ***Analitkul*** could help you, if not someone else.

As well, ***Analitkul*** is written so you have a better feel of who I am so that hopefully you won't think I'm just some crazy cat who likes to blast any and everything Black, white or anything that ain't Afrikan. I didn't choose to be this (but then again, I probably did, destiny-wise). This is who I am and I accept my role, as well as my purpose — or Personal Legend as author of *"The Alchemist,"* Paulo Coelho noted. I sat on what you are about to read for a long tyme, fearing no one would really understand. But I realized it's my duty to be consistent and thorough, therefore, my keeping it to myself would be a dishonor to the Ancestorz not to speak of my experiences because there's a big chance my experience is not authentic and I could possibly not be the only one who's experienced something like this.

I'm also writing this book for my benefit. In case the theory of reincarnation is true and I *do* return and forgot that I once knew (Transition 13), this can be a tool to help me remember.

Lastly, when dealin' with spirituality, metaphysics, history and global white supremacy, we must get in the habit of eliminating the belief in coincidences. Everything happenz in divine tyme and for a reason. If one takes the tyme to make tyme to dissect it, the reason will often be revealed.

Intro

My life changed in 1991. I was 21, in Pittsburgh, Pennsylvania, attending the University of Pittsburgh, my junior year. What happened to me Tuesday, February 19th, is responsible for the person you will get to now know. I owe it all to those omnipotent thingz that make up the entire Poly-verse and our Ancestorz who chose to communicate to me through a vessel named Kris Parker, aka, KRS-One. I call it the *Poly*-verse and not *Uni*-verse because all life exists in duality; positive and negative; up and down; right and left; light and dark; woman and man, etc. We have been duped to believe there is but one universe and all life exists inside it. If you take a visit to your nearest Planetarium, you might evolve and expand your mind *(more on this later in the book)*. Now back to KRS-One…

It is not a coincidence that some 13 yearz later, it is KRS again who exposes me to a realm that enabled me to further know and define who I am, which led me to change my name to M'Bwebe Aja Ishangi.

- **M'Bwebe — (M)**ind and **(B)**ody **(W)**orking **(E)**qually exudes **(B)**lessingz **(E)**ternal

  Meaning, if I continue to have my Mind *and* Body (along with Spirit) work together; the blessingz will continue to come eternally in abundance.

- **Aja** — Information, definition, explanation, facts; An Orisha (God) in Yoruba mythology.

Polyverse versus Universe
Author, Anthony Browder once said to me that we are *"Spiritual Beingz having a human experience who chose to come back for a purpose."* I believe we're all microcozmz of the macrocozm — a smaller part of a bigger thing. And just as we live in part of a polyverse, there are polyverses in each of us.

I choose to call it a 'poly' — meaning 'many' — instead of uni-verse because We actually live in a poly-verse. If you study the fourth Djhuitic Principle, Polarity, it states, *"everything has its pair of opposites,"* meaning there's duality in everything; 2 legz, eyes, brainz, physical/non-physical, etc….
Using the 'Microcozm of Macrocozm theory', it proves there isn't just one or a uni-verse, but many poly-verses!

If you were to zoom into yourself, it looks just like the polyverse! Look at the skin on your hand, we do not realize there are over 6 trillionz acts of movement goin' on at any one moment that our naked eye cannot see. Just because we cannot see it, or even feel it, does not mean it does not exist. If you were to get a high-powered telescope and focus on your hand, the deeper you get, you'd be able to see movin' objects. Just as if you were to look at a plants' soil, you'd see crawling lifeformz livin' their lives on this "plant". So is the same with the living organizmz that crawl on you.

These thingz help protect and maintain your physical and as these lifeformz work to maintain their lives, they are in fact, maintaining yourz! To them, your body is their "Earth"; just as we walk on this planet.

This makes the perception of what we are much bigger than the illusionary parameterz the european-based western society wants us to see.

• **Ishangi** — Gatekeeper. A name created by Baba Ishangi, head of the Ishangi Family Dancers, caretaker and preserver of the culture. His focus was the appreciation and understanding of Afrikan culture through history, philosophy, life-style and the arts. I aim to echo his efforts in the field of multimedia.

Finally, again I ask that you look over my preference of writing style. Over the yearz with the magazine, I've received numerous letterz and emailz about my use of '*z*'s instead of ''*s*' in wordz, as well as my occasional fondness to use what has been classified as Ebonics. I humbly ask that you overlook this; be that Evaluative thinker not getting caught up in *how* I'm sayin' it, but *what* I'm sayin'. I ask that you cease to allow non-traditional standardz stifle not only your mental and spiritual development, but the maturity of our people as a whole. Besides, English ain't our native language anyway! So Y should I feel the need to preserve it?! I represent a new generation — or better yet, resurrected era; the rebellious vanguardz who have chosen to protect a post that has long been abandoned… Alternative Thought.

I urge that you read with an open mind. Enjoy the journey, spread the knowledge 'cause it ain't ourz to keep anyway!

May the Ancestorz and Supreme Force of the Poly-verse guide and protect you as you venture on the road of righteousness.

Reespek,

—

M'Bwebe Aja Ishangi
fka Jehvon Buckner
November 2005

Prologue

Déjà vu [dé·jà vu (day zhä voo) *n.***]**
1. *Psychology.* The illusion of having already experienced something actually being experienced for the first time.

2. An impression of having seen or experienced something before.

Up ‘til now, I only told this to a couple people…

This is a true story…

**It must be noted there was no kind of drug use (including weed) throughout this experience. It is this encounter that taught me the power of "gettin' high" naturally...*

Déjà vu

the first weeks of my re-awakening…

Chapter One

My life changed on a cold winter night, Tuesday, February 19, 1991. I was 21, in the city of Pittsburgh, Pennsylvania, attending my junior year at the University of Pittsburgh. What I experienced that evening created the person you will get to know reading this book. I owe it all to our Ancestorz who patiently waited for me to become mature enuff to comprehend a spark that was emitted through a vessel named Kris Parker, aka, KRS-One.

That night, I'm on campus at the Student Union. I'm amped 'cause Boogie Down Production's own, KRS-One is s'posed to perform tonight.

I can remember the first tyme I heard *'Criminal Minded'* back in '86. I was sixteen drivin' home from track practice in a 1969 Buick LeSabre convertible (the shit was a big steel tank bein' held together with duck-tape!). That song blew my mind, yo! Needless to say, I was ready to see "The Teacher" in person.

As I entered the main ballroom in the Union, I thought, *"I must be in the wrong room 'cause there's too many chairz in here, like it's gonna be a lecture or somethin'."* I see a mic — but it's behind a podium. Where's the turntables and the speaker boxes?!!? Yo, Sun, I ain't in no mood for no lecture! I be in class ALL day! I came to see 'The Teacher' *teach*, but through *music* not a lecture, feel me?

But I decided to stay — at least for a lil' while. After he was introduced, it was evident there wasn't gonna be the show I came for. Kris walked up to the podium wearing a charcoal grey hoody and a navy blue New York Yankee cap, a bottle of water and what appeared to be some notes and a couple books under his left wing. I thought to myself, *"Oh shit! Kris is gonna really teach! I didn't know he did lectures!"*

Up until that point, the only speakerz I saw were white and madd boring. I never saw an Afrikan perform a lecture in person, B. So I was naturally intrigued. I decided to stay awhile and hear what he had to say.

The lecture was entitled, *Revolution of the Mind*, and it was that evening I re-evolved, Sankofa ala Déjà vu style back into possibly a former-self. I say this because after that night, strange thingz started to happen to me and what's even crazier is that I was somewhat familiar to what was goin' on.

He spoke of several thingz with the breakdown of the Emancipation Proclamation serving as one that stood out. What seemed to be minute drops from the infinite abyss of knowledge today were like immeasurable oceanz of deep quantities, enuff to make my dome feel like it was submerged, even drowning! That evening KRS re-introduced me to my mind perhaps *'Transition 13'*-style.

As I listen to his taped lecture over 10 yearz later, I realize for someone hearing what he said for the first tyme has the makingz of really driving one crazy! Y? Because of the truthfulness.

Immediately following the end of his lecture that evening, I didn't rush the podium wanting an autograph like the other hedz that were there. As I looked down at the 27 pages of notes I had written, my hand continued to shake; as if I had hacked into the ancient papyrus vaulted chamberz written by scribes who learned from Griots. For the first tyme in my educational life, I felt I really attended class!

I exited the Student Union in somewhat of a stupor. *"Sun just blew my mind, B!"* I thought to myself. *"Now how am I gonna deal with that?! I cain't act like I just didn't witness that! Shiiiit, the 27 pages of notes I wrote won't let me! Denying it would contradict the person I've challenged myself to be!"*

I somehow made it back to my dorm without sayin' a word to anyone along the way (which was somethin' unordinary). When I made it to my dorm, I opened the door, quickly stepped in and closed it as if someone was spyin' on me. Little did I know that feeling was true. *"Trust ya gut, duke!"* I thought to myself.

At the tyme, I was a confused Christian who got baptized the summer before of my own accord. I say confused because I couldn't actually say I was a believer and follower of something I couldn't really understand. See, I like learning; it's how and what we're taught I got beef with.

Like many, I joined a Church and got baptized because I had been taught since my youth it was the right thing to do. I can recall myself prayin' to Jesus and touchin' my head, lower stomach, left shoulder and then right shoulder — invisibly drawing the crucifix on me as I approached the starting line before I ran the 800 meterz at each Track & Field meet. I really didn't know Y I would do it. Again, I thought it was the thing you were s'posed to do — somethin' we are taught since birth, if not in the home, certainly in society. I think back at all 'The Exorcist' and 'Damien Omen' movies and realize I was "shook" or scared into believing this shit!

My grandmother bought me a King James Bible one Christmas and I brought it to college with me. I alwayz wondered Y Grandma gave me this book, yet she hardly ever stepped inside a Church (at least during my life — not that that was a bad thing).

After locking the door to my dorm, I quickly reached for my copy of the Bible. I dropped my bagz, the notes I took and quickly started pacing the rectangular room from end-to-end clutchin' the Bible askin' internally, *"What am I gonna do?"*

KRS didn't speak much on religion, but what he did speak on shattered my foundation of beliefs, yo! I was now alone for the first tyme in my life. Not knowing my next step, I paced the floor hoping for some sign from the Bible to assure me that everything was ok and what KRS spoke of wasn't that deep. The problem was that it *was* deep!

So deep that I — a person who adopted the belief of never letting the Bible touch the ground because if it did, it would mean it was too close to hell — thought about tossing it out the window, which would mean it would most certainly touch the ground. Later, as I mentally matured, I realized using logic and common sense that, (1) if you live in a building, one person's floor is another one's ceiling and (2) since the Earth is circular in design, what's down is up and what's up is down!

I've been told knowing too much can get you into trouble. On the contrary, not knowing enuff, or just plain ignorance is deadlier!

Before I decided this book's fate, I opened the cover to the front page desperately lookin' for some kind of epiphany. My eyes fixated on two wordz, **"RE-EDITED VERSION."** Until then, the wordz never meant much to me. In fact, I didn't recall ever really seein' it. But tonight it glowed bright like a "Eat At Joes" diner sign. The only reason I would even go to that page was because at the top my Grandma wrote, *"To Jehvon, love Grandma."*

I alwayz thought there was just one Bible. At least that's what I was led to believe. But then again, I did alwayz hear, *"the King James version."* I started wonderin' what does 're-edited' mean and Y is it written in the Holy Bible?! Even an idiot knowz to edit something is to go back and make changes to something already written. And if it's *re*-edited, it meanz this has happened more than once! And what about 'version'? If this is a 'version', what version is it number or kind-wise?? I mean, just how many versionz of the 'word of God' are there?! I could now see that these wordz were resoundingly clear… somebody been fuckin' with this book for a looooooong tyme!

I continued to pace my room pondering who had the right to make these changes and for how long. Think about it… Someone or a group of hedz felt and still feel they have the authority to go in a change the word of 'God' on a consistent basis!

Then, without a thought, I dropped the Bible into my trashcan. Although I knew I did it, it was as though I was not in control. It was as if something took over me, loosened my grip and dropped it in the can! This was big because you *know* if before tonight I wouldn't let my Bible touch the ground, I certainly wouldn't throw it next to an old Burger King cheeseburger wrapper!

I stared at the container askin' myself if I realized what I just did and the possible repercussionz of doin' so. I could hear my sisterz echoing in unison, *"ooooooooh! You gonna get it!"*— like they used to alwayz say when we were little. But by whom was I gonna get it from? God? Jesus? Was a bolt of lightening gonna suddenly strike me 'cause of what I just did?

I stood frozen like the perfect target for that lightening bolt for a few secondz, then I started to think… My mental and spiritual foundation had just been blown to smithereenz, yo! Just hourz ago me and 'God' was cool. I had no questionz, well I did have a couple questionz, but it seemed 'God' was too busy to answer them so instead, there was some idiot reverend who acted like he was 'God's' personal assistant and was authorized to be a stand-in. I was a nobody, a number, living like everyone else, not creating any waves, just livin' off faith. Now I'm questioning the whole dam thing, callin' 'God's' bluff! *"Where you at God? Show yourself! Talk to me! Lemme know you're real, 'cause you 'bout to lose a follower!"*

Obviously, 'God' was a no show… After accepting my fate, I went to bed... I was tired... more so, my *mind* was tired. I guess God'll get me tomorrow…

This walk proved to be the craziest quarter-of-an-hour I had experienced to that point, but again, this was just the beginning...

Chapter Two: The Godz Know…

I didn't have morning Track practice the next morning so I slept an hour over before I had to get ready for class. This was the day it was on the other side of campus, so that meant about a 10-15 minute walk down Forbes Avenue from Lothrop Hall.

This walk proved to be the craziest fifteen minutes I had experienced to that point, but again, this was just the beginning…

As I walked down Forbes Avenue, I was approached by a Christian with a flyer talkin' 'bout, *"Jesus loves you."* I sarcastically responded, *"mm hmm, yeah. I know,"* as I took the flyer. Soon after I folded up the flyer to put in my pocket, I was approached by four more men of different faiths one literally after the other: a Buddhist, a J-Dub (Jehovah Witness), one of them orange-dressed, tambourine-playin' Hari Chrishna cats, and an Ansaar Muslim.

It became somewhat comical as I knew with each step I took towardz my class, anutha religious cat would approach me as if I had a t-shirt that said, *"Help me, I'm looking for God."* I mean, I walk down this street at least twice a week and I been seein' these cat's for madd semesterz and they *never* spoke to me — as if the look on my face was non-inviting (which it was). So Y today?! What did I do different? On top of that, Y did *all* these religious hedz want to step to me on the same day?!!?... the very next day after I threw my Bible away?

It was as if the Poly-verse had made public on the spiritual grapevine wire that I was a 'Spiritual Free-Agent', 'cause yo, they was tryin' to recruit a brutha, harder than my college Track & Field coach did before I graduated high school, B!

As I walked down the auction block, I mean, street, there stood a figure I'd seen dozenz of tymz, but he never spoke nor even made a gesture to approach me. So it caught me by surprise when this skin-headed white dude tried recruiting me by attempting to sell me a book on Buddhizm. I tried to be cordial, but simply could not see myself dressed in a baggy orange garb and sandles, head shaved with a tambourine skippin' down the street and whatnot. All I could think of was what all my peeps would think if they saw me lookin' like a tangerine in Jesus sandles… not too masculine for a brutha, feel me?

I politely replied, *"No thanks,"* and continued toward my class although I gave him a look like, *"keep on playin' your tambourine, yo! Don't even think about comin' over here wit dat!"* After stutter-stepping towardz me, he obliged. I was runnin' a lil' late which was a ritual, 'cause I loathed goin' to class. I was too tired from bein' a student/athlete where we were expected to uphold the rigorous schedule of bein' a full-time athlete *and* full-time student. It's not that I couldn't handle it, I was just tired of it!

Not even 10 meterz away stood a Jehovah Witness. I already knew about them 'cause the male my spirit chose to come to this planet through's mother is a J-Dub (I won't define him as my Father because he chose to abandon my two sisterz, my Mother and me). I remember the couple tymz my Mother would let my sisterz and I stay with her on weekendz and she'd take us to the "Hall" — we'd be there *allllll* day, yo! On top of that, at the age of 21, she was *still* sending me the J-Dubz magazine, Awake. She would send a note with the magazine highlighting articles like, *"How to deal with peer pressure."* I would say to myself, *"this is shit teenagerz s'posed to read!"* I know she meant well, but don't every religious person be tryin' to get you to convert to their beliefs? I kept walkin' with a smirk on my mouth.

When this J-Dub walked up to me, I was quick and swift with my reply, *"Haaaaaiiiiiilllll naw, yo."* I snapped, *"Get tha fuck away from me with that shit!"* It still amazes me today the ballz they have ringin' your doorbell on an *EARLY* Saturday morning and expect you to let them in! Gotta give it to them though, 'cause their brainwashed beliefs must be strong to be that person out on the street in Bed-Stuy, Brooklyn ringing doorbellz, Sun!!

Back to my walk to class down *'Religious Auction Blvd'* — then came something so bizarre, it made *me* stutter-step. About 50 or so meterz down the path stood a brutha, about mid-twenties, dressed in all white with an army fatigue jacket on. He seemed not as eager to "recruit" me. Instead, he was more laid back lookin' as though he wasn't lookin' for me, but that I was lookin' for him. Little did I know how true that was.

"I heard you threw away your bible last night," he blurted out with a gentle yet confident tone at a pitch that shutdown every other sound I was hearing at the tyme. What made it more ill was that I had already passed him and was a few steps beyond him when he decided to speak. My pace stuttered to the point where I almost tripped as though my ankle was about to give out from gettin' shook from an Iverson or Hot Sauce crossover.

I turned and looked at him with a ill stare as if he just talked 'bout my momma and countered, *"What?! What'chu just say?!!?" "I heard you threw away your bible last night!"* This tyme with more certainty in his voice. How'd he know this? I never, EVER spoke to this cat before, and I was pretty sure he never saw me! Honestly, the brutha looked like he was some kind of ex-military/ex-pimp who probably was tryin' to hustle me something — but it was somethin' 'bout his swagger. His spirit seemed pure; his vybration high, I mean, *real* high (or was it that I started to know there were different levelz of high).

"I'm here 'cause you asked for me," he further stated. *"I been standin' here waitin' on you."* I'm like, what da hell is goin' on, Sun?! Inside, I'm havin' a conniption, but I can't let this cat see me gettin' all open and whatnot 'cause he's gonna eventually ask me for some money.

After that thought, I came down, sensing this was where all this was gonna lead to — *"yeah, he just spittin' game actin' like he know me and shit,"* I thought to myself, *"then he gonna bring in his sales pitch to buy some book from him and if that don't work, he gonna try and sell me some incense, oilz or bean-pies and try and rope me in that way. And if that don't work, he gonna come with the sob story 'bout needing a nickel to catch the bus — as if it that's all it cost!"*

But that didn't happen. I wound up not goin' to my class as he talked about my just emerged quest to want to know more than what society had taught me; more than what college could ever teach me. I was drawn to his vernacular. Despite his appearance bein' somewhat suspect to me, it was not the visual that interested me; on the contrary, it was the essence of *Word, Sound, Power* at its finest. I was a dry sponge before an ocean of 'New Thought' and I must admit, for the first tyme, I was very interested in learning more!

His name was Nasir and he was an Ansaar Muslim, a follower of the infamous spiritual chameleon, Dr. Malachi York. At the tyme, I was oblivious to Dr. York and his manipulative movement; even Elijah Muhammad for that matter.

For the first tyme, I was hearing a Blackman talk about the whiteman with historical context and didn't seem to be all that scared to do it.

Of course, I was drawn to this like a magnet. Every Black person in America, whether "conscious" or not, knowledgeable of the Black Nationalist movement of the 1960s or not; we all had beef with YT. I had come from a 99% Black high school and now I was on an all white college campus with nearly 40,000 students — with only about thirteen-hundred Black students. Did my affection toward YT increase? Hell no! I hated my all-too-often bigoted white professorz who said I would never be a writer givin' me D's and F's in my Basic and General Writing courses; my white tricknologically racist Track coach and his Black 'step-n-fetch-it' assistant coach, the historically racist white-based city of Pittsburgh, Pennsylvania… pretty much any and everything white! This growing hate was based on personal and observational incidents that started to happen as soon as I set foot on campus back in 1988.

Around this same tyme, my girlfriend, Michelle and I were gettin' back together and she had begun speaking to me about thingz we never spoke of before. I recall one night I was over her apartment. She was lying in her bed and I was on the floor next to her (as I said we were in the midst of gettin' back together). With her arm extended I caressed her hand as she spoke about seeing and feeling spirits. I must admit, I thought she was loosing her mind, talking about spirits and demonz, when before our breakup, this was never a topic. I was sure she wasn't "on" somethin', which made it more ill, but I cared for this woman deeply and felt I needed to be there for her. So I would listen, nodding my head, but not *really* listening to what she was saying, just tryin' to console her and make her feel safe.

The cypherz became deeper, longer and more powerful with all of us buildin' together now...

Chapter Three: A Common Link

A couple weeks later, it turned out the topics Michelle talked about had a common source. She wanted me to meet this guy her roommate Subeam and one of my teammates, Chop, had been building with… turned out to be the same cat I met the day after KRS-One shook me, Nasir!

This gave even greater significance to what was goin' on 'cause I hadn't told anyone about my meetingz with him. I hadn't shared any of my thoughts since KRS' lecture with nobody at that tyme, not even Michelle. Then I find Sun had already been in contact with someone *very* dear to me. It was both an elated as well as weird kind of feeling 'cause it seemed so strange.

The cypherz became deeper, longer and more powerful with all of us buildin' together now. I became less and less focused on school and track, finding myself more occupied with 'knowledge of self' than what my scholarship paid for me to do. Some practices I would just skip and pay the consequences later with my coach 'cause the cypherz were so intense, I didn't realize we had been reasoning (anutha word for building or cypher; a group of hedz talkin' about thingz in a group) from the night before — straight!

Although I felt myself becoming dependent on the building sessionz I had with Nasir, the feeling started to shift when he said to us one night, *"I'll never leave ya'll unless you tell me."* See, we had no way of contacting Nasir, no phone number, no address. He would just show up. Sometymz he'd come to my dorm at night and call me, I'd come down and we'd build, but most of the tymz he would just pop up at Michelle's apartment. This, of course, bothered me.

He started visiting almost everyday. Now, I had class and track practice everyday and would leave every Thursday or Friday through Sunday because we were in the beginning of the indoor season. His visits were becoming too frequent; he would come late, unannounced and would basically try and stay as long as he could. I knew duke liked either my girl or her roommate Subeam, I just wasn't sure which one and I didn't want to let Michelle know unless I had a good enough reason to speak on it.

I'll admit, I was a little insecure 'cause on the outside, it seemed Nasir was well received and was hanging out a lot with Michelle and Subeam. My perception of him also started to change when I noticed he was always talking about the freedomz we had that he no longer had because he was an Ansaar. It was as if he was envious, but it puzzled me because "his way" (Dr. York's) was s'posed to be *the* way.

I was sure he wasn't born Ansaar, so he probably lived similar to us at one tyme, and I know temptation can be a tumultuous fight, but it made me wonder Y he yearned to be like us so much. What initially appeared to be a flawless spiritual man had now taken on the shape of swiss-cheese filled with holes of unfulfilled happiness and lust for a former lifestyle.

This made me look at him different, 'cause at first, he seemed all brick about his faith, talking to us as though *we* were the lost one's and that salvation was only achieved through bein' an Ansaar (just like how all other "organized" religionz do).

He made it clear he was in search of a wife, one that he could convert, and because he was showin' up at my lady's spot so much, I felt he had his sites on one of them. I began to believe he had an altered motive.

One night he came to my dorm in his usual way, late and unannounced, called me and I came down. I never signed him in to my dorm, we alwayz met in the lobby or outside and talked. We were outside and two sisterz walked by entering the dorm. I knew them and spoke. After they passed, he nudged on my left arm and said, *"I'd like to have them in the Green Room!"* I looked at him, on the surface agreeing for the sake of seein' where he would go with this, but on the inside, I saw the layerz of who he really was peeling off.

Previously he had told me what the 'Green Room' was all about. It is a room couples/mates use to have intercourse, mainly for the purpose of having a baby. He told me of this when I first met him when he was contrasting the life society lives (including me and company) with the way of the Ansaar. In the beginning, his way was right and the rest of the worldz way was wrong; he spoke of how casual sex was meaningless and wrong and that family building was right. I would later learn how Dr. York most likely spoke the same shit while he impregnated many women followerz, with no regard to fulfilling his fatherly duties. This is the same shit I would soon learn anutha early cat I admired did, Elijah Muhammad.

Comin' from a broken fatherless home myself, this form of abuse and neglect was something I despised. Growing up without a father — especially with a father who is not dead, that consciously chooses not to partake in his own offspringz life — is a plague that vexes me to no end!!

So, not even a month knowing this kid, Nasir talkin' 'bout how he'd like to "sex" these college girlz in their *sacred* Green Room. He then went on tellin' me tales of adventures he had in the Green Room as well as stories of his comradz. Now, I wasn't appalled about him talkin' about women, I mean, I do it with my peoples all the tyme just like the next. It just shocked me, 'cause this cat started out sayin' it was practically an abomination to view and use women for sexual escapades.

I later learned that of all the religionz I studied, the Ancestorz and 'Energy' (my name for God) had a way of drawing me to a belief system, show me the good and then reveal the bad allowing me to make the decision whether to move on or join.

It is this spiritual protocol that has enabled me to grow into the being I am today; a firm believer of the unknown, bound to no man-made religion or theory on 'God'. I strive to be a true free-thinker, not afraid to elevate my definition of what I follow the moment a jewel is revealed.

Gettin' back to Nasir, it seemed there was a shift. No longer did I feel I needed Nasir; it felt like Nasir needed me (Michelle and Subeam specifically). Don't get me wrong, Nasir opened me up to a world of alternative thought. If you've read any of Dr. York's often noted as plagiarized works, there's some real deep shit in there — *Leviathon666*, *The Making of the Paleman*, yo, those are classic's filled with split-dome information!

Along with the Ansaarz perception of women, it was the lifestyle I couldn't get with. I mean, I wasn't ready to wear all white garbz, army fatigues (which is what they wore at the tyme) and sell books, incense and oilz all day standing on the corner. Fuck that, yo!

Although Nasir put a bad taste of Ansaar in my mouth, I still was interested in learning more about Ansaar. I never said I was in the process of converting and I was sure Michelle wasn't either; we were just developing free-thinkerz yearning to know more about it. But Nasir's unannounced visits began to get on all of our nerves. Michelle was telling me how he would pop up more frequently at her and Subeam's apartment at odd hourz in the day — not only in the evening, but during the day. Either he felt my vybe or it was mutual, but Nasir didn't come to see me that much anymore. This made me even more suspicious of his intentionz. I'm sure he was aware of my being in the middle of indoor Track season just by pattern alone. When Michelle told me how she was becoming irritated by him showin' up so much, I knew a split was coming...

I've heard of all the alleged great men of our tymz, while hearing little-to-nothing of the women who supported them...

Chapter Four: The Split

It was now March, so the weather was gettin' a little warmer. One late Thursday afternoon, Nasir, Michelle and I were building and he invited us to go with him to evening prayer. We decided to go. When we were together, we alwayz talked, but mainly would listen to Nasir. We took our conversation on the road and walked about 3 miles downtown to the U.S. Steel Building. One thing I noticed is when you build, tyme doesn't exist, nor space for that matter, for the 3-mile walk had no physical impact on us at all and we got there in what seemed a short period of tyme.

As we walked around the back of the skyscraper, we saw several of Nasir's Ansaar bruthaz preparing for prayer. This was our first encounter with other muslim memberz so I was bit nervous wondering if I'd be accepted or not. Old and young, and all men, I saw them rolling out their prayer rugz facing east. Of course Michelle and I didn't have rugz, so we used our coats as substitutes.

Simultaneously, I heard the chime of a nearby church… it was six o'clock; tyme to pray. On cue, everyone faced east kneeling down. Michelle and I immediately felt out of place not knowing what to do. Nasir on my left, asked us to join. With Michelle to my right, we both began to kneel down when Nasir sternly yelled, *"No! She has to pray behind you!"* I looked at him like *"What?!"* I suddenly had a brief mental moment, hearing infamous quotes like *"behind every great man standz a great woman,"* — the key word bein' *'behind'*. I was raised by my mother with no male presence in the house until I was 14 (my mother remarried a man who was in the early-to-mid stages and eventually became a full-blown alcoholic).

"She can't be beside you, she has to be BEHIND you," he quickly snapped again. My look was that of what a woman might look like, being degraded to 'less than' in comparison to a man. My look was of protest, but I did nothing. Because prayer was beginning, Michelle and I complied without haste although my focus was now shifted from praising Allah to thinkin', *"Y the fuck did he just diss my lady and ALL women like that?!"* As they spoke in their Arabic tongue, I knew there was no way I was gonna be down with bein' an Ansaar. I was raised by my Momz and two sisterz.

My respect for women was the level of gender balance, even back then before I knew this was the last of the Seven Djhuitic Principles, Gender *(Gender is in everything. Everything has its masculine and feminine principles. Gender manifests on all planes.).*

Being raised by my mother and having two sisterz is probably one of my greatest blessingz. I've witnessed the pain and struggle Afrikan women go through living in a male-dominated-eurocentric society.

I've heard of all the alleged great men of our tymz, while hearing little-to-nothing of the women who supported them — as if they weren't the *backbone* of these men! Afrikan women have been holdin' it down for a madd long tyme, Sun!! And to this day they *still* aren't given the credit they deserve. If it weren't for Afrikan women, we men would not be; so how could I go along with Sun tellin' me Michelle had to pray *"behind"* me?!

At this point and throughout prayer, Michelle and I kept lookin' at each other like, *"what tha fu__?!"*, as if Nasir had just spoken in a tongue unknown to us. Not to create controversy, Michelle took a few paces back and kneeled behind me. We didn't know Arabic or what they were praying about and frankly, at that point, I didn't care. I was through with these cats, B! As I doubled-over, mocking prayer, I looked at Michelle knelt behind me, under my right armpit. I thought of how humiliated she might've felt. I felt Nasir gave me the reason needed to speak to her about ending our relationship with him and the Ansaarz. This shit wasn't right and there was no way I was gonna be involved in somethin' like this. As soon as prayer commenced, Michelle and I excused ourselves both feeling the same way… it was tyme for a split.

Although our relationship with Nasir was appearing to be comin' to an end, our cypherz continued with Chop, Subeam and Missy. Shit was getting' deeper and deeper and I started havin' strange encounterz that started to scare me. It made me start wonderin' what had I gotten myself into...

Our mindz have been trained to accept bullshit answerz to our most innate questionz, 'cause they know we only exercise a small percentage of our intellect!

Chapter Five: The First Encounter

I was beginning to believe the visionz Michelle had been tellin' me about. It had been several weeks since KRS-One bent my reality and since that night, I began to notice I had been experiencing a lot of déjà vu's — at least two each day! I even started havin' déjà vu's of havin' déjà vu's! Yo, I was buggin', Sun!!

If you're unfamiliar of what a déjà vu is, it's defined as *"the illusion of having already experienced something actually being experienced for the first tyme."*

Now this is YTs definition, but if you've had a déjà vu or two in your life, and you're a free-thinker like I aspire to be, you cannot accept this definition. For one, it sayz it classifies it as an 'illusion' or as additionally defined in the dictionary as *"an erroneous perception of reality, concept or belief."*

If you take a second look at the definition YT gives for a déjà vu, the meaning they give contradicts itself. In fact, it's an oxymoron! Be the 'Literal Thinker' Afrikanz and ask yourself how can you have an illusion of experiencing something you feel already occurred, yet you really didn't experience it before 'cause it's happening for the first tyme?! How does this make sense? If you didn't have some recollection of this incident in the past, how would you recognize it as somethin' you experienced before in the first place?!!? This is a pure example of how this system is designed to think for us and we accept it without question. Remember, be the Evaluative Thinker. Our mindz have been trained to accept bullshit answerz to our most innate questionz, 'cause they hope we only exercise a small percentage of our intellect!

I was havin' so many, I started playin' the "vu's" out: *"-ight, this seemz familiar. So I should turn right... then go straight a couple steps then turn left..."* and BAM! I'd run into somebody I needed to see, was meaning to call or I would see somethin' that helped complete an earlier thought I had! Shit was crazy, B!

I was beginnin' to think I was developin' some kind of power. This easily added juice to my ego but somethin' in me echoed the importance of humility 'cause as they say, *"with great power comes great responsibilty."*

Well, eventually I realized I had no power — at least no more than the next hed who's tryin' to be intuned with their inner-self.

As if *that* wasn't enuff to deal with, I started feeling like I was bein' watched! Now, let me remind you, I know hedz probably forgetting what I wrote in the beginning of this book, so I'll repeat it... Absolutely *NO* drugz of any kind was bein' used during this tyme, not even cold medicine!! So I wasn't trippin' off some skunk ganja, mushroomz or weed brownies, I was completely sober and conscious throughout this entire experience! So Y was I suddenly havin' these crazy encounterz?!

For example, one afternoon, Chop and I was building. Our cypher took us from Pitt's campus to downtown — again, about a 3-mile walk. I can remember hedz tellin' me before I started gettin' into this shit, *not to,* because I'd become all paranoid and shit. Well, I did! But not to the point where I felt the need to stop. On the contrary, this paranoia increased my curiosity!

I felt paranoia wasn't so bad. I mean, what's so bad with becoming aware?! I began to realize this was a scare tactic made into legendary folklore. I imaged the countless Sunz who were 'on the path' and let someone scare them off it. *"Fuck that, B!"* I said to myself. *"I'ma see this shit through!"*

I began training myself to be more visual; to start lookin' at thingz, then lookin' beyond what it was I was seein'! I also made a point to be aware of who was around me. I mean, if there *were* any 'agents' following me, I focused on being aware of it.

Case in point, back to me and Sun buildin'. We started walkin' from the Cathedral of Learning toward Forbes Avenue. We were talkin' 'bout how wicked YT is and we weren't at all quiet about it — not that we were shouting, we were speakin' in the same public tone as anyone else. I say this because I often found when hedz would build, they would whisper when heard by otherz as if they were worried about otherz hearing them. I felt that was some plantation shit. I mean, Y we gotta be scared to reason?

When we got to the corner, as we waited for the light to change for us to cross, I felt this sensation behind me. I looked over my right shoulder and *"whoa!!!"* The wickedest woman I ever seen was staring at me with a ill grill!

She had to be at least in her 80s. She was a small old white lady, perhaps just over 5 feet tall. She had a hump in her back which made her crouch over. To compensate her stance, she used a cane for balance. It wasn't so much that she was lookin' at me; it was *how* she was grillin' me! The hump made it difficult for her to look directly at me so her head was tilted and slightly turned to the left. Her nose was flared with one side of her mouth slanted open showing the left side of her yellow-tinted upper teeth.

I was a little startled cause she looked just like a witch without the hat, yo! Instead, I replied aloud to Chop loud enuff for her to hear, *"See, there go one of 'em right there!"* Sayin' that, I felt an adrenaline rush which boosted my courage levelz, not 'cause I was dissin' someone, who probably was a sweet old lady; but that I was refusing to bow down to somethin' I felt was s'posed to scare me off 'the path' I was traveling.

The light changed and we crossed the street. I looked back as I crossed and she kept lookin' at me as she slowly crept across the walkway. I calmed as we kept walkin' thinkin' it was over 'cause our pace was much faster than herz.

When we reached downtown about an hour later, we were on the corner of Grant and Smithfield. It was early in the afternoon so there were mad hedz still out on their lunch break. Suddenly, I felt that same sensation! I looked over my left shoulder and there she was again!! Standing in the same stance, ice-grillin' me, Sun! I was like, *"What tha fu__?!"* How did she get down here at the same tyme when Chop and I *walked!* She couldn't have walked! Maybe she caught a bus, but I wasn't sleepin' the coincidence of me gettin' the vybe and her bein' in the same position with all these people around!

This was one of many episodes I encountered. As I mentioned at the beginning of this book, I felt I was experiencing thingz I had experienced before — I remember havin' several ill encounterz starting when I was about five yearz old. Some of them included out-of-body experiences!

It's crazy to explain, but I remember I'd bug-out and wind up screaming and my momz would come in the room to console me. If you can imagine goin' from lookin' in front of you (like how you're seein' the page of this book), then suddenly you sorta jump out of yourself and see yourself from behind, lookin' at the book, then, like a movie camera, feel yourself "panning" out or moving away, still lookin' at yourself look at this page of the book. At five, Sun, that's a lot to take in and I would bug-out feelin' like I had no control and could possibly not get back and reconnect to my body.

In addition, if that wasn't enuff, I would see people's spirits! One ongoing incident I remember started happenin' when I was about six sittin' at home in our living room on the couch. I was watchin' somethin' on tv and I noticed on my left, with my peripheral vision, seein' a ghost-like figure walk right by me! I didn't move, wasn't even afraid. It was a man, but he wasn't a brutha and the only white men I saw at that age were either on tv or my school teacherz!

He didn't do or say anything to me; he just walked by as if I, the room and the house weren't there. It made me start thinkin' about tyme and space. I started wonderin' how long this house I lived in had been here. I wondered what was here before. Was it anutha house? A road of some sort? Maybe it was a busy street block. I started ponderin' on what was here 100 yearz ago; 1,000 yearz ago! 100,000 yearz ago!! I thought of all the living thingz that occupied the same space I was occupying and if there were some sort of celestial remnants of their existence still here. It was then I embraced the notion that there are no such thingz as ghost's — as *Hell-y-wood* (Hollywood) would want you to believe, but there certainly are spirits!

These experiences had been suppressed in me as I grew up in this society. Yeaz later, after reading Malidoma Soma's *Of Water and the Spirit*, I learned there is a connection between early youth and Elderz. The connection is simple. When asked the question where we come from, we usually start from our Mother's womb or even Father's penis. Which *is* true, but not necessarily truth! There's a physical and non-physical you. The non-physical you come from some place, *some*where beyond the world we live in. It's this place many believe an Elderz spirit ascendz to once they "die" — Some call it heaven (my guess is that this also applies to a being that dies at an earlier age).

In my later yearz recalling these experiences, I came to the conclusion, due to Malidoma's book, that in our early yearz, we are closer to where our spirts came from. As youth's, we are not fully corrupted from this worldz imbalances yet. So we are able to "see" and feel thingz grownups may have tuned out.

If life is cyclical, this "place" is the same dwelling a child's spirit comes from. This "place" must be where all spirits evolve from — or this place may be one of many places that create spirits. And this "place" does not have to be just one place, which would be the perfect example of linear thinking. There could be an infinite number of spot's where spirits are born and come back just like how starz are born out of Nebula's. How and when we will know for sure probably comes when our Earth tyme is up.

A child is still connected to this "place" and not entirely corrupted by the physical world simply due to them not bein' here physically long enuff.

An Elder is often noted near the 'end' of their physical life as senile or "out there" at tymz in their later yearz. I think, as Malidoma mentioned, they are reconnecting with that realm. It's deep when you really think about it! It's a cycle, you leave the non-physical, enter the physical, leave the physical, and re-enter the non-physical! Does the cycle repeat itself? Inquiry mindz want to know!

Have you ever wondered Y it seemz the polyverse gives the impression life is only on planet Earth?! Y IZ Dat?! YT realizes there's more to life than what's "inside the box". While they raise large sumz of money for fellowships on studies and debates of the possibilities of life "outside the box", they want us to remain inside the box, caught up in tryin' to pay rent, feed our families and deal with racizm. And while they research our ancient scrollz, we forget that we, melanated people, have the ability to know these answerz if we tuned into our higher frequency.

One of the easiest wayz to prove this is by using the Djhuitic Principle, 'Correspondence'. By simply realizing everything is connected, from micro- to macrocozmically, it's easy to realize that we can understand the thingz we don't know simply by studying the thingz we know. We are, just as everything is, a mere consumption of elements of a bigger thing(s).

You will learn more about this in the 'Microzom of the Macrocozm' series later in this book.

The Power of Self Definition:

"Those that can define you can confine you..."

Chapter Six: The Maturation: From Body to Mind

It seemed tyme conspired with me because this search to find myself made me question everything I had been doing. Sorta like a blessing in disguise, my junior year I had a lingering injury that started in October but was not diagnosed until February. I honestly think when they told me, after four months of asking for an X-ray on my right femur (thigh bone), that it was cracked a third of the way in deep, I woulda quit the track team and school altogether, and this was big for me, 'cause I never ever quit anything before!.

Y? Because I was madd, yo! Anyone who's been exposed to some level of knowledge of self can attest. When you find you've been deceived, you become heated because you can't understand Y someone would devise a system that could do such a thing!

It didn't help that I already had a shaky relationship with my white track coach and an even worse one with his "step'n'fetch it" black assistant coach who didn't like me 'cause I *"reminded him of someone else,"* I was told by a fellow teammate.

They say thingz happen for a reason, so my bein' injured freed me from havin' to leave every weekend for track meets. It also allowed me more personal tyme 'cause all I had to do was report to the trainer for treatment. I wouldn't have 2-a-day practices for a while; I had to let my leg heal.

Admittingly, I was loosin' interest in college. I knew how to get by and did what I had to do to pass examz, so I was freed up enuff to really get into this knowledge thing. What made it easier was havin' the support of Michelle, Subeam, Missy and Chop goin' through this together.

Our cypherz became longer and deeper each day to the point that I wasn't even attending my classes and sparingly went for treatment for my leg. My coach started to beef with my lacking attendance and after learning the shit I was bein' exposed to, I was about to sound on duke! I started thinkin' 'bout how my worth to him was strictly to win races, like I was a thoroughbred or somethin'.

He didn't give a shit about me. From the beginning of my injury that November, I told him I should get an X-ray. He had me see the team trainer who misdiagnosed me with a groin pull. Thinkin' she knew what she was talkin' about, I continued to train despite the pain, mainly because my coach made me feel I would be failing the team if I didn't. I will admit, it was hard to not want to run. At that point in my career, I was at my highest. I had run a 4:09 indoor-mile and was in the best shape of my career. How you gonna tell someone to sit out and let your leg heal when you're in the best condition of your life, not to mention, your tyme keeps dropping every race?!

I kept running until the Big East indoor championships in February. About a week before, I was in the middle of practice, running a timed 600meterz. By then, my form had considerably changed; I had an obvious limp in my walk and even more so in my stride, however I was still strong and my tymz kept dropping. As I entered the curve as I passed the 200-mark of the 3rd set, my leg gave out! I fell flat on my face! I heard a crack-like sound and immediately thought I broke my leg!!

It wasn't broken, but after finally getting what I asked for, for the last four months, my X-ray revealed my femir had a crack a third of the way deep! Meaning, the crack was so deep, I coulda been walkin' downhill and my thigh bone could've broke in half!

I felt cheated that my coach didn't believe my injury until I could barely walk. What made it worse was now he was comin' at me like, *"I knew there was something wrong! I knew it!"* I was like, this punk muthafucka thought I was fakin', now he believes me because of an X-ray, somethin' he denied me of for four months! Had it gotten looked at back then, my injury and recovery woulda been addressed and I'd be ready for the rest of the season and probably woulda had my greatest season to date. Now all that shit's down the drain 'cause I can't run and can barely walk!

I was physically drained. Comin' back from a leg injury in Track & Field is major — especially if you're a middle-distance runner! See, Track is basically a 9-10 month-a-year sport. You begin trainin' for cross-country in August — if you're not competing in Track & Field championships which can be as late as August. Cross-country season lasts until late October-early November. Indoor season beginz in November and lasts until March and outdoor goes from April to July/August. That's a lot of wear-and-tear on your legz, Sun.

Because my injury was not a muscle pull or strain but a cracked bone, I couldn't do anything, not even ride a stationary bike to keep up my conditioning! So I basically lost all my endurance built up over the previous summer and fall.

I participated in sports since I was seven yearz old and this was the first tyme I had an injury that barred me from playing. I didn't know how to handle it.

In addition to all that, I was spendin' more tyme buildin' and one day came across an old political cartoon that was published in a black magazine. It was two pictures, one depicting a professional sports draft with an athlete standing in his briefs with white hedz takin' his measurements. The second picture was pretty much drawn the same except it wasn't an athlete, it was an enslaved Afrikan! And in addition to him standin' in his briefs, his armz and legz were shackled. The political cartoonist who drew this was depicting the similarities between professional sports drafts and the Atlantic Slave Trade auction docks!

This picture spoke volumes to me, 'cause I really did feel like a slave! I was an asset to good 'ol massa-coach as long as I was runnin' but as soon as I was injured, I was of no use to him! It was at that point I decided trying to make my career with my body was over. It was now tyme to use my mind. I soon began workin' on a piece called, *"Athletics versus Slavery"* which later appeared in one of my first editionz of Da Ghetto Tymz.

The cartoon also reminded me of a similar ill situation I experienced in high school. I played three sports each year, football each fall followed by basketball (my luv), and then track in the spring. In 1993 the head Track & Field coach died. After his death, I soon found out that before my 11th grade year, he met with the head football and basketball coaches to decide my athletic fate.

I was vying for the starting free-safety position with a senior havin' had significant playing tyme as a sophomore and as well was a lock for the varsity b-ball squad. The three coaches conspired to allow me to try-out but to cut me from the football and basketball programz, with no reason other than to appease my track coach, never giving me a reason other than that I wasn't "big enuff."

The July, before my Junior year when football camp started, on the first day I had a meeting with the head coach. He informed me I shouldn't bother trying out 'cause I was too small. I was 5-10, 155 lbs. That's more than the average size for a defensive back! I was like, *"what?! I'm too small?!"* Where'd this come from? He was adamant about my not makin' the team suggesting I don't even waste my tyme. I was pissed and was like *"fuck it!"*, told my track coach and he consoled me tellin' me not to worry and to concentrate on running cross-country instead. I didn't hesitate joinin' the team; I kinda did it in spite! I felt, at least this coach cares about me!

That fall I suprised a lot of hedz, winning the city championship and second in the District. Havin' such a successful first year, Coach naturally wanted me to run indoor track, but my heart was set on makin' the basketball team. Same shit went down come basketball season! But this was worse because basketball has and alwayz will be my favorite sport! Instead of discouraging me from the door, this coach allowed me to go through two of the five-day try-out period and then cut me.

I was devastated. I was just gettin' over the football thing and now I'm bein' cut from b-ball?! Yo, I never cried so hard as I walked home. I felt worthless! After speakin' with my uncle, he suggested I be a man, approach the coach and ask for a second try-out. On the following day, I was madd nervous, but was

Although todayz Black Athlete has had more financial success than ever before, they still maintain the role as 'player' and not where the real money is made, as 'owner'. If you were to watch two of america's most popular sporting drafts combines (Football and Basketball), you'll see a close resemblance to what happened on the slave docks of the period in which Afrikanz were kidnapped and brought to the america's and caribbean to be sold off to the highest slavemsater.

College athletic's has probably the closest likeness, where hundrez of millionz of dollarz are made by universities through alumni boosterz and tv endorsements. After the millionz dispersed for athtletic program facilities improvements and high paying salaries to coaches, what does the athlete get? Oh, yeah right, *a full-ride scholarship!*

Every season, the bowl games and tournament's alone bring in millionz to schoolz with top athletic programz. But who really makes these winning programz so successful? Sure, the coach designz the playbook, but it's the athlete who executes the play! It's the athlete who should be allowed to receive financial compensation for sacrificing their body for free! Sure, they have an opportunity to make their millionz if, and that's a *big* if they make it to the pro's!

If this isn't a model of modern day slavery, what is?!!?

determined to prove them all wrong, that I was a good athlete!

Coach granted me the remaining two dayz of camp, had me play dummy-defense the whole tyme and he cut me, yet again! By then, I didn't wanna play for him, so I flipped him "the bird" and came running to indoor track. Coach, of course, welcomed me with open armz. Little did I know they all conspired to appease my track coach 'cause he wanted me to run cross-country and indoor track, which ran simultaneously with the football and basketball seasonz.

How was I to know there was a conspiracy of sorts behind this whole thing? My sophomore year in track, I had a break-out season. I went from a slow 110meter hurdler to a 2:00-minute 800meter runner. My Coach saw I had promise to be a good middle-distant runner and after his death, I found out he wanted me to exclusively run cross-country and track, Y? For various reasonz: (1)he had a winning program with a city championship winning streak at stake; (2)he was a successful athlete himself, and thus had a reputation he wanted to preserve in creating top high school runnerz; (3)at the tyme, we had no starz on the team due to a couple seniorz graduating the year before and (4)he saw potential in me.

He thought I would develop into his next star runner, which I did. The next two yearz, our team dominated all the track meets and invitationalz and even got national press in USA Today and Track & Field News. My high school career ended with numerous Cross-Country and Track & Field City, District and Regional titles in the 800 and 1600 meterz cappin' it off with Track & Field Athlete Of the Year. His gamble paid off. But yearz later after finding out about this conspiracy, I began to wonder how many other kidz he gambled on. I thought how unfair it was to decide a student-athlete's fate without consulting them. I wondered how he could sleep at night using us the way he did.

As mentioned two paragraph's up, I used me as last in my coaches reasonz for wanting me to run instead of playing football and b-ball 'cause I later learned he never, EVER helped any of his athletes get to college on any level! He didn't make no callz, send out any letterz or newspaper clippingz, nothin'! He didn't even help us prepare for college-entry examz. Basically, it was four yearz of service and that's it! Meanwhile, it was his name that continued to be in the paper once you graduated, applauding his tenacious coaching ability as he rode the back of the next outstanding athlete on the team!

I must admit that I was blessed to have someone who did care. The assistant coach did whatever he could to get me and my teammates into school. After my junior year in which I won a ton of races, he put together a portfolio of all my newspaper clippingz and race results and sent to colleges across the country. He truly believed in me and because of this portfolio, I was able to not only attend a Division 1 college on a track scholarship. He also helped me prepare for the ACT test. I was recruited by several top programz around the country including University of Georgia, Tennessee, Arkansas, Purdue, Ole Miss and Ohio State. I chose the University of Pittsburgh.

This was an invaluable experience, for I soon realized after reflecting on my athletic career that if you don't use your mind, hedz will determine your life for you.

It was evident, the more we exercised the mind, fatigue became a factor...

Chapter Seven: Spring Break '91

Spring break was approaching; I was busy makin' cheat sheets gettin' ready for pre-final examz. With these past several weeks my focus had totally shifted. I finally was diagnosed by the Track team physician that I had a cracked femir, so Track was out; and I could give a fairy fuck about school right now, so I was basically free to concentrate on my new studies, 'knowledge of self!'

We all felt the same way. Throughout each day and nite we would basically stay up and vybe, askin' questionz we had never heard nor thought of until now. These questionz led to logical answerz, answerz that led to other questionz... and well, you can see the ongoin' process it creates.

We began to trust our intuition while at the same tyme shedded layer 'pon layer the euro-controlling theories and concepts-turned into belief systemz that has crippled our mental growth for centuries.

Think about it, YTs entire fortress is sustained by our *ignor*ance — or should I say, our choice to *IGNORE* the fact we have the ability to think and process a thought ourselves, first. Unfortunately we live in a world where too much is done for us, hence the shit we're in now!

There's a certain feeling of bein' free when you start your quest of questionz (or should I say *re*-start 'cause the quest first beginz when as a child you're askin' questionz about *everything*).

But with this freedom comes the flipside... disappointment! I soon realized damn near everything I believed in was questionable — the bad *and* the good!

At the same tyme we were learning YTs historical lies about history and religion. We also started reading books on health. *"Dam, you mean I cain't eat pork no more?!"* Sadly, I fathomed never eatin' bacon or the juicy flavor of Jimmy Dean sausages!!

Michelle introduced me to Anthony Browder's first book, *'22 Essays From The Browder File'*. Now I wasn't much of a reader. And I admit, I was among the fraternal memberz of the stereotypical notion that reading is like kryptonite to black people. But this book was different. It was somethin' 'bout the way Browder writes, it's like he's talkin' to you; simple, a smooth flow, like he's havin' a conversation with you (this was a style of writing I was comfortable with and have since. adopted it since my first writingz).

Among many articles he put together in this book, I was particularly drawn to the one's he wrote on health. After readin' the entire book in one day (my first from front-to-back), I knew it would be hard to continue eatin' this slave diet knowin' what it does to the human body.

The joy I initially felt thinking freely quickly morphed to anger and rage! It was hard for us to believe the thingz we learned... it was too much, too soon; I just saw KRS not long ago, yo! It was like we just took a weekend cram course, *'Knowledge of Self 101!'* Taking in info like this is taxing on the mental, spiritual *and* physical!

It was evident, the more we exercised the mind, fatigue became a factor. Just after a few weeks, we all became suddenly irritable and tired. Part of me began to wish I didn't know this stuff. Y? 'cause I didn't wanna change! Y shit gotta be like this?! How am I s'posed to survive?! My foundation has been ripped right from under me 'cause I'm learnin' dam near everything I believed in is a lie! If I continued to ignore this info, I could be like everybody else and not so dam *analytical!*

But I knew I needed to know, I tried to base my life on learning, thinking and knowing; somethin' the majority of males in my family, for whatever reason, didn't do. I'm so muthafuckin' pissed while at the same tyme, so, so tired...

Almost two weeks into buildin' nite and day, signz of fatigue started to take over. Not only did I feel it, the mental and spiritual overload was evident in all of us.

Little beefs were more frequent; the littlest thing sparked the biggest of arguments. We would snap at each other 'bout the most petty of thingz. We were unaware that these can be symptomz of mental, spiritual and physical fatigue. Our sessionz were intense, yo! Mainly 'cause there were no boundaries. We were free to explore any and everything! I was totally engulfed in wanting to know.

The deep thing was that we didn't have any kind of curriculum! Aside from Nasir's influence, our "curriculum" was created from just askin' questionz. We'd pose a question and build on it… for hourz!! I mean, we'd ask questionz about anything and we swore we could break it down to its very last compound!

It was then that I realized there exists an Ancestral memory bank of sorts. I wasn't a big reader at the tyme, but the thingz we were sayin' were thingz we didn't know we knew, feel me? For example, have you ever found yourself in a profound discussion and you say somethin' and didn't know where it came from? That's that shit, yo! Your Ancestral memory bank at work! Everytyme this happenz I get madd chillz up my spine!

Takin' this on an even deeper note, like how a woman and a man can naturally create a baby, the education or science behind this happenz because everything that's needed to make this creation comes from within. The same can be applied to knowledge. Everything there is to know can be drawn from within. All it takes is humility, patience and the ability to listen silently… *(More on this in my 'Freequencee' series)*

We were so open we could find some kind of subliminal in practically everything we looked at. Now some may think we were just reachin', lookin' to make somethin' out of nothin'. At tymz we even did! But isn't that what the search is all about? You search *everything,* for in everything lies a story; information about its past, present and possible future. The Djhuitic principle of correspondence *(as above, so below; so below, as above)* teaches that all things are relative.

The first being "The Universe is Mental," is defined as *"(S)he who grasps the truth of the mental nature of the universe is well advanced on the path of righteousness and mastery. The all is mind, the Universe is mental. When an idea exclusively occupies the mind, it is transformed into an actual physical state."* As mentioned earlier, with knowledge comes great responsibility. What I forgot to add was that repercussionz soon follow. Afterall, every action has a reaction. We were about to witness just how powerful the poly-verse is...

Don't go to sleep, I need for you to protect me...

The Luciferian Conspiracy
In 1770, Adam Weishaupt was a professor at Inglecot University when he embraced the Luciferian conspiracy. He began writing the master plan that was designed to give ultimate world domination to Satan. He completed the task May 1, 1776, setting out to destroy all existing governments and religionz. That same day in America, thousandz of miles across the Atlantic, *before* it was the United States (and 2 months before July 4th), 50 of the 56 signerz of the Declaration of Independence, joined the Luciferian Conspiracy. This is commemorated on the back of the $2 bill.

It would be reached by dividing the masses of people into opposing camps on political, social, economic and other issues. They would then be armed and incidents would be provided causing them to fight and weaken themselves, gradually destroying national governments and religious institutionz (soundz like the United States present state, huh?).

In 1784 Weishaupt issued his orderz for the French Revolution. Zwack, a German writer, had put the entire plan into a book. A copy was sent to the Illuminates in France, who were headed by Robespierre, Weishaupt had delegated to instigate the French Revolution. The carrier was struck and killed by lightning as he rode on his way from Germany to France. The police found the documents on his body, and turned them over to the proper authorities.

After a careful study of the plot, the Bavarian Government ordered the police to raid Weishaupt's lodges and homes of his most influential associates.

In 1785, the Bavarian Government outlawed the Illuminati and closed their lodges. In 1786, they published all the detailz of the conspiracy, called *"The Original Writings of the Order and Sect of the Illuminati"*. Copies of the entire conspiracy were sent to all the headz of Church and State in Europe. But the warning was ignored and Weishaupt was already ahead of the game. He had already ordered Illuminates to infiltrate into the lodges of Blue Masonry, and form their own secret societies within all secret societies.

Because the warningz about the Illuminati were ignored, the Revolution broke out in

Chapter Eight: Don't Go To Sleep…

Spring break was finally here and I was gonna go with Michelle to her home in Philly. We left on a gloomy Thursday afternoon. As we boarded the Greyhound bus, we both were extremely tired and somewhat lifeless, physically and mentally. Neither of us were in the mood for the nine-hour treck we were about to endure, but I did feel by us bein' on the road, we'd at least be able to get some much-needed rest.

The awkwardness of the past weeks made it virtually impossible to get more than an hour or two of sleep. Just as I was tryin' to situate myself in this tight-ass coach seat, Michelle layz across my legz and faintly whispherz, *"Don't go to sleep. I need for you to protect me."* I looked first thinkin' *"protect you from what?!"* Instead I gave her the facial impression okaying her, while inside I knew there was no way I'd be able to… I was too exhausted, yo!

Once the bus took off, a sort of ease came over me, feelin' that for at least nine hourz we'd be in motion and therefore, somewhat safe from any crazy encounterz.

"I'm serious, don't go to sleep, I REALLY need for you to protect me." Michelle blurted out, now more sternly, almost sounding desparate.

When she said that to me I started to realize how serious she was. I started wonderin' maybe this tyme it was *her* that was havin' some kind of spiritual encounter, not me, and that she needed me to be alert to wake her in case somethin' happened.

That was enuff to keep me up for the duration of the trip. When we arrived in Philly that early Friday morning, I couldn't help shake an eerie feelin' that came upon me.

See, Philly's an old town; one of the original 13 colonies, so I couldn't help but focus on the fact that I was in a city where the concept of colonializm and the Luciferian Conspiracy was born.

You can still see colonial remnants especially if you look at their cobblestone roadz. I started gazin' on what it might've been like some 200 yearz ago on the very street we were walkin' on. I envisioned Afrikanz shackled bein' transported from the docks off South street. Yo, I could feel the wickedness ease into my bones as we left the Greyhound station downtown.

We gathered our bagz off the bus and caught a cab headed for Mount Airy, Michelle's crib. It was my first tyme bein' here without havin' a track meet. I had been here every year we compete at the Penn Relayz held at the University of Penn but I never got to chill. As soon as the meet was over, we were back on the bus to Pittsburgh.

Michelle still looked drained and you know I was madd tired, so as soon as we stepped into her home, I got ready for bed.

I couldn't shake this ill feelin' though. I still felt a little uneasy with the amount of reasoningz we had done over the past weeks, the strange encounterz as well as the nine-hour bus ride. This trip to her house was s'posed to be to relax, regroup and recharge; but it didn't end that way and in fact, shit started as soon as we arrived!

1789, as scheduled by Weishaupt.

Weishaupt died in 1830, but prior to his death, he prepared a revised version, which, under various names, was to organize, finance, direct and control all international organizationz and groups by working their agents into executive positionz at the top.

In 1834, the Italian revolutionary leader, Giuseppe Mazzini, was selected by the Illuminati. He later enticed an American general named Albert Pike into the Illuminati. Pike ultimately became the head of this Luciferian conspiracy.

Between 1859 - 1871, Pike worked out a military blueprint for three world warz and various revolutionz throughout the world which he thought would forward the conspiracy to its final stage in the 20th Century. (Pike was also the founder of the KKK and the U.S. government honorz this follower of Satan with a statue in downtown Washinton, DC at 3rd and D Streets, N.W.)

World War I was to be fought to enable the Illuminati to destroy Czarism in Russia. After the war ended, Communism was to be built up and used to destroy other governments and weaken religionz.

In the U.S., immediately after WWI, the Illuminati set up what they called the Council on Foreign Relations (CFR). This CFR is actually the Illuminati now operating in the U.S. Its hierarchy are descendants of the original Illuminati even though many have changed their names to conceal this fact.

There's a similar establishment of the Illuminati in England, called the Royal Institute of International Affairs (RIIA). There are also Illuminati organizationz in France, Germany, and other nationz operating under different names.

The Second World War was to be started by using the controversies between fascist and political Zionists.

The Third World War is to be started by stirring up beef between political Zionists and the leaderz of the Moslem world. Their hope is that all of Islam and Zionism, will destroy each other while, at the same tyme, the remaining nationz, once more divided on this issue, will be forced to fight themselves into a state of complete exhaustion — physically, mentally, spiritually, and economically. The stage will then be set to put the one world government into operation.

In the final phase, the one world government is to consist of a key dictator — the head of the United Nations, the CFR, a few billionaires, the Communists and scientists who have proven their devotion to the great conspiracy. All otherz are to become total slaves of the conspiracy.

I now saw the figure that cast the shadow on the wall floating toward me...

Chapter Nine: Déjà vu: Was It A Dream Or Reality?

I slept in Michelle's old bedroom while she slept in one of her older sisterz room about 20 feet down the hall.

To help me sleep, I turned on the tv that sat to the right of the top of the bed. As the tv subdued me to sleep, I felt myself begin to slip... into the abyss of the unknown... The feeling I felt is really hard to explain, but I'll try.

Have you ever felt, when first starting to fall asleep, like you're on a roller-coaster swooping deeper and deeper, then even deeper, looping downward as though you're beein' pulled down some kind of spiral drain? It feelz is as if you are the wind or a current rhythmically diving-down-then-evening-out then diving-down-then-evening out and so on; coasting and repeating this graceful yet seemingly dangerous sequence over and over again. There were several soundz at once, but none I could focus clearly on, other than the tv that was on. I was descending at what appeared to be a rapid pace, yet gliding so smooth; I couldn't focus on the setting other than the worm-like black hole that seemed to be suckin' me in. The rate of speed made me feel like I was bein' stretched.

I knew that if I *was* sleep, I wasn't totally. I was somewhere in between because I could distinctively hear the television show that was on in Michelle's bedroom. I was conscious of all of this and felt as though my body was bein' stretched like I was plasticman. I could feel my mouth expand wide open due to the excessive rate of speed.

I was experiencing this for the first tyme so I was madd scared, yet not so scared that I wanted to "wake up"... I wanted to know where this was going.

I guess what I was experiencing was a form of what they call REM (Rapid Eye Movement) sleep. This flight seemed to last about a minute or so. Allz I know is that it felt angelic, yet the combination of fear and curiosity vybrated throughout me. I had a sense this was no ordinary "dream". This incident had substance.

I hadn't recalled a feeling like this since my earlier dayz when I was about 4 or 5 when I would constantly jump outside myself looking down (which meant I was floating) seeing myself lying in my bed appearing to be sleep, yet couldn't understand

Y I could see myself. This would happen for several yearz off and on and it would totally freak me out each tyme! I never told anyone until now. I guess it happened to prepare me for wha'gwan now.

As the "flight" came to a sudden halt, my vision began to come into focus. During the descent, it was all feeling with basically nothing to see. This is what made it somewhat difficult for me to tell whether this was a dream or reality. I mean, it *felt* like I was awake, but I wasn't sure because it seemed so weird, and I couldn't put my finger on what it was that made it so crazy. Suddenly I had vision. And what I saw was even more mystifying.

The setting was in black and white, so there was no color. In fact, it was like I was in one of those old black and white movies. What I saw was confusing; I was still in Michelle's bedroom laying on my left side but I knew I was somewhere else. See, everything that was movable in her room was there, it was the wallz that were different!

The tv, her dresser drawer, everything that could be moved was there, but the wallz were made of stone! I could hear the echoing sound of water dripping not too far away. The drops sounded like I was in an enclosed setting, inside some place.

I then detected the sound of burning wood crackling like you'd hear from a small campfire. Although I couldn't see it, I could see the light of the fire flickering off what I now recognized as wallz made of rocky stone. It was then that it struck me... I *wasn't* in Michelle's house anymore, somehow I was inside a cave!!

Although a panic came over me 'cause I didn't know how in the hell I got there, I didn't try to move. Instead, I continued to just lay there and use my eyes to navigate where I was.

There was no sound, just the fire cracklin' in the background. It was too calm! That's Y I decided not to try to move; somethin' might be watchin' me and waiting for me to move. Then I saw somethin'…

Now, we Afrikan people have seen enuff horror flicks to know when somethin' don't feel right, you don't investigate, you get's the fuck outta there, yo! But I B-S you not, B, when I saw what I saw, it was hard to move!

The flickering flame cast a shadow of a figure calmly, slowly and gently gliding toward me. After a few secondz, I was convinced I had seen enuff and was ready to jump out of the bed and start runnin'. But when I tried to move, I couldn't!

I wasn't strapped nor shackled down or nothin'. Just usin' my eyes, I gazed down to see my body with my eyes, I could see there was nothin' holdin' me to the bed, it was just me in a t-shirt and shorts!

Inside I was fidgetting to sit up and jump off the bed, but my body was numb, paralyzed as if almost dead, just laying there as the shadowy figure on the cave wall continued to glide towardz me.

I was sitting prey; like that deer on the road that stops and stares at the headlights of a car before it gets hit. Fifteen yearz later, I learned this is associated with the feeling of "paralysis" author of '*Soul Traveler*', Albert Taylor, PhD. wrote about in this profound book on the spiritual significance of visionz and other esoteric experiences when we sleep.

Focusing my vision by gazing at a point, I was able to see more with my peripheral now activated. Just when my vision expanded, from the bottom of the bed, I now saw the figure that cast the shadow on the wall floating toward me. The image seemed to float because it was dressed in an oversized soft white cloak that appeared to be light as life. It also gave this illusion because my view was restricted to a letter-box-type view you see at the movie theater which is more wide the high.

Lying on my left side, the mattress I was on prohibited me from seein' the ground and I could only see up which, because I was lying down, is really lookin' right. By now, I knew this wasn't a dream because the detailz were so vivid. Usually when you dream, there's so many thingz goin' on — as if you're fast-forwarding a scene only picking up the detailz. This was different. Everything was flowing, minute-by-minute; second-for-second; moment-to-moment; just like it is when you're "awake."

I lay still on my left side on the same bed facing the same tv that now had no picture, just snow on the screen like when a channel is out. I was motionless not because I didn't want to move, I was shook 'cause I didn't know where I was, so naturally I was ready to be out! The thing was, I *couldn't* move!!

The figure continued to gently and quietly glide in my direction. You pretty much can sense danger and my radar was on high, and not only could I not move, as far as I knew I couldn't speak so I couldn't yell out anything...

Suddenly, the scene changed. Color had returned to my vision and I was back in Michelle's bedroom. Michelle was kneeling on the floor in front of the bed, hysterical! *"Jehvon, wake up!"* She was shaking as much as she was tryin' to shake me awake.

"I was layin' in my bed and somethin' told me to wake you up, NOW!", she said. I looked at her confused yet relieved because a flash of where I was came to mind.

I asked her to tell me again what happened. She was trembling with tearz rolling down her cheeks. *"I don't know what happened... I was asleep and a voice told me to come and wake you up! It told me to wake you up NOW!!"*

I shook my head puzzled; what the fuck is goin' on?! Y do I feel like it's *'A Nightmare on Elm Street'* and I can't go to sleep 'cause Freddy Kruger is waitin' in my dreamz?!!?

I tried to remain calm but I was scared, yo! I honestly didn't know what to do and because of examz, the last few weeks we been buildin' and the long bus ride here to Philly, I was madd tired and needed sleep! *"Now what am I gonna do?"* I pondered.

I tried to play it off tellin' Michelle I was alright — *knowin'* I wasn't — just so she could go back to sleep. I told her to go on back to bed and that I'd watch a lil' tv thinkin' the distraction may calm and assure me this is some 'make-believe' type shit.

She went back to her room, lookin' back at me. I knew that look, that was the look of *"yo, somethin' is about to happen!"* I didn't want her to be anymore scared than I was, so I assured her I was ok. I'll just watch some tv and everything will be ok.

I flipped through madd channelz that mainly showed either some type of violence, monster or demonic shit. *"Damn,"* I thought, *"I can't get a win tonight!!"*

The only show I found I could even consider light enuff was 'The Three Stooges'. Fighting sleep, I decided to sit up. But as the moments passed, I was soon laying on my side battling my heavy eyelidz. *Please... don't... fall... asleep...*

Moments later, I felt the rollercoaster ride again; swooping deeper and deeper down this dark tunnel, whirling through sudden and abrupt tight curves mixed with aggressive yet graceful turnz... I realized I was on my way back to that cave!

Like a sudden scene change in a movie, I was right back where I was before Michelle "awakened" me earlier. Everything was as it was before I "left". I could still hear the dripping water; still see the flickering flame dance on the rocky wall; and yes, I was laying in the same position, unable to speak nor move. All I could do is see... and... wait.

The crazy shit was that the figure that was approaching me before was still there, yo! Just like TiVo, he was in pause. And as soon as I realized he was here, it seemed like someone pressed "play" 'cause he started gliding towardz me again!

As said before, I was limited to only to a letterbox-kind of view, I could not see who or what the figure looked like, only that it was wearing a white oversized cloak and that it was moving gently towardz me. It was the kind of movement that was eerie, yo! It made you contemplate on what was about to happen and because it was walkin' — rather gliding — so slowly, it made my hair raise!

Sure enuff, my instincts were right. As the image glided to the point where it was now right in front of my face, it made a military left turn… I'm just sittin' there, yo, like dead meat!

Suddenly, with a quick move, *"SLAM!"* a pair of handz smacked the mattress right in front of my eyes… *"JEHVON, JEHVON, YOU GOTTA WAKE UP! WAKE UP NOW, JEHVON!!!"* Next thing you know, I'm seein' Michelle literally smackin' me silly in the face to wake up! I "came to" with a gasp of air as if I was under water down to my last ounce of breath.

As soon as I realized I was no longer in that cave and could move, I stood up in the bed and began jumping and shouting at the top of my lungz, *"You can't get me! You tryin' to fuck with me, but you can't kill me!! I know you tryin' to 'cause I'm on to somethin'! But you can't kill me!!"* I was so scared I had to say somethin'! I will say I didn't believe exactly what I was yellin' but I wanted whoever was listenin' — including whatever it was that slammed its handz on the bed — to hear me!

You gotta realize, I didn't know what was happenin'. From that point-on, I was literally afraid to close my eyes, even to blink! At the same tyme, I was so open, all the scary movies I ever saw was goin' through my head makin' me wonder if this shit is really real!

I wouldn't bow to this without a fight. So I shouted, hoping that would hype me up to conjure up the courage to believe this "thing" wasn't gonna get me.

After doin' this for about what seemed to be ten minutes or so, I started to calm down. Now I started to think…I was awake, or was I? *Where* was I and how was Michelle able to know I needed to "come back" at that moment?

As I reflected on what just happened I pictured the images' handz. It happened really quick; the handz slamming onto the bed, then I was "awake" lookin' at Michelle crying for me to wake up. But I remembered those handz…

Even though the setting was in black and white as I stated earlier, the handz seemed to be a deep, dark red, maybe burgundy. Even more ill was that the handz were very, very thick and muscular with short, sharp black clawz! *"Were these the handz of a demon or even the devil himself?"* I speculated. If you asked me, if it wasn't, it definitely was a relative!

This only added to my shouting in the air. At what, I had no idea, but it did give me a little more nerve to deal with the task at hand. Frankly, I was shook, Sun! What little hair I have on my back was standing upright, yo! I didn't know if this figure would just remain in that place, 'paused', waiting for me to "go back to sleep" — this tyme, right in front of me with its handz on the bed makin' it easy for it to grab me — or could it possibly materialize in this world and come after me while I'm "awake". I didn't know what to do, nor did I have anyone to talk or go to for guidance or protection…

"What do I do now?..."

I felt like I was down to the last moments of my life, fearing that this tyme that thing would be able to do whatever it wanted...

Chapter Ten: What Do I Do Now?

All I could think was, *"what do I do now?"* I was too afraid to go to sleep; I was too afraid to even think what I was gonna do next! Again, I felt like that deer in the middle of the road staring at the headlights before I'm hit.

Needless to say, I didn't go back to sleep that night. I was too wired up! All I could think was that I needed to speak to Nasir; he had to be the key! Afterall, he's been there since the day after I heard KRS-One speak and he's been fillin' my head up with all this shit, so he *had* to know somethin' about this! The problem was, it was our first night in Philly for springbreak and we were gonna be there a whole week! So I would have to survive the week before I could reach Nasir and at that point, I feared I wouldn't survive the night!!

Michelle and I spent the remainder of the night tryin' to figure out what was goin' on. I turned on the radio hoping it could lighten the mood and calm me down a bit. I remember thinkin' what she was sayin' to me when we were on the Greyhound on our way here, *"don't go to sleep, I need for you to protect me..."* Although I somewhat believed her before, there was a lil' doubt as I thought she might be loosin' it. But after what we just experienced, I was now a firm believer!!

I paced up and down the room thinkin' out loud. I was jumpin' from topic to topic, blurting out *"fuck you's"* and *"you can't get me!"*, then I'd jump to scannin' all the discussionz we all had over the past weeks. Before I knew it, a beam of sunlight broke through the window… it was morning.

I didn't feel any safer now that it was daylight but there was some comfort. Afterall, what killer strikes during the day? I wasn't at all sleepy — nor hungry for that matter. You gotta understand, I really thought this was some 'Freddy-Gruger-Nightmare-on-Elm-Street' type shit, B!

Michelle and I spent the day reasonin', tryin' to figure out what we were facing. Would it return tonight? Would it be in the same position I last saw it; with his handz placed firmly on the bed mattress right in front of my eyes? Would 'it' or somethin' else even come after Michelle? Afterall, she too experienced somethin' and it was some *thing* that told her to come down the hall and wake me up twice! Just thinkin' of that made me feel we weren't totally alone, but how much help could or would it grant us in case we were faced with this thing again?? We had a million-and-one questionz and not one answer or even a lead. So I had to resort to stayin' awake and not goin' to sleep.

I stayed up a total of three dayz before I was too weak to stay up. The first two, although I was still too shook to even think about bein' tired, I had to literally fight to stay awake. When I felt myself fallin' to sleep, the same rollercoasting-like feelin' would happen and I'd jump right up and try to occupy myself with somethin'. I mainly would turn on the radio or listen to cassette mixtape's I made to keep me up.

Instead of sleep, as a diversion, we tried doin' other thingz to take our mind off of what happened that Friday night. We chilled on South Street, went to the museum, parlay to some other spots downtown; shit like that. We made a point not to talk about it, nor do any reasoning — even though we were "jonesin'" to build. We tried to just be 'normal'; like everybody else, livin' life.

By Monday afternoon, the fatigue was settin' in; I needed sleep, but I was still too scared to close my eyes for more than a second. I felt like I was down to the last moments of my life, fearing that this tyme, because Michelle and I were more tired than before, that thing would be able to do whatever it wanted — which I believed was tryin' to kill me. But there was nothin' I could do. We didn't tell anybody, so there was no one to consult, I spent so much tyme bein' scared, I didn't think about the repercussionz of stayin' up and that eventually, I would succumb to the natural forces of sleep.

This tyme, Michelle lay next to me. I couldn't expect her to wake me up like she did last tyme 'cause her eyes were as bloodshot as mine. We were so tired, to the point where I no longer cared. *"Fuck it!"* I said to myself. *"If he gonna get me, then come and do it!"* Tryin' to syke myself up yawnin' in between thoughts.

The street lights were on, it was nighttyme. I had been listenin' to jazz musician Joe Sample over the past few weeks, so I threw him on along with some other deep tracks I made that was the kinda music we'd build on: some Sample, Mr. Fingers, Caron Wheeler, some undaground house and afrobeat tracks, shit like that. If I'ma go out, I'ma go out with beats and rhyme!!

We entered a spiritual marathon with absolutely no training nor clue of what it would take to partake in this experience…

Chapter Eleven: A Sleep Like No Other

I bullshit you not, we slept nearly 15 hourz, yo! And the plus side to it was that there was no 'demon', no Freddie and no 'Nightmare on Elm Street!' I woke up feelin' truly refreshed, and as soon as I realized nothin' happened and that Michelle and I were ok, it hit me! I figured out Y all this shit was happening! Like a subliminal fax from our Ancestorz, the reasoning made all the sense in the world!

I remember learnin' from our cypherz that life exists at least on three different planes: the mental, physical and spiritual planes. Knowin' this, I know all are diverse planes yet they interact with each other cohesively.

For instance, when we go out and play ball all day or go running, what eventually happenz? You become physically tired. What do you do then? You lie down and may eventually fall asleep. What happenz after you wake up from your sleep? You feel recharged. Just like your mp3 player or cell phone battery, when it's low, you have to plug it in to charge before you can use again. And although you don't have to have a full charge for it to work — or, in my case, get a full 8 hourz of sleep — you can get it to work, but nothin' beats a full charge! It's basically the less-discussed and misunderstood act of sleeping that allowz us to recharge. We've overlooked how little we know about this phenomenon.

Ponder this for a moment! We don't have to plug ourselves into a wall socket to regenerate power. Each tyme we sleep we plugg ourselves into the mysterious dominion of sleep!

We go through this cycle practically everyday ending each night in our bedz and rising the following morning with the energy needed to go about our day. Now… apply that to the spiritual realm.

Just like a long distance runner who buildz endurance with each training session, s/he get's stronger and is able to run farther and longer. See, we — Chop, Subeam, Missy, Michelle and I were just babies — sprinterz if you will, with no endurance at all. We entered a spiritual marathon with absolutely no training nor clue of what it would take to partake in this experience. Oh you may *look* good the first quarter of the race, but once you hit the wall… and that fatigue sets in due to improper training, you gonna *have* problemz, Sun! All we had was the raw will of sincere curiosity; wanting to *know* the *unknown*.

Yearz later, I was told by several Elderz that frankly this shit is no joke! People have literally lost their mindz and even their lives dealin' with Spirituality and Metaphysics. I wondered had I known this back then, would I still have chosen to walk this path…

What came to mind (the subliminal fax sent from the Ancestorz) simply relayed to me that I was vulnerable to this — what I now call 'entity' — because I was spiritually fatigued. Remember, for almost two months I had been buildin' consistently, day and night, since the night KRS-One bent my reality enuff to make me throw my bible in the trash. That alone was a blow to my spiritual foundation! And I really didn't take the tyme to analyze what I did, I just did it, went to sleep and the next dat met Nasir. Within those first 24-hourz I had done a 180-degree turn and the dayz following had been sort of a crash course in many of the other religionz and philosophies that existed.

I realized our spirit has a guard. Each night when you sleep, you "go" to a place other than the realm we know when we're awake (read *'Sleeperz'* piece later in this book). When falling to sleep, there is a transition from the physical realm to what's called "the non-physical realm" — where your body recharges while these "dreamz" allegedly occur. In this realm there's both positive and negative forces and I believe your spirit is protected from total interaction with these forces, which gives the illusion of it bein' a dream.

If your spiritual guard is fatigued, these entities or forces have the ability to interact with you on a higher (or lower) spiritual and energetic level. Perhaps you've had a 'dream' that seemz so real, you swore it was! Remember those 'fantasy' dreamz you had 'pon the height of your puberty? Bruthaz, remember how it felt so real, your physical body "reacted" in the form of an erection and sometymz even the remnants of a sexual act (discharge or ejaculation, also known as a 'wet dream')? Maybe you may have had what's called an out-of-body experience where you left your body and you saw yourself float or fly to anutha place. Of all the episodes that's been told, you may have heard of some bein' killed in their sleep.

Because we had been buildin' for so long with no guidance nor rest, both me and Michelle's spiritual guard were beyond the point of exhaustion; so much that we had been havin' spiritual encounterz both awake and 'asleep'! I started to realize we showed symptomz of spiritual exhaustion from reasonin' before we left for spring break, when we started beefin' at each other over small, petty reasonz. We were too naïve to know we really were just spiritually tired.

As soon as we returned to school that Sunday, I knew I had to meet Nasir. The problem was I didn't have a way to contact him. Whereas lately, before springbreak, I was beginning to look at duke like he was a cat I shouldn't fuck wit, I now waited in my dorm pacing, wondering how many dayz would pass 'til he called.

Outside of class and practice, I confined myself to my dorm, frontin' like I was studyin' — but how could I? I needed answerz, B! And I wasn't sure my unproven solution theory was the right way to deal with these encounterz or not. Y hadn't Nasir called?! Luckily, I was no longer sleep deprived havin' gotten proper rest each night since Sunday. I made sure I followed my newly found ritual of playin' music before I went to sleep and if I felt that rollercoaster-like feeling, I'd fight my way back to consciousness (in this realm) and quickly turn the music back on.

Still, I was jonesin', Sun! Neither of us had gotten together to build since before springbreak — and *that* was somethin' I both wanted and needed badly. As shook as I was, I still wanted to reason, and I couldn't shake the urge to want to know more!

Over the last couple nights before we left to come back to Pittsburgh, I simply had been preparing my thoughts so when I did eventually meet with Nasir, I wouldn't leave anything out. I backtracked to the first night with me hearin' KRS-One on up to that crazy night in Philly.

I made sure my temporary "cure" was precise so I could explain it fully to him. Because my spiritual guard had gotten too weak to protect me, I was approached by what appeared to be a negative entity. Neither of us possessed the endurance to continue building at the rate we were goin', so we were bound to experience some wild shit 'cause we weren't ready and quite frankly, not worthy! We were rookies, yo! Tryin' to play in the major leagues!

I realized, just like I train to run the 800 meterz in track, so must I train to be able to go deeper and deeper in the realm of metaphysics and KOS (Knowledge of Self). And no, my trainin' wasn't gonna be me runnin' any more miles than I had to for track! My trainin' would come mentally and spiritually; from reading (internal and external), discussionz, proper diet and rest, and most important — KNOWING WHEN TO STOP AND CHILL!

No one can train at anything everyday all day and not eventually develop some kind of problem or setback. This is what I experienced. That trip to Philly was when I was officially tapped out and because I exceeded my level of endurance, I was vulnerable to the natural law of repercussionz.

So knowing that I have a limit, I realize I can extend my limit simply by some form of paced-training. But there remained a question. How would I know when I've exceeded my limit? Further, what would I do if I already went past it? How would I protect myself and not experience a visit from this entity again?! I mean, I was lucky the first tyme with Michelle bein' there. What if it happened and she wasn't there?

I remembered one of the thingz that helped me calm down somewhat that night was that there was music playing. I didn't think much of it at the tyme, but it was starting to make sense to me. Because I was a music hed, somehow, my luv for music proved to actually be my savior!

It was music that was bein' played while we were buildin' about the 'unknown', shit. I was even "re-awakened" by a musician in KRS-One! I'm not a musician, but I did play the jhembe drum often as a youth. Music had always played a significant part in my life. Music was a way for me to reconnect and in this case, it brought balance, calming me and allowing me to evaluate what was happening to me… But I still needed to talk to Nasir.

You brought me into this shit! What tha fuck is happening?!

Chapter Twelve: No, Let Me Tell YOU What Happened!

Two nights later, that Tuesday at about 11:30, I'm pacin' my dorm, end-to-end wonderin' Y this cat ain't called yet. Suddenly, *"Ring, Ring!"* my phone goes off! I clumsily make a dive for it, fumbling with the receiver while at the same tyme findin' myself entangled with the cord. *"Yo, who dis?"* I blurted out, hopin' whoever it was didn't hear any of the commotion. *"It's Nasir, I'm downstairz..."* My heart started thumpin', *"I'll be right down,"* I countered, simultaneously puttin' some boots and a coat on.

I lived on the fourth-floor, so instead of waiting for the elevator, I literally ran, jumped *(and fell)* down to the main floor; I didn't care who saw, I was focused on seein' him and tellin' him what happened to me.

I reached the main lobby and walked outside, he was to the left where the benches were. Surprisingly, it was moderately warm, enuff for me to take off my coat.

He had on an army fatigued hoody on top of his usual Ansaar-dress. He looked real calm, too calm, as though he had come to tell me somethin'. No sooner that I opened the glass doorz did I yell out, *"Yo, I gotta talk to you! Somethin' hap..."* He interrupted, *"hold up, I know somethin' happened to you. Sit down and I'll tell you what I know."*

I sealed my lips closed, still a little confused about what was about to transpire. He stood up in front of me as I sat down. *"I know somethin' happened to you recently,"* he said calmly. I looked puzzled, *"And I'm gonna tell YOU what happened,"* he reiterated. I'm still lookin' at him like, *"what da f... is he talkin' 'bout?!"* Immediately, I started havin' regrets for meetin' with him. Afterall, following that episode downtown during their prayer, I was done with him. Y was I meetin' with him now??

"You were in a cave the other night, right?" He blurted out like he could sense my interest fading. Suddenly gettin' my attention, I looked toward him and screamed defensively, *"What?!!?"* I had a flashback to the day I met him. It was the same kind of vybe I felt when he said he heard I threw away my bible the night before. He had my undivided attention now. I knew this was the discussion I was waitin' to have with

him since Philly!

He went on, *"you were inside a cave, right?"* I said, *"yeah..." "the setting wasn't in color, it was black and white like an old picture movie, right?" "Yeah!"* I replied now sittin' on the edge of the bench. *"Was there somethin' approaching you?"* I jumped off the bench, *"Yo!"* I was becomin' hysterical, and I started walkin' up and down the length of the bench — just like I did in my dorm holdin' my bible that night after I heard KRS-One's lecture.

"This thing was floatin' towardz me, yo! Michelle woke me up, I fell asleep again and he was still there!" I was now shoutin' not carin' if any of the students walkin' by heard me. *"Yo, you brought me into this shit! What tha fuck is happening?!"*

He told me to calm down and sit. I'll admit, it wasn't easy for me to 'cause I was seein' him as the reason for my troubles. I wanted to lash out on him, but that wouldn't give me the answerz I needed, so I decided to chill. Breathing heavy, voice cracking and tearz flowin' down my face, I pleaded with him, *"Tell me. How do you know this? What's happening to me? I'm afraid to sleep, I'm afraid to build. This shit don't seem real!"*

"It is real, brutha," he explained. He went on to tell me, *"I know this is real because I experienced the same thing only it was my girlfriend who was approached, not me."* He explained to me there was this demon — whose name he told me but I've since forgotten — who came to his girlfriend and killed her in her sleep!

"What?!!?" I blurted out! *"Wha'chu mean, she was killed in her sleep?!"* He then went on to tell me verbatim, step-by-step how he had had the same "dream", seein' her inside this cave with something in a white cloak gliding slowly towardz her as she lay on a bed unable to move. That "thing" then slammed his handz on the bed and quickly grabbed her by her throat and choked her until she was lifeless.

I looked at him as he had a blank stare into the night's sky. He was calm, but I could tell he was still deeply saddened and even scared himself. I wondered Y that thing didn't come after him, afterall, he saw the whole thing. He couldn't explain it either. He, too, was unable to move and all he could do was watch. When he "woke up", he realized his girlfriend, who was layin' beside him, had no pulse. She was *really* dead!

I felt for him, but was even more scared for myself! I feared this "thing" would someday come back for me and try and finish the job! If Michelle wasn't there back in Philly… I wouldn't be here right now!

I was starting to hyperventilate. My mind was scanning. I became uncertain how long my temporary solution would hold off this thing from eventually gettin' me. What was I gonna do? I needed answerz. I totally forgot to ask him how and Y he knew what happened to me, and quite frankly, it didn't matter. My focus was now on how to survive this and remain alive! Then I remembered I did come up with at least a temporary solution!

I told Nasir what I did that has allowed me to sleep since that night. I explained to him one needz to build up their spiritual endurance when dealin' with this shit, 'cause if you exhaust yourself, this shit can happen, and so far, it was music that makes this entity go away. I tried to make light of the situation, tellin' him I guess, in this case, music *can* soothe the savage beast. I was laughin', but it wasn't your average laugh, I was terrified, yo! I told him I believed as long as I didn't cross my limit "It" can't get me…

He told me he has yet to have been approached by this entity and doesn't feel he ever would. He just couldn't figure out Y he was there to witness his girlfriend die. After that night, I never spoke to him again…

I will never forget this brutha, and although our acquaintance was but for a season, I couldn't have asked for a better usher or head start onto the road of 'knowledge of self'.

If you have not trained to obtain a certain level of endurance, in some way you will be tested and I believe if you are not worthy... well, let's just say there are repercussionz to that.

Chapter Thirteen: When I Am Strong Enuff, I Will Be Able To Face It

Not that every entity that exists will hurt you, which you will read about in the chapter, *'Soul Traveler'*, but if you have not trained to obtain a certain level of endurance — which is tallied by hourz, dayz weeks and even yearz of study — in some way you will be tested and I believe if you are not worthy... well, let's just say there are repercussionz to that.

We were babies at that tyme, fresh out the incubator! We didn't know what spirit's we were conjuring up as we posed question after question. It's like we didn't have an advisor or a curriculum to follow, we were pretty much alone which meant we had no idea whatsoever what we were dealin' with!

Since that season I have used my temporary solution of playin' music and it still is effective, however, I know I'm only delayin' the inevitable… I must face it.

Havin' never forgotten what happened, I never told anyone until I decided to write ***'Analitkikul'***. More importantly, I started writing ***'Déjà vu'*** about seven yearz ago and even though it's taken me this long to write this book, there was reason behind it. I simply did not have the courage to write it.

Basically, I feared if I wrote about it, hedz would think I was off my rocker! Moreover, I felt writing about it would give the spirit of this entity the energy it needed eventually enabling it to kill me. Afterall, I really had no one I felt I could bring this up to. I thought I was alone and therefore no one could protect me, much less overstand my ordeal.

I have alwayz been a firm believer in thingz happening in 'divine tyme'. Over the yearz, as I mentally and spiritually grew, I felt my soul begin to travel. My writing style started to take on topics other than joints on global white supremacy and conspiraceez.

Up 'til this point I mainly wrote about conspiraceez. Topics like the Boule', the Illuminati and Masonz usually graced the pages of each edition of DGT. But now my style elevated to an esoteric level. Following my 2002 piece, *'The God Complex'*, I wrote *'What Frequency R U On?'*. It turned into a series of other pieces *['Free-*

Quencies of Tyme,' 'Free-Quenceez of Tyme, Pt.2: The Art of Travel', 'Free-Quenceez of Tyme, Pt.3: The Star of A Story,' 'Degreez of Separation', 'Evolution? or Nebulution!', 'Recharging the Revolution', 'A Revived Vybration', and *'Sleeperz'* (as of December 2006)]. Also, I created one of my favorite three-part lecture series, *"Afrikan Spirituality: The Microcozm of the Macrocozm"*.

This new thought I came into — what's been dubbed 'Alternative Thought' — got me back into Spirituality and Metaphysics, which is how I came into all this in the first place! I felt like I had come full circle and was now gettin' ready to embark on a journey that would take me on a whole new level. The will to write this book became one of the most paramount thingz I needed to do in my earthlife!

I started writing less and less about conspiraceez and more about spirituality...

Chapter Fourteen: Soul Traveler

Over the past fifteen or so yearz, I have continued to have these mysterious encounterz when trying to sleep and it was not until a dear friend of mine invited me to see it from a different perspective.

Since 1991, any tyme I would feel that now infamous rollercoaster kinda feeling, it reminded me of what happened that night in Philly. I was convinced that demon was still there paused; standing there waiting for me. I promised myself I'd never give it the chance.

This 'feeling' only happened when I was spiritually fatigued mainly from writing, editing, designing the next edition of DGT or the website or after I did a lecture. I had come to believe that I had it under control knowing what to do whenever that feeling came along. For yearz, I just accepted it and prepared myself to live with it for perhaps the rest of my life. Then one evening in 2003 I was politicin' with my friend.

I've alwayz been a fan of astronomy and space believing there *has* to be somethin' more than what we know here on earth. My friend let me borrow this book written by Dr. Albert Taylor called, '*Soul Traveler'*. She recommended it 'cause I had told her about my experience in Philly. She suggested this book a must read, so I basically engulfed it like it was my last meal!

I must admit, I'm really not good at borrowing books. She didn't give me the book to have, but to read. I have this habit of takin' notes inside books, so I actually ended up writing and highlighting notes throughout the book. Sorry Chelsie… I know I still owe you a new copy!

See, all these yearz, I had spent my tyme makin' sure I learned as much about the unknown by knowin' the known (Correspondence), yet I wouldn't go as far as tryin' to understand Y I was scared to deal with this "entity" whenever I was spiritually exhausted.

After readin' Taylor's book, it made me think of a movie that was made not too long ago. In 1993, Universal Pictures put out the movie *Dragon: The Bruce Lee Story*, a movie about the life of Bruce Lee. Legend has it Bruce had numerous spiritual encounterz and that it was possible a spirit from his dreamz actually killed him and not the other numerous and unproven wayz, makin' the official determination of his death still a mystery.

There were several scenes in the movie where he had encounterz with this omnipotent Shogun warrior. In the beginning of the movie, this warrior emerged in Lee's father's dream when Bruce was a child. This warrior did not speak, however, his actionz were clearly evident he came to fight. The challenge was toward his father with the prize bein' he'd possibly kill little Bruce. The problem was Bruce's father was not a fighter. And because he chose not to confront this spiritual encounter, the warrior promised to haunt Bruce. This, of course worried Bruce's father. So he took little Bruce to be taught by a Master Martial Arts teacher. Hence, the legend of Bruce Lee was born.

According to the movie, it wasn't until Bruce had his own son, Brandon (who's also believed to have died a mysterious death although it's documented as him being shot by a prop-gun with real bullet's on the set of his movie, *The Crows,* also in 1993) that he started to have encounterz with this Shogun himself.

Right after seeing this movie, I felt it spoke to me. But today, I *now* believe that was the day I was sent into an even deeper spell of Hell-y-wood. To this day, when I'm spiritually fatigued and experience that rollercoaster-like feelin' I can feel myself elongate, like I'm bein' vertically stretched or like my soulz bein' stripped from my body like how a sticky piece of candy clingz on to a candy wrapper. I'd frantically fight to reconnect with my body by tryin' to close my mouth which would feel like it was wide open due to me bein' stretched and pulled into this roller-coaster vortex.

Each tyme, it's a struggle to 'wake up' 'cause I could feel myself bein' between two dimensionz, half sleep-half awake. I would struggle to close my mouth which helped bring myself back together so I can reconnect and wake up.

Other tymz when I'm able to catch it before I'm too into my sleep, it would feel like I was floating and suddenly did a nose-dive a couple hundred feet, evened out, floated a little, then did anutha dive! This was that roller-coasting feeling! When I was aware, or not too into my sleep; enuff to not go through too many nose-dives, I'd jump right out of bed and turn on some music. After a couple hourz, I'm good!

Since the start of writing ***Analitikul*** and particularly ***Déjà vu***, I've had an increase of these episodes. Before, whenever this would happen, I'd be too scared to continue writing so I'd shelf my book and come back to it after a while. But since reading *Soul Traveler,* I realize this book had to be written no matter what, because writing this could possibly free me.

I've been' livin' this ever since 1991, but I now realize I can't live my life in fear. Back in 2003, I realized I needed to confront this entity, but realized it would take some training. I believe thingz happen at the right tyme and if you ask "*then you shall find.*"

Like many, I have been influenced by a series of movies, books and speakerz over the yearz. The movies *Contact* (1997), *Mission to Mars* (2000); books *Ancient*

Future, The Kybalion, The Alchemist, Parable of the Sower and authorz Anthony T. Browder and Wayne Chandler to name a few.

As I said, 2003 was a pivotal breakout year for me 'cause my writingz started to change. I started writing less and less about conspiraceez and more about spiritual shit. The thing was, this was different. The conspiracy shit I had to do major research on — attend lectures, listen to audio and videotape, read transcripts, books, the whole nine; but the spiritual pieces just flowed!

One of the major reasonz for this was because I started askin' those very seldom heard questionz again. My quest of questionz re-emerged after visiting the Hayden Planetarium in New York City, late October of 2002. They had a state-of-the-art, fifteen-minute three-dimensional mapping digital sky screen exhibit from the solar neighborhood to the grand structure of the universe entitled, *"Passport to the Universe"* narrated by actor Tom Hanks.

After the first tyme I went, I walked out dazed, yo! One part in particular was responsible for the birth of my whole *"Microcozm of the Macrocozm"* lecture series. I learned about Nebula's and how much they resemble, macrocozmically, the birth of human beingz.

See, a Nebula is a combination of dust and ice. Starz are actually born from Nebula's. The Starz that are born from a Nebula looked to me like sperm. Suddenly, because of the panoramic view of the planetarium, it looked like we were inside the Nebula and it made me think of us bein' inside a womb where fetus' (or Starz) are born!

Starz give birth to planets via explosionz and implosionz and makes these planets rotate the Star because of its gravitational pull; and planets? Well, let's just say Earth can't be the only place in the poly-verse that holdz life as we know it. To think that severely limits the comprehension of 'Correpsondence'.

That first tyme, after leavin' the Planetarium, I was just walking. I was literally on some outer space shit, yo! I was sort of here, but not here. My daze led me out of the buildin' and over to the adjacent park which happened to be Central Park. I didn't have a destination; I was just walkin' really feelin' connected to the stratosphere. I was lookin' up then, *"wham!"* I bumped into a sign. It was a Central Park map. My eyes gazed to the center of the map. Next to the wordz, 'The Great Lawn', I saw 'Obelisk'.

Was this the obelisk I heard about yearz before in one of Tony Browder's lectures? Was this one of the artifacts that was stolen from Kemet, dragged down 5th Avenue by masonz and erected in the middle of New York City's Central Park?!

I followed the map walkin' through 'The Great Lawn'; I couldn't see it. All I could see was madd treez. Then a gust of wind went before me and I looked up and at the top of the treez swayin' left from the wind and saw some kind of structure with a pointy top. *"Is that it?"* I thought to myself.

I ran towardz the structure. I had to go around a-round-about and as the dirt road curved left, I got my first glimpse of the obelisk, or the correct name, tekhen. I was floored, B! This was the first ancient relic I could actually see and touch that was from Afrika!! I was havin' a mini-conniption thinkin' *"first the planetarium, now this?!"*

Watch this Video Article (VA), *'Secret In the City'* on my .tv site, DGTv: Conscious Webvision @ *www.daghettotymz.com/dgtv/videoarticles2.html*

The tekhen was sittin' there 'up in the cut' hidden from the surrounding treez. I walked up the steps brushin' the tree branches away from my view. It was standing there, so peaceful, almost too peaceful, as if it was there hidden rather than out for all to see like it should be.

I walked up to it, climbed over the surrounding metal fence and climbed the first layer. Standin' on my toes, I placed both my palmz on its side. Man! The feelin' was so dope! I was feelin' the very stone our Ancestorz built! Two of the sides still had readable Medu-Neter, or heirglyphs on it. The other two sides had eroded from the tekhen once havin' fallen from what's been said an earthquake leavin' it to lay on its side for several hundred yearz (you can see the Video Article I did on it on my website DGTv: Conscious Webvision. The piece is called, *"Secret In The City"* [www.daghettotymz.com/dgtv/videoarticles2.html]. I was overwhelmed, eyes all watery and shit, 'cause, again, this was the closest thing to ancient Afrika I ever felt!

Goin' to the planetarium and then to the tekhen became my monthly ritual keepin' me connected with thingz that are bigger than global white supremacy! This, of course, helped me see that the period we are livin' in now is but a centimeter on the tymelined ruler of life.

The astral body is just that, a vehicle for the astral plane. But in order to transition beyond the first level, I would need to shed yet another outer shell...

- Albert Taylor, Soul Traveler

Chapter Fifteen: Styles Upon Styles

Now after bein' exposed to Dr. Taylor's book a couple month's later, I realized that all these yearz of bein' afraid to fully experience this roller-coaster ride feelin' and possibly bein' confronted by this entity, I may have been lied to by both Hell-y-wood *and* Nasir. Taylor pointed out, *"...[P]rior to traveling and during soul travel,* (remember) *that you are a being of light and nothing can harm you unless you think it can. Even then, after the experience you will emerge unblemished."* He went on to say, *"I have found that my worst enemy during out-of-body experiences is my own uncontrolled imagination. I have learned that whatever I imagine — devils, demons, or pink elephants — will be created instantly." "...[I]t is important not to prejudge or guess what is going to happen, because you might be the one creating it."*

When I read that, all I could think of was my encounterz. As real as I thought it felt and because of all the buildin' we did on dam near everything, perhaps my thoughts sparked and have continued to give this "entity" life? What if, when I felt the roller-coaster feeling comin', I thought of somethin' positive? What would my encounter be like then?

Dwellin' on this newfound perspective on life made me realize the thing I feared most probably wasn't anything to fear at all. But I wasn't fully convinced. Besides, Nasir tellin' me this is how his girlfriend died made it even harder to see it differently.

When I play back what went down that night in Illadelph (Philly), I remember how shook I felt layin' there on the bed unable to move. I remember that thing floatin' towardz me. Yeah, I know we was all tired and whatnot from buildin', which could've contributed to me bein' so open.

To this day I try to trick myself into thinkin' the muscularly-clawed bein' that slammed its handz on the bed before Michelle woke me up, was actually a peaceful and even perhaps funny bein, like, say, Mr. Rogers... or even Mudfoot from Fat Albert.

I admit, because of how real it felt back in Philly, it's been a challenge to believe I thought all this up. I mean, in order for me to know if this is true or not, I'd have to let myself go entirely through this experience; meanin' I'd have to take what seemed to be a treachorous and possibly life-ending ride down that roller-coaster again, and if Dr. Taylor is wrong, I could be at the mercy of this entity!

The most important thing I know I must continue to be is humble to the Djhuitic law, Cause and Effect. Before I could consider any kind of revisit, I'd have to be able to control my movement as well as defend myself in any way in case this thing did try to kill me.

I need to know more before I can even think about facing my fate…

Dreams are the language of the soul, and because we dream every night, it is important we learn this language!

—Ruth Montgomery

Chapter Sixteen: Facing My Fate

Some may ask, Y even feel the need to face it? I seemed to have been able to manage since 1991, so Y take that chance now? The reason goes back to the Planetarium. There's so much more "out there" than we know. Although we might find it hard to come by textbooks or classes that deal with this shit, it doesn't mean it doesn't come 'cross the mind as do all the other questionz, like "how did we get here?"

We are a microcozm — or smaller thing — of a bigger — or macrocozmic — thing and bein'that we are part of it, it's only natural to be curious. The challenge is if you're willing to satisfy this curiosity. If I chose not to further investigate Y this shit happenz to me everytyme I get spiritually tired, I could be missin' out on somethin' beautiful! And I don't think I could live a full life not tryin'. I can face it willingly or perhaps be forced to confront it when my earth tyme is up.

Ruth Montgomery's quote couldn't have made more sense to me now. I now felt compelled to deal with this. Before I read Dr. Taylor's book, I felt there was no one I could talk to about my experience. Further, I wasn't about to give anyone the notion I needed to be locked up somewhere!

In addition, I thought about that Bruce Lee movie. I didn't want my unborn children to inherit somethin' I was too scared to face. I feel if you're exposed to somethin', now you know and you cain't act like you don't. There's some responsibility hedz don't wanna accept, but I feel there are actionz, better yet, repercussionz once you know.

Dr. Taylor's wordz became the literal guide to the path I've been on now to finally face what happenz after this roller-coaster-like feeling. That entity may *still* be there waiting and if so, I'm sure *somethin'* will happen! The question is, will it be positive or negative?

Like Bruce had to face his spiritual entity, eventually, so must I (and for those that share anything similar, you may too!). But I am not goin' in a rookie like I did the first tyme. I'm pacing myself. I'm gonna build my endurance mile-by-mile.

Of course, I'm not one-hundred percent convinced this'll work. Thinkin' positive thoughts when that roller-coaster feeling comes isn't as easy as it soundz. Over the past few yearz, I have been trainin' myself to think this way whenever I'm spiritually drained. To date, I've yet to completely let go and ride this roller-coaster to wherever it leadz, although I've been close. I let the ride go a little more each tyme. I feel with proper training, humility and focus, one day I will be ready to go the distance.

The more I read Dr. Taylor's book, the more I felt I wasn't alone. He wrote, *"Another peculiar thing that happened during sleep is what I used to call "waking up in my dreams." Although sound asleep, I became cognizant that I was dreaming or at least aware of what I thought was a dream. Scientific and metaphysical circles refer to this as "lucid dreaming."* When I read this, I was like, *"YO! This is what happened to me!!"*

He went on, *"After waking up in my dream, I had the ability to change the dream!"* This is when I realized that perhaps, there's a slight chance I have been scaring myself out of what could actually be a positive experience. The last sentence in his introductory Taylor wrote, *"I soon learned that fear would be the bars in a prison of my own creation. If I wanted to soul travel, I would have to break free of that prison. Only then could I explore the limitless world beyond the constraints of everyday life."* ***Déjà vu*** *had* to be written and more importantly, I had to begin preparation for one day facin' whatever lies waiting for me in my "sleep".

This is one of a couple books you'll hear me champion over and over again, this book has proven to be a vital piece in my now spiritual quest. Of the many parts of the book I felt spoke directly to me, one particular was how he handled an encounter, *"...[S]uddenly I could see, but my physical eyes were not open. I noticed an eerie, nondirectional lighting radiating inside our bedroom. There was also an intermittent, high-volume buzzing sound. I thought to myself, "Is this it?" I decided to get up physically, but I could not move an inch! I was paralyzed!... Without warning, a humanoid shape appeared about eighteen inches away from me. Startled, I mentally told it to move away. It did not respond, though it did become increasingly transparent. I panicked! I began moaning, hoping that my wife would wake me up, which she did. I noticed that the lighting in the room changed as I reconnected with my body.*

After waking, I told my wife about the ghostly apparition. She said I had not moved physically, and when she nudged me awake, my head was approximately nine inches from the headboard.

Thinking about it afterward, I decided I hadn't exactly been afraid of the figure near me. I think that the buzzing sound, the lighting, floating into the air, the paralysis, and finally the figure had all overwhelmed me... Did I astral project out of the top of my head?"

I later learned there's somethin' called the 'crown chakra' which is at the top of the head in Paramahansa Yogananda's book, *'Autobiography of a Yogi'*, Dr. Taylor may not have been shook, but when that shit happened to me, I sure was!!

Taylor's book proved to be more of a connection than just an interesting read. Readin' it made me realize what I have been experiencing is not original and that there are otherz who've had similar encounterz. To not only learn this but to also read another personz experience removed all fear I had before in tellin' otherz.

Most importantly, this book served as a crossroadz for me. For as long as I feared havin' to face that roller-coaster feeling again, I would never know. Even though the quest of learnin' had become my life's work, I took numerous precautionz makin' sure I was never too spiritually tired that I was vulnerable to these "visits". Taylor wrote, *"...[F]ear became a prison of my own creation. I believe the majority of my fearful reactions stem from having grown up conditioned by controlling religious beliefs. My Catholic upbringing primarily taught fear rather than love and faith. I always thought that something nonphysical and intelligent had to be evil! Boy, was I wrong."*

Now, I wasn't brought up in the church, but I still fell victim to the various religious brainwash mechanismz perpetuated by this society. I began to wonder maybe that thing out to get me; maybe it is... but how would I ever know if I remain afraid of it? Perhaps of what I've been blessed to learn over the yearz about our legacy, consciousness and spirituality, I've stunted my growth because of my fear to face this entity?

At the same tyme, there's the notion that everything happenz in divine tyme. Perhaps I was s'posed to "stay away" to learn what I've learned now. Maybe Chelsie introducing me to Dr. Taylor's work was a part of that divine order. This could conceivably be the tyme for me to prepare myself to finally confront whatever this thingz to be.

As eager as I am to do it, I realize I must prepare myself — remember the sprinter who wants to run a marathon? As I mentioned, I'm a space nut! I luv any and everything about astronomy and space. I often go to the Planetarium and watch worthy movies about space [not that Star Trek bullshit, although they did have several episodes where they talked about antimatter a lot (somethin' I'll get into later)].

I mentioned two of my all-tyme classic movies are *Contact*, which starred Jodi Foster and Don Cheadle starred in the other one, *Mission to Mars*. In Mission to Mars, one of the most profound phrases said was, an astronaut's quest should be to *"stand on the edge of a new world looking at the next."* My personal translation meanz it's tyme I leave my comfort zone, if you will, and open myself up to what else is out there both physically and in this case, non-physically!

These encounterz were not new to me. I have vivid memories from when I was as little as 3 and 4 yearz old. Although I had two sisterz who shared a room, I had alwayz had my own, so you can imagine how big a room can be to a toddler. It would sometymz scare the shit outta me because I thought the room was too big and I'd sorta have panic attacks.

I remember often literally jumping outside myself, pannin' out like a movie camera does. I would pan out so far, I could see myself lying in my bed. I would panic and then suddenly swoop back into myself. I'd open my eyes, feel my heart racing, hear this very high-pitch sound — so high it sounded faint — and begin crying. My mom could tell you I was a cry baby when I was little, but it was because of that room and the experiences I had in it! I thought it was haunted, yo!

One night, I jumped outside myself and was floating a couple feet above where my physical body was lying. Something had gotten my attention floating in the top corner of the room. It was a small tiny figure. Although it was so tiny the naked eye could not see the detailz of this figure, I could see it clearly and I knew who it was. I was about 4 yearz old, so I had never really been nor could comprehend church (I was lucky my family wasn't into it that much) and knew very little about God or any man-made religion.

Not really knowing any concept of God, I knew it *was* God, but in the form of a man. Lookin' back I can say the deep thing about YTs brainwashing mechanizm is even at age 4, havin' not much exposure to religion, I pictured 'God' as a white man; kind of like the experiment where Black kidz chose white baby dollz instead of black ones. I also must remind you that this was in the mid-1970s, so the concept of a Black Jesus wasn't popular as of yet.

This lilly-white, stringy-haired white man peacefully stood there, floating in the corner across the room from where I was floating with his armz stretch out and palmz turned up as if he was gesturing for a hug. It was real peaceful for a minute as we both sorta stared at each other. Then I suddenly heard a loud siren-like noise which startled me. I looked around, 'God' was gone! I started to cry and next thing you know I was back in my bed lookin' up at the ceiling, the siren noise stopped and still no sign of 'God'. It was so quiet, you could hear that very dim, yet high-pitch tone. I remember hearin' this pitch everytyme I awaken from these encounterz. To date, I still don't know what it meanz, but I'm sure it has some significance. Perhaps if and when I am worthy, it will be revealed to me.

Dr. Taylor discovered that you can control these encounterz. If you invite fear into your 'dreamz', thingz that scare you will manifest. Since then, I've gotten good at blankin' out some fearz, but have yet to master it. One thing I did learn was that I would have to go through this alone and back then, I wasn't confident enuff to tell anybody about this.

This takes me back to some of the cypherz I had with my professor, Rob Penny, a well-respected Pan-Afrikan poet who would later introduce me to Garveyizm. In addition to buildin' with Nasir, Michelle and I often visited Rob during his off hourz.

He was one of those cool Elderz, one of the few I really felt was spiritual in the whole Black Studies department. A short man with vibrant grey locks who possessed one of the coolest, calm and collected voices. I remember he used to alwayz wear a button on his shirt that was of Marcus Garvey. No matter what he wore, everyday, he would put that button on the shirt he would wear for the day. I didn't know much about Garvey then, but as I became more aware, I was glad it was Rob who introduced me to him.

Rob was very sarcastic and was as much a good listener as he was a speaker. He would let me rant and rave about the Ansaarz and their knowledge and all he'd do is propose questionz with a wise smirk; questionz he knew I did not have answerz for, which made me feel compelled to study more and speak less until I knew what I knew. He was a father figure I never had, for I wanted Rob to see my progression into Pan-Afrikan consciousness.

I continued to visit Rob even after I was out of college. It wasn't like there was this job waitin' for me, and my rebellion to society was growin' everyday. I had a small gig workin' for NASA's (National Aeronautics and Space Administration) Education department at Pitt, so I was still on campus a lot so I would go by Rob's office.

I remember one tyme we were reasoning about how otherz may take what I've grown to embrace. He told me the first people who will doubt you will be your friendz and family. He said that this is the test to see if you have perseverance to continue your quest alone. Rob was so deep 'cause he never rebutted what you "thought" you knew. He simply proposed questionz that eventually led to you answering some of yourz on your own.

I remember for one of my final examz in college I wrote my first paper about consciousness. It was entitled, *Quest for an Afrocentric Society; Society, an Afrocentric Quest,* for one of Rob's Black Studies courses.

Although the 13 page paper was heavily based with Dr. Malachi York's Ansaar rhetoric, Rob gave me an "A-" and wrote at the top of the cover page, *"You're close and almost home!"* I asked him what he meant by this. He explained to me the information I was using was not Afrikan but muslim-based. At the tyme, I thought he was crazy. I had about six of Dr. York's books under my belt and I let my youthful arrogance get the better of me. I would realize a short tyme later after reading Chancellor Williams, *'Destruction of Black Civilization'* and watching lecture videos of Dr. Yosef ben-Jochannan and Dr. John Henrik Clarke, just how wrong I was. I look back at that and realized, as with every other religion I sampled, they were levelz that would lead me home to Pan-Afrikanizm!

That paper was my first crack at really writing. Throughout high school and college I received "D's" and even "F's". I was even told by one of my college professorz in my Freshmen General Writing class that I should probably never think about becoming a writer. I later realized it wasn't that I *couldn't* write, I just didn't like the writing style these corny white professorz wanted me to write like. Not that I wrote how I write now in my magazine with ebonic spellingz and 'z's at the end of wordz. I was actually quite the speller, it was just a challenge writing wordz together to explain my thoughts. Besides, I come from an all Black neighborhood, havin' lived with my people all my life, so my expression was through Black talk and it is this dialect that is often not welcomed in the world of academia.

Anywayz, I was extremely proud of my 'A-' I earned, even more so of the content, for it was a theology in development. I brought my paper home during the summer break anxious for my mother to read it. I wanted everyone in my family to read it 'cause I believed it was info they may have never heard and would automatically gravitate to it like I did.

It was a hot early afternoon in June. My mother was sittin' in the back yard catchin' some Ra (sun). *"Opportune tyme,"* I thought, so I went and got my paper and brought it to her. *"Mom, here's a paper I wrote that has changed my life. I'd like you to read it,"* handing it to her proudly. She took it, lookin' at it with an unsure look. I told her I was gonna get somethin' to drink and that I'd be right back — I was ready to be on site to answer any questionz she may have had.

A couple minutes later, I returned puzzled to see my mom lying back in the chair with her eye's closed. I looked for my paper, it was on the table next to her, closed. I wondered if she even read *some* of it. I asked her fairly disappointed, *"so, what did you think?"* She replied, *"Your father used to be into that shit and look at him now. All he does is drive a bus!"* I overstood what she meant. She never, ever talked bad about him to us, but I could feel the rage of him leavin' us at the age of five or six, left to starve; never paying child support even after the court ordered him to (I cram to understand to this day Y they didn't garnish his wages); replacing me and my sisterz with anutha family of two girlz and a son who was named after him (which hurt me dearly); all the while living a mere fifteen minutes away from us.

Her reply felt like she just shut me down. I would soon learn to realize that in the realm of building a higher self, you must not be afraid to travel this road alone. Your loved one's may not feel you and the test will be in order to maintain your focus (which I later coined the acronym **FOCUS** - **F**rom **O**neself **C**omes **U**ltimate **S**acrifice), you may have to travel it alone.

My momz rejection would serve as a growing determination to show, any and everyone who dare test we, wrong. I was 21 and going through a lot of changes, so I can understand her thinkin' this may be a fad with me. Today, I am happy to say after yearz of dedicated and consistent focus, my mother is open to some of the thingz I share with her. I love you for that momz!!

There's no such thing as a black greek!

Chapter Seventeen: The Greek Myth

A lot had happened my junior and senior year. After all this shit I was exposed to a couple months. Later that fall I pledged Alpha Phi Alpha Fraternity, Inc. Some seven yearz later proved critical in placin' me on a path of controversy you may have heard of when my name or DGT is mentioned. If you haven't heard, you're about to find out.

When I was a youth, I remember seeing a group of black men in suits that were responsible for creating a community housing project that developed new apartments for families in the hood. My cousin and his dad were one of the families who were movin' in.

I didn't have too many positive images of black men in my life so seein' these bruthaz was like lookin' at God! I found out they were memberz of some fraternity called Alpha Phi Alpha. Not knowin' what a frat even was, I swore one day I'd be one.

Fast forward to my high school yearz, I was invited by anutha uncle of mine to go to a weekend cookout with his sonz. We were all close and my uncle assured me there'd be plenty of tyme to play basketball and swimming. What kid could say no to that? See, this uncle was my fatherz older brutha and he did whatever he could to be some kind of male presence in my life since my real father abandoned us.

I alwayz liked visiting my uncle and my cousinz. In my eyes they were rich, but were probably upper-middle class. I often envied my cousinz, havin' both parent's most importantly a father that invested quality tyme with in his sonz. Plus, it didn't hurt that they had thingz we couldn't afford like a basketball court in the backyard, Atari, Commodore64, Coleco Vision and Nintendo! Other than my other first-cousin on my momz side, these were the only "bruthaz" I had growin' up… and all I needed.

So we go on this weekend trip and I find out it was an Alpha regional conference and my uncle's a member of the graduate chapter. I was so excited because before then I really hadn't thought of pledging Alpha, nor attending college for that matter. After that weekend, I tried to find out as much as I could about Alpha from my uncle.

I felt like an Alpha Legend — which is someone who's a son of an Alpha, even though I wasn't. By my junior year, I was already doin' steps in high school talent showz and even came to college my freshman year stepping!

I didn't do it to disrespect anyone. I later learned you were not "allowed" to step unless you were in a frat. The bad thing was when I attended the University of Pittsburgh in the fall of 1988, Pitt's chapter — one of A-Phi-A's oldest chapterz, Omicron — *'Bloody O'* as hedz called it, had their chapter suspended indefinitely with no date of bein' reinstated! I was vexed!! I wanted to be an Alpha and by the second semester of my freshman year, everyone knew it.

Although the chapter was suspended, there were still a few Alpha's on campus. There were two I got real cool with and a third was more of a moody bitch who once told Michelle he didn't like me *"just because."* That's that old mind trick, wanna-get-you-to-swing-on-my-nuts-if-you-wanna-be-frat shit!

This cat was hypocritical 'cause as much as he hated me, there were at least two occasionz we're at a hyped-up student union party, there's no otha bruthaz there for him to step with, so he asked me to step with him. This is a no-no for a greek to let a GDI, or God Damn Indivual, step with them. Of course I did it, Y? 'Cause deep in my heart, I was an Alpha and although it seemed I'd never get a chance to pledge because of the chapter bein' gone, hedz looked at me sorta as an honorary Alpha.

By my junior year, a group of us had begun inquiring about when Omicron chapter would be reinstated. We checked with the University as well as Nationalz and the local Grad Chapter. The University told us the ban could be lifted yet Grad and Nationalz was somewhat against it.

The accusation of excessive hazing was a serious issue fraternities were facing in the early 1990s. Some were facing major lawsuits and there were even some fatalities. So you can understand Y there was some hesitation in reinstating the University of Pittsburgh's Omiocron chapter.

Several interested hedz and I petitioned to have a meeting with Grad and eventually they met with us. After several months of meeting, we got the nod, all the while, we maintained contact with the few undergrad bruthaz that were still around.

Although we didn't like that we had to go through grad to get our letterz, that was the only way we could get 'em. Because the remainin' bruthaz of Omicron had been expelled along with the chapter, they didn't have the power to pledge then give us our letterz and be recognized by the national headquarterz, so we had to go through grad.

According to the grad chapter, they were indefinite suspended memberz of the frat and therefore had no power or authority to neither reinstate nor run an undergraduate chapter. This was going to be done with the grad chapter holding our handz.

Before all this shit went down with Grad, we met and decided to go a step further. We wanted both the letterz *and* the respect of our undergrad bruthaz, plus the respect of the campus! It just wouldn't be right to get these letterz without pledging. Besides, Omicron is an undergrad chapter, so it would be wrong to get letterz from a grad chapter that doesn't have the legacy as a single-lettered chapter. In addition, bein' on an undergrad campus, we had to deal with other undergradz, not older hedz. We determined our rep on campus was more important than what those old farts thought of us!

See, grad chapter was made up of 'old hedz' and anyone who got their letterz through grad and not undergrad was seen as weak in the eyez of undergrad, 'cause grad chapterz don't haze! Oh, they may do a couple errandz, but they're not physically pledged like undergrad, mainly 'cause these are grown ass men many in their 40s and 50s with careerz and families. I couldn't see them standin' in line gettin' wood (hit with a wooden paddle), holdin' bricks and fightin' off ambushes from visiting bruthaz from other chapterz.

We knew if we got our letterz through grad, we would not be respected and trust, you don't wanna be known to not've pledged or earned your letterz! This was called 'skating', and you gets no luv from any frats, let alone your own frat for skating! To be a line that skated would be the talk of campus for yearz, not only would your line be seen as soft, but your whole frat would!

This happened to the AKAs, right after my line crossed where one line promised undergrad they'd pledge after grad had them go through a 48-hour process. They were given their letterz and these sistaz had the audacity to change their mindz when it came to reporting to undergrad to be pledged — or did they plan this all along?

The whole campus knew! The older AKAs publicly denounced them, ostracizing them to bein' the laughin' stock on campus. Beef continued when grad took on anutha line of AKAs and these sistaz reported to the undergrad sistaz and pledged. Needless to say, the two new lines had major beef, verbally and physically!

Me and my line bruthaz all agreed pledging was the honorable thing to do. So on the night of our initiation, we meet with grad and some ill shit happenz. At the beginning of the 48-hour process, we're on campus in this room and they have us sign this sheet that basically states that we are not to, in any way, form or fashion, allow ourselves to be hazed or hit by any Alpha and if we are, we are to report them to Nationalz immediately! If Nationalz found out we were and we told no one, we would basically lose our chapter and be suspended from the frat.

We all signed, knowin' as soon as our 48-hourz are up, we're gonna report to undergrad and begin our 6-8 week pledge process with no one on campus knowin' we're already Alpha's.

After we signed these waiverz, we were taken to this church in Wilkinsburg. We were now officially sphinxmen — what an Alpha pledge is called when on line. It was a cold November night, late in the evening which gave the church a sort of eerie-like feeling. We were outside in the back of the church blindfolded. Earlier, we were told to bring a brick with us. One voice told us to told hold this brick over our headz, armz reachin' upward towardz the sky. Soundz simple, right? Try holdin' it for 20-30 minutes! I heard hedz to the left and right of me grimacing in pain and every couple minutes hear one of my line bruthaz name called.

Then my name was called, *"Buckner, Jehvon! Come with me!!"* I stepped towardz the voice but was hesitant because I was blindfolded and couldn't see where I was walking. I started to drop my armz to reach out for guidance, *"hold that brick above your head, magget! That's brick's your name, so hold it high!"* I quickly raised it as high as Ben Wallace reaches for a rebound!

I felt someone grab the side of my torso and guide me toward the voice. He guided me inside the church and down the stairz. I could hear a loud smack followed by someone wincing in pain. *"Someone's gettin' hit,"* I thought. But this can't be happenin', we're not s'posed to be hit, they had us sign this letter!

I was at the bottom of the steps and led a couple steps more and stopped. I was then asked to lower my 'name' (the brick) and remove my blindfold. I saw one of my line bruthaz gettin' hazed by a grad member with a wooden paddle! I didn't show my shock. I thought to myself, *"these hypocritical muthafuckaz!! They tell us not to allow ourselves to be hazed and look at this, these 45+ year-old school hedz is down here with their sleeves rolled up!"* I was in! I was scared, but I was in!! I thought this would only help us, respect-wise! Yo, these old greyhoundz could throw some wood, B!

Needless to say, by the end of the night, my ass was literally so swollen, I could barely fit my pants! We pretty much got hazed throughout the weekend and at the end when they gave us our letterz, the grey-haired grad chapter president had a sneaky grin on his face as he reminded us to not let anyone pledge us!

We all gathered after and walked over to who would be our dean (of pledges) house. The real shit was about to begin. My overall pledge process was memorable, mostly consisting of reciting historical facts and poemz while bein' hazed, runnin' errandz while bein' hazed, damn near no sleep at all 'cause we was bein' hazed, gettin' hazed by visiting bruhz from other chapterz, and since they found out I liked to draw so much, I had to design several graffiti sweatshirts for bruhz. About a month and a half later, on December 21, 1991 at 10:37 pm, me and my 9 line bruthaz crossed.

Contrary to what some may tell you, I have no personal ill feelingz about my pledge process. I do, however, about the historical and psychological impact it has on young and impressionable Afrikan mindz.

After I started lecturing and writing about the Boule', some would say I alwayz talk bad on black greeks. Let me make it clear, I luv'd Alpha; ever since I saw those bruthaz open up those homes in my neighborhood. And although most will tell you they pledged for the service they do in the community, they won't tell you about the additional perks of bein' in frats, likes, the women, the women, and did I already say the women?!

We would go on road trips and meet all kindz of people and get madd luv 'cause we wore those 'greek' letterz!! I look back now knowin' I was caught up, yo!

There were several other thingz that drew me to Alpha over the other frats. Among them were the symbolz, like the sphinx (which I later learned is actually called Her-Em-Akhet — keep readin' I'm about to get into that!). Before I pledged, seein' a bunch of bruthaz adopt two of the seven wonderz that happened to be in Afrika, gave me a source of ethnic and historical pride. At the tyme, I was beginning to know about my history and I felt through Alpha I could.

Up 'til this point, I hadn't done a written piece exclusively on my pledging experience, not purposely however. In several of my lectures, I mentioned that the whole pledging process in undergrad fraternities dealt with lettin' the public see you messed up. This sorta validated you were pledgin' and not 'skating'.

I'm not sayin' frats don't physically work over their initiates, because most do. But I think the biggest scam that all of 'em participate in is to make you believe there's these deep secrets.

In a nutshell, before I tell you, I have to let you know that all initiationz are not identical to the 'T'. Most chapterz have their own ritualz, yet there are some universal ones that find its origin in white fraternities like the first chapter of the Illuminati, Phi Beta Kappa and the second chapter, Skull and Bones at Yale University.

In my lectures, debates and conversationz, I have alwayz maintained that the secrets people are intrigued to know about in frats is that THERE SIMPLY ARE NO SECRETS!! The only secrets that exist are some historical facts (that anyone can research using the library or internet) and ritualz. How deep is that? The secret is there are none!

For example, one ritual I experienced was being "tarred and feathered". Me and my line bruthaz had Karo maple syrup poured on us, then we had to strip naked and roll around in cornflakes (we couldn't afford real feathers so cornflakes had to do). We then were instructed to get dressed and we were driven somewhere far from where we were all stayin', dropped off and left to find our own way back.

Underneath our outside clothes we wore these tight grey-colored longjohnz. Because they were so tight, it allowed the cornflakes and syrup to stay in place and dry. After a couple of hourz, the syrup and flakes began to stick and rip our skin as we walked tryin' to get home to the point where it became very painful to walk ripping and tearing hair and skin apart. But we had to keep movin' 'cause we had to be back in a certain amount of tyme.

Once we reached home, gettin' it off was even harder, especially if you had hair on your body. One after the other, we all took turnz showerin' tryin' to wash it all off. Needless to say, my line number was 9, so I was next to last to wash myself. By the tyme it was my turn to shower, the tub was clogged with soggy flakes, watery syrup and dirt! Plus the water was madd cold so that made it even harder to wash the syrup off!!

There were a lot of stupid ritualz like the candle wax on the skin burningz, shit done just to put fear in your mindz. Other thingz we experienced throughout our pledge process were beatdownz. There were a lot of physical attacks. Often we were jumped by out of town bruhz, where you might be "kidnapped". But we had to "earn our respect" so this is what had to happen.

We were often up late during the week and the entire weekend, runnin' errandz for big bruthaz (as they were called), cleanin' up their apartments, cookin' 'em food, wake up callz, shit like that.

Don't get me wrong, I was not against hazin', just excessive hazing! During my process we did a lot of physical shit. I mean, we had our history to know, but by the 3rd-4th week, you pretty much knew your shit 'cause it had been beaten into our collective memory! Now what do you do with the rest of the 2-4-plus weeks? "Let's just haze 'em (again, not just physically, mentally as well)!"

I wasn't vexed because of that. My pledge process taught me a lot. I did, however, make sure I didn't do what was done to me on lines after me. But, every man has their own way.

Anutha ritual is called the 'Alpha Dinner'. This was actually a funny one 'cause it's something like the last supper. We had to eat a mixture of cat and dog food, limburger cheese, different salad dressingz, all kindz of shit! Our Dean of pledges mixed it up, made us sit in a circle and we had to eat it. All this mixed up pretty much looked like vomit! So, of course that's what we ended up doin'. One by one, we pretty much watched each other dry heave to the point where we pretty much threw up in unison.

This ritual is the openin' event before goin' into what's called "hell", or the last week an initiate must go through before crossing. This is the tyme where anything goes! What's good is that we are allowed to defend ourselves, 'cause we ain't got nuthin' to lose 'cause we gonna take an "L" (loss) anywayz!

Right before we went into "hell" our names were changed. We were no longer called Sphinxmen, but APEs! Get that! We're now called a type of primate!! Even though 'APE' was an acronym that stood for 'Almost Pledged Entirely,' and although there's some subliminal symbolizm behing bein' called an APE, it still showz the severity of our conditioning!

The symbolizm behind bein' called an APE is that the entire pledge process is meant to degrade or break you down as a person or individual, down to your lowest point — an APE — then build you back up which is what's s'posed to happen when you go through "hell" week.

So, although one can see there's a purpose behind it all, I still wonder what sick and anti-Afrikan hed created and okayed such ritualz? I mean, peep this, in addition to bein' called an APE, we had to wear a banana around our necks and was only allowed to speak like apes do, 'grunting', 'oooohin', 'aaaahin' and 'eeeeking'!! Think how this looks to YT on a predominately white campus! This act does more than validate their stereotypical viewz of Afrikan people!!

At the end of hell week, we're about to "cross the burnin' sandz". We had the "Alpha Smoke" ritual, where we got high off smoking some cigarz in a small bathroom with the windowz and door closed. After we're high enuff, one by one, we came out and went through a process where we were given madd wood, grabbed, pulled, kicked and punched, while trying to answer questionz and recite poetry and history. We're then walked over what felt like sand, but actually was a kitty-litter box with sand in it to resemble us being on a beach crossing the "burning sandz of Egypt". **[*NOTE:** So I won't have to repeat the significance of crossing the burnin' sandz and its relation to masonry's depiction of the fable, Adam and Eve, you can read it later in this book in part 2 of the Boule' series *'2B or Not 2B... Greek!,'* you will read how the role Afrikan pledgeez play in crossin' the burning sandz by foot payz homage to something we didn't know.]

The 'crossing over' ritual is quite tense when you're blindfolded. Madd hedz are swingin' and shouting, you don't know whether you're gonna get clocked in the jaw or gut-checked! All this isn't to hurt you, it's an initiation of sorts.

I will admit that throughout my process, we were never taught anything about white supremacy, nor was the word "Boule'" ever mentioned. It wasn't until many yearz later, after I started doin' the math on masonry, Skull & Bones and the Boule' that I started to see the connection.

I reiterate, I didn't think any of this was bad. At sometymz it was excessive, but overall our dean kept us safe. I look back now and still harber no bad feelingz. However, I will admit its kinda sick to think that way and most, if not all frat memberz embellish this same feeling.

Just think, the average frat hed would love to have a slave(s), I mean, pledges for 6-8-plus weeks to do as they like; clean their homes, run errandz, even get them to collect money to buy them shit. In addition, how well the ego is stroked when the public seez they got 'em in check! Then after beatin' you for a month or two, you're now my brutha!

To many, it gives them a power rush! I didn't get caught up into that. Ask any pledge I came across and they'll tell you I never touched them. My kind of pledging was mental. I got in your hed, yo.

Overall we weren't taught to hate, it was subliminal. See, when you join an organization, you have to uphold it. When there are "rivalz" or other organizationz (like Kappa Alpha Psi, Omega Psi Phi, Phi Beta Sigma and other frats that make up the original eight fraternity and sororities), to the public, this is a form of competition of who's the largest.

We spent so much tyme biggin' up ourselves we didn't/couldn't realize we were doing exactly what YT wants us so-called "talented 10th," collegiate-post-high-school-educated negroes to do: SEGREGATE!! Go to a stepshow. It's all about how good you are while dissin' otherz organizationz. At student parties, we would step around the party and was ready fi romp if the Kappa's mistakenly bumbed into one of us; ready to bum rush anutha 'cause he tried to break our line as we stepped around the party. We were almost like gang bangerz aspiring for degreez.

Although I admit I was probably one of the wildest stepperz on campus, I enjoyed every minute bein' an Alpha until I met Steve Cokely. Most black frats are on white campuses and we're too ignorant to see that YT seez us, witnessing our inability to get along. On most collegiate campuses, you'll find that the black greeks are not united.

Someone created these stereotypes that have been handed down chapter to chapter, pledge line to pledge line. We call the Delta's of Delta Sigma Theta Sorority, Inc. "jiggabooz"; the AKAs (Alpha Kappa Alpha Sorority, Inc.) "wannabe's". If you know your history, you'll know a "wannabe" is a term that was used in the early 1900s for Afrikanz-in-america who didn't like their Afrikaness and did everything they could to be more 'white'; from bleachin' their skin and straightening their hair to the extreme of not bein' seen eating watermelon!

For a long period of tyme they — along with the Alpha's — used to have what was called the 'brown paper bag test' where you could only be considered to pledge AKA if your skin was lighter than a brown paper bag. "Jiggabooz" was a term used in the likeness of bein' called anything negative that was Afrikan: 'negro', 'colored', 'jungle bunny', 'monkey', 'nappy', 'coon', etc.

The Alpha's were called faggot's, the Kappa's of Kappa Alpha Psi Fraternity, Inc. called "pretty boyz" and often were made up of light-skinned blacks; and Ques of Omega Psi Phi Fraternity, Inc. took pride in wearin' dog collarz while barkin' like a dog as their signal call.

These are the 'Talented 10th' WEB DuBois spoke so highly of. This is the (cess)pool our current and future leaderz have come from.

I also went as far as gettin' branded! But not for your usual reason. It was my way of payin' homage as I tried equating my pledging process to what our Ancestorz who were involuntarily brought over here and imprisoned and turned into slaves. One of the first thingz YT did when our kidnapped Ancestorz got off the ships was brand them with a hot branding iron so they could keep track of them, as if they were cattle — in fact, this form of slavery was called 'chattel' which is defined by the absolute "legal" ownership of a person or personz, including the right to buy and sell them, as defined by the Wikipedia Encyclopedia. See, they used the word 'legal' because our Ancestorz were not seen as people; not even human. They were seen as intellectual goodz.

So I got branded to pay tribute to what they went through — even though I knew my pledge process was but a 'teaspoon' compared to the 'ocean' of events they endured. Bein' broken down to "nothing" is easy, bein' able to build yourself back up is special. I wanted to honor their legacy and although I wish I was wise enuff back then to not use greek letterz and instead use somethin' like the Medu-Neter or even adopting one of the Adinkra symbolz, it has proven to be somewhat of a marketing tool.

Whenever I'm approached by frat 'cause they see my brand on my arm, I politely tell them, *"I'm not in the frat anymore and if you'd like to know Y,* (if they have tyme) *we can talk about it or you can log on to my site and read about the Boule'."* Simple as that…

See, this is my reason for speaking and writing against black fraternities and sororities. We are simply not told the whole story, most importantly, the origin of Y these organizationz were founded. On one hand, I do give them credit for raising large sumz of money and their successful canned-food and clothes drives. This is somethin' that can still be done, but it should not continue to be under the banner of our enslaverz.

I find so many hedz refuse to shake their allegiance to something that has dishonored our Ancestorz who were stolen from, enslaved and murdered for over a century!

If you don't know, it needz to be known now! THERE IS NO SUCH THING AS A BLACK GREEK!! This historical relationship between Afrikanz in the Nile Valley and the plagiarizing greeks was not harmonious in any way! So Y do we, nearly two-milleniumz later, continue to honor or wear the letterz of an invader?! I say honor because these letterz payz tribute to the era greeks occupied the Nile Valley. Therein lies a serious form of mentacide (mental suicide — coined by historian Dr. Bobby Wright) when a descendant chooses the culture of their oppressor rather than their own!

Y haven't these "historically" black organizationz — who've had the opportunity to reveal the stolen legacy of, what George GM James wrote, *"greek mythology bein' stolen Afrikan history"* to millionz upon millionz of what's s'posed to be the most intelligent our race has to offer — not felt the responsibility to change the letterz from greek to somethin' Afrikan?!!?

Many argue they are not tryin' to be greek and that although they're a black greek-lettered organization, they are not greek. Well let's just say this... if they're not tryin' to be greek, or rather, honor the greeks by continuin' to wear their letterz and identifyin' their fraternal names with their language, we can also attest for certain THEY ARE NOT TRYIN' TO BE AFRIKAN!!

Callin' yourself a black-greek lettered organization is nothin' but semantics, B! I mean, ask yourself, if the Ku Klux Klan opened their doorz to black membership, would it now be ok to join? The KKK has a history of murdering Afrikanz, and guess what, so do the greeks! The only difference is the Klanz murderz are more recent!!

So if the Klan professed to no longer hate and discontinued murdering Afrikanz, would it be ok to join the local Klan chapter now? Too soon? Ok, how about one-hundred yearz from now? How about five-hundred yearz?! Sensible hedz would emphatically respond "HELL NO!" Y? Because we are familiar with the KKKs deedz. It's still fresh in our mindz and for that, we'd do whatever to ensure no generation EVER forgets nor forgives!

But it seemz because what happened in the Nile Valley millenniumz ago has been forgotten and even somewhat forgiven. Most have adopted the philosophy, *"When in Rome, walk like the Romanz!"* Many believe because it was so long ago, the effects from it aren't as blatant. But what is this a form of? White supremacy — the act of one race enforcing dominance over another race purely because they feel they're superior based on skin complexion.

Now ask yourself, are we still livin' in a world where white supremacy exists? Are we still experiencin' discriminationz and inequality where YT still benefits? Is their wealth today not derived from the embezzlement of Afrikan culture?!

For those that paused to consider this, it's very clear there's no way you could be an asset to our legacy because it is obvious you've been totally assimilated to the mindset of a 'wannabe'!

In summation to all this greek frat shit… the biggest hype about fraternal secrets is: THERE ARE NO SECRETS!!!! Think, if I'm an outsider and I can make the public think we're all prestigious, have a long history, get all the fly women, step the best and do this enclosed secret handshake that no one is s'posed to see, to the average hed, he'll think, *"I want in, yo! What do I hafta do?!"*

My experience is only on the undergrad level, but I've been told on the grad level, shit gets serious. I'm not sure to what degree but from what I've learned of the Boule', the game is raised. Whereas the hazin' shit's gone, the click is solidifyed and the segregation heightened as these negroes push to further their careerz to work for YT, becomin' "leaderz" of Afrikan people, whereas the ideology of Marcus Garvey and his proclamation of Afrikan self-reliance becomes but a dream deferred.

I was dedicating my life to the advancement of Afrikan people. But could I continue to do so bein' an Alpha? Could I remain bein' a member in a black greek-lettered organization that gave recognition and homage to Greece, in good conscience, knowin' what I now knew was all a lie?

Chapter Eighteen: Adhere To The Message, Not The Messenger

As said before, I luv'd Alpha and enjoyed bein' one for six yearz until about 1997, when I met Steve Cokely.

I was still livin' in Pittsburgh and one of my best comradz, E.D. invited me to go to West Virginia to listen to this lecture on secret societies. Me and E.D. just got into the science of global white supremacy, so anything that was about conspiracies, we was on it!

I had become enamored with the study of global white supremacy and how YT came into power. I was in my mid-twenties and shoulda still been into club hoppin', but I wasn't. I was into lecture hoppin'! I would travel to DC, Virginia, Philly and New York to listen to all kindz of lecturerz: Dr. John Henrik Clarke, Dr. Yosef ben-Jochannan, Naim Akbar, Francess Cress-Welsing, Anthony Browder, Runoko Rashidi and the like.

I remember thinkin' my old college professor Rob Penny would be proud of me. *"I'm home Rob!"* I'd think, knowin' now that I was wrong thinkin' that Dr. York and Islam shit was me.

So E.D. and I drove down to West Virginia to hear Steve Cokely talk about this organization called 'the Boule', aka Sigma Pi Phi, Fraternity, Incorporated. At that tyme, I was still an Alpha and when he stated the Boule' was founded before the Alpha's, my greek-laced ego kicked in. I had never heard of the Boule' and as far as I knew, we were taught Alpha was first, starting December 4th, 1906. I learned that night that Sigma Pi Phi was founded in Philadelphia, May 15th, 1904, the first black fraternity in the united states.

I listened to Cokely speak for about three-and-a-half hourz, breakin' down their origin and link to the notoriously wicked Skull & Bones, aka the 2nd chapter of the Illuminati better known as 'The New World Order'.

When he finished, I looked down at my notepad and my hand was shakin' again, just like it did when I heard KRS-One speak yearz before. I hacked into the papyrus vaults again, Sun! And I needed to know more!

Not a month went by that E.D. befriended Cokely and got him to come to Pittsburgh to do a series of speaking engagements. One lecture, he brought along with him historian/lecturer Ashra Kwesi, a Pittsburgh native. In this four-to-five hour lecture they got into the symbolizm of the Boule's shield, explaining that the 3x3 square or tetragrammaton (defined as *"the Hebrew word for God, consisting of the four letters yod, he, vav, and he, transliterated consonantally usually as YHVH, now pronounced as Adonai or Elohim in substitution for the original pronunciation forbidden since the 2nd or 3rd century BC"*) on the bottom of the Boule's logo stood for the eight black fraternity and sororities, with the 9th square (the one in the center), bein' the Boule', the founder of them all! *(I won't get into the history of the Boule' here, I wrote a whole series on it that you can read later in this book, 'The Boule' Series'.)*

Learning this brought me to a crossroadz, DGT was in its fourth year of production and I considered it a Pan-Afrikan publication. In addition, I was dedicating my life to the advancement of Afrikan people. But could I continue to do so bein' an Alpha? Could I remain bein' a member in a black greek-lettered organization that gave recognition and homage to Greece, in good conscience, knowin' what I now knew was all a lie?

I had read *Stolen Legacy* by George GM James book as well as Carter G. Woodson's, *The Miseducation of the Negro* before, but none of it rang more resoundingly clear than after I heard Cokely and Kwesi speak!

Cokely was big on callin' people out and that they needed to be exposed for their involvement. He often spoke about how black greeks need to tell the secrets of their organizationz, and that anything less was criminal and basically a slap in the face on our Afrikan legacy.

I was faced with makin' a decision. I luv'd Alpha, but could I now respect what I claimed to luv? From Anthony Browder's books, I learned the real name of the Sphinx is called Her-Em-Akhet, meanin' "Heru on the horizon." I learned the story of the riddle of the Sphinx and Oedipus. GM James quote, *"Greek mythology is stolen Afrikan history,"* rang loud and clear in my mind!

I had to make a decision… I couldn't remain an Alpha — a black 'wannabe' greek — knowin' it was the greeks, along with the persianz and romanz that went into Kemet (erroneously called Egypt), and stole virtually everything, changed the names and authorz and claimed it as their own. Knowin' this is what also gave me the idea of changin' my name because it was they who tried to erase the origin of our people so that we would become better slaves.

As much as I wanted to remain an Alpha, I felt perhaps they weren't aware of this. Before I would leave this organization, I thought maybe they should know about what I found out and would possibly make this change after bein' exposed. I even thought perhaps Alpha Phi Alpha would be the first to abolish its greek letterz and adopt Afrikan one's. I was syked! I had to let Nationalz know!

I wrote and sent the General President a certified letter detailing what I had learned and proposed a motion to change the name pledgeez are called from 'sphinxmen' to perhaps 'Her-Em-Akhet-men'. I also proposed to get rid of the greek name and change the frat's name to somethin' usin' a language indigenous to our homeland, Medu-Neter (hieroglyphs), Adinkra, Woloff, anything Afrikan. I know my suggestionz were bold. I did think if they were not aware of this info, they would give it consideration, but my gut was tellin' me somethin' different. But who am I? How can I expect them to listen to a young-buck like me who's not even a decade deep in the frat, tryin' to change a what's about a century-old organization?!

Sure enuff, my gut was right. Approximately two weeks later, I received my letter. It had a big stamp on it that said 'Return to Sender'. I knew the several page letter I sent had been read because on the top left edge, the page were stapled. The top edge were look like the pages had been flipped over while reading. In addition, havin' sent it certified, I knew if not the General President, *someone* high-up, got the letter, read it and sent it back.

By them returning the letter with no response spoke volumes and made me realize I had to accept what my gut had been tellin' me all along. I mentioned before I alwayz had this experience where I would join a group or organization, learn their wayz and then somethin' wicked would reveal itself and I'd end up removing myself from the group. It happened religiously with christianity and islam and now it was happenin' with Alpha.

I spoke to my line bruthaz about the Boule' and the letter I sent. I thought, if *anyone* would feel me, my line bruthaz would! Several of them had also been walkin' the path of 'Afrocentricity'. Of those, a couple moved on with their lives to other cities, but I remained in contact with about five of them. Out of them, only two seem to be somewhat interested.

I was disappointed to say the least. It looked like I was gonna be doin' this solo. On top of that, I knew hedz on campus was gonna look at me like I was now a hypocrite because for so long, I was so public about my luv for Alpha and we had gone through great lengths to bring Alpha back on Pitt's campus.

As soon as I got that letter back from the national office, I followed, submitting a letter declaring my wish to dissolve my membership. I told several of my line bruthaz what I was doing — that I was no longer gonna be an Alpha, but it wasn't that that was gonna disturb them. It was what I was about to tell them next.

They told us we were bein' miseducated by YT, but didn't tell you exactly who was responsible.

Chapter Nineteen: 2B Or Not 2B… Greek!

One of the thingz that weighed on me was the stories of George GM James, Carter G. Woodson and W.E.B. DuBois. James, a master mason; Woodson a member of the fraternity, Omega Psi Phi and DuBois an Alpha, and both were also exiled memberz of the Boule' *(again, all this can be read in my series on the Boule' later in the book).*

James wrote *Stolen Legacy* knowin' it would most certainly cost him his life for revealling secrets on masonry. Woodson and DuBois, havin' once been pawnz of global white supremacy *(DuBois was the first negro to write for the Illuminati's, Council on Foreign Relationz magazine, 'Foreign Affairs')*, were used to belittle the rise of the Marcus Garvey movement of the 1930s. In their latter yearz Woodson wrote *The Miseducation of the Negro* and DuBois did a one-eighty, becoming an outspoken voice for the Pan-Afrikan movement as well as livin' his last dayz in Ghana.

What these bruthaz did in their latter yearz is admirable, BUT… they couldn't bring themselves to do what GM James did. See GM James named names! He informed us of Aristotle's and Socrates theft of our knowledge from the ancient 'Egyptian' mystery schoolz. Woodson and DuBois, although they eventually were outspoken about white supremacy, NEVER, EVER NAMED ANY OF THEM! This clearly proved their pledge to live out the oathe of the Boule' — even though they were by now, exilded from the organization — to never reveal the names of those who run the world!

They both had financial ties with the Illuminati. Woodson received large sumz of money from the Carnegie, Lord-Spellman and Rockefeller families — all memberz of the Illuminati. DuBois was one of the poster faces of the NAACP. We're told he was among the several 'negroes' who found this organization — who also receives large contributionz from the Rockefellerz as well as Cecil Rhodes. But DuBois bein' a founder is not the truth. The fact is the NAACP — what I call 'the National Association for the Advancement of *CERTAIN* People' — was formed by two jewish spies of the Round Table Group or Illuminati, Rabbi Steven Wise and

Jane Adams *(again, all this is covered later in the book. Read the piece on the origin of the NAACP).*

It's obvious these spineless, noodle-back negroes feared their lives, so instead of comin' out with the entire truth, they gave us 'leadz'. They told us we were bein' miseducated by YT, but didn't tell you exactly who was responsible. That's like someone tellin' you someone shot your momz, you ask who and they tell you "they" or "them" instead of a specific name.

I didn't wanna go out like that. And although I believe my situation wouldn't necessarily cost my life, I understood the principle, *"you're either part of the solution or part of the problem!"*

I informed some of my now ex-line bruthaz as well as other Alpha's I knew that I was no longer a member of Alpha and that I was gonna start writing and lecturing about the Boule' and it's affiliation with 'black greeks' — as if there's such as thing!

Ok. Lemme go back a bit. Initially, hedz didn't really seem to care, but the buzz suddenly changed when I had an altercation at Hillman library on Pitt's campus.

I was in the library doin' my usual daily study (I stayed on campus even though I was out of school. I was utilizing the universities services to both publish DGT and do my research), and I was approached by a friend of mine who recently pledged and crossed Omega Psi Phi. He was a neo — which is defined as someone who just finished his pledge process but hasn't pledged anyone yet — and as with all neo's, they're engulfed in wanting to get the scoop on other frats.

One of the biggest jokes about frat life is how hedz try to hide their "respective" grip's. A grip is a secret handshake shared by frat memberz. When they meet in public, this handshake is performed to both cause attention as well as conceal what they're doin'. It's like *"hey look at us, we're about to greet each other with this secret handshake, but don't look at us doin' this secret handshake!"* Foolishness! But I admit, I too was caught up I my day.

So I'm sittin' at this table talkin' to my boy, who just crossed, about the Boule'. Then one of my frat bruthaz approached the table we were sittin' at. He was my 'spec', pronounced 'spesh', short for special. A pledgee is anointed this title by a member of the frat who intendz to look out for him while he's on line. It's a way to build a bond with an older frat member.

See, before I left Alpha, we had this ill dilemma at my chapter. Remember the older frat memberz I told you we went to be pledged undergrad after we got our letterz from grad? Well two of the three were still in Pittsburgh. It wasn't long after my line crossed that dissention and chaos erupted in our chapter.

There's a side of frat life outsiderz don't know. Hedz used to tell me that Alpha specialized in creating leaderz. Well what happenz when you have a room full of leaderz? No followerz! Because everybody wants to be the leader! Ego's run rampant, there's controversy, hedz don't get along and even pick sides or 'clicks'. All this is s'posed to be done internally. Most do a good job showin' unity publicly, but I assure you, most if not all sorority and fraternity chapterz got beef with each other! It's because we too busy tryin' to out negro each other! But that's anutha story…

So! Back to my chapter. My line took on a line of bruthaz the following year (1992) but grad chapter found out and the line had to be dissolved, mainly 'cause we had shown our commitment was to the bruthaz of Omicron chapter instead of grad, who had to power to dissolve our chapter. We decided to listen to the two remainin' undergrad bruthaz that pledged us instead of dealin' with grad 'cause basically, we didn't respect grad. On top of that, Omicron is a single-lettered chapter. So we're never s'posed to be pledged by any chapter other than Omicron!

See the dilemma we faced?? It was well known undergrad didn't respect grad memberz because they simply do not pledge like undergrad. On top of that, bein' a single-lettered chapter, we were bound to continue the legacy of "Bloody O" as our chapter was called, not some skatin' grad cats! The only hedz who could pass the legacy of the chapter was through those two bruhz.

As much as we felt the grad chapter was weak, we had to drop the line because they had the power to take away our chapter and we just got it back. So midway through their pledge process, we dropped the line. We assured them we would get them in, it would just have to be through grad first, like we did.

Weeks later, I get a phone call from one of my line bruthaz tellin' me the two older bruthaz, the one's who pledged us, took this line down to the University of West Virginia and crossed them without tellin' me nor any of my line bruhz! They basically pulled rank and took them without our consent nor did they respect that we were the only active memberz of the frat!

Now this was a massive diss, one, 'cause those two were not even active bruhz, so they had no authority to cross anyone; second, they crossed them on West Virginia's campus through *their* chapter, Pi Mu, so they weren't Omicron! Yet I was told I had to now embrace these cats as memberz of my chapter because hedz on campus already knew (before we did) that they crossed! They were already on campus celebrating and wearin' the letterz!

Needless to say, when I saw them and they was like, *"whattup Frat?!"* I had to publicly embrace them, but I was sayin' to myself, this shit was fucked up! They totally disrespected my line and more importantly the history of our chapter. Further, they weren't official 'cause they never received their pinz nor certificates from Nationalz, so as far as Nationalz was concerned they didn't exist. These young bucks couldn't even see it. This gave me even more reason to wanna leave the frat!

Back to the library where I'm with my neo comrade. My 'spec' (one of the cat's that crossed without our knowledge until it was too late) decides to sit in on my tellin' them about the Boule'. Soon, about fifteen hedz were at the table listenin' to me talk of how we had been miseducated about 'greek life'.

Towardz the end, I was hopin' they'd reconsider their membership to their organizationz and join me in lettin' other hedz know. I told them I wasn't gonna be like

Woodson and DuBois, and that I would answer any question and/or reveal any secret anyone wanted to know not for the sake of creating controversy, but to be a livin' example of George GM James and hold nothin' back!

Funny thing is you never know what goes on in people's mindz. The neo who just pledged Omega asked me a question, and it was certainly not an intelligent one, but a predictable one! I have to attribute him bein' a neo as to Y. Right after I said I would reveal anything anyone wants to know, he blurts out, *"show me your grip!"* I look at him crazily.

I was put on the spot, I talked it, now I had to walk it. Immediately, hedz, greek and GDI's (again, 'God Damn Indivualz' or non-greeks) looked at me, eagerly awaiting my response. This is a cardinal sin! You're never, ever s'posed to give away the grip!

I immediately turned to my spec and spoke gently, *"look, what I'm about to do, this is in no way in disrespect to you as an Afrikan. I hope that you understand that what I'm about to do is in the spirit of GM James. We are not greeks, we're not black-greeks, we're Afrikan, and I hope you can respect that. I hope that you can see my intention is to honor our Afrikan legacy and denounce all greek associationz we've adopted."*

I didn't wait for their response; I immediately did my hand gesture for everyone to see. Following that, after a couple "ooh's" and "ahh's" — not because they were able to see the grip but because of the gossip this would make — my spec walked away, he was obviously heated!

Before I convinced myself I was gonna go public with what I learned, I knew that eventually, hedz would probably ask me somethin' like this. As an Afrikan who now knew bein' a black-greek is an oxymoron (or contradictory) — 'cause history proves the greeks came into Kemet as pirates, stealing, murdering and plagiarizing our story and claimin' it as their own — I have nothin' to hide. I've given out the secret handshake, I've also asked and gotten a few of the other frats handshakes over the yearz.

If you look at the older hedz, they usually do the shake so openly, you can virtually see it with your own eyes! Second, in undergrad, one of the infatuationz of keepin your frat on top is by letting the other frats know you know their secrets! This usually kept the fire of rivalry burning between black organizationz.

Right after I showed the grip, I quickly said to the crowd, *"now what frat or soror is ready to reveal some of their secrets?"* Of course, there was no response and I respected that. I realize how devastating this shit can be.

Although there was a lump in my throat the entire tyme, 'cause I had no clue how my now ex-frat bruthaz would take it. It coulda got physical, but I knew I had to make a choice... I could either choose to emulate the actionz of Woodson and DuBois, or do the honorable-much-bigger-than-me-thing, GM James!

If there is no passin' of the torch of knowledge to the next generationz, those babies of the 90s will have no clue of our legacy. Now what will you think will happen to our story when they are elderz?!

Chapter Twenty: Passing Of The Torch, Or Not!

I knew my ex-frat bruthaz would have beef with me! After I showed the grip publicly, my ex-spec stormed out of the library with no wordz. I knew he was heated, and I knew he was goin' to tell the other bruhz, and I prepared myself for it.

It was my hope they could see I wasn't tryin' to create some kind of controversy — although I knew this was a controversial act. I also knew that at any tyme physical harm could come to me. Doin' this didn't make me feel invisible, on the contrary, I was somewhat paranoid. But I knew I had to stand my ground. I also knew I had to make it clear that my intent was of no disrespect to anyone who regarded themselves as an Afrikan; but for anyone who felt the need to protect somethin' 'greek', disrespect *was* intended!

Other than the embarrassment I emposed on my ex-frat, it wasn't much they could do other than express their displeasure. I knew most of these cats before I pledged and quite frankly, I wasn't cool with most of them before and wasn't really cool with them while I was in the frat, so I didn't expect us to be cool now that I was publicly denouncin' my affiliation.

Fortunately, it never got any farther than verbal. I made sure I reasoned with them, makin' sure I explained this was not an attack on any of them personally. This was a focus on the founderz of these organizationz, and I made it known I intended to find and reveal any and everything I found on all the fraternities and sororities. Quiet as kept, I honestly felt there were some that agreed with me, to a degree.

Not long after this happened, I published my three-part series on the Boule'. I got a copy of the Boule's national roster and decided to put them all on my website. I thought of the repercussionz of doin' such a thing, but I tried to maintain an alignment with the spirit of GM James, pondering on the pressure and fear he might've felt writing his book *knowin'* they'd kill him. He gave his life to tell us the truth. If he hadn't, we wouldn't know the greeks, persianz and romanz were the main culprits that slaughtered and tried to conceal of our history by changing history to 'their'-story. I didn't feel my life was in danger, but I did feel compelled to decide who I was goin' to emulate. Walkin' in the steps of GM James made me feel I was doin' our Ancestorz proud!

The campus was buzzin', B! Greeks left and right started to disassociate themselves with me. Even the majority of my line bruthaz who were still around as well as the memberz of our auxiliary group, the Alpha Angelz. I must say I wasn't surprised. I basically summed it up as anyone who wasn't feelin' me because I chose to be Pan-Afrikan and sever my ties to organizationz that were mainly founded to keep Afrikanz from bein' truly Afrikan, they were never really my friendz in the first place.

Although I found it hard to believe so many chose to remain greek without even attempting to do the research themselves, I didn't judge them. I only hoped that one day they might feel they owe it to themselves to investigate it so that they could make a clearer determination to stay greek or not.

I continued to speak about the Boule' whenever there were a few willing to listen. They were mainly GDI's consisting of freshmen and sophomore's and a few older hedz.

I did maintain cordial relationships with some greeks. One brutha was a member of Omega Psi Phi (a Que). He suggested we set up a speaking engagement for students to hear this information. I agreed to write up a lecture. It was entitled, *"Who Iz the Boule'?"* Both E.D. and I spoke, breakin' down the origin of global white supremacy, the Illuminati, white fraternities and it's need to create black greek societies.

Although we did madd promo for the joint, it wasn't until a second lecture/panel was created that the campus showed up in large numberz. This tyme with a panel of greek memberz! Because only about thirty or so hedz showed up to the first lecture, I felt at a disadvantage because this was a panel where we would have to share the tyme as a rebuttal to my arguments. Most didn't attend the first lecture where we made the connection to global white supremacy, so the task would be an even harder challenge to convince the masses.

The night started off just like I expected. Greeks from the surrounding colleges came. Before the event even started there was one Que from a college outside the city of Pittsburgh walked up to the front of the stage callin' me all sorts of M-F's and whatnot. Luckily we had campus police there in case of a situation like this. The brutha was told to sit, and throughout the beginning of the program, he kept interrupting the flow, throwin' 'F-bombz' toward me.

I remained calm replyin' to the audience that this was not an attack against anyone in this room. I was unearthing its origin and although a lot of egoes was about to be challenged, I assured them this thing originated some one-hundred yearz ago; obviously before any of us was even thought of!

This at least composed the temperz of most greeks that were there, except for that one Que — who was later ushered out by campus police.

Although the presentation went well with the students showin' much interest in the information I presented, I couldn't get any greeks to cross back over from greekhood to Afrika. I just couldn't understand what continued to make them remain faithful. Was it because of the oathe's they took? I dunno. But hedz did finally know where I was comin' from! And I knew the work was just beginning! I realized there were college students on campuses that embrace greekdom all over the country. They deserved to know an alternative side before choosin' to join. So I began my college tour speakin' about the Boule'!

Puttin' the Boule's roster on my website was one of the most controversial thingz I'm proud of. This empowered hedz, enabling them to look these culprits up in their own home townz. But this also seemed to have created an issue with Steve Cokely.

Cokely was a giant to me, B. I looked up to this cat! I studied Cokely not 'cause I wanted to be him, but because I respected his work. He had the true spirit of GM James, yo! He wasn't afraid to name names! That courage inspired me to publish the roster and begin speakin' at local colleges about the frat-soror-connection. I shared part two of the Boule' series I wrote with Cokely much to his approval. He informed me I was the first person who was in a frat to talk about the experience. The streets was watchin, hedz couldn't wait for the next edition! Emailz were pourin' in and the DGT phoneline was blazin'! Hedz around the country was as eager as I was to know more and DGT became a source for that kind of info. Then it happened…

E.D.and I had financed Cokely's trip to Pittsburgh to do anutha lecture a couple months later. I remember when he was leavin' he was kinda standoff-ish towardz me. I didn't think much of it, I just registered it and moved on.

After he left, E.D. told me Cokely had pulled him to the side and told him not to trust me 'cause I was an "oathtaker". *"Now, where did that come from?!"* I thought. He told him that I needed to *"confess"* about my membership to Alpha and submit a letter to him stating so, and ask for repentance. He said if I did this, through his direction he promised he would make sure my magazine would blow up!

I wasn't tryin' to steal Cokely's shine, I was only tryin' to put more light on the topic! Steve wasn't a writer, he mainly did lectures that were recorded on VHS tapes. I knew the internet was catchin' on and it would be a vital tool for hedz to know about this quicker and easier! I even remember pleaing for Cokely to put this info in writing so I could include in DGT before I even thought to write about it myself!

Somethin' wasn't right. This wasn't about me repenting, I had already did that in part two of *'The Boule' Series'*, where I made the connection between the Boule' and black greek-lettered organizationz. This was a takeover, Sun! A fellow conscious magazine publisher and comrade of mine out of Chicago told me he tried to do the same thing to him! He wanted to take over DGT!

Cokely also had a rep. He was known to have created a lot of enemies. Mainly 'cause he didn't trust nobody! And because of this mistrust, he was very moody with people who support him and because of his acts, he didn't have too many allies.

E.D.'s my boy for life, yo! He assured me there's no way Cokely's gonna come between us. I just sat there bewildered, wondering what I did to make him feel that way. Over the next couple months, our relationship dwindled basically to an end. Before I put the Boule's roster on my website, I knew Cokely had a copy. I requested a copy simply so I could put it on the internet so they would be exposed to the world. Cokely never honored my request, much less returned my phone callz.

What's worse, I started gettin' phone callz from around the country from fellow supporterz of DGT, including some magnificent guidance from the late, great historian/lecturer, Del Jones, who basically told me somethin' similar to what Richard Pryor told Eddie Murphy, in *'Eddie Murphy's Raw'* on Bill Cosby, who didn't like Eddie using curse wordz in his act... *"Tell Cokely to suck my d__k and have a coke and a smile!"* Jones said.

I got callz from Virginia, North Carolina, DC and Philly tellin' me Cokely was talkin' about me at his lecture's callin' me a spy!! He was beefin' 'bout how Jesse Jackson was 'created' to replace Martin Luther King (which is true), and how I was basically doin' the same thing!

I wasn't tryin' to replace Cokely! And I certainly don't work for, nor know of any hed in the Illuminati! I've alwayz respected his work. If you read my series on the Boule', I constantly gave him credit for the info!

So you know I couldn't let that shit go! Since he wouldn't return any of my callz, my only other choice was to confront him in person, but before that, I had to make a statement on my site letin' hedz know wha'gwan. This led me to writing the piece, *"Letter 2 Steve Cokely" (included in this book).* I wrote this in the spirit towardz a lot of our Elderz reluctance to pass the torch to the next generation enabling the fight to continue.

The piece basically drew a parrelel to our people's historical reluctance to pass the torch to ensuing generationz for the salvation of our people. Cokely's no exception, there are many of our Elderz who've lectured over the yearz who still frown at a younger lion respectfully standin' on their shoulderz.

I created DGT in that spirit. I know that readin' is like kryptonite to Afrikan people! I know the volumes of books our Elderz wrote — you know, those books that are two-three-hundred pages plus with no pictures — are not bein' read by the younger masses. We need to accept that there is a generation gap between the civil rights family — who will soon move to the non-physical realm, or death — and the 80s baby; and there's certainly a gap with the 90s baby!

If there is no passin' of the torch of knowledge to the next generationz, those babies of the 90s will have no clue of our legacy. Now what will you think will happen to our story when *they* are elderz?!

DGT was created to bridge street hedz with scholastic mindz. That is Y my writing style is in ebonics! It's not dumbed-down language, it's what we speak! We don't speak academia, we speak skreet (street)! And unless there's some adaptation to this translation, the information will be lost; and that's a condition I vow not to let happen.

In addition to the piece I wrote to Cokely, I had at least two occasionz to confront him when he came to speak at the United Afrikan Movement's (UAM) lectures which used to be held every Wednesday at the Oberia Dempsey Center on 127th Street in Harlem, New York.

I attended every Wednesday until it ended in, I think 2003. During its operation, I was priviledged to see an All-Star cast of Pan-Afrikan heavy hitterz like Dr. Ben, Del Jones, Ashra and Meri Ra Kwesi and Kwame Toure to name a few, as well as UAMs founder, Attorney Alton Maddox. I was even blessed to be a featured speaker at UAM four tymz. I remember on two occasionz speakin' about the Boule' and everyone was hyped and ready to go after hedz on the roster!

Cokely spoke there often as well. The two tymz I saw Cokely come and speak, I made sure I was there early enuff to perhaps steal a few secondz from him to hopefully squash this alleged "beef".

The first tyme I saw him it was about an hour before he was to speak so there weren't a lot of people there yet. He was settin' up his table of his taped lectures he intended to sell. When I walked up to him, it was just him and I. He looked at me as like he didn't know me. I thought Sun was tryin' to play me, it wasn't that long ago E.D. and I had him speak in Pittsburgh. I greeted him and he suddenly acted busy, refusing to look me in the eyes.

As he fumbled to make sure his VHS tapes and cassettes were lined up, I reached in my bag and pulled out an edition of my magazine and said, *"maybe you don't recognize me, but I'm sure you recognize this!"* He looked at it, then look at me and replied, *"Oh! What's goin' on good brutha?"* I responded wanting to know if it were true that he considered me a spy and was goin' around the country sayin' this. Instead of givin' me an answer, he literally turned his back on me and signaled somebody down the aisle and began speakin' to him. Soon after, one of UAMs security guyz walked up to me askin' me to move on.

I was left with the magazine in my hand and my mouth open. I couldn't believe it! Cokely just dissed me to my face!! Rather than cause a scene, I took his ignoring me as his choice to disregard what just happened. I left putting the magazine on his table on top of his tapes opened to the page I wrote the article about him. To this day there's been no contact and although I continue to do lectures on the Boule', I continue to pay homage to his works.

I will say since then, I have not heard any rumorz of him callin' me a spy anymore. Maybe he read the piece I left for him? And although I doubt we'll ever speak again, I guess, in some way, whatever beef he had with me is somewhat squashed. If he ever readz this, I hope he understandz it was never my intent to compete with him. I simply wanted to further his works by lettin' hedz know about this group of men who willingly continue to be pawnz for global white supremacy.

I remember waking up one morning shouting out the word, "M'Bwebe!"

Chapter Twenty-One: Comin' N2 Self

As I continued to work on elevating myself, I alwayz had an interest to change my name. There wasn't an urgency to do it and I wasn't even exactly sure if I ever would, but havin' thought of it sparingly before had now become increasingly a constant on my mind.

Knowin' the premeditated separation of our culture brought on by white supremacy — and not just Afrikanz that were stolen from Afrika and brought over to the Caribbean, North and South America. There is evidence Afrikanz were in the America's well before the so-called 'Indian' or 'Native American'; but because of global white supremacy, it's proven to be quite difficult for any melanated, kinky-haired, broad-nosed person to really know their legacy.

I say this because at one tyme, a personz name held weight. The name had a meanin'; one a person was to live up to. What really got me thinkin' about a name change was the last name I was 'born' with. I don't know much about the history of the name 'Buckner', but I did know it's origin comes from Germany, and of little I know of my family tree, I was never told I was related to any Germanz.

I also had beef with my first name (not blamin' my mother, she's a victim like the rest of us.). She named me 'Jehvon' because my father told her he didn't want any child to be named after him. So she named me 'Jehvon' which is French for Jeffrey (his name). Other than that, 'Jehvon' has no bearing, no history, no meaning.

Around the summer of 2000, I remember waking up one morning shouting out the word, *"M'Bwebe!"* I don't remember Y I said it 'cause I had no recollection of what I was dreaming before I woke. I just know when I said it I liked how it sounded. I didn't think much of it, not even as a name, I just made a mental note not to forget it.

As said before, I feel everything happenz in divine tyme. Three yearz later, I still hadn't found a name I liked and never really gave 'M'Bwebe' much thought. I went through a lot of name books, yet didn't want to settle for your ordinary name that was defined as *"A Prince born on the sixth day", "Warrior on a Wednesday"* or made up names like *"knowledge", "cypher", "science"* or *"explanation point"* like some of these cat's on the street. It had to have meaning, somethin' I would have to live up to.

That summer, I was takin' a trip to Jamaica with some extended family. This was gonna be my first vacation from everything since before 9/11. A couple weeks before the trip, I heard that KRS-One had written a book called *'Ruminations'.* Since I wasn't bringin' my laptop which prohibited me from doin' any work on my site, I bought it and decided I'd be a good read during my trip. This 'divine-tyme' thing is deep 'cause 2003 happened to be the 10th year anniversary and 100th issue of DGT. And before that year started, I had projected that year to be a one where I would step my game up. So I find it hard bein' reconnected with KRS-One through his book to be a coincidence.

I'm in Harbour View, Jamaica, takin' in some Ra (Sun), sippin' a Red Stripe and I crack open KRS' book. The revelation came when I came to a part where he defined his name. 'KRS-One' is an acronym that standz for 'Knowledge Reigns Supreme Over Nearly Everyone'. Right when I read that, a voice spoke in my head, sayin', *"M'Bwebe — Mind & Body Workin' Equally exudes Blessingz Eternal!"* In other wordz, if I keep my mind, body (and I include spirit) working together equally, the blessingz will continue to come in abundance! I swear to you not, kid, it came like one of those subliminal faxes from the Ancestorz, Sun!

I was madd excited! — and a lil' buzzed, I admit, from the Red Stripe. I finally had a name that had meaning! Simply livin' up to its definition was a pledge I made to apply to my life daily.

Havin' renamed myself has given me a measuring stick of sorts to align myself to which I believe will make me a more humble and focused being. I encourage you to challenge yourself mentally, spiritually and physically in whatever way you find will make you a better person. I feel if we all started demanding such thingz from ourselves, not only will we be better individually, our families will be more sound and our offspring will have a more firm foundation — which is a gateway to knowledge of self.

What you've read thus far is but a short-biography of what I perceive to have been a fruitful path of alternative thought I continue to travel. There was a need for me to share this with you so that you would now know the author before you read the articles that make up the rest of ***'Analitikul Cogitationz'.***

References and Suggested Readingz

From the Browder File, Anthony Browder

Nile Valley Contributions to Civilization, Anthony Browder

Survival Strategies, Anthony Browder

Soul Traveler, Albert Taylor, PhD

Ruminations, KRS-One

Ancient Future, Wayne Chandler

Of Water And The Spirit, Malidoma Patrice Some'

100 Amazing Facts About the Negro, J.A. Rogers

Conscious Rasta Report, Keidi Obi Awadu

Homosexuality and the Effeminization of Afrikan Males, Mwalimu K. Bomani Baruti

Nutricide, Llaila O. Afrika

Destruction of Black Civilization, Chancellor Williams

Blueprint for Black Power, Amos Wilson

Black Man of the Nile, Dr. Yosef ben-Jochannan

The Isis Papers, Dr. Francess Cress-Welsing

Yurugu, Marimba Ani

The Historical Jesus and the Mythical Christ , Gerald Massey

The Came Before Columbus, Ivan Van Sertima

Rule By Secrecy, Jim Marrs

The Secret Of the Great Pyramid, Peter Tompkins

Analitkul Cogitationz

Analitikul Cogitationz is a selection of some of my favorite perspective writingz that appeared in *Da Ghetto Tymz magazine* from its inception in 1993 through 2006.

The history presently taught in most public and private school systemz will not be the same history our children and grandchildren will learn, it will be worse! I believe if Generation X does not step up, the future of our people will be lost to "multiculturalizm' also known as 'the melting pot theory'.

Multiculturalizm is defined as *"relating to, or constituting several cultural or ethnic groups within a society."* Soundz nice readin' it, but the real-life definition meanz, *"the grouping of all ethnic groups except the Afrikan race where this group portrayz or passes themselves off as Afrikanz, while the Afrikan continues to be taught self-hatred."*

Long definition, but you can see it happening everwhere! There are more europeanz movin' into Afrikan neighborhoodz as we witness gentrification around the country; white rapperz — or any white person in Hiphop period — have become accepted; they showin' up at our most sacred of ceremonies (like the annual tribute to our Ancestorz at Coney Island every June).

I believe the current generation, Generation X (those born after 1965 and before 1980) is the last generation that has had the benefit of exposure of the civil rights and Black Power movements as well as the current technological era.

We are not too old to remember the stories and images of Martin Luther King, Malcolm X, Medgar Evers, Huey Newton and the Black Pantherz, and so on. We can remember the era where conscious Hiphop reached its heights in the late 90s with groups like X-Clan, Brand Nubian, Tribe Called Quest, when Queen Latifah was really actin' like a Queen (remember U.N.I.T.Y.? Today her hair *stay* blond!) and the infamous Black medallion with the Red, Black and Green Afrikan continent on it.

We are also the first to join the business world, where we are privy to thingz our Elderz daydreamed of. We are making *and spending* more money than we ever had! Yet, we continue to remain ignorant of this potentially lethal and effective combination.

If we, the memberz of this generation do not take lead on the preservation of our culture, it will be lost. As you can attest, the Elderz of the 60s are makin' their transition to the non-physical realm (dying) and with them goes an abundant amount of our story. Soon, gone will be the one's who can best tell the story of our continuous fight for liberation; gone will be those who could best teach the wayz of our Ancestorz; and gone will be the spirit of race pride as Amerikkka seeks to eliminate Afrikan people through the ideology of the melting pot theory — where the thickest and last part of the stew used, which in most cases are burnt (black) by then, are at the bottom;

symbolic for Afrikan people.

Analitikul Cogitationz represents the first chapter in the resurrected legacy of our people. This book's attempt is to be a link, bridging the historical heritage of our people conveyed in a modern way generation X, Y and beyond can comprehend. And although a lot of the following pieces are controversial, we warn you to read with caution. Some of this may disturb you, inform you and hopefully compel you to contribute somethin' to our story.

I ask again, that you read with an open mind. I don't expect you to agree with everything you will read in this book. Some info you'll read you may agree with and some you may totally disagree. I challenge you to go beyond the disagreement and use this as an opportunity to make it a conversation piece with your friendz and/or family.

By talkin' it out, one goal could be for you, the individual, to find out what it is you do believe because most of us never had the opportunity to be enlightened to an alternative thought, so we were forced to choose the one perspective given to us. Many of us, including myself at one tyme, grew up with this one perspective and when someone comes with an alternative thought, we shut it down, not because of truth or falsehood, but because we've been programmed to believe what we were taught before, accepting no other viewpoints.

My writingz reflect the *'9 Areas of People Activity'* authorz Neilly Fuller and Francess Cress-Welsing spoke so eloquently about in each of their works. They are as followz: (1)Economics, (2)Education, (3)Entertainment, (4)Labor, (5)Law, (6)Politics, (7)Sex, (8)Religion and (9)War. After havin' numerous discussionz with Bro. Keidi of *LIBRadio.com*, we both agreed that a tenth one needed to be added... (10)HEALTH!

It is my hope that you, the reader, will find somethin' inside the rest of this book that may assist in your growth and awareness. Maybe conspiraceez ain't your thang, then maybe the health pieces will grab you. Perhaps you're into metaphysics, well there's a wealth of pieces in this book! Whatever your interest's, if they fall within the 9 Areas, ***'Analitikul Cogitationz'*** got it covered!

Now that you know the person behind DGT and how it came about, I welcome you to the rest of ***'Analitikul Cogitationz'.***

2006

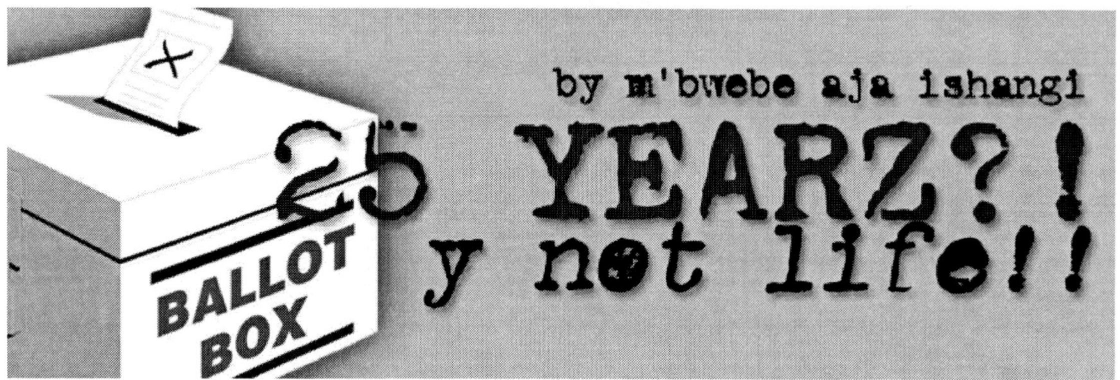

It's almost 2007, and hedz still think our government isn't racist! On Thursday, July 13, 2006, the 1965 Voting Rights Act, which opened booths to millionz of Afrikanz-in-america (Black people), was "granted" a 25-year extension from Congress as Republicanz sought to improve their standing with us so-called "minoriteez" before electionz this past fall.

The Senate turned in a 98-0 vote count the week of July 17th after the previous week's House passage vote count of 390-33. Can you believe there were actually 33 hedz that wanted to abolish Afrikanz the right to vote?!

The next step is for good-old George W to sign the legislation, which, by the way, was not a coincidence that he finally showz up to speak at the National Association for the Advancement of CERTAIN People's (NAACP) national conference after refusing to the invitation for five yearz in a row. (more info on NAACP later in this bok). President Lyndon Johnson signed the Voting Rights Act into law in August 1965 after efforts to fully integrate Afrikanz produced violent reactionz in Southern states.

The law declared a nationwide prohibition against voting discrimination based on race, eliminated poll taxes and literacy tests, and other election devices that were used for decades to keep us from voting.

The 33 who voted against the Act were obviously Republican. They wanted to shorten the renewal from 25 yearz to 10!! But that don't shouldn't make the Democrats our boy neither!

We should all be askin' ourselves, "25 yearz?! Y not LIFE!" This is Y I am a proud NON-registered voter! That's right, I don't vote, 'cause it's a game designed for you to believe you have a say when you actually don't!

I mean, ask yourselves, Y are Afrikanz-in-america the only group of people who has to ask if we can partake in voting every 25 yearz?!!? Not Asian-American, not Latino's, us Afrikanz!! Y have our "so-called" leaderz allowed this shit to happen? Y aren't they informing the people of this fact?! Oh, forgot, they're all part of the game – they're not our leaderz, the system appointed them as our leaderz for us, we didn't choose them!

This Act and every election should be seen as an insult to us – especially for those who call themselves "american" because the truth is we're "leased" americanz!

The fact the government makes this a part of legislation serves as an even greater diss because it meanz come 2032, hedz will convene again and decide if Afrikanz should be "granted" the permission to partake in voting again!! I mean, what's the big deal with trashin' the 25-year contract and make it life?! It's clear to me they still see us as 2nd class and thus not worthy of full citizenship and in the next 25 yearzthey will decide if we're worthy to join in their reindeer games again!

No other race, including Asian- and Latino-americanz have to have congress pass a bill allowing them the right to vote in the country they reside.

We are the only hedz who have to go through this shit despite the large percentage of us that make up this country's armed forces as well as having the largest spending power – well over $761 billion ($1 trillion by 2010)!

Ask yourself, what you think woulda happened had they not passed the Act? Take a sec and marinate on that vision… I think all hell woulda broke loose, Sun! In fact, it actually woulda finally freed us because we woulda finally wised-up! Once and for all, we'd see how they truly see us; we'd ultimately give the ax to the co-conspiratorz of our ignorance – our so-called negro leaderz – and develop new leadership, creating our own systematic government!

We also need to make as many hedz possible aware of this. And those we contact, if they're not with us, then we will call 'em out — grouping them with the other supporterz of this inhumane policy. We will allow no one to ride the fence! You're either a supporter of the bill bein' revisited in 2032 or not. Either way, the masses would know their status and the interests would be severely damaged if the public knew they were supporterz. Now *that* would lead to a global boycott and a total collapseof YTs corporate infrastructure!

I guess YT ain't fully ready fi war yet! But that don't mean we shouldn't be gettin' prepared. It shoudn't take anutha 25 yearz to go by 'til we speak on this again, 'cause come 2032, they might be ready to deal with the repercussionz of abolishing the Act.

So instead of celebrating YTs permission to play in his reindeer games for the next 25 seasonz, we should be organizing our own game plan which would include a Nationality that would give us both dual citizenship and exemption from the 2nd class rights they instilled on us post-1865.

There needz to be more than speeches, marches, protests and boycotts, there needz to be a strategic 5-10 year plan devised or revised to develop our own government – a system that unites all melanated Afrikanz 'pon di world!

Ok, enuff of the readin', "let's all go out and get this movement started!!"

The Encyclopedia Africana Scandal: For Us, By Us?

by m'bwebe aja ishangi

It seemz everytyme you think we come out with something "for us, by us", it ain't... Back in 1999, an encyclopedia for the Afrikan diaspora was released. It was a remarkable feat for it was the first of its kind – a set of volumes that told our story... or did it?

It should not be a surprise when we find out this project had the financial and, I'm sure, creative guidance from a shadow influence. To most who may have seen the volumes, are under the assumption it came solely from Kwame Anthony Appiah and Henry Louis Gates, Jr. when actually, like with most of "our" thingz, there's an overseer.

Gates has long pledged his allegiance to the mythological greek life. From his affiliation with the Boule' (Sigma Pi Phi), on up to and including now, his partnership with The Perseus Books Group.

One only needz to look through the first couple pages of the first printed edition to find out more about this secret overseer. Here you'll find the wordz, *"Copyright 1999 Kwame Anthony and Henry Louis Gates, Jr."* Under this you'll see a logo of the Basic Civitas Books, a subsidiary book publishing company that promotes Afrikan authorz.

What's under that you'll see *"A Member of the Perseus Books Group."* This is where it get's interesting... This is s'posed to be a project for and about Afrikan people. So who are they, Y did Gates choose to not show this shadow corporationz real logo and Y didn't he use his fellow Boule' brother John Johnson of JP Publishing Co. or even Oprah to finance the project instead?!!? Then it would at least be an all black project.

If you go to the Perseus Book Group's website, you'll find their logo is based off Perseus – a greeky mythological "god", the son of Danaë and Zeus and husband of Andromeda who killed the Gorgon Medusa (again, I stress, "myth" 'cause this shit ain't really happen!). They refused to mention their historical origin from the caucus mountainz, so instead to make them appear to evolved from this prestigious heritage, they made up Godz (Zeus, etc) and legendz, that over tyme became believed by the masses.

My question is Y did they choose not to put this logo in the book? I have to believe this isn't a coincidence 'cause when you're dealin' with white supremacy, there aren't any coincidences! So I must believe The Perseus Books Group, Gates and Appiah would know that any person that knowz their history, is fully aware the greeks were among two other pirates (that bein' the persianz and romanz) who stole our identity through our culture and history as well as murdered and enslaved our Ancestorz.

They all had to know this link bein' known, Afrikanz would not support such a project because it is an example of yet anutha ALP – an "Al Jolson Project"(a white financed and governed project that's marketed as an Afrikan project.) After all, it was the white-racist Winston Churchill who said, *"History is going to be good to us because I'm going to rewrite it."*

LIK SHOT

Nigga versus Spik

So many tymz on the train I hear young gunz shootin' out the word *"nigga this"* and *"nigga that."* True, we've all had the *"we ain't niggaz"* lecture, but I realize there's a whole nutha generation that hasn't. I've had to recondition myself over and over again to not say this word and just when I thought I had it licked, Dave Chappelle popularized the word again!

Not to blame Dave, there's been madd hedz strugglin' with the word.

Although Black people have adopted this as part of the vernacular, I feel we must again look at this closely because it has become acceptable for even otherz to use this word!

You probably sayin', *"if a white person sayz nigga, they dead!"* But Y is ok for Latino's to use it?

If we get so offended and ready fi war when the word is uttered by YT, Y do we give a pound to Latino's when they don't see themselves as Afrikanz (most do not acknowledge their connection to the Afrikan bloodline)?!

The jokes been on us Afrikanz and its tyme to stop! True, Latino's have their injustices, but they also have a word that ignites the same rage as the word *'nigga'*. The fact is if you were to ask a Hispanic person if they were a nigga, they'd look at you like you were crazy. Everyone knowz the history of the word and everyone knowz it only applies to Afrikanz-in-America. So again I ask, Y is it ok for you to be buildin' with a Hispanic person and the word 'nigga' is thrown loosely throughout the conversation?!

Here's an experiment, next tyme you're polyin' with a Latino cat, substitute *'nigga'* with the word *'spik'* each tyme you'd say nigga and peep the reaction... Maybe then we'd take note how everyone's cool with bein' us when it's convenient. By the way, like nigga is a negative word, 'Spik' is an offensive term for personz of Hispanic descent. Funny, I've never heard 2 Latino's callin' each other that...

KATRINA: WAKEUP CALL 4 AFRIKANZ?

BY M'BWEBE AJA ISHANGI

With the latest string of natural disasterz over the past couple yearz, it would make one wonder if we really are in the last dayz. But this piece isn't about *"God's wrath"...* this is about how humanz treat humanz in tymz of disaster.

Not even 5 yearz ago, the aftermath of 9/11 reminded me of the 1993 movie, Demolition Man which starred Wesley Snipes and Sylvester Stallone. For several dayz (and possible weeks) there was no crime, everyone dropped their stereotypical differences and saw each other as one; a country united who needed to bond if we were to get through this. Everyone suddenly started dawning red, white and blue flagz under the illusion they can cover up their fearz by feelin' patriotic. This was a tyme where everyone was affected and thus, everyone participated in the rehabilitation to bring calm.

	NEW YORK	NEW ORLEANS
POPULATION	8,008,278	484674
WHITE	44.6%	28.05%
AFRIKAN	26.59%	67.25%
OTHER *(Asian, Hispanic, etc)*	28.81%	4.7%

SOURCE: 2000 US Census www.neworleans.areaconnect.com/statistics.htm & www.newyork.areaconnect.com/statistics.htm

Fast forward to Hurricane Katrina; although there weren't alleged terrorist planes attacking skyscraperz, we find ourselves as victimz to yet anutha uncontrolled attack. The reaction this tyme? Not the same…

I started to think, other than this bein' a natural disaster instead of a man-made and planned attack, what was the difference? I started doin' some searching for stats 'cause before I can make my obvious claimz, for all those naysayerz who are quick to say I try to make everything a black-white issue, I needed stats to verify what I know to be true. I went to a website *(www.newyork.areaconnect.com/statistics.htm & www.neworleans.areaconnect.com/statistics.htm)* to search for the amount of black people that live in New York and compare it with those of use that are in New Orleans.

According to the 2000 US. Census, New York City has a total population of over 8 million people with 44.6% being white, 26.6% Afrikan and 28.8% other. New Orleans has approximately 485,000 with 28.1% white, 67.3% Afrikan and 4.7% other.

Now, after marinating on the numberz, it's safe to say that New Orleans is predominately Afrikan with just over 30% consisting of whites and other ethnicities. Now, am I wrong to think there's somethin' racial about US Government's response 4-5 dayz after Katrina hit the hood?

Next comes a barrage of questionz: 1)Y were all the Newz stationz able to get there to cover the story as it developed and throughout the aftermath, yet there were none that would bring supplies 'til dayz after?

2)Of all the helicopterz and Newz teamz that covered the story, Y didn't they just put some supplies in those copterz to give to the victimz?

3)Y would the National Guard show up heavily armed and given permission to shoot anyone "looting" for supplies to survive on?

4)Y did it take Bush so long to come to see the aftermath and Y did he just go to Biloxi, Mississippi where, according to the 2000 US Census, 71% of the population is *white* and not New Orleans – where our people dwell? Biloxi wasn't even hit as hard as New Orleanz!

5)And Y didn't Bush take at least one person with him to safety when he left?

6)Y did Jesse Jackson and Elijah Cummings nut-up when Larry King asked if the US. Government's delay in relief was racially motivated?

7)Where are our so-called leaderz? Y haven't we heard Farrakhan say anything about how the victimz have been treated? What about Al Sharpton?

8)Y is everybody tryin' to tie God into this? Farrakhan stated Katrina was *"God's punishment for the war in Iraq."* What parties responsible for the war in Iraq live in New Orleans?!!? Evangelist, Michael Marcavage stated Katrina *"destroyed a wicked city"* favoring the hurricane because it caused the cancellation of an annual gay festival (which I'm in agreement of the cancellation, but I'm sure it was on the next year!)

9)If this "God" shit is true, Y would "God" destroy a city where a lot of Black people live and label it a wicked city, yet not destroy DC which is the symbolic headquarterz of the most wicked clan that's responsible global white supremacy?

10) Where were all the helicopterz in the nation that could've dropped off supplies starting the day after the storm?

11)Knowing that the eye of Katrina had passed over Florida Thursday, August 27th and that it was headed toward New Orleans, Y didn't the US Government take any preventive measures before the storm?

12)Y hasn't anyone come down on the press for its blatant racial epithet it showed when they released two photo's, one with a white couple *"finding"* food from a local grocery store contrasting it with a young Afrikan doin' the same exact thing, yet the media claimz he's *"looting"* a grocery store?; and

13)Y are hedz blastin' Kanye West for speakin' the truth?!!?

These are but a few questionz that may never be addressed by the actual parties that need to answer them, and that's not my purpose for addressing them. The questionz are for you, the reader to look at and ask yourself Y you think they'll ever be addressed. All this points to two logical points: 1)Afrikan people, even in America, are still considered less-human than whites and 2)Our so-called Black leadership is so weak, we are virtually paralyzed to do anything ourself, *for* ourselves.

In a tyme where fellow Americanz, no fuck that, *Human Beingz* are in need of help, other living beingz chose to ignore, then because of tv coverage, finally stepped in – I mean, why'd it take damn near a week to finally have a nationally televised relief program?!!? Racizm is the answer. The statistics support my claim, for if it were a New York City or any other predominately white populated city, relief would've come much sooner – remember the hurricanes in Florida? What about the Tsunami?!

The lengthy delay our people have endured since August 28th, 2005 is the longest and most inhumane atrocity done on modern US. soil. The way the government chose to both relieve and gain control in New Orleans also showz just how they feel about Afrikanz-in-America. To show up with gunz before food and water verifies my claim.

Friday, September 2nd, Kanye West did what those who know him well, would do. He spoke the shockin' truth. Stating Bush didn't care about Black people, YTs massa-media has again flooded the waves clamin' Kanye attacked Bush, when he was only echoing what several other reporterz as well as New Orleans officialz were saying – especially mayor Ray Nagin. I applaud Kanye's courage to actually say somethin' many think about doin'! Nagin should be commended as well.

Nagin has gone on record with CNNs WWL Radio, demanding the federal government get off their ass and do something! Nagin also revealed in the interview that they've requested in the past, the governor, homeland security, FEMA, etc. to fix the 17th Street Canal where a pumping station that's used to keep the city dry because it's 6 feet below sea level. Because this plea was ignored, it probably killed thousandz more, because the pump station also pumped the cities water supply through the city. You can read more of his interview at *www.cnn.com/2005/US/09/02/nagin.transcript/index.html.*

He was asked what could people do to help and his first response was to keep talkin' about it, which is Y I wrote this piece. We need to keep talkin' about this Afrikanz! At the dawn of the possible historic Millionz More March this October, we must begin to see that what happenz to Afrikanz anywhere in the world affects us all globally! We must make it our business to know what's goin' on abroad as well as in this country because you'll find that YT discriminates against us all equally. If you thought not before, hurricane Katrina should be your wakeup call!

Keep talkin' about it Afrikanz, keep talkin'!!

I shoulda known on October 21, 2002 when I read the USDA (United States Department of Agriculture) and the organic industry merged with the new organic label, organic food was well on the course of being ushered into the class of unhealthy foodz. Actually, I shoulda known before that after realizing the sudden surge of hedz wanting to eat healthier foodz in the 1990s.

All the industrial, pharmaceutical (including hospitalz) and government industries saw this comin' well before the public: if the masses suddenly move to eat healthier – meaning, eating less and less red meat and dairy products – they would suffer tremendous financial losses because, let's face it, sick and dead people simply make money! (For reference, read *"In Sickness & in Health? Or Potential Wealth!")*

Have you noticed over the last couple yearz your local supermarket now features an organic produce section? Currently, organic foodz represent a small part of overall grocery sales in the united states, but the market is growing fast. In 2001, sales of organic foodz and beverages grossed more than $9 billion.

If you're familiar with then-president Jimmy Carter's Global 2000 project launched in the late 1970s – which called for the slow deaths of some 2 billion people before the year 2000 – you'd be able to connect the dots on the tyming of organic foodz. There is no way the Meat & Dairy industry, the hospital administration, the Food & Drug Administration (FDA) and countless other groups could achieve Global 2000s projected goal if everyone was suddenly eating healthy! So they had to infiltrate the organic industry!

Many of us – even me until recently – thought by eating organic foodz, we were safe. But, again, we shoulda known – those who became vegetarianz and veganz because of how toxic "regular" food is – that the energy of the world for some tyme has been vibrating predominantly on a negative or death frequency, not life… so the move for organic food market to be infiltrated was inevitable.

One only needz to look at the corporation Monsanto to see how major their influence has been on how foodz are made today. Monsanto's not only a manufacturer and distributor of agricultural chemi-killz (chemicalz) and developerz of plant biotechnology, they are also the worldz leader in producing genetically modified seedz. Over the past several yearz larger and brighter-colored produce has been introduced as passed off as 'food'; but it's genetically modified. If you've wondered Y the fruits that had seedz (like cherries and grapes) are almost a thing of the past replaced with seedless fruits, it's because they're genetically modified; and if you're a farmer or you know one and you have to constantly buy seedz to replant your crop, it's because the seedz you are forced to now buy have been scientifically made to be unable reproduce, yet promises to be the size resembling what might be on Fred Flinstone's plate.

We are livin' in an era where the very sustenance needed to sustain our lives are bein' polluted with man-made technology all in the name of profit and population control. Remember when you could actually drink water from the faucet?!

SERIOUS AS CANCER...

Have you noticed the sudden rise of cancerz? Todayz fast-paced society is full of fast-food joints, microwaveable and genetically modified foodz. We take less and less tyme to eat actual mealz makin' it harder to digest. On top of that, the kindz of foodz we eat are less healthy mainly because it *"simply ain't momz cookin' no mo!"* Patience and luv in making food has been replaced with haste, population demand and profit.

This year, according to the National Cancer Institute website, there will be more than 1.3 million cases diagnosed and more than 500,000 hedz will succumb to the disease. It's estimated by 2020 cancer could be responsible for the deaths of over 10-15 million people every year, that's nearly half the amount of Afrikanz livin' in America today!

As veganz and vegetarianz, we thought we escaped this treacherous man-eating dis-ease by givin' up the Jimmy Dean sausages, Oscar Mayer weinerz, macaroni & cheese, barbequed ribz, honey-glazed ham, kool-aid and peach cobbler (to name a few of my childhood favorites) for we surely were on the path of various health ailments. But it stingz even more when you left all that shit to find out some of the shit we been eatin' as alternatives is just as, if not even more, worse!

THYROID CANCER ON THE RISE

With the most common cancerz – colorectal, breast and prostate – declining, thyroid cancer has risen sharply. The reported number more than doubled from 3.6 per 100,000 hedz in 1973 to 8.7 per 100,000 in 2002 and about 24,000 newly diagnosed thyroid cancerz have emerged nationwide according to the "*Journal of the American Medical Association.*"

Not to scare you, there *are* cancerz that grow so slowly they pose no threat to life. But of those that are, there seemz to be a connection to a particular ingredient that's been embraced by the vegetarian community… no not canola oil, it's SOY!

THE SOY STORY

The fact that soy causes several formz of cancer is clearly a cover-up. For every book or website claiming this destructive food product, there's probably several hundred that speaks different. For those confused I'd consider in the meantyme, because soy isn't unanimously clean of these allegationz, give soy up until you have information that undoubtedly clearz soy of these accusationz. Don't do what I did for nearly 3 yearz ignoring what I heard because I felt I've given up so much, I don't wanna give anutha thing up. Denial can only hurt you. So please, once you finish readin' this, if you're not convinced, do the proper research to complete your curiosity so you can come to a complete decision on whether to give it up or not…

I strongly suggest you read Kaayla T. Daniel's, *"The Whole Soy Story: The Dark Side of America's Favorite Health Food."* In it, Daniel unveilz hard-to-find cover-up material the american press refuses to publish.

Over the last 10 or so yearz, the vegan/vegetarian community has witnessed a boom in a new "food" source that quickly has become america's favorite "health" food to eat. With the assistance of positive write-ups in "massa"-media, it's believed by most that soy is the key to disease prevention and can add yearz to your life – all the while never shedding an ounce of proof that it is so.

What exactly is soy? Soy foodz come in many formz including many products that go through a massive processing procedure. "Massa"-media's done an excellent job in deceiving the public soy is a major part of the Asian diet – although it's been reported the people of China, Japan and other countries in Asia eat very little soy. The claim that soybeanz have played a major part in of the Asian diet for more than 3000 yearz is simply not true.

In Daniel's book, she states their consumption ranges from *"9.3 to 36 grams per day. That's grams of soy food, not grams of soy protein alone."* A cup of tofu is about 252 gramz and a glass of soy milk is about 240! Most hedz in america eat not just tofu and drink soy milk throughout the day, they also eat veggie burgerz, Textured Vegetable Protein (TVP) nuggets that taste like chicken nuggets, soynuts, soy yogurt, soy ice cream, soy energy barz and the list goes on!!! What's more dangerous are infants who are fed soy formula and soy milk. Mainly because the amount ratio is more because they are smaller in size and body weight. Most hedz don't even realize they've most likely eliminated or severely lessened the nutrients calcium and vitamin D 'cause they think they gettin' it in soy milk, when their actually added in some, not all, so it can compete with dairy products. I'm sure you've seen the boxes that highlight calciumz added.

On the contrary, soy studies have shown links to malnutrition, digestive problemz, thyroid dysfunction, reproductive disorderz, infertility, heart disease, immune-system breakdown (which is AIDS, when your immune-system becomes deficient or unable to no longer work) and heart disease.

"Americans rarely hear anything negative about soy," states Daniel, *"Thanks to the shrewd public relations campaigns waged by Archer Daniels Midland (ADM), Protein Technologies International (PTI), the American Soybean Association, and other soy interests, as well as the Food and Drug Administration's (FDA) 1999 approval of the health claim that soy protein lowers cholesterol [and] maintains a "healthy" image."*

THE WAY IT'S MADE

You've heard the sayin' *"too much of anything is bad for you."* This ringz true and also applyz to the vegan/vegetarian diet. Y? Because processed "health" foodz have made it so (this doesn't apply to naturally made foodz although thingz have changed ever since companies like Monsanto monopolized the seed industry making dam near everything GM or genetically-modified.). We've seen so many different kindz of soy products – soy sausage, hot dogz, salad dressing, lunch "meat", smoothies, etc. – we don't realize in one day we might ingest so much soy our diet's are probably worse than non-vegetarianz because they have the luxury to choose from various different kindz of toxinz better known as food.

Here in america, over the last decade or so the industrial processing system of making soy has enabled scientists to develop cheaper meat substitutes. What many aren't aware of is the soy revolution is also in pharmaceuticalz and used as a plant-based resource that replace petroleum-based plastics and fuel.

Initially, soy left over from the soy-oil extraction went to animalz and poultry. But since food scientists have found wayz to disguise the color and flavor of soy, it's now bein' aggressively marketed as "people food." They accomplish this by simply adding toxic additives like sugar, salt, artificial flavorz, colorz and monosodium glutamate, that's right, MSG!

Todayz food products contain soy in nearly 60% of foodz found in your local supermarket. What's shockin' is it's also present in hamburgerz sold at fast-food joints!!

DIFFERENT KINDZ OF SOY

Soy is made into different kindz which had even me thinkin' perhaps there's good and bad soy. WRONG! All are bad! Take textured soy protein for example. It's made by forcing defatted soy flour through a machine called an extruder under conditionz of such extreme heat and pressure that the very structure of the soy protein is changed. Production differz little from the extrusion technology used to produce starch-based packing materials, fiber-based industrial products and plastic toy parts, bowlz and plates.

Another kind is soy protein isolate (SPI) which is first mixed with a corrosive alkaline solution to remove the fiber, then washed in an acid solution to speed up the depletion of protein, yet it's still called soy PROTEIN isolate! Next the "protein" curdz are dipped into another alkaline solution and spray-dried at extremely high temperatures. All this to erase the beany taste while sacrificing all vitamin, mineral and proteinz and increasing the levelz of cancer-causing ingredients like nitrosamine.

SPIs are abundant in so many products we eat and as mentioned earlier, YTs media has done a good job hiding info on an organization like the Federation of American Societies for Experimental Biology (FASEB) who in 1979 published that the only safe use for SPIs was for sealerz for cardboard packages.

THE SCIENTIFICAL MADNESS OF SOY

There's madd studies done by scientists who report the use of soy protein in animal feedz cause malnutrition, digestive problemz such as pancreatitis and other health issues. Phytates block mineral absorption, causing zinc, iron and calcium deficiencies;

lectinz and saponinz have caused leaky gut and other gastrointestinal and immune problemz; oxalates causes problemz for people prone to kidney stones and women suffering from vulvodynia – a painful condition marked by burning, stinging and itching of the external genitalia; and finally, oligosaccharides give soy its notorious reputation as a gas producer.

Soy allergies are on the rise for 3 reasonz: (1)the growing use of soy infant formula which is reported to be some 20-25% of the formula market; (2) the increase in soy-containing foodz in grocery stores, and (3) the possibility of the greater allergies due to the creation of genetically modified soybeanz.

Soy is one of the top allergenz that cause immediate hypersensitive reactionz such as coughing, sneezing, runny nose, hives, diarrhea, difficulty swallowing and anaphylactic shock which can result in immediate death! Delayed allergic responses are even more common and occur anywhere from several hourz to several dayz after the food is eaten. Sleep disturbances, bedwetting, sinus and ear infectionz, crankiness, joint pain, chronic fatigue, gastrointestinal woes and other mysterious symptomz are also linked to the consumption of soy.

THE RIZE OF THYROID PROBLEMZ

According the Daniel, there's more than 70 yearz of human, animal and laboratory studies that show soybeanz put the thyroid at risk. The chief culprits are the plant hormones in soy known as phytoestrogenz or isoflavones. The United Kingdomz Committee on Toxicology has identified several populationz at special risk: infants on soy formula, veganz who use soy as their principal meat and dairy replacements, men and women who self-medicate with soy foodz and/or isoflavone supplements in an attempt to prevent or reverse menopausal symptomz, cancer or heart disease.

Since the mid-1940s, scientists have known that phytoestrogenz can impair fertility. Fertility problemz in cowz, sheep, rabbits, cheetahz, guinea pigz, birdz and mice have all been reported. Recently they discovered soy lowerz testosterone levelz too! Could that be the reason for the rize in homosexuality?? Humanz and animalz appear to be the most vulnerable to the effects of soy estrogenz before and during pregnancy, the youth's infancy, puberty and lactation as well as during the hormonal shifts of menopause. Of all these groups, infants on soy formula are at the highest risk because of their small size and developmental phase, and because formula is their main source of nutrition.

"A crucial time for the programming of the human reproduction system is right after birth – the very time when bottles of soy formula are given to many non-breastfed babies," Daniel's writes. *"Normally during this period, the body surges with natural estrogens, testosterones, and other hormones that are meant to program the baby's reproductive development from infancy through puberty and into adulthood. For infants on soy formula, this programming may be interrupted."*

Baby boyz experience a testosterone surge during the first few months of life and produce androgenz – a male sex hormone like testosterone – in amounts equal to those of adult men. A lot of this testosterone is needed at such a tender age to program the body for puberty, the tyme when the sex organz should develop and begin to express male physical traits such as facial and pubic hair as well as a deep voice.

With soy estrogen in the diet thus replacing testosterone, the appropriate development may never take place, hence instead of developing into a "he", he'll develop characteristics of a "she". In the yearz since soy formula has been in the marketplace, parents and pediatricianz have reported growing numberz of boyz whose physical maturation is either delayed or does not occur at all. They've reported these youths havin' breasts, underdeveloped semen to reproduce, testicles – male ballz – that never come down from the abdomen into the scrotum (called cryptorchidism) and steroid insufficiencies are increasingly common and on the rise. Sperm counts are also falling. Open your eyez people! This is Global 2000 at work!!

Soy formula is bad for little girlz as well. Natural estrogen levelz approximately double during the first month of life, then decline and remain at low levelz until puberty. With increased estrogenz in the environment in the diet, an alarming number of girlz are entering puberty much earlier than normal. 1% of girlz now show signz of puberty, such as breast development or pubic hair, before the age of 3, yo! And by the tyme they turn 8, 14.7% of Caucasian girlz are affected, whereas nearly half (48.3%) of Afrikan girlz born in american had one or both of these characteristics. Y IZ Dat?!

Y does it attack our sistaz in larger numberz than YT has yet to be determined although we have reason to believe racial discriminationz behind it. According the Daniel, of all the estrogenz found in the environment, soy is the likeliest explanation of Y our young sistaz reach puberty so quickly. *"Since its establishment in 1974, the federal government's Women, Infants and Children (WIC) program has provided free infant formula to teenage and other low-income mothers while failing to encourage breastfeeding. Because of perceived or real lactose intolerance, black babies are much more likely to receive soy formula than Caucasian babies,"* writes Daniel.

Early puberty creates reproductive problemz for them later in life including a period that no longer comes, anovulatory cycles where eggz are no longer released, eggz that fail to mature and develop into healthy eggz and several other hormonal dilemmaz. In addition, because the mammary glandz depend on estrogen for their development and functioning, the presence of soy estrogenz at a vulnerable tyme might expose young girlz to breast cancer – another condition on the rise and definitively linked to early puberty. If they continue to induce soy, they can most likely count on a life of continued painful menstrual periodz, possible development of allergies, asthma, higher rates of cervical cancer, polycystic ovarian syndrome, blocked fallopian tubes, and pelvic inflammatory disease.

Those who become motherz and feed their children soy formula expose them to higher levelz of aluminum, fluoride and manganese. These metalz have the potential to affect brain development. Children have been found suffering from attention-deficit disorderz, dyslexiaz and other learning problemz.

DO YOU BELIEVE?

Over recent weeks since I found out about this, I've heard several hedz say this is not true and that soyz bein' attacked by the Meat & Dairy Industry 'cause so many are givin' up their products and moving towardz a more healthy diet. The argument is further made difficult because finding research on soy is scarce – mainly because soy hasn't been part of our diet long enuff. Even health authorities are somewhat baffled recommending the public to "wait and see" what happenz in a couple yearz.

Several hedz have sung to me the "too much of anything can hurt you" theory. But I believe waiting to see what happenz – meaning, I'ma continue to eat this shit and once it's been a part of the diet long enuff that there's an adequate amount of cases to prove or disprove these allegationz – would be the biggest of mistakes. To me it's just plain ignorance, IGNORing the hazard signz we have today. Y choose voluntarily to be a guinea pig for these industries that see us – as they classified humanz are in the Global 2000 project – as "Useless eaterz"? What happenz if these claimz are true and soy does cause all these thingz you just read? If we find out 5, 10, even 20 yearz down the line, when not only did we continue to consume soy products, we also fed it to our babies, what then? Cry to the hippocratic hospitalz for a cure?!

Daniel M. Sheehan, formerly the senior toxicologist with the FDA's National Center for Toxicological Research, has called the soy-eating experience as a *"large, uncontrolled and basically unmonitored human experiment."* There's anutha choice you can make. How 'bout just give this shit up altogether and continue to do the research until you there's sufficient evidence to clear soy of these charges. Not only will you save your life, but otherz as well!

The choice is yourz…

Scenario: Annual West Indian Labor Day Parade
Location: Brooklyn, New York, Eastern Parkway
Attendance: Several Hundred Thousand
Agenda: Party and Bullshit

Throughout the year we plead with YT to help us with aid, reparationz [which they've made apparent they will *never* pay], jobz, medical care, etc. Hence, "freedom" has been "granted" to Afrikanz-in-america for several hundred yearz yet we continue to show up at the meeting table, first, entering through the backdoor, and then sitting at the table with our handz out. The only thing we bring to the table is our strategically inherited drama as we beg for otherz to throw us a few bread crumbz.

While we continue to dwell on the bottom of the socio-economic ladder, we continue having parades, carnivalz, fairz and festivalz where the only interpretation of the word 'wealth' is from an individual perspective.

Take for instance, the Annual West Indian Labor Day Parade held in Brooklyn, New York every Labor Day where several hundred thousand Afrikanz get together to biggup which colonized sect is better than the rest. We are a long wayz from realizing we are not Jamaican or Trinidadian but Afrikan by way of the *Maangamizi or Middle Passage.

I'd like to add a different perspective to these parades 'cause I believe the theory of building collective wealth is a reachable concept.

How much money do you think could be raised if someone organized to have collection baskets that asked for a $1 minimum donation every 20 or so meterz apart on Eastern Parkway (where the parade is held). The several-hundred-thousand-to-millionz raised could be used to finance our needz in a particular country in the Caribbean, Afrika and even here in america for the year. How many hospitalz are needed in our homelandz? How many homes could be built? How many jobz could be created to build these homes?!

Each year a country could be the focus as we work on building the United States of Afrika using our own resources controlling our own destiny. Something as big as that can start with something as little as setting up collection boxes at each and every gathering we have, and of course material (like this piece) dispersed so that everyone knowz the importance of their involvement.

Not takin' advantage of our people comin' together and collecting fundz to finance our liberation is simply not Kuji, yo! meanin', not Kujichagulia which meanz "Self-Determination!"

NOTE: I do acknowledge that all Afrikanz on the planet did not fall victim to the Atlantic Slave Trade, but collectively, we have! In the eyes of the world, we are powerless, yet we are the main ingredient to the world's — and especially america's — economy. It's this disunity (one group saying they're not descendants of "slaves" therefore implying they're "better" than those who were") that keeps us in disarray collectively. This mindset was implanted by those who've been taking advantage of the rape of Mama Afrika for centuries! As victimz of this atrocity when is enuff enuff?! *"Afrikanz are not free until Afrika is free!"*

Also note that there are hundredz, if not thousandz of Afrikan cultural events around the world throughout the year. If a list of specific needz for specific countries was created and at every festival took a collection, within 20 yearz, Afrikan people *globally* would be in a better position!!

This can happen! Go to your local organizerz of these events and drop this jewel! There's no reason we can't start to see the liberation of Afrikan people and our homeland in this lifetyme!

MORE FIE-YAH!

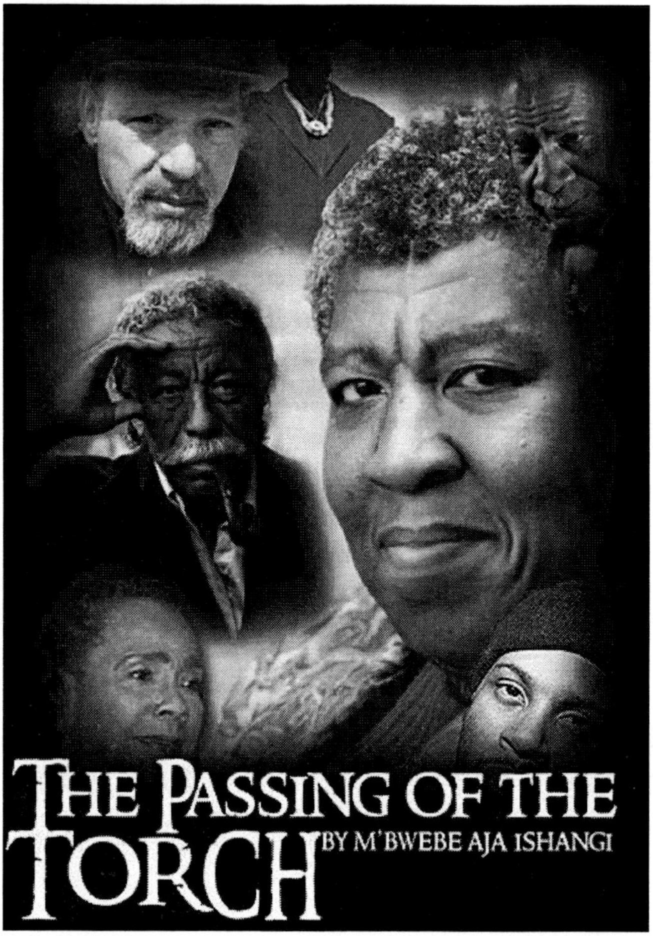

THE PASSING OF THE TORCH

BY M'BWEBE AJA ISHANGI

If you've noticed lately, we've lost some major influences over the past couple yearz. As *'Generation X'* becomes *'Generation Now',* I find we have some very large shoes to fill. With the recent deaths of Gordon Parks, Octavia Butler, J Dilla, Rosa Parks, Coretta Scott King, Ossie Davis, August Wilson, Del Jones, Johnnie Cochran, John H. Johnson, Richard Pryor, Nipsey Russell, Professor X, Lou Rawls, Luther Vandross, Barry White, Floyd Patterson and Shirley Chisolm, we should all reflect on the deedz of these and those not mentioned.

The historical biographies of those spoken of are large indeed. Many of them were actually the first to do what they did; many did those thingz during a tyme when racizm and segregation wasn't as camoflauged as it is today; many accomplished those deedz in the midst of fear but realized the importance of takin' on such a task and pressed on; and many silently ached with disappointment from the lack of vision and support from the very hedz their work was dedicated to...

I venture on to say that as of now, these may have been the last crop of freedom fighterz and pioneerz we may ever see again. And I say that because the world is ever-changing. As the world embraces – better yet – swallowz the Afrikan experience, there are too few of us willing to be the next group of griots, much more, there aren't enuff of us even equipped with how to take on such a role as vanguard.

There are a couple reasonz for this. First is beef on the part of the Elderz and second is on my generation.

Ever since the fall of the Civil Rights movement, of those that didn't take the gratuitous jobz, stayed on the streets. But they too found they still needed to eat. Out came the numerous 'Africentric Pimps' conducting 6 hour lectures for $15 bucks, tellin' you a lot of history but equippin' you with nothin' to change your situation. These same scholarz became infatuated with the fame and chose rather than take tyme in groomin' up-and-coming youths who also had a voice, to bast in the glory of popularity while preying on a young sista or two.

Generation X also shoulderz some blame because we've somehow lost sight of what's important. We are the first to experience the 'illusion of inclusion', not bein' able to detect that our presence is bein' literally 'whited-out'!

There are more interracial and homosexual couples than ever while the numberz on householdz with an Afrikan mother and father continue to fall faster than Wall Street stock!

Race-pride has been co-opted with Reggaton; we have more whites that care about poverty in Afrika than I & I; and thanx to 'Reality TV', MTV and BET, the youth are now experimenting with gay *"rights"?!!?*

On the flipside, a positive about us is that we could be the best and possibly the last to do anything that would really be effective. We are but one generation removed from the dayz of a segregated america, while also able to acquire the secrets of corporate america. The weight of our legacy is heavy and I believe it fallz solely upon *our* shoulderz. For 'Generation Next's' been alienated to experiencing any kind of physical segregation (they didn't experience growing up with neighborhood community centerz, shit, there's hardly any all Afrikan hoodz in major cities these dayz!) so to them, they are living the 'melting-pot theory' – even though we're still on the bottom of the kettle gettin' burnt!

It truly fallz on my, our generation (X), to finally merge identity culture with corporate culture and finally enterprise our way of life to where we start creating and receiving some of that over $700 Billion we loosely spend each year. Far too many other ethnicities have profited off our story, it is tyme we create the benefits for ourselves!

And even if you don't see yourself as one to lead but to follow, pursue somethin' that's worth following and don't *just* follow, support!

What will be our generationz legacy? More importantly, what will be yourz individually? I only hope in 50 yearz, someone will be able to comment on how our efforts allowed the torch to be passed.

LIK SHOT!

The mind is truly a physical phenomenon. It's just that it's hard for us to really realize because it works, in large part, on automatic.

We truly are not aware of the kind of work we put our mindz through each day; we never "think" how the mind knowz how to govern so many thingz at once; we "forget" to wonder how somethin' can work literally all day as well as all night without a break – even when we sleep! Dreamz are proof that your mind is still at work. Let's face it; the mind is the perfect employee!!

Because of our oblivious disconnection, not only do we make it difficult to reach the "summon bonum" or "greatest good" our Ancestorz taught during the dayz of the Nile Valley, we actually lead our mind to a premature cancellation – meaning death, be it physically alive but 'brain-dead' or actual death of the entire body.

After a long day at the plantation (job piece or whatever your day comprises of), you come home madd tired. But exactly what part of you is tired? You, physically. What do you do to recharge? You lie down and rest, eventually falling asleep.

It gets deeper when asked, "When do you actually sleep?" We do these thingz automatically so we've never took the tyme to breakdown the science of sleeping.

From the moment you fall asleep to when you awake, that period of tyme no one's able to account for. When you sleep, most tymz you can recall having dreamz. What we don't recall is the process it takes to get from right before we sleep to that actual "place" where dreamz happen.

Seldom spoke of; there is a route or process of departing one dimension to enter anutha. What is the course of leaving the present/physical realm and enter the non-physical realm where we 'sleep'?

If you've ever lifted the eyelidz of someone sleeping without waking them, you will recall that although their eyes are open, if they remain "sleep", they will not be able to see you (if you've never done this, try this exercise on a luv'd one tonite!). Now, if they're unable to see me right in front of them, where are they and what are they seeing?!

We've been taught the basic function of our eyes is to see. It's your eyes that allow you to read this piece. If you close and then open your eyelidz back up, unless you turn to look at something else, you will still see this article.

But Y doesn't this happen when you're asleep?! Y can't the person sleepin' see you lifting their eyelidz?! My point is once your eyes are open you're s'posed to see what's in front of you, right? Or is it??

But again, I say, we were taught the basic functionz of our eyes. If you're able to lift a sleeping personz eyelidz without them seein' you, we have to admit there's has to be a higher science, thus clearly the eyes must have advanced capabilities.

Like computerz, 'sleep mode' is a realm between the physical and non-physical [the 'used' and 'not used' (the computer)]; conscious and subconscious; alive and dead.

As the body recharges during 'sleep', the mind ventures to realmz the physical cannot go. Many want to believe dreamz are nothin', but they say this because they cannot comprehend Y it exists.

I believe 'sleeping' is one of the many realmz we have to consider where life can exist.

If we looked more into this, sleeping could be where we're able to learn more and even communicatae with the unknown.

The brain, coupled with melanin could be a gateway to understanding life on higher dimensionz than the three we know of.

Our Ancestorz were more than likely were able to connect to these realmz and manifest it on this planet. Some examples of this can be seen in the building of the Pyramidz and Her-Em-Akhet — two structures YT can't figure how they were built.

The creation of the world wide web can also be traced to the Nile Valley. When you type in a web address, you begin with the letterz, 'http'. What's interesting is YTs infatuation with *Our*story.

Our Ancestorz of the Nile Valley wrote using consonant's only without vowelz. So when lookin' at the URL prefix, we actually see the greeting 'Hotep' short for the name of the ancient Afrikan multi-genious, Imhotep.

THE ALL SEEING EYE(S)

I'm sure you've heard many hedz speak about seeing with your "3rd Eye", yet very few actually elaborate on what this is all about.

The 3rd Eye is that inner-vision that vybrates on a frequency higher than your normal eyesight. Its alleged function is to assist in seeing what our eyes can't see. It's been said the 3rd Eye has the ability to see thingz on a deeper level in addition to a subliminal or esoteric plane. With all that said, only the ability is spoken of and rarely will you find a discussion buildin' on the phenomena it truly is.

Have you ever had a conversation that spoke of the role the mind playz in seeing? Is it solely our eyes that observe or does the mind also have the capability to see? Take a moment and think of something that happened in the past. Did you notice while reliving this moment, you could see it although it wasn't your eyes that was seeing it? Did you also realize that while you were "seein'" this mental picture transpire in your mind, your eyes were seein' what was in front of them? It's like your vision was multi-tasking – one busy viewing your past experience in your mind while the other examined what was in front of it.

Further, how do you explain the site that's used in your dreamz? It's not your eyes seein' what goes on. Your mind has the capability to project images inside your head. Again, the mind is truly a physical marvel.

THE DREAM STATE

Just literally walking through each phase we each go through everytyme we go to sleep gave me a larger appreciation of how special living beingz are.

If you look at basically every man-made thing, it's modeled off the human body – especially electronics! Look at your typical mp3 player or computer. It runz off an electrical outlet but also has an internal battery. This allowz you to listen or work without being plugged into a wall – but only for a certain amount of tyme.

Eventually the power (or energy) is used up and you have to use the outlet to recharge the battery. Over tyme, the battery will eventually die out and have to be recycled.

The same can be applied to us. Sleep serves as that outlet in the wall. We "plug" ourselves into a place that recharges us physically. After a few hourz, we're refreshed and good as new! But, as with the mp3 battery, eventually sleep will not be able to recharge our battery (ie, heart, soul, etc.). This is where we will go through a bodily transformation from the physical to the non-physical realm. Many have been miseducated, calling this death but nothing ever dies, it just transformz into something else.

I like to equate the process of sleeping to a trip, 'cause if you really look at it, it really is a trip. We're about to leave one realm and enter anutha and in a couple Earth hourz, return!

When we eventually lie down, our body must first prepare itself for the "trip". First the body must be in a relaxed state, so it must slow down. This is accomplished by a series of deep breathes. Now notice, all this is done automatically! You don't have to tell yourself to do anything, all you have to do is lie down and close your eyes.

Life is preserved by breathing so it's not a coincidence it's this rhythmic breath fluctuating on its native mantra-like level that escorts us from the physical realm into this dream state.

The most intriguing phase to me is the actual occurrence of slipping from physical consciousness to sleeping. I've tried many tymz to maintain some kind of coherence when starting to dream – still being able to hear the refrigerator cut on and off, for example.

It's been well documented that there are 6 stages of sleep, with the first 4 being non-REM stages. Stage 1 sleep is the period of drowziness you feel. Polysomnographic tests showz a 50% reduction in activity between wakefulness and stage 1 sleep. The eyes are closed during Stage 1 sleep, but if aroused from it, a person may feel as if he or she has not slept. This stage is estimated to last 5 to 10 minutes.

Stage 2 is a period of light sleep during which polysomnographic readingz show intermittent peaks and valleyz, or positive and negative waves. These waves indicate spontaneous periodz of muscle tone mixed with periodz of muscle relaxation. The heart rate slowz and body temperature decreases. At this point, the body prepares to enter deep sleep. I can recall after havin' played b-ball (Basketball), I'd lay down to rest and as I'm spiraling down to "la-la land", I'd replay in my mind how I played that day and in most cases I'd make sudden jerks and move as though I was actually playing at that moment.

Stages 3 and 4 are the deep sleep stages. These stages are known as slow-wave, or delta, sleep. During slow-wave sleep, especially during Stage 4, tests record slow-waves of high amplitude, indicating a pattern of deep sleep and rhythmic flow.

The period of non-REM sleep is comprised of Stages 1-4 and lasts from 90 to 120 minutes, each stage lasting anywhere from 5 to 15 minutes. Surprisingly, however, Stages 2 and 3 repeat backwardz before REM sleep are reached. So, a normal sleep cycle has this pattern: waking, stage 1, 2, 3, 4, 3, 2, REM. Usually, REM sleep occurz 90 minutes after sleep has begun.

The 5th is the REM stage marked by extensive physiological changes, such as increased brain activity, eye movement and muscle relaxation, heart rate and respiration speed up and become erratic, while the face, fingerz and legz may twitch. Intense dreaming occurz as a result of heightened brain activity. Paralysis also occurz in the major voluntary muscle groups, including the sub-mental muscles of the chin and neck. Because REM is a mixture of brain states of excitement and muscular immobility, it is sometymz called paradoxical sleep. It is generally thought that REM-associated muscle paralysis is meant to keep the body from acting out the dreamz that occur during this intensely cerebral stage. It's this phase I speak of in my book, Analitikul, where I experienced several spiritual encounterz that, at one tyme, made me fear for my life. (This part is revealed in Analitikul so I won't get into it now)

The first period of REM typically lasts 10 minutes, with each recurring REM stage lengthening, and the final one lasting an hour.

The 6th is called the 'Waking' stage in which a person fallz asleep. The waking stage is referred to as relaxed wakefulness, because this is the stage in which the body prepares for sleep. When falling asleep our eyes are moving erratically. Then, normally, as a person becomes sleepier, the body beginz to slow down. Muscles begin to relax, and eye movement slowz to a roll.

It's been reported the 6 stages of sleep, including their repetition, occur cyclically. The first cycle, which endz after the completion of the first REM stage, usually lasts for 100 minutes. Each following cycle lasts longer, as its respective REM stage extendz. So we may complete 5 cycles in a typical night's sleep, hence havin' numerous dreamz in one night.

It seemz stage 6 is the period that's the hardest to "wake" a person up. This is where you can perform the "eyelid lift" experiment I spoke of earlier. In some cases, it's also the stage where the person sleeping is less likely to hear anything like you sneakin' up on 'em – which further proves that the sleeper must be somewhere else because our earz alwayz hearz and never turnz off, however, there's some kind of phenomena where the brain sorta "mutes" your hearing as your focus is now centered to the dream state.

DON'T SLEEP ON SLEEPIN'

Y we're unable to see what's in front of us with our eyes when someone lifts up our eyelidz when sleeping is definitely a deep mystery. Anutha example of proof – which should be noted as an obvious oversight – that we're somewhere else when someone's yellin' at you trying to wake you up and you don't "hear" them. As I said, "in some cases," our hearing isn't totally mute when sleep. Have you ever slept with a tv or radio on and you found segments of the broadcast playin' out in your dreamz? This is also a phenomenon because the mind is somehow able to allow you to exist in 2 dimensionz and incorporate the 2 to play as 1! Clearly your consciousness is somewhere else and that place seemz to be a mystery merely because we rarely, if ever, build on it!

As we fall asleep, the mind goes through a process of shifting its awareness from the present to the past, future or possibly some other unknown dimension or dimensionz all-together. The realm we're in now is the present, but like in the first Matrix movie, what we think is the present could possibly, not be. We could be asleep right now caught in the Matrix! If this is so, it still showz the Matrix doesn't control us entirely because we're able to escape it when we fall asleep!! Still wit me?

In contrast to the Matrix theory, while we sleep we venture into innumerable dominionz of existence. Here we can relive past experiences with the possibility of altering what happened as well as encounter thingz that may play out in the future. And of course, this is also the place we can play out fantasies that would never happen in our current lifetyme (keep it clean ya'll!!)!

I perceive this dimension to be a place where we have the least control like when we're awake. This logically meanz this is the tyme the mind is possibly most free to create thingz the physical would have a challenge comprehending.

This also points out a very important fact. In some instances – especially when sleeping – you are not in control! Better put, we are not in control because we haven't been trained how to control our mind when sleeping! This is exciting because it openz the door to anutha form of mental development!

The book '*Soul Traveler: A Guide to Out of Body Experiences and the Wonder's Beyond*' by Dr. Albert Taylor, goes into depth on the phenomena of multiple dimensionz one can train themselves to not only experience, but control!

I believe there are different realmz of consciousness. In particular, we live in the physical which is the realm we spend what seemz to be the most tyme in (present-day life). One other is the non-physical realm. Now this is the place I feel we go to when we sleep. This place is very real for if it weren't we'd be "awake" in this realm permanently. In fact, hedz would never die – better yet, hedz would never be born 'cause this would be the only place where life existed! Ask yourself, where do spirits or soul's come from at birth and ascend to at death? It's not a place on Earth for if it were, with all of life that has experienced tyme here since the planets creation (including animals, insects, etc.), past, present and future, Earth woulda been over populated!

I'm not sayin' the non-physical realm is the place we go when sleeping, but it definitely is a place we can connect ancestrally. This also supports my claim that life exists outside of our solar system, but we'll have to get into that in anutha piece.

I'm a strong believer that mysteries are only that because they have not been investigated. After reading this, what maintenance can we conduct to ensure our mind stayz healthy?

With proper study and training, we may truly be able to know if life exists elsewhere. And as long as we embrace the notion that life exists on at least 3 planes – mental, physical and spiritual – some of these mysteries will be revealed.

Reespek!

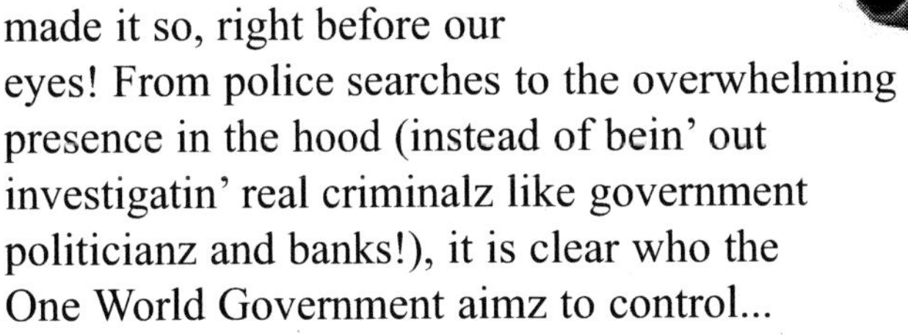

Have you noticed that we're livin' in a police state?! YT (for those that don't know after 13 yearz of DGT, say it faster, also standz for Yakubian Tribe) has deceitfully and silently made it so, right before our eyes! From police searches to the overwhelming presence in the hood (instead of bein' out investigatin' real criminalz like government politicianz and banks!), it is clear who the One World Government aimz to control... *"We, the People..."*

Some 10 yearz ago probably the only tyme you'd see a military tank was on a tv commercial. Today places like Wall Street looks like Iraq! And speakin' of domestic's, YTs qlobal quest to maintain power extendz in regionz that bug me out, yo! Take for instance the recent buzz about the US. now wanting to attack Iran because they are makin' nuclear weaponz. How and with what does the US. plan to attack them with? NUKES!! So, is that not hypocritical that this nation can also have – and use – artillery on otherz but no one else can have it?! Shit like this makes me so ashamed to be reapin' the benefits of livin' in this country.

YT obviously doesn't believe in karma. In the 2004 movie about global warming, *'The Day After Tomorrow'* with Dennis Quaid, as the United States started to freeze and everybody migrated south, they wanted to enter Mexico. Well, of course the Mexican government wasn't havin' it, afterall, it was the US. who didn't want anyone enterin' *their* country, now they have the audacity to want to enter Mexico?! The US. counter-offered to, get this, forgive their debt to the US. if they'd let US. citizenz cross the border.(?!) Hell-Y-wood show'd its arrogance writing this script 'cause who in their right mind would accept such a crazy offer? All the Mexican government had to do was decline the offer and let the US. citizenz freeze to death and there'd be no debt to think about! But of course, they accepted the offer. This also showz how YT feelz they are intellectually superior and can get over on anyone at anytyme regardless of how long they've shitted on 'em.

It's YTs fear that drives their insanity. The other nite Bill O'Reilly had NY mayoral candidate and old-school Black Panther, Charles Barron talkin' about the newly proposed immigration lawz and Barron but Bill on blast! Barron pointed out what immigrants are doin' here "illegally" today is no different than what the european did when they came over to North America.

It was this cracka that felt the need to separate countries and devise the game of Nationalism. We ALL live on this freakin' planet! Y do I need a passport to go to anutha part of the world?!

The bottom line is YT is scared! Scared of havin' to be equal, to share and scared of the karma that inevitably will visit them. It's our goal, bein' that we're part of this society, to make sure we don't receive the blunt of the blow (hint, look into Nationalism, for most of us do not have a Nationality and are thus deduced as property of the US government – proof bein' our birth certificates, social security numberz, etc.).

MORE FIE-YAH!

2005

The Bible, said to be the holiest book ever written, also "passes" as the alleged *"word of God"*. We at DGT feel it is important to attempt to prove the continuous tampering of this book by passages that seem to contradict one another, thereby leading to the assumption that a book such as this continues to be degraded by the pen stroke of man (YT) makin' it not as holy as it may seem – for if it was, it would never go through the contininuous re-editionz this text has already undergone – not counting the infinite number it will continue to experience.

If I can show you over 100 contradictionz in the Bible what would you think then? What would that do to your religious foundation? If you dare, read on. Many thingz which we may have taken for granted as being true – without question – may not be necessarily so.

The Bible has been considered the most reliable source that exists regarding the concept of this man-made version of "God". After reading these contradikshunz, if you are a free-thinker, your thoughts may change...

If someone were to give testimony in a court of law and s/he were found to give 101 contradictory statements under oath, the testimony of that person would be rejected (it wouldn't take 101 contradikshunz, by the tyme they told their 2nd lie they'd be thrown out!). So Y can't we use the same standard when judging the reliability of the statements of The "Holy" Bible?

As you read each contradikshun, keep in mind to use your mind and not be guided by emotion alone. We all have brain power and it's about tyme we use it.

Contradikshun #1 Who incited David to count the fighting men of Israel? (a) God did (2 Samuel 24:1) (b) Satan did (1 Chronicles 21:1).

Contradikshun #2 In that count how many fighting men were found in Israel? (a) Eight hundred thousand (2 Samuel 24:9). (b) One million, one hundred thousand (1 Chronicles 21:5).

Contradikshun #3 How many fighting men were found in Judah? (a) Five hundred thousand (2 Samuel 24:9). (b) Four hundred and seventy thousand (1 Chronicles 21:5).

Contradikshun #4 God sent his prophet to threaten David with how many yearz of famine? (a) Seven (2 Samuel 24:13). (b) Three (1 Chronicles 21:12).

Contradikshun #5 How old was Ahaziah when he began to rule over Jerusalem? (a) Twenty-two (2 Kings 8:26). (b) Forty-two (2 Chronicles 22:2).

Contradikshun #6 How old was Jehoiachin when he became king of Jerusalem? (a) Eighteen (2 Kings 24:8). (b) Eight (2 Chronicles 36:9).

Contradikshun #7 How long did he rule over Jerusalem? (a) Three months (2 Kings 24:8). (b) Three months and ten dayz (2 Chronicles 36:9).

Contradikshun #8 The chief of the mighty men of David lifted up his spear and killed how many men at one tyme? (a) Eight hundred (2 Samuel 23:8). (b) Three hundred (1 Chronicles 11:11).

Contradikshun #9 When did David bring the Ark of the Covenant to Jerusalem? Before defeating the Philistines or after? (a) After (2 Samuel 5 and 6). (b) Before (1 Chronicles 13 and 14).

Contradikshun #10 How many pairz of clean animalz did God tell Noah to take into the Ark? (a) Two (Genesis 6:19, 20). (b) Seven (Genesis 7:2). But despite this last instruction only two pairz went into the ark (Genesis 7:8, 9).

Contradiction #11 When David defeated the King of Zobah, how many horsemen did he capture? (a) One thousand and seven hundred (2 Samuel 8:4). (b) Seven thousand (1 Chronicles 18:4).

Contradikshun #12 How many stallz for horses did Solomon have? (a) Forty thousand (1 Kings 4:26). (b) Four thousand (2 chronicles 9:25).

Contradikshun #13 In what year of King Asa's reign did Baasha, King of Israel die? (a) Twenty-sixth year (1 Kings 15:33 - 16:8). (b) Still alive in the thirty-sixth year (2 Chronicles 16:1).

Contradikshun #14 How many overseerz did Solomon appoint for the work of building the temple? (a) Three thousand six hundred (2 Chronicles 2:2) (b) Three thousand three hundred (1 Kings 5:16).

Contradiction #15 Solomon built a facility containing how many baths? (a) Two thousand (1 Kings 7:26). (b) Over three thousand (2 Chronicles 4:5).

Contradikshun #16 Of the Israelites who were freed from the Babylonian captivity, how many were the children of Pahrath-Moab? (a) Two thousand eight hundred and twelve (Ezra 2:6). (b) Two thousand eight hundred and eighteen (Nehemiah 7:11).

Contradikshun #17 How many were the children of Zattu? (a) Nine hundred and forty-five (Ezra 2:8) (b) Eight hundred and forty-five (Nehemiah 7:13).

Contradikshun #18 How many were the children of Azgad? (a) One thousand two hundred and twenty-two (Ezra 2:12). (b) Two thousand three hundred and twenty-two (Nehemiah 7:17).

Contradikshun #19 How many were the children of Adin? (a) Four hundred and fifty-four (Ezra 2:15). (b) Six hundred and fifty-five (Nehemiah 7:20).

Contradikshun #20 How many were the children of Hashum? (a) Two hundred and twenty-three (Ezra 2:19). (b) Three hundred and twenty-eight (Nehemiah 7:22).

Contradikshun #21 How many were the children of Bethel and Ai? (a) Two hundred and twenty-three (Ezra 2:28). (b) One hundred and twenty-three (Nehemiah 7:32).

Contradikshun #22 Ezra 2:64 and Nehemiah 7:66 agree that the total number of the whole assembly was 42,360. Yet the numberz do not add up to anything close. The totals obtained from each book is as followz: (a) 29,818 (Ezra). (b) 31, 089 (Nehemiah).

Contradikshun #23 How many singerz accompanied the assembly? (a) Two hundred (Ezra 2:65). (b) Two hundred and forty-five (Nehemiah 7:67).

Contradikshun #24 What was the name of King Abijah's mother? (a) Michaiah, daughter of Uriel of Gibeah (2 Chronicles 13:2). (b) Maachah, daughter of Absalom (2 Chronicles 11:20). But Absalom had only one daughter whose name was Tamar (2 Samuel 14:27).

Contradikshun #25 Did Joshua and the Israelites capture Jerusalem? (a) Yes (Joshua 10:23, 40). (b) No (Joshua 15:63).

Contradikshun #26 Who was the father of Joseph, husband of Mary? (a) Jacob (Matthew 1:16). (b) Heli (Luke 3:23).

Contradikshun #27 Jesus descended from which son of David? (a) Solomon (Matthew 1:6). (b) Nathan (Luke 3:31).

Contradikshun #28 Who was the father of Shealtiel? (a) Jechoniah (Matthew 1:12). (b) Neri (Luke 3:27).

Contradikshun #29 Which son of Zerubbabel was an ancestor of Jesus Christ? (a) Abiud (Matthew 1:13). (b) Rhesa (Luke 3:27). But the seven sons of Zerubbabel are as follows: I. Meshullam, ii. Hananiah, iii. Hashubah, iv. Ohel, v. Berechiah, vi. Hasadiah, viii. Jushabhesed (1 Chronicles 3:19, 20). The names Abiud and Rhesa do not fit in anywhere.

Contradikshun #30 Who was the father of Uzziah? (a) Joram (Matthew 1:8). (b) Amaziah (2 Chronicles 26:1).

Contradikshun #31 Who was the father of Jechoniah? (a) Josiah (Matthew 1:11). (b) Jehoiakim (1 Chronicles 3:16).

Contradikshun #32 How many generationz were there from the Babylonian exile until Christ? (a) Matthew sayz fourteen (Matthew 1:17). (b) But a careful count of the generationz revealz only thirteen (see Matthew 1:12-16).

Contradikshun #33 Who was the father of Shelah? (a) Cainan (Luke 3:35-36). (b) Arphaxad (Genesis 11:12).

Contradikshun #34 Was John the Baptist Elijah who was to come? (a) Yes (Matthew 11:14, 17:10-13). (b) No (John 1:19-21).

Contradikshun #35 Would Jesus inherit David's throne? (a) Yes. So said the angel (Luke 1:32). (b) No, since he is a descendant of Jehoiakim (see Matthew 1:11, 1 Chronicles 3:16). And Jehoiakim was cursed by God so that none of his descendants can sit upon David's throne (Jeremiah 36:30).

Contradikshun #36 Jesus rode into Jerusalem on how many animalz? (a) One - a colt (Mark 11:7). Luke 19:35). And they brought the colt to Jesus and threw their garments on it; and he sat upon it." (b) Two - a colt and an ass (Matthew 21:7). They brought the ass and the colt and put their garments on them and he sat thereon."

Contradikshun #37 How did Simon Peter find out that Jesus was the Christ? (a) By a revelation from heaven (Matthew16:17). (b) His brother Andrew told him (John 1:41).

Contradikshun #38 Where did Jesus first meet Simon Peter and Andrew? (a) By the sea of Galilee (Matthew 4:18-22). (b) On the banks of river Jordan (John 1:42). After that, Jesus decided to go to Galilee (John 1:43).

Contradikshun #39 When Jesus met Jairus was Jairus' daughter already dead? (a) Yes. Matthew 9:18 quotes him as saying, *"My daughter has just died."* (b) No. Mark 5:23 quotes him as saying, *"My little daughter is at the point of death."*

Contradikshun #40 Did Jesus allow his disciples to keep a staff on their journey? (a) Yes (Mark 6:8). (b) No (Matthew 10:9; Luke 9:3).

Contradikshun #41 Did Herod think that Jesus was John the baptist? (a) Yes (Matthew 14:2; Mark 6:16). (b) No (Luke 9:9)

Contradikshun #42 Did John the Baptist recognize Jesus *before* his baptizm? (a) Yes (Matthew 3:13-14). (b) No (John 1:32, 33).

Contradikshun #43 Did John the Baptist recognize Jesus *after* his baptizm? (a) Yes (John 1:32, 33). (b) No (Matthew 11:2).

Contradikshun #44 According to the Gospel of John, what did Jesus say about bearing his own witness? (a) *"If I bear witness to myself, my testimony is not true"* (John 5:31). (b) *"Even if I do bear witness to myself, my testimony is true"* (John 8:14).

Contradikshun #45 When Jesus entered Jerusalem did he cleanse the temple that same day? (a) Yes (Matthew 21:12). (b) No. He went into the temple and looked around, but since it was very late he did nothing. Instead, he went to Bethany to spend the night and returned the next morning to cleanse the temple (Mark 11:1-17).

Contradikshun #46 The Gospelz say that Jesus cursed a fig tree. Did the tree wither at once? (a) Yes. (Matthew 21:19). (b) No. It withered overnight (Mark 11:20).

Contradikshun #47 Did Judas kiss Jesus? (a) Yes (Matthew 26:48-50). (b) No. Judas could not get close enough to Jesus to kiss him (John 18:3-12).

Contradikshun #48 What did Jesus say about Peter's denial? (a) *"The cock will not crow till you have denied me three times"* (John 13:38). (b) *"Before the cock crows twice you will deny me three times"* (Mark 14:30). When the cock crowed once, the three denialz were not yet complete (see Mark 14:72). Therefore prediction (a) failed.

Contradikshun #49 Did Jesus bear his own cross? (a) Yes (John 19:17). (b) No (Matthew 27:31-32).

Contradikshun #50 Did Jesus die before the curtain of the temple was torn? (a) Yes (Matthew 27:50-51; Mark 15:37-38). (b) No. After the curtain was torn, then Jesus crying with a loud voice, said, *"Father, into thy hands I commit my spirit!"* And having said this he breathed his last (Luke 23:45-46).

Contradikshun #51 Did Jesus say anything secretly? (a) No. *"I have said nothing secretly"* (John 18:20). (b) Yes. *"He did not speak to them without a parable, but* *privately to his own disciples he explained everything"* (Mark 4:34). The disciples asked him "Why do you speak to them in parables?" He said, *"To you it has been given to know the secrets of the kingdom of heaven, but to them it has not been given"* (Matthew 13:10-11).

Contradikshun #52 Where was Jesus at the sixth hour on the day of the crucifixion? (a) On the cross (Mark 15:23). (b) In Pilate's court (John 19:14).

Contradikshun #53 The gospelz say that two thieves were crucified along with Jesus. Did both thieves mock Jesus? (a) Yes (Mark 15:32). (b) No. One of them mocked Jesus, the other defended Jesus (Luke 23:43).

Contradikshun #54 Did Jesus ascend to Paradise the same day of the crucifixion? (a) Yes. He said to the thief who defended him, *"Today you will be with me in Paradise"* (Luke 23:43). (b) No. He said to Mary Magdelene two dayz later, *"I have not yet ascended to the Father"* (John 20:17).

Contradikshun #55 When Paul was on the road to Damascus he saw a light and heard a voice. Did those who were with him hear the voice? (a) Yes (Acts 9:7). (b) No (Acts 22:9).

Contradikshun #56 When Paul saw the light he fell to the ground. Did his traveling companionz also fall to the ground? (a) Yes (Acts 26:14). (b) No (Acts 9:7).

Contradikshun #57 Did the voice spell out on the spot what Paul's duties were to be? (a) Yes (Acts 26:16-18). (b) No. The voice commanded Paul to go into the city of Damascus and there he will be told what he must do. (Acts 9:7; 22:10).

Contradikshun #58 When the Israelites dwelt in Shittin they committed adultery with the daughters of Moab. God struck them with a plague. How many people died in that plague? (a) Twenty-four thousand (Numbers 25:1 and 9). (b) Twenty-three thousand (1 Corinthians 10:8).

Contradikshun #59 How many memberz of the house of Jacob came to Egypt? (a) Seventy soulz (Genesis 46:27). (b) Seventy-five soulz (Acts 7:14).

Contradikshun #60 What did Judas do with the blood money he received for betraying Jesus? (a) He bought a field (Acts 1:18). (b) He threw all of it into the temple and went away. The priests could not put the blood money into the temple treasury, so they used it to buy a field to bury strangerz (Matthew 27:5).

Contradikshun #61 How did Judas die? (a) After he threw the money into the temple he went away and hanged himself (Matthew 27:5). (b) After he bought the field with the price of his evil deed he fell headlong and burst open in the middle and all his bowelz gushed out (Acts 1:18).

Contradikshun #62 Y is the field called "Field of Blood"? (a) Because the priests bought it with the blood money (Matthew 27:8). (b) Because of the bloody death of Judas therein (Acts 1:19).

Contradikshun #63 Who is a ransom for whom? (a) *"The Son of Man came... to give his life as a ransom for many"* (Mark 10:45). *"...Christ Jesus who gave himself as a ransom for all..."* (1 Timothy 2:5-6). (b) *"The wicked is a ransom for the righteous, and the faithless for the upright"* (Proverbs 21:18).

Contradikshun #64 Is the law of Moses useful? (a) Yes. *"All scripture is... profitable..."* (2 Timothy 3:16). (b) No. *"...A former commandment is set aside because of its weakness and uselessness..."* (Hebrews 7:18).

Contradikshun #65 What was the exact wording on the cross? (a) "This is Jesus the King of the Jews" (Matthew 27:37). (b) "The King of the Jews" (Mark 15:26) (c) "This is the King of the Jews" (Luke 23:38). (d) "Jesus of Nazareth, the King of the Jews" (John 19:19).

Contradikshun #66 Did Herod want to kill John the Baptist? (a) Yes (Matthew 14:5). (b) No. It was Herodias, the wife of Herod who wanted to kill him. But Herod knew that he was a righteous man and kept him safe (Mark 6:20).

Contradikshun #67 Who was the tenth disciple of Jesus in the list of twelve? (a) Thaddaeus (Matthew 10:1-4; Mark 3:13-19). (b) Judas son of James is the corresponding name in Luke's gospel (Luke 6:12-16).

Contradikshun #68 Jesus saw a man sitting at the tax collectorz office and called him to be his disciple. What was his name? (a) Matthew (Matthew 9:9). (b) Levi (Mark 2:14; Luke 5:27).

Contradikshun #69 Was Jesus crucified on the daytyme before the Passover meal or the daytyme after? (a) After (Mark 14:12-17). (b) Before. Before the feast of the Passover (John 13:1) Judas went out at night (John 13:30). The other disciples thought he was going out to buy supplies to prepare for the Passover meal (John 13:29). When Jesus was arrested, the Jewz did not enter Pilate's judgement hall because they wanted to stay clean to eat the Passover (John 18:28). When the judgement was pronounced against Jesus, it was about the sixth hour on the day of Preparation for the Passover (John 19:14).

Contradikshun #70 Did Jesus pray to The Father to prevent the crucifixion? (a) Yes.

(Matthew 26:39; Mark 14:36; Luke 22:42). (b) No. (John 12:27).

Contradikshun #71 In the gospelz which say that Jesus prayed to avoid the cross, how many tymz did he move away from his disciples to pray? (a) Three (Matthew 26:36-46 and Mark 14:32-42). (b) One. No opening is left for another two times. (Luke 22:39-46).

Contradikshun #72 Matthew and Mark agree that Jesus went away and prayed three tymz. What were the wordz of the second prayer? (a) Mark does not give the wordz but he sayz that the wordz were the same as the first prayer (Mark 14:39). (b) Matthew gives us the wordz, and we can see that they are not the same as in the first (Matthew 26:42).

Contradikshun #73 What did the centurion say when Jesus dies? (a) *"Certainly this man was innocent"* (Luke 23:47). (b) *"Truly this man was the Son of God"* (Mark 15:39).

Contradikshun #74 When Jesus said *"My God, my God, why hast thou forsaken me?"* in what language did he speak? (a) Hebrew: the wordz are *"Eli, Eli..."* (Matthew 27:46). (b) Aramaic: the words are *"Eloi, Eloi..."* (Mark 15:34).

Contradikshun #75 According to the gospelz, what were the last wordz of Jesus before he died? (a) *"Father, into thy hands I commit my spirit!"* (Luke 23:46). (b) *"It is finished"* (John 19:30).

Contradikshun #76 When Jesus entered Capernaum he healed the slave of a centurion. Did the centurion come personally to request Jesus for this? (a) Yes (Matthew 8:5). (b) No. He sent some elderz of the Jewz and his friendz (Luke 7:3, 6).

Contradikshun #77 (a) Adam was told that if and when he eats the forbidden fruit he would die the same day (Genesis 2:17). (b) Adam ate the fruit and went on to live to a ripe old age of 930 yearz (Genesis 5:5).

Contradikshun #78 (a) God decided that the life-span of humanz will be limited to 120 yearz (Genesis 6:3). (b) Many people born after that lived longer than 120. Arpachshad lived 438 yearz. His son Shelah lived 433 yearz. His son Eber lived 464 years, etc. (Genesis 11:12-16).

Contradikshun #79 Apart from Jesus did anyone else ascend to heaven? (a) No (John 3:13). (b) Yes. *"And Elijah went up by a whirlwind into heaven"* (2 Kings 2:11).

Contradikshun #80 Who was high priest when David went into the house of God and ate the consecrated bread? (a) Abiathar (Mark 2:26). (b) Ahimelech, the father of

Abiathar (1 Samuel 21:1; 22:20).

Contradikshun #81 Was Jesus' body wrapped in spices before burial in accordance with Jewish burial customz? (a) Yes and his female disciples witnessed his burial (John 19:39-40). (b) No. Jesus was simply wrapped in a linen shroud. Then the women bought and prepared spices *"so that they may go and anoint him* [Jesus]*"* (Mark 16:1).

Contradikshun #82 When did the women buy the spices? (a) After *"the sabbath was past"* (Mark 16:1). (b) Before the sabbath. The women *"prepared spices and ointments."* Then, *"on the Sabbath they rested according to the commandment"* (Luke 23:55 to 24:1).

Contradikshun #83 At what tyme of day did the women visit the tomb? (a) *"Toward the dawn"* (Matthew 28:1). (b) *"When the sun had risen"* (Mark 16:2).

Contradikshun #84 What was the purpose for which the women went to the tomb? (a) To anoint Jesus' body with spices (Mark 16:1;Luke 23:55 to 24:1). (b) To see the tomb. Nothing about spices here (Matthew 28:1). For no specified reason. In this gospel the wrapping with spices had been done before the sabbath (John 20:1).

Contradikshun #85 A large stone was placed at the entrance of the tomb. Where was the stone when the women arrived? (a) They saw that the stone was "Rolled back" (Mark 16:4). They found the stone *"rolled away from the tomb"* (Luke 24:2). They saw that *"the stone had been taken away from the tomb"* (John 20:1) (b) As the women approached, an angel descended from heaven, rolled away the stone, and conversed with the women. Matthew made the women witness the spectacular rolling away of the stone (Matthew 28:1-6).

Contradikshun #86 Did anyone tell the women what happened to Jesus' body? (a) Yes. *"A young man in a white robe"* (Mark 16:5). *"Two men... in dazzling apparel"* later described as angelz (Luke 24:4 and 24:23). An angel — the one who rolled back the stone (Matthew 16:2). In each case the women were told that Jesus had risen from the dead (Matthew 28:7; Mark 16:6; Luke 24:5 footnote). (b) No. Mary met no one and returned saying, *"They have taken the Lord out of the tomb, and we do not know where they have laid him"* (John 20:2).

Contradikshun #87 When did Mary Magdelene first meet the resurrected Jesus? And how did she react? (a) Mary and the other women met Jesus on their way back from their first and only visit to the tomb. They took hold of his feet and worshiped him (Matthew 28:9). (b) On her second visit to the tomb Mary met Jesus just outside the tomb. When she saw Jesus she did not recognize him. She mistook him for the gardener. She still thinks that Jesus' body is laid to rest somewhere and she demandz to know where. But when Jesus said her name she at once recognized him and called him

"Teacher." Jesus said to her, *"Do not hold me..."* (John 20:11 to 17).

Contradikshun #88 What was Jesus' instruction for his disciples? (a) *"Tell my brethren to go to Galilee, and there they will see me"* (Matthew 28:10). (b) *"Go to my brethren and say to them, I am ascending to my Father and your Father, to my God and your God"* (John 20:17).

Contradikshun #89 When did the disciples return to Galilee? (a) Immediately, because when they saw Jesus in Galilee "some doubted" (Matthew 28:17). This period of uncertainty should not persist. (b) After at least 40 dayz. That evening the disciples were still in Jerusalem (Luke 24:33). Jesus appeared to them there and told them, *"stay in the city until you are clothed with power from on high"* (Luke 24:49). He was appearing to them *"during forty days"* (Acts 1:3), and *"charged them not to depart from Jerusalem, but to wait for the promise..."* (Acts 1:4).

Contradikshun #90 To whom did the Midianites sell Joseph? (a) *"To the Ishmaelites"* (Genesis 37:28). (b) *"To Potiphar, an officer of Pharoah"* (Genesis 37:36).

Contradikshun #91 Who brought Joseph to Egypt? (a) The Ishmaelites bought Joseph and then *"took Joseph to Egypt"* (Genesis 37:28). (b) *"The Midianites had sold him in Egypt"* (Genesis 37:36). Joseph said to his brotherz *"I am your brother, Joseph, whom you sold into Egypt"* (Genesis 45:4).

Contradikshun #92 Does God change his mind? (a) Yes. The word of the Lord came to Samuel: *"I repent that I have made Saul King..."* (1 Samuel 15:10 to 11). (b) No. God *"will not lie or repent; for he is not a man, that he should repent"* (1 Samuel 15:29). (c) Yes. *"And the Lord repented that he had made Saul King over Israel"* (1 Samuel 15:35). Notice that the above three quotes are all from the same chapter of the same book! In addition, the Bible showz that God repented on several other occasionz: i. The Lord was sorry that he made man (Genesis 6:6). *"I am sorry that I have made them"* (Genesis 6:7) ii. *"And the Lord repented of the evil which he thought to do to his people"* (Exodus 32:14).

Contradikshun #93 The Bible says that for each miracle Moses and Aaron demonstrated the same by their secret arts. Then comes the following feat: (a) Moses and Aaron converted all the available water into blood (Exodus 7:20-21). (b) The magicianz did the same (Exodus 7:22). This is impossible, since there would have been no water left to convert into blood.

Contradikshun #94 Who killed Goliath? (a) David (1 Samuel 17:23, 50). (b) Elhanan (2 Samuel 21:19).

Contradiction #95 Who killed Saul? (a) *"Saul took his own sword and fell upon it...*

Thus Saul died... (1 Samuel 31:4-6). (b) An Amalekite slew him (2 Samuel 1:1-16).

Contradikshun #96 Does every man sin? (a) Yes. *"There is no man who does not sin"* (1 Kings 8:46; see also 2 Chronicles 6:36; Proverbs 20:9; Ecclesiastes 7:20; and 1 John 1:8-10). (b) No. True Christianz cannot possibly sin, because they are the children of God. Every one who believes that Jesus is the Christ is a child of God ... (1 John 5:1). *"We should be called children of God; and so we are"* (1 John 3:1). *"He who loves is born of God"* (1 John 4:7). *"No one born of God commits sin; for God's nature abides in him, and he cannot sin because he is born of God"* (1 John 3:9). But, then again, Yes! *"If we say we have no sin we deceive ourselves, and the truth is not in us"* (1 John 1:8).

Contradikshun #97 Who will bear whose burden? (a) *"Bear one another's burdens, and so fulfil the law of Christ"* (Galatians 6:2). (b) *"Each man will have to bear his own load"* (Galatians 6:5).

Contradikshun #98 How many disciples did Jesus appear to after his resurrection? (a) Twelve (1 Corinthians 15:5). (b) Eleven (Matthew 27:3-5 and Acts 1:9-26, see also Matthew 28:16; Mark 16:14 footnote; Luke 24:9; Luke 24:33).

Contradikshun #99 Where was Jesus three dayz after his baptizm? (a) After his baptizm, *"the spirit immediately drove him out into the wilderness. And he was in the wilderness forty days..."* (Mark 1:12-13). (b) Next day after the baptizm, Jesus selected two disciples. Second day: Jesus went to Galilee — two more disciples. Third day: Jesus was at a wedding feast in Cana in Galilee (see John 1:35; 1:43; 2:1-11).

Contradikshun #100 Was baby Jesus's life threatened in Jerusalem? (a) Yes, so Joseph fled with him to Egypt and stayed there until Herod died (Matthew 2:13 - 23). (b) No. The family fled nowhere. They calmly presented the child at the Jerusalem temple according to the Jewish customz and returned to Galilee (Luke 2:21-40).

Contradikshun #101 When Jesus walked on water how did the disciples respond? (a) They worshiped him, saying, *"Truly you are the Son of God"* (Matthew 14:33). (b) *"They were utterly astounded, for they did not understand about the loaves, but their hearts were hardened"* (Mark 6:51-52).

THE 3 MUSKATEERZ: FAST-FOOD, MONSANTO & THE FDA BY M'BWEBE AJA ISHANGI

You can remember when Chicken George, I mean, MC Hammer danced for KFCs popcorn-chicken about a decade ago. This was the beginning of the industrial strong-arm of tv product placement into the rap game. Well, thingz are about to heat up again!

According to Advertising Age, McDonald's has offered to pay popular Hiphop performerz if they mention their Big Mac sandwich in their lyrics. The agreement offerz no advance on royalty cuts, but will pay each artist $5 everytyme the song is played.

Already geared to promote Mickey D's obese-causing "food" are Kanye West and Busta Rhymes. So if you do the math, a track with only 10 airplayz comes to about $50. This openz the door for price warz.

As they auction on the price of our health replacing it with profit, you can expect Burger King to up the price, for example, to $7 with McDonald's countering with $10. Sure, this is an opportunity for mceez to make a few extra pennies, as well as broaden their market value to a more non-urban audience, but what about the flipside. What bad can come of this?

One of america's rising epidemics is obesity. The rise of overweight people in this country is alarming, yo! There are several combinationz that contribute to its growth. One, the taste. If you read Eric Schlosser's *'Fast Food Nation'*, you'll read about the IFF – International Flavors & Fragrances, Inc. The IFF is responsible for how most thingz on the market taste the way they do. What they don't tell you is how they are able to make practically anything taste like something it isn't, like making a piece of spoiled, intoxicated and decayed flesh taste like a "fresh" beef pattie (as if old meat can ever taste fresh)!

The IFF, along with Monsanto Corporation and the FDA (Food AND Drug

IFF International Flavors & Fragrances Inc.

Administration) should be Public Enemy #1 for there's no tellin' what we're actually eatin' because it's camouflaged by the flavor! I'm sure these scientists have the capability to make a piece of shit taste like apple pie!

Second, the availability. There are more Fast Food chainz opening up – predominately in urban areas – on the daily! Couple that with continuous radio, tv-play and rock bottom prices, I'm sure these chainz thrive in even the poorest of communities.

And third, the effect. If you are addicted to the taste, you don't care of its nutritional value (or lack of). If you saw the 2003 movie, *'Super Size Me'*, you saw how a personz health deteriorates with the continued consumption of fast food.

So how can Kanye or Busta's continued pursuit for paper help us? It simply won't. If anything, it will draw more of our youth to these slaughter houses causing young Afrikan females to have earlier menstrual cycles; reach puberty quicker, increasing the aging process and possibly support the continued rise of homosexual habits in especially Afrikan boyz (Y? 'cause over 40% of the burgerz hedz eat are from cattle injected with recombinant Bovine Growth Hormone or rBGH).

What hedz don't know is that rBGH is banned in Europe and in February 1999, after an 8-year scientific review, Canada rejected Monsanto corporation, the creator of rBGH. Animalconcerns.org revealed even more wicked drama when it was found Canadian health officialz claimed Monsanto tried to bribe them as well as government scientists testifying they were being pressured by "higher-ups" to approve rBGH against their better scientific judgement. Y? Because it's directly linked to Mad Cow Disease!

Briefly, rBGH is a genetically engineered copy of a natural occurring hormone produced by cowz. The drug is sold to dairy farmerz under the name 'Posilac'. It also goes by the name BGH, BST or rBST. When rBGH is injected into dairy cowz, milk production increases by as much as 10-15%. Of course the Food AND Drug Administration (FDA) won't tell you it's bad for you because it increases production, which increases profit both for the meat and dairy industry and the hospital administration (read *"In Sickness and In Health? Or Potential Wealth"*).

It must also be noted that Monsanto is responsible for practically all genetically engineered foodz (soybeanz, tomatoes, etc.)! Today, they control an estimated 99% of food "creation" leaving less than 1% to organically grown crops. Word is they're even tryin' to get the label "organically grown" on their products. With the recent merger of the FDA and organic farmerz, it seemz it has already happened.

What's worse is Monsanto's latest technology called the Technology Protection System, also called "Terminator Technology". Developed with taxpayer money by the US Department of Agriculture but patented by Monsanto, terminator technology is a genetic technique that renderz the seedz of crops sterile after one or two yearz.

This assures that Monsanto's seedz cannot be illegally saved and re-planted year after year, forcing farmerz to purchase their genetically-altered seedz from Monsanto.

This easily puts them in control of our very lives. *"...[I]t appears the US. Government my view genetically modified crops as a powerful new arm of US foreign policy. Nations whose staple foods are grown from seed that they must purchase year after year from a handful of US. Corporations are nations likely to see the world the way the US. Wants them to see it. When asked, they are likely to play ball, whether they want to or not. A new world order, indeed."* (animalconcerns.org)

Now do you think these mceez will make a responsible decision and choose not to partake in this form of suicide sacrificing the lives of millionz for a few thousand George Washingtonz? We'll see...

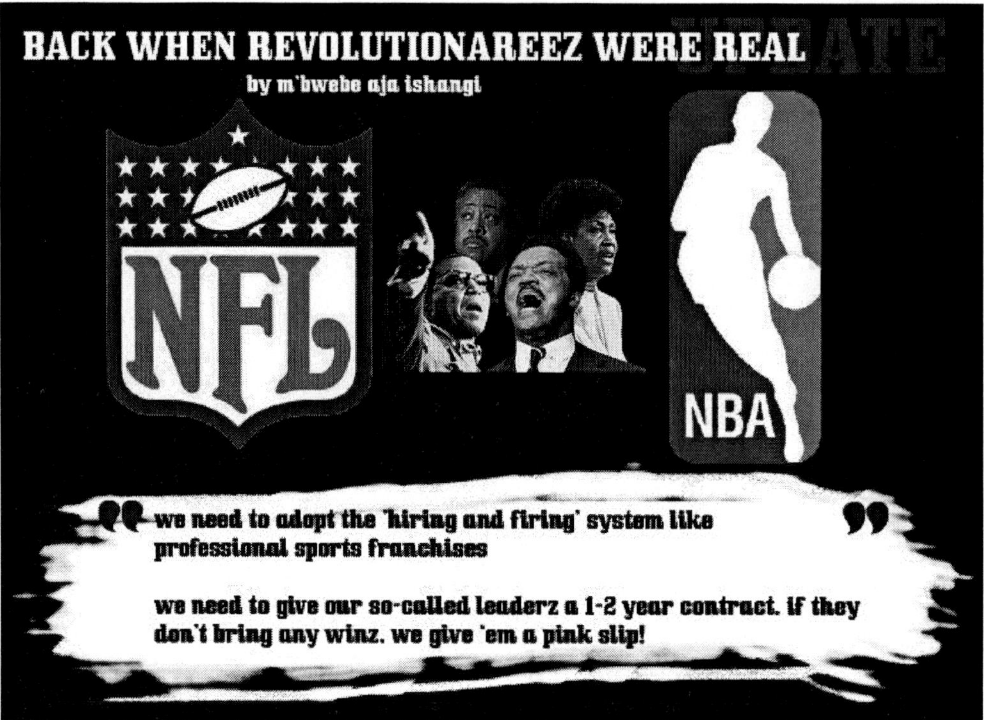

A while back I wrote the piece '*Back When Revolutionareez Were Real'* which spoke in comparison of our current self-appointed leaderz versus those of the past. Now that we have yet anutha charade of an election upon us, we have to seriously see how messed up our situation is. Many who still believe in the vote merely voted for John Kerry and Edwards mainly because he wasn't Bush, despite Kerry's faithful allegiance to the same white supremacy cult as Bush, Skull&Bones (read '*Bush, Kerry: Bloodbrotherz to the Core*'). I ask you, Afrikanz, where's our leadership in these tymz?!!? Hedz voted for Kerry thinkin' he's like Clinton (as if *he* was all that). Where's our alleged leaderz and their stance for the future of Afrikan people in america? Who does Farrakhan, Jesse, Al Sharpton and the like endorse? [NOTE: Back in 2000 Farrakhan urged followerz of the the Nation of Islam and black muslimz alike to partake in voting. He also warned politicianz this would be the only tyme they would vote for a candidate they did not endorse themselves promising by 2004 they'd have one they'd have their own candidate. To this day, there's been no other candidate while black muslimz gear up to partake in yet anutha voting scam!]

Afrikanz, we are long overdue a revamped plan of our future here. We've allowed hedz like the aforementioned to "lead" us to nowhere for decades with no pressure nor request of vision they may have for our future. If you want my opinion, we need to adopt the philosophy of professional sport teamz. For example, take the National Football League (NFL) and National Basketball Association (NBA). Some 10-15 yearz ago we began to see a difference in the demandz of head coaches and even general management.

Prior to that, a coach's job was secure for as long as he wanted to coach. Up until the early 90s, you had some that were a frachise's first and only coach. Dallas Cowboys head coach, Tom Landry was there for 29 yearz, winning the Superbowl 2 tymz; Chuck Knoll of the Pittsburgh Steelers reigned 22 yearz, winning 4 Superbowlz. These coaches remained at the helm despite a winning or losing season. Come the early 90s, the business of sports changed and patience faltered. Franchises became infatuated with winning at any cost and if it meant firing a coach despite their winning system or even trading half the team, they'd do it for an immediate winning season.

I think we Afrikanz should adopt the same strategy. WE NEED A WIN NOW!! The "coaches" or "leaderz" of our people in this country haven't delivered us a victory since they were self-appointed by YT (of course, we know they have been effective in doin' their job which is to stall our liberation. Read *'Scam: How the Black Leadership Exploits Black America'*, by Rev. Jesse Lee Peterson).

For too long we have allowed the Jesse's, Farrakhanz and Sharptonz to CON us into thinkin' we're makin' progress while their pockets get fatter and links with the enemy get stronger, while we continue to suffer generation 'pon generation. Y do we continue to blindly support these agents yet refuse to demand a progress report?!

We should hold our current so-called leaderz to a 1-2year contract. If they provide no victories from what they proposed, we pull from a pool of 'free-agents' who'll be ready to fill their shoes and implement improved strategies. As simple and maybe farfetched as this may seem, it really is practical and can be implemented immediately! This would not only involve the people more in the decisionz and directionz we plan to go, it will also enable us to hold accountable any and all parties who we put in positionz of leadership and power.

Got any other ideas?!!?

LIK SHOT!

Tyme. What is tyme? It takes Earth 24 hourz to rotate once around the Sun; giving us 24 hour dayz. Pluto however, circumnavigates the Sun once every 247.7 Earth yearz equating a Plutonian day at 5,944.8 Earth hourz – think of how many life lessonz you would experience if you were there!

But what about outside our solar system, our galaxy, nebula and even star cluster?? If the Djhuitic (erroneously called Hermetic) principle of 'Correspondence' *(As Above, So Below, So Below, As Above)* applies to everything, there is tyme everywhere in various mathematical formulaz. The question is, is tyme really real or is it a man-made concept? And if this is a concept, how has it segregated us from the universal vybrating frequency of life itself?

To be a free-thinker, one must have the capability of reaching their mindz beyond the illusionary borderz YTs educational system dictates. Bein' a *free*-thinker allowz you to think on higher *free*-quencies. The word 'education' should be a word under close scrutiny because the meaning totally contradicts how it's utilized. The root bein' 'educere' meanz, *"to come from within."* So how is it we base our knowledge on accumulative grade point averages and diplomaz?!

Free-thinking is just that, Afrikanz, FREE! The curriculum is life and there are no professorz (at least in human form). Your classes are the lessonz experienced. The more "tyme" or commitment one puts in, the more jewelz manifest. I can truly attest!

Since March of 2003, when I wrote *"What Frequency R U On?!"* I can say my confidence in free-thinking has grown enormously! I say this because even the notion of thinking different can alienate a person and if that person is not confident or sound in mind and spirit, what the mind revealz may be too much to handle causin' mental regression. I give thanx every moment of every day and ask for continued will to continue this ancient path.

BEYOND OUR PAST

Yes, we do have an illustrious past, with one of them being in the Nile Valley. Yeah, our Ancestorz were/are dope! But I find most wind up romanticizing the past instead of breaking those illusionary borderz I spoke of earlier. Y do we think our story starts and stop near or around the Nile Valley?! Common logic and free-thinking would tell you our Ancestorz had Ancestorz. The same way we speak of Afrikan civilizationz millenniumz ago, so did they speak of cultures before them! Our ability to think past our immediate Ancestorz stiffenz our ability to see life beyond Earth, our solar system, our galaxy, the nebula and star cluster we are a part of mainly because its been estimated the Sun in our solar system has is been burning for 93,000,000 yearz yet we've only documented our story probably no more than 50,000. We've only tapped a *fragment* of life on this planet!

One reason because of this points to manz need to create tyme. Look around you, everything is run by this creation called tyme. It tellz you when to get up, what tyme to catch the train, what day you get paid, what day billz are due, the list goes on.

I'm not sayin' tyme is a bad thing, although man-made, it has enabled us to put thingz in perspective, which may be a necessary tool for one to have direction. What I am implying is our concept of tyme has overwritten everything else. It has kept us earth-bound. It has limited our ability to use more than the estimated less than 1/3rd of our mindz; and most importantly, it has almost severed our connection with the perspective that, as I pointed out in one of my latest lecture series, *"all thingz are Microcozmz of the Macrocozm"*, or smaller parts of a bigger, relative thing.

BREAKING FROM THE MENTAL SHACKLE

Let's take the example I spoke of in the beginning of this piece. A full day on Pluto is about 6,000 Earth hourz – that's about 8? months! Thingz that happen on Pluto are obviously different here on Earth, going further, thingz that happen on *other* planets in *other* galaxies are different as well. Blame hell-y-wood (Hollywood), the "educational" system and the religious diocese, not me, for thinkin' *"M'Bwebe talkin' 'bout some Parliament-spaceship shit!"*

It is hell-y-wood who makes these visual decisive and destructive miscalculationz in the form of movies, for they know we have relied more on our sight than using logical reasoning. Logical reasoning would tell you that of all the alien movies they've made, when the settingz were on their planet, the plants were green and more important, they breathed oxygen!! Even if they were in a spaceship, when they encountered humanz (ie, Star Wars, Star Trek), they were breathing what we humanz use to sustain our earthly-life… OXYGEN! Let's be thinkerz, Afrikanz, Y IZ it Dat all the necessary elements we need for life can be present on an alien frontier, yet the "alienz" themselves are little gray men with 3 fingerz and huge eyes?!!? Hell-y-wood been hoodwinkin' us for a century, yo!

It is the educational system that refuses to acknowledge the microcozm of the macrocozm principle when they teach health/social studies and astronomy separately. They teach us about ourselves before our very eyes in the form of chemistry ('chem' = khem = KMT = black, carbon or melanin; '-istry' meaning *"the study of"*). They base their foundation on the Periodic Table, yet cease to make the connection to anything outside our universe.

Lookin' at it macrocozmically, everything inside you exists because of the bigger you, or the vessel where these inside thingz reside. These inside thingz are affected by the bigger you. This also works inversely where the macrocozm is affected by the microcozm. The food you internalize becomes a part of the bigger you.

Now visualize yourself bein' planet Earth. Think of all the thingz that are on Earth. All *appear* to be workin' individually, but are really in unison – whether good and/or bad. Step outside the shell of Earth and become the Milky Way galaxy. Think of the infinite number of thingz that go on on that level: imploding and exploding starz, blackholes, meteorz, planetary formationz, etc.

Don't stop there Afrikanz – or should I say 'Elements' because we're no longer earth-bound. Become the Nebula responsible for creating the galaxies that inhabit this particular vicinity of the poly-verse. Better yet, become the Star Cluster who simply creates Nebulas that creates galaxies!! Continue, continue, continue to expand macrocozmically and you will see everything is connected as you come full circle onto the level we currently exist in as seen in the first 5 minutes of the movie *Contact* (released in 1997).

THE NON-PHYSICAL SELF VS. THE PHYSICAL SELF

As said before, the foundation for the use of tyme is a man-made concept utilized to create and record an order of experiences. I believe Ancient cultures like that of the Dogon used (and still use) tyme, but not in the way of YTs eurocentric system. YTs system got us enslaved to tyme. They lock us down to worry about havin' a payin' wage to live off instead of the wayz of our ancients who created and invested in Nature and the land.

This binding grip to YTs concept of tyme has handicapped our ability to see beyond our sight. Our vision is blurred and because of this, we feel we cannot find our way without our eyes, but Afrikanz, don't we have, as YT sayz, 4 or even 5 other senses? Who's to say we don't have more than that? (the white)Man?!!?

Author of '*Nile Valley Contributions to Civilization*', Anthony T. Browder once said to me, *"we're Spiritual Beingz having a Human experience who chose to come back for a purpose."* To say that is to acknowledge there is more to "life" than what is experienced on Earth and in this lifetyme. The analogy of a car comes to mind everytyme I think of what Browder said.

A car is considered a vessel. It moves, but not without a driver (unless parked in neutral on a hill). The same pertainz to the human body and the spirit. We are taught to believe they are one, and to a certain degree, they are, but not exactly. Society has a way of tellin' lies and half-truth's and we take them whole.

Case in point, if we acknowledge we have living Ancestorz, where are they? We know they are not in physical form. So where are they? What are they made of? Some believe in seein' ghosts and spirits. If they are visible, then they are made of molecular and chemical structures. What are they?

If our Ancestorz exist then we must concede they are separate from the physical earthly body. This concept has been termed the non-physical self and the physical self. We can say we are somewhat familiar of the physical self or world, but there's anutha part we have not. The ancient Djhuitic principle, *Polarity*, speaks of everything havin' an opposite. In this case, converse the physical realm lays the uncharted, less exhumed non-physical self.

For example, author of '*Ruminations*', KRS-One, pointed out when you silently read, although you are not using your mouth, tongue, larynx and lungz to produce physical speech, you are still speaking. Repeat the lyrics of your favorite song without using your mind. Go ahead, try it. This is done without your tongue. But where does this internal voice/sound come from? "Who" produces such a sound? The Non-Physical Self!

It gets more interesting when you realize you can also *hear* the wordz of your Non-Physical speech. Even if you closed your earz, there is still hearing. You can still hear yourself reading without reading out loud.

The same notion can be applied to your sight. What is sight? We're *alwayz* seeing. Even when we sleep we are seeing! The phenomena of lifting a "sleeping" personz eyelidz and they not be able to see you is soooo deep!! For those free-thinkerz, you can't help but wonder *"if their eyes are lookin' right at me, yet they're sleep, what are they lookin' at? What are they seeing, 'cause they're not seein' me!"* Even better, *"where are they to have such vision?!"* I've pondered this since my early childhood, B. I've been told in my "dreamz" that dreamz are the language of the elements many mistakenly call 'God' (this led me to write the piece, *The God Complex*).

Ponder this… without the use of your 2 physical eyes, there is still sight! Your non-physical eyes see thingz your 2 physical eyes have yet to see and in some cases, your inner-sight is more accurate than your outer vision! Your 'inner' can see the past, present and future while your outer only sees the present! We all truly need to get back in balance and genuinely get to know ourselves, THOROUGHLY, the way we s'posed to, with Polarity.

Listen to self. If you scramble the letterz in the word 'LISTEN' you get 'SILENT'. How often do we listen silently to the rhythm of the most constant messenger in this physical realm – the heartbeat. In the Kemetic text, '*The Book of the Dead*' or '*The Book of Coming Forth By Day*', the phrase *"Be still and know that I am"* sparks my pineal when speakin' on this topic. That pulsating tempo our heart makes is more than just sound, it is imbedded-encrypted data reminding us of our kinetic connection to the frequency of 'The All' or 'Energy' as I call it.

Talk within yourself while being quiet. Hear the soundz and ideas within, see with your eyes closed. What world/realm/dimension does this exist in? Definitely not the physical realm! It is your inner-voice that empowerz or animates your physical voice. It is your inner-ear that really hearz. It hearz physical events long after they physically exist. It hearz music, speech and soundz *before* they physically manifest in the present. Think of how a musician makes music, a writer writes. It hearz all from the past, present and future at will.

Inner-sight also sees the past, present and future at will. Inner-sight directs and interprets the display of your physical eyes. Ask yourself Afrikanz, what and how are you seeing when you are dreaming or even daydreaming? What is the sight that is used to see your imagination?

When we speak of dreamz, we are talkin' about the non-physical realm at its best. Here you see, hear and even touch in the non-physical world. It is at this juncture the existence of the non-physical realm exists. A good book to read is *'Soul Traveler: A Guide to Out of Body Experiences and the Wonder's Beyond'*, by Albert Taylor, PhD. Out of body experiences (OBEs) are very real, in fact, when you think about it, for every dream you had, most placed you somewhere other than where your body was sleeping, right? There Afrikanz, lies a simple example of an OBE. We have so many "dreamz" yet remember so few and are able to interpret even less, clearly showing more "tyme" must be put towardz the non-physical. We only know one side of ourselves Afrikanz, and that's the side that makes us think we are *only* Afrikan, *only* beingz on this planet and the *only* species that was so clever to record our experiences with this invention called tyme.

By gaining a deeper inner-standing of 'correspondence' *(as above, so below; as below, so above)* and 'polarity' *(duality; the union of opposites but only differ in degree)*, it makes perfect sense to realize this dream-like presence we frequent nightly for mid-to-long hourly sessionz, have more significance in the reason we exist than we'd like to think!

We cease to acknowledge that along with our being made of blood and oxygen, we are also electrical. In hospitalz they have a procedure called an Electrocardiography that traces electrical activity of the heart. An Electrocardiogram (ECG or EKG) can be used for checking currents in various parts of the body, including the brain.

Like the heart, which we take for granted as it continues its rhythmic beat even when we are at "rest" or sleep (when our consciousness is altered into anutha realm most call dreamz), the mind persists at a rate that, I believe, goes beyond the heart. The heart, we know will eventually stop beating. The mind, however, is a different case – especially if you still believe your Ancestorz are real!

The electrical sparks that derive from the human brain is not just electrical shocks you may feel from a poorly-wired socket. They are images, soundz, probably even gatewayz to dimensionz only our imagination (mind) would allow to see if and only while in this dream-like state. It is here we have not applied the principles of Correspondence and Polarity, for we have not spent enuff "tyme" exploring it.

As I wrote in the piece, *"What Frequency R U On,"* I noted that while YT got us locked into the physical matrix worried about Kobe Bryant, Michael Jackson, un- and under-employment and the last episode of *Friends*, they continue to break barrierz the world won't know for decades through corporationz like CERN (European Organization for Nuclear Research) and Lockheed Martin. We are out of balance, Afrikanz, and our individual and collective tymerz are tellin' us we are running out of tyme, if not, at the very least, *waisting* our tyme weighin' too much on the physical side and not enuff energy towardz the non-physical.

LIFE BEYOND

There is more to seeing, hearing and speaking than physically looking, listening and talking. Your inner-movements and senses direct most of your physical (outer) movements and senses. We simply give the physical realm too much credit, when in fact the physical body does very little on its own. Even the will to live doesn't originate from the physical body! If this were the case the body would choose to live forever!

Even if 'you' wanted to die, the body would choose to preserve itself and live on. Command yourself to die right now…….. nuthin' happened, right? Your heart didn't stop beating, brain function didn't cease. If you were to hold your breath, because the human body needz oxygen to exist, you will find your body tightenin' up and eventually forcing you to take in air.

As I said before, the body doesn't live, it functionz, only the spirit lives, learnz and expandz. Like the car analogy spoken of earlier, without the spirit commanding the body, it is literally lifeless and without direction. This is Y many believe that physical death is not the end.

So knowing this, ask yourself, If you don't need the physical body to have speech, sight, hearing, ideas, emotionz, will, personality, consciousness, then Y wouldn't these abilities exist without the body altogether?!

To me, death is more like the separation of one's physical senses from one's non-physical senses. We microcozmically experience this every nite we go to sleep and have these thingz called "dreamz". The thing about "dreamz" is that it seemz so real. And to be quite honest, it *IS* real, non-physically!

We literally cut ourselves off from what lies beyond the Earth, our Solar System [which is but rocks called planets rotating around a star – and there's an infinite number of starz in the universe/poly-verse (Polarity states duality, so maybe the concept of 1 uni-verse is also incorrect)], our galaxy we reside in called the Milky Way, the one Nebula responsible for creating the Milky Way, the Virgo Cluster NASA (National Aeronautic & Space Administration) sayz we're a part of, and so on…

Using rational and logistical thinking, one would find that of all the religious and spiritual movements – including those that evolve from the Nile Valley of Afrika – none could prove they are as old as the planet Earth or the Sun. Sayin' this should lift the barrierz that block free-thinking. Ask yourself, Afrikanz, do you *really* think soulz and spirits didn't begin to live eternally until man-made religion came about?

Of the 3 major western-religionz (christianity, judaism and islam) – which are no older than 2000 yearz and some change – that's not even one centimeter on the ruler of Earth's existence, do you really think the soulz of our Ancestorz Ancestorz did not experience eternal life until the so-called biblical Jesus?!!? If you believe this, the diagnosis is clear, YT has entrapped your mind.

The concept of a "dream"-world or non-physical realm co-exists with the physical world. Many of us spend our lifetyme wondering what happenz after death. The mind is bamboozled by religionz who ask you to trade your ability to think in exchange for the unproven theory of everlasting life through their 'God'. But what actually is everlasting life? It cannot be physically because the human body does not have the capacity to stay in tact eternally. So this leaves the spiritual or non-physical.

Buckle your seats, the journey has just begun…

LIK SHOT!

FREE-QUENCEEZ OF TYME, PT.2
THE ART OF TRAVEL

BY M'BWEBE FKA JEHVON BUCKNER

"The mind is the most underrated organ of the human makeup. It is only the mind that has the ability to connect your physical questionz with the non-physical answerz. If one would only break the illunsionary barrierz or "the glass jar" society has encased our mind in, we'd have the ability to travel to places far beyond the reaches of this planet."
– M'Bwebe Aja Ishangi

Before I can even begin speakin' of the art of travel, initially I choose to reveal the microcozm of the macrocozm concept as it applies to the human body. As done in part 1, I will further explore the concept of being what I term, a free-thinker. What is a free-thinker, or better yet, what *isn't* it? A non-free-thinker is a person who believes without question. It is a person who commits to a mindset because of tradition or because it is what the majority believes. A free-thinker is not one who confines all their knowledge base on one, or a few books or a just over 2000-year-old man-made religion and feelz there are just some questionz that aren't meant to be known.

A free-thinker is one who encompasses viewz, constructively and critically, from various perspectives. A free-thinker also thinks outside the illusionary borderz the norm's mindset is imprisoned in. A free-thinker is not afraid to stand alone on a concept. And more importantly, a free-thinker will not betray nor relinquish what their heart knowz even if it meanz bein' ostracized, deemed an outcast or seen as "out there."

This is important because when Baba and author of *Nile Valley Contributions to Civilization*, Anthony T. Browder, said to me, *"We are Spiritual Beingz havin' a Human experience who chose to come back for a purpose,"* a non-free-thinker would not be able to grasp such a concept. This theory has a resounding appeal because it (1) separates the physical from the non-physical (as spoken about in '*Free-Quencies of Tyme, part 1*'. Second, it openz up a whole new realm for in-depth elaboration since it speaks of our "choosing" to come "back" for a purpose.

To "choose" is a sign of intelligence and will. Does our spirit exhibit this ability? If Browder's statement is true, it applies. And what about the part of coming "back"… *back* from where?! This "place" is a realm seldom spoke about. Y? Probably 'cause if someone heard you speaking of some unknown realm that no one really knowz how to get to, you might find yourself in a padded room strapped in a straight-jacket.

This concept, though on the thin line of bein' presumed 'off your rocker', has been virtually swept under the rug in most think tanks. Most would rather speak of miracles and visionz from "God" rather than explore the dimensionz each of us journey to, on a nightly basis.

Every night, when you go to 'sleep', you do what has been deduced by western science as merely 'dreaming'; a make-believe dimension that is of no significance other than purposeless visionz while you sleep. Many believe dreamz are meaningless episodes and fantasies of our lives, a movie reel of our experience, if you will. This definition, adopted by the masses, has left the people of this world plugged into the matrix of linear-thinking. YTs training system (school) are one of the main culprits responsible for the mindset we people of 'Planet E' have. Their training has confined us, making us believe we are the only intelligent life in an ever-expanding poly-verse. Not to play with wordz, but uni-verse seemz limited and therefore incorrect because if you study the Djhuitic (erroneously called Hermetic) principle of Polarity, it speaks of everything having its pair of opposites. More on that as I introduce the concept of matter and antimatter later.

If you've seen the 1997 movie *'Contact'* with Jodie Foster, you might remember the scene where her father said if space is infinite and we're the only one's in it… what a waste of space! We've let Hell-Y-wood define our perception of life (if we believe there's life) outside our planet. Many can't even grasp the concept of life past our solar system (past Pluto)!

I don't know how to say it any simpler Afrikanz, we are a microcozm of the macrocozm. What you see is not everything. The duality of 'seen' is 'unseen'. There are so many books and movies that talk about life elsewhere, giving us the idea that they're little grey or green men with big eyes, 3 or 4 fingerz – and what buggz me out *– can speak English!!*

'MASSA'-MEDIA'S CONTROL OF YOUR PERCEPTION

"When you control a man's thinking, you do not have to worry about his actions. You do not have to tell him not to stand here or go yonder. He will find his proper place and stay in it. You do not need to send him to the back door. He will go without being told. In fact, if there is no back door, he will cut one for his special benefit."

This quote from Carter G. Woodson (fellow Boule' member I might add) transcendz the color line when speakin' about the impact good ol' 'massa'-media has on the public. Not only do they have us believing "alienz" fly into Earth, breathing oxygen and speaking English, on what has been termed flying saucerz or disc-like aircrafts [do a little research and you'll find it doesn't take much to make a flying saucer right here on Earth. I mean, if YT can put a plane up, Y can't they put the same interior design (motor, valves, etc.) into a saucer-like body?!!?], in the same breath they downplay the tenacity of "dreaming" and the connection to the physical realm it has.

Some 20 yearz ago, actress Shirley McClain got public attention for her alleged out-of-body experience where she claimed to have been able to leave her body with a life-line or physical-to-spiritual umbilical chord attached to her so that her spirit may find its way back to the body. She claimed that as long as the line was intact, you were "alive". However, if the line became severed, you had no way of returning to your physical body which meant you died in the physical realm. Never before had anyone gone on tell-a lie-vision (tv) speaking of this. The hype it created had many in disbelief with very few ready to give it a deeper look.

Although I can't say I am a firm believer in McClain's "life-line" theory, it was then in my early teenz that I became fascinated in the unknown. This subject was an untraditional theory that can be deemed "outside the box" of normal thought. I was very much interested in knowing more of this as a youth but (1) I didn't know how because I had no cultural/spiritual base and (2) I didn't have access to McClain or anyone that shared this interest. So it was suppressed, or better yet, stored away until I began my deprogramming and then process of mental maturation.

MENTAL STIMULANTS

Take one trip to your local planetarium and, if you're a free-thinker, you will start thinkin' "outside the box". With the help of the 7 ancient Djhuitic principles, you will realize that we are truly the microcozm of the macrocozm; a smaller part of a bigger thing(s) (duality).

We are of the universe; therefore, there are universes in us. Microcozmically, if you were to zoom into you, it would look just like the universe (again, go to your local planetarium for reference). When you look at the skin on your hand, we do not realize there are billionz, probably trillionz of moving activity goin' on that our naked eye cannot see.

Just because we cannot see it, or even feel it, does not mean it does not exist. It's been estimated some 6 trillionz thingz goes on at every moment in our body. If you had a high-powered telescope and focused on your hand, you'd be able to see movin' objects. Just as if you were to look at a plants soil and see crawling lifeformz livin' their lives on and around the plant, so is the same with the living organizmz that crawl on you.

These thingz help protect and maintain your physical existence and the duality is that some work to destroy you. This is called balance. What's an even deeper concept is to these crawling lifeformz, your body is their "Earth"; just as, macrocozmically how we walk on the Earth. We are macrocozmincally those crawling lifeformz dwelling on the "scalp" or "skin" of the Earth. Look at the wrinkles and crevaces in your hand. These lifeformz as they work to maintain their lives are in fact, maintaining yourz! These lifeformz, too finite for the naked eye to see, these crevices are valleyz — perhaps as big as the Grand Canyon! This makes the perception of what we are much bigger than the illusionary parameterz the european-based western society wants us to see.

Macrocozmically, what we do to sustain/destroy ourselves sustainz/destroyz our household, community, city, state, nation, country, planet, solar system, galaxy, nebula, star cluster, and whatever else come after. The same applies inward. These should be primary thingz taught to us from our youth but because we've put our trust in, as Dead Prez say, *"They Schoolz"*, we continue to poison our universe first through misleading 'boxed-in' and eurocentric-based information; second via an improper diet; and third opting to choose linear thinking instead of free-thinking. One of the key strategies used to make us think this way is man-made religion, but I will have to deal with that in anutha piece.

SPIRITUAL BEINGZ HAVING A HUMAN EXPERIENCE

Again, Baba Browderz statement bringz relevance to the topic because too many obstacles have been placed to keep us from truly knowing an alternative way of who we are which would/could enable us to define what our purpose for being here is. Afterall, this is probably the one poly-versal question, *"Why am I here?"* (for those interested, I suggest reading *The Alchemist,* by Paulo Coehlo).

As a likkle yute, what was one of your first questionz after learning about health in school? *"Where did I come from?"*, *"Why do I have to die?"* and the infamous, *"Where is heaven?"* All 3 are literally lengthy articles in themselves. The first 2 I dwelled on in my lecture, *'Afrikan Spirituality: the Microcozm of the Macrocozm'*. For this piece, I will focus on the where is heaven question.

Our perception of heaven is man-made consisting of just a physical concept and not a non-physical, or spiritual notion. From all the stories of what heaven is like, most speak of the same concept: a bright light, you walking towardz this light and on your way, relatives are there to greet you. Ok, then what? How many hedz do you know that actually went to heaven then came back giving full detail of what it's like? It's been said that in heaven everyone is happy and everything is all good. Now, free-think Afrikanz, of all the people that ever lived and will live that are dead and will die, quite a few have/will be murdererz and pirates. They all came/will come from a place where thingz aren't all good, in fact somewhat chaotic and you are a product of this environment, how long you think you'll be able to adjust to such a place without corrupting it? I'll let you marinate on that for a lil' bit........................

Ask yourself who came up with the policy of who gets admitted into heaven and who doesn't? Oh, forgot. It's said that all you gotta do is accept jesus christ as your lord and savior and you in! So again, I ask, how many corrupt hedz who repented at the last minute just so they could get into heaven, are there and while there have regressed back to their wicked wayz? If they've been wicked and corrupt all their Earth life, what makes you think they won't their 'Heaven' life?! Accepting this would be pure linear-thinking. It's also madd material for a comedian!!

Everytyme you've asked this question about where's heaven, more than likely you were told it's *up* or *out* there. This society is not in the practice of tellin' you heaven is *inside* you. This gives a feeling of detachment because you have to look outside of you, leading you to develop a feeling of exclusion. The same goes for the concept of "God". We feel we're that high-powered toy everyone wants that can do all the hottest thingz… yet no batteries are included and "some assembly may apply."

Because of our conditioning, we've been programmed to settle with an answer that does not answer our question. Oftentymz we are told, *"you're not s'posed to know everything"* or *"God is the only one who knowz."* This has become acceptable, relinquishing the ability to be that free-thinker because if there were *more* free-thinkerz, we'd ask that person who told us we're not 'sposed to know, who told *them* we're not?! There are 2 types of people who give such answerz. Either they're a linear thinker, who takes everything at face value due to stunted curiosity; or they're someone who may have tried to seek an answer but gave up settling for ignorance (again, read '*The Alchemist*').

If you know you are a microcozm of the macrocozm and the macrocozm is "God", you will know that you *are* "God", microcozmically *and* macrocozmically, thus giving you the capability to know more than you think. We totally ignore the tenacity our brain possesses. Our mind has worn illusionary shackles thanks in part to YTs school system plus religion and 'massa'-media/propaganda. Think of how most would react when you say you are God and that you *can* know all. They'd call you blasphemous, egotistical and out of your mind, as if to imply the human mind is incapable of knowing "all". But ask yourselves Afrikanz, if the universe is mental and everything that has ever been created on this earth was first in the mind then brought into physical manifestation; better yet, if wo/man can create aircrafts, cloning and antimatter (again, more on this later), Y do we feel we cannot know more?

I'm sure you've heard of the saying, *"Know thyself."* But have you heard the entire phrase? *"Know thyself and thou shalt know the Universe and God."* If we have the ability to procreate – something that's taken for granted is the amount of encrypted data that goes into creating a fetus – Y do we continue to downplay our ability? Because we have been programmed. Just like a computer programmed to work efficiently for 1-2 yearz before it starts actin' up, so have we been duped to believe our efficiency is at 100% when we're probably, collectively, at the 30% range.

What we fail to realize is that this program can be deleted. If you read my piece, *What Frequency R U On?,* you'd be aware of the constant energetic vybration emitted from what I believe is that realm that's been demoted to be called dreamz. If we were to heighten our awareness and tune into that higher frequency just as you would change to anutha tv or radio station, we would be able to hear this frequency and assist our conduit (instrument) of this info exchange, the brain, as it tries to override YTs program of mental arrest.

See it is the brain that is the vital organ that truly run tingz! Physically, yes the heart is regarded just as vital, but this is only in the physical realm, what about the non-physical realm (refer to *Free-quencies of Tyme part 1*)? When you lay down to sleep every nite, everything is pretty much at rest except your heart, respiratory system and your brain. All are needed and rely on each other to function, but only the mind has both the key and access to the non-physical realm. In this realm you are spirit, not needing oxygen to breathe nor a beating heart, not even legz that walk for that matter, because when you break us down (microcozmically) that is exactly what we are… MATTER!

The mind is truly the most underrated muscle. We work so hard to maintain physical fitness, but cease to exercise the greatest organ we have. Many are not aware that the mind is different from the brain. See, the brain exists in our head and governz our body whereas the mind exists in our environment and governz our lives. We have the mind, including the environment, in the spirit while the body, including the brain, is in the mind. We should all know the brain exists in our head and governz the body but the mind is beyond our physical space and tyme for it has the ability to exist in the realm of the spirit where past, present and future are all one event.

In part 3, I will continue exploring the mind, show it's relation to the notion of traveling (dreamz) and introduce the conceptual duality of matter and antimatter.

LIK SHOT!

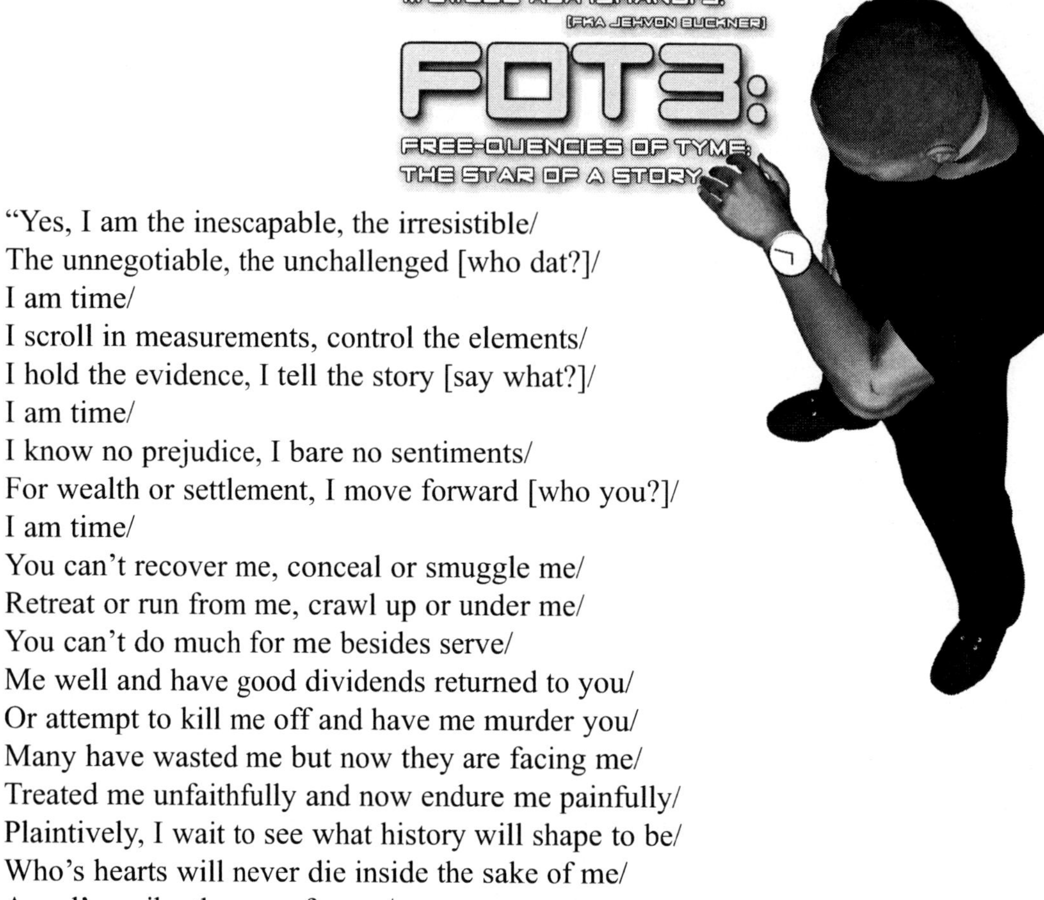

"Yes, I am the inescapable, the irresistible/
The unnegotiable, the unchallenged [who dat?]/
I am time/
I scroll in measurements, control the elements/
I hold the evidence, I tell the story [say what?]/
I am time/
I know no prejudice, I bare no sentiments/
For wealth or settlement, I move forward [who you?]/
I am time/
You can't recover me, conceal or smuggle me/
Retreat or run from me, crawl up or under me/
You can't do much for me besides serve/
Me well and have good dividends returned to you/
Or attempt to kill me off and have me murder you/
Many have wasted me but now they are facing me/
Treated me unfaithfully and now endure me painfully/
Plaintively, I wait to see what history will shape to be/
Who's hearts will never die inside the sake of me/
Angel's scribe the page for me/
Keep a full account of all the names for me…

Artist: Mos Def | Song: Hurricane | Album: The Hurricane soundtrack

---

"Our mindz are massive harddrives with a speed concentration infinitely faster than the calculated level of exa-hertz. The speed it takes to tell your index finger to scratch your head goes beyond the speed of light."

- M'Bwebe Aja Ishangi

I'm gonna get a lil' trivial with you. If you've read my 2 previous pieces of this series plus my articles, *'What Frequency R U On?'*, *'Evolution? or Nebulution!'*, *'A Revived Vybration'* and *'The God Complex: Microcozm of the Macrocozm'* you should be familiar with where this is leading…

This is free-thinking, Afrikanz. Meaning, throw away all the earthly concepts of life as you know it. Break the illusionary borderz this western-eurocentric society has placed on your mind and think… THINK, for most, for the first tyme… Now consider this…

When did you actually come into existence? I mean really ask yourself this.

When did you actually come into existence?? Was it in your motherz womb? Was it your pop's penis? Or was it when they THOUGHT of you? Perhaps it was when your mother wanted to be pregnant? Or maybe when she realized she was pregnant. Did you exist when your parents reached puberty?

Had some or none of these sequences happened, you wouldn't be, BUT, you were not created just by a sexual act alone. So I ask again, *when did you come into existence?*

Let's dig deeper… Did you exist when your parents did? How about when *their* parents did? All this and we haven't even considered the food our parents ate in order to physically exist? As they say, *"you are what you eat"*, so those foodz each person in your lineage ate was a part of them just as they are to you.

I want to bring up the ancient axiom again, *"Know thyself AND THOUGH SHALT KNOW THE UNIVERSE AND GOD."* The part underlined is the element seldom, if ever heard! Feel like you askin' God-like questionz now [which is a form of free-thinking]? or is this blasphemy your preacher told you never to research. This is our birthright to know everything that makes us who we are. Would you purchase a complicated electrical appliance without the manual?! There *is* a manual for us Afrikanz, and this manual resides inside you, it's just that we've been tricked by YT to think only they could tell us who we are.

YT knowz that when you know your capabilities you can succeed in them. To know your potential/PURPOSE, you will move towardz it with confidence, it's mathematics, yo! Erase what you think you know and focus on who you are without the titles, labelz, opinionz and perceived notionz of reality you picked up while growing up. BEND YOUR REALITY by unlearning what you've been taught and re-teach [re-wire] your self [mind]. You are your truth. Study your Self. Here you will learn to know God and the Universe. It is merely our social training that confine our mind to our headz.

BEND YOUR REALITY: A JOURNEY

Bending your reality is a journey in itself. To begin to analyze and re-analyze everything down to the basics is not something done [correctly] overnight. It takes patience, discipline and focus [**f**rom **o**neself **c**omes **u**ltimate **s**acrifice]. It is an often solo-trekked journey with madd sublime lessonz. But there's only one manual and it lies within you. Being *'Analitikul'*, as my book is titled, challenges your willingness to accept without question or because *"it's what I've been taught since I was little."* Being analitikul meanz you dare to go against the norm and fear not to question societal-appointed authorities on any and all subjects. And lastly, bein' analitikul meanz even what I'm spittin' doesn't have to be the gospel. My truth is my truth, if we share this truth, cool. If not, it should be your mission to find *your* truth.

I say all this because tyme is much, much older than wo/man. Tyme itself has a story we have yet to translate into our level of comprehension. It is from this perspective 'the microcozm of the macrocozm' concept is born.

I've referred to the movie *Contact* with Jodi Foster several tymz; the intro scene is

Read 'Do U Believe Me?' by E.D. Johnson on daghettotymz.com R-kyvz section

about the deepest visual I've seen on film! Starting from Earth, the camera zoomz slowly out of our atmosphere into space and zoomz past every remaining planet in our solar system; past our galaxy, the Milky Way; beyond the visible universe ending as a visual coming out of a person's eye. Of course the person should've been Afrikan [this is Hell-y-wood y'kno], so you know she *had* to be white! But you can get the principle regardless… that we are a microcozm of the macrocozm; an independent, functioning smaller part that is both an individual [microcozmically] as well as part of a collective [macro] of the whole.

A universal principle that was used several tymz in the movie was *"If space is infinite and we're the only ones in it, what a waste of space!"* It would be complete arrogance as well as ignorant to believe that an infinitely-growing universe [actually should be called 'poly-verse'] has the ability to inhibit life in a dense space .1 of 1% of its mass. Just because we haven't physically left this solar system – or planet for that matter – does not mean life as we know it only exists here. I encourage interested readerz to logon and read *Do U Believe Me?* by Daawiyd Johnson on my site: www.daghettotymz.com/rkyvz/articles/doubelieve/doubelieve.html.

EXERCISE THE MIND

The mind is truly the most underrated muscle. We work so hard to maintain physical fitness, but cease to exercise the greatest organ we have. Many are not aware that the mind is different from the brain. See, the brain exists in our head and preside over our body whereas the mind exists in our environment and governz our lives. We have the mind – including the environment – in the spirit while the body, including the brain, is in the mind. We should all know the brain exists in our head and overseez the body but the mind is *beyond* our physical space and tyme for it has the ability to exist in the realm of the spirit where past, present and future are all one event.

All that you see, hear, touch, taste and smell are all part of your existence. When you smell a foul odor, you are not just smelling an invisible scent, you are inhaling the particles of the physical object it came from. You actually eat not just through your mouth but through your nose & ears!

We eat and digest the life circumstances of those around us every day eating through our conscious awareness just as we eat through our mouth. You might be askin', *"alright, what da hellz M'Bwebe talkin' about?!"* I'm speaking of Metaphysics, meaning *'after or beyond physical nature'*.

Metaphysics addresses questionz, about the ultimate composition of reality including the relationship between mind and matter. We are born free of ignorance of the non-physical world, all the while naïve of the physical world which leaves us both vulnerable and impressionable.

In Malidoma Soma's book, '*Of Water and the Spirit*', he wrote about how soon-to-pass Elderz and youths [in their first 4 or so yearz] are closer to the non-physical world than those aged in between. While in the womb, we are at the highest and closest element of creation both physically and metaphysically. During your 3 trimesterz in mom dukes womb, think of the daily genetic coding, wiring and encrypted data that happened manifesting in the physical transformation of fetus to wo/man forming armz, legz, eyes, two brainz [left and right hemisphere]. All this is done automatically and consistent with every woman who becomes pregnant.

A perfect comparison would be the building of a house. After the foundationz built, the electrical wiring must be put in so that everything works. The same transpires plus more inside your mother. There is a spiritual connection that goes beyond Earth.

Degreez of Separation
If you're aware of the 7 Djhuitic Principles, Correspondence is one of my favorites. It speaks of how everything is linked, both a smaller part of a bigger thing and vice-versa. It got me thinkin' 'bout how fragile life as we know it, is on this planet. We worry about natural disasterz, from hurricanes to man-made atrocities. YTs carved up the planet overruling the fact that we're all citizenz of this planet, first and foremost, and should have access to anywhere on this planet without the worry of passports. With all this man-made nonsense, it can make one feel separated from the unknown and thus, segregate amongst each other. This is purely a european mindset. A feeling of separation anxiety from the bigger picture. But if we applied Correspondence, we would see we are not alone. In fact, every earth-minute that passes is a blessing. We seldom dwell on what goes on outside the atmosphere. You think your local crack-corner is dangerous – space is a danger zone where anything can happen; comet's crash into mega-ton blocks of rock, a star explodes or implodes, or a galaxy is engulfed by an adjacent over-powering galaxy causing bright colorz that blaze across the dark space of the universe. What many don't know is that most of these colorz are remnants of colliding matter far more destructive than the A-Bomb here on earth. Yes, we have been blessed, for it only

MICRO AND MACRO COMPARISONZ

On a macrocozmic scale, if you look at how starz are created in the [poly-] universe, it closely resembles the stages human life goes through from incubation. For you to actually see what I'm talkin' about, I again suggest you visit your nearest Planetarium.

There you can learn of Nebula's. Nebula's are places deep in space where starz literally are born. From the combustion of dust, gases or both that can take on any shape, illuminate all kindz of colorz. This bein' a place where starz are born is but a macrozmic womb! Microcozmically, a womanz womb is a Nebula!! And I haven't even begun to speak about black holes!!

Some may think this is not taught in schoolz or universities so what makes is a legitimate argument?! Simple, you apply the Djhuitic principle 'Corrrespondence' – *"As above, so below, as below, so above,"* talked about in-depth in Wayne Chandler's, *'Ancient Future'.*

Microcozmically, when you stare into a bright blue sky, you see molecules that look like transparent, ghost-like cellz. These cellz are elements in probably their most natural state; floating freely attaching and detaching from other elements to make or change at will. This element could bond with otherz and eventually manifest as something physical like a blade of grass, a drop of rain or even mentally, as a thought. Each element containz an abundance of intelligence. This is seen micro- and macrocozmically in the formation of a fetus and the creation of starz.

Looking at our body, visualize it as a vessel, or a carrier of some sort that houses something like a car does to a human body. Now, the spirit is inside the body, just like you inside a car. Your body travelz taking you places. Just as a car can take you from New York to California, the same can be said microcozmically if you were to take a walk from your house to the food market. That journey alone could be like trillionz upon trillionz of light yearz traveled for elements inside us.

The Djhuitic Principles teach that with the principle of Vybration, nothing rests and that everything moves as well as vibrates. The molecules, electronz and neutronz inside us move. The principle is universal as it applies to each and every thing. Slower movement makes thingz appear to be harder like a desk, chair, tree or metal door, etc. These same elements in these thingz are inside you!

For example, a tree. It is a scientific fact there is a human/tree relationship where we count on each other to survive. We breathe out carbon dioxide which the tree needz to survive. The tree in turn exhales oxygen, which we need to survive. See, these are but two of many elements that are in both I&I and trees. So Y do hedz wanna *smoke* 'em?!!?

We are, just as everything is; a mere consumption of elements of the bigger thing. There are many of us who may have some difficulty accepting this due to the YTs school and religious system, where they separate science from spirituality. Many of us become imprisoned behind the transparent prison barz of trained thought. It is in these systemz we are taught that God isn't within but outside ourselves "up there" somewhere [refer to *The God Complex: Microcozm of the Macrocozm*].

THE PHYSICAL PHENOMENA

Because there are so many people in the world, we've never looked at our physical makeup as a phenomenon. Truly, the human body is one of *the* greatest creationz. Basically every man-made invention is based on the structure of humanz. From the car to the computer, practically every inventionz blueprint starts with the human body. It's hard to think a cordless; free-willed; electrical; no battery-needing just needz sleep to recharge; self-multiplying; self-governing appliance known as wo/man is a physical phenomena, but we are!

Lookin' at our physical evolution is mystifyin' enuff! To think, somethin' that's as feeble male semen is. Once ejaculated out of the penis, if it is not inside a womb the sperm will die within' minutes of contact with oxygen. Once this practically transparent group of elements – carryin' 50% of the data needed

takes a solarwind powerful enuff to move us a fraction of a degree off our current axis of 23.5° and life as we know it would be severely different, probably eliminated! We experience 4 seasonz because of how the Earth rotates around the Sun. If the Sun cooled down or was to rise a fraction of a degree, we could either freeze instantly or singe! This is somethin' YT could never control, because space is too large – it's infinite! Everything moves, so we have no clue what's floating towardz our direction. This isn't to scare you, it's to make you appreciate what we are and the tyme we have to be an asset to our existence rather than one who sit's on the sideline and wonderz when "God's" gonna come and save us. Live life, 'cause tomorrow *really* isn't promised...

R We Alone?

Ask yourself, are we alone? If space is infinitely expanding, do you know how big space is? Better yet, in order for space to expand, it has to expand 'over' or 'in to' something. What is it that its expanding to?! In other wordz, what was *before* space?? These are a series of questionz I've had since the dayz of my youth. And although I haven't been able to answer them yet, I believe applying 'Correspondence' has helped me remain on the path of eventually knowing. Of all the space programz on Earth, none are older than 100 yearz old. We're led to think because we haven't been able to prove there's life elsewhere in the poly-verse that there isn't when in fact, it may take hundredz, even thousandz of more Earth yearz before we're able to contact anyone or something else. So remain open, keep studyin' and applyin' those principles!!

to create us – breaks through a womanz vaginal wallz and fertilizes the egg something mind-blowing happenz! This development eventually transformz itself into dense matter creating a human being complete with independent functionality plus the ability to reproduce! Again, we take this for granted, but it truly is a phenomenon! We are truly a physical marvel! Everything the human body will need to create itself is there from its essence. In comparison to appliances, the physical body can also wear down and has its own way of recharging its "battery" so to speak… It's called sleep [refer to '*Free-Quencies of Tyme pt.1*' and '*Sleeperz*'].

There is a need for a total re-evaluation of the human body and it should *not* be done in YTs linear-thinking school systemz! There is a need for Afrikanz to be re-introduced to who we are and how we became. This will only allow us to see and fulfill our *"summon bonum"* or *"greatest good"* our Ancestorz in KMT [Kemet, aka Egypt] taught. From this analysis, we'd find that the body is fully capable of healing and maintaining itself if you allow it. But YT doesn't want us to know this. We are not aware that one of the safest thingz an Afrikan can do is stay away from hospitalz!

The hospital administration is a corporate entity that preyz on the masses ignorance and reluctance to apply the principles of cause and effect and correspondence to developing and maintaining our lives. I know it's hard to see this Afrikanz 'cause to even see a doctor you need insurance. YTs school system stripped us of this uni- [poly]versal law. In cases of emergencies a hospital may suffice, but what I'm talkin' about is preventive medicine aka LIFE Medicine! Meaning, the principle of cause and effect compelz you to take care of yourself now so that you can eliminate major problemz later. It's like choosing to be a vegan 'cause you know if you keep eatin' meat, white sugar, dairy products and canola oil (to name a few), you will develop serious mental and health problemz in the future.

When we can *inner*stand how infinite the mind is and its connection to everything, we can begin to overstand that we are truly limitless… just like space. However, YTs 'massa'-media machine and learning system blocks both our awareness and willingness to welcome such a concept. Lookin' at it on a level of wavelengths, our ignorance can be attributed to YTs takeover of the vybrationz in airwaves! They're constantly blasting their lifestyle via radio, tell-a lie-vision and the internet! Take a walk in your community. Look at all the billboard adz, fast food restaurants and drugstores that have no positive significance to our living a prosperous and healthy life! It's enuff to make you think this is what is normal and tryin' to be Afrikan or spiritually-based [minus all man-made religionz] is a waste!

We choose to stay in this illusionary box refusing to cross the boundary of what's known because someone or some-THING told us there *are* boundareez, but there aren't. They instilled the fear of Afrikan Liberation by assassinating Lumumba, Malcolm, Medgar and Martin, while infiltrating Garvey, the Panthers and MOVE and today, we have the intelligence to sit here and talk 'bout the Illuminati and Ancient KMT, but have yet to come up with a whollistic and strategic combative plan without some agent snitchin' on us to 'ol massa! We have reduced ourselves from *Active* Activist's to oral Activist's!

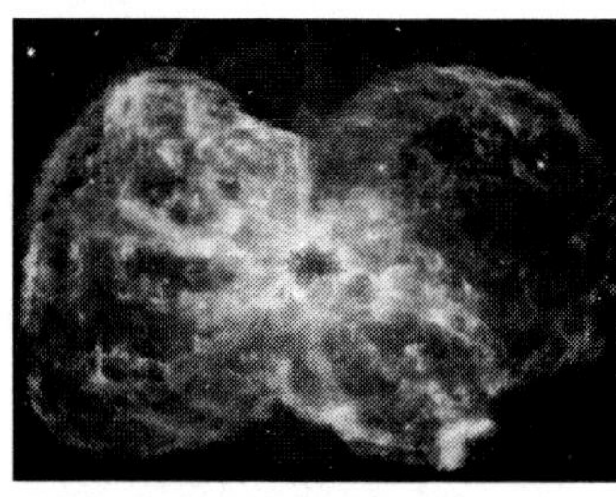

KOS vs. Chaos: Not for Everybody! Naturally, Knowledge of Self (KOS) makes you want to save otherz. But how do you save someone who doesn't believe they need to be saved?! You're gonna want your family and friendz to learn what you've learned and it hurts when they don't gravitate towardz it the way you do.

Realize, (1)KOS ain't for everybody; and (2)not everybody's ready for it. It's best to just drop a seed and keep it moving. Besides, if you waste tyme tryin' to convince otherz you could postpone your progression for there's more for you to experience and learn.

Some may eventually gravitate toward it, otherz may never. See, Earth could just be this place where imbalance dwellz. Otherz may call it 'Will', I'll also call it the choice of 'KOS vs Chaos'.

Look at it microcozmically, there are spots in your city where you know you will find trouble, no matter how many yearz go by. Just like on Classon & Putnam Avenue's in Bed-Stuy, Brooklyn, you will find real live crackhedz, and in other spots in NYC, you'll find pimps and prostitutes.

And on the opposite end, there are places on this planet that's real dope; places that are safe, peaceful and calm.

YT got us thinkin' there's no life out in space and that we're the only one's in this vast and ever-expanding space.

They say they have proof because of their NASA SETI (Search For Extraterrestrial Intelligence) program they once operated (they cancelled the program in 1993 and was later by the private, non-profit SETI Institute, and a smaller

One thing we cease to realize is that we are electrical beingz, with currents flowin' in and out of us steadily. See, YT teaches us that we're mainly blood and oxygen. But what about the rest of us?! We're also elements. We are conduits, emitting and transmitting energy and data at all tymz. What do you think it is that enables you to stick a balloon on the wall after rubbin' it on your hed? What is it that allowz you to shock someone by just touchin' them after you rub your feet on a carpet floor? Electrical energy. Start to see yourself as a machine and you will be able to comprehend how electronics and machines work. They are all based off the human body and all these inventionz were created first, in the mind. And just like a battery, we have a positive and negative side.

THE REAL POWER YOU

Think of your body as a remote controlled machine or computer. Instead of pluggin' yourself in a wall, your battery — or body — is recharged when you sleep. For every movement you make, realize there are electrical currents flowin' throughout your body enabling you to do these actionz. These electrical currents are bits and pieces of intelligence flowin' from your brain to a particular body part of region, tellin' it to move.

When you place your hand on a hot stove, your hand sendz a message to the brain that it's hot, the brain receives this signal and replies, sending data to tell the hand to rise and shake wildly, tryin' to cool it off. At the same tyme, the brain already sent a message to the neck to move forward, the mouth to open, the lungz to inhale and blow on the hand, while the vocalz yell out, *"Mutha__"!!"*

All these thingz seem to happen simultaneously but there's a frequency of tyme that transpires that's so fast, using a stopwatch would be senseless – all the while not recognizing that this phenomena happenz naturally. I really believe had we been taught this type of Health & Science in school, trust, I&I'd be in a much better situation, globally. But we should realize in knowing our enemy, their schoolz are institutionz of mental-training, not mental and spiritual development.

If we were to use their education only as a meanz of makin' it through this society [until we re-create ours] and balanced our tyme using free-thinking as a curriculum, we'd realize there are teacherz and professorz all around us. No, they may not all be in human physical form, the Djhuitic principle of vybration proves everything moves, and there's some kind of intelligence to this movement. We could learn so much about our own body by just lookin' at a microcozmic replica like a computer.

You think computerz today are fast? You sit at your computer typin' shit, switchin' from Microsoft Word to Photoshop to iTunes, and you're impressed by how swift your computer performz under software applicationz demandz that require more RAM and memory from your harddrive. A 100GHZ [gigahertz] processor [not yet released on the market as of today] on a computer would seem to be *lightning* fast as if lightning is really that SLOW! In comparison, the speed of the human processor is infinitely higher than 999EHZ [Exahertz. After gigahertz is tera-, peta-, then exa-hertz; think of cordless phones that have recently been marketed in the GHZ level.].

To date, there's no man-made machine that can exceed the level of exa-, while the human body far surpasses it, to a word not even used yet. Havin' an inner-standing of this also points out how information is transferred by electro-magnetic frequenceez. Not only do they transfer data, or matter; they can also instruct and decisively control a thought or action. So I ask you, *'What Frequency R U On??'*

More on this in Free-Quencies of Tyme pt. 4 where I will introduce the theory concept of antimatter.

LIK SHOT!!

part by the non-profit, grassroots SETI League).

Just like there are good parts and bad parts in cities across the world, I see Planet Earth as that spot (or neighborhood) in the universe where chaos dwellz. As big as Earth is, it really is small, macrocozmically.

Sayin' this bringz comfort in my knowin' I can't "change" everybody. Everybodies not gonna be down with KOS, this happenz to be the place of free will.

This also makes me realize that this 'mythical' God is not gonna come and bring vengance on the wicked on behalf of all the innocent's that have fallen victim to global white supremacy. Besides, the poly-verse is infinite, so how do you think 'God' has tyme to keep track of the Illuminati when there are starz exploding and imploding at random obliterating everything in its path. I'm sure there are victimz there as well...

This makes my decision to cope a lot easier and quite frankly, more realistic. With all the ill thingz going on in this world, all you can really do is focus on surviving as long as you're allowed and continue to elevate self by bonding with otherz on the same path.

I believe the test of livin' here on Earth is for you to keep your hed, elevate, tune in to the frequency and not get caught up!

If life never endz and it just changes, then surely there's somethin' after this. So spend your tyme masterin' KOS so that hopefully you'll be worthy of graduating to the next level, 'cause comin' back here (resurrection) I don't think is a blessing, it's probably a curse for not gettin' somethin' right in a previous life.

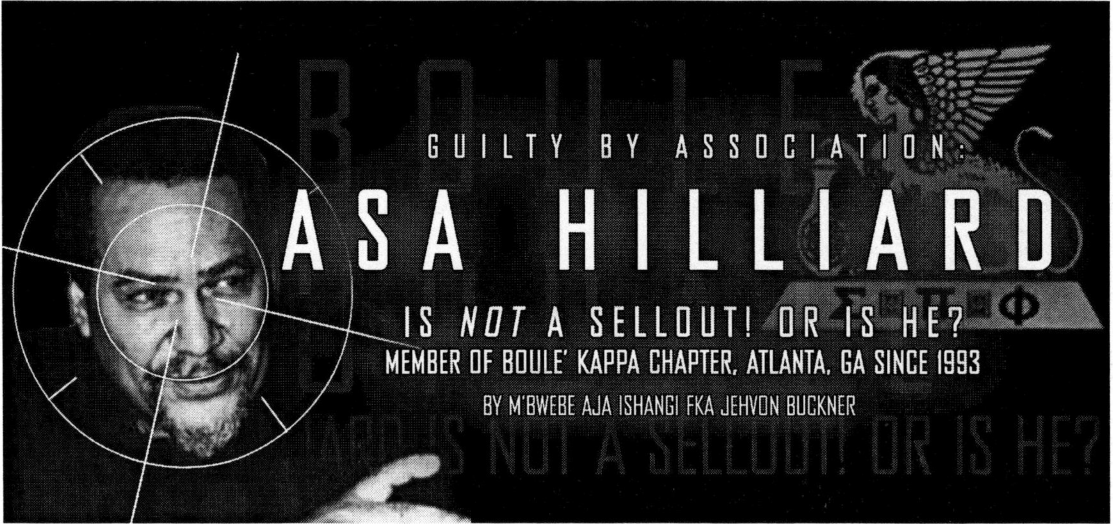

Many people walk through life riding the fence choosing whatever side when it is convenient for their benefit. This happenz a lot not only on personal levelz, but also with our so-called leaderz. The people that surround these chameleonz unknowingly serve as a buffer because they choose not to check them. So not only does this dampen the direction these leaderz are s'posed to lead the people in, it creates an even greater dependency and eventual immunity from doin' any wrong because the people refuse to step up and challenge this now deified God.

As Historian, Ashra Kwesi sayz, *"The enemy has become our deity!"* This case is no different. For example, December 6th 2000, Asa Hilliard — a so-called Africentric scholar (should be called Negro-centric scholar) was in Harlem speaking about the need for a more structured stance on Pan-Afrikanizm.

Through our studies of the Boule', aka Sigma Pi Phi, america's oldest fraternity of elite negroes founded May 15, 1904 [read *Boule' Series*], we are aware that this organization, whose principle founding was to be a black version of the notorious Skull & Bones secret society [read *Skull & Bones Series*].

Now it doesn't take an idiot to realize that if a group of Afrikanz who think like negroes (or wannabes) and want to create a secret society based on a society of white supremacists, what kind of mindset do you think these negroes have?! Logic will tell you they are ANTI-Afrikan or better yet, anti-THEMSELVES! This is what the Boule' was founded on and is still today!

Now we, at DGT, weren't gonna allow this brutha to address an all Pan-Afrikan audience on how to be more effective Pan-Afrikanz. So we came prepared to address this Psychologist publicly about his involvement and his answerz were expected, yet a lil' startling.

My request to the Ancestorz – more specifically the spirit of the author of *Stolen Legacy,* George GM. James – was that I be given a chance to address him after he did his presentation during the question & answering session. Unfortunately that wish was denied. So I was left to see if I could steal a few moments as the rest of the audience applauded and ignorantly showed their gratitude of his presence when his presentation ended.

I waited patiently, watchin' several Afrikanz give him biggups and praise. After the last one finished jockin' him, I moved into position. *"Asa,"* I said sternly as he shook my hand (I held tight to his, in case he tried to walk away as I questioned him. *"I wanted to know if you were still an active member in the Boule'"*, gettin' right to the chase.

He suddenly looked shocked, backed up a bit and said, *"Well yeah, but all that stuff that was said about us is not true."* He suddenly looked as though he was tryin' to find a way out. Quickly sounding like a politician, he replied, *"I don't know everything THEY'RE doin' I just attend certain functions. We mainly throw banquets and social get-togethers. I don't know anything else."*

My anxiety and naivety showed as I pressed on for him to confess Y he would be involved with an organization with such allegationz. He kept replying he didn't know much because he only attended *certain* meetingz and was quick to separate himself by saying *"Them"* and *"They"* when I asked him Y he wasn't aware of everything else they did, as if he was a limited member, privileged to only certain info and benefits. But common sense would tell you that a person with such a reputation both in the Afrikan community and his profession of Psychology must have *some* intelligence enuff to not join an organization he knew little of, in addition to giving part allegiance to it.

The Boule' is too big! Trust me, I'm sure they wouldn't allow a part-tymer in their crew. I then asked if he would be willing to set the record straight about the Boule' and their wrong-doing (knowing he wouldn't), he replied, *"I don't know nothin'. I told you everything I know. If THEY are doin' somethin', then GOOD FOR THEM. I only go to certain meetingz. But if you know of something I should know, then we should talk!"*

I looked at him like, you SELL-OUT! You don't even have the ballz to back 'em up! That's what I mean by ridin' the fence, yo! He admits he's a member, but claimz to only have limited info on what they're about. Are these the actionz of an intelligent man or a negro coverin' somethin' up? Either way, he's guilty by association!

A NOT TOO POPULAR DISCUSSION ABOUT AGENTS IN DA HOOD
» Case #009: Asa Hilliard is not a sellout! Or is he?

[This is an excerpt of an email sent to DGT responding to the article about Asa Hilliard]

"What is your basis for carrying this completely wrong message about one of our greatest scholar warriors besides Steve Cokely tarring him with the Boule' brush? I happen to know Baba Asa personally and can tell you categorically he is not a sellout.

Rather, he has devoted his adult life to advocating Africentric education as the ONLY solution to educatin' Afrikan youth. In doing so, he has received death threats and has been attacked from ALL sides.

Have you read ANY of his many books on the subject? Posing as an Africentric scholar? Check it. He is a founding member of ASCAC. On July 23, 2000, Dr. Asa Hilliard and his wife were enstooled as development chiefs at Mankranso Village in the Ashanti Region of Ghana. This honor being bestowed on him because of his HARD WORK in getting money and educational materials to the people. He co-developed the ever popular educational television series "Free Your Mind, Return to the Source: African Origins".

He proposed and largely wrote the Afrikan American Baseline essays for the Portland public school system in the early '80s. He worked in conjunction with the National Black United Front on the this project. Their work was so impressive that it was roundly attacked from all sides as pseudoscience. Yet, these same essays served as one of the fundamental documents used by the Africentric movement.

He, along with Dr. Ben, Dr. John H. Clarke and others, were attacked by [Henry Louis] *Gates on behalf of certain Jews. Remember the full-page article Gates took out in the the New York times in the 90's attacking the Africentric movement? Remember that it overlaid a star of david? Baba Asa's wife is the current mayor of East Point, GA. An attempt was made at one time to attack his wife by attacking him as a crackpot and anti-white.*

Baba Asa makes frequent trips to Afrika, taking many along on tours to many places that tourists NEVER go. For example, he took a group to visit the Dogon and was able to get info that no one else was able to get because of the relationships he has established there. AND, he made sure his informants were WELL PAID as recommended by Ayi Kwei Armah.

This is a bunch of bullshit!! If it's not, ya'll will have to come with something stronger than merely attacking him for being in the Boule'. Do your research; don't just accept something blindly from Cokely. But then, I can remember chastising you several years ago for saying that the term "dreadlocks" was created by whites or YT as you say which is bullshit. It seems you are still a mile wide and an inch deep. Ya'll are wrong about Bill Cosby too.

- from Cheikh Diop via email

M'BWEBE's RESPONSE: I know enuff about Asa and the Boule' to know that although he has done great works, it still does not exonerate his membership to an organization that's a black version of Skull & Bones! On the contrary, do *your* research! Look into the background of the Boule', and no you don't have to take Steve Cokely's worked for it, nor mine, just look at the affiliationz.

Yes, I've read Hilliard's scholastic works, even sat front row in several of his lectures. But his admitted membership with the Boule' is reason enuff to go after him. Have you read the Boule's history book (a book he himself as a member is required to read thoroughly each and every May as a ritual)?

You can believe what you want, I KNOW HE'S A SELLOUT! I had an encounter with him publicly about his membership back in the Boule' in 2000, and he tried to act like he didn't know nothin' about it. His response was that they were just a social organzation who threw parties and picnics.

Ask your boy Y would he would lie like that? What is he coverin' up? The way I see it, he's simply doin' EXACTLY what Boule' memberz are s'posed to do, they have sworn to never let you know who the rulerz of Global White Supremacy are. So of course he'd play the run-around with me sayin' he didn't know much about the group! He couldn't deny he was a member of the Boule's tenth chapter (Kappa) out of Atlanta, because the roster has been public on my site for nearly 10 yearz!

When you know the story of the Boule', it don't matter what "deedz" one has done! The work of Carter G. Woodson, Alain Locke, WEB DuBois and yes even Bill Cosby... deserved to be dissed because it just doesn't make sense to be "PanAfrikan" or for the advancement of the legacy of our people, then in the same breath, be associated with the very conspiratorz who've done everything they can to harness and conceal the truth of our history. That's like bein' a civil rights leader while also bein' a member of the Ku Klux Klan (KKK)! Unless he professes to be a *'spook sittin' by the door,'* it's oxymoronic!!

Asa is a sellout *not* for the volumes of work and research he's done on our legacy, but for his continued refusal to (1)admit he knowz much, much more than he leadz us to believe about the Boule'; (2)tries to play it off by belittling his role in the Boule' when common sense would tell you no elite group of men would allow partial membership. If you in the Boule' you in ALL THE WAY!; and (3)as he remainz an active member of the Boule' he continues to honor the sacred ritual of concealing secrets.

Since you're so high on protectin' him, Y not ask him to come clean about his entire involvement in the Boule'? Ask him to share with everyone and prove Steve Cokely, Ashra Kwesi, myself and all otherz that believe the Boule' to be co-conspiratorz to global white supremacy, wrong? Doing this only clearz not only him, but the Boule's overall perception by the PanAfrikan community. Y wouldn't he want hedz to see the Boule' as an ally instead of what we've found them to be?

And if the Pan-Afrikan community is as important as he claimz, he would want to tell us of these "secrets" and not follow the path of fellow Boule' concealerz, WEB DuBois and Carter G. Woodson [read *Boule' Series, Part 3*]

So since you seem to be his #1 fan, contact him about this and see what he has to say. But first, I suggest you do your own research on the Boule'. You are welcome to use my research as a source, but it's even more important to do your own investigation. *Then* contact him and see what he has to say. If you choose to do nothin' to clear this up simply validates the research and our claimz.

You can do what you will, just as we at DGT will continue to lift the skirt of ANY and ALL perpetratorz who defile the Red, Black & the Green!

MORE FIE-YAH!

Inner-Thoughts Series

As of 1997, I've dwelled in the realm of conscious game for 14 semesterz and I've seen 'em come and go. One day we wearin' Afrikan black medallionz, the next we wearin' versace and hilfiger; you got peeps who just "know" what tyme it is while doin' nothin' and those who can't even tell tyme but ready to die (for anything – really NOTHING); we got hedz who went from beef, pork and chicken to vegetarian and back; and of course we got those "righteous" bruthaz who say they all about us while, on the low, beatin' their Queen and neglectin' their youth. Amidst the elements of negative stress, I parlay on. Although the illmatic whisperz of wickedness are constant, I persist to exist on a higher level.

Everybody speaks to themselves, askin' *"Y"* and *"should I or shouldn't I"*. It is with questionz that we find balance; for it is what separates God from doG (beast), so eloquently encoded in the structure of Her-Em-Akhet (most call the Sphinx) of Kemet (egypt). But this battle remainz confined between the wallz of my mental. How can we manifest consciousness physically??

Like a feen searchin' for his pipe, I yearn to politic on relevant issues of Afrikan advancement, but I keep runnin' into pimps and pretenderz. Abandoned, alone, yet still motivated, I find my pineal my safe haven. Since there ain't many doin' shit, I'll do it myself. Since no one else will interview me, I'll interview myself...

What made you embrace consciousness?
Excuse me sir, lemme redirect that question, what makes one not?!!? Dependency! Since I was a shorty I was independent. With consistency, The Creator kept throwin' subliminalz at me and when I turned 21, I was re-awakened. This was only a process of reconnecting me to my youth. See, when you're a child, you want to know everything. Every other word out your mouth is, *"What's this, What's that, Howz that? and Y?"* As a seed, this marks your closest connection to the natural elements that make up the universe. Because western civilization, which we are products of, is of a dominant, controlling, oppressive nature, our people have been stripped of the will to ask Y and to research yourself. That was wiped out our first day of kindergarten!

The day we entered their mental re-training institutionz (schoolz), our connection to Nature was severed. I embrace consciousness because that is who we are originally. It is our consciousness that gave the world what it has today. Todayz technology is only an artificial contraction of what we have naturally, including computerz. All that shit comes from our melanin! We don't have to "log on" to a computer to get "on line"; by the proper meditation we can connect with otherz mentally anywhere in the galaxy! That's the shit I'm about!!

Y Do you choose to exist in a not too popular field of business — that being the field of liberation?
Hmm, good question. This is a field that is in the Want Adz hedz will most likely *not* apply for. It offerz no vacation dayz and no medical benefits! Being conscious is an everyday affair. I can't just turn it on for 8 hourz and go home and chill. I live this everyday!

Of course, it's not popular because our values have been whitewashed. We've removed the word "we" and replaced it with "I". "We" know shit is hectic for black people, yet we won't stand up and make it right for ourselves! We got wizardz on the other squad. We send our Afrikan mindz to white institutionz where they graduate and get drafted for the opposing team.

For example, over 70% of the people that enable space missionz to leave the earth for NASA are black scientist's! We got hundredz of thousandz of black engineerz, lawyerz and doctorz all working for the "away" team, whereas the "home" squad has but a few, if any at all! I chose this field because in the realm of education for generation X and so on, there aren't many young Afrikanz who care just as much about the streetz as they do with education — no not school, knowledge of self education!

Are you saying you're against the public school system?
Are you sayin' you're for it?! C'mon yo, especially when these institutionz are not run, financed and owned by black people! From day one we are told of George Washington never tellin' a lie and some cherry tree bullshit. They never teach us about his connection to the Luciferian Conspiracy and Masonry, but oh, he was an "honorable" man. Along with that, you know how much they disrespect our people by not including us in *their*-story until slavery! Yo, that's mentacide! I went from K-12, and damn near all of college not knowin' shit about my people and culture!!

You wouldn't be doing this if you felt it wasn't worth it. What do you think will happen in the future?
Life exists in cycles. If you study astrophysics, or cosmology, the starz are revealing we are going into anutha stage: the age of Aquarius. We are entering an age where the quest to know will be intensified. The information age is what is going to lead us back to where we were when we built the pyramidz and created electricity with the use of our ancient symbol, the Ankh. Information bringz power and because, right now, many don't have this urge to know, it affirmz the age we're in currently. As the new millennium nearz, more and more of our people will awake from our 6000-year-hibernation. I'm not pressed about all this hype of the "new world order", I just study it because I want to know what YT has planned. Doesn't mean tingz a g'wan. The

pendulum is swingin' towardz positivity and guess who's system isn't included??

What is your opinsion of today's leaderz?
Oh, shit. My opinion?? The one's society wants us to acknowledge are weak, noodle-back's. The real leaderz are the one's who get no prop's, the George G. Jackson's, who dedicated his life to our people but died alone and broke; John Henrik Clarke's, Dr. Ben's, Ashra Kwesi's, Khallid Muhammad's and Eraka Rouzarhondu's.

It's dedicated hedz like FRONTLINE magazine, outta of Chi-town and THE BLACK TRACK outta Brooklyn, who pump madd info the air that oftentymz go unnoticed by our people. This is so because we haven't decided to think for ourselves yet. We haven't decided to choose our own leaderz, develop and fund our own institutionz and, yes, reconnect ourselves with our original spiritual identity. But no worry, the age is coming. As far as the "leaderz" you're talkin' about, the Jesse's and Farrakhan's, don't have much luv for 'em. I'm all about economic strategy but when you wearin' a phat diamond and got golden ceilingz in your castle, well, let's just say, I question your agenda.

How can you really be for the people when you lavish in materialistic luxury. True, we are the originalz of this planet and everything in it is ourz, but yo, if 99% of your people don't have, Y you flauntin' it so? Of all the so-called "Black" leaderz we have had, NOT ONE HAS PUBLICLY CALLED FOR A BOYCOTT OF NON-AFRIKAN MADE GOODZ! Not one has talked of the importance of entrepreneurship so that we can contend with the existing entities. No, they want us to keep singin' *"We shall overcome"* and *"No Justice, No Peace"* and attend anti-police and klan rallies. The real battle is economics, and not one of those noodle-back need-to-growz are gonna tell you that! Y? Because they'd be bitin' the hand that feedz them, point blank! Besides, with "black" organization's like the Boule' and NAACP preserving the eurocentric values it makes me wish I remembered the D.R.O.P. Squadz 1800 number! (A Spike Lee movie)

In your writngz, you often refer to your readerz as "God", "Goddess" and "Sun". Y?
I am not of the 5%, nor muslim for that matter. These termz originated before that. I do credit them for makin' 'em popular though. Because of the history of Her-Em Akhet, what YT callz the sphinx, I know the math about the God and also the beast within' each of us. I refer to ourselves as Goddess' & Godz because that is the part of you I am connecting with. When we politic on mental stimulation, we are simply suppressing the beastly nature within us that is often provoked by the imbalance society we dwell in. "Sun" is a play off the word, "Son". I've seen many refer it to the star because our ancients knew the importance of the sun, along with carbon — which is melanin — and that all life if fueled by it's radiant energy. Am I an originator of this term? No. I say this just so hedz don't think there's some ego to it. One tyme this kid emailed me talkin' 'bout usin' "Sun" was here before me. I agreed. I didn't start this, I'm talkin' 'bout when I started usin' it.

I overstand. People do like to get petty don't they?
Yeah, they do. But that battle is not on my agenda. Trust me, if I'm destined to invent somethin', it ain't gonna be no word!

Word.
Huh? Oh, *"word!"*

Whta's your view of religion?
Man-made Religion?

Yeah.
I look at it as one of the toolz YT uses to control the masses. Religion is a very touchy subject when it comes to blackfolk. Many won't even get into an educational debate with me. I'm not invincible, I'm just a humble student who wants to learn more. But I keep findin' these preacherz, church goerz and even muslimz that don't want to talk about how the Koran and the Bible haven't even been around for 1500 yearz! When we are humble enuff to realize that life existed before these texts, we may see some mental elevation in our people.

Well, do you believe in God?
No question, I do believe in myself! I AM GOD! But, I am NOT The Creator or 'Energy' as I call it. I believe God has the ability to also be a doG — to parlay on what I spoke about earlier about Her-Em-Akhet. As far as a belief in a higher entity? I do. Is it a man or woman? No. When you break us all down we are simply matter; carbon, molecules and atomz. Energy. Energy is that; Energy is in everything; and I am of this Energy; therefore everything is me, both good and evil, it's just that I have a choice.

Religion has taught us to look for Energy outside of you, whereas our Ancients taught us Energy is within. If you think Energy is outside of you, you've already been disconnected with Energy. This is Y our people feel so helpless and are so quick to *"leave it up to God to take care of"*.

Naw, that's bullshit, "God" helps those who helps themselves! We've been separated from our natural, spiritual powersource. All those feel good sessionz thatta g'wan every Sunday is only a mind fuck, because the only one's truly happy are the reverend — who just got paid — and white supremacy, because we still remain awaiting for this mystery God to come flyin' over the sky to take us away from this hell. Our leaderz make sure they put that shit in our sistaz hedz so they won't wanna hook up with a freethinking, self educator who has a thirst for the truth and ain't afraid to blaze a trail alone if need be.

Whoa, whoa, I felt a little more energy in that last statement. Could it possibly be that I pushed a button?
Yeah Sun, you did. Because I'm tryin' to do what the forces will me to, but yo, I must admit, shit ain't really gonna be tight until we win our sistaz back. A lot of our sistaz

are gone, without a trace! I be tryin' to wake my bruthaz up and they are, semi. I mean, they readin' books and condunctin' deep cypherz, but is there any physical manifestation, hardly! I can't entirely knock these kidz because I'm not the one to keep a brutha in check, that's what a sista can do! It's sorta like a cat chasin' it's tail: Bruthaz are readin' but ain't doin'; a sista can make a brutha do, but she's caught up into either religion or materializm. Yo, shit is madd hectic! But, as said before, I am soothed by the subliminal faxes I receive from the starz: *"keep doin' wha'chu doin'; like will attract like"*. My efforts of today only add to those Ancients that got me here today, it is now my tyme to add my spice to the pot.

We could go on and on about quamz, beefs and biggup's about our people and consciousness. The most important factor is that tyme is dictating a change; a change for the good. We will cross the bridges of blacks and religion, leadership and consciousness; tyme wills it. It is not a race, and when I'm around a circle of free-thinkerz, the thought of the new world order manifesting isn't so real to me. What's real is the resurrection of our mindz dictated by the universe; what's real is being in touch with my inner thoughts.

LIK SHOT!

Inner Thoughts 2: more questshunz, more answerz

by m'bwebe aja ishangi

Fast-forward…the dawn of a new millennium, 2001. 22 semesterz in the realm of Afrikan-consciousness and it *still* mystifies me. Just over 3 yearz ago, I felt a need to be heard unlike anyway I have ever before. *"What better way",* I thought*, "than to speak in a way to the masses seldom read!"* I decided that since there were many media outlets that refuse to hear Afrikan-centered expressionz, the best way to be heard was to do it miself. That's right, a one-on-one interview with miself, *by* miself.

The game hasn't changed, there's still madd hedz out there who disgrace spirituality; still hedz who belong to "organizationz" yet they continue to "tion" or "shun" away from organizin'; the streets still crawl with peeps who feel their consciousness is based on the variety of Afrikan garb they have, goin' natural or locks, blazin' incense and oilz and buyin' a book (they never crack open) a month. The extreme challenge of maintainin' a not too popular way of life that venture capitalists are on the verge of commercializin' again, becomes even more complex as the humble continue to seek truth.

Like our Ancestorz who refused to leave their ancient land the wicked mindz behind the Aswan Dam buried them under, my feet stand rooted on the quest of truth.

Still, to this day, the footsoldierz voice go unheard mainstream. The dayz of undaground cella dwellaz need to be numbered. In order for us to win back di youth from the clawz of commercialized stereotypes, we must surface above ground. If there are no outlets that will listen to our voice, we must create our own outlets.

"Like a feen searchin' for his pipe, I yearn to politic on relevant issues of Afrikan advancement, but I keep runnin' into pimps and pretenderz. Abandoned, alone, yet still motivated, I find my pineal my safe haven. Since there ain't many doin' shit, I'll do it myself. Since no one else will interview me, I'll interview myself..." – from Inner Thoughts, 1997

What is your take on conspiraceez?

Actually, I believe there's a conspiracy on conspiraceez. I mean, for the last 10 or so yearz, many Afrikanz have started doin' further research on the topic of white supremacy. This lead to books like *'Behold A Palehorse',* madd books on the Illuminati and New World Order pamphlets. It particularly escalated as we were approaching the end of the 1990s, where many felt – including myself – that we were probably in the *'Last Dayz'* of life as we know it.

Y I believe there's a conspiracy on conspiraceez is because it is a multi-million and soon billion dollar industry! Just think of all the cheddar that was made during the

Y2K scam! Books upon books, cypherz upon cypherz, the message even got out through the music industry.

I needed to ask myself, as protective as YT is about his world, he couldn't possibly think of lettin' blatant, Afrikan-centered hip hop hedz like Boogie Monsters, X-Clan and KRS drop what they did on wax unless they thought they could make a profit and not lose their empire. As big as Time Warner is, with all its backin' from white supremists, there's no way they would allow this to be heard unless they thought they could get paid!

Don't get me wrong, I still believe there are conspiraceez, but I also believe they realize there is a market out there for people with 'Afrikan-consciousness'. It's bizness, B. See, this pool of people could be their ultimate demise, so it is essential for the survival of white supremacy to be in control of what we are exposed to. This would consist not only in the music industry, but the entire entertainment industry as a whole. See, Neely Fuller, Jr, and Dr. Francess Cress-Welsing made reference in their books respectively, *The United Independent Compensatory Code/System/Concept* and *The Isis Papers*.

In addition, we have to acknowledge the arrogance of YT as he is convinced through the actionz of our Ancestorz that within the last 150 or so yearz in America, there have been a 30-yearz surge towardz Afrikan-consciousness leading them to believe that they can exploit us because we will go through this just like any other "fad", – look at how we went from jheri curl, to the fade, to the box-cut to ball head and now dreadlock; all in a matter of 15 yearz?!

To a large degree, I kinda believe Afrikanz look at liberation as a fad. How else could we allow a potato chip company to sell Malcolm X chips after the movie came out?! How we allow there to be a million 'Million-"blank"-Marches' to happen when all we get from it is an increase in Farrakhanz bank account a million tymz over?! Face it, the conscious community has not – to date – exemplified solidarity any more than the Black Church or Nation of Islam; and because of that, white-owned industries have made millionz sellin' us -ish like they've done to everyone else! Personally, I think this conspiracy on conspiraceez is used to delay us from what we really should be studyin', Knowledge of Self.

Even though knowing your enemy (YT) is vital, we consume ourselves in knowing them. Hedz can recite numerous Illuminati families but cannot name 5 countries in Afrika. They can mention all the warz America has been in, but never heard of Menelek and the battle at Adwa, which was just over 100 yearz ago. I think it serves 2-fold. While makin' loot for themselves, they derail our progress by gettin' us to get caught up into Y2K, 5/5/2000, the Mayan calendar in 2012, Jesus' 2nd coming and the next so-called catastrophe they decide to dream up we're s'posed to face. Trust me, since the 5/5/2000 meltdown didn't happen, the religious theologianz and Roman Catholic Church will conjure up some other Armageddon dates to get the masses to fear. We'll be hearin' a new date some tyme soon.

Author of *Ancient Future*, Wayne Chandler stated, *"As we approach the 21st century, we find ourselves morally bankrupt and spiritually destitute,"* namely because we believed the end was comin' and when you break it down, who told you it was... YT! If it wasn't through his literature, it was through his religion!

I speak of this from personal experience. For several yearz I was "caught up", buyin' a book on the New World Order every week, doin' madd research on , Lord Rothschilds, Cecil Rhodes and Rockefeller – don't get me wrong, this *is* very, VERY vital info, but there needz to be balance. Studying YT and not enuff of us is imbalance, just as studyin' too much of ourselves and not enuff YT – our #1 enemy!

What's your take on Farrakhan?
Farra-who?? FarraCAIN'T is more like it! I mean, after the Million Man March of '95, I was given this tape with all the Afrikan-centered heavy hitterz that spoke the night before and they were blastin' Farracain't. Dr. Clarke, Ben, you name it. I wish I knew about it 'cause I woulda rather been there than at the March, though it was a special spiritual experience to see the soulz of a million-plus Afrikan men. All Farracain't did was get our loot, oh and for us to be sorry for shit we allegedly did, but no solutionz, not one! I began to suspect a change in him after this, even though most hedz were sayin' Farracain't must be infiltratin' the establishment so he can destroy the cracka from the inside (a 'spook behind the door' tactic). But after this past year with his change to orthodox islam, refusin' to give props to his leader(z) Master Farad, Elijah, and his all-being creator, Allah after his alleged bout with cancer, I know he's converted! He seemz to be too busy tryin' to be like Jesse – a safe Negro, more than the firey motivational, INDEPENDENT, speaker he used to be. He claimed he was able to get through his bout with cancer because of the prayerz he received from the very people he used to bash.

I mean, look at him. We've seen him increasingly quote from the Bible and not the Koran. The Nation used to never vote. Last election in '96, he spoke of gettin' muslimz registered to vote so that next election (2000), they'd have their own candidate. What happened? He registered them to vote and since there was no muslim candidate, they voted for either Gore or Bush! He's also met with Illuminati member, Edgar Bronfman tryin' to open hotelz he said would be black-owned, but after a little diggin' found these hotelz would be owned by Bronfman with the workerz bein' Black. Most importantly is his refusal to acknowledge the enslavement of Afrikanz by Muslimz in Sudan, Afrika. After 2 reporterz from the Baltimore Sun proved this was goin' on after purchasing enslaved Afrikanz themselves, Farracain't still claimz it ain't true. What's worse is, like Jesse, he won't even look into it himself! Probably because he's on the Khartoum Government's payroll.

What buggz me out is wonderin' how it seemz most if not all of his clones, oops, followerz in the Nation have accepted this change not only in his life, but have done so in theirz as well. It goes to show that if a member of the Nation of Islam no longer speaks what Elijah taught, calling YT a blue-eyed devil and whatnot, they are truly brainwashed. I guess if Farracain't told the world he's a member of the KKK, he'd still probably pull a large percentage of followerz with him!

I've heard there are memberz of the NOI that do not agree with his 180° philosophical turn, but the sad thing is that there are still memberz who choose to follow Farracain't and not the Nationz version of Islam. This proves to be a pure example how Afrikan people have been conditioned to deify the speaker and not intuit the message.

That's what gets me red, because people don't study! I mean, first off, Islam is responsible for the enslavement of Afrikan people just like Christianity and Judaizm! Second, if you look at the history of the Nation, you'll find that their spiritual foundation is based on a white man! 2 good books to read about the Nation have been written by Karl Evanzz. Yeah, if you look at a picture of Master Farad, you can see his pale white skin and jet black, STRAIGHT, hair! The excuses that have been told as to Y he is white is crazy, yo! The bottom line is you have this organization that is against the cracka, yet their leader is one! What type of –ish is dat?!!?

Y do people get on you about sources?
It's funny, people will question a fellow Afrikan but never question their teacher in school or reverend in church. I'm always asked, where I get my info from, claimin' they have a hard tyme believin' what I'm sayin'. Let me ask you somethin', what is a source? You mean to tell me that you will not believe somethin' I say unless you read it somewhere else?! In other wordz, in order to feel what I'm sayin' you need to have validation from someone who's been published? Well what about them??

Information mainly comes from within. Of all the books who provided sources from where they got material from, it links down to an individual that THOUGHT something. A thought starts somewhere.

A large percentage of my writing come from within. This source is connected with our Ancestorz and plain old common sense. A source can come from within. In fact, I am a source, we're all sources! Everyday you may say or think something that was channeled from your inner thoughts. You mean to tell me it can't be believable unless you read it in someone else's book?! Shit, you either feel it or not!

What's your definition of a successful boycott?
Well, I think we need to get back into the spirit of the 60s movement when hedz boycotted for months instead of one day. Ask yourself, Y do you boycott? Because you are not satisfied with a certain situation. So Y do we boycott and then give up before we get satisfaction? Mainly because our self-appointed leaderz take us off track. See the goal of a boycott should not be equality but self-reliance. That's what we need. I don't wanna be equal to those racist pirates, we want liberation and that can only come with self-reliance!

We see that Harlem is being taken over by YT with their Walt Disney, Old Navy's, fast-food restaurants and Blockbuster Video stores, while we stand and watch it happen. Today, our self-appointed leaderz enjoy boycotting Burger King and Mitsubishi, for a couple dayz instead of calling for the creation of Afrikan-owned restaurants and car manufacturerz.

See, you can't boycott somethin' without offering an alternative. I can't tell you to boycott Old Navy and not offer an alternative store, compatible in price, to shop at. Our people ain't on that level yet. The majority of our people are asleep, so they don't care to hear of our $600Billion spending power in the US, all they want is a pair of jeanz!

The Selma, Alabama bus boycott of 1955 lasted 381 dayz forcing YT to see over a 12+month period how much money they lost due to Afrikanz carpooling instead of ridin' in the back of the bus. See, their alternative was the carpool. We need to create competitive outlets before we boycott the existing ones.

More importantly, we lack endurance because we lack vision. Every year, from November 1st to February 1st, there's a 90-day Selective Buying Boycott, calling for all Afrikanz to refrain from frivolous buying from non-Afrikan people during the holiday season. This is the end of the year YT makes most of their money, slapping 3 holidayz back to back. We need to add an additional mid-year 90-day boycott, maybe in the summer. As the word gets around, in conjunction with Afrikan-owned stores used as alternatives, we could see in a matter of a couple yearz, the effect on YTs economy.

Oh, they'd go through severe tactics to get your dollar. Trust me, you'll see sale after sale after sale. This is where we have to be vocally aggressive about the mission. See, YT can drop their prices but so low. After that, they will crack. We have to be willing to see this to the end. I'm not sayin' spend all your money with Afrikan-owned stores, that's my eventual wish. Initially, we can see dramatic effects by just takin' 15% of what we spend on YT and spend on us! It's that simple! C'mon Afrikanz, liberation ain't that hard to attain. We just need to stop deifyin' these false leaderz and deal with the agenda at hand! You want freedom, then 'free' your 'dome' – which is your mind – and let's do this! But, relatively speaking, only a small percentage of us are ready fi do sum*ting!*

You diss our leaderz alot. What are your major problemz with them?
I can never express enuff how effective the puppeteer/puppet theory works on our people. We are not critical about our "leaderz" enuff. True, no one is perfect, but we let too many blatant atrociteez go by.

Take the latest catastrophe with Jesse. Now this so-called righteous leader got busted. Now he's a "baby-daddy". True, that's between him and his family, but what we should be critical about is how he's getting' the loot to pay for this child. I heard on the radio he's giving his mistress up $6000 a month! Question, Jesse ain't never had no job, so how is he payin' for this? Who and where is he gettin' the loot to pay for it? Ain't nobody checkin' him on this shit! We too busy forgivin' him for stickin' his Johnson in anutha woman. In addition to forgiving him, we allow him to simply pay for his act, instead of bein' a father to this child. This child will have money, but lack in what's more evident, this child needz a father presence in his life.

Same –ish happened with Elijah Muhammad and even Bill Cosby a couple yearz back, and what happened to his daughter he still claimz ain't his? She's in jail while Cosby goes on with his life. Ben (Chavis) Muhammad did his part in continuously sexually harassing our sisterz, as he made a complete mockery of the already melting pot, Million Family March.

Face it, our leaderz aren't our leaderz, they're pimps, pimpin' us, who're bein' pimped by YT, the puppeteer. Because our unwillingness to be critical about them, we allow them to derail us from liberation. Not one of them has called for an economic boycott. In fact, it was Jesse who told Clinton NOT to apologize for the enslavement of Afrikan people on behalf of the United States!

All they've done is take our money and spend it on their habits, refilling their pockets every session with a boycott on this, boycott on that. And we faithfully support their habits by givin' their front organizationz money. A leader is a leader because the people supports that leader. A leader is s'posed to be a spokeperson of the people, therefore, s/he should represent the collective consciousness of the people. If we stopped financially supporting Farracain't, Jesse, even brutha Sharpton and made demandz on what it is we actually want, they would be forced to deliver or be stripped of their leadership.

It's tyme we take responsibility of our progress and quit takin' the lazy route, leavin' it to these "leaderz". They should earn their money just as hard as we give it. If you don't produce results, you fired! Maybe then they won't be occupied with which young sista they can manipulate and focus on the task at hand, the emancipation of Afrikan people worldwide!

Your predictionz on the future...

Shiiiit, after Y2K didn't happen, I had an epiphany, yo. As I said before, YT tries to keep the people baffled by conjuring up these catastropheez, meanwhile they go on with mischievous planz. Living in fear is not living in control. We get too caught up in the future that we forget the present. Although we are living in drastic tymz, we are still living! Since we've decided we are not at a stage of physical war – because as much as we talk about how "the man" is holdin' us down, we ain't out riotin' or organizin' – so it's safe to conclude we don't see ourselves backed into a corner just yet, so Y not live a little? I'm sayin' this based on our actionz.

Lemme break it down. There are a total of 168 hourz in a week. Of that week, the majority of us only spend a couple hourz a week "fightin' the power". This may include reading books about our history, goin' to see speakerz speak or goin' to town rallies. The rest of the week is spent workin' at the plantation, which is about 40-50 hourz a week. That roundz out to about 60 hourz. With over 100 hourz left, that leaves us to about 50 hourz for sleep, and let's say 20-30 for just chillin'. We still got 20 or so hourz where we do…NOTHING!! So if you don't wanna dedicate some of that tyme to uplifting yourself first and people second, live life! Take advantage of the tyme you have permitted on this earth because we don't know what happenz after this.

So what are you sayin'?

Personally, I use that extra 20 or so hourz to develop self. After a recent session with Tony Browder, thingz that were parlayed simply confirmed thingz I was already feelin'.

I don't follow...

Listen up Star. See, life is a quest and on this 'quest' lay infinite 'questionz'. Hence the root word, 'quest'. This journey, though a challenging one, only openz to more questionz. This is where one has to learn the benefits of listening.

One of the most profound thingz about listening is realizing that in the word "listen" is also the word "silent" (scramble the wordz). Listening silently to your inner thoughts can also be equated to meditation. See, I've known that long before I read the works of Chancellor Williams, Dr. Clarke and Ben, Kwesi and Browder, I knew consciousness. I think we all experience that intuitively. It is the burning desire to know more of thyself that bringz us to these scholastic works. When I reawakened in 1991, I didn't read my first book, '*From the Browder Files*' until a year later. For most of that almost 2 year span, most of my knowledge came intuitively.

As I started to read book after book, I noticed that what these authorz wrote, I had said or thought before. It was these inner thoughts that assured me I was not alone; that there was an Ancestral connection with seen and unseen forces.

After vybin' with the author of the first book I ever really read, Browder, I realized we are all, as he would put it, "conduits". What is a conduit? A natural or artificial channel through which something is conveyed. For yearz, even as far back as when I was a likkle yute, I can remember having spiritual encounterz. See, consciousness is alwayz around and when a person focuses on that channel, growth happenz.

We are not just blood and oxygen, we are the blueprint to all of man'z creationz. Take the car for instance, the heart of the car is the engine. The gasoline that flowz through the valves fuel the engine to move just as the blood flowz through our veinz propelling our parts mobility. Even the computer is designed off the hueman body. Browder related the movie *Matrix* with our ability. Just like they were able to download software into their hard drive, or brain, to learn karate or pilot a plane, so are we able to download the power of our Ancestorz, as well as the power of our Ancestorz enemies.

So you sayin' we gotta slide disks into our ass or somethin'?!
C'mon, yo. Be serious! These downloadz happen through electromagnetic waves. Y'kno, just like how music is transferred to your stereo via the antenna. As I said before, we're just not blood and oxygen, we are also made of electricity. Y do you think they use electric volts to restart a heart with a heart respirator? As conduits, we receive all kindz of wavelength activity imbedding all kindz of thoughts.

Have you ever been in a deep discussion with someone and you wound up sayin' somethin' you thought you didn't know? This happenz because you have the ability to tap into your inner-self where there lies a connection to the lineage of the first mastermindz of the earth. Some may also equate it to hearin' voices. Whatever you call it is irrelevant, what *is* is that we are not alone and YT knowz it! That's Y they use radio and tv as diversionz.

Be it the lies television tellz to our vision or radio, our mindz are constantly bein' stimulated with thoughts and behaviorz, and just like anything else, the one you hear/see of most, you begin to adopt. Think of all the hourz our people spend on emulating black life from music videos and adopt poor dietary habits due to the countless Coca-Cola and McDonald's commercialz. See, we're only losing because negative thoughts are downloaded 24-7. We can see it by just watchin' the behavior of our people. We are truly actin' like niggaz! No, I'm not sayin' we *are* niggaz, I'm sayin' we ACTIN' like niggaz! Y and how are we actin' like this? Because the subliminal influence of livin' in a eurocentric society is chauffeured by the european mindset.

Day in and out we hear and see images propelling europeanz on the top of the ladder with us on the bottom and when they do portray us, we're either shakin' our ass, dancin', makin' someone laugh, playin' a criminal, pimp, drag queen, homosexual, dead-beat dad, unfaithful husband or dumb athlete. We are more than entertainerz. Overstanding this is the challenge. Although there currently is no way for me to stop Wendy's, Pepsi and Hilfiger from poisoning us, we can still combat this by using some of that 20 or so extra hourz a week we have to focus on our inner power.

We have to literally learn how to tap into that intuitive force to create balance. Browder spoke of how this mindset, once activated, can be heightened to the point where otherz will function on that level. He pointed out the importance of consciousness over culture. The consciousness of a people is witnessed through the creation of how they live.

An example is the 1000 monkey syndrome where 1000 monkeyz were divided into groups and spread across an island miles apart from each other. They were left to fend for themselves with yamz imbedded in the sand for them to eat. Most just dug up the yamz and started eating them despite the salty taste. One monkey in particular was seen diggin' up a yam and would go over to the edge of the ocean, washing it off and then eating it. This allowed the sweetness of the yam to come out because the salt was washed off. Soon after, the other monkeyz of that particular group began doin' the same. The startling thing was, before long, the other groups of monkeyz, though separated by many miles – too many to be exact for them to communicate with each other – began doin' the same thing. Without any kind of verbal communication all of the other groups began diggin' up and washin' off the yamz before they ate them. How was this habit spreaded throughout each group without verbal communication? Simple, it was not verbal but mental communication.

Consciousness can be spread throughout despite tyme or space simultaneously. How do you think Afrikan people across the Diaspora have been able to maintain our spiritual connection to our past? Think about it, not even 150 yearz ago we were not allowed to read, in addition to the countless books that were burned and plagiarized, so how were we able to still possess the knowledge of our past? We have the same ability to communicate with each other worldwide, just like those monkeyz did. One way to heighten the connection would be through a more healthy diet.

It is my wish that those on the path concentrate on enhancing the consciousness of our people. This way our consciousness will be move us to create a culture that will emulate our consciousness – just like our Ancestorz did in Kemet. This guiding force is omnipotent in its presence, alwayz whispering solutionz to our challenges. If only we be 'silent' and 'listen'… to our inner thoughts.

MORE FIE-YAH!

"One day we wearin' black medallionz, the next we wearin' iced jesus-pieces; you got hedz who just know what tyme it is and do nothin' and those who those who can't even tell tyme but 'Ready to Die' for anything; we got cats who went from beef, pork and chicken to vegetarian and back; and of course we got those "righteous" bruthaz who say they all about us while on the low, beatin' they Queen and neglectin' they seedz.

Amidst the elements of negative stress, I parlay. Although the illmatic whisperz of wickedness are constant, I persist to exist on a higher level. Like an addict feenin' for a hit, I yearn to politic on relevant issues of Afrikan advancement. But I keep runnin' into pimps and pretenderz. Abandoned, alone, yet still motivated, I find my pineal as my safe haven. Since there ain't many doin' shit, I'll do it myself... Since no one else will interview me, I'll interview myself..."
M'Bwebe Aja Ishangi – *Inner Thoughts* (1997)

One who seeks, continues to find. *Inherent* – meaning somethin' innate, deep-rooted or built-in – *Nuances* – defined as a subtle difference in a meaning or expression – is exactly what started me on this *quest* of *quest*-ionz some 25 semesterz ago. I continue to search for answerz to inquiries many gave up on once we entered instutionz of higher programming (school). These are but some I need to get off my chest...

Ok, I'ma shoot straight from the hip –
By all meanz, go right ahead...

If someone were to read the articles you write in your magazine, one might think you don't have much love for, as you call it... 'YT'. So I'ma flat-out ask you, do you hate white people?
It's easy to think so, but it isn't true. What it is, is I really don't like is anyone who masquerades as somethin' they're not, and mainly will do it only when it benefits them. This doesn't just go for YT, it's for every other culture whose sucked from the Afrikan cultural breast of creation; changin' their vernacular, posture, apparel and even residence just so they can be 'close' to Black people. We can see this now more than ever with all the white folks movin' into predominantly Afrikan neighborhoodz like Bed-Stuy, once called 'Do or Die', now called Stuyvesant Heights. Today, we see more and more snow flakes movin' into parts of Brooklyn they once would never come to even if escorted by po-po! Now they walkin' Fulton & Nostrand like they belong, yo!

Yeah, shit's gettin' crazy in Brooklyn. And I'm sure it's like this around the country.
Of course it is! YT tired of commuting to work from the suburbz, plus, they've alwayz had this attraction to our people. I mean, I know our shit is hypnotic, but I feel other ethnicities go beyond admiration to the point of blatant disrespect especially when I see white girlz tryin' to drop it like its hot *tryin'* get they eagle on and whatnot. It doesn't stop there. I can't tell you how upsettin' it is to hear Hispanics call other Black people and even themselves 'nigga' and it's ok. I mean, what would the conversation be like if we substituted the word with 'spik' do you think they'd overlook it? How many Hispanic hedz you know don't mind you callin' 'em that?! Admittedly though, we are the reason it's tolerated. We allow asian hedz to infiltrate our culture. I mean, Vietnam was almost 50 yearz ago, so bruthaz was over there havin' relationz 'cause they was stuck over there and not here with our Sistaz. But today, everywhere I turn, I see a brutha with an asian chick! I turn on music videos and see madd asian-lookin' females in the video! Do you know how many so-called Rasta's be with Asian chicks?! I mean, wha'gwan? Afrikan women ain't in style no more?!!?

So is it safe to say you don't like any other kindz of people than Black?
Yes and no. Again, it's not because of their skin-tone or cultural background that I don't like them. Look at it this way… If you were a very creative person – so creative that you didn't realize how good you were, not realizin' it's evident by the number of hedz who mock you – and everytyme you came up with somethin' there was someone tryin' to imitate you. Not just here and there, but *everytyme* you originated something. Some tyme goes by and you start to see madd hedz tryin' to be like you, but the catch is that they start claimin' it's theirz! Other cultures have been "borrowing", "stealin'", whatever you wanna call it from Afrikan people for millenniumz, yo! What hedz do today ain't no different then what Persianz, Romanz and Greeks did in Kemet during the Nile Valley age!

Ok –
Please, lemme finish… I don't have a problem with sharing with otherz, I just think everyone else does more than borrow our shit, they blatantly steal it! Now, a lot of that fallz on us for not stakin' claim in the first place. You'd think we learned that by now. I mean, we're the creatorz of the hottest music, but don't own shit; we the most dominant athletes, but don't run shit; we the dopest designerz, engineerz and architects and still can't come together and design the first Afrikan-owned car – or even smaller, a damn color tv!! Y IZ Dat?! When we're allegedly almost 70% of the brainpower at NASA that puts people and satellites in space, can't come together and own a tv or radio station?!!? This is 2005, and it's insane for us to be the spending power of this country yet don't aspire to own nothin'! This goes back to what I said before, we just create and create and create while at the same tyme, lay ownership to none of this shit, so it's easy for a vulture to come and eat what you prepared! Look at how YT was able to steal our shit from Kemet! We didn't write shit down, we committed it to memory. YT devised a way to take ownership of our philosophies by

simply validating the importance of literature, and had the audacity to also come up with the term 'plagiarizm'!

Ok, I wanna make sure we stay on point –
But we are Brutha. We just buildin', there doesn't have to be a linear structure to buildin'. I know I get on tangents. My goal and intent is to show that this is all interwoven into one. All this –ish is relevant.

I feel you. I just have these questionz I wanted to ask you 'cause I've had these conversationz about you and your philosophy with otherz and I have a list of general questionz that seem to be asked by most of 'em.

That's cool…

Now, I hear you, but I still think you got away from my question. And I ask you this because it seemz you're alwayz talkin' about YT in a negative way. If I were white and I read your articles in Da Ghetto Tymz, I would definitely think you ain't feelin' me 'cause I'm white!
Well, you might think that if you're unwilling to hear what my beef is really about. Again, I don't hate white people; if there was a white person who collapsed in front of me, I wouldn't just walk over them – even though I probably would've 10 yearz ago…

Yeah, me too!
Uh… yeah…, right. Seriously though, the base of all my statements is because when you look at the playing field, they have all the advantages. Yes, even the sport's playing field. I mean, yeah, we the strongest and quickest, but who's smarter, the player – who's at risk everytyme they step on the field and once retired, has to find anutha hustle to survive? Or the owner who governz all this shit, not to mention and most importantly, has a safer and longer chance of livin' financially well.

Despite the percentage we are in this country, this shit is all around the globe where, numerically, we have the largest! Yet every corner of this earth has some caucasian runnin' shit! Are they *that* smart? Is it a science? Yes it is, it's called *Global White Supremacy!*

So if you wanna know Y I diss YT so much, it's because they seem to be the only ethnic race that can't seem to see everyone equally and thus share equally. And yes, there are other 'races' that discriminate too, like the Mexican government who issued those fuckin' stamps depicting Afrikan people as monkey's and Aunt Jemima! But I find that they have been poisoned by YTs plague and are simply tryin' to be white, just like the Dalit in India where dark-skinned people are discriminated only because of the tone of their skin.

So, it's not that you diss 'em 'cause they white, it's because –
It's because they are master plagiarist's! My feelingz toward them isn't based on me

just feelin' this way. Historically, they've given validation to not be liked. While they steal everyone else's shit, they create these lawz called copyright, trademark and patent's! I mean, how many logo's – better yet, author of Nile Valley Contributions to Civilization, Anthony Browder showed how basically all the buildingz in Washington, DC were stolen designz from ancient Kemet! It's like what historian Steve Cokely called it, they like to *"double-cross"* you by sayin' one thing and doin' anutha. They say it's unlawful to plagiarize, yet the curriculumz taught in school is stolen information and they will not give credit to its origin which is mainly from ancient Afrikan civilizationz!

Yeah, it's a shame we don't know while in school that Afrikan people created shit like math, chemistry and science. We all know what the history books leave out, the problem is we don't know until after we're out of school and gotta now get jobz to survive.
It's like they make it a struggle for you to even want to learn more 'cause we so caught up in tryin' to make endz meet, who has tyme to exercise their mind?!

True. So, Y do you write the way you do? I mean, I've heard people say your use of 'z's and broken english takes away validity to your message. Do you think it degrades the level of intelligence we strive to maintain?
Yo, I'm glad you asked that. I been hearin' this since the first edition in '93. I used to wonder, damn, is my writing that hard to read or is it what I'm sayin' that's hard to swallow? I know I make it easy for critic's to shoot my message down because of my choice to write freely. Yeah, I've had several teacherz tell me they can't let their students read my shit 'cause of my spelling errorz. I tell them they ain't errorz, they're blatant "misspellingz". No, I'm not tryin' to teach hedz how to read. I assume if you readin' DGT, you already know how to read!

True (laughing)...
So, that leaves me with *what* I'm sayin'. I mean, is it really confusing for me to put a 'z' at the end of a word that soundz exactly like that when you read it?! Any other word I spell different is so easy, all you have to do is sound it out. Isn't that how we were taught to read in the first place? So Y are hedz bitchin' 'bout the way I write. 'Cause it's different, and hedz don't like change. But I know the audience I'm tryin' to reach feel me and they're intelligent enuff to know not to write this way on their homework, report or application.

The beef with your writing style is like hedz who didn't like Rock'n'Roll in the beginning or Hiphop for that matter...
Exactly! It's different, and I think, attractive. I mean, I look at a lot of artists who write this way. Take the musician Music Soulchild. On his last album, Soulstar, he gotta track entitled, *'infatueighties'*. His first two albumz were called *'Juslisen'* and *'Aijuswanaseing'*.

So you don't think it's really about the way you spell thingz, it's somethin' else –
Oh hell yeah! See, I've alwayz wanted to write exactly how I feel despite the repercussionz. I mean, of course I care about how I come 'cross, but I realize as with any artist, if you try to appease everyone bein' what they want you to be, then you're not really an artist, you're impersonating someone else! How can I explore the depths of my creativity if I'm afraid of how I'm received? If Jimi Hendrix didn't make the music he did, would you even know of him? Would we know of Prince and all the other cat's he influenced?? I ain't tryin' to be no legend, I'm just aspiring to be M'Bwebe Aja Ishangi, nothin' more and definitely nothin' less! I think the challenge is *what* I'm saying. As I challenge those who ready my pieces, I challenge myself. The challenge is if you do not agree with what I write, find out what you do agree with. See, we're afraid to address issues that may cause us to see somethin' different. We are comfortable in our ignorance. We continue to *ignore* the fact we can continue to learn beyond the 12th grade, or even Masters degree for that matter. I often wondered what makes one a Master because you paid an extra ten-thousand or so for a couple more yearz after a Bachelorz. Shiiiiiit, I'ma life student, been learnin' more now than I would ever learn in any institution of higher training. And I'll keep aspiring to earn more degreez until I am physically no longer. Oh, and by the way, there's a study that validates my writing style. It's called Ebonics or Black English, and Professor, Ernie A. Smith, PhD out of Charles R. Drew University of Medicine & Science in Los Angeles did an extensive study on it back in the early 1990s.

It's 2005, do you think Afrikanz-in-America are better or worse?
It's so interesting how one can beef about one thing and settle for anutha. I'd like to compare our plight here in American, and basically around the world, to those million-dollar lawsuits we hear about. What we don't know is that many of these suits don't even make it to court because most settle out of court for a much smaller amount. How many tymz have you heard someone suing this person for millionz and wind up settling for a couple hundred thousand? That's us! For example, hedz still talk about how effective the civil rights movement was, when we demanded equality or else and "or else" was backed by public transportation boycotts, marches and even riots. The problem *I* think is, we walked in there in the 60s and didn't have a clue how we wanted to be treated equal, we just wanted equal treatment. Because we didn't have an agenda, we were spoon-fed results, and today we ain't no where's full. In fact, they still servin' us from the same plate, we ain't had secondz, thirdz, nothin'. It's like goin' to an All-You-Can-Eat buffet and all you eat is hors d'oeuvres!

Look at tv today and ask yourself are we treated equal? I ain't talkin' 'bout the poor programming and modern minstrel showz, just look at tv ratio-wise. For every Afrikan you see on tv, how many whites do you see? From commercialz to actual tv showz, take 5 minutes, get a pen and piece of paper, make a column for us and one for YT and count! We're that lawsuit that never happened. We think 'cause we dominated sports and 'News-at-11' highlights, we're equally accepted.

If we continue with this bullshit pace to gain equality, numerous generationz will be morally and spiritually robbed of their natural right to be a human being! I mean, Y do we no longer call for local, regional, national and/or global boycotts of bare essentialz this economy banks on? Y wouldn't we want to have a study that lists the majority of corporationz Afrikanz support and use those numberz to our advantage calling for a boycott of these products and services until our demandz are met?

More importantly, Y wouldn't we then use this tyme of boycotting to launch alternative products and services made by ourselves? After all, a boycott doesn't necessarily mean you have to stop using the product – not if the product is now made by ourselves!! When are we goin' to implement a simple idea Dr. John Henrik Clarke always spoke of?! He said if Afrikan people took care of just themselves, by buying our essentialz from ourselves – who also ownz, creates and distributes, we'd be able to employ the world-over! We wonder if we're treated equal… does hurricane Katrina prove we are?!!?

What is your comment to Kanye's remarks on national tv right after Katrina…
Yo, Sun is my hero! He basically said what a lot of hedz feel but are afraid of the repercussionz. What he said was noble, 'cause he has so much to lose now, I mean, he was just on the cover of Time magazine, right? And he just dropped his second album! He risked all that to speak the truth! How many cat's done that? Of course, there's plenty of Step'n'Fetch It's who blasted him like Usher and Master P…

You been publishing Da Ghetto Tymz for almost 13 yearz. What keeps you going and what can we expect in the future from you?
I think I'll have somethin' to write about as long Afrikan people are in the situation we're in. It's sorta depressing 'cause I wonder what I would write about if global white supremacy didn't exist – not that everything would then be all good… but I sometymz wonder what it will be like when the rhythmic swing of the pendulum of tyme swingz in our favor. See tyme exists in a cycle; what once was, will be again, and again, and again. Meaning, there was a tyme when global white supremacy didn't exist and we were balanced with nature; that tyme will return. The other side of the lesson is that as we rise, we will fall again… It's somewhat puzzling because it makes one wonder Y do we fight for somethin' we're gonna end up losing again?! To date, the only logical reason is that it is what it is. We experience the cycles many wayz daily – we experience morning, afternoon and nite daily and seasonally – spring, summer, fall and winter just to name a few. I don't think our rise and fall from liberation will happen as quickly as the seasonz change, but it is inevitable – whether we like it or not. Tyme is much older and wiser than any wo/man, civilization and era. Tyme is at least one thing we cannot control. Knowin' that gives me assurance that YTs grip on the world is loosenin' as every minute ticks away… our tyme is comin', but it's not gonna be a smooth transition, knowin' YTs 'fight-to-the-death' mentality, many will most likely perish before the dust clearz…

So you're predicting a world war of sorts?

Not predicting, it's already happening! Can you not see how quickly the United States' is decaying? If it's not attacks on U.S. soil, it's attacks from hurricanes. America's bein' attacked from the outside and inside! The U.S. government is quickly loosing the faith of its citizenz. We are closely reliving Vietnam with Bush refusing the withdraw troops from Iraq; the number of enlistments into the armed forces are dismal; the treatment of our people in the Gulf Coast of Louisiana, Mississippi and Alabama gave everyone a clear indication where the government has its priorities; who will America be able to call on when he really needz it? Will we help 'cause we believe or because we don't want to victimz. Not just pinpointing the U.S., corrupt governments have alwayz existed. With advanced technology like the internet and the recent boom of documentaries to the silver-screen, we are able to be informed in wayz that didn't exist 20 yearz ago. I'm talkin' about the internet and computerz that allow everyday people to film their own documentaries – oh, by the way, a couple documentaries to peep is 'The Corporation', 'Life and Debt', and 'The Fourth World War'.

So this comes back to my question from before. I'm assuming since you've been in the field of propaganda for awhile, you have some thingz you got lined up...
Yeah, I do? Guess you readin' my mind... I mean, I love Steve Jobs, owner of Apple Macintosh computers. Because of him and other developerz, I can purchase a mini-DV camera, go out and shoot what I want and bring it into Final Cut Pro and bring it to the people in wayz we thought only Spielberg could do! It is true when they say we are in the information age of Aquarius! As more and more info becomes available for the masses, a global consciousness will be reawakened! It is said the age of Aquarius will be a tyme where the concept of individual nationz will fade and that humankind will join together as one – only if global white supremacy is destroyed. That's where I find my purpose, my 'Personal Legend' as Paulo Coelho, author of *The Alchemist,* would call it. We are in the planz of adding an additional angle to DGT. Our biggest challenge in modern tymz has been gettin' Afrikan people to read. We've been stuck on this bein' the only way to convey a message. There is never only one way to get to something! This winter we will be launching DGTv, a website where one can log on and visually see web broadcasts of our kind of propaganda. See, before we had to rely on YTs multimedia outlets to know wha'gwan. We watched their news stationz where they constantly showed Afrikan men bein' arrested; we read their newspaperz and magazines and listen to their radio stationz. With the advancement of the internet where broadband is becoming more affordable over dial-up, we will be able to broadcast a message without havin' to pay millionz of dollarz to be on one of YTs tv stationz. In the very near future, hedz will be loggin' on websites to watch their favorite program instead of the tv. Knowin' that presents a golden opportunity to address issues to a global community! I'm not gonna speak too much on it...

Yeah, I feel you...
It's too much to go into now, I'd rather just do it. So stay tuned, DGTv will launch this winter!!! [NOTE: DGTv was launched January 2006. Visit the site at

www.daghettotymz.com/dgtv/dgtv.html]

What are some other thingz you're planning?
My goal is to find a way to create somethin' I love doing and be able to live off it! Pure and simple. Y are we gettin' up every mornin' to keep someone else rich?! Y am I not utilizing my talents to better serve me, my family and my community? I know I personally have madd ideas, just like everyone else, but how many actually go about manifesting them?! That's my challenge, so I'm putting shit together now. Next year I'll be releasing my first book, *Analitikul,* I told you about DGTv, I have a design company with a new name, what once was called *DGT D'Zynz* is now *Nebulution Studios* and I'm about to do the second volume to my series, MicCheck: The Series, an event that showcases independent artists, urban fashion designerz and young Afrikan-owned vendorz. I created an interactive CD to compliment each show that includes mini-websites of each artist, samples of their music, the ability for you to purchase their products with an electronic order form and some classic back issues of DGT. I tell hedz all the tyme, the technology has made it possible for us to create what we want ourselves minus the large investments it would usually take. I want to create a strong depiction of Afrikan life via multimedia that serves as a worthy opponent to the platformz YT uses continues to showcase the stereotypical negro. We live in an era where perception come before content; what we see sticks to the mental more than what we read. As they say, a picture paints a thousand wordz, if the wordz are negative connotationz of our people, if there's nothin' set up to counter this view using the same mechanizmz to do it – movies, videos, etc, the viewer will 1) begin to believe it's true and 2) modify their life living exactly as the message portrayed.

Yeah, for too long our culture's been presented from one point of view – YTs view! It seemz you really focused on liberating Afrikan people. Y then, do you feel so many of us are reluctant to what you call, 'alternative thinking'?
I once heard someone say that it's hard to save a people who don't think they're sick. Now, I'm not sayin' my was is *the* way. We're all individualz and interpret thingz our own way. So I think it's wrong to tell a person their way of thinkin' is wrong if they can back up Y they think the way they do. The answer cain't be, *"I've thought this way all my life,"* or *"my momma taught me this..."* I find that the majority of our beliefs are based on ideas that were given/forced on us without question or alternatives. And I can sorta understand this. I mean, children in some cases should be on a need-to-know basis, the trick is once they become old enuff, can they find the mental strength within to make their own decision. True, old habits are hard to break, but if one truly wants to be the best person they can possibly be, they must be willing to thoroughly analyze themselves often. This only makes them better...

You know they say we're our worst critic...
I don't believe that. I think that's a scare tactic used to keep you from knowin' yourself. I mean, think about it... Y would you be your worst critic when you know

yourself best?! The magic behind this is you can see just how many don't know themselves because they heard this and when they reach their 40s they bug-out tryin' to find themselves 'cause they know they done lived half they life and *still* don't have no direction!

I don't think many know this side of you 'cause everyone tellz me you don't like nuthin', you hate YT and you bitch about all the black leaderz.
Hedz perceive me as this cat who just hates everything black, white and in between. They think I don't like Maulena Karenga or Farrakhan just because, but they refuse to read Y I feel the way I feel. I've asked a million tymz, our so-called black leaderz are leading us where? While we shower them with material wealth and pack every building they speak in, can we honestly say our conditionz are gettin' better? We're conditioned to deify these leaderz while never confronting them when they do wrong 'cause quite frankly, most of us blindly support and believe in them regardless. My choice is to challenge them just as I would the next man, for they are just human and can be wrong. I think we need to redefine what a leader is. A leader is nothin' without someone to follow him or her. So, in actuality, the power comes from the people. The leader should carry out the aspirationz of the people, not the other way around. If we developed a platform consisting of needz and a direction, we'd be more involved in the progress of our people. We need a playbook for our liberation. Amos Wilson's, *'Blueprint for Black Power'* is a start. Since we're natural sport enthusiast's, Y not adopt the 'team' philosophy? I mean, I don't know 'bout you but I want a victory! I want liberation! I want food, clothing, shelter and opportunity for every Afrikan the world-over!

I feel you...
And if these leaderz don't deliver results, they need to be fired like an NFL or NBA coach would!

So, we've found that you really don't hate YT, you don't like that they plagiarize our culture; we learned Y you write the way you do; that we're disillusioned thinkin' tymz are better as far as racial equality; and that you publicly endorse Kanye West for President –
Yeah, (laughing) Kanye for President!!

Racizm is alive and well in marketing products to the masses. This past spring, Reebok launched the campaign, *"I Am What I Am"*. But when you look at how Reebok defines Afrikanz opposed to everyone else, you know we still facin' discriminatin' dilemmas.

Several yearz ago we wrote about Reebok's egotistical marketing promo that yelled out the compelling notion that this was *"My Planet"*. Using a younger Shaquille O'Neal and other athletes, Reebok used the dominant play of these athlete's to lay out their claim of 'King of the Hill' in the continuinin' war against the likes of Nike, adidas, Puma and the like.

To the average hed, this is just harmless fun tryin' to get in the mindz of the consumer to pick them over everyone else. But to those who know better, what was done then was possibly a prototype to the ever-growing mind-control advertising that exists in todayz market.

We all know – or rather *should* know by now – that consistency is key to successful marketing. The more you hear a song or see a specific commercial advertising a specific product like Sprite, eventually, a large majority of onlookerz will fall into the trap of wanting what the tv and radiowaves are flashing before them. Think about how blatant Sprite has become when they tell you to *"Obey Your Thirst"* and drink their "soft"drink as if an *acidic* beverage is *soft*.

Reebok's recent ad campaign is no different... in fact, its worse! One who uses their 3rd eye could see the blatant racizm in their adz when you look at the entire series of adz and athletes they used to promote *"I Am What I Am."* If you logon to www.reebok.com you'll see the entire *"I Am What I Am"* series if you refresh the page.

There's one with Allen Iverson. Next to his picture (fig.1) you see what appearz to be some kind of devil or demon... *"I Am What I Am."* So I guess they sayin' AI's evil. Next (fig.2), and even though there may be some truth to it, they got 50 Cent with fingerprints next to him... *"I Am What I Am."* So I'm guessin' they're sayin' he's a criminal.

THIS AD IS AN ACT OF WAR: ASK Y THE ONLY AD WE'VE SEEN IN THE HOOD IS EITHER THE ALLEN IVERSON OR 50 CENT AD?!!? THERE'S CERTAINLY A REASON AND I'M SURE IT ECHOES THAT OF A CERTAIN DISCRIMINATIN' DILEMMA.

Then we have Houston Rockets center, Yao Ming (fig.3) who has an image of a basketball goin' inside the rim... *"I Am What I Am."* So I guess they sayin' he makes shots... or do he??

Next we have Lucy Liu (fig.4) most noted from the movies series 'Charlie's Angels'. They simply have next to her a picture of her as a child smiling appearing to be sliding down a sliding board on a playground. *"I Am What I Am."* So she's basically the cute little Asian girl, you know, so pleasant; so gentle; so pure...

And last I found one of tennis player, Andy Roddick (fig.5). And what do they have next to him? A championship trophy. *"I Am What I Am."* So I guess the white guy'z a champion.

Now let's recap. We got 2 Afrikan men – 1 a devil, the other a criminal; 2 Asianz – 1 a b-ball master??, the other a cute, cuddly likkle girl; and a champion who, you guessed it, is a white guy.

Am I reachin'? You think about it. Decisionz are made when it comes to advertising, and these firmz are certainly tryin' to convey a message. If they can get you under their spell to invest in their products while at the same tyme continue illegitimate stereotypes, don't they even think they'd pass it up. Ask yourselves, Y they couldn't have AI with the same kind of graphic used for Yao? And AI's much more accurate and the ultimate example of a clutch playe! How many games has Yao taken over??

Or better yet, ask Y they decided on these images. Or even better, ask Y the only adz we've seen in the hood is either the AI or 50 ad?!!? The people of our neighborhood are constantly shown images – via the advertisement of products like shoes, clothes, alcohol and movies – that reflect a negative image. Our youth see these images constantly. It's no wonder they grow up to think doin' a (jail) bid gives you juice! There's certainly a reason and I'm sure it echoes that of a certain discriminatin' dilemma.

LIK SHOT!

Ten yearz ago, October of 1995, a million-plus Afrikan men met in DC for what seemed to be the beginnin' of a long awaited change… Bruthaz were finally gonna get it right! I can recall coming off the train onto the monumental stretch of land that led up to the nationz capital. All I could see was bruthaz. *"Dam, yo!"* I said to my comradz, *"This shit feelz great!"*

As we walked toward the sea of Red, Black & Green flagz, we noticed a truck to the right of us. It was one of those trucks that opened at the side and sold food. I noticed 30 or so bruthaz standing at the side of the truck waiting for the merchants to slide open the side panel. I thought, it's early, hedz is hungry, they just waitin' for them to open. But as we got closer, I overheard some cats sayin' *"Not today… they ain't gettin' our money today!"* and *"Y they gotta always show up at OUR functionz?! They just tryin' to get our money!"*

No sooner that I heard last Sunz remark, the side door was lifted and who did I see? Some Asian cat tryin' to sell fried chicken and egg foo yung, B! In unison, we all yelled out, *"Hellllll naw! You ain't gettin' no money today!!"* Hedz was madd rowdy! We started hittin' the side of the truck, tryin' to top it over. The Asianz quickly shut the side panel hopped into the front and sped off. I was surprise 'po-po' didn't give 'em a ticket, nor us for that matter!

As the tires screeched when they turned the corner, we began givin' each other poundz and soul grips (a handshake whose meaning has long been forgotten and co-opted by non-Afrikanz), proof that although we didn't know each other, we were focused and came here for a purpose… to be lead by Farrakhan to independence!

Fast forward a decade later… we are more off track now than ever before! Not to put blame solely on Farrakhan ('cause you know I have in the past), but when I heard late summer of 2004 hedz were wonderin' if there was gonna be a 10th Anniversary Million Man March, I thought to myself, *"Y?!"* I mean, hasn't the 'million-somethin' march idea been played out?! On top of that, after Farrakhan's last Million Family March of 2000 with the Rev. Sun Myung Moon, I thought, this million man shit had gone way past commercial!

Just a couple yearz prior we had the Million Woman's Mall – I mean, March – where the women were distracted by the amount of vendorz who were there instead of focusin' on activist's like *Jada Pinkett-Smith?!!?* I mean, they couldn't get someone real like Francess Cress-Welsing, Meri Ra Kwesi, Marimba Ani or Eraka Rouzarhondu?

So when I was asked the question would I support the 10th Anniversary this October, at first I thought, HELL NO! I mean, what has it gotten us? I *still* don't think Farrakhan's come clean of the whereabouts of all that loot they collected in '95. Trust, I was there when he asked for us to raise $1 over our hedz so that the usherz could pass madd collection boxes around, because Farrakhan claimed the collection was to *"pay for the costs it took to have the march."* It was well over one million Afrikan men there and hedz weren't holdin' $1 billz over their head, they were holdin' $10s, 20s, I even saw a couple Benjaminz floatin' bein' held to the sky!!

After the march was over, on my ride home, I thought to myself, what did I get out of this march? What plan or orderz did Farrakhan actually leave us with? When I thought about it, his speech was nothin' we hadn't heard before – excluding the heavy Masonic overtone and codes with illusionary promissory notes. I started to think, *"Man, we got jacked!"* I blurted to mi bredren. *"And they got paid! They had to have collected over a million! Now what they gonna do with it? Add more solid gold ceilingz in Farrakhan's mansion* (from last I heard when he was asked about that, he allegedly replied that this was still Elijah Muhammadz house and not his – *but Elijah been dead since '75, yo!)?!"*

On top of that, I copped a tape of a lecture that happened the night before the march where several Afrikan-centered scholarz, authorz and speakerz like Dr. Yosef ben-Jochanan, and Dr. John Henrik Clarke met and spoke about Farrakhan's deliberate refusal to use the march as a mechanizm to address issues on a global scale. The taped conference revealed Farrakhan's snub to anti-slavery movements that would address the continued enslavement of Afrikanz by the Sudanese government. Hearin' this tape on the drive back, I was vexed and felt betrayed by a person I then vowed to print whatever info I could find on him in my magazine.

Fast forward to April 2005, I'm informed by a comrade of mine that Farrakhan's speakin' at this town meeting in the House of the Lord church in downtown Brooklyn off Fulton Ave. Havin' no interest in hearin' him, I realized it had almost been a decade to the day since I last took interest in what he had to say. I decided to go to the town meeting not because of him, but because two comradz of mine were scheduled to speak before, M1 of Dead Prez and Lumumba Bandele of the Malcolm X Grassroots Movement.

I walked into the church already disturbed by the Nation of Islamz security guardz (the Fruit of Islam or FOI) cocky demeanor. I think to myself, how can they act all authoritative-like to their own people as if we were criminalz?? I don't see them bein' that way to the real enemy! After bein' frisked, like, *too* many tymz, I decided to just breathe and go find a seat. I was in the balcony and recognized several hedz in the audience. I didn't want to show my skepticizm so I made a point not to say anything *negative* 'cause for one, there was security everywhere and I didn't want to cause a ruckus.

The only thing I dreaded until Farrakhan spoke was the hour or so they use to literally *beg* for money. I've alwayz had trouble with millionaires askin' everyday people for money. I mean, just how they different from the many Reverend Cash's and Deacon Dollar Billz??

By the tyme Farrakhan was to speak I had pretty much had enuff and was thinkin' 'bout bein' out, but somethin' in me kept tellin' me to wait and at least hear what he has to say, after all, it's been 10 yearz since I last lent an ear to his wordz…

For about an hour-and-a-half, he spoke about the usual thingz: bruthaz need to get off drugz, respect their women, don't be physically nor verbally abusive; for women to uplift themselves and not settle, y'kno, the usual bodda-boom, bodda-bip. But I was only interested in what he was gonna say about the Million Man March anniversary, I've had enuff cheerleadin' lectures about how *"we need to uplift ourselves 'cause our tyme is comin'."*

But then somethin' happened. You gotta admit, Farrakhan's got charm and a lil' bit of humility. I did a double-take when I heard him say he made a mistake with the first march and wasn't gonna drop the ball again. Just hearin' him say that was like him sayin' the first march didn't reach the potential it should have – a feeling I've felt ever since I left DC 10 yearz ago.

After all the other million-"somethin'-marches, Farrakhan seemed tired of taking a militant, pro-Black stance as he spoke of his planz for October. As the crowd got hyped, I clutched myself, tryin' not to get caught up in his wordz. But the energy was too strong. So I momentarily shelved my opinionz and allowed Farrkhan to paint a picture of what could be. The picture he envisioned echoed the likes of many Pan-Afrikan leaderz like Dr. John Henrik Clarke and Dr. Yosef ben-Jochannan – who was there in attendance. More importantly, I agreed.

After he spoke, it dawned on me that although he's *still* probably the only person at this moment who could call or such a march, he wasn't the only way it could get done. Just when that thought was completed, it was complemented when Farrkhan announced his position as but a tool for this to happen and it not bein' his march. Again, he's an eloquent speaker, so I felt the sincerity, although my skepticizm was summoned.

As I stood there clapping at the end of his speech I thought about a piece I wrote yearz ago entitled, *"Back When Revolutionareez Were Real"*. I wasn't sure about Farrakhan; I didn't feel I could totally trust *him*, but his trust is not what's really important at this point, what happenz from now 'til October 15th *is.* Havin' heard Farrakhan's response to what could've and should've happened in and since '95 felt as though it was a plea for redemption. It seemed he now knew how powerful an impact it'd be if this platform is used to address these issues globally.

I STILL DON"T THINK FARRAKHANZ COME CLEAN OF THE WHEREABOUTS OF ALL THAT LOOT THEY COLLECTED IN "95. TRUST, I WAS THERE WHEN HE ASKED FOR US TO RAISE $1 OVER OUR HEDZ SO THAT THE USHERZ COULD PASS MADD DONATION COLLECTORZ BOXES TO HELP, AS FARRAKHAN STATED, *"PAY FOR THE COSTS IT TOOK TO HAVE THE MARCH."* IT WAS WELL OVER ONE MILLION AFRIKAN MEN THERE AND HEDZ WEREN"T HOLDIN" $1 BILLZ OVER THEIR HEAD, THEY WERE HOLDIN" $10S, 20S, I EVEN SAW A COUPLE BENJAMINZ FLOATIN" BEIN" HELD TO THE SKY!

Every person deserves a chance to redeem themselves, so to be fair, I felt Farrakhan deserved that same chance. However, just as forgivin' as we should be, should we also be unwavering if he deceives again? See, this compliments the updated piece I wrote on Revolutionareez bein' real (Read *"Back When Revolutionareez Were Real – update"*).

It is tyme we put our leaderz on blast!! They should be treated like coaches in the NFL and NBA (personally, I think the current leaderz should be given a lifetyme ban for all their yearz in leadership and bringing no significant victories whatsoever!). To summarize the article, basically contracts should be given for an amount of tyme long enuff for them to complete their mission.

We, the people, should be the one's who create the agenda and pass on to our "leaderz". Bein' that most of "our" current leaderz have been self-annointed, appointed or strategically positioned by groups from other ethnicities and interests [ie, Jesse Jackson and his affiliation with the Boule' – which is the breeding pool the One World Government or New World Order (the Rothschilds/Rhodes secret society) created and pullz candidates from].

So all of our current leaderz, Farrakhan, Jesse, Al, Kwame Mfume, etc, are given notice. I call for a committee of elderz *and* serious young Afrikanz to create an agenda of our needz, submit them to these "leaderz" with a 6 month – 1 year deadline of implementation. If we see no results or significant progress, they will be fired, not demoted, FIRED! During this same tyme, this committee will be examining applicationz for replacements.

It's been long over due, these "leaderz" have been leadin' us nowhere! We haven't had any victories in a madd long tyme! The current leaderz have been in position of this power well over 30 yearz and we ain't had a winnin' season yet!! It is tyme we hold them accountable. Instead of them bein' the usual reactionary leader; comin' in to speak and march *after* a catastrophe against Afrikanz, let's put them at the forefront and be the *active* activist's they're s'posed to be!

We can start with Minister Farrakhan. For one, this Millionz More March should finally be the pod that will link all Afrikan people's struggles, *globally!*

Since the march is so close, it's probably too late to dictate the agenda, so we should concentrate on the aftermath: (1) Links must be made with other Afrikan countries in the fieldz of knowledge/information transfer; technology – get all countries web-access so that global e-commerce can be established; and trade and tariffs – distribution of all goodz and services nationally and internationally. (2) Industrial enterprise joint ventures in the realm of electronics, automobiles, farming, travel – so we can become transcontinental citizenz of here and abroad, etc. Basically, as the late Dr. Clarke once said, *"We could employ our people the world over if we just took care of ourselves."* (3) Establish national and international educational schoolz and universities that has an aggressive student-exchange program allowin' our people to reacquaint ourselves with the many cultures we hail from; and (4) probably most important, in order to protect what we collectively create, we need an army to protect it all. We don't want anutha Black Wallstreet happenin'!!

These are merely a few suggestionz we could start workin' on. A lot of these tasks can be accomplished using the internet as a medium. I challenge you the reader to take if not these suggestionz, come up with suggestionz of your own. Organize a crew of serious hedz, get the appropriate number of signatures and call town meetingz across the country and world demanding these "leaderz" review our agenda.

I know you might feel this is bigger than you, which may make you feel there's no way it can be done *through* you. Many who feel this continue to do what we've been doin'… *waiting!!* No, this ain't some overnight-type shit. It's gonna take work, consistency, dedication and most importantly, your involvement! If we cease to do somethin', how can we actually believe we can have a say on what happenz to us next?! More importantly, the work we choose not to do will be even heavier for the next generation to take on. We can use the battles the generation I belong to (Generation X) as an example of what happened after the Black Power and Civil Right Movement's were co-opted and faded out!

I intend to collab with cats on an agenda and submit to these leaderz and wait to see if they incorporate these ideas at length.

In addition to Farrakhan – who again, seemz to be the only Blackman who can call for such an occasion effectively – there are some questionz that should be answered after the Millionz More March. For one, he should voluntarily be forthcoming about the moneyz that will be tallied from the donationz from the march. An account of what those moneyz will be used for and lastly, he must give a full explanation of his position of Sudan and the continued enslavement of Afrikanz by the Khartoum government as well as (personally) his stance on Kola Boof. If he does these thingz, I would have no problem at all truly callin' him a leader of Afrikan people!

It is tyme we decide our leaderz are no more powerful than the people who anoint them. It is truly the 'final call'; the summonz has our name on it, our future dependz on it! Get involved, make this shit happen!!

LIK SHOT

"Whoever controls the image and information of the past will determine what and how future generations will think; and, whoever controls the information and images of the present, will also determine how these same people will view the past."

— George Orwell, author of the book 1984

"At the time we came into this ship, she was full of black people, who were confined in a dark and low place in irons...many of us died everyday. When our prison could hold no more, the ship sailed."

— Slave story about Middle Passage

The so-called jew talks of the holocaust they went through during World War II at the handz of adolf hitler. They estimated a couple million of their kind were viciously murdered by oppressive, experimental meanz. Not long ago, they constructed a museum so the world will never forget what was done to them.

Where's *our* museum so the world never forgets *our* holocaust?! The descendants of Afrika at home and abroad have been experiencing an ongoing holocaust for thousandz of yearz, including the invasion of the Persianz in KMT, up until this very second as you read this piece.

Afrikanz have been victimz of malicious, callous murderz ever since the caucasoid realized we were the children of the founderz of mathematics, arts and sciences, chemistry, astronomy and so on. One startling stat is a 25 year period during the Atlantic Slave Trade cost over 100 million deaths of Afrikan people, averaging about 4 million deaths a year who never made it to land after leaving the 'Door of No Return', in Senegal, West Afrika. 4 million per year for 25 yearz, B! Think about that! Our entire race coulda been completely wiped out! It woulda only took about 3-4 yearz to exterminate Afrikanz that reside in the united states! Some were suicides but the majority came from illness or murder.

There was the belief that a sail ship leaving Afrika should sail on the sabbath day (Sunday) for there was a popular saying that *"God will bless the journey."* It obviously was not our God they were speakin' of.

There was a practice they had, when a slave ship began loading Afrikanz. Oftentymz the first two on board would be male and female who would be recorded in the log as *'Adam and Eve'* and the rest were numbered 3, 4, 5 and so on. They were packed into the slaveship as if they were sardines.

Because of the enslavement, we do not know what to call ourselves. According to a survey done in 1990 by the Joint Center for Political Studies, 72% of Afrikanz-in-america preferred to be called black; 15%, African-american; and 2% negro. Historian Tony Browder feelz, *"The name that a people call themselves must provide them with an understanding of their history by religion, a philosophy and so on. If a people's name fails to accomplish these tasks, then their name is useless."*

There is a reason virtually every other ethnic race chooses to use a name that has a geographical existence on the globe. Italianz are from Italy, the French are from France, Polish from Poland, Europeanz from Europe, etc. But what about Afrikanz?!!? Where on the map do I see a land called *"Blackland"*; even the land called *"African-american"*?? It simply does not exist! Malcolm X once said, *"if a cat had kittens in an oven, you wouldn't call them biscuits.* So Y would one call an Afrikan, who had been kidnapped and transported across the Atlantic Ocean, *"Black"* or *"African-American"?!*

THE STORY BEHIND THE ATLANTIC SLAVE TRADE

The first european settlerz came to the America's in search of freedom and a better life. With them, however, they brought kidnapped Afrikanz. There were many overseerz who believed in the motto, *"We came here to serve God and the king, and also to get rich!"*

The Slave Trade began in 1502 and ended in 1808. It was rooted in YTs craving for goodz seen for the first tyme during their crusades (from 1095-1200s) over Arabz, Indianz and Chinese. There they competed for goodz but couldn't overtake Muslimz inland routes, so they were left with using unventured all-water routes from Afrika to Asia.

An internal slave trade existed in the United Snakes ran by overseerz who still needed workerz for the then booming cotton business. In 1820 an internal slave trade was created in the Upper South states, Maryland, Virginia, Kentucky, North Carolina and Tennessee. By 1830, these states were selling 80,000 Afrikanz a year over what was called the Cotton Belt.

Slave traderz packed Afrikanz aboard ships in voyages similar to those of the Middle Passage, unloading them in cities like Charleston, South Carolina and New Orleans, Louisiana and marched them to plantationz. It's funny how everyone get's on christianz for their involvement in using the bible as a tool during the enslavement process, but few are aware that christianz were not the first the enslave our Ancestorz. In fact, the first to do this has shown a resurrection in the Afrikan community over the last 60+ yearz! Yeah, dat's right, I'm talkin' about islam!! Muslemz were stealing Afrikanz several decades before YT got involved.

YT wanted in on the profit making scheme of selling Afrikanz just like you would sell spices and furz; so they aggressively began to compete. However, YT was unable to take from the Muslimz the land routes to Asia and as a result, YT began looking for all-water routes. One route was around the tip of Afrika, an area where no European ship had ever sailed more than a few hundred miles along the coast. Sailorz feared the Atlantic Ocean, calling it a "green sea of darkness."

Led by Prince Henry the Navigator, the Portuguese began voyages into the coast with hired, sellout Afrikan navigatorz and guides and encountered their first Afrikanz they wanted to kidnap in 1444, where they literally stole 200 Afrikan Moors and took them back to Portugal to be sold at a public auction. Within 10 yearz, Portugal was stealin' over 1000 Afrikanz a year.

Most Afrikanz came from an area bordering a 3000 mile stretch on the West Coast coming from over 1000 villages and townz, including tribes like the Hausas, Mandingos, Yorubas, Ibos, Efiks, Krus, Fantins, Ashantis, Dahomeans, Binis and Sengalese.

When you look at someone from Portugal, you can see the Africoid features, which may lead you to believe they are black. Well actually they are because they had stole so many Afrikanz, the whites were soon outnumbered.

The Portuguese saw possibilities for trade in Afrika and as they pirated along the west coast, they renamed parts of the continent after the leading product from each region. The area with an abundance of pepperz and spices were called the Grain coast; the Ivory coast had madd elephants whose tusks were/are sold for profit; the Gold coast and Slave coast which are self explanatory.

Because the slave trade was becoming very lucrative, Afrikanz were seduced by YTs greed and got involved. This has become an argument mainly with white historianz and scholarz who claim their foreparents weren't the only who enslaved Afrikanz. It must be made clear that there was a very small percentage of Afrikanz who were involved, but there were many, like King Almammy and Captain Tomba who forbade their people to take part in it.

As well, some of these same scholarz claim we did the same in Kemet. This is not so. True, there was some type of system but not like what our Ancestorz experienced here in the US. The difference is that our Ancestorz did not practice what's called 'Chattel slavery'. 'Chattel' is greek for cattle, which is moveable property. We were labeled as moveable property and could be exported to anyone the overseer chose; kinda like how the NBA and NFL works today. With free agency, you could be playin' with the New York Knicks one year and the LA Clippers the next week! In Kemet, the form of "slavery" was synonymous to todayz labor force. You work for x-amount of hourz and receive compensation. What you do on your off-tyme is yourz. Chattel slavery was the complete opposite; you weren't paid, and your off-tyme (if there *was* off-tyme) was not yourz. While a partnership was forming with white kidnapperz and few Afrikan sellouts, this enabled missionaries to set up camp and convert Afrikanz to christianity.

With the discovery of the new world, there was a large demand for labor. The number of europeanz who came as workerz could not meet the growing demand so the Spanish enslaved the 2nd Native Americanz (because Afrikanz were in the new world thousandz of yearz before the so-called Indian) to work in the mines of Peru and Mexico and sugar plantationz of the Caribbean islandz. There became a problem when YT realized the natives could not endure the hard labor needed as they started dying by the thousandz.

This turned YTs attention towardz our Ancestorz. It was said that 1 Afrikan was worth 4 natives and the same money that would buy an Irish or English servant for 7 yearz would buy an Afrikan for life. The enslavement of Afrikanz emerged from the Caribbean which then spread to the new world. It is said that the slave trade yielded such high profits that Afrikanz became known as "Black Gold"

THE DEMONZ BEHIND THIS MESS...

One, John Hawkins, lived among our Ancestorz for 30 yearz, all the while gaining our trust before he began his tricknology. When he wanted to show off his fine ships, our Ancestorz trusted him. When they invited us aboard their ship, we thought they were safe, but we were so naïve. Our Ancestorz were held captive and brought across a grueling 3-6 month travel across the Atlantic Ocean. This was called the 'Maangamiza' or 'Middle Passage'.

On the ships, our Ancestorz were made to lie very closely together just like how cattle are packed tightly in trucks today. What's deep is the the Pope and the catholic church gave blessingz for the Portuguese to enslave our Ancestorz. Pope Eugenia IV, in 1442, granted the request. In 1452, Pope Nicholas V gave King Alphonso of Spain general powerz to enslave 'paganz', a term that meant any Afrikanz who hadn't been converted to the white version of christianity.

In 1588, the English navy smashed the Spanish Armada, ending their control of the Atlantic. In the next century, England planted 13 colonies up and down the Atlantic seaboard of North America. By controlling the eastern border, the english received all royalties of international trading.

After being stolen from villages, traderz marched our over Ancestorz 500 miles to the coast over mountainz, through forests and across riverz...BAREFOOT and naked and sold to their enemies! Soundz just like what was done to YT some 5500 yearz earlier — Read *"IZ YT Hueman? or Mutant!"* Series. Those who rebelled were killed. Those who fell ill were left to die.

CONDISHUNZ OF OUR HOLOCAUST

The men who fastened irons on the mothers, took the children out of their hands and threw them over the side of the ship into the water. Two of the women leaped overboard after the children...One of the two women was carried down by the weight of her irons before she could be rescued; but the other was taken up by some men in a boat and brought on board. This woman later threw herself overboard one night when we were at sea."

— From the Book, Before the Mayflower.

Other injustices during the voyage were frequent brutal whippingz; forced feeding, where many instances occurred where Afrikanz, who protested by not eating, had their jawz and teeth broken from the overseer forcing food down their throats; because our Ancestorz had to lay in their waste, blood and the oftentymz dead brutha or sistaz lyin' next to them, the stench of death and funk could be smelled miles before even seeing the slaveship. Sea sharks and vultures followed these ships in hopes of a meal for hundredz of miles.

The actual layout of the ship would make even the ruffest neck cry in fear and agony. Each stolen Afrikan were paired off with shackles at the arm, legz, ankles and sometymz neck. They were packed on the bottom of the ship like you would see a pack of sardines: one over each anutha. Because of these unsanitary conditionz, this was the breeding ground for madd diseases such as smallpox, yellow fever and hookworm. This caused them to lose sometymz half the human cargo they started out with. But YT knew this and in fact, planned it!

They purposely overstuffed their ships with 50% more than what they actually needed for obedient and pleasure purposes. They could rape, castrate and murder thousandz of Afrikanz as long as they reached their destination with the right amount of captives.

The holdz of most slave ships measured only 5ft high. But the spaces was cut in half by a shelf that extended about 6ft. The Afrikanz were chained by the neck and legz to the shelf or to the deck below and had only about 20-25 inches to sit up. On storm-tossed seas, they banged into one another, and the chainz cut deeply into their flesh. Amid the suffering, many Afrikanz went mad. Some killed each other fighting and clawing for breathing space. They had deduced us to act like a pack of hungry wolves.

YTs NEED TO VALIDATE THEIR ACTIONZ

YT needed to create 2 steps to divide themselves with our Ancestorz to justify slavery. Using religion, they first created an ideology of racizm that would justify subordination of Afrikan people. They dreamed up the notion that Afrikanz are a little better than lionz, tigerz and other wild beasts, which Afrika produces in great numberz. So because Afrikan had so many Afrikanz, it was ok to enslave *some*. This was their rationale!! This is the excuse they used to rape thousandz of women and killing men!! As if to say, *"because there was so many of us, it's ok to take a few (million!)"*

They tried solidifyin' this wicked mindset by rewriting the "Holy" Bible so that many would cherish; as well as incorporating a Slave version of the Bible for our future children to follow.

The number of Afrikanz were rising, so was the fear of some type of revolution. By 1710 there were over 50,000 Afrikanz; by 1776, 500,000; and by the Civil War, over 4 million.

Over a course of 64 yearz, they were finally able to break the first group of Afrikanz they kidnapped. There were numerous tactics used to break us down and we were broken down in a similar fashion as to how YT breaks down a horse. The process wasn't easy though, madd resistance was rampant. We did not conform to their wayz easily. One theory is that an overseer by the name of Willie Lynch, in the late 1770s devised a way to enslave us and guaranteed it to last at least 300 yearz. Enslaved Afrikanz outnumbered their overseer 50-1. This proved how potent the Willie Lynch program was (and still is, Afrikanz and Latino's outnumber all races, yet we're at the bottom end of the stick).

In 1863, during the Civil War, good ol' Abe Lincoln declares nergroes *"like other people."* Exhilarating, huh. To know that Abe was a person who liked us negroes so much, he wanted the world to know that he saw us as equalz...NOT! There's a catch. He wasn't talkin' about all Afrikanz. He was explicitly referring to those enslaved Afrikanz-turned-soldierz for the Union, and of course, it was temporary!

Pure and simple, Abe was a racist like the rest of 'em, not a liberator. The Civil War had nothing to do with slavery. In fact, slavery wasn't even recognized as a situation until the war! The 13th Amendment doesn't even mention slavery. It dealz with the right to vote and in section 2 you'll find the 3/5ths clause, an idea from the southern overseerz.

Abe was seen as cunning, a liar and a cheat. It was not until after his death they made him a saint — just like they do all of 'em! Before 1863, Lincoln never spoke of freeing Afrikanz, because he knew 90% of the soldierz would rebel. In fact, he followed Thomas Jefferson's attempt to send Afrikanz back to Liberia, Afrika and replace them with European servants but they realized it would be too costly.

It was Abe who later blamed Afrikanz for the Civil War. Right before the Emancipation Proclamation, he met with several free Afrikanz and told them that they may think they are free but they are not. He wanted them to go back to Afrika (where he hoped they would die) because he knew if they stayed they would be a threat to the country. And today, in school, we are taught that Abe was a man who loved us so that he wanted to free us from bondage.

The truth is out there, it's hidden in those thingz YT think Afrikan people are afraid to use...BOOKS! No other race of people have endured such pain and strife as Afrikan people! The key is that only we can cease the pain and begin healing the woundz, but this can only happen through self-study, cultural awareness and a factual chronological analysis of the historical relationship of Afrikan people with the rest of the world. Can U handle it? Let's hope so.

LIK SHOT!

The Rothschilds wasn't their original name, for they went by several before choosin' this one. One of their earlier names was the Bauers — one of the most notorious cult bloodlines of Middle Ages Germany.

The name Rothschilds became in the 18th century (note the close resemblance to "Red-Shield") when a working member of the Illuminati, one Mayer Amschel Rothschild, took the name from the red-shield or hexagram; y'kno, the Star of David or Seal of Solomon.

The masses ignorance to history enables pirates to literally rewrite their story. Most are not aware the Star of David did not become affiliated with the so-called Jew until after Rothschild adopted it for themselves. So-called Jewish resources will tell you the star has a connection to David or Solomon, but the very ones who started them using the symbol made it clear who their allegiance was with...EVIL!

According to author of *'Ancient Future'*, Wayne Chandler, *"Many people have seen the symbol that represents the axiom; it is now referred to as the Star of David or Solomon's Seal, the hexagram of Judaism. Its origin and meaning are far more auspicious than that of an emblem used to categorize a particular creed or group of human beings. What is ironic is that this symbol has been regarded as officially Jewish only for about a century. The hexagram reached Judaism via the eastern Tantric influences on medieval Jewish cabalists, who chose to elaborate on the union of God and his female counterpart, Shekina. Historically, at the time the biblical stories were being spun about David and Solomon, this star had nothing to do with the Jewish people, but had been previously employed in cultures such as India and Egypt for more than 2,000 years."*

In India, its earliest appearance was discovered in the Indus Valley civilization (3000BCE, and soon after was regarded as a jain philosophical symbol. It would later be utilized by the Buddhists and Tantrikas of India to symbolize divine sexual energy and union of the male and female elements in creation. The linguistic originz of the word 'sex' is rooted in mathematics, as in the biblical reference to *'six days of creation.'*

Sex in Sanskrit means six. Currently, in India the six-pointed start is called the Star of Vishnu. The Rothschilds had long had a plan to create a religion of their own for the Illuminati in Palestine and that plan involved manipulating so-called Jewz to settle in that area.

One, Charles Taze Russell, of the Illuminati-reptilian Russell bloodline (the Russell's were one of the creatorz of the Illuminati) was the man who founded the Watchtower Society, also known as the Jehovah's Witnesses. He was a Satanist, a pedophile according to his wife and most certainly Illuminati. His new religion was funded by the Rothschilds as he was a friend of theirz, just like the Mormonz who were also Rothschild-funded through Kuhn, Loeb, and Co.

This is where shit get's hectic! Now, movin' on up to World War II, we find that Adolf Hitler and the Nazis were not only funded by, but CREATED by the Rothschilds!

The Rothschilds arranged for Hitler to come to power through the Illuminati secret societeez in Germany like the Thule Society and the Vril Society. They later funded Hitler through the Bank of England and other British and American sources like one of their many financial houses, Kuhn and Loeb bank.

We also find America's own Ford Motor Company as the ones who built the tanks the Germanz rode, with Rockefeller's, Mobil Oil providing the fuel for the tanks. In essence, we find the Rothschilds clan as the hidden force behind Hitler; a so-called "Jewish" bloodline which claimz to support and protect the "Jewish" faith through organizationz like the B'nai B'rith and Anti-Defamation League (ADL), financed a monster out to kill so-called Jewz. Assinine, right?!

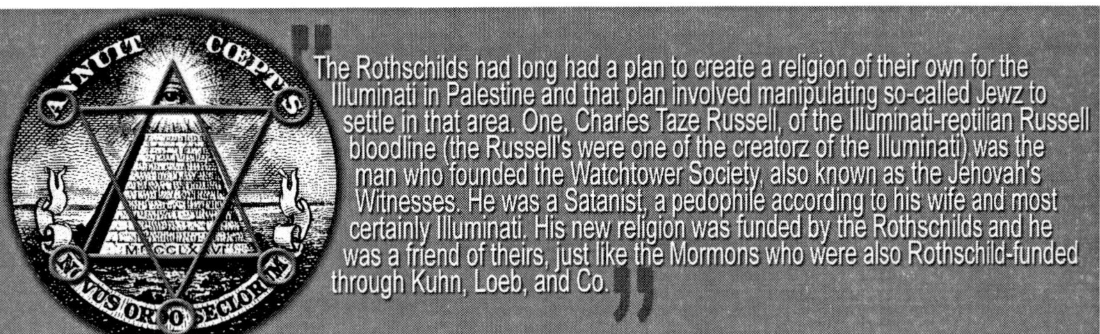

Oh, but it gets deeper... Writer, David Icke said, *"...the Illuminati are so utterly obsessed with bloodline, because of this reptilian genetic code, that there was no way that someone like Hitler would come to power in those vital circumstances for the Illuminati, unless he was of the reptilian bloodline. This is the bloodline that has produced ALL 42 of the Presidents of the United States since and including GeorgeWashington in 1789. It is the bloodline of...George W. Bush. The World War2 leaders, Roosevelt, Churchill and Stalin, were of the bloodline and also Freemasons and Satanists."*

The Rothschilds and the Illuminati produce many offspring out of wedlock in their secret breeding programz and these children are brought up under other names with other parents. Peep, like ex-president, Bill Clinton, who is most certainly a Rockefeller, produced in the same way, these "ordinary kids from ordinary backgrounds" go on to be extraordinarily successful in their chosen field.

2004

DAILY NATURAL LAWZ

The following are lawz one can recite and add to their daily lives. I've found them to be profound and a vital element to my stayin' FOCUSed (**F**rom **O**neself **C**omes **U**ltimate **S**acrifice).

You are a Physical Extension of that which is Non-physical.
"All-That-Is", or "God", (I call it 'Energy') is not finished and waiting for you to catch up. You are the leading edge of thought, here seeking more: more of all that feels good to you, more of that which is fresh and gloriously uplifting. (You are, in essence, bringing heaven to earth.)

You are here in this body because you chose to be here.
You wanted the opportunity to experience this delicious contrast in tyme and space, and with great anticipation you came to co-create with other joy-seeking beingz, to fine-tune the process of deliberate thought. (What, where, when and with whom are your choices, too.)

The basis of your life is Freedom; the purpose of your life is Joy.
You are free to choose to discover new avenues for joy. In your joy you will grow, and in your joyous growth you will add to the growth experience of 'Energy'. (However, you are also free to choose bondage or pain.)

You are a creator; you create with your every thought.
You often create by default, for you are getting what you are giving your attention, to wanted or unwanted but you know by how it feelz if what you are getting (creating) is what you are wanting or if it is not what you are wanting. (Where is your attention focused?)

Anything that you can imagine is yourz to be or do or have.
As you ask yourself Y you want it, the essence of your desire is activated, and the Universe beginz to bring it to you. The more intense your positive feelings, the faster it is coming to you. (It is as easy to create a castle as a button.)

You are choosing your creationz as you are choosing your thoughts.
Your loving, Inner Being offers guidance in the form of emotion. Entertain a wanted or unwanted thought and you feel a wanted or unwanted emotion. Choose to change the thought and you've changed the emotion and the creation. (Make more choices in every day.)

The Universe adores you; for it knowz your broadest intentionz.

You have come to earth with great intentionz, and the Universe constantly guides you on your chosen path. When you are feeling good, you are, in that moment, allowing more of that which you have intended from your broader perspective. (You are Spirit Incarnate.)

Relax into your natural Well-being. All is well. (Really it is!)
The essence of all that you appreciate is constantly flowing into your reality. As you find more thingz to appreciate, your state of appreciation opens more avenues to more to feel appreciation for. (As you think you vibrate. As you vibrate you attract.)

You are a creator of thoughtwayz on your unique path of joy.
No one can limit where you can direct your thought. There are no limits to your joyous journeyz to experience. On the path to your happiness you will discover all that you want to be or do or have. (Allowing others their experiences allows you yourz.)

Actionz to be taken and money to be exchanged are by-products of your focus on joy.
On your deliberately joyous journey your actionz will be inspired, your resources will be abundant and you will know by the way you feel that you are fulfilling your reason for life. (Most have this one backwardz, therefore most feel little joy in their actionz or their possessionz.)

You may appropriately depart your body without illness or pain.
You need not attract illness or pain as an excuse to leave. Your natural state coming, remaining or leaving is that of health and of Well-being. (You are free to choose otherwise.)

You can not die; you are Everlasting Life.
In grace, you may choose to relax and allow your gentle transition back into your Non-physical state of pure, positive Energy. Your natural state is that of Foreverness. (Have fun with all of this. Lighten up! You can't get it wrong.)

P.S. It is not necessary for even one other person to understand the Lawz of the Universe or the processes that's offered in order for you to have a wonderful, happy, productive Life Experience for you are the attractor of your experience. Just you!

— *author unknown*

A REVIVED VYBRATION

BY M BWEBE FKA JEHVON BUCKNER

I want you to travel with me... as you read these wordz, become these wordz and visualize. Visualize yourself rising; rising from the chair you're sittin' in; visualize yourself elevating into the air, visualize yourself flowing freely about the air like incense midst... Now, elevate to the frequency of Correspondence. Visualize yourself standin' on the edge of a new world lookin' at the next. You there? Good! Now, let's have a conversation!

It is at this level I'd like for you to see thingz from the macrocozm (the bigger), 'cause when you vybratin' on the microcozm (the ground level), it's difficult to see outside the illusionary parameterz of global white supremacy. See, the station (frequency) we should be tuned into has been blacked out by YT for a long tyme. Their ability to increase this hold has increased each year since the creation of the radio and tell-a lie-vision. At this higher level, we can look down on his earthbound hold and see beyond. This is about realizing our purpose.

What is your purpose for being, Afrikan? It isn't to make 6-figures, drive an Escalade and attain all the material wealth you can before you die, that's YTs focus, it shouldn't be ourz. We are in the Age of Aquarius, the information age; the age where there's a revived vybration tellin' us of our purpose for being. It was said to me once by Anthony Browder, *"when the student is ready, the master teacher will manifest."* This teacher comes in various formz, most notably, yet most ignored, is in the form of a current, frequency or vybration. Take for instance, music.

Did you know that sound has the ability to communicate in other wayz in addition to what you hear? If you saw the 1997 movie *'Contact,'* with Jodie Foster, or *'Mission to Mars,'* (2000) with Don Cheadle, you know sound can be translated into numberz, and what are numberz? The universal language able to be translated by all formz of life/energy. Everything is assigned a number. So as you sit and bounce your hed to a track that moves you, realize, if you tune-in, the music itself can be transmitted information despite the lyrics. This is Y I still have a luv for Hiphop, 'cause although madd hedz ain't sayin' shit other than pimpin', trickin', bakin', sellin' and cappin', *some* of these beats still be bangin'! (shouts to Pete Rock, 9th Wonder, and J-Dilla)

I can't even write without some music on. Y? Because music allowz me to travel into my inner-self and pull out subliminal faxes from our collective memory. It is from this rhythm we can draw a message from.

I'm a firm believer it is at this frequency, The Djhuitic principles of Rhythm and Vibration are speakin' to us. Like a repetitive signal with no ending, this signal is constantly reachin' out to those willing to hear. For a complete inner-standing of what I'm speakin' on, read Wayne Chandler's, *'Ancient Future,'*.

This message/signal never waverz, it repeats the same rhythmic pattern, and we've heard it several tymz in our life tyme — some call it your conscience — yet so many tymz the message was blurred or cluttered due to the blocked, counter-signalz sent out by YT not to "know thyself!"

NATURE: THE MASTER TEACHER

Think about it Afrikanz, whenz the last tyme you looked at nature and appreciated how everything works in natural order? Take for instance, a house plant. I have a plant in my home that sits' next to my window. This plant does not go through the temperature changes the outside vegetation experiences, so this plant knowz no winter (the tyme cycle of death or sleep). This plant only knowz the constant feeling of a consistent 70 - 75° (degreez).

This plant was given to me one late summer and it had white budded leaves with a sprout inside in addition to the green ones. I assumed the plant was healthy and as soon as fall set in, I noticed the white leaves and sprouts started to turn brown and eventually, one after the other died, yet the green leaves remained green. Now I have basically little to no knowledge of plants, I don't even know the name of this plant, but I can recognize when a plant seemz to be dyin' — or so I thought.

Soon, the white budz completely fell off, I didn't know what I did wrong, maybe I watered it too much, maybe too little, was it gettin' enuff sunlight? I basically accepted it for as long as the green leaves are there, I guess she's ok.

Winter went by and on comes spring. I was surprised when I saw the white sprouts return!! Now, feel me... this plant is indoorz, livin' in a climate that's like a warm July day, *everyday!* So it couldn't have been the cold of winter that caused the leaves to wilt because it never felt the cold! Maybe it wasn't the 'cold' of winter, but winter itself.

See, we forget that the planet Earth rotates in a divine pattern around the Sun. In addition, the Earth is tilted, so on one extreme, when it's in a particular position, we get winter, and when it's in an opposite extreme, due to the tilt, we experience summer.

Ask yourself, melanated Afrikanz, how is it that every spring the grass growz and turnz green, the budz sprout from the branches and even the smell is different?! If you live in a region where you experience winter, even in March when it's still too cold for spring, you can see the budding beginning! What thing is responsible for that? Or is it 'a' thing? Could it be an ensemble of 'thingz' workin' coehesively, yet appearz to be independently? If we are microcozmz of the macrocozm, then everything is connected and there's no one 'thing' working independent of the rest.

This is divine law. Nature followz a cycle in-discretely, and it took this phenomena for me to realize, everything in its natural state followz a divine rhythm or pattern governed by a certain vybration or frequency.

I once worked for NASA, and asked a scientist what it sounded like in space and he replied, *"there's no sound 'cause there's no oxygen to carry it."* Even then I didn't believe him, but I was not yet ready, nor exposed to the innerstanding of what I termed the 'God Complex'.

Yearz later, after writing the piece, *'The God Complex: Microcozm of the Macrocozm,'* I realized there *is* sound in space because all the elements on Earth ARE in space, because Earth is a micro-replica of the macrocozm — space; just as our human bodies are a small blueprint of the Earth. It is with the blessingz to know, one can think outside the box that one can define their reality the way our Ancestorz did; not the way the linear-thinking european has. It is through YTs thinking that we doubt what is taught innately because YT told us if it ain't written in a book — and written by them then it's nonsense.

This plant, like all plants, knowz it's purpose and functionz as such, adhering to the repetitive cycle of life. It never dies because it is intuned to the signal and the signal never dies. It gets clouded by the lower frequencies governed by YTs man-made frequencies, but it never dies. We could take several lessonz from nature and this should probably be the first. What is your purpose? What frequency are you vybrating on? Who do you listen to, 'massa'-media or your inner-voice??

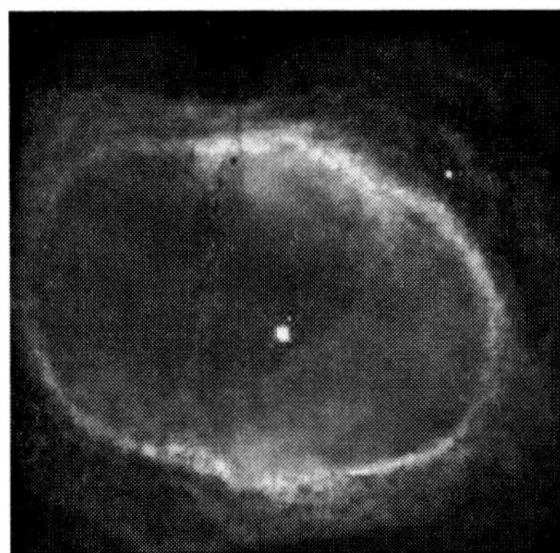

This plant, like all plants, knowz it's purpose and functionz as such, adhering to the repetitive cycle of life. It never dies because it is intuned to the signal and the signal never dies. It gets clouded by the lower frequencies governed by YTs man-made frequencies, but it never dies. We could take several lessonz from nature and this should probably be the first. What is your purpose? What frequency are you vybrating on? Who do you listen to, 'massa'-media or your inner-voice??

BALANCE

Now, don't get me wrong, I'm not sayin' we have to stay "afloat" on this level indefinitely. What makes us different from a plant is that we have will. A will that can choose to disconnect themselves from this frequency. Because we are flesh and spirit, we must co-exist in both realmz, BALANCED!

We currently do not live in balance between the 2, largely in part because of YTs blocked signal, sending confusion amongst the Diaspora. As I wrote in *'The Terrorist Factory'* series, YT winz by using the strategy, *'Ordo Ab Chao,'* or *'Order out of Chaos.'*

You tell me YT ain't settin' us up to go buck wild with the constant rise of the cost of living while at the same tyme navigating the decline of the ability to earn a living. They're fighting madd hard to instill fear after fear, broadcasting war updates, rising unemployment and rising gas prices, causin' us to become reactive to our situation instead of pro-active.

Think about it, we are fueling their victory by reacting to every Y2K, anthrax, and biochemical threat they can think of, not to protect us, but for us to stay tuned into their propaganda worryin' about DYING instead of Nature's propaganda which is about LIVING!

Look at Nature... you see the vegetation not growin' because the threat of Nuclear war or the Greenhouse Effects lurks among the tabloidz?!

No, I'm not sayin' completely tune YT out, afterall, you gotta keep your enemy close, but I am sayin' we need balance. So quit jumpin' up and buyin' plastic and duck tape 'cause tell-a lie-vision told you to! While they got us worried about terrorist attacks (and we should know who the real terrorist's are), they have us dying without them even touchin' us. The brain is strong enuff to manifest a sickness even though there initially wasn't one.

Hedz might say, *"M'Bwebe's writing is on some next, crazy shit! We used to him writin' about 'conspiracy this, conspiracy that."* It's called balance dictated by a flow, and the flow has been guiding me to write about shit like this now...

Trust me, I luv learning and writing about conspiraceez, but there's also the other side of me (balance), the side that's been on a continued 'quest' of 'questionz' for almost 15 yearz now. It is this side that asks me to clear my thoughts, don't think... listen... listen to the signal, can you hear it?

THE ART OF LISTENING

The one key aspect of learning balance is the art of listening. Flowing often requires one to have the ability to just flow. Thingz abide by the lawz of Nature indiscretely, they don't ask questionz, when they do that, the signal becomes unclear. I'm even guilty of this, too often I try to analyze thingz instead of just flowing. When I do act on my gut instincts, instead of re-acting off one of my thoughts, thingz fall into divine order.

"I know the 100th issue and the event is a couple of dayz, and I still got a ton of shit to do to make it jump off," I say to myself, But when I relax and say, *"what will be, will be; don't dictate, just flow,"* it works out (and it did too! The issue and event was a success!). This is not to say it alwayz works out in the way you'd like it; if it is meant to be, it will be. If it was meant to be a 100th issue of DGT, it will be; if the event we threw, *'A Nite of Expression'* was successful, it was meant to be. All we can do is be 1000% focused on the task at hand. That is how you manifest your purpose...

It isn't an easy task, tunin' out YTs broadcast. I mean, we're surrounded by his propaganda: magazines, radio, music videos, and the sudden wave of "reality tv". Overstand we need to practice what Dead Prez said, *"Turn off the Radio!"* and tune into balance. For if we continue to function at this imbalanced vybratory rate, our youth that ensues us will experience a far greater hell than we can attest!

In addition, when one dwellz on this level of reality, it stallz spiritual growth takin' you away from your original purpose of bein' here. And if one becomes a permanent resident on this level, they are simply preppin' themselves for a return visit to this world.

I believe we all are hedz who didn't get the lesson in our past lives and are thus repeating this level. See, while we're playin' YTs game of survival, we're ignoring the vybratory frequency our Ancestorz used to create physical manifestationz like electricity, astrology, music and all other sciences that emerged from our collective conscience (con-science, 'with' intuitive knowledge). The question is, what is your purpose for bein' here? Mine? You ask, to graduate to the next level; to stand on the edge of a new world and look at the next.

LIK SHOT!

by m'bwebe aja ishangi fka jehvon buckner

the UGLY truth about the

They made Jesse repent for his infamous 'Hymie-town' remarks during his election run in the 1980s; spied on american Black Muslimz to South African spies (revealed in 1990), the NAACP, Rainbow Coalition, United Farm Workers, among otherz totalling up to 950 political organizationz; have bribed countless police and sheriff departments country-wide, illegally obtaining classified government data on at least 20,000 American citizenz; sold info on antiapartheid groups to agents of the South African government; enjoying tax-exempt status from the IRS; their known — well unknown — memberz who are also in the KKK as well as their historic collusion with arab terrorists; and now they want you to believe that as they put in their latest ad campaign running throughout the streets of New York City, "Anti-Semitism is anti-everybody."

Pick a copy of '*The Ugly Truth About the ADL*', by EIR (Executive Intelligence Review), you'd find this is but anutha fraud by the Anti-Defamation League, ADL for short — who really serves, as the book stated, *"nothing more than a protection racket for the drug cartel."*

You will find that the ADLz foundation is *"more closely aligned with the Ku Klux Klan than with Judaism; more closely aligned with the murderous Medelin Cocaine Cartel than with any civic group,"* as stated in the book.

Its partner in crime, the International Order of B'nai B'rith have a lengthy marriage that dates back to 1865, playing pivotal roles in the British Freemasonic plot to destroy the Union of the United Snakes before and during the Civil War.

Since 1948, the ADL has devoted over 1/3rd of it's legal efforts to support activity that may rightfully be called *'the plot to kill God.'* The ADL as filed dozenz of briefs in legal cases often settled by the US Supreme Court, whose results have included banning school prayer, banning released tyme for religious instruction and banning celebration of the celebration of religious 'holy'-dayz, causing federal, state and local governments to be neutral on religious issues, but turn around and contradict themselves when they have you swear on a stack of bibles!

Havin' been on the hush for some tyme, they've re-emerged with an ad campaign claiming *"Anti-Semitism is Anti-Me."* They have the *audacity* to use an Afrikan woman (supermodel, Naomi Campbell) in the premiere launch seen across New York City! Since when has a jew gave 2 shits about Afrikan people *especially* with their often down-played role in the massive enslavement of Afrikanz during the

Maangamizi and the Atlantic Slave Trade!

Yet here they are, throwin' a curve-ball, tryin' to conceive the notion that *they* are victimz of an atrocity with their *'never forget'* campaign; a holocaust immeasurable to that of which our people continue to suffer to this day!

The question that should come to mind is exactly who is the *'me'* that they're talkin' about?! Afterall, this is an organization that went against Dr. Abdul Alim Muhammad and New York City physician Dr. Barbara Justice, who treated more than 600 patients who were HIV positive with a drug they brought back from Kenya, Immuviron.

As seen in the streets of New York City

The list of pirates associated with the ADL is proof enuff of their wickedness: Edgar Bronfmann [read *'Vivendi Universal: Industrial Vampires'* on my site*daghettotymz.com*], George Bush, the Rockefellerz, the House of Rothschilds, Kuhn, Loeb and Company; Metro Goldwyn Mayer (MGM); are but a few.

These pirates should be charged with perfidy (treachery or deceit) for it seemz what they sayin' is if you ain't down with them and all their wickedness, then you da enemy! But because the masses are ignorant and they *know* this, they can put out a subtle ad out like this, implying that everyone who's semitic is good when in fact it's the opposite!

Bein' anti-semitic really can be defined as one who believes in a system that predates the 3 major western religions: christianity, islam and *judaism.*

And if that's not good enuff, find out the numerous definitionz of the word. What does anti-semite mean? If you look 'anti' up, in addition to meanin' *'opposed to'*, it also meanz *'unlike the conventional form'*. Now *who* was the original Jew? Were they not descendants of Afrika??

Remove the lies and uncover the truth!

MORE FIE-YAH!

Since working on my latest lecture series, *'Afrikan Spirituality: the Microcozm of the Macrocozm',* the research has challenged me to address several topics we were taught as youths. One in particular is the age-old theory of Evolution.

YTs claim is that man came into bein' from the family of apes/monkeyz. When we use YTs dictionary of wordz, they say 'evolution' meanz, *"(1)The theoretical process by which all species develop from earlier forms of life; (2)the gradual development of something into a more complex or better form."*

'All species develop from earlier formz of life'. Now lets build on that. If something evolves or develops from something before it, that could also be seen as something that replaced its predecessor. Now, if we evolved from apes and/or monkeyz, common sense would lead you to believe — based on *their* definition of Evolution – apes and monkeyz would no longer be here.

So, suffice it to say, this theory should be thrown out the window! It makes sense to me Y YTs schoolz would want us to believe this because this theory bindz you to the physical earth, totally disregarding what exists outside our atmosphere. It is this type of thinking that has cut us off spiritually and metaphysically makin' it virtually impossible to "think outside the box."

Here at DGT we profess the will to be open to "alternative thinking." This type of thinking, I believe, has the potential to open gatewayz to a realm that I'd like to introduce as a replacement of 'Evolution', I call it 'Nebulution' (for reference, read *'The God Complex'*

See we're really microcozmz of the macrocozm. What is the macrocozm? I'd like to refer it to the ever-expanding universe. Afterall, if you look beyond the gravitational pull that keeps you grounded on Earth, the planet itself seemz to "float". But there's actually some kind of gravitational pull that keep the earth afloat and inside the solar system which "floats" inside the Milky Way galaxy which "floats" in our Star Cluster and so on…

Planet Earth circles the Sun — which is a star among an infinite number of other growing starz. By studying the Hermetic (should be called Djhuitic) principle, Correspondence, you will find that if we live *in* the universe, we are *of* the universe, and if we are *of* the universe, there must be universes *in* us, because we are the microcozm (smaller part) of the macrocozm (the whole).

The definition of the principle is *"As above, so below, as below, so above."* It's the study of nature of the first rung on the ladder to greater understanding and eventual overstanding self knowledge is the basis of all true knowledge. Mastery of the passionz allowz higher thought and action. To free the spirit, control the senses, the reward will be clear insight. We are what we eat, physical food becomes a physical body. What we take in mentally becomes our mental body.

If we could zoom into ourselves, it would look just like the universe! If you were to look at the skin on your hand, we weren't really taught that there are billionz, probably trillionz of moving activity goin' on that our naked eye cannot see. It's been estimated some 6 trillionz thingz goes on at any moment in our body. If you were to get a high-powered telescope and focus on your hand, the deeper you get, you'd eventually see that we are but molecules, electronz and chemical compoundz!

These same molecules, electronz and chemical compoundz also exist in space (again, because we are the microcozm of the macrocozm). Think about how planets are created. To date, astronomerz and scientists have been able to hypothesize the creation of life wasn't actually how the Bible stated. To believe the "story" of Genesis literally, totally goes against how the rest of the universe continues to exist. Journey with me...

We look at the sky at night and don't realize we are witnessing the birth, change (not death) and rebirth of starz before our eyes. Ever wondered what gives birth to starz? Nebula's. Nebula's are a cluster of gases and dust that appear as a cloudy patch of light. Nebula's are probably creationz greatest because they come in all sorts of colorz, shapes and sizes.

I'd like to refer to Nebula's as parents who give birth to starz as their offspring. These starz wander out of the womb of a Nebula and begin their journey into infinite space expanding in size and energy over tyme. No one really knowz how long the life of a star is, it is estimated our Sun is 93million-earth-yearz-old and should burn another 93million.

The older a star becomes, the bigger it gets and beginz to take on a white color — which, by the way, in the ancient Nile Valley of Afrika, the color was seen as the color of death, or the ending hence, the 'white' snow of winter givin' off the presumption that the earth is dead (or quiet) when it's really sleeping. Anutha analogy is the 'whiteness' of flour, sugar and other deadly products that bring nutrition to an 'end' when consumed.

In relation to a 'dying' or changing star, the beginning/birth is symbolized by the blackness of its carbon-based core and the death or change of the star comes as the star turnz white. This same concept microcozmically can be applied to a piece of dog shit seen in the park — alright, if you got irresponsible neighborz like me, you've seen in front of your house.

When first vacated from the host (dog), the feces have a dark brown to even green appearance (depending on how much vegetation you include in the dogz diet). As it sits there on the soil, an exchange beginz to happen. The earth starts to pull the nutrients from the manure and engulfs it into itself. What it does not need, it leaves. It's like suckin' the marrow out of a bone (I know you know someone in your family who sucks on chicken bones!!).

The earth sucks what it needz and what's left is the white nutrition-less piece of shit. Over tyme, the feces beginz to dry up and eventually becomes one with the elements of the air as the breeze of oxygen and other elements flow throughout.

Macrocozmically, some starz explode at their change (death) while otherz implode creating what's known as Black holes, which is believed to be a portal to other parts of the universe. For those starz that explode, the outer core that shoots out are pieces of the star now independent of the star. Of these, there are some that get caught up in the gravitational pull of the now new nucleus formed from the "old" star. This new nucleus creates an energetic gravitational pull forcing the "new" pieces of debri to circle around this new nucleus.

The temperature in space is said to be -273°C, which meanz, it is so cold, if you were to step out of a space vessel into space in a turtleneck and a bubblegoose, even wrapped in an electric blanket, you would freeze solid immediately like glass! And because everything is moving so fast in space (giving off the appearance that nothing is moving, because everything is moving relatively at the same speed), a particle of debri as small as a grain of sand could shoot right through you and shatter your frozen corpse to pieces!

However, if you take the heat of this new nucleus/star/sun, the heat plus the cold of space can create steam and eventual water! Now what is the molecular structure of water? H_2O!! Hydrogen and OXYGEN. Now, YT will have you believe there is no oxygen on any other planet, nor in space for that matter, other than planet Earth. This arrogant and ignorant belief is a vital part to the people of this planet's belief that we are the only life in space. In the movie, *Mission to Mars,* Don Cheadle was able to prove that oxygen existed on Mars. I believe this to be true not only on Mars but throughout space! Y? Because if you believe in the microcozm of the macrocozm, what's on the smaller scale is the same (only different in degree) to what is on the larger scale.

The water blendz with the space debri [which is most likely frozen (with ice which is also H_2O)] circling the new sun and, coupled with heat and water, softenz some of the rock into soil where in other parts of this new debri (which is actually a new planet forming), the ice glacierz melt into oceanz, seas, lake and swamps. Using common sense, you can now see how vegetation, fungus, bacteria and other living organizmz manifest, on up to human life as we know it.

Many of us can't clearly see this due to this societies programming system called school and the church (religion). This is a place where they separate science from spirituality; a place where many of us are held captive behind the transparent prison barz of trained thought.

Coupled with YTs ongoing slaughter of truth with all the blockbuster alien movies they dreamed up in Hell-Y-wood, it's quite a challenge to get someone to believe there may be life elsewhere and that this intelligence isn't necessarily little green or gray men with big eyes, long fingerz and wants to kidnap and perform tests on you.

Reespek!

One of the messages we at DGT have alwayz conveyed is when dealing with Global White Supremacy (the Illuminati, Rhodes/ Rothschilds, Phi Beta Kappa and Skull&Bones to name a few), there is no such thing as a coincidence! We have also echoed Gary Allen, author of *'The Rockefeller Files'*, belief that the Illuminati alwayz play both sides of the fence. Meaning, while they may have the masses believe two people or parties are against each other, in secret, they are in fact, comradz; thus makin' it impossible to lose.

For example, while they may have you thinkin' McDonald's is better than Burger King; Mobil One gas is better than BP; or even Byron Allen is "blacker" than Wayne Brady, the fact is, more tymz than none (at least for the first 2 examples), corporationz are not in competition of each other.

On the upper echelonz of power, above the CEOs and COOs – I'm talkin' 'bout the Board and the Financial investorz who are the backbone of these companies – there is an allegiance between these parties to "share" the wealth. As long as they can maintain control of the diverse choices conveyed to the masses as competition (KFC, Popeye's Chicken, WalMart, Target, etc.), they win. This is about winnin' regardless of who's "on top."

Case-in-point, last presidential election, many felt Al Gore was stripped of his chance to be president. His competition being George W. Bush, Jr. (Skull&Bones class of 1968), in most eyes won because of his father George, Sr. Whether true or not is not the point, the point is regardless, if it were Bush or Gore, BOTH were memberz of the same elite 2nd chapter of the Illuminati, Skull&Bones located at Yale University.

Flash forward 4 yearz later, anutha so-called election is upon us and the masses have been duped again to believe they have a say in who the next elect will be. As big a sham the last one was, the drama was not authentic. The Trilateral Commission have been choosing this country's president at least since the dayz of Woodrow Wilson. Make no mistake about it, the Trilat's have not shunned from countless reports that have proven their selection of the president yearz before the next election.

So 2004s election should not come as a surprise when we find that Bush's so-called foe is also Skull&Bones. That's right, Senator John Kerry is Skull&Bones class of 1966!

"The only agenda of Skull and Bones is to get its members into positions of power and then to have those members hire others to positions of prominence. The

You may have heard about it by now, P. Diddy done thought of anutha campaign slogan in his constant conquest to biggup his already 'superstar' status. Not that I can't tip my hat off to the brutha for his energetic creativity, but if I didn't dissect his concept of *"Vote or Die!"* I wouldn't be bein' the analitikul cat that I am. As a person strivin' for consciousness and innerstanding, I must look at this concept.

First off, I overstand in order to get someone to pay attention, you gotta use some sort of shock treatment. The government uses it with the yearly threat, *"you betta pay your taxes or you'll go to jail"*; Religion uses the *"you better get saved or you goin' to hell"* method – and now we got P. Diddy tellin' us we betta *"Vote or Die!"*

I'm sure he doesn't mean it to that extent literally. As much as he idolizes the mafia, he's not able to carry orderz if it was physical retaliation. His meanin' would probably be that too many of our Ancestorz died for the right to vote (as if we non-voterz never heard that). However, this message still merits an investigation.

Now that it seemz Hiphop will not only influence but may possibly anoint the next President of the United States in 2008, Hiphop can soon find itself at the Supreme Court level as well as those "unseen" political/governmental agencies. This was tried before but with a not-so genre-specific movement, remember "Rock the Vote"? It is true no one or nothing can shake

organisation has an enormous superiority complex that partly fuels their secrecy," argues Alexandra Robbins, author of *'Secrets of the Tomb: Skull and Bones, the Ivy League, and the Hidden Paths of Power'.*

As Ron Rosenbaum, a classmate of Bush's, wrote in a famous Esquire article in 1977 the idea behind Skull and Bones was once that of *"converting the idle progeny of the ruling class into morally serious leaders of the establishment"*. An article in Bush's 1968 yearbook recounted, *"the initiate faces the delegation and the alumni alone and is physically beaten. Next he is stripped and made to engage in some form of naked wrestling."* Later in the year the fledgling Bonesman would be *"quite brutally evaluated by the others"*. You figure out what they meanby *"brutally evaluated"*.

It is said S&B have a strict code of silence, to the point that if someone bringz up a topic regarding S&B, memberz are to literally walk away from that person – even if it's live on CNN! The other choice is to deny membership in such a way that his denial both confirmed his membership and brought the discussion to an end, but I'm sure the latter, though not seen publicly as of yet (maybe someone brave enuff will during the presidential debates later this year), for S&Bs interest, is the better choice.

In recent interviewz, NBCs Tim Russert asked both men about their membership in the society. *"Is there a secret handshake? Is there a secret code?"* he asked Kerry. *"I wish there were something secret I could manifest there,"* replied the Democratic candidate. Bush for his part, quipped, *"It's so secret we can't talk about it."*

Yale's Bonesmen swear they'll carry the secrets of Bush, Kerry and their other brothers to the grave. In a March 23rd, 2004 article written by Ellen Gamerman of the *'Sun National Staff'*, she mentioned inside the tomb, as the society's meeting place is called, the two men bared their souls. Decades later, only select detailz about their experiences rise from the crypt – and most sound closely to their official campaign script.

"John used to say, 'I'd like to be president of the United States some day,'" says William "Chip" Stanberry, who rememberz a young Kerry proudly voicing his lofty ambitionz.

But inside that windowless stone building on High Street in New Haven, Conn., more than 35 yearz ago, a handful of students saw what many voterz now crave – the unguarded side of the men who would one day fight for the presidency.

The misconception about S&B is that many think it is a secret society memberz join in ther last year and upon graduation, that's it. On the contrary, as Ron Rosenbaum, author and columnist for *The New York Observer* who has written extensively about the secret society as well as a classmate of Bush's at Yale who has long been curious, stated *"You often see news reports that say Bush and Kerry were in Skull and Bones, but in fact they still are in Skull and Bones."* If Kerry winz, three of the last four presidents will have hailed from Skull & Bones.

There are some tapped memberz who later regretted their membership. In the late 1960s, anti–Vietnam War activist the Rev. William Sloane Coffin Jr. took aim at the club and its male bonding ritualz, regretting that he'd ever belonged in the late 1940s. *"It's an awful indictment that you have to disappear into a tomb to have a meaningful relationship,"* he told The New York Times in 1967, when he was quoted in a front-page article about the selection of the next crop of Bonesmen, a group that included Bush.

Other men dissed S&B, finding it flamboyant in its secrecy and its embrace of the establishment. Kingman Brewster Jr., Yale's president when Bush was a student, was a hero on some parts of the campus for turning down Bones when he was tapped nearly three decades before. Former Baltimore Mayor Kurt L. Schmoke said the society seemed uncool as anti-establishment feeling swept the Yale campus in the 1960s and 1970s; he rejected Bones on Tap Night BUT later on accepted the black version, the Boule' aka Sigma Pi Phi (read more on the Boule').

For Bush and Kerry, the Bones relationships are still strong. Memberz of Bush's group gathered for his wedding and celebrated most of his political triumphs together. Eleven of Bush's 14 brotherz have visited Camp David during his presidency, according to the White House, which lists them simply as friendz or donorz. *'The New Yorker'* reported that one of his first social functionz at the White House was a gathering with the Bonesmen of 1968.

Similarly, Kerry still hangz tight to the crypt. A decade ago, he orchestrated one of the biggest reunionz his Bones class had ever had. The Massachusetts Democrat gathered almost all 15 together to mark the 25th anniversary of the death of their fellow Bonesman, Richard Pershing, Kerry's close friend who was killed in action in Vietnam. Kerry credited Bones for the strength of their friendship.

Kerry told his friends about a picture taken yearz before in the Senate president's chamberz with then-Vice President George H.W. Bush, the late Rhode Island Republican Sen. John H. Chafee

the magnetic touch of Hiphop, the question is, who in Hiphop will be steering this movement? Thus far, I must say, I am dissatisfied with the Pilot (Russell) and co-Pilot (Diddy).

Y? Because neither of these cats stand for nothing. They have not revealed what party they're loyal to, they just want cat's to register and vote, but for *who* I ask?! Stic.man from Dead Prez said it best in a recent inner-view in XXL 'zine, *"the thing is, people like Russell Simmons, they running around trying to get people to vote and say that's how you participate in making a difference. But they ain't educating people on how the system works. And to me, that's criminal."*

Registering and placing a vote is not a form of activizm as they may have you believe. True, our Ancestorz *did* die for the right to vote, but with this right is "choice." See, their valiant effort has enabled our people to walk up to the pollz and cast a vote if we choose. Some may think there is an obligation to vote because of what they did, but do you really think they'd still be out there takin' rocks to the head, singin' *"we shall overcome,"* if they knew our vote didn't count? Wha'chu mean "wha'chu talkin' about?!" Lest we forget what happened almost 4 yearz to the day?!!?

See, I really don't see how Diddy, rapper 50 Cents, Usher (who's seen wearin' his *'Vote or Die!'* shirt with the raised Black Power salute fist – like he knowz the first thing about the movement!), Russell; any of them are helpin' you or I. What they are doin' is placing false hope in young hedz who know the vote ain't shit, now they see them talkin' about they should vote, and you know how influential young mindz are.

What these cats are doin' is placin' the youth on a conveyor belt of deceit as these politicianz devour our hopes and dreamz, thanks to their pawnz, black celebrities.

If Diddy and the like wanted to really be effective and they chose to do it through the vote, I would hold these politicianz accountable! Ask them about serious shit like, *"what the hell is goin' on with this Biochip technology?!"* Jobs and education are important but this biochip shit is ill! I mean, if you gonna get all these youths registered to vote, you'd want them to vote for someone. Go to that "someone" and demand (on tape, contract, whatever to make it binding so that the moment they deviate from this agreement, they are impeached and must step down) they address issues that pertain to our needz.

If Diddy and crew do not step up with these stances, then we must become "Active Activists" and remove Diddy and Russell from their position and anoint a new Pilot and co-Pilot! That's the only way we can have an influence through the vote. If we choose to remain as is, this voting thing will eventually fail and I can't say I would not be happy, 'cause pretty soon, hedz will see the hypocracy of the vote, maybe sooner than we think, like this November 2nd – a repeat of 2000? Very likely.

and then-Sen. David L. Boren, an Oklahoma Democrat. According to a fellow Bonesman, Kerry had the photograph snapped because all four power brokerz were in Bones.

"John has been one of the major conveners" of his Skull & Bones group, sayz Dr. Alan Cross, a Bonesman with Kerry and now a professor of social medicine and pediatrics in the school of medicine at the University of North Carolina at Chapel Hill. Cross sayz his friend enjoyz their shared past, planning reunionz with a mellow, rich atmosphere: *"A bunch of us [Bonesmen] had dinner at his house in Boston four years ago at his birthday party. We had a great time – nice wine, good food, good companionship, pretty house."*

Four yearz ago, classmates say, Kerry confided to his Bones brothers that should Bush become president, he would challenge him in 2004. A victory in the presidential election would be the fulfillment of a goal that Kerry had been telling his friendz about since college. Classmates say Kerry was tapped for Skull and Bones largely because of his prominence as head of Yale's political union and his near-perfect record as a member of Yale's debate team, whose discussion topics included not just politics but also lighter subjects – like Y *"a woman is just a woman but a good cigar is a great smoke."*

Many are not aware that the current president initially had no aspirationz of following in the footsteps of his father and grandfather much less bein' president of the united snakes. He was not picked because of intellect, he was simply what some would call a legacy tap. Though he didn't meet some of the usual member characteristics – otherz in his group were standout students and athletes. It was his own father, then a congressman, who reportedly came to Bush's dorm room one night and asked him to join the Bush tradition at Yale's oldest secret society.

"George was very aware of being a Bush – it didn't stop him from being an individual, but the thought of damning the family name I'm sure would have been abhorrent to him," Dr. Kenneth Cohen, an Atlanta dentist and a fellow Bonesman with Bush, recalled during Bush's first presidential campaign. *"He joined because he was asked."*

But friendz recall him soon warming to the club, spending more tyme in the tomb than the mandatory twice-a-week meetingz required. Inside the *"Firefly Room,"* where men drank from skull-shaped cups at dimly lighted official gatheringz, Bush offered his pals a glimpse of his softer side and surprised those who saw only his bravado on campus.

One classmate called that inner sanctum a *"microcosm of a better world,"* where the men saw themselves changing the future. Bonesmen don't recall Bush, then president of the hard-partying fraternity Delta Kappa Epsilon, showing much interest in politics or being highly outspoken on the subject of the war. In 1968, Bush joined the Texas Air National Guard and was not sent to Vietnam.

Kerry, the son of a diplomat who was never so much a part of the campus "in" crowd as a world-weary observer of it, spent his tyme in the tomb focusing on politics, his classmates say. He discussed foreign affairz – even inviting William Bundy, a senior State Department official and an architect of the war in Southeast Asia, to address the group about the escalating conflict in Vietnam.

Classmates also remember Kerry taking refuge behind the society's triple-locked doors when, a few weeks before delivering his Class Day speech at graduation, he ripped up the standard platitudes and rewrote his address. In his remarks he reportedly called for a restricted U.S. role in Vietnam – though he also spoke of the duty to serve. A few months earlier, Kerry had enlisted in the Navy; he would serve two tourz in Vietnam.

Kerry's friendz say he knew of Bush, though the president is said not to have remembered Kerry. But both knew the secrets of Bones, like the mysticism surrounding the number "322" (legend has it that the club's secret number unlocked former Bonesman Averell Harriman's briefcase when the presidential adviser was shuttling classified documents between Allied leaders during World War II).

Both men know Y the Bones clocks are always five minutes fast and Y there's a rumor that Bonesmen lie in coffinz for initiation and what all those nicknames mean (Bush's reportedly was *"Temporary,"* because he never chose one; Kerry's remainz a mystery). Skull&Bones began admitting women in 1992. Barbara Bush, the president's 22-year-old daughter and a junior at the school, was either snubbed by the society on Tap Night or rejected the request to join, depending on which tabloidz are doing the reporting. Regardless, it's too soon to tell whether Bones will work any similar magic for women on the path to power.

Today, a number of Bones alumni can be found around Washington. Some have taken jobz in the Bush administration, including two from the president's class. Dr. Rex Cowdry is the associate director of the National Economic Council and Robert McCallum Jr. is serving as the associate attorney general at the Department of Justice.

Kerry's connectionz to Bones appear strongest in his personal life. He met his first wife, Julia Thorne, through her brother, David Thorne, a fellow Bonesman and, later, a political adviser to Kerry. The candidate's second wife, Teresa Heinz Kerry, was first married to another member of the society, the late Republican Sen. John Heinz of Pennsylvania.

The success of Bonesmen is likely to breed more success for the club. *"With two presidential candidates, they probably won't need major recruiters after this,"* says Rosenbaum, the occasionally Bones-obsessed columnist. *"For those who are looking for a ladder up, it sure looks promising."*

For the rest of us, it's obvious it doesn't look so promising – if you continue to support this system! But knowing the masses who choose to remain ignorant, will disregard the fact that Kerry comes from the same satanic lair as Bush, they will still vote for whom they think as *"the lesser of two evilz"* Afrikanz, there aren't levelz of it, evil is evil!

LIK SHOT!

For more info on Skull&Bones, peep these links:
• *http://www.bilderberg.org/skulbone.htm*
• *http://www.matrixmasters.com/world/usnews/skullandbones.html*
• *http://www.cbsnews.com/stories/2003/10/02/60minutes/main576332.shml*
• *http://www.prisonplanet.com/010104kerryadmits.html*
• *http://www.geocities.com/CapitolHill/8425/BONES.HTM#list*
• *http://www.nomorefakenews.com/archives/archiveview.php?key=367*
• *http://www.bilderberg.org/skulbone.htm#proof*
• BUSH FUNDED HITLER – *http://www.bilderberg.org/usglobal.htm#nazi*

frequency – (noun)
1. A wavelength on which radio or television signal is broadcast and to which receiving set can be tuned.

This will be a selfish piece; a piece I'm hopin' you feel to be a necessary discussion 'cause these thoughts have been brewin' in me for some tyme now and the wordz have maturated to the level that I must release them. I promise you as I write this, I simply sat down and started typin', knowin' no format of this piece; I am freely allowin' the corridorz of my spirit to express itself…

I make a point to note that everything happenz in divine tyme; nothin' is ever early nor late. When dwellin' within a moment, the 'order' of everything happenz at its right tyme and place. I say this because I find it not a coincidence that the thoughts that have taken me through this incubation (slow development of somethin', especially through thought and planning) process is in divine order with my magazine's 10th year and 100th issue.

Prior to last April 2003 (our 9th Anniversary), I realized I had to step it up. Although I proclaim to sit on the shoulderz and works of the John G. Jackson's and John Henrik Clarke's on up to present and living, Dr. Ben's, Kwesi's and Browder's, I realize, in order for me to really reach the hedz in the streets (where most of us dwell), physical manifestation of overstanding self MUST happen. Face it, hedz ain't livin' in the past, so they really don't give 2 shits about *"how great we were"* back in the dayz of the Nile Valley with pyramidz and whatnot. On the real, I feel the same! I mean, what can attainin' all this knowledge, buyin' the books, goin' to the lectures, knowin' the facts, how can that help me today?!

For myself, I pledged I would not come into my elder yearz just spittin' knowledge and doin' 4-figure lectures. I've alwayz felt I was "close," yet still felt so distant from my initial goal when comin' back into Pan-Afrikan-centered consciousness: to physically manifest somethin' from the mind. All this knowledge meanz nothin' if you cannot take it from the mind (the 4th-6th dimension) and bring it into the physical (the 3rd dimension). In order to do that, for myself at least, the principle of Correspondence (*'As Above, So Below; As Below, So Above'* — or, in order to understand the unknown, study the known), led me back to the mind.

THE ALL IS MIND

"The ALL is MIND; The Universe is Mental."

– The Kybalion

Everything starts in the mind and the mind is as infinite as the Universe. In the Hiphop track, *'2000 Seasons,'* by Talib Kweli, his first verse was madd profound. He said he was a *"Spiritual (being) remanifested as a human..."*

Thoughts are spirits. Once these spirits are physically manifested, they live. Think, when your mom and pops got together to make you (be it planned or unplanned), the genetic DNA codes of each came together and conferenced on a thought of makin' you. After they determined how many X and Y chromosomes there'd be, the incubating transition began to slowly turn this thought, which was as fragile as a tear drop to manifest into somethin' weighing over 100 poundz, with everything from strong, sturdy bones, to velvet-like mahogany skin. Approximately 9 months later, this thought/spirit manifested into the physical realm as a baby you! This is a universal example, 'cause the same can be applied to how one can create somethin'... like my creating Da Ghetto Tymz magazine. This thought now has life, 10 yearz strong!!

THE PHYSICAL PHENOMENA

Truly, the human body is one of the greatest creationz. To think, somethin' that is so frail as male semen and a womanz egg, can transform itself into dense matter (a living being) and function independently and reproduce! Everything, I mean, *everything* the human body will need to reshape itself was there from its essence — from shootin' out the males penis, to breakin' through the vaginal wallz of the womb, fertilizing the egg!

This concept is hard to grasp because YTs school system stripped us of this Universal Law. And rightfully so, for had they not, how could global white supremacy exist??

When we can innerstand how infinite the mind is and it's connection to everything, we can begin to overstand that we are truly limitless. We refuse to cross the boundary of what's known because someone or some-THING told us there are boundareez, but there aren't Afrikanz. They instilled the fear of Afrikan Liberation by assassinating Malcolm, Medgar and Martin, while infiltrating Garvey, the Panthers and MOVE, and today, we have the intelligence to sit here and talk 'bout the Illuminati and

Ancient KMT, yet cannot come up with a wholistic and strategic combative plan without some agent snitchin' on us to 'ol massa.

One thing we cease to realize is that we are electrical beingz, with currents flowin' in and out of us steadily. What do you think it is that enables you to stick a balloon on the wall after rubbin' it on your hed? What is it that allowz you to shock someone by just touchin' them after you rub your feet on a carpet floor? Electrical energy!

Start to see yourself as a machine and you will be able to comprehend how electronics and machines work. They are all based off the human body and all these inventionz were created first, in the mind.

Just like a battery, we have a positive and negative side. Just like the meanin' behind Her-Em-Akhet (erroneously called the Sphinx), whose reason for havin' Khafre's head on top of a lion was not because there were human-faced lionz walkin' the landz of the Nile Valley, but that it was symbolic, an ill-type subliminal. See, in every person, there's a higher-self and a lower-self; a God-side and a devilish-side; a positive side and a negative side — just like a battery. Our Ancestorz taught that if you could suppress your lower-self or beastly nature — with the king of all beasts bein' the lion — you could elevate yourself to the higher level of God. In order to achieve the '*Summom Bonum*', KMTic for *'Greatest Good,'* your frequency must be elevated to the level of God, not THE God, because I don't think there is ONE; there's Energy.

So when we talk about real revolution, we need to redefine our innerstanding of what we are sayin'. See when you break *'revolution'* down, we get *'RE-'* (which meanz to do over) *'-VOLT'* (if you remove the 'u', which is energy, matter) and *'-TION'* (which meanz action). In other wordz, Afrikanz, <u>WE NEED TO RECHARGE OUR FOCUS WITH ACTION!</u> But in order to do that, we must assess what frequency we are vybrating on. What frequency are you on, Sun?!

The higher side is usually on top (if your balance is right) and the negative on the bottom. In any case the 2 poles are opposite in charge. In some cases, the highest point transmits and the lowest point consumes or takes in, case-in-point, shockin' someone with a touch after rubbin' feet on carpet. As well, there are cases where the highest part (where your brain sits) receives frequenceez. This high point also can be described similarly to how an antenna functionz.

Back in the day, before cable, how did you get a picture on your favorite tell-a lie-vision (tv)? There was an antenna on top of the roof, which is the highest point of the house. See, after all the temple break-inz in Kemet, YT has learned SOME thingz. One in particular is that you can transfer information using wavelengths, aka frequenceez. Knowin' this has enabled YT to create all kindz of info transmitterz, exchanging data without us even seein' it, provin' the point that just 'cause you don't see it, don't mean it don't exist.

Think about it, when you're in your ride and you turn on the radio, most do not think about the phenomena of takin' a current — that is unseen nor heard — and have it change into sound, which is heard. The only challenge is how does one change the vybratory level? It is very clear the currents most of our people tune in to is *'Self-*

Destruction Power 120FM,' (1+2=3, or 1/3rd the wholistic knowledge; 120°) with *'The Wannabe and Jigaboo show'* startin' the day from 7a-11a, *'Close Your Third-Eye'* takin' up the lunch hour 'til 3p, 'DJ Sellout' comin 'on strong at 3p 'til 6p, 'DJ Snitch' on the wheelz of steele (mind stealerz) 6-10p, with 'DJ Kill Dat Nigga' warpin' your mindset from 10 to 1a, closin' with the quiet storm, lullabyin' yo ass to an even deeper mental sleep is none other than 'DJ Comatose'.

It is my belief that there are a number of Ancestorz that still try to communicate on these higher frequenceez, much, much higher than *'Self-Destruction Power 120FM.'* I'd like to call it *'Power 360 FM'* or better yet, *'Power 720FM'* (notice the numerology? 360 bein' 'whole' and 720 bein' both positive and negative and both equally 9)!

THE RELEVANCE

You may think this is perverted numerical masturbation of the Djhuitic Principles, but I assure you, as life exists at least on the 3 planes (mental, physical, spiritual), there is a reason for this sudden madness that has had a serious impact on how we carry our daily lives. With calculated catastrophe after calculated catastrophe I see more and more of my fe/male comradz shook; shook to the point they have become idle, and an idle mind is clearly the biggest foe to Pan-Afrikan liberation.

Peep, we have an alert or scare practically every 2-4 months now! Before, around 9-11, hedz was like, *"Yo, the sky is falling!"* thinkin' we were in the last dayz. In a way, we are. But WHOSE last dayz is what should be the next question! If you remain on their level, operating off *their* frequency, then this could very well be your last dayz. But as for me? This is the beginning. The beginning of my life, havin' the ability to exist on both the higher plane, converting downloaded subliminal faxes expressed across the esoteric wavelengths of the universe. In this life, I intend to maintain a strict code: *know thyself and thy enemy!* Just doin' this is somethin' different than what our Elderz have done. Throughout this process I intend to prove one can take one of our most ancient principles *(the Universe is Mental)* and bring into physical manifestation.

THE REAL POWER YOU

Think of your body as a remote controlled machine or computer. Instead of pluggin' yourself in a wall, your battery — or body — is recharged when you sleep. For every movement you make, realize there are electrical currents flowin' throughout your body enabling you to do these actionz. These electrical currents are bits and pieces of intelligence flowin' from your brain to a particular body part of region, tellin' it to move — sorta like a message delivery boy — then the signal is transferred back to the brain.

When you place your hand on a hot stove, your hand sendz a message to the brain that it's hot, the brain receives this signal and replies, sending data to tell the hand to rise and shake wildly, tryin' to cool it off. At the same tyme, the brain already sent a message to the neck to move forward, the mouth to open, the lungz to inhale and blow on the hand, while the vocalz yell out, *"Got dammit!!"*

All these thingz happen simultaneously, yet we do not recognize this phenomena because it happenz naturally. Had we been not taught this type of Health & Science in school, trust we, I&I'd be in a much better situation, globally; but we should realize in *"Knowing Thy Enemy,"* that, as Dead Prez said, *"They Schoolz,"* are institutionz of mental-training, not mental development.

We have microcozmic replicas of the human body all around us. You think computerz today are fast? You sit at your computer typin' shit, switchin' from Microsoft Word to Photoshop to iTunes to watchin' a DVD, and you're impressed by how swift your computer performz under software applicationz that require more and more RAM and memory from your hard drive. True, a 100GHZ (gigahertz) processor on a computer seemz lightning fast (as if lightning is that *SLOW*), but the human processor is infinitely higher than 999EHZ [Exahertz. After gigahertz is tera-, peta-, then exa-hertz. An exabyte (EB) is a large unit of computer data storage, two to the sixtieth power bytes. According to the dictionary, the prefix 'exa' meanz *"one billion billion, or one quintillion, which is a decimal term. Two to the sixtieth power is actually 1,152,921,504,606,846,976 bytes in decimal, or somewhat over a quintillion (or ten to the eighteenth power) bytes. It is common to say that an exabyte is approximately one quintillion bytes. In decimal terms, an exabyte is a billion gigabytes."*].

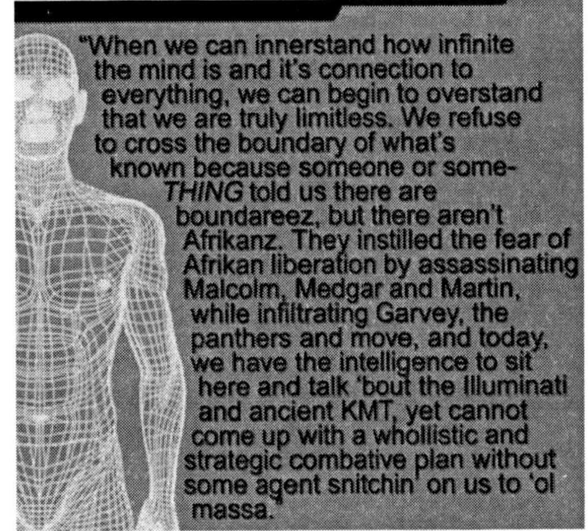

To date, there's no man-made machine that can exceed the level of exa-, but the human body far surpasses it, to a word not even used yet. Havin' an inner-standing of this also points out how information is transferred by electro-magnetic frequenceez. Not only do they transfer data, or matter; they can also instruct and decisively control a thought or action. Case-in-point, the nature of this piece, *'What Frequency R U On??'*

WHAT FREQUENCY R U ON??

There is a reason we are in the mindset we are in. There is also a reason Y it is so hard to break the dependence this mindset has become addicted to. Even hedz who claim they deep are as deep as the book they just read, because quite a few can retain shit they learned because of the lack of linkin' the importance of mental callisthenic's with physical and spiritual callisthenic's, but YT does. That's Y we can look at probably our greatest foe and their greatest weapon, 'massa'-media (mass-media)! 'Ol 'massa'-media basically consists of practically every thing you see and hear on tell-a lie-vision and radio.

How effective are they? Corporationz put billionz of dollarz in advertisement each year tryin' to win your confidence and convince you to purchase their products. The most successful meanz of doin' this are tv, magazines and airplay. Take, for example, how successful the *"Got Milk"* project has been. They've used everyone from athletic starz to

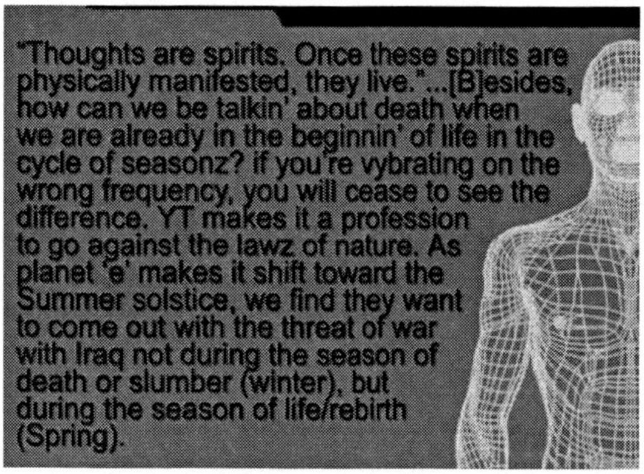

"Thoughts are spirits. Once these spirits are physically manifested, they live."...[B]esides, how can we be talkin' about death when we are already in the beginnin' of life in the cycle of seasonz? if you're vybrating on the wrong frequency, you will cease to see the difference. YT makes it a profession to go against the lawz of nature. As planet 'e' makes it shift toward the Summer solstice, we find they want to come out with the threat of war with Iraq not during the season of death or slumber (winter), but during the season of life/rebirth (Spring).

movie starz to convince you that this radioactive piss and feces, called milk, does a body good.

How many of you eat at fast food joints? How do you know about them? They're blazed across the tv-screen and radio day after day, hour after hour. If you hear somethin' long enuff, you will begin gravitating to it.

How many wack songz have you heard on the radio, but since the radio played it almost every half-hour, you find yourself singin' the melody while you wash the dishes. YT overstandz that repetitive consistency is the motivating factor to submission and success. This is a strategy we Afrikanz fail to exert. We hold madd functionz, but we're not consistent, nor do we do these projects collectively. There's madd hedz tryin' to reach the same audience with the same message yet refuse to link because of ego, sharin' the shine, or not wantin' to split the proceedz.

'MASSA'-MEDIA, THE WEAPON OF CHOICE

YTs mental brainwash through 'massa'-media has our frequency on idle. We sit and wait for YT to tell us what's goin' on in the world. They fill our mentalz with fear of war, biochemical terrorizm, a slumping economy, increasing unemployment ('cause we still ain't figured out we can create our own jobz), a non-existent social security plan; and now businesses no longer matching 401(k) contributionz. They got our mindz stuck in the present while they plan our future.

We sit here, with our mindz on a blank screen; a silent signal, awaiting instructionz. As soon as the puppeteer deliverz their next staged catastrophe, like robots, we react. Cypherz have changed. When I build with my people's, hedz talk about them not knowin' what we gonna do and how we gonna survive this. I say, we gonna survive, 'cause we gonna change our frequency and tune into a higher one and LIVE, PRODUCE and MANIFEST! Anything else is a form of what author Dr. Bobby E Wright coined, *'Mentacide',* which is mental-suicide (four yearz before Dr. Wright's untimely death in 1982, he wrote a profound article entitled, *"Mentacide: The Ultimate Threat To The Black Race."* In defining *"Mentacide,"* Dr. Wright explained that it is *"the deliberate and systematic destruction of a person's or group's mind [which] may give a clue to why the Black race, after developing such an advanced civilization, has for the last 400 years been assisting in its own destruction and the nearly total subjugation of Africa by foreign invaders."*

Besides, how can we be talkin' about death when we are already in the beginnin' of life in the cycle of seasonz? If you're vybrating on the wrong frequency (watchin' YTs tell-a lie-vision, listenin' to YTs radio and 'ol "massa"-media), you will cease to see the difference.

YT makes it a profession to go against the Lawz of Nature. As Planet Earth makes it shift toward the Summer solstice, we find they want to come out with the threat of war with Iraq not during the season of death or slumber (winter), but during the season of life/rebirth (Spring).

Realize that this is a carefully designed scene in a play called *"Life: Under YTs Control."* I'm not sayin' become oblivious to wha'gwan in the world. If you wish to attain 720° of Knowledge of Self, half of that is knowledge of your enemy. As much tyme as you wanna study Ancient KMT or the Illuminati, we need to apply balance, for tyme is in a constant need to rise above all the bullshit so we can plan our lives and our childrenz-childrenz lives. Anything else would be *'Mentacide'.*

We will survive this Afrikanz! Like Dead Prez said, just *"Turn off that Radio"* and elevate your frequency. Through the balance of MAAT using in particular, the Djhuitic Principle of Rhythm (everything moves, nothing rests) and literally "keep it movin'" with MIND, SOUND, POWER!

LIK SHOT!

It's been said just as a coin has two sides, so can a person; like yin and yang if you will. Although they are opposites, they should compliment each other. Like the swing of a pendulum, the force that makes it swing to the right is the same force that moves it to the left, this is a form of complimentary balance. This same principle can be applied to humanz via self-awareness. However, the imbalanced society we live in stifles our ability to reason and because of this, instead of complimentary balance, we have convoluted contradiction.

Take Boule' member, Bill Cosby. At a Washington, DC gala commemorating the 50th anniversary of the Brown v. Board of Education earlier this summer, Cosby put the financially lower-classed Black family on full blast as he compared us with the 60s civil-rights movement. *"These people marched and were hit in the face with rocks to get an education, and now we've got these knuckleheads walking around... The lower economic people are not holding up their end in this deal."* He added, *"These people are not parenting... I can't even talk the way these people talk: 'Why you ain't,' 'Where you is'... You can't be a doctor with that kind of crap coming out of your mouth!"*

Although some of this may be valid, his critique was one-sided. Bein' that he's been financially wealthy for decades, it seemz he strategically left out the apparatus responsible for instillin' this lethargic state of mind: Propaganda; designed, financed and implemented by YT.

Lest we forget Cosby once tried to buy NBC and was denied most likely because to "them" no matter how much money and clout you have, you still a nigga! He also was very blunt about the virtually non-existent presence of positive, serious roles for Afrikan actorz on tell-a lie-vison and movies. I would think Cosby would be aware of the false images of Black culture that are displayed through YTs propaganda mechanizm everyday, all day. So Y would he blast just us?

Lest we forget, Bill that his depiction of todayz use of ebonics is no different than *"Far out," "I'm a split,"* and *"Ya dig;"* wordz he used in his younger dayz [and no one could hardly understand what Mushmouth would be sayin']? The contradiction is that the use of street lingo and "ghetto" wayz was showcased at it's highest for over 10 yearz with his creation, Fat Albert of the 1970s. Here, Cosby created a vehicle for the entire nation to see Black life; the struggles, pain and abstinence of wealth, yet was still able to *"nah, nah, nah, gonna have a good tyme"* as the Cosby kidz made instruments out of a radiator and trash cans with spoons for drum sticks. This was us makin' the most out of a fucked up situation. Bill has forgotten that.

Cosby has gone on to make several tv series and cartoonz depicting Afrikanz in more successful roles. No beef with that. But up until 2002 – when the first production of the movie, Fat Albert was in production – We read all about his books and cartoonz on Nickelodeon [Lil' Bill and Fatherhood], but Fat Albert was left out... until recently...

It seemz greed has Bill reachin' back to a realm he wanted us to forget. Before production of the movie when you look his bio up on the web, you rarely read anything about him in association with the Fat Albert franchise. But I guess he realized the success of Scooby Doo and superhero movies like Batman, Spiderman, The Hulk, Catwoman and The X-Men, that he too could rack in several million. Can't blame duke for capitalizin' on his own invention, it just seemz he virtually abandoned the series after the last season in 1984.

Rightfully so [in his eye's I perceive] if he did. Afterall, The success of NBCs "The Cosby Show" and the short-lived "Cosby" on CBS perceived Afrikanz in more positive roles. But it seemz Bill has been hangin' 'round the rich and privileged too long. After beefin' about us and these comedic or negative roles, he comes out with Fat Albert: ghetto youths havin' fun, bein' silly and whatnot.

In addition, what buggz me is to alwayz see Cosby wearin' Morehouse and Lincoln sweatshirts, Y can't you keep your creationz Black?! One would think he would have our people workin' on his projects. But sadly, this isn't so. Like his white crew behind 'Fatherhood', he had Forest Whitaker as director of the movie, 'Fat Albert' back in 2002 but because of creative differences, split with him and now has some other white cat's, Joel Zwick and Charles Kipps. I'm sure there are hundredz of Afrikan directorz and writerz waitin' for a chance!

What's drivin' him to resurrect 7 ghetto youths – slang and all – month's after he criticized the youth of today showz the bitch in him. On one hand chastises us for bein' who we are and the next he wants us to buy tickets for his movie! He's no better than YT criticizin' us for bein' who we are and then turn around and wanna cake off us to see his movie!

LIK SHOT!

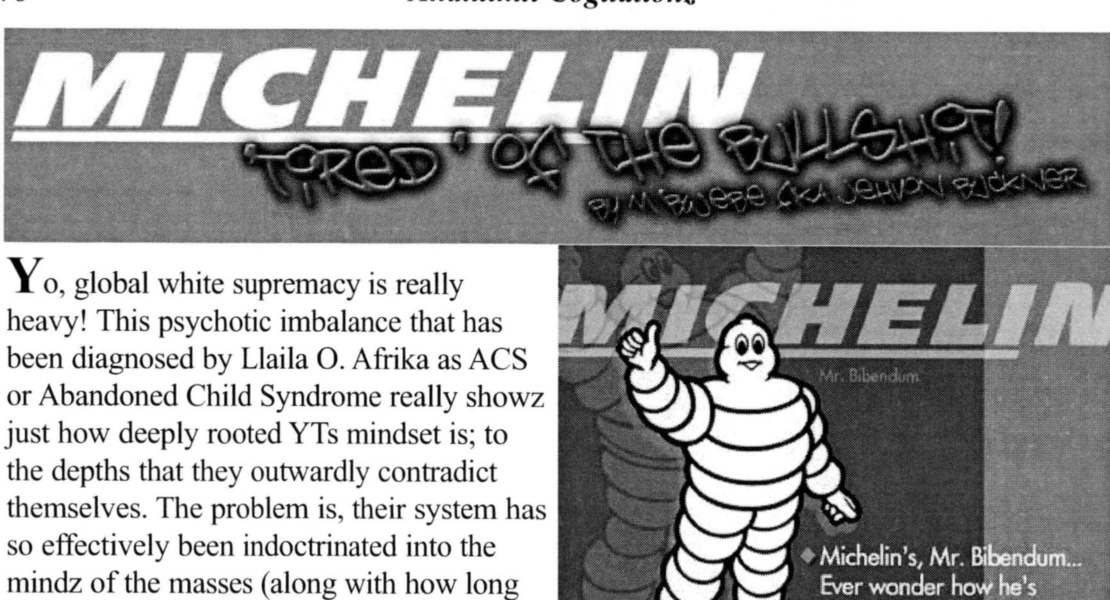

Michelin's, Mr. Bibendum... Ever wonder how he's s'posed to be made of tires, and last tyme I checked, tires are BLACK, yet Mr. Bibendum is WHITE!! Hmmm, global white supremacy at its best!

Yo, global white supremacy is really heavy! This psychotic imbalance that has been diagnosed by Llaila O. Afrika as ACS or Abandoned Child Syndrome really showz just how deeply rooted YTs mindset is; to the depths that they outwardly contradict themselves. The problem is, their system has so effectively been indoctrinated into the mindz of the masses (along with how long this system has been in place), most are blind to the fact.

If you've been readin' DGT for awhile, you should know by now that the majority — if not all — the wealth of the US. Economy is based on the theft of natural resources, murder and free labor from Afrikanz and the continent of Afrika. Knowin' this, you should also be aware that Fortune 500 Corporationz take special interest in Afrika, especially with satellites like NASAs LandSat7, which has the ability to scan the globe and locate which regionz are the richest in natural resources — which point directly at Afrika. So suffice it to say, YT knowz business cannot be successful without resources comin' from Mama Afrika. Knowin' this not only indicates YTs schizophrenic personality where they luv to hate us, yet wanna be us. Still, I'm literally TIRED of this blatant disrespect and rape of our people and homeland.

Case in point, ever really took a look at the corporation, Michelin?! Now they're a tire company, right? Started in France in 1891, they have used a man made of rubber tires called Mr. Bibendum as their logo. Ever looked at Mr. Bibendum?! Notice his color?!!? Now ask yourself Afrikanz, what color are tires??? Aren't you TIRED of this bullshit?! Tires are BLACK, not white; so Y is he white?? This is where it gets even deeper.

Thanx to some *good friendz of DGT, we got our handz on a comic newsletter that was a fable as to how Michelin started, written in french. After translating it, we found this story to be very startling.

(Screen#1) The fable starts out with a well-educated man on a mission in the Sahara desert (in Afrika). He got so tired that he fell asleep in the sun. **(2)**Along came an ostrich and saw the man's bald head. Because of the desert windz, the sand buried the man up to his bald head. The ostrich mistook the head to be an egg, so instinctively, **(3)**the ostrich sat on the manz head as if to hatch the egg. Sure enuff, the egg (head) hatched and out comes a baby Mr. Bibendum shouting out *"A Boire, A Boire"*, or *"Feed me, feed me!"* as would any newborn whine. **(4)**Mr. Bibendum is "adopted" by Moroccanz. His nurse (or nanny, who's depicted as such) fed him through her large Afrikan breast's while she ate nailz. Eating these nailz made him immortal. As she continued to nurse him, he got bigger. **(5)**He eventually grew big enuff from sucking the life out of his "nanny" who gave him his power (just like how YT is leachin' the nourishment of Afrika's natural resources), **(6)**that he took the cup of nailz she fed him and stuffed himself, leavin' her to wilt away. **(7)**He steps out into the world and goes after 2 brotherz, who were, at the tyme, the best in the tire business. He murderz them and embarks on his global quest to destroy all competition, mainly through death. **(8)**He got an old car and began building tires. **(9)**A statue of him was erected in honor(?!) of him slaying the 2 brotherz and **(10)**caused havoc in June 1902 in Vienne, where classical music and bakeries brought them fame. **(11)**He went on to conquer Madrid, Spain and successfully murdered the competition throughout Europe. **12)**Crossing the Atlantic, he took over America and returned to France with trophies of his massive takeover. **(13)**He was hailed by driverz around the world as King of the world.***(end)***

VIE & AVENTURES DU CÉLÈBRE BIBENDUM

Vélautobiographie transcrite par O'GALOP

screenz 5 & 6 blownup

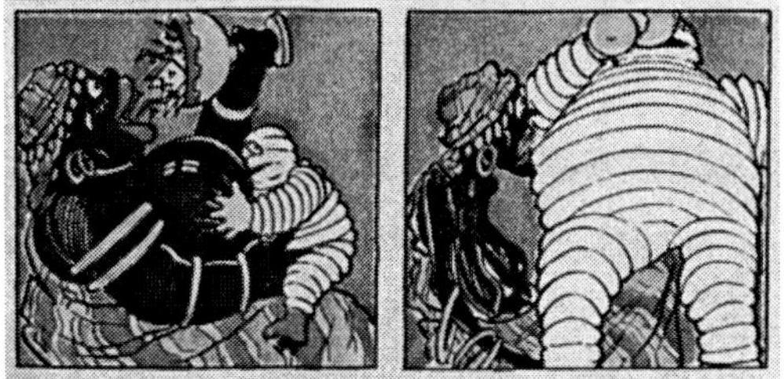

Recueilli par des Marocains, il fut confié aux bons soins d'une plantureuse nourrice nommée Boi-ta-Klou, qui raffolait de clous et de verre pilé; l'enfant profita énormément.

Mais, bientôt réduite à l'état de squelette, la nounou vous eut de ces genoux aigus auxquels force fut à BIBENDUM de s'habituer; parfois, arrachant des mains de la nounou le verre d'obstacles, il le buvait d'un trait gloutonnement.

Now of course this is a made-up story, but there are certain points that I believe to be true. First, YT ain't stupid, they're arrogant. They brag about how they conquered the world and make it no secret that they were willing and able to kill if need be (which has proven to be their initial preference. We know YT don't like to negotiate with no one!).

Second, how the source of their strength comes from Mama Afrika, which in the story was characterized as the Moroccan nanny. Y the Afrikan mother who nursed Mr. Bibendum ate nailz is symbolic for Michelinz claim that their tires are so durable, nailz cannot penetrate; therefore their claim of immortality.

And third, they luv to hate us, clearly showing Afrika (highly melanated people) as the source to their success yet their intentionz, relationship wise, is very clear: they will suck us dry getting everything they need (ideas, lifestyle, resources, soul, etc) to survive and conquer, then leave us to wither, but not die because we can still be of use.

I wonder Y we Afrikanz still can't figure that out?! I for one, am literally 'TIRED' of this shit!! The history of Michelin tires is ILL! The subliminalz are even "ILLer!!"
NOTE: The main ingredient to make a tire besides rubber is CARBON. Carbon is Black! Tink 'bout dat, Afrikanz!!
**biggup to carla, chelsie and moussa for all your help!*

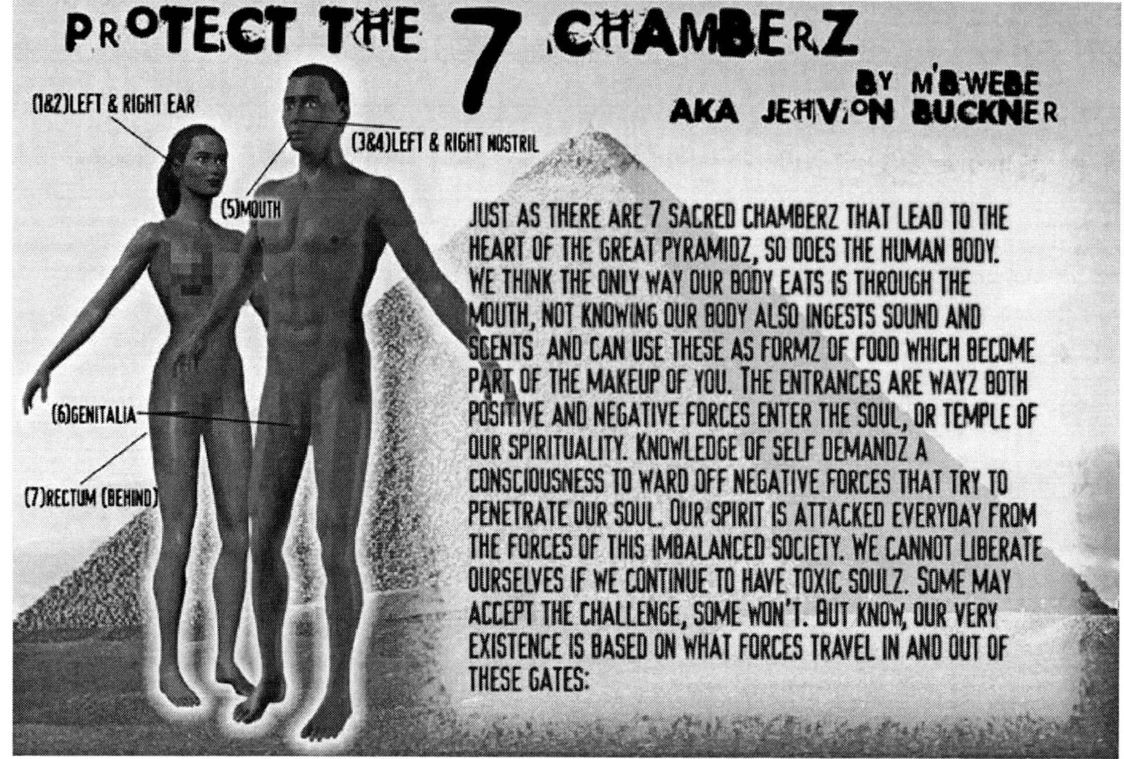

(1&2)
Dealz with whether your spirit hearz positive or negative soundz

(3&4)
Consists of smoke, unscented gases and radiation from electro/radioactivity

(5)
The eating of decayed flesh (meat) and products from animalz (dairy) and using this to fuel the body

(6)
Unprotected sex and participation in homosexual activities like oral sex anal penetration

(7)
Having this most sacred chamber(z) in contact with perfumes, toxic soaps (which are s'posed to be CLEAN), tamponz for women and colored/scented toilet paper, to name a few. These products damage the digestive system. Most importantly, the absence of having regular colonics to enhance bowel movement. Without a healthy digestive system, your body is unable to rid itself of waste, therefore, causing the entire body to eventually shutdown.

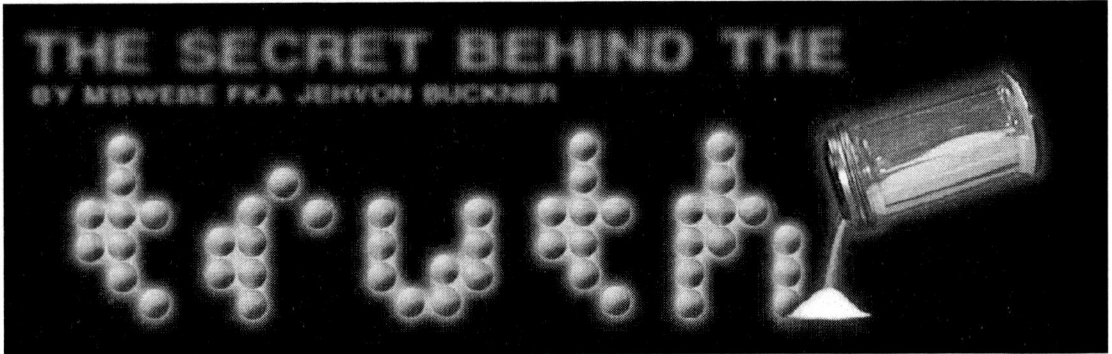

"the truth is, it isn't the nicotine and tobacco that's killin' you in cigarettes, it's refined sucrose, mistakenly called white sugar."
— M'Bwebe Aja Ishangi

Have you seen the commercialz put out by the website company, **truth.com**, where they have people droppin' off body bagz at tobacco industries?

They claim the addiction nicotine has on smokerz are responsible for the over 400,000 annual deaths in America. After researching cigarettes, it seemz the truth.com isn't tellin' you the *whole* truth!

The food processing industry is the biggest sugar customer, putting as much as 50% in processed food. What's shockin' to know is filling the #2 slot is the tobacco industry. The Surgeon General has commissioned all cigarette manufacturerz are required to tell you on the cigarette box that smoking is hazardous to your health, but they are not required to tell you any further info. In fact, cigarettes are probably the only substance that does not print its ingredients on the box! Most have been misled to believe it's only made of tar, nicotine and filterz, but they do not tell you about the tobacco.

The history of tobacco didn't start until after Columbus got lost and landed in the America's. The "Red man" had been blowin' peace pipes for centuries before their encounter with YT. (The "Red man" or so-called 'Native' American was not the first in the America's, it was Afrikan people! In fact, the first chief's of tribes were Afrikan!).

The tobacco plant wasn't brought to Europe until 1558, by the spanish physician, Jean Nicot, where nicotine is derived from.

According to the March 1973 edition *Medical World News,* there's an average of 5-20% sugar that's added to cigarettes, up to 20% in cigarz and as much as 40% in pipe tobacco, mainly in the form of molasses. The truth is the presence of sugar in cigarettes is the main source of lung cancer, based on experimental studies.

This was done by conducting experiments in environments where cigarettes were processed with sugar in landz where they

Watch this Video Article (VA), *'The Secret Behind the Truth About Cigarettes'* on my .tv site, DGTv: Conscious Webvision @ *www.daghettotymz.com/dgtv/videoarticles.html*

used tobacco that wasn't laced with this addicting drug.

They found that cigarettes made in Britain have the highest sugar content of any in the world at 17%. American cigarettes came to about 15%, with Russia, China, Formosa and other countries where they're made from air-dried tobacco – which is the closest to what the Red man smoke – barely had, if any. From this group they were unable to find any cases of lung cancer correlated to smoking.

What was found was that the tremendous excess of sugar and artificial chemicalized animal protein eaten is the link to causing lung cancer. So if you eatin' meat and smokin' you're a sure shot for gettin' it! This bringz the addiction cigarettes have to a deeper level. Not only are you fightin' the addiction of the nicotine, you're also combattin' the even stronger addiction of refined sucrose (white sugar).

If you are a smoker, or know someone who does, think how many tymz you heard them say they needed to relax so they lit up; or in the morning, as soon as they woke up, they light up; or after a meal, or sex. Then think of how challenging it is/was for them as they tried to kick the habit. Just as with sugar, the longer a person goes without a puff, the more uneasy they become. If they hold out long enuff, they will begin to resemble a crack hed lookin' for his next hit!

Author of *Sugar Blues,* William Dufty said, *"On the one hand, the government informs us that smoking depletes our systems of certain vitamins. On the other hand, the government assures us we don't have to worry since the average U.S. diet supplies these essential items in quantity aplenty."*

This is where the mind fuck beginz. After readin' the piece, *'In Sickness & In Health? or Potential Wealth!',* you'll see that the hospital administration along with the Food & Drug Administration has every intention to kill us all slowly through malnutrition.

These industries have ties with the sugar monopoly and tobacco industry and they all realize they can financially capitalize by givin' us a slow death by tellin' us what we should eat, processing these foodz which eliminate the vitaminz and mineralz our body need to stay healthy, and makin' it hard to stay away from refined sucrose because of its presence in so many foodz. After we develop problemz over the yearz we then come literally crawling to the local hospital they pump us with other addictive-slow death drugz, never gettin' us healthy. Y do you think they take the Hippocratic Oath?! What's the root word of Hippocratic... Hypocrite!!

This leaves the question as to Y the website *'truth.com'* chooses to not reveal the sugar connection. If you are an avid reader of DGT, you would most likely realize there is literally no company that is prepared to announce a widespread campaign against the sugar industry. Doin' this would literally cripple the entire economy to its core!

It makes me wonder if the *'truth.com'* is really out to reveal the truth, the whole truth and nothin' but... nah, if they haven't by now it's very clear they intend to keep this a secret!

LIK SHOT!

DECEMBER 15TH, 2003, BED-STUY, BROOKLYN, NEW YORK, FULTON STREET, APPROXIMATELY 5:45PM.

I'm sittin' in a Senegalese restaurant with a friend, gettin' a bite to eat. Now, this is an Afrikan-owned restaurant, and I'm in the majority and historically inhabited, BLACK Bed-Stuy. My friend and I walk in; we immediately notice 2 arabic-muslimz sitting at a table. The restaurant provides its customerz with a tv and it seemz the 2 arabic cats have the remote control. We sat down and waited to make our order…

I noticed they were watching a foreign channel that was talkin' of the capture of Saddam Hussein. I don't know about you, but I alwayz feel uncomfortable when in a setting surrounded by people who speak a language I do not understand. Not that I'm phobic or nothin', but *this* situation was awkward.

The 2 muslimz were then joined by another muslim, who was just as loud speaking as the other 2, I thought to myself, lookin' at the tv of Hussein bein' checked by doctorz after bein' captured, *"I wonder what they're saying?"*

Now, again, I do not speak their language, but by the nature of the tone of their voices, it didn't seem they were in a pleasant mood; not that they were angry, you just get that feelin', ya know?

We constantly surveyed the situation, lookin' with our peripheralz at the muslimz, lookin' at the tv and lookin' at how the restaurant's young Senegalese host is oblivious to wha'gwan. Both my friend and I felt VERY uncomfortable, especially since we were directly in front of the muslimz view of the tv. As the foreign newz station aired footage of middle-easternerz livin' under american military rule, I began thinkin' of how these muslimz cats may be feel, probably even vexed at the american presence in what was possibly their homeland.

As I longed for the station to be changed to an english-speaking station, I started realizing how detached Afrikanz-born in-America are. My yearning to hear the english (or the biased american version) of what's goin' on over there made me feel like a sell-out somewhat. I mean, where's my allegiance?! On top of that, how much of a factor has YTs negative view towardz arabic-muslimz played on my psyche?

The tone of their conversation aired a not-so pleasant vybe in the restaurant, so we got the host's attention and asked to change our meal to go.

As we walked down Fulton street, it was 6 o'clock; prayer tyme for the muslimz in the neighborhood. I heard the chants of islamic prayer bein' blasted from speakerz on top of what appeared to be a brownstone-turned-into-mosque. I gotta admit, I can't stand hearin' that shit everyday, several tymz a day! Not that I have anything against Islam – ok, I do, read *IZ Islam 4 Afrikanz*, but I think it is very, VERY arrogant for them to blast their gender-imbalanced belief's in a predominantly BLACK and non-muslim-based community.

Hearin' the islamic chants echoe throughout the adjacent streets, I asked myself, *"Dam! Are we in Brooklyn or Iraq?!"* This made me feel like I was in Iraq, B! Muslimz of various shades of color, bowing in reverence to a male created god who, according to master scholar and researcher, Dr. Yosef ben-Jochannan, at first was worshipped as a woman (the original name of Allah was a woman, named Allat). These men egotistically promote their chauvinistic belief system as if it were the chosen way of life. I wondered while walkin' by, just how many Afrikanz who were muslim had any idea how islamic origin was and to this day *is* as destructive as christianity has been to our people globally, if not *more* than christianity.

Then it hit me… amidst all of this confusion between america and the middle east, where's *my* allegiance?!!? As an Afrikan-in-america, was I glad or mad that they caught Hussein? As an Afrikan-in-america, was I hatin' on muslimz for freedom of religious expression? I mean, everyone else does it. I even had to catch myself wishing they would realize they are in america and not in their homeland, so assimilate! I later realized, to an extent I was right, but at the same tyme wrong.

See, everyone has a right to worship their own belief system in whatever way they choose. I just think muslimz in Bed-Stuy, Brooklyn — specifically — are arrogant in their worship. They are really not respecting all the thousandz of other people that live here that has to hear that shit on their bullhorn numerous tymz a day!

But that is not the nature of this piece, I bring myself and all other Afrikanz in this country to the fact that as Afrikanz, we are caught in the middle, yet on the outside of a situation that directly affects us. Saddamz capture made me realize how the possible vengeance the US will most likely feel will take, along with YT, quite a few of us as victimz, or even "guilty by association," bein' that we live here!

As these 2 groups continue the millennium-long beef between the Knights Templar and the Arabic muslimz — read Terrorist Factory series or get the DVD lecture, *"The Metaphysical Repercussionz of the World Trade Center Bombing"* — we are but spectatorz, but in this case, we are not on the sideline watchin', eatin' popcorn and drinkin' soda, we're smack dab in the middle of it; at the 50 yard line, with YT on one end of the field and the muslimz on the opposite 20 yard-line, both charging toward each other with us in the middle.

Which side do we choose? America's side because we live here or the people of the middle east because — in this case only — they happen to be under attack by the same clan who continues to attack Afrika (I say 'in this case only' because again, the arabic muslimz are just as, if not more guilty as YT in the continuing slaughter and degradation of Afrika and Afrikan people)? Or, do we have to choose a side at all?

The tyme has long passed where sittin' on the fence makes us negligible to our stance on this "war." The both of them are fighting for power that resides in Afrika! It continues to puzzle me as I see the many Shoshana Johnson's who go sacrificing their lives for countries that have every intent to keep Afrika down!

Bottom line, regardless of whether I am pro or anti- YT and Arabic muslimz, they continue to infiltrate wherever Afrikan people live, somethin' must be done Afrikanz, who's gonna take the weight?

To Be Continued…

2003

I'ma make it clear, this topic will be an ongoin' series because this has turned out to be one of the deepest research topics I've come across. At first I wanted to approach the effects of sugar from a health perspective, but I was soon led to the historical significance sugar has had on the enslavement of Afrikan people. So before I can even get into what sugar does to our bodies, I must dive into just how far the greed for this drug has extended.

First and foremost, I must quote author of *'African Holistic Health'*, Dr. Imhotep Llaila Afrika, *"White sugar is sweet, it is delicious, it is good, however, it is a drug!"* Due to the mischievous deedz of the european, sugar has been purposely put in the same category as natural sugarz found in cane or beets. It must be noted that we are not speakin' of natural sugar but 'refined sugar' – that is what that white crystal stuff is really called.

According to William Dufty, author of *Sugar Blues*, *"Sugar is nothing but a chemical. They take the juice of the cane or beet and refine it to molasses and then they refine it to brown sugar and finally to strange white crystals."*

White sugar, or refined sucrose, is a highly refined carbohydrate that is technically classified as a drug. Refined sucrose is a drug. If we look it up in Webster for a definition, it sayz, *(1)A substance used as a medicine in treatment of a disease. (2)A narcotic, which is a drug that dulls the senses.* And when you look at this society and the need for YT to keep the masses "in check", you can see that this substance has proven to be one of their most lethal weaponz.

SUGAR: A LINK TO THE ENSLAVEMENT OF AFRIKANZ

Dr. Afrika speaks of white sugar bein' used as a weapon for the enslavement of Afrikan people. Not only does refined sucrose enslave the internal organz of the body, destabilizing our inner bio-chemical balance, robbing our body of essential vitaminz and mineralz, it literally was one of the reasonz that lead to the enslavement of our Ancestorz!

Sugar has an addicting taste and with addiction comes greed. Natural sugarz found in almondz, chestnuts, walnuts, pistachios, apples, figz, grapes, olives, barley, wheat, rye, millet, cucumberz, melon, carob, mint, onionz, garlic, lentilz, mustard, ginseng and honey existed as long as wo/man, but refined sucrose was not present until millenniumz later.

The use of sugar cane appearz to have first surfaced in 600BC East India and it

Watch this Video Article (VA), *'White Sugar: The Mark of Cane'* on my .tv site, DGTv: Conscious Webvision @ *www.daghettotymz.com/dgtv/videoarticles9.html*

was chewed. By 325BC, when Nearchus, appointed admiral of Alexander the (not so) Great's army, explored the East Indies, we find the Greeks first encounter with it, describing it as a kind of honey growing in canes or reedz. Many of the natives of the Indus Valley made it into a sweet cane juice as a fermented drink. According to Dufty, *"sometimes it was called 'Indian salt' or 'honey without bees' and imported in small quantities at enormous cost. By 300BC, the Greeks it was used as medicine and by 600AD, in Persia it was seen as a miracle drug in dealing with pestilence. Remember, I'm referring to sugar that is heated, refined and then solidified into sugar cane juice, not the other white powder stripped of all the natural elements."*

Due to research done, enabling the refining of the cane juice into a solid form that would last without fermenting, at the University of Djondisapour, of the Persian Empire (circa 600AD), the Persianz began growing sweet cane on their own, opening the doorz to global trade. The chinese imported loaves of what was called "stone honey" from Bokhara, where careful skimming of the liquid and the addition of milk contributed to the eventual appearance of it being white. Author of *Food in History*, Reay Tannahill writes, *"Roman writer Discorides gave it a new name, saccharum (later called saccharin), describing it as a "sort of concrete honey which is called saccharum found in canes in India and Arabia Felix; it is consistence like salt and brittle between the teeth."*

At that tyme, a piece of saccharum was considered a rare and precious miracle drug, heavily in demand in a tyme of plague and deadly dis-ease. This term was later changed to 'khanda' – eventually becoming the English word, 'candy', after surviving the further invasionz of the Muslimz with their Latin tongues.

After the rise of Islam, sugar became a potent political form of bribery, where all kindz of people would sell their very soulz for it. This is where the greed came in. European invaderz of Kemet found that their ambassadorz of the Kemetic court were being corrupted by the sugar habit and won over by bribes of costly spices and sugar.

In 1306AD, Pope Clement V headed a resurging wave of christian crusades against the world [you will recall the dayz of Constantine (circa 1000AD) when he raided indigenous villages, enforcing 'christianity or death' on the natives]. Their strategy was summed up by Dufty, *"In the land of the Sulta* [in

Afrika], *sugar grows in great quantities and from it the Sultans draw large incomes and taxes. If the Christians could seize these lands, great injury would be inflicted on the Sultan and at the same time Christendom would be wholly supplied from Cyprus."* What followed was 7 centuries of torture, leaving a trail of slavery, genocide and organized crime.

British author of *The History of Sugar*, Noel Deerr said, *"It will be not exaggeration to put the tale and toll of the Slave Trade of 20million Africans, of which two-thirds are to be charged against sugar."*

At first it was the Portuguese who were out in front. Henry the Navigator of Portugal explored the West Coast of Afrika searching for fieldz of sugar cane outside Arab dominion. Instead of finding sugar fieldz, he found what he deemed an even greater "thing" to exploit for profit, our Ancestorz! In 1444, this wicked pirate kidnapped 235 Afrikanz from Lagos to Seville where they were sold into slavery. So not only did YT find the perfect crop to sell for profit, he found the perfect hueman able to endure the demanding physical strength needed to cultivate this crop. This was the beginning of the 'Maangamiza' or 'Middle Passage'.

10 yearz later, the Pope extended his "blessing" to the slave trade. He gave authority to all crackuz ordainin' them to attack, subject and reduce to slavery the Afrikanz and other enemies of christianity. The scriptures of the alleged "Holy" Bible were perverted to provide solace for slave-holding christian sugar (drug) pusherz. American-Afrikan poet, Jean Toomer in his 1923 work, *Cane*, wrote *"The sin what's fixed against the white folks...they made the Bible lie."*

By 1456, the Portuguese had control of the european sugar/slave trade, with Spain not far behind. After the Moorz (who were Afrikan) were ousted out of Spain, they left behind large cane fieldz in Granada and Andalusia.

In 1510, after Columbus' second voyage to the New World, he negotiated the transportation of Afrikanz in the West Indies to work on the Spanish sugar cane plantationz. King Ferdinand called for the kidnapping of a large amount of Afrikanz to satisfy this need. By this tyme, the Portuguese were growing sugar cane with Afrikan slave labor in Brazil.

In 1515, Spanish monks offered $500 in gold as loanz to anybody who would start a sugar mill. The Dutch got into the game around 1500. Because they were skillful seamen, they were able to transport a large portion of our Ancestorz. They used our Ancestorz as credit to start their sugar empires in Antwerp, which was shipped from Lisbon, the Canary Islandz Brazil, Spain and the Barbary Coast, then exported to the Baltic states, Germany and England. By 1560, Charles V of Spain had built magnificent empires in Madrid and Toledo, Spain off the exploitation of Afrikan free labor.

Because of the greed for sugar and Afrikanz, the Portuguese and Spanish empires rose swiftly in power. But sugar had its own planz. With all their power these empires rapidly went into decline, because as I stated earlier, it is a drug. Sugar is a drug that is not prejudice. It only seeks to destroy anyone who befriendz it.

After the fall of the Portuguese and Spanish, the British were next in line.

As Dufty stated, *"In the beginning, Queen Elizabeth I shrank from institutionalizing slavery in the British colonies as 'detestable,' something which might 'call down the vengeance of heaven' on her realm."* But by 1588, she quickly turned from God-fearing to power-hungry, establishing the 'Company of Royal Adventurers of England' into Afrika, creating for them a huge monopoly in the West Afrikan slave trade.

What's deep is how YT never, ever saw us a huemanz, but as a product they could "use" for "trade". And we got Negroes today who still think we can civilize them, who continue to refuse seein' us as beingz. Rev. Ishakamusa Barashango commented on our relationship with YT: *"If we couldn't civilize this white man when we were at our highest, during the Nile Valley days, why we think we can get them to change now?!"*

This group came to West Afrika exclusively to kidnap Afrikanz, who were transported to the West Indies, sold to sugar planterz. This was mainly done to establish trade with the mistakenly called "Native Americanz" (Afrikanz were here before the Red man), because they were now turning the fermented raw sugar cane juice into rum. They gave this rum to the Red man in trade for furz, ('cause it's madd cold in europe, yo!!) the furz and sugar went to YT in europe and molasses went to the colonialz in the New World. This triangle trade went on until the land in Barbados and other British stolen islandz were unable to produce anymore crop because the land was exhausted.

Dope, I mean, sugar pushing became so profitable by 1660, and the British were willing to go to war. They created the Navigation Acts of 1660 claimed the prevention of the transport of sugar, tobacco or any product of the American Colonies to any port outside England, Ireland and British possessionz. The Colonies wanted to be free to trade with all European powerz.

While American historianz like to argue that it was the British tax on tea that started the War of Independence, otherz point to the Molasses Act of 1733, which levied a heavy tax on sugar and molasses coming from anywhere except the British sugar islandz in the Caribbean. What happened was the ship ownerz of New England had cut themselves in on the rewarding trade of Afrikanz, molasses and rum. They would sail off with a cargo of rum to the slave coast of Afrika to exchange for kidnapped Afrikanz whom they hauled back to the West Indies for sale to the greedy British plantation pirates. From there they took on a load of molasses which they hauled back home to be distilled into to rum to sell to their heavy drinking wino's.

Long before the Boston Tea Party, the annual consumption of rum in the American colonies was about 4 gallonz for every man, woman and child. The Molasses Act posed a serious threat not only to the colonies involvement in the trade game, but also to their addiction to get drunk. See what this white devil, called sugar did to these crackuz? The constant, addicting need for it started to turn them on each other. As Dufty stated, *"...[W]ant had become need. Gluttony had produced necessity. Sugar and slavery were indivisible. Therefore, they were defended together."*

The French took the lead in the game in the middle of the 18th century. Sugar was everywhere by now. It had become a source of public wealth and international importance. Each government kept their allegiance to this organized crime by making sure they got their cut through taxes.

The ill shit is just as with tobacco, the soil can be ruined after extensive strain on the land. By the mid-1850s, British sugar planterz in Barbados and Jamaica were ruined. This caused the British government to raise the price of enslaved Afrikanz to cover for the sugar loss. This created an intense, almost exclusive focus on the slave trade.

Although other demandz were created for our enslaved Ancestorz, the first POWs (Prisonerz of War), *"[S]lavery of one kind or another never went out of style as far as sugar was concerned. The sugar industry was the model for other agribusiness conglomerates that were to follow decades later. Sugar beets had still to be planted, thinned and topped by hand. Growing sugar cane required backbreaking labor under the hot sun of those climates where the cane thrived. Tending and cutting of sugar cane could not be mechanized. It had to be done by hand. Most of the hands were black.",* Dufty.

As I started, I wanted to write about the health effects sugar has on our bodies, but as I dug deeper, the Ancestorz willed me to speak of a story seldom, if ever told; to make a connection the masses may not be aware of. It is vital that we overstand that the origin of refined sucrose, that other "white stuff", more addictive than any other drug (including crack-cocaine), has played a significant part in the historical, physical and mental enslavement of Afrikan people worldwide. A role that it still playz today.

Refined sucrose didn't create itself. Natural sugar probably has been here since the first plants started grow. It is the wicked, imbalance mindset of the white man that decided to create this addictive drug. Part 2, we will continue the historical evolution of sucrose and begin to breakdown the effects this crystallized powder has on your body.

MORE FIE-YAH!

"White sugar is sweet, it is delicious, it is good, however, it is a drug!"
– Dr. Llaila O. Afrika

In part 1 of this joint, we dealt with the historic genesis of white sugar, datin' it's primary function as the key component behind the beginning enslavement of our Afrikan Ancestorz and the notorious Atlantic Slave Trade. Noel Deerr said it best, *" it will be not exaggeration to put the tale and toll of the Slave Trade of 20million Africans, of which two-thirds are to be charged against sugar."* For more in the history of white sugar, peep part 1. Part 2 will deal with the exact affects of this drug that continues to kill us sweetly…

HOW WHITE SUGAR AFFECTS YOU

Back in 1964, a book written by a Japanese natural healer, Sakurazawa, wrote, *"Western medicine and science has only just begun to sound alarm signals over the fantastic increase in its per capita sugar consumption, in the United States especially. Their researches and warnings are, I fear, many decades too late. [They] will one day admit what has been known in the Orient for years: sugar is without question the number one murderer in the history of humanity — much lethal than opium or radioactive fallout..."* Puttin' it bluntly, the human body cannot handle man-refined sucrose erroneously called sugar!

William Dufty, author of *Sugar Blues* said, *"the difference between life and death is, in chemical terms, slighter than the difference between distilled water and that stuff from the tap."* The brain is likely the most sensitive organ in the human body. The difference between feelin' up or down, sane or insane, calm or bugged out, inspired or depressed dependz largely on what we put in our mouth. In order for normal function, the levelz of glucose in the blood must balance with the amount of blood oxygen, an operation supervised by the adrenal glandz. Dr. E.M. Abrahamson put it best when he coined the phrase, *"Body, Mind and Sugar* (instead of Soul)*."*

Dr. Linus Pauling, an orthomolecular psychiatrist, stated in *Orthomolecular*

Psychiatry, "The functioning of the brain and nervous tissue is more sensitively dependent on the rate of chemical reactions than the functioning of other organs and tissues." He goes on, *"I believe that mental disease is for the most part caused by abnormal reaction rates, as determined by genetic constitution AND DIET..."*

What happenz when one eats white sugar? It starves the body's cellz especially in the brain. When one induces white sugar, because of its close resemblance to glucose, it foolz the body, evading the chemical process goin' directly into the intestines where it becomes "predigested" glucose. This then is absorbed into the bloodstream where the glucose level drastically increased — some may refer this to the "rush" or "pick up" in energy they may feel — where balance is destroyed. Now you may feel this rush is a good thing and harmless to your body, but if I were to equate this to someone takin' a hit of crack or heroin, the rush is fast and quick and a soon as it's over, you come crashing down... HARD and even further away from balance. We begin to feel even more tired and listless. We become irritable, jumpy and unable to focus. What do you do to feel better, you take anutha "hit" of crack, I mean, white sugar, by drinkin' some soda, eatin' a candybar or some chips.

When you eat white sugar, one of the most vital vitaminz is destroyed, vitamin B12. Deficiency in B12 has proven to lead to mental illness. Since the brain is the most sensitive organ, white sugar attacks there first. And because we cannot see our brain, the mood swingz, nausea and hallucinationz are overlooked. By the tyme the dis-ease is spread throughout and beginz affecting the body, the brain has already been poisoned. When I say mental illness, you think of someone in a straight-jacket, which is true, but if you really look at the world we live in, the straight-jacket is put on someone who's be diagnosed as a disturbance. This illness is seen in various degreez. Depression is one of the most notable symptomz. You may think, *"ev'rybody get a lil' depressed ev'ry once and a while."* Yeah, and hedz get got every day too! Read the tabloidz and see all the sex and violence... all these are symptomz of mental illness.

The chemi(kill) breakdown of white sugar is $C_{12}H_{22}O_{11}$. White sugar is considered an empty carbohydrate, meaning it has no value whatsoever! How does this affect the human body? Y do you eat? Not because you hungry but because it is fuel for your body to operate. Without food and water, the body will eventually cease to function and lead to eventual shutdown and deterioration of the body. The ending result is death, but, as any process, there are stages.

Many think a person that's starving is one whose skeletal bones are showing. If you were to see a walking skeleton, you'd say that person was malnourished and sick. Although in most cases, this is true, we've stereotyped what a starving person looks like. Never have we visualized a slim, mid-size or even obese person as one who's sick or malnourished and believe me, the FDA (Food & Drug Administration), the WHO (World Health Organization), the AMA (American Medical Association), HEW (Department Health, Education and Welfare), the government, Hospital Administration and a string of other constituents are hopin' you continue to see sickness this way. Our ignorance to health ensures their wealth (read *'In Sickness and In Health? Or Potential Wealth!'*).

So what happenz when you continue to eat empty carbohydrates? Are you familiar with what cancer is? Lemme break it down. Just cause you eat 3 mealz a day don't mean your body is gettin' what it needz to sustain itself. When you continue over the yearz to feed your body food that has no nutritional value, it inevitably leadz to cancer. See, cancer isn't just a tumor, cancer is developed after eating foodz that offerz the body nothing it needz to continue flowing like calcium, all the vitaminz A to Z, chromium, magnesium, zinc, and all the other elements on the periodical chart. When your body does not get this from the food you give it, it has no choice than to get it from its own reserves. Yes, the body does create the nutrients, but it cannot continue to do it if it doesn't get any help from you (the foodz you choose to feed it). See, we take our body for granted. We expect it to do thingz on demand, yet most of the tyme we do not nurture and maintain it.

Funny how we can have more luv for a car than the most important ride we'll ever have, that bein' the human body! Think about it, we'll splurge on some deep-dish rimz, wash it every week, even throw in the dope coconut air freshener, yet the only thing we do to maintain the real ride, which *should be* our body, is a daily shower and a cut. What about the inside? I mean, if we gonna vacuum the inside, wipe the inside windowz, make sure we maintain consistent oil changes, tire pressure and radiator pressure, Y don't we for our very own insides?!!? Hedz is deathly afraid of colonics! We feed our body cheap fuel in the form of fastfood, fried foodz, and (nuclear) microwave dishes, yet we wouldn't dare put cheap gas in our whip!

But I can't blame ya'll. The health education we got in school didn't deal with the importance of diet. On top of that, the imposter food that's manufactured (cause it ain't natural) has chemi-kill additives to make it taste good, makin' it even harder to give it up! Breakin' down chemicalz or 'chemi-killz', 'chem' meanz black. So chemicalz actually attack and seek to kill blackness!

What we're not told is where this road of careless eating leadz to. See, we've been told to expect deteriorating health as you get older. We are not taught we have an option that enables us to live a prosperous life as elderz with clean kidneyz, thin blood and a strong heartbeat. The road of careless eating, in particular, one that is heavily laced with white sugar leadz to cancer.

Again I ask, what is cancer? When the body beginz to eat itself alive, so much that the body can no longer replenish what it needz. Huh? What I'm sayin' is when you eat a lifetyme of white sugar, white flour, white rice, white bread and basically any other thing that's white (including dairy), your body *will* digest it, but when the food goes through your intestines, it's not only forming waste (shit) it does not need, there's s'posed to be some type of exchange where the food, as it passes through after bein' digested in the stomach, the stage where it passes through the intestines is where the nutrients are to be sucked out of the food. What the intestines does not need is compacted into shit and of course, emitted out when you sit on the toilet. However, many are not aware that 100% of the waste is not out of you. Approximately 20-30% of it stayz in your colon, and you KNOW how bad shit smellz! Over the yearz, your colon becomes a gravesite to all the corndogz and happy mealz you ate, rotting more and more in the 98.6° oven our body's temperature maintainz.

The body wants and needz food to give it nutrition. When you give the body empty foodz it still craves nutrition which is one reason people gain weight. The other reasonz are addictionz to certain foodz (e.g. white sugar, salt, caffeine, etc.) and the lack of exercise. White sugar moves very slowly out of the stomach. This creates over-acidic conditionz in the stomach which influence the secretion of enzymes and hydrochloric acidz to help digest our food. This over-acidic condition also affects the entire body.

Back to the cancer. Since none of the nutrients are in the food you ate, the body pullz it from it's reserves. After yearz of this continued exchange, the body, after givin' you madd symptomz something was wrong (most people get real sick a couple tymz a year — I can attest that since I've lived a vegetarian and now vegan lifestyle goin' on 12 yearz and the elimination of white sugar for 5 yearz in particular, I have not had a cold, gotten sick, nor even vomited), the body, no longer bein' able to supply the demand of vitaminz and nutrients it needz, bottomz out and cancer develops. Actually, cancer can be equated to AIDS, 'cause the immune system becomes deficient (Acquired Immune Deficient Syndrome) leavin' you open for other dis-eases to settle in. On top of that, when one is diagnosed with cancer, they are given 'kill-o', I mean, chemotherapy, which is s'posed to kill the cancer. But what it really does is charges it because the radioactive treatment expedites the growth and strength of the cancer. But the Hospital Administration won't tell you this, for if they did, they'd be out of business!

One of the most vital organz affected from yearz of white sugar consumption are the adrenal glandz. Not from overwork but from continued whiplash! The overall production of hormones is low, the entire endocrine circuit (glandz that secrete hormones directly into the lymphatic system or bloodstream) is shot and the brain may soon begin having trouble tellin' the unreal from the real. Sound like Alzheimerz Disease to you?

Alzheimerz is the deterioration of intellectual functionz such as memory and other senses. *"Day-to-day efficiency lags, we're always tired, never seem to get anything done. We've really got the sugar blues,"* Dufty states. He further notes, *"...Doctors won't tell you that since the cells of the brain are those that depend wholly upon the moment-to-moment blood sugar level nourishment, they are perhaps the most susceptible to damage."*

I'm not tellin' you this to scare you. We've just been misinformed of what the worldz most addictive drug does to us. You ask, Y do I say white sugar is a drug? Because of it's addiction. You may say it is not addictive. I say it is more addictive than crack-cocaine! The only reason this is hard to prove is because white sugar is legal and in basically EVERYTHING! If white sugar were a banned substance, you'd see just how addictive white sugar is!

C12 H22 O11: THE MARK OF CANE

Refined sucrose, erroneously called white sugar has no food value and containz no nutritional value. For the sake of familiarity, we will call it white sugar, but keep in mind we are talkin' about refined sucrose, not natural sugar or cane sugar!

The process of making sugar comes from both the sugar cane and beets. They are heated and calcium hydroxide (lime, and a know toxin to the body) is added. This process is done to remove all ingredients that hinder the complete processing of sugar. Carbon dioxide, which is another toxin, is then used to remove the some of the lime. Now, just starting out, we already have 2 highly toxic chemi(killz), that bein' calcium hydroxide and carbon dioxide.

The sugar then turnz from a sticky black substance to a clear juice which is further heated to remove other impurities. In addiction, I mean addition, if that's not enuff, the sugar is then bleached white with a chemical solution that uses pork by-products primarily based with blood albumin and/or animal charcoal. By the tyme we see it as we recognize it, the sugar has been processed at least three tymz.

According to brutha Arron Muhammad, white sugar is used for different purposes. There's the grade that's commonly used for table sugar, the grade used in processed food (such as cakes, ice cream, candy and soft drinks) and the sugar that's used for non-food purposes such as making plastic, cement mixing, and leather tanning. Muhammad stated he's used table sugar along with white flour for yearz to make glue for hanging posterz. So if you don't mind having your intestines glued shut, then feel free to continue eating this deadly substance.

WHAT WHITE SUGAR DOES

The chemicalz used in white sugar processing are phosphoric acid, acid calcium phosphate among otherz. They are potent and health-debilitating. White sugar has a tremendous amount of carbonic acid which disturbz the nutritional balance in the body. White sugar robz the body of almost all nutrients, especially the mineralz chromium, zinc and calcium, and vitaminz C and B-complex.

White sugar also destroyz food digestion enzymes in the mouth, stomach, the small intestines and the pancreas. It also reduces the amount of hydrochloric acid — a necessary digestive acid in the stomach. Without it, the food doesn't get broken down properly, thus inhibiting the body from properly absorbing the nutrients. A symptom of this is frequent bouts with constipation.

White sugar interferes with activities of the small intestine which digests the food. The small intestine pushes the waste along and most importantly releases the nutrients in the food to give us energy and nourish cellz. But when we eat white sugar, digestion is disturbed. According to Muhammad, the amount of food nutrients available to the body are limited.

In addition to this, white sugar is released into the blood. This toxifies the blood, putting too much carbon in it which further damages the body cellz. Since there's no real nutrition in white sugar, it represents a toxic waste material in the blood that the body will try to get rid of. The lymphatic system will grab some of this waste in an attempt to purify the blood. When the lymphatic system becomes overloaded, health problemz occur, which could have been avoided. Too much white sugar, salt, and starch can work together to create an excessive appetite. These food cravingz create an imbalance in the body. I was recently told that over 60% of Afrikan women in America are obese. The amount of food that is consumed by us is sickening! In this country alone, the average hed consumes entirely too much white sugar, more than 125 poundz of it annually! Even deeper is the fact that many may not be aware of it. That's 'cause white sugar is hidden in many foodz such as cerealz, ketchup, canned foodz, frozen foodz, etc. In fact almost 70% of the white sugar that we consume is hidden in foodz! For instance, a typical 12-ounce soda containz 10 teaspoonz of white sugar. The typical candy bar is almost all white sugar. Even pizza has a considerable amount of white sugar in it. The sweetness of the pizza is hidden by putting in a lot of salt and other ingredients which give a semi-sweet taste. As I mentioned before, we do not know what malnutrion looks like. When you see somebody walkin' down the street and their gut is so big they can't see their nuts or womb… THAT'S MALNUTRITION!!

The body really desires nutrition. Cravingz are but the body tryin' to tell you what it needz. But we have not been taught how to listen to our body. If you continue to ignore your body's warningz, such diseases as cancer, diabetes, high blood pressure and otherz are the results of eating too many highly acidic foodz.

THE CORPORATE CULPRITS BEHIND WHITE SUGAR

For those who are career boycotterz need to gather Jesse and Sharpton to boycott The Nutrition Foundation. Who are they? They're a front organization for the leading sugar pushing corporationz in the food business. This front operation includes multi-billion dollar businesses like the American Sugar Refining Company, Coca-Cola, Pepsi-Cola, Curtis Candy Co., General Foods, General Mills, Nestles Co., Inc., Pet Milk Co. and Sunshine Biscuits to name a few. In total there are about 45 companies.

In the 1930s, Dr. Weston Price, a research dentist traveled across the world (from Alaska to the South Sea Islandz and from Afrika to New Zealand). He wrote a book entitled, *Nutrition and Physical Degeneration: A Comparison of Primitive and Modern 'Diets and Their Effects'* in 1939. In this book, he concluded that people who live under what YT classifies as "backward primitive conditionz" or hedz who live in 3rd world countries, had excellent teeth and exceptional general health. What's deep is that after these regionz became in contact with YTs civilization and they started importing their poison (white sugar), the physical degeneration was so fierce, it was easily visible within a single generation. Harvard professor, Earnest Hooten said in *'Apes, Men and Morons', "Let us cease pretending that toothbrushes and toothpaste are anymore important than shoebrushes and shoepolish. It is store food that has given us store teeth."*

Most of these researcherz who published their findingz in numerous books — that, by the way, were not publicized to the public — the serious effects of white sugar, were financed by sugar corporationz. But when the researcherz went to reveal their findingz, the funding suddenly dried up and their work was silenced. *'Time magazine'*, in 1958, reported that a Harvard biochemist had worked with mice and the effects of white sugar and how it causes dental cavities for over 10 yearz. They were financed by the Sugar Research Foundation, Inc. What the biochemist found was that there was no way you could prevent white sugar from causing dental decay. After the findingz, the chemist and his crew reported their finding in the 'Dental Association Journal,' soon after, they lost all their funding.

Because there was research after research disclosing the severe problemz white sugar caused, the drug, I mean, sugar pusherz had to rely on marketing adz to get their product out. Author of *'The Magic of Findhorn,'* Paul Hawken, wrote, *"...[T]he more you see a product advertised, the more of a ripoff it is."* Little did we know back then, just how effective the advertising campaign of sugar-laced products would be over the next 50 yearz...

COCA-COLA: THE REAL THING

Of all the sugar-laced products that are on the market today, none has been more successful than Coca-Cola. Y? Mainly because they been the sole-source of this madness since day 1.

Many are not aware that Coca-Cola containz known poisonz, destroyz teeth and the stomach, yet at the same tyme has one of most successful ad campaignz in the history of YTs reign. Dufty stated, *"...This unreal amount of money creating an illusion — the illusion that 'Coke is the real thing.' Now young America is searching for what is real, meaningful in this plastic world, and one bright ad executive comes up with the idea that it is Coke. Yep, Coke is the real thing and this is drilled into the minds of 97% of all young people between the age of 6 and 19 until their teeth are rotting just like their parents' did."* He further addz, *"There's nothing truthful about advertising. Imagine a young pimply faced kid in front of a camera telling folks how clear his complexion was before he started drinking Coke; and even though he knows it's bumming his social life, he just can't seem to get off the stuff. That would be truth in advertising. Or how about a young girl holding up a can of orange drink made in New Jersey saying the reason it's orange is because of the food coloring. The reason it is bad is because we use coal-tar artificial flavors, and the reason we would like you to try it is because we want to make money. Truth in advertising would be the end of three major networks, 500 magazines, several thousand newspapers, and tens of thousands of business. So there will never be truth in advertising."*

So what is Coca-Cola? For one, it containz a high amount of phosphoric acid. In 1951, a Navy nutritionist, Dr. McCay found at the Naval Medical Research Institute, that human teeth softened and started to dissolve in a short period after sitting in a cup of Coca-Cola. McCay stated the acidity of cola beverages is about the same as vinegar, only its masked by the sugar content. I guess this gives meaning as to Y they call soda "SOFTdrinks," 'cause it can soften your teeth, including our other bones — which is what? Osteoporosis!!

McCay documented he was later speaking to an unnamed Congressman who asked if he had any findingz of the effect of cola beverages on metal and iron. McCay said no and the Congressman told him a friend of his once dropped 3 tin penny nailz into a cola bottle and 48 hourz later, the nailz had completely dissolved!! McCay added that you could drop phosphoric acid on iron and even limestone and it would dissolve, even concrete steps!!! That was 1951. Today, shit's even more ill! There are figures that show that almost 30% of sugar consumed in the United States comes in the form of softdrinks! Look around you... everywhere you see Coke and Pepsi machines. We blast hedz for all the churches and liquor stores in our community but after all our yellin' at the boycott rallies, how do we reward our thirst? We *"obey our thirst"* and drink Gatorade — who's owned by PepsiCo, who ownz Pepsi, Quaker Oats, FritoLay and Tropicana — or any other liquid-cocaine-laced drink! Dufty couldn't have said it better, *"our addiction to drink —from the cradle to the grave — is an addiction to sugar."*

COKE: FROM GENESIS TO REVALATIONZ

In the early 17th century, an Italian voyager to South America found the second-native Americanz (second because they were not the first in the Americaz, Afrikanz were. They're also mistakenly called Indianz) there constantly chewing on the leaf of the coca plant; at work, on trips, they carried it in small pouches and kept it in their mouths with a small amount of ground lime or ashes of the quinine plant. Three or four tymz a day, everything stopped for the coca break. For the Peruvian Indianz, it had been the pause — from tyme immemorial — that refreshes, stimulates, sharpenz the mind and increases physical ability. Through the refinement of the South American coca leaf, a constellation of alkaloid drugz, called cocaine, were derived. Today, the coca plant is now grown in the West Indies, Java, Sumatra and other parts of the tropical world. In North America, the second-native Americanz chewed or smoked tobacco, while in West Afrika, the natives had a habit of gettin' high from chewing kernelz of the cola nut, which contained caffeine.

In the ol' dayz of the South, many hedz used Coca-Cola as a remedy for headaches. Back then, drug pushing was a multibillion dollar LEGAL operation. *"Opium, cocaine, morphine and later heroin were advertised on the front pages of newspaperz and magazines as a cure for everything form syphilis to bad breath,"* writes Dufty.

The Coca-Cola addiction became the driving force, becoming a multimillion dollar business in the South. In the 1890s, Coca-Cola was advertised as "A Wonderful Nerve and Brain Tonic and Remarkable Therapeutic Agent." In 1906, after the passing of the first Pure Food and Drug Law, the federal government took a look into this liquid "Coke" phenomenon. The Bureau of Chemistry of the US. Department of Agriculture analyzed the drink and brought charges against Coca-Cola, charging misbranding against the manufacturerz and dealerz.

The main cat behind this was the BOC (The Bureau of Chemistry) founder and chief, Dr. Harvey W. Wiley, who later wrote how Coca-Cola got around the indictment, *"Those who adulterated our food and drugs foresaw that if they could cripple the activities of the Bureau of Chemistry, they could save themselves from indictments. They proceeded with successful lines to effect this paralysis."* None of the higher authorities in government would co-sign the BOC's findingz. Finally, the Bureau was ordered to override Wiley's case and cease and desist in its activities in trying to get

Coca-Cola to the court system. How did this happen?

Well, a newspaper owner from Atlanta, Mr. Seely, came to Washington to ask Wiley Y he was pressing criminal charges against the manufacturerz of ketchup and sting beanz yet was layin' off Coca-Cola. He showed Seely the orderz from the secretary of Agriculture and Seely shot right over to the secretary's office to beef. He threatened to publicize all the gory detailz in his paper unless the secretary recalled the order. After a lil' pressure, Wiley was allowed to continue his prosecution. But here's the catch, publicly the DOA (Department of Agriculture) gave the go-ahead to prosecute because they had no choice. But on the private tip, they did every dirty and mischievous deed they could to derail Wiley's case.

Wiley wanted to try the case at Coca-Cola's bottling headquarterz, Chattanooga, Tennessee. After a hot-contested trial, the attorneyz of Coca-Cola moved to dismiss the case on a mere technicality, citing caffeine, the deadliest substance in the drink, was not an added substance under the law because it was part of the original formula. The judge granted the dismissal and Wiley tried it on the Supreme Court level. The Supreme Court gave them static, citing that caffeine was an added substance and that Coca-Cola was a descriptive and not a distinctive name. Coca-Cola was in deep shit. *"What Coca-Cola undertook to do behind the scenes to save its corporate life, we can only surmise. When brought back into court in Chattanooga in 1917, Coca-Cola pleaded no contest."*

Check what their sentence was… The company was ordered to pay all costs of the suit and the 40 barrelz and 20 kegz of the drink that were seized from them, given back with the provision that they cannot sell or dispose of it outside of its founding state, Georgia. In addition, the judge added a safety valve clause: *"…Judgement of forfeiture shall not be binding up on the said Coca-Cola Company or it's product except as to this cause, and the particular goods seized herein…"* Say what?!!? We all know how YT likes to use tricknology and the English language can be one of the most at tymz. So, here's the DGT translation: in other wordz, this noodle-back, paid-off judge tellz Coca-Cola they can't sell the 40 barrelz and 20 kegz of Cola that were seized before the trial in no other state than Georgia, BUT were free to go ahead and sell OTHER barrelz and kegz in states in and outside of Georgia! What a mind fuck!!

Yearz later, Wiley reflects, *"…Owing to a lack of these proceedings, the Coca-Cola Company has its stock now listed on the New York Stock Exchange. Its sales have been enormously increased, invading the North, as they previously invaded the South. The effect of drinking caffeine on an empty stomach and in a free state are far more dangerous than drinking an equal quantity of caffeine wrapped up with tannic acid in tea and coffee. The threat to health and happiness of our people is reaching far greater proportions due to this expansion of trade. The governors of the New York Exchange have admitted the stock of the Coca-Cola Company, the products of which have been condemned by a United States court as both adulterated and misbranded."*

When will we realize see there's a massive attack on our health?!

LIK SHOT!

The war against your immune system is on and is hasn't stopped!! This is a part of the ongoing saga to elevate the Afrikan warrior to the level of *"Summon Bonum"* or *"Greatest Good"* our Kemetic Ancestorz practiced as a way of life. As said before, if you do not have your health, you are not as free as you think! If your temple (body) is filled with toxinz, your mind is. Yes, even you 'Afrocentric kid', who thinks he got all da knowledge but won't stop eating decayed flesh, drinking soda and smokin' blunts!

Y, we all pretty much know we have been in a messed-up situation for millenniumz, have we not gotten ourselves out of it? Y did Martin fail us? Y is Jesse failing us?? Y are the so-called black organization's (NAACP, Urban League, Churches, etc) failing us??? Because they do not realize we are POWz! That's right, Sun, we are prisonerz of war and still think someone's (namely the mystery god) is gonna pay our ransom! Would it shock you if I told you there IS NO RANSOM??!! No one's gonna save us *but us,* so let's get in on!

The next culprit on the map of Afrikan dissection is the fluoride conspiracy. The National Fluoridation Campaign of the late 1940s, launched by the Rockefeller Foundation, is enthusiastically supported by the nationz dental profession. Through research and study we find the principal source of fluoridation is the poisonous chemical 'sodium fluoride', also known as RAT POISON!

This poison can be found in our nationz public drinking water! We also found there were unsafe levelz of chlorine, lead and other toxic substances in the water as well. Over some 38 million Americanz have been drinking unsafe water for 50 yearz!

Aluminum, Sodium and Fluoride are the primary elements of poisonz. What would make you think these 3 lethal substances combined does not have a dramatic effect on your immune system? The reason this conspiracy was developed was, of course, because the wicked white beast, aka the Illuminati, have been on a global conquest since their origin!

We find it is very expensive for aluminum companies to dispose of aluminum because it does not degrade. It also accumulates in the body. Each day you add a little more to your sodium fluoride reserves each tyme you drink a glass of water or brush your teeth with fluoridated toothpaste.

U.S. PUBLIC HEALTH SERVICE ALLOWS THIS TO EXIST

We see that the origin of the sodium fluoride conspiracy stemz from close allies of the

Chase Manhattan Banks and other Rockefeller interests.

The source of much of this substance is ALCOA, a $5 billion a year corporation. The present chairman (as of '92), William H. Krome George was an active director of the well-publicized US USSR Trade and Economic Council intended to rescue the Soviet Union from economic oblivion. ALCOAs president, William B. Renner, who is also director of Shell Oil Company – now controlled by Rothschilds interest, and John A. Mayer serves as director of HJ Heinz Company, Mellon Bank, and Norfolk & Western Railway.

USPHS noted in Washington Post (April 20, 1988), *"...the PHS estimates that each year (the aluminum manufacturerz) $2 billion is saved through water fluoridation."* What is saved? The estimated $2 billion it would take to dispose aluminum.

The head of the USPHS during the entire fluoridation campaign was Oscar Ewing, a graduate of Harvard Law School, who ran a profitable Wall Street practice, can be linked as a close associate with the Rockefeller Foundation. He also served as then president, Truman's head of the Federal Security Agency – which encompassed the USPHS, the Social Security Administration, and the Office of Education. Ewing is most noted for his campaign for greater government control over the citizenz of the US. In Eustace Mullin's, Murder By Injection, *"He (Ewing) was particularly anxious to increase control of medical education, a prime goal of the Rockefeller interests since 1898."* Of Ewing, Mullins also states, *"Mr. Ewing is one of the highly paid lawyers for the Aluminum Company of America (ALCOA). It was hardly accidental that Washington, DC, where Oscar Ewing was king, was one of the first large American cities to fluoridate its water supply. At the same time, Congressmen and other politicians in Washington were privately alerted by Ewing's minions that they should be careful about ingesting the fluoridated water. Supplies of bottled water from mountain springs then appeared in every office on Capitol Hill; these have been maintained continuously ever since, at the taxpayers' expense." The key words are "these have been maintained continuously"*, meaning the recent hot-trend of people buying bottled water is some 50 yearz late!!

In fact, one Senator carried with him a small flask of spring water whenever he dined in DCs most fashionable restaurants assuring his companionz that *"not one drop of fluoridated water will ever pass my lips."* These are the people most of us voted for; the people some of ya'll choose as your leaderz! Ewing is also responsible for enrolling the US in the United Nations' World Health Organization (WHO).

Chase Manhatten Bank (front-name for another Rockefeller operation) showed crucial concern in overseeing the installation of sodium fluoride equipment in most of the nationz largest cities. Fluorides have long been a source of contamination in the US. Large quantities are produced by the giant chemical firmz:

1)American Agricultural Products Corp.
2)Hooken Chemical
3)ALCOA – Aluminum Company Of America

The American Agricultural Products Corp. produces enormous waste quantities of fluoride in preparing fertilizer from phosphate rock. Some of the waste is used in pesticides, until the Department of Agriculture banned their use of being too dangerous to the public. As if to say as long as the danger is not 'too' dangerous, it's tolerated by the government. Because, of course, if people started dropping like flies, their operation would be blown; therefore the approach of a 'slow-kill' is more suitable because it will not be seen as an epidemic. As a result, they pumped the waste into the ocean despite the Department of Agriculture's prohibition. It is clearly evident these beasts' have no respect for Nature (The Creator), which in turnz, meanz they have no luv for you, Afrikan, for we are the children of Nature.

Hooken Chemical became part of Rockefeller network when Blanchotte Hooken married John D. Rockefeller, III; and ALCOA is another Rockefeller operation. Hooken Chemical, for example, pumps 100,000 tonz of fluorides into atmosphere a year. They pipe another 500,000 tonz into the nationz water supply each year in addition to the amount of fluoride used in "treating" our drinking water.

IMMEDIATE AND LONG-TERM EFFECTS OF FLUORIDE AND ALUMINUM

The immediate and long-term effects fluoride has on people denotes crucial attention. Fluoride slowz down the vitally important DNA repair enzyme activity of the immune system. Once the enzyme becomes inefficient, AIDS is developed. As you can see you can develop AIDS without having sex, keep drinking public/tap water. Fluoride is effective even in concentrationz as low as one part per million, the standard dosage which the USPHS set for our drinking water. At this concentration, fluoride can cause serious chromosomal damage changing normal cellz into cancer cellz. It also causes interference with the body's production of important neurotransmitters in the lowel level of the brain. Neurotransmitterz protect you against seizures, strokes and brain damage.

Some immediate effects fluoride has on the body are sudden mood changes, severe headaches, nausea, hallucinationz, irregular breathing, night twitching, damage to fetuses, and various formz of cancer. Fluoride depletes the energy reserves and the ability of white blood cells to properly destroy foreign agents by the process of phagocytosis. As little as 0.2 ppm fluoride stimulates superoxide production in resting white blood cellz, virtually abolishing phagocytosis. White blood cellz serves as very vital elements of your immune system fighting diseases of all types. However, if consuming fluoride, it confuses the immune system and causes it to attack the body's own tissues, and increases the tumor growth rate in cancer prone individualz. Fluoride also is know by many doctorz to depress the process of thyroid activity, as well developing bone cancer, causing premature aging of the human body and, according to Dr. William Marcus, show *"evidence of (causing) bone fractures, arthritis, mutagenicity and other effects."*

When scientists found that one part per million dosages of fluoride transformz normal cellz into cancer cellz, the fluoridation program should have been halted immediately. The government agencies realized if they did, they would open the door for thousandz of lawsuits against the government.

The death rate among elderly people from kidney and heart disease began to rise steadily in the first cities to begin fluoridating their water. This was the "final solution" to the problem of social security payments. By the government knowing most will die before reaching the age to receive social security, as well as those so sick that their checks go right to the hospitalz, they have been able to pull of one of biggest 'pimp tricks' the world has ever known!

FLUORIDE USED AS A 'CONTROLLING' MECHANISM

Ewing and his crew were also aware of Soviet studies showing that fluoride was extremely important in introducing a docile, sheep-like obedience in the general population. It is a little known fact that fluoride compoundz were added to the drinking water of prisonerz to keep them docile and inhibit questioning of authority in both Nazi prison camps in WWII and in the Soviet gulags in Siberia.

The passivity and unwillingness to challenge any authority is merely the first achievement of the fluoridation campaign. This is its initial effect upon the central nervous system and the further deadly effects on the kidneyz, heart and other organz, as well as the widespread development of new and fast spreading cancerz is yet to come. This is probably Y the Afrikan community feelz helpless in the fucked-up situation we're in. Many are upset, but a very small percentage have actually walked what they've talked. That is Y we can talk about revolution and never do nothing about it (also because we do not come with an economic agenda – besides boycotting, which we know, cain't last if there are no Afrikan business' as an alternative)!

To speed it up, not only are American kids given fluoridated water, they are told to brush their teeth at least 3 tymz a day with heavily fluoridated toothpaste. Toothpaste containz 7% sodium fluoride. Children habitually ingest about 10% of the solution each brushing giving them a daily dose of 30% of the 7% solution in toothpaste.

WHAT CAN WE DO??

In the true spirit of holistic studying, it wouldn't be right to leave ya'll with no solutionz after the shit I just laid on you. If we continue to study the negative situation we habitually, as a people, have found ourselves in, we will find solutionz that will break the chain!

For one, some may think we should start buying our water from the store and we'll be better off! WRONG! I used to think that...until I saw an expiration date on the container! Ask yourself, *"If the spring water is natural, Y is there an expiration date?!"* Evidently it ain't as natural as we're led to believe.

And if you continue to think about it, we didn't see the water come from the mountainz, for all we know this is tap-water with a price tag on it!! Go one step better...

1)START BOILING YOUR WATER!! And most importantly, DO NOT BOIL THE WATER IN ALUMINUM POTS!

2)Have you and your seedz start brushing your teeth with unfluoridated toothpaste. Just because you may find the Food AND Drug Administration (FDA) won't approve it does not mean it is not good for you. Afterall, if any food product does not have drugz in it, they won't approve it anyway, that's Y they're called FOOD *AND* DRUG!

The FDA tellz you fluoride fights cavities, but it actually creates them! The contents of a family-sized tube of fluoridated toothpaste is enuff to kill a 25 pound child!! In 1991, the Akron (Ohio) Regional Poison Center reported that *"death has been reported following ingestion of 16mg/kg of fluoride. Only 1/10 of an ounce of fluoride could kill a 100 pound adult. According to the Center, fluoride toothpaste contains up to 1mg/gram of fluoride."*

Even Proctor and Gamble, a known white supremacist cult and the makerz of Crest, acknowledge that a family-sized tube theoretically containz enuff fluoride to kill a small child.

Think about it, if everyone had perfect teeth, would your dentist have a job? Now do you see Y he gives you fluoride at your checkups?! We must overstand government (facilitated by the Illuminati family) like the FDA and the ADA (American Dental Association – also started by Rockefeller) does not want you to take your health into your own handz. Our Kemetic Ancestorz had their teeth while building pyramidz, so Y should you feel we couldn't now?!

3)Discard of all aluminum pots, panz and cooking utensilz! Toxinz go into foodz cooked. If you choose to still use aluminum pots, do not leave cooked foodz in them for more than a few minutes. Foodz cooked in aluminum pots, along with fluoridated water, quickly forms a highly poisonous compound. According to Dr. McGuigan's testimony in a famous court hearing on aluminum effects, the Royal Baking Powder case, he revealed that extensive research had shown that boiling water in aluminum pots produced hydro-oxide poisonz; boiling vegetables produced hydro-oxides as well; boiled eggz produced a phosphate poison; and meat produced a chloride poison. Any food cooked in aluminum containerz would neutralize the digestive juices producing acidosis (gas) and ulcerz.

The use of these pots may be responsible for the widespread indigestion in America, which the necessitated the ingesting with large amounts of antacids containing even more aluminum! A study showed that people, after cooking with aluminum pots over a period form 20-40 yearz, began to experience serious memory loss. Their mental capacities then deteriorated rapidly until they were totally unable to fend for themselves or to recognize their spouses of many yearz.

This is Alzheimerz Disease, Sun!! 2.5 million Americanz have the incurable Alzheimerz disease. The disease strikes the neurotransmitterz of the brain (done by fluoride). The principle agent is the accumulation of aluminum deposits on the principal nerves of the brain. Alzheimerz causes more than 100,000 deaths a year, ranking as the 4 leading cause of death in the US. We find Americanz have been ingesting aluminum since 1920s!

4)Try to eliminate purchasing canned (aluminum) goodz and sodas. They contain high levelz of sodium along with being sealed in aluminum for long periodz of tyme – sometymz over 3 yearz!! Purchase fresh fruits and beanz.

5)Some other thingz to stay from: a)Women, stay away from douches! They now contain aluminum, which injects this toxin directly into the system and can cause a miscarriage or stillbirths.

b)Painkillerz or aspirin like Bufferin and Advil. They contain enormous levelz of aluminum. Many sistaz take Advil during their menstrual cycle. This, along with a poor diet, is the main reason Y your cramps hurt so much!

c)Baking Powder (Soda) used in cake mixes, frozen dough, self-rising flour and processed foodz. If you know cake rises with heat, Y don't you think it will continue to rise once in you when your body maintainz the temperature of 98.6°??!!'

d)Antacid products like Mylanta and Pepto-Bismol which are loaded with aluminum; and

e)Aluminum foil (ie. Reynolds Wrap), toothpaste tubes laced with aluminum, aluminum sealz on food and drink products and soda canz. Y do you think they want you to recycle aluminum? 'Cause they can't dispose of it and it also continues to make these white supremacist families and organizations rich!

LIK SHOT!!

"There are negroes who will never fight for freedom. There are negroes who will seek profit for themselves from the struggle. There are even some negroes who will cooperate with their oppressors. The hammer blows of discrimination, poverty and segregation must warp and corrupt some. No one can pretend that because a people may be oppressed, every individual member is virtuous and worthy."

— Martin Luther King, Jr.

First, let me say this… I am an extremist. Although we live in a society with other ethnicities including europeanz, there is no reason Y we Afrikanz should allow them join with us in everything we do. Can't we Afrikanz have at least ONE thing for us without YT bein' there?!!? So before you pass judgment, ask yourself, Y IZ it Dat everytyme we have a function, there's at least one european amongst us?!

I write the piece in the spirit of millionz of Afrikanz who perished during the Middle Passage as well as author/historian/activists Dr. Francess Cress-Welsing, Del Jones, Nielly Fuller, Phil Valentine, Kola Boof and Bobby Hemmitt.

This past June 14th, the annual tribute to our Ancestorz who endured the Maangamizi, or Middle Passage was held at Coney Island, Brooklyn, New York. I awoke to the vybrating heat of Ra (the Sun), with the sound of birdz spittin' the word for their flock. I arose still emitting high frequency charges from the subliminal movienite I attended the nite before. Needless to say, I was ready for what the day was to bring me...

I linked up with my peeps and ventured to Coney Island to pay respect to those Ancestorz who physically perished during the crossing of the Atlantic Ocean, several hundred yearz ago. Little did I know my day would awaken me to somethin' more vital than celebrating our Ancestorz…

Upon reachin' the beach, I saw from afar a mighty red, black and green flag waving, serving as the welcoming spot for the congregation. It was nothin' but luv, poundz and handshakes as I made myself a part of the vybration. After watchin' a few poets spit wordz of truth on our legacy, I ventured onto the beach.

" ...[T]hey further consolidate white nationalism under 'The New World Order.' They're talented in disrupting, destroying and dismantling other cultures. This fact has never been truly dealt with. In fact, they propagate that the highest achievement to reach for is global integration, while making it impossible to obtain."

— Del Jones, Culture Bandits

CULTURE BANDITS

As I began my trek from the boardwalk down to the edge of the North Atlantic, I thought my eyes were seein' white spots, because as I drew closer to the drummerz circle — where a congregation of Afrikanz were dancing and chanting encircling a collage of Afrikan drummerz, I saw a not so pleasant site... WHITE PEOPLE! Crackuhz to the left of me, crackuhz to my right, sprinkled throughout! Some with jembe drumz, and many dressed in Afrikan garb!!

I've notice over the yearz, europeanz showin' up at events that are blatantly and exclusively for Afrikanz. Even at my magazine's 10th Year/100th Issue celebration a few crackuhz came! Dam yo, cain't Afrikanz have just ONE THING EXCLUSIVELY FOR OURSELVES without YT showin' up?!!? But this was only the beginning...

My spirit changed, it went from celebrative to defensive-mode. I suddenly felt our culture was subtly bein' attacked and, as alwayz, we were to asleep to recognize it. I've found this tolerance to be accepted amongst all events created around Afrikan celebrationz. Over the past year or so, I been starting to realize a lot of our Elderz are passing on to the next level of life, therefore makin' us next in line in the realm of the heirz of our legacy, so it was not a coincidence that my vybration turned to "battle-and-protect" mode.

As the apparent distaste was evident on my face, a couple of my peoples spoke and grimaced as well as we spoke under our breaths about the bullshit we was seein'. I was vexed and even after a couple agreein' facial nodz of *"I know, this is wack, but don't let it stress you,"* I chose to let it stress me... as stolen descendants from Afrika, we were out there paying homage to our Ancestorz and the very descendants of the culprits responsible for this tragedy flocked amongst us willingly! Our culture was under attack and somethin' had to be done!

I tried envisioning what our Ancestorz woulda thought had they seen what we were doing. Even though we were from various tribes on those ships, we understood one universal thought... we were kidnapped and it was these pale-skinned europeanz who did it! The rage that must've ran through their veinz long ago — seein' their mates, daughterz, sonz, brotherz, sisterz and elderz chained up and stuffed inside the bottom of the box like luggage on a Greyhound bus; watchin' countless Afrikanz, tied to large stones and dragged off the side of the ship, left as shark bate; the chopping off of the limbz, armz and handz, the castration of the Elderz used to instill the fear so there'd be no uprising on the ships; and the trail of blood, the stench of death, mixed with a concoction of fear, not knowin' if you'd be the next example — began to race through my veinz. What would they do if they saw us appearing to let them be amongst us in celebration of their tragedy? There is no mistake in my mind they would attack these crackuhz knowin' their intentionz were to steal us away! Our culture was under attack!!

There was one situation where an inebriated white female that walked in and out of the circle, botherin' Afrikanz left and right, yet everyone seemed to ignore her. Now, this woman was already possessed by "spirits", so I looked at her as an immediate threat! I noticed her peripherally from my left. I watched as she walked up to each Afrikan tryin' to get close and probably speak some nonsense. And of course, I was in her path. As each Afrikan stepped aside ignoring her, passing her off to the next like a hot potato, she began to walk towardz me.

I said to myself, "I ain't movin'! I'm not going to yield to this wicked spirit!" Sure enuff, she came up to me and began to slur somethin' to me. I told her simply not to speak to me and to keep it movin'. Of course, as with any wicked spirit, they don't back down easily. So this woman continues to walk closer to me and this tyme, in front of me! Before she could utter another syllable, I raised my voice on purpose, *"Yo, get the fuck away from me!"* I said it loud thinkin' otherz would see that you can tell YT what you really feelin'. But I was faced with a dilemma, see, she STILL didn't move! She took another step toward me, this tyme, she was inside my circle, a foot or two in front of me. Initially, I felt I was within' my rights to check her chin, but instead, I mooshed her in the face, pushing her backward. She regrouped and began to walk toward me again, I clutched my fist, ready to defend myself, and she walked away callin' me everything in the book, except the 'N' word (no matter how drunk she was, she knew that was not the place to say that!).

After the small victory, I thought maybe the next Afrikan would be just as adamant as I as the woman continued to approach another Afrikan a few steps away. To no avail, I found no one took such action. Everyone else pretty much tolerated her presence by ignoring her. This is where the mistake is made.

See, as we continue to ignore YT as they come to our sacred events, they seem to get the notion they are welcome. Although the consensus (based on facial gestures) seemz we do not want them there, very few — to none, dare do or say something about it.

I can recall yearz back when I first noticed YT comin' to Coney Island for the ceremony. At first they stood on the outside of circle, as if they knew they could not just walk up and join the festivities. Nowadayz, they're wearin' garb, leading chants and even dancing in front of the drummerz circle, while we watch and do nothing. If we keep this up, in the next couple of yearz, they will be numerically the majority at the tribute! Now how backwardz is that?! A majority white audience "paying homage" to our Ancestorz?! Don't believe YT would try to a take over? Need we yet anutha lesson?! Have not the theft of jazz, rock & roll, their current taking of Hiphop?? Makes me wonder if they'd actually be thankin' them for makin' it over here, for had they not, they (YT) would not have the wealth they have! But the shit didn't stop there…

As individualz made peace with our Ancestorz in their own way — some standing along the shoreline staring out as far as the eye could reach, others dancing, as well as some standing in peace, praying — I noticed there were several white photographerz taking shots. There were some amateur photographerz, but there also were, what looked to be, professionalz. What really did it was when I saw an entire film crew zoom in on many of us as we "ignored" the oppressorz descendants capture us on film — without our permission! I mean, they had the big cameras as well as carrying big stage lights! This wasn't no fashion shoot, these were Afrikanz tryin' to have a moment with our Ancestorz, this shit didn't need to be filmed. What, they gonna put it on DVD and sell it back to us or somethin'?!

Standing next to a good friend of mine, we both were like, *"What da fuck?! These hedz are takin' pictures and filming, disturbing our vybration, without even askin' us if we mind!!"* No one, I mean, NO ONE was sayin' shit to them, yet you'd see a look of displeasure on many faces. It was then that she was like, "yo, handle that!" It was as if Queen Tiye had summoned me for a mission. She emphasized, "that's what we need you Bruthaz to do... defend us!" Up until that point, I was doin' exactly what everyone else was... NOTHING! Without hesitation, I headed directly toward the cameraman.

I asked him who gave him authority to come out here and film us without askin' our permission. He was shook, 'cause obviously he felt (1) ain't nobody gonna say nothin' and/or (2) every Black person wants to be on tv or print! We're born to entertain!

I made a point to be loud, loud enuff that otherz would hear, so that they would no longer fear! After makin' enuff of a scene, I was approached by Muriel A. Stockdale, producer and director of New York Spirit. I directed the same question to her regarding her authority. I made it known that we all did not feel comfortable with them bein' here filming without asking and not knowing Y they were there. With her fake soft-spoken, *"I-don't-mean-to-harm"* voice, she stated she had gotten permission from the creator and promoter of the Tribute to the Ancestorz, Tony Akeem.

Shocked that Bro. Akeem would have this white crew out here and not an Afrikan one, she further stated she thought he made us all aware they'd be there, which I find would be impossible unless you disclosed this on the flyer (which it wasn't). She explained she was using the footage as a documentary on the different wayz people in New York worship and practice their spiritual belief system. As enlightening as that may sound, I still felt their presence should not have been there and in a non-threatening way, let her know it.

Within a couple minutes, they packed up and left. Right after, several Bruthaz walked up to me sayin' how they felt the same way, that they shouldn't have been here. I said to myself, *"Y didn't ya'll say shit?!"* I couldn't be mad 'cause before that Sista "checked-me," I was doin' the same thing they were!

This made me immediately think about the 3-point program, the elite white supremacist's put out during the 60s. They noted that (3 being the highest and most threatening) any organization ran by men received 1 point; any organization ran by men AND women received 2 points; and any organization ran by women received 3 points!!

It took an Afrikan woman to check me, making me realize that we Afrikanz (men especially) need to standup and be the protectorz of our culture we're s'posed to be!! No longer should we hold our tongues when we plan events for our people. YT wearz clothes the way we do, try to speak the way we do, sleep with our women, sleep with our men, try to sing and dance to our music, again I ask, *"can't we Afrikanz have at least ONE thing exclusively for ourselves?!!?"* This will only happen if we demand it!

If YT wants to atone for what their foreparents did to us, they need not do it with us. They should have their own ceremony amongst themselves, one-on-one with THEIR ancestorz dishonoring the horrendous deedz they did across the globe. When Afrikan people decide to 'Never Forget' as the so-called Jew does, we will no longer allow them to be amongst us. They will be ousted on some straight up on some, as Dead Prez puts it, *"RBG (Revolutionary But Gangsta) shit!"*

Follow up on the status of the white group who's responsible for "documenting" this past tribute to our Ancestorz at Coney Island. The party responsible is Muriel A. Stockdale, Director/Producer of New York Spirit (www.newyorkspirit.us), Manech Ibar and Casey Fitzpatrick. Muriel can be reached at 810 Broadway, NYC 10003, (212)475.1875 | email: muriela@nyc.rr.com. Swarm them with questionz of what they intend to do with the footage, do they intend to make a profit/are they receiving some kind of funding/corporate support and if so, how do they plan on compensating those used in the footage (without permission).

As the next generation of vanguardz to the Afrikan legacy, we must ask overstand that if we continue to stand idle, YT will come and colonize our culture just as they colonized Afrika.

LIK SHOT!

RHYMIN': REALITY OR ILLUSION

BY M'BWEBE AKA JEHVON BUCKNER

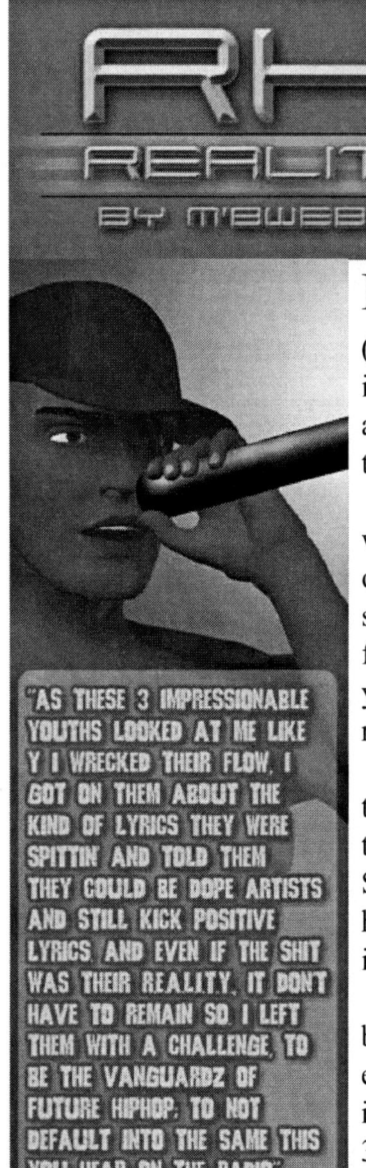

I can recall a joint KRS-One did called R.E.A.L.I.T.Y. (Rhymz Equal Actual Life In The Youth); when I first heard it, I felt the acronym applied. But when really lookin' at life as it today, the rhymz (or vybrationz) our youth are hearin' today has become more destructive than productive.

Take for instance, we all can attest to the reason we hear what we hear on the radio 25-8 (not 24-7). The ones mainly responsible is obviously the white corporate structure who pour in millionz of dollarz to these stationz – from record labelz to gear, to fast-food chainz – ensuring yet anutha week of bling-bling, bang-bang and kill dat nigga joints. And this shit is addictive yo!

Even to the most conscious hed, if they listen enuff, they will find themselves chantin' the latest WACK cut from the Hot Boyz, Master P or yes, even JayZ (lyrically/morally). So think, if it affects your subconscious so easily, think of how effortlessly it affects the "reality" – which is actually an illusion – of our youth?!!?

It doesn't take a brain surgeon to realize the forces behind this. The white corporate structure allots millionz each month to ensure that the troposphere is filled more immoral HipHop. Take a survey yourself! For 1 hour, even 30 minutes, listen to HOT97, Power 105.1 or any other HipHop station around the country. Make sure you listen between the hourz of 3 and 8pm weekdayz or any tyme Saturday. Y? Because these tymz represent the hourz our youth have the most access because they are not in school (as if *that's* a better place!).

As you write down each song, take the tyme to actually listen to the lyrics. Percentage-wise, you will find that well over 90% of the lyrics you hear will mention blazin' some weed, extacy, bitches, hoes, hustlin' drugz, benjaminz, some bangin' ice, 20-inches, SUVs, gunz, thugz, criminalz, gangstaz, niggaz, some kind of alcoholic beverage and all other termz and acronymz under the same family.

The society we live in today revolves around money. Paper allowz you to get thingz. Most equate anything to money and the average hed seez that as success. The unfortunate thing is the ethics behind gettin' this cash is simply there are no ethics.

Forreal, hedz ain't lyin' when they say, *"I'ma do what I gotta do to get this c.r.e.a.m.* ('**C**ash **R**ules **E**verything **A**round **M**e', a phrase created by Wu-Tang)*."* What that entailz, well, if you don't have a clue, you are actually given hundredz of testimoneez via the airwaves everyday ALL day (although most are ficticious).

One Friday eve around 7pm I was drivin' home down Fulton Street, in Bedstuy, Brooklyn, when I thought I'd give HOT97 anutha chance. FunkMaster Flexx is on speakin' with a married so-called "heterosexual" female who called in talkin' about how she was bein' fondled by another female homosexual and was *"likin' it!"* I mean, she was goin' all into detail, over the air, yo! And Flexx was geesin' her on, gettin' her to dwell into specifics!!

Within' the first few secondz, I switched to the cassette player, but then thought I should listen just to see how far Flexx would go. The ill shit is that all of New York gotta hear yet anutha Sista get caught up in the wicked-imbalanced-european-originated act of homosexuality.

I thought to myself, it's evident Funk Flexx don't give 2 shits about how many youth's are listening to this. On top of that, think of how many impressionable hedz – not just youth's, but even adults – that may get the message that, *"yo, participatin' in homosexual acts ain't so bad."* [NOTE] This piece ain't about homosexuality (including bisexualz), but I do have just one thing to say about it: Homosexuality is ANTI-LIFE! The primary use for sex is for procreation. Now how you gonna have a baby with 2 guyz or 2 girlz?!!? And because of the backward nature of europeanz, they felt they could handle that problem by developing artificial insemination – but isn't it like YT to create somethin' that goes against the lawz of Nature?!

Not only are our youths bein' sent confusing sexual lifestyles, they're being taught what success is based on.

Case in point, I drive up to the local gas station to fill up and I'm approached by 3 shorteez, no younger than about 8, no older than 10. They step to me sayin' they rap for money and if I'd like to hear some rhymz. I was like, -ight. Plus I admired the fact that they seem to be true HipHop hedz who were focused on earning a lil' cash for somethin' they dedicated themselves to.

So, the first shorty starts, and he immediately talks about how much ice he got, how many *"Bitches"* he's sexed, how many glocks he's popped and no sooner than I was able to digest what he just said, shorty #2 flowz in. He spittin' 'bout bakin' bricks, poppin' Crystal and chillin' at the VIP with all the loot he got!

YO! These youth's were 8 and 10 year oldz, Sun! They all sounded like little Prodigy, Nelly and Beanie Sigel's!

I wasn't gonna give shorty #3 a chance. I immediately butted in, *"Yo, yo, yo! Shorty, what'chu sayin'?!"* I thought to myself, they talkin' 'bout how much paper they got yet they at the gas station askin' *me* for money to rhyme, plus he about 12 semesterz from even bein' legally able to even sit behind the wheel of an SUV!!

Rhymin' is a vital part of growin' up for young Afrikan men in America just like playin' basketball. It's one of the several thingz that help define our manhood. Even more profound is recognizing the innate power of creativity the Afrikan Diaspora possesses. Just like how we've been able to have the world embrace our interpretation of what basketball is, so have we revolutionized music. The difference can be seen in just one generation. Look at white parents and how they dress, talk and walk and look at their kidz; take a look at Orientalz, how many young Orientalz do you see wearin' their custom clothin'; they wearin' RocaWear and FUBU!

I knew they did nothin' they spoke of, but I also knew they felt if you rhyme, this is what you gotta rhyme about. This is not the R.E.A.L.I.T.Y. KRS is speakin' of; this is the ILLUSION!! The sad shit about it is that although they may not be doin' this shit now, a large percentage of youths will eventually gravitate to it.

So what do we, who see this madness, do about it? For one, the airwaves must be attacked! Afterall, this is one of the main sources (music videos included). Stationz like HOT97, need to be changed or as Chuck D used to say, *"Shut 'Em Down!"*

Second, and in the meantyme, as parents, cousinz and/or friendz, we *are* the balance. We need to speak with those youths in our lives and ask them who they like to listen to and how does their lyrics affect them.

The youths pick up after what they see and hear. If we set the example of being critical analyst's of HipHop – OUR creation – plus with computerz bein' able to burn your own CDs, we owe it to our future to give them balanced HipHop. Purchase the joints MTV and BET don't play, pull out those old CDs and make a copy for your peoples. And most importantly remain vocal. Devise a plan to get these stationz to hear our plea. If boycotts is your thing, organize them, but not without givin' alternatives! Because if we don't do nothin' soon it will be your 5 year old spittin' Mobb Deeps, *"Kill That Nigga!"*

As these 3 impressionable youths looked at me like Y I wrecked their flow, I got on them about the kind of lyrics they were spittin' and told them they could be dope artists and still kick positive lyrics. And even if the shit they were sayin' was their R.E.A.L.I.T.Y. it don't have to remain their reality.

I left them with a challenge, to be the vanguardz of our future, to not default into the same shit you hear on the radio and dare to be different, to sound different, which in this case, is to sound POSITIVE!

They looked back at me with both a look of wonderment and *"whatver, yo",* I broke 'em off with $7 each and gave them a copy of my magazine. I felt my seed had been planted for the day. Hopefully they'll be able to cultivate it.

LIK SHOT!

It should not surprise you when you hear that when the persianz, romanz and then the greeks came into Afrika, along with the murder and plagiarizm, they helped themselves to the wealth and monumental structures of the Nile Valley.

The limestone from the Pyramidz of Giza, for example, were stripped and used to build virtually all the churches in Rome. It's been documented of the 14 or so obelisks (originally called Tekhen) that were stolen still standing erect today in places like the Vatican and in the middle of New York City's Central Park.

The fight for the return of these monuments had been a tumultuous battle until recent when in 2002 Italy agreed to return an over 2500 year-old, 200-ton, 78-ft. Obelisk of Axum which stood in downtown Rome for some 70 yearz. The Obelisk served as a constant reminder of one of the 20th centuries most vicious war crimes as Mussolini invaded Ethiopia, putting under his rule from 1935-41 and introducing the first use of an aerial assault using poison gas on civilianz and soldierz [it must be noted that Mussolini, like Napoleon – who, in 1899 came to KMT and saw the Afrikan features of Her-Em-Akhet (erroneously called the Sphinx), saw that KMT was as, if not more civilized than the land he came from – Mussolini went on what he considered a mission to 'civilize' darkest Afrika only to find evidence of a civilization that thrived during the same period as the Roman Empire].

In July, 2003, after several decades of pressure on Italy to return the Obelisk from the African Union, Italy finally began to dismantle the solid granite pillar to be returned to its native Axum in northern Ethiopia .

A 22-ft. piece weighing 40 tonz was removed from the top for the "eventual" voyage back to Afrika. I say "eventual" because, as of June 28, 2004, according to writer, Nicole Martinelli, they've dismantled it, but have yet to send it back home to Ethiopia. Officialz have left the Axum obelisk sitting in three sectionz in an airport warehouse for over six months.

"The trouble?," states Martinelli, *"According to Italian officials, the destination airport in Axum can't handle a landing by cargo planes large enough to transport the pre-Christian era obelisk. Shipping by boat was also considered but nixed because the nearest port – now part of rival neighbor Eritrea – is not considered safe."*

Italy had agreed to give back what Fascist troops took from Ethiopia in the 1930s, but intentionz don't always match actionz as the Afrikan country learned in 1998 after printing commemorative stamps in vain for the expected return of the obelisk. Once returned home, the obelisk would have crowned a UNESCO-protected heritage site of the same name.

Now, as the government ponderz building a monument to Italian soldierz and civilianz killed in the Nov. 12 bombing in Iraq where the Ethiopian obelisk used to stand in Rome's piazza Carpena, those who spent yearz campaigning to get the monument back, wonder what will happen as the dust collects.

"To Ethiopia it is like the Statue of Liberty," teacher Nicola DeMarco stated. *"All the technical excuses made by the Italian government are delay tactics. If Silvio Berlusconi can build a bridge from Calabria to Sicily , he can bridge the gap between Italy and Ethiopia with this small gesture."*

Head of the Axum Obelisk Return Committee Richard Pankhurst sayz it's time to end the foot-dragging. He says the airport in Axum , recently expanded and reinforced, is capable of handling the precious but weighty shipment. *"After so many years we are tired of such excuses, it shouldn't take another half century to get back what is ours,"* said Pankhurst, 75. *"Many of us would like to see it in its rightful place in our lifetime."*

The question is, will we? Knowin' the wicked wayz of YT (including pale-imposter italianz who deny their Moorish origin), many of us won't.

UPDATE: SHOULD WE BE SATISFIED?! Y NOT RETURN THEM ALL!

After 68 yearz, the ancient Axum obelisk – properly called Tekhen (Tekhenwy for more than one) – was returned to it's home in Ethiopia.

The first piece of the 1700 year-old obelisk was stolen from Benito Mussolini and his Italian troops in 1937. The 58-ton middle section came from the Circus Maximus in central Rome to the northern town of Axum, April 20, 2005. Axum was once the center of the Axumite kingdom that lasted just before the tyme of "alleged" birth of the biblical Jesus.

I say alleged because many authorz, including Gerald Massey – who wrote *'The Historical Jesus and the Mythical Christ,'* and Anthony T. Browder proved the biblical Jesus' life is identical to the life of Heru erroneously called Horus of the original trinity, Auset, Ausar and Heru (which is also incorrectly called Isis, Osirus and Horus). In fact, the original trinity is some 4100 yearz *before* christianity!

Now if you're familiar with the legendary Ausarian Drama, it's a story of how Ausar was murdered by his brotha Set (origin of the word 'Satan'). After trickin' Ausar to lay in a coffin, Set murdered him and then cut his body into 14 pieces spreading them everywhere across the world. His wife, Auset, walked the four cornerz of the planet finding every piece of her husband with the exception of one, his penus.

This story is not of a pornographic tone. The Tekhen is symbolic for Ausarz penus. Our Ancestorz of the Nile Valley realized the penus is a vital piece to the creation of life. His son Heru (where the word 'Hero' derived) avenged his fatherz death by fighting Set. From this battle, Ausar was resurrected from death.

Our Ancestorz didn't erect these wonderz in pieces, they were made from one piece of solid stone, hence the reason so many statues and other artifacts are still intact today. Even Her-Em-Akhet is still well carved despite Napoleonz order to blow off the broad Afrikan nose and lips so the world would have trouble seein' Afrikan people were behind the building of these sky scraperz.

When it was stolen by Mussolini's troops, the obelisk was broken into fragments after being toppled during a 16th century Muslim rebellion. Once in Rome, it was restored with metal rodz embedded in concrete. To return to Ethiopia, the obelisk had to again, be dismantled in 2003.

Watch this Video Article (VA), *'Secret In the City'* on my .tv site, DGTv: Conscious Webvision @ *www.daghettotymz.com/dgtv/videoarticles2.html*

Since 1947, after Italy signed a pledge to the United Nationz to return all property stolen from Ethiopia, it wasn't until nearly 70 yearz this relic returned. But after having waited all this tyme, two questionz should follow: (1) Has everything stolen been returned and (2) Y hasn't everything *else* stolen by europeanz, italianz, asianz and the like been returned?!!?

If you were to take a visit to any museum in a major city like New York City or The British Museum, or even if you were to walk down the street, most likely you'd see somethin' that was stolen from Afrika that has yet to be returned.

Browder in his book, *'Exploding the Myths Vol.1: Nile Valley Contributions to Civilization'* revealed several ancient Afrikan artifacts that were stolen from colonialist's who erected these monumental structures still standing today, which in essence continues to celebrate the theft, exploitation and murder of Afrikan people. Many pieces were stolen from the notorious Giovanni Battista Belzoni in the early 1800s, who would later be referred to *as "the greatest plunderer of them all." "Within a period of three years,"* Browder writes, *"Belzoni excavated the Temple of Abu Simbel, gained entry into the Second Pyramid of Giza, discovered the royal tomb of Seti I (father of Rameses II), recovered a statue of Amenhotep III, an obelisk from Philae Temple and a host of numerous other artifacts."*

Browder published a written account of Belzoni's exploits as a tomb raider as well as him describing his reason for living: *"My purpose was to rob the Egyptians of their papyri; of which I found a few hidden in their breasts, under their arms, in the space above their knees, or on the legs, and covered by the numerous folds of cloth."*

Browder pointed out there's tekhenwy at the following places:

1) One pair of Tekhenwy which formery stood at the entrance of the first pylon of the Philae Temple. Belzoni sold it to William Banks for 1000 sterling

poundz. It currently standz on the groundz of the Kingston Lacy House in Dorset, England.

2) There's one right in the middle of St. Peter's Square where the pope gives his annual easter sunday speech.
3) There's the Tekhen of Rameses II in Paris
4) Tekhen of Thutmose III in London
5) There's also one stuck in the middle of Central Park in New York City

Where are our movements to have these historically ital fragments of our legacy returned? Oh no, we should not be satisfied with the return of just *one* stolen piece of our history. Along with the fight for reparationz, we must *insist* that *ALL* of these structures be returned and properly placed where they originated.

And although YT will do everything in their power to delay the return of every item stolen 'cause it would cost them not only a fortune, it would be a confession of their guilt.

It is obvious YT has no intent to return such itemz thus we should've retaliated long ago. I suggest we use the recent momentum gained from the 'Live 8 Concert' which focuses on the AIDS epidemic in Afrika, to publicly put YT on blast and demand for the return of stolen property. This would serve as a warning...

2002

I was buildin' with pham a while back and whatnot and the topic of what God and Jesus looks like came up. Jesus is included because he is said to be the son of God, made in his image. So, takin' this literally — even though bible believerz would say the Bible shouldn't be taken literally — Jesus, bein' a man has identical physical attributes as you would your father and/or mother (as if there's anutha way to take it. I mean, the other way is individual interpretation, now how can I get you to overstand what I'm sayin' if I leave your individual perception to be your guide? If I want you to feel me on what I'm sayin', my best bet is not to confuse you and tell you directly what I mean).

Many of us, when presented the question of God/Jesus' looks, first visualize a picture of the lily-white chi-chi mon with long, straight brown hair. This image can be attributed to the picture-Bibles and framed drawingz on your Grandparents wall. Of course, this is incorrect. After you shake that off, you may envision the black version. Although we've seen black versionz, the physical characteristics are not that different than the white one (ie, locks/dreadz opposed to the long, stringy brown hair). This search for a black identity in white images is a symptom we still suffer from stemming from mentacide (mental suicide). This too is incorrect. Y? Because we allow ourselves to be limited in our thinking. Think outside the mental parameterz society placed on us.

What makes up our environment? Broken to it's origin, it's molecules, electronz and neutronz. These same elements exist not only on Earth, but they do in you; even greater, they exist outside the Earth, that's right, in space! Space has a reading of –273°, which is the frozen state because it is too cold for the molecules to move so they stop (freeze). What makes thingz move if space is so cold are the starz like our star, the Sun. The Sun radiates energy that makes thingz move, like the planets that orbit around it. What happenz when cold meets heat? You get steam! What's the molecular code for steam? H_2O, or water! So, as I said, we are the microcozm of the macro. If there's water on Earth, there is in space and every thing that's of space. The same elements "here" are "out there."

If God is omnipresent (everything), that meanz how we've been programmed to perceive "him" (from here on, I will refer to "God" as "Energy") as human, limits what God is. We are basin' this perception on what's we are used to seein' and not what we haven't seen. Think, the Force is much bigger than our Earthly perceptionz. What makes up the force? Everything on Earth is in space.

An ancient principle our Ancestorz followed is the principle of "Correspondence" which also translates as "as above, so below." In other wordz, if you wanted to understand the unknown, study the known because everything is a microcozm of the macrocozm (everything is a smaller part of a bigger thing).

Watch this Video Article (VA), *'The God Complex'* on my .tv site, DGTv: Conscious Webvision @ *www.daghettotymz.com/dgtv/videoarticles3.html*

For example, when you look at the skin on your hand, you do not realize there are billionz, probably trillionz of moving activity goin' on that your naked eye cannot see. Just because we cannot see it, or even feel it, does not mean it does not exist. It's been estimated some 6 trillionz thingz a'gwan at any moment in your body.

If you were to get a high-powered telescope and focus on your hand, the deeper you get, you'd be able to see movin' objects; moving object with legz and everything. Just as if you were to look at a plant's soil, you'd see crawling lifeformz livin' their lives on the plant, so is the same with the living organizmz that crawl on you. These thingz help protect and maintain your physical! Hard to believe, and even more to perceive, but it is true!

See, to these crawling lifeformz, *your* body is *their* Earth; just as *we* walk on the Earth. Look a the wrinkles and crevaces in your hand. To the lifeformz to finite to see with our eyez, these crevaces are valleyz — most likely as big as Grand Canyon! This makes the perception of what we are much bigger than the illusionary parameterz the european-based western society wants us to see.

If you were to look even closer, you'd see the skin and crawling elements disappear and become what everything is in its natural state... elements. Elements like molecules, electronz and neutronz. We are, just as everything is, a mere element of the bigger thing. I believe at birth, comin' out of the womb and probably our first yearz we are aware of this. Once the reprogramming system beginz (school), where they separate science from spirituality, many of us become imprisoned behind the transparent prison barz of trained thought. It is in school (and church) where we are taught that God isn't within but outside ourselves "up there" somewhere. But in every lie there is truth.

See, they separate science from spirituality, yet studyin' chemistry [root word *"chem"* or *"Khem"* as in *'Khemit'* or Kemet (KMT) meaning *"Black"*; and *"-istry"* meaning, *"the study of"*; hence, Chemistry is, *"the study of Blackness"* or YOU], we find truth. So this bringz me back to the conversation I was havin' with my people, *"What does God look like."*

See the transparent prisonbarz, Afrikanz. Pry them open... Start to erase everything you were taught and start to think from your (inner) self. What does logic tell you?

To me, what "God" or "the Force" looks like does not matter because I feel I cannot picture somethin' that is the macrocozm. Well, lemme change that, actually, if I *were* to picture "God", it most definitely would not be what we've seen in the picture Bibles or stained-glass windowz at the cathedral.

Again, if "the Force" is omnipotent, logic would tell me that if I wanted to picture it, I'd have to include the *"all,"* the only thing I believe that symbolizes anything close to that would be the Periodic Table.

Look at it, it entailz every element allegedly found here on Earth to date. But these same elements can be found in space and I'm sure more! Think about it... and no Ma, I ain't high, I do not puff lye; this is pure spiritual high!!

LIK SHOT!

In December of 2000, I wrote a piece entitled, *'In Sickness & In Health or Potential Wealth'*, and followed up in January 2001 with part 1 of the joint, *'White Sugar: Killin' You Sweetly'*. In my ongoing investigation of the US Government, the USDA (United States Department of Agriculture) and the FDA (Food & Drug Administration), we now find there's yet anutha culprit... the FFI (Fast Food Industry)!

It's not like one should be surprised of the FFIs involvement, afterall, they've been the primary mechanizm used to accelerate the declining health of people worldwide. But I will admit, never did I expect to find out the shit I've found out! This all fits into the One World Governments (aka New World Order) plan to maintain population control. It should be noted that the OWG callz all people who are not part of the OWG *"useless eaterz"* and this includes even whites!

Before I dig into this piece, lemme hit you with some stats: In 1970, America spent $6Billion on Fast Food. In 2000, just 30 yearz later, more than $110Billion was spent. Just 1 generation ago, 3/4 of money earned was used to buy food to prepare mealz at home, whereas today, 1/2 is now spent in restaurants, mainly fast food restaurants. In order to meet such a demand, one must come to conclude the meat industry *HAS* to be doin' somethin' to have enuff meat to meet such a demand.

McDonald's Corporation — 'cause it *is* a Corporation, a multi-billion dollar Corporation, not just a restaurant — is responsible for 90% of the United States new jobz. Now that's real scary if you realize most of the countreez job creation is comin' from a fast food chain that specializes in payin' extremely low wages mainly to teenz.

McDonald's is the nationz largest purchaser of beef, pork and potatoes, as well as the second largest buyer of chicken. Think about this, with all the beef they purchase, Madd Cow Disease could easily be spread 'cause the beef is gotten from several different slaughterhouses. I'll parlay on that later.

In addition to Mickey D's bein' the largest owner of retail property in the world — because of its 28,000 plus restaurants — they are the United States largest distributor of toyz through their 'Happy Mealz'. The infamous golden arches are now more widely recognized than the christian crucifix.

It shouldn't shock you that Americanz spend more on fast food than on higher education, personal computerz, computer software, new carz, movies, books, magazines, newspaperz, video & recorded music COMBINED!

The typical American now consumes approximately 3 hamburgerz and 4 orderz of fries each week. The scary thing is did you ever wonder Y they can put the ingredients on food that you buy from the supermarket, but not on food you buy at fast food restaurants? If I were to tell you what goes into what makes a hamburger or a french frie, you might consider givin' this shit up for life! Which is the reason I'm writin' this piece! I promise you, this piece will be part of my continuous effort to expose the dangerz to poor eating habits… Scalpel please…

WHAT'S IN THE MEAT

Ever heard of Escherichia coli 0157:H7, aka E.coli 0157:H7? It is a foodborn pathogen. A pathogen is somethin' that can cause disease such as a bacterium or a virus. Everyday in the US. roughly 200,000 people are sickened by a foodborne disease. Most of these cases are never reported or properly diagnosed. Viruses like E.coli can cause heart disease, inflammatory bowel disease, neurological problemz, autoimmune disorderz and kidney damage.

E.coli 0157:H7 was first discovered in 1982, the year before HIV. Just like HIV, cattle infected with E.coli can appear healthy for yearz showing few signz of illness. With the rise of huge feedlots, slaughterhouses, and hamburger grinderz seemz to have provided the meanz for this virus to become widely dispersed in the nationz food supply. American meat production has never been so centralized. 13 large packinghouses now slaughter most of the beef consumed in the US. *"The meat packing system that arose to supply the nation's fast food chains — an industry molded to serve their needz, to provide massive amounts of uniform ground beef so that all of McDonald's hamburgers would taste the same — has proved to be an extremely efficient system for spreading disease,"* author Eric Schlosser.

Today the US Government can demand the nationwide recall of defective softball bats, sneakerz, stuffed animalz, and foam-rubber toy cowz. But it cannot order a meatpacking company to remove contaminated, potentially lethal ground beef from fast food kitchenz and supermarket shelves. In 1996, the USDA found that 7.5% of the ground beef samples taken at processing plants were contaminated with Salmonella, 11.7% were contaminated with Listeria monocytogenes, 30% were contaminated with Staphylococcus aureus, and 53.3% were contaminated with Clostridium perfringenz.

Millionz after having consumed these agents have proven to generally require hospitalization with fataliteez in 1 of 5 cases. I couldn't have said better when Schlosser said, *"In the USDA study 78.6% of the ground beef contained microbes that are spread primarily by fecal material. The medical literature on the causes of food poisoning is full of euphemisms and dry scientific terms: coliform levels, aerobic plate counts, sorbitol, MacConkey agar, and so on. Behind them lies a simple explanation for why eating hamburger can now make you seriously ill: There is shit in the meat."*

To make thingz even more trivial, to know what goes down in the meatpacking process is crazy, yo! Animalz that can be seen with the naked eye as diseased are routinely slaughtered, the use of chemi-killz such as borax and glycerine to disguise the smell of spoiled beef, the deliberate mislabeling of canned meat, the tendency of workerz literally pissin' and shittin' on the kill floor, where the animalz have their necks slit.

YOU THINK YOU EATIN' JUST BEEF

The FDA will have you thinkin' all cattle do is graze on hay and grass. That was then, today it's about business and they need for these cattle to get fat quick. About 75% of the cattle in the US were (are) fed livestock wastes — meaning the remainz of dead sheep and cattle. In addition, dead pigz and horses have been added to the diet. They are also fed dead cats and dogz purchased from animal shelterz. Hard to believe how they taught us in grade school that cowz were grass eaterz, realizin' they're cannibalz that even are fed their own kind.

This past year there was a sudden breakout in Great Britain. It was scientifically called bovine spongiform encephalopathy (BSE), aka Mad Cow Disease.

THE BUG THAT KILLZ DI YOUTH

Ever wonder Y our young teenage Sisternz have been lookin' more like they're in their mid-20s? It is a known fact the anabolic steroidz and bovine growth hormones injectionz that became the daily diet of the animalz meat come from have become part of the genetic makeup of our children.

The average ignorant hed will think it's cool that a 13 year-old will have nice perky mid-size to large breasts, a tight backside with hourglass hips. Much to ones delight to see, it has a flipside. If you look like you 20-somethin' at 13, when you 20-somethin', if you maintain the same poor diet of eatin' fast food, you'll appear to have the body of a 30-40 somethin' year-old. What about when you reach your early 30s and your body starts to show the deteriorating effects of the several decades of eatin' toxic shit and drugz.

One fungus in particular, E.coli 0157:H7 releases a powerful toxin that attacks the lining of the intestine. Again, one can go along tyme bein' effected while showing no outer physical effects. Otherz suffer mild diarrhea, severe abdominal cramps, watery, then bloody shit that goes away after a week or so, but returnz as one continues to eat fast food. Many of you readerz may have experienced this.

E.coli consumption can lead to kidney failure, anemia, internal bleeding, and the destruction of vital organz. It can also cause seizures, blindness, brain damage and strokes. The younger the size of the eater, namely children, the more effective E.coli is. E.coli has been the perpetrator to countless infants who dies after eating Happy Meals or a Whopper. Otherz have had brain damage, even gone blind.

The scary thing is because of the FDAs unwillingness to police the toxinz that are in the meat industry, you never know when if next burger and fries may be you or your childz last.

In order for me to do this topic any justice, I must end it here and continue next month where deal more in-depth with what goes in the slaughterhouses across the country, how Wall Street and the Illuminati got involved and Y french fries taste the way they taste. More Fiyah!!

Over the last 30 yearz, fast food has infiltrated every aspect of American society. Just within the past 2 decades, we've seen the American influence of poor eating habits, via fast food, expand across the globe, even to "Third World" countries.

Today, fast food's are now served at restaurants, stadiumz, airports, zoos, elementary schoolz, high schoolz and universities, on cruise ships, trainz, airplanes, bus terminalz, at K-Marts, Wal-Marts, gas stationz and even, of all places, *hospitalz?!!?*

America's main streets and mallz now encompass the same McDonald's, Burger King's, Pizza Hut's and Taco Bell's. Almost every part of American life has been franchised or chained and this chain leadz to the same pool of physical, spiritual and mental termination. Much of the taste and aroma of American fast food has been manufactured at a series of large chemi-*kill* plants off the New Jersey Turnpike for yearz! Fast food has been carefully designed to taste good, hence the addiction. This plan is both inexpensive and convenient.

THE ORIGIN OF THE FIRST FAST FOOD CHAINZ

McDonald's was the first to start the global chain business industry. Back in the early 1940s, after World War 2, in the state of southern California, and mainly Los Angeles, the government spent nearly $20 billion building airplane factories, steel millz and military bases.

Richard and Maurice McDonald left New Hampshire for southern California at the start of the depression hoping to find jobz in Hell-Y-wood. In 1937 they opened up a drive-in restaurant in Pasadena. They mainly sold hot dogz. They started to get rich when they moved to a larger building in San Bernardino calling it, the MacDonald Brothers Burger Bar Drive-In. Located near a high school, it didn't take long for the success. But they had a bigger vision…

"In 1948, they fired all their staff, closed their restaurant, installed larger grills, and reopened three months later with a radically new method of preparing food," stated author of *Fast Food Nation: The Darkside of the All-American Meal*, Eric Schlosser . They got rid of dishes, glassware and silverware, replacing everything that had to be eaten

with a knife, spoon or fork, and everything else as paper cups, bagz and plates.

Otherz soon followed, William Rosenberg opened up Dunkin' Donuts later that year; Glen Bell, Jr. opened Taco Bell, Keith Cramer and father-in-law, Matthews Burns opened up Burger King in 1953 in Florida; Dave Thomas opened up Wendy's in Ohio; Thomas Monaghan created Domino's Pizza in Michigan; and Harland (Colonel) Sanders opened up Kentucky Fried Chicken (now called KFC because they don't fry real chicken, it's genetically mutated meat) in 1952.

By the early 70s, these companies were not only makin' money hand-over-fist, they were revolutionizing the way America eats. As family values plummeted, the economy was booming! So, in 1973, the Illuminati via Wall Street jumped on the bandwagon by first firing many of the early pioneerz and replacing them with corporate pioneerz. Today, even in the most impoverished of places in the world, you'll still see an old McDonald's french frie box or cheeseburger wrapper.

HOW DO THEY WIN? TARGET THE KIDZ

The corporate pirates behind soft drinks are targeting the youth and are using strategic war tactics to accomplish the task. With the growing costs of textbooks and schoolz havin' little-to-no budgets at all to finance this need, they've turned to corporate-sponsored teaching materialz. This has proven to be the path allowing them to flood the gates with soda!

What do the corporationz want in return? The right to sell their products (like McDonald's and Coca-Cola) in the schoolz as well as dictate what's in the textbooks. For instance, the Consumers Union found in a 1988 study that 80% of the teaching material were biased to benefit the corporate sponsor. Schlosser noted, *"Proctor & Gamble's 'Decision Earth' program taught that clear-cut logging was actually good for the environment; teaching aids distributed by Exxon Education Foundation said that fossil fuels created few environmental problems and that alternative sources of energy were too expensive."* Dam, YT got NO conscience, yo!!

Today, at least 20 school districts in the US have their own Subway store. Taco Bell products are sold in about 4500 school cafeterias along with McDonald's, Pizza Hut and Domino's. To date, approximately 30% of public high schoolz have fast food chain stores and this number is growing… FAST! (so are the sizes of these students! More on that later)

KILL DI YOUTH

The nationz 3 major beverage manufacturerz are now spending large sumz to increase the amount of soda that the youth consume. Coca-(Cocaine) Cola, Pepsi and Cadbury-Schweppes (who makes Dr. Pepper) control 90.3% of the US. market. Today, Americanz drink approximately 56 gallonz of soda per person a year!

The cocaine dealerz who poison our youth with each and every can (the aluminum is also a toxic — read *'War vs. Your Immune System'*), pledge to raise it's consumption at least 25% each year (hence their ongoing target of Afrikanz, using Common, Mya, Busta Rhymes, and any other Hiphop icon to influence the addiction). *"The adult market is stagnant; selling more soda to kids has become one of the easiest ways to meet sales projections,"* said Schlosser.

In the 1999 issue of *'Beverage Industry,'* an article stated, *"...[I]nfluencing elementary school students is very important to soft drink marketers... [B]ecause children are still establishing their tastes and habits."* It further stated, *"Eight year-olds are considered ideal customers; they have about sixty-five years of purchasing in front of them. Entering the schools makes perfect sense."* I've long said one of names the Illuminati callz the people of this country is "Useless Eaters." This clearly showz their continued refusal to see us as humanz and instead as dollar billz... ALL OF US! WHITES INCLUDED!!

THE LIQUID ADDICTION

In a 1999 study by the Center for Science in the Public Interest, an article on soda, which should be called "Liquid Candy" was written. It showed that in 1978, the typical teenage boy in the US. drank about 7oz. of soda a day. Today that number is 3 tymz the amount!

So about 9% of his daily calorie-intake is from soft drinks. Teenage girlz level is about 12%. Between the 2, an average of 5 or more canz of soda are being drunk a day by our youth. Where at? Home, the corner store AND SCHOOL!

Each can of Coke, Pepsi, Mountain Dew and Dr. Pepper containz about 10 teaspoonz of sugar — who's real name is called 'refined sucrose (read *'White Sugar: Killin' You Sweetly'* and *'White Sugar: The Mark of Cane'*). These sodas provide empty calories. If excessively taken (which is oftentymz the case), it can lead to calcium deficiencies, bone fractures and osteoporosis. I guess this is Y they call it *"soft drinks"* knowing the high sugar amounts in these drinks makes your bones *soft* (which is osteoporosis)!

Even deeper, softdrink consumption has become commonplace among toddlerz between the ages 1 and 2! About 1/5th of the nationz tot's drink this shit!!

Y DOES IT TASTE SO GOOD?!

Y does McDonald's have such a large rep on the taste of its french fries? How is it that they taste the same no matter what McDonald's you eat at, anywhere in the world? It's not the potatoes 'cause every other fast food joint buy their potatoes from the same processing companies. So what's the secret? It's the kind of cookin' oil they use!

For decades McDonald's cooked their fries in a mixture of approximately 7% cottonseed oil and a whopping 93% BEEF tallow. These fries have more saturated beef fat per ounce than one of their hamburgerz! So you can bet a large percentage of hedz who've had cholesterol problemz can point the finger at "Mickey D's." This would be such a large lawsuit if the people decided to sue fast food joints, the economy would virtually be turned upside-down!

In 1990, they switched to using vegetable oil, but they needed to maintain the consistent original flavor the fries first had. To do this, they started using a catch-phrase word that has fooled the masses the world over! Have you ever wondered exactly what it is they mean when you look on the ingredients of a food substance and you see *"natural flavor"* written on it? Exactly what is "natural flavor?!!?"

Open your kitchen cupboardz, your frig and freezer; look at the labelz on your food, most if not all will either say "natural flavor" or "artificial flavor." Both are man-made additives that give most processed food it's taste. About 90% of the money Americanz spend on food is used to buy processed food. We've found there's really a fast food conspiracy 'cause the flavor industry is highly secretive. Its leading companies will not reveal the formulas that make food taste the way it does, nor will they expose the identities of the parties involved, but we have been able to pinpoint where the factories are.

According to Schlosser, the New Jersey Turnpike runz through the heart of the flavor industry. A company named, International Flavors & Fragrances (IFF — www.iff.com), the worldz largest flavor company, has a manufacturing facility off Exit 8A in Dayton, New Jersey. Givaudan (www.givaudan.com), the worldz second has a plant in East Hanover. Haarman & Reimer, the largest German flavor company, has a plant in Teterboro, as well as Takasago, the largest Japanese company. Flavor Dynamics has a plant in South Plainfield; Frutarom is in North Bergen; Elan Chemical is in Newark. All of these joints lie within Teaneck and South Brunswick, New Jersey.

The foodz 2/3rdz of America tastes is created from this area. Companies like IFF "create" flavorz from beverages, to dairy, sweets, coffee, black pepper, ginger, grill flavor, honey, lemon, nutmeg, potato and corn chips, breadz, crackers, breakfast cerealz, toothpaste, mouthwash, sport drinks, bottled teas, wine coolerz, all-natural drinks in practically any flavor (peppermint, raspberry, spearmint, tropical, strawberry), beer, malt liquorz and even "organic" soy products — to name a few.

Schlosser visited the site and one of the first thingz he had to do was sign a nondisclosure form, binding him to keep secret the brand names of products that contain IFF flavorz.

The IFF was formed in 1958, through a merger of 2 smaller companies. Today, it has manufacturing facilities in 20 countries.

FOOLING YOUR NATURAL DEFENSE MECHANIZMZ

Our craving for flavor has historically never really been studied. Royal empires have been built, uncharterred territories explored and man-made religionz created because of the spice trade. One of the major thingz the pirate, Christopher Columbus, was lookin' for in 1492 were spices and seasoningz.

The flavor industry emerged in the mid-19th century, as processed foodz began to be manufactured on a large scale. The early flavor companies turned to the perfume industry for help. The large perfume houses of England, France and the Netherlandz produced many of the first flavor production. It's been said German scientists discovered methyl anthranilate, one of the first artificial flavorz accidentally while mixing chemi-killz in his lab. Suddenly, the lab was filled with the sweet smell of grapes. This compound later became the chief flavoring of grape Kool-Aid.

After WW2, many of the flavor companies moved from Europe to the US. The flavor additives were used mainly in baked goodz, candy and sodas until the 1950s when the sale of processed foodz began to rise. By the 1960s, the American flavor industry was makin' chemi-kill compoundz supplyin' the taste of Pop Tarts, Bac-Os, Tab, Tang, File-O-Fish sandwiches, and literally thousandz of new foodz.

According to Schlosser, the American flavor industry now makes about $1.4 billion annually, with about 10,000 new processed food products each year. They make this loot not by givin' the masses what we need to maintain good health, body, mind and spirit; no, they *know* we are like a dog who trusts his sense of smell rather than it's eyes; as long as it smellz good, we eatin' it, despite it's appearance.

I've longed smelled a conspiracy and the 2 major parties involved is the Fast Food Industry (FFI) and the Hospital Administration. Smelling these products — although lethal health-wise — is probably the least of woes. What do these chemi-killz do to your body after you eat them (on top of the substance you just ate that you THINK is meat 'cause it smellz like it)?! This way proves to be the easiest of wayz to slowly kill someone.

Ask yourself, 30-40 yearz ago there were no health planz; just about anyone could walk into a hospital and receive treatment. Nowadayz, you cain't get no attention unless you're insured. It's deep how they create the addiction in the form of food and once the body cannot take any more punishment — in the form of empty calories and nutrition — they stick it to us again (financially) with prescriptionz drugz that do not cure the ailments, and makes the patient now dependent on the prescription drug! Most internal ailments we get come from how well or not we maintain our body — and the kindz of food we eat is the most vital piece to our health.

I can't tell you how many hedz I know who'll tell me they ain't changing their diet 'cause the food(?) they eat taste so good! And I'll agree, it does! You know it does!! When I walk by Burger King, I reminisce on the many Whoppers I used to eat. When my neighbor cooks bacon Sunday morningz, I wake up like, yo, I MISS that, B!! But I know what it does to my body, so I stand firm.

The nose is the doorway to your stomach. Hedz like the FDA (Food AND Drug Administration; blatantly tellin' you they put drugz in our food), the FFI, the Hospital Administration and particularly the company, IFF, are aware the nose is the most sensitive part on the human body. A nose can detect aromas present in quantiteez a few parts per trillion. Scents like coffee or decayed flesh (meat) usually consist of over 1000 different chemi-killz. To make the smell of strawberries takes about 350 different chemicalz.

What's deep is no one can clearly tell what's in these processed foodz. *"The FDA does not require flavor companies to disclose the ingredients of their additives, so long as all the chemicals are considered by the agency to be GRAS (Generally Regarded As Safe),"* Schlosser wrote. This allowz companies to maintain their secret formulas, thus sustainin' their relationship with the Hospital Administration, continuin' to make madd loot off the ignorance of the people and their diet.

Aroma and food are generally linked to each other and YT is well aware of it! In addition, the smell of food can be responsible for as much as 90% of its flavor. These madd scientists believe that we acquire our taste as a way to avoid bein' poisoned. Think about it, you ain't gonna eat nothin' that stank! In nature, those plants that were edible generally taste sweet, whereas deadly ones taste somewhat bitter. Taste naturally helps us differentiate food that's good for us from food that isn't. *That was then...*

If we were to examine the real ingredients that make food taste the way it does, you'd literally have to have a chemistry background. Amyl acetate, amyl butyrate, amul valerate, anethol, anisyl formate, benzyl acetate, benzyl isobutyrate, butyric acid, cinnamyl isobutyrate, cinnamyl velerate, cognac essential oil, diacetyl, dipropyl ketone, ethyl acetate, ethyl amylketone, ethyl butyrate, ethyl cinnamate, ethyl heptanoate, ethyl heptylate, ethyl lactate, ethyl methylphenylglycidate, ethyl nitrate, ethyl propionate, ethyl valerate, heliotropin, hydroxphrenyl-2-butanone, ionone, isobutyl anthranilate, isobutyl butyrate, lemon essential oil, maltol, 4-methylacetophenone, methyl anthranilate, methyl benzoate, methyl cinnamate, methyl helptine carbonate, methyl naphthyl ketone, methyl salicylate, mint essential oil, neroli essential oil, nerolin, neryl isobutyrate, orris butter, phenethyl alcohol, rose, rum ether, undecalactone, vanillin, and solvent; all these make up a simple strawberry Burger King shake.

These cats at IFF are mad scientists, yo! They can make a simple compound smell and taste like anything you want! Ethyl-2-methyl butyrate, for example, smellz just like an apple; methyl-2-peridylketone smellz like popcorn; and ethyl-3-hydroxybutanoate makes anything — even a piece of wood — smell and taste like marshmallowz!!

There's been research that revealed how IFF has smell and taste tests. One report stated there were a dozen small glass bottles from the lab. *"After he opened each bottle, I dipped a fragrance testing filter into it. The filters were long white strips of paper designed to absorb aroma chemicals without producing off-notes. Before placing the strips of paper before my nose, I closed my eyes. Then I inhaled deeply, and one food after another was conjured from the glass bottles. I smelled fresh cherries, black olives, sautéed onions, and shrimp... After closing my eyes, I suddenly smelled a grilled hamburger. The aroma was uncanny, almost miraculous. It smelled like someone in the room was flipping burgers on a hot grill. But when I opened my eyes, there was just a narrow strip of white paper and a smiling flavorist."*

Afrikanz, they can now literally feed us poison and we won't know the difference because it will be camouflaged by the smell! This is truly a war tactic!!

Knowing this, we now know the FDA lies to us when they put on food labelz, "natural flavor," because these are man-made flavorz created in labz, not nature. If they were to put the real scientific names on food labelz, there'd be no room the name of the product!

A natural flavor is not necessarily healthier or any more pure than an artificial one. When benzaldehyde (almond flavor) is taken from natural sources such as a peach or apricot pit, it containz traces of hydrogen cyanide, which is a deadly poison.

McDonald's recently changed the ingredients of their fries after it was leaked out about their use of pork and beef tallow. To date, although they've alleged changed to a different chemi-kill, yet the fries (as I recall doin' some of my own sampling research) still taste the same. Hmm, makes you wonder, they may have stopped using one particular pork or beef compound, but whose to say they just altered the formula a lil' bit, while still using some kind of other inexpensive animal product?

A lot of "foodz" that you would think has no beef or pork in it, do. So many hedz say proudly, *"I don't eat pork,"* yet they eat beef. Would it surprise you if I told you, you were STILL eatin' pork when you eat chicken and beef?? For example, Wendy's grilled Chicken sandwich containz beef extracts.

Be wise and on alert, there's never been a tyme more important to live by the cliché, "You are what you eat!"

LIK SHOT!

You wanna really know wha'gwan?? Watch the Wall Street ticker! Notice as of October 2, 2001, Federal Reserve chief, Alan Greenspan – the unelected, yet secretly known Governor of the United States – issued yet anutha interest rate cut, putting it at the lowest level in almost 40 yearz! Howz does that equate fi we?

War is STRICTLY about makin' money! Although I really don't think the Illuminati felt no one was bold enuff to do what the so-called "terrorists" did, they ARE prepared to make some dough by goin' to war. Afterall, this ain't 'bout revenge for knockin' down the modern Babylon Towerz (ok, maybe it is…a little), this is about takin' over the oil reserves in Afghanistan!

Everyone talkin' 'bout how it's the Bush-wack clan that's behind this, but to think it's them and them alone would be complete ignorance! Remember the countless Skull&Bones pieces we've done? These cat's ain't in this alone! Besides, ev'ryone talkin' 'bout how big an idiot Bush, Jr. is, yet you get on him for decisionz that are bein' made. Now who's the idiot, Bush? or you, the one who feelz he's intellectually challenged, yet you think he's actin' on his own accord. Bush, as was Clinton, as was Bush, Sr., as was Reagan, on down (to at least) Carter, have all been groomed, trained and instructed by the not-so-famous, Trilateral Commission.

Y can't negroes get it? Since we've been bumped down off the top spot for hedz who could jeopardize YTs rule, we suddenly wan fi be patriotic. This cracka don't give two saltines about us! Like brutha Malcolm X eluded to, *"what does the whiteman call an educated Blackman?...Nigger!"*

This rang loud when we found that during, immediately after 9/11, Washington, DCs Mayor, Tony Williams (who's black), didn't even receive a call! As usual, Afrikan people are the first to be exploited and the last to do anyting 'bout it! We've seen our paranoid and confused bredren and sistren suddenly wan fi wave 'Ol Glory. Y? Cause you don't know if you gonna lose your shack on good 'ol massa's plantation??

It's well past tyme we leave this plantation and create our own, yo! Most of ya'll who have put up the Star and stripes — the same starz our Ancestorz saw after bein' bashed in the face and bloody stripes on our backs — not because you patriotic, but because YOU SCARED!! Scare to lose the state you livin' in which is HELL! Face this fear Afrikanz and build up your strategic defense through intuit observation and knowledge. Ready? –ight, turn your 3rd eye on, we goin' in!

ON HALLOWED GROUND

How do you feel knowing your Ancestorz were buried under humongous skyscraperz? Within dayz of the fallen towerz, already, hedz were speaking of rebuilding the towerz. Although there were some who felt the area should be left as some kind of memorial, I shook my head a the audacity of these mindsets.

I thought to myself, YT will only memorialize some shit they claim to be "victim" to, so they're really not in the practice of honoring slain people at all, for if they *were,* the towerz, shit, *lower Manhattan as a whole* would not be where it is!! Y you ask? Because Lower Manhattan used to be an Ancient burial ground for enslaved Afrikanz!

Those kidnapped Afrikanz who endured the 6 month + Middle Passage journey to the America's arrived first in New Amsterdam, later changed to New York when the British took the city from the Dutch. They were then brought to an auctioning block in the area that we know today as Wall Street. This was where slave traderz placed their bidz.

New York, had the second largest population of enslaved Afrikanz on the eve of the American Revolution! Enslaved Afrikanz were used in the city to accomplish the backbreaking work of creating an industrial urban center. Enslaved Afrikanz were also used to work on lengthening and widening the city's main streets, like Broadway Avenue. When Afrikanz died, no recordz were left of them except their age, gender, and physical condition, which were marked into a slave ledger.

No Afrikanz were allowed to be buried in the town's Trinity Church graveyard. All blacks were to be placed instead in the African Burial ground, just outside city limits, where perhaps 20,000 blacks would eventually be laid to rest over a period of 78 yearz.

The history of this graveyard is heavily embedded in the history of one of the largest cities on Earth. New York grew from an "island of rolling hills" (that's what Manhattan translates to) into a bustling metropolis.

As the city ran out of space to spread, it began to grow upward. Each generation of buildingz was stacked on top of the last and the skyline rose higher and higher. It was not rare that on one city block, ten or twelve different buildings stood on one spot at different tymz in New York history. The graveyard became a row of stores and even a parking lot before the US Government decided to bulldoze the lot and the land underneath, to build a new federal building.

Bulldozerz don't belong in graveyards, and skyscraperz shouldn't be built upon corpses. In 1992, this destruction of the first African burial ground in the United States occurred in the heart of lower Manhattan. Continuing with their lack of respect for Afrikanz, the government wanted to build a skyscraper in this busy financial district to house organizationz like the FBI, CIA and EPA (Environmental Protection Agency). On top of that they took all the remainz and they are currently at Howard University in DC, for what they call scientific observation, when for all we know, they just threw their remainz in the trash or better yet, up in some museum where hedz'll pay money to see like our Ancestorz of the Nile Valley of ancient KMT (Egypt)!

And those nearly 500 hundred skeletal remainz of our Ancestorz have not been able to rest because of it.

The large federal building was built, minus a small grass area that has now been sectioned off and identified as a site of the African burial ground. This insulting "memorial" meanz nothing when the masses are unaware of what is now called the Financial District — yeah, money — especially when the so-called white designed pieces of artwork in commemoration to our Ancestorz are placed inside the Federal building, which is pretty much off limits to the public unless you're being led on a guided tour and are willing to pass through an X-ray and security checkpoint.

And, of course, WHO is currently responsible for the continued cover-up? The Financial District's co-creator, the Rockefellerz!

THE SIEGE

Just like in the movie, *"The Siege",* in which Denzel Washington starred, the US Government is responsible for the training these hijackerz received! If the attacks can be linked to Osama bin-Laden, this is, as been said, a simple case of 'Chickenz comin' home to roost'. Afterall, it was the CIA that trained bin-Laden, think of how many other bin-Ladenz they've created, and multiply that by how many bin-Ladenz returned to their homelandz with the knowledge and technology to teach their countrymen.

You can't hate on that! If it's bin-Laden, he simply pimped a system that was out to pimp him! When you wan fi deal wit war, it is war! The arrogance of the US. to think they can go pull some "3rd world useless eater" as they may call him, teach him how to strategically wage war against the very people they put there to war against him (the Palestinianz vs. Israelis) then EXPECT them to contain their battle over their and not go for the puppeteer (the US.) is complete egotizm!

Just like the movie, *'Wizard of Oz'*, it took someone considered small and therefore overlooked to pull up America's skirt, showin' the punk-bitch he is!

In addition, now that the US. has to show some kind of resilience, they go over to Afghanistan threatening to strike back, but not to fight by himself, oh no, see, that's not how a bully works. He tryin' to bring his serpent siblingz along through NATOs Article 5: the centralization of worldwide people. Their motto is *"they bombed me, they bombed US!"* But ask yourself, what makes you think your highly publicized leave to fight on their home turf, makes you think there aren't hedz here positioned to attack/counter attack?!

In addition, Y don't you wan fi stage this war in Saudi or Egypt where all the "terrorist" and terrorist factoreez are said to be?!!? Simple, this is not about bin-Laden, this is about takin' over the land of Afghanistan. What's in Afghanistan, you ask? Remember, the Russianz fought the Arabz there for 10 yearz and lost. What YTs after is black tea, aka, OIL! I mentioned yearz ago how NASA has this telescope, LANDSAT7, the scopes for the Earth's natural resources (gold, silver, copper, oil, etc.) and the largest abundance is in Afrika, but the Illuminati got control of that through illegitimate billion dollar corpationz like Oppenheimerz, DeBeer Diamond Co., but the neighboring Afghanistan has yet to fall under YTs rule, hence the possibility of war.

However, in the absence of the Afrikan Revolution, the recent attacks have YT second-guessing the power of the people! Although I got no luv for no Arab Muslim 'cause I know they gots no luv for we (peep the enslavement of Afrikanz in Sudan, by Arab Muslimz), their belief — no matter how insane — to die for their 'cause is one to recon with. They call it a jihad, or holy war, but "Holy" and spirituality got nothin' to do with this.

The concept of 'God' got not a ting fi do wid it! This preliminary act of war is not ordained by 'God', it's initiated by man and his greed! If it ain't YTs greed to rule the world, it's the Muslimz will to die so that they will allegedly be rewarded 100 virginz in the afterlife. Is this about Freedom or about the usual 'Cash money and hoes?!'

WHERE WAS EVERBODY?!

On the morning of 9/11, 4000 Israeli employeez didn't report to work at the World Trade Center. After the towerz fell, the international media, particularly the Israeli one, started mourning for Israelis who work at the two towerz. Then suddenly, no one ever mentioned anything about them and later it became clear that they suspiciously took off the day the incident took place! Y? Who got the word out?

Arab diplomatic sources revealed to the Jordanian al-Watan newspaper that those Israelis remained absent that day based on hints from the Israeli General Security Apparatus, the Shabak, the fact which evoked unannounced suspicions on American officialz who wanted to know how the Israeli government learned about the incident before it occurred, and the reasonz Y it refrained from informing the US authorities of the information it had. Suspicionz had increased further after Israeli newspaper Yadiot Ahranot revealed that the Shabak prevented Israeli premier Ariel Sharon from traveling to New York and particularly to the city's eastern coast to participate in a festival organized by the Zionist organizationz in support of the "Israel".

To this day there's been no further investigation on this matter. It is clear that it was more than just the alleged terrorists behind this conspiracy! The 4000 that took off are guilty by association!

THE US's FUNNY LINKS…

The United Nationz held the Conference on Racism in Durban, South Afrika, from August 31st to September 7th, but did you know who was really behind it? The Rockefellerz! It was the Rockefeller clan who also formed the United Nationz, wrote the Treaty for the UN in San Francisco, literally created Lower Manhattan, where we find what is called the Financial District built on top of the Enslaved Afrikan Burial Ground; yet they wanna point the finger at otherz about Racizm and take the side of the Is-it-realz (Israelites) — when we know it was Rockefeller along with his Illuminated

Bredren who created and continues to instigate the war between them and the Palestines — and walk out the conference, as if to say they haven't a racist bone in their body!

Khadam Gishogi, who is the American Business Representative for Saudi has immediate-direct family relationz to Osama bin-Laden. But Y IZ it we find, according to historian, Steve Cokely, that he ownz mallz in Dallas with the Bush pham?!!? Just how personal an attack on the US, was this for bin-Laden, that's IF it was him?! The answer we may never know…

As mi Bredren, Kamou Voudon wrote, *"We should know that the devil likes confusion, because confusion leads to ignorance, hate and other wickedness on that end of the pendulum. We know the Illuminati is trying to spread One government, One currency, One nation, & mostly overlooked One language. With these recent terrorist attacks the illuminati and George W. Bush will look at the evolution of the computer processing unit chip (CPU). That shit started out huge now that shit fits into watches, pens, hearing devices, etc. The world powers are putting financial and political pressure on countries to pledge their allegiance to them. And if you look even deeper you'll see the Rothschilds right there behind it all. The chess pieces are almost all in place. Now one that many are ignorant to is the one world language. That language is english period."*

Our focus over the next 90dayz should be on ourselves! We should be creating a systematic operation dealin' with food, water reserves (I been blazin Mos Def's New World Water joint on the regular!) medical supplies, survival skillz (in the outdoorz — in case hedz gotta run for the hillz), weaponry (including the gat, knives, makin' bullets, etc), homeschoolz, etc. Basically we need to build our own counter-terrorist factoreez and not to defend the red, white & blue, but the Red, Black & Green, ashe'!!

I know you scared Afrikanz, I am too, but this is our destiny, UHURU! WE WILL WIN BUT ONLY IF WE PREPARE!! PRAYER IS GOOD, BUT ACTION MAKES A MU'FUCKA KNOW YOU FORREAL, FEEL ME??

Reespek!

Take a breath Afrikanz…a deep one, because this shit is more intense than YT wants us to know! Just as with all the other pieces I've written about Secret Societeez, in order for you to get an inner-standing of this, you will need to rid yourself of the notion of coincidences, because when studyin' these cults, it is your ignorance they count on to maintain their "secrecy", which is the essence of their power.

The war on terrorizm is proving to have more secret corridorz than the pyramidz of Giza, yo! If you stay glued to the idiot box (tv) or base your info on what 'massa'-media's sayin' in their newspaperz, you'd think the attacks, although planned for some tyme, were random with no real significance than to instill fear in the mindz of the masses.

Make no mistake about it, whoever and whatever parties are behind this shit wanted to connect an ancient Middle Eastern secret society, 'the Order of the Assassinz'. In addition, it had to be on that day, September 11th, or 9/11, because if you take the year the secret society, Knights Templar was founded (1118AD — 1+1+1+8=11) along with the 9 founderz of the Templarz, we get 9/11 or 911. Again I ask you, Afrikanz, to take a deep breath, 'cause this shit is subterranean!

THE MYSTERIOUS #9 AND 11

To my surprise, several newspaperz came out with the consistent repetition of the number 11 during the Pentagon and World Trade Center attacks. Here's some additional notes:

- Each World Trade Center had 110 floors, a multiple of 11
- The aircraft that hit the Pentagon was American Airlines Flight 77, a multiple of 11
- American Airlines Flight 11, the first plane that hit World Trade Tower 2, had 11 crew memberz. A total of 65 (6+5=11). If you minus the crew, there were 54 passengerz, the #9
- The second plane, Flight 175, hit the World Trade Tower 1 at 9:02am* (9+2=11) (*This raises suspicion, because the ability to strike a point at an

exact tyme takes pure Wile E. Coyote, "Super Genius")
- 9/11 is the 254th day of the year 2+5+4=11
- After 9/11, there are 111 dayz left in the year
- New York City (where 2 planes hit) consists of 11 letterz
- New York was the 11th state admitted into the Union
- President Bush ordered flagz to fly at half mast until 9/22, making an 11 day period of morning

Now you may feel all this is mere coincidence, but I told you Afrikanz, YT operates on sciences stolen from the tymz of the Nile Valley (they use it negatively though). So when we dealin' with conspiracies, *there is no such thing as coincidences!!*

Additional numberz we will prove to be in the coded language of Masonic communication are 33 (relating to the highest degree a Mason can attain), 39, 19.5, 19.

Y was this day of all dayz chosen? If you go back in history, September 11th is also the New Years Day in the ancient Kemetic or Egyptian Coptic Christian calendar. This date serves of additional significance with it being the day Egypt drafted its new constitution in 1971.

THE MASONIC CONNECTION

Most have been misinformed to believe the start of Masonry was around the 18th Century, when in actuality it stemz back to ancient Kemet. However, like YTs done with everything else — probably due to their lack of melanin, affecting their mental balance — they turned somethin' good into somethin' bad. Back then they weren't known as Freemasonz, they were known as the Knights Templar. Who are they?

This "recent" War on Terrorizm — as 'massa'-media would have you know — is not somethin' new; not even recent. This war between these two is nearly a millennium strong!

In 1095AD (note 19.5), Pope Urban II declared a Christian jihad (holy war) on the Muslim invaderz of the Holy Land (even though they, themselves were invaderz), in Jerusalem. This is where we find the beginning of the war between the Christianz and the Muslimz.

4 yearz later they won the advantage and in 1113, the Catholic Church was reformed into a new cult. This cult became known as the "Knights Hospitalerz." One of the original memberz, St. Bernard also created a monastery in Seborga, Italy that same year. Documents found in the monastery said it was built to protect a "great secret."

As with all other secret societeez, there were inner differences. In 1118 (1+1+1+8=11) 9 Knights split from the Hospitalerz and met with King Baudoin I of Jerusalem requesting the duty of keeping Christian pirates — oops, pilgrimz safe on the roadz and highwayz leading to the holy city from the port of Jaffa. We later find this was not their true intentionz. Once they arrived in Jerusalem, they went to the Temple Mount — the ancient site of the Temple of Solomon — and began diggin' out the ancient ruinz, stealin' anything they could. For this burglary, they received the name, the 'Knights of the Temple', or shorter, *'Knights Templar'*.

THE TEMPLE OF SOLOMON

According to research about the Hiram Key, the Temple of Solomon was a structure designed under the teachingz of sacred geometry by the earliest founderz of Freemasonry, and was made in such a way as to raise the essence of the Ausarian Drama — the legend of Ausar, Auset and Heru (mistakenly called Isis, Osirus and Horus).

In 1867, British engineerz found a secret room beneath the Temple Mount. What was it? Legend has it the Ark of the Covenant was there before the fall of the Roman Empire. Those 9 Knights mission was not to save Christianz but to locate the Ark and bring it back to Europe. After the mission, they returned to their native landz. 2 were from Rosslyn, Scotland (probably where the Scottish-Rite Masonz were born) and set up a headquarterz.

For their theft — oops, successful mission they were given the official seal of the Roman Catholic Church. This increased their membership; with many bringing wealth with them.

After this, they enjoyed numerous victoreez against the Muslimz, along with stealin' madd wealth. It was believed by many, the Knights Templar could attribute their power to the fact that the secret they stole from Solomonz Temple was a piece of the true cross of the alleged "crucifixion" of Christ. It was said they never lost a battle while in possession of the cross. This streak ended when they lost to the Muslimz in the battle of Hattin in 1187.

Then the Templarz became a threat to the Catholic Church. The Pope and the King of France, Philip le Bel, plotted to fight against the Order and seize their stolen wealth. On Friday, October 13th, 1307, they moved in to arrest the Knights (this is Y Friday the 13th is considered unlucky, not Jason Myers of Camp Crystal Lake, the madd serial killer of the *'Friday the 13th'* horror flick series).

Most of the Order was wiped out. The leader of the Order, Jaques de Molay, was burned at the stake. If you're familiar with de Molay, the Masonz have an auxiliary organization for youths called the Knights of Pythagoras. The black version of Skull&Bones, the Boule' (Sigma Pi Phi) makes reference to de Molay as well.

Surviving memberz went underground and re-emerged as the "Freemasonz." What's deep is the official date the Templarz were recognized by the Vatican is 1118AD (1+1+1+8=11, anutha 11!).

THE ORIGIN/ADOPTION OF WICKED WAYZ

As mentioned before, this war on terrorizm is not new and it dates back to the beginning of the first millennium. From what we've discussed so far, you would think only YT uses Masonic practices as a part of society, but remember, these Arabz and crackuhz been fightin' each other for a long tyme. The person(s) behind this attack has brought an ancient battle to center stage between the 'Assassinz' and 'Masonz'. And throughout this period certain war tactics have been implemented into each otherz strategy.

Mustafa al-Amin, author of *'Al-Islam, Christianity & Freemasonry'* states,

"During the period of the Crusades, many of the ideas and practices of the Muslim groups were adopted by the European Christian warriors. More specifically, it was through the Knights Templar that most of the Eastern secret societies' methods were introduced to Europe. The Templars were influenced by the Order of the Assassins."

So what we have is a learned behavior YT adopted, not somethin' they originated — which is their exact nature, master plagiarist's! So what about these Arab terrorists?

Osama bin Laden has been referred to as the modern day Saladin — the Islamic general who defeated the Templarz at Hattin. Before there was the Templarz, there was the "Assassinz". Formed in 1090 by al-Hasan ibn-al-Sabbah, the Assassinz were a murderous sect who called themselves defenderz of Islam. They came out of Kemet (note that by then the Afrikan presence had been completely shifted) but soon moved to the mountainous region of present day Iran. Most of their battles were fought against the Knights Templarz as each other tried to overthrow and steal each otherz wealth, in particular the search for the Ark and the biblical Jesus' cross. One of the key strategeez that instilled fear into their foes was their willingness to sacrifice their own lives for the cause — just like the Muslimz of today.

What also must be noted is how they were able to get people to commit themselves to the point where they would take their own life. According to explorer, Marco Polo, who visited the Assassinz castle in Alamut in 1273, they used a variety of techniques that would today be called "mind-control". They did this by drugging the initiate with hashish and placing the recruit to, as Polo stated, *"a sumptuous garden filled with beauty, feasts and women."*

In this drug-induced state, when the recruit woke up he was convinced he had literally gone to Paradise. Once the drug wore off and he returned to the real world, overtyme the recruit's original beliefs in Islam were replaced with a version called "Nizari Ismailis" which convinced him he would return to Paradise if he sacrificed himself for the cause and its leaderz.

So it all makes sense now Y we hear of how young their soldierz are willingly ready and able to give their life to "Allah". If they were reprogrammed to believe, what person wouldn't sacrifice their life if they were promised paradise and 100 virginz as their reward to suicide! They're used to livin' in underdeveloped regionz (rocks and caves) and hear gun claps everyday, who wouldn't want paradise?!

History notes that the Assassinz were present during the battle Hattin. When lookin' at the origin of the word 'Assassin', we find the word 'Assasseen' and in Arabic it meanz *guardian*. What exactly are they guarding? Perhaps whatever the Knights of Templar stole during the crusades and break-inz into Solomon's Temple in 1118, and bringing it to Europe, then Scotland and eventually America.

THE NUMERIC CONNECTION AND ASTRONOMY…

Most would think the reason the Trade Center's were hit was because they were the biggest and most visible structures that would get the worldz attention. True but not entirely the truth. True, if you wanted to make an impression, the Towerz was it (remember it was also a target in '93). But as I stated earlier, this is a long enduring battle and to keep the tradition goin', what we will soon see is these parties are playin' a much deeper game than we, the outsiderz, know. If you look at these attacks, you will find Islamic/Masonic code written all over it! Let's take a look at the Trade Center's.

Just like how our Ancestorz built the pyramidz using mathematics — bein' placed at the center of the Earth's landmass, positioned at the apex of the Nile Delta, with its base twice its height yielding the infamous number 'pi', or 3.14 — math was used in the design of the Towerz.

Freemason/Templar mythology speaks of the legend of Jachin and Boaz, aka the Twin Pillarz of Atlantis. In all Masonic lodges, you will find these 2 pillarz. Inside these pillarz was said to be engraved all the then known sciences to preserve them from destruction by fire or flood. These secrets allegedly came from the children of Lamech of Atlantis.

Jumping up to the American Revolution, these 2 pillarz were made of brass to represent the pillarz erected at the entrance of Solomon's Temple. It is said these pillarz contain the source of the deepest Masonic secrets, conveying in detail the end of dayz and the Masonz role to preserve and strategically tyme the redissemination of this knowledge to maintain their power.

After knowin' this about the 110-story Towerz, even an idiot would think they resemble the modern Jachin and Boaz. But if you are in need of additional suspicion, take into the fact that the Towerz were designed *by* a Mason (Minoru Yamasaki)!

Yamasaki on the Towerz, *"There are a few very influential architects who sincerely believe that all buildings must be 'strong'. The word 'strong' connotes 'powerful'— that is, each building should be a monument to the virility of our society."* Yamasaki's belief in the strength of a structure happenz to be the very meaning to one of the pillarz of Solomonz Temple.

The pillar, Boaz, sits on the left or north, representing strength. Lookin' at the attacks, we find it was the left or strength portion of the pillarz, I mean Towerz, that was hit on the 11th, by Flight #11. So subliminally, or metaphysically, the terroists' went to attack the strength of America FIRST.

On top of that, when you look at the design of the Towerz, due to their height, 110 (where we see the #11) feet, they were designed to sway on wind bracing columnz, called a prefabricated steel lattice, that were 39 inches. The floor construction of the lattice was only 33 inches in depth spanning the full 60 feet to the core. So let's see, we mentioned the numberz 110, 39, 33 and 60.

39 is twice 19.5 (will elaborate in a sec); 33 is the highest degree in Scottish Rite Masonry as well as the (get out your calculatorz, for those good in trigonometry) 'sin' or 'sine' of 19.5°. THIS IS WHERE IT KEEPS DEEP!

There are certain constellationz that become of significance now. Sirius, which represents the goddess Auset (greeks call Isis), the 3-belt starz of Orion, which represents Ausar (Osirus), and Regulus, the "heart of the lion" of the constellation Leo.

Leo also happenz to be symbolic for Heru (Horus), the son of Auset and Ausar.

What is significant is the positionz of these starz during the attacks. When we apply these same numberz to these constellationz, we find madd tingz a'gwan when the starz were at 33° and 19.5° above or below the horizon. The horizon itself symbolizes the passage between life and death.

THE DATES, TYMZ & FLIGHT NUMBERZ

American Airlines Flight #11 struck the first Tower at 8:45am. It was at this tyme Sirius was slightly above 32° over the horizon. It must be noted that although it technically was not at 33°, it was but 1° off, Sirius never really got as high as 33° that morning. When doin' these stellar calculationz, there is a 1/2° margin of error. However, when we look at Giza, Kemet (Egypt) at this tyme, which is the home of the Assassinz as well as the birth of the Templar/Masonic system itself, it showed the belt starz of Orion we well within the half degree margin of 33° at the tyme of the first hit.

In Kabul, the capital of Afghanistan, Regulus, the heart of the lion, was dead on the horizon, which could be translated as the western death, or the day American dominance died. Now, Regulus or Leo represents Heru, who avenged his fatherz death. Could it be whoever is behind these attacks see themselves as avenging a millennium-long beef??

The 4 involved planes were numbered 'American Airlines Flight 11', 'United Airlines Flight 175', 'American Flight 77' and 'United Flight 93'. Notice a pattern? In addition to the 9's and 11's, Flight 77, which slammed into the Pentagon, the 3 belts of Orion was precisely at 39° over Washington, DC.

And?!!? You may be sayin'… Orion, the representative of Ausar, overseer of the dead, judge of the underworld and resurrection of the dead, was at 39°! However, the longitude of DC was at 77°!! What was the latitude? 39°!! As stated earlier, 39 is twice 19.5. These numberz are key code numberz in what is called Templar Magic. If you go back to the architecture of DC you can see it.

In part 3 of this series, we continue to bring di fire as we cover how these numberz were also influential in the design of the Nationz Capitol, how the National Aeronautic Space Administration (NASA), planet Mars and how these all tie into when and where there are military strikes and counter-strikes in each and every war America was involved in.

Until then, continue to study and don't use tell-a lie-vision and 'massa'-media as your primary source!

MORE FIE-YAH!

Last piece, we spoke about the Masonic numerical principles in the design of the Twin Towerz as well as using astrology to show the longitude and latitude of certain places at the tyme the planes hit New York and DC. Hopin' I left your mouth's droolin' for more, I promised part 3 would entail even more, shall I say, coincidences (even though it should be, as a golden rule, as a researcher of truth, there IS NO SUCH THING AS COINCIDENCES!).

After 9/11, YT urged us to *"go out and live your lives", "spend your dollarz",* and *"support the slumping economy."* It is the establishments wish that we do this to diverge our questionz and convert into intructionz, havin' us be caught up into bein' patriotic rather than findin' out just who is takin' advantage of this "patriotizm."

Within dayz after 9/11, Bush flooded the airwaves with *"getting back to normalcy."* But exactly what is normalcy?! Normalcy is how "we" got in this shit in the first place!

Exploitation of the land, reserves and impoverished people/countries, racizm, material hording and tricknology have been the practice of "normalcy" for the US for centureez!

Goin' back to this practice gives YT the ability to continue with its scheduled final acts of instituting a One World Government, somethin' that has been in motion since May 1st, 1776 — the day the Luciferian Conspiracy was ordained, as well as the birth of the Illuminati, in Bavarian, Germany. NOTE: Those same wicked men who signed a pack with the devil (LUCIFERian Conspiracy), met 2 months later, July 4th to meet about signing this countreez Declaration of Independence, although it actually wasn't until the following month in August (5th) that they actually signed it. So Y isn't YT lighting firecrackerz in August instead of July?? More on this later…

As I stated last piece, the inner-standing of YTs structure is purely deep indeed — especially when we see that the root is of an Afrikan Deity, Ausar, Ausar and Heru. Imitation is the highest form of flattery and flipping it is the ultimate form of DISRESPECT.

Everything we've researched has nothing to do with us, yet they're using our science for destruction. What we will find is that the founding fatherz of this nation, Washington, Franklin, Hancock, and everyone else who signed the Luciferian Conspiracy were intimately connected with and the original Knights Templar who fought against the Islamic forces over half a century ago.

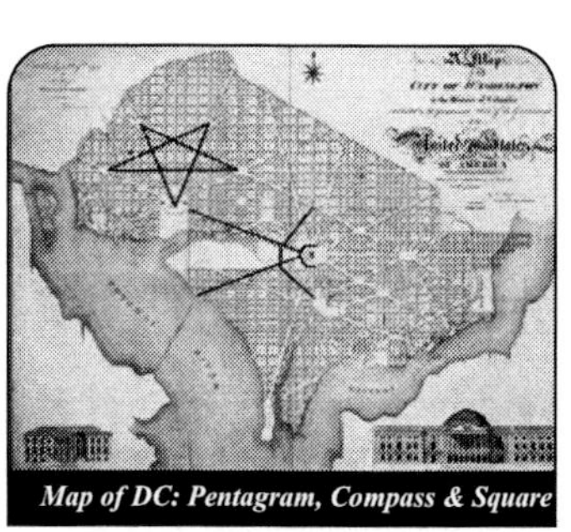

Map of DC: Pentagram, Compass & Square

For the past months we've heard YT call these people Terrorists' as if America never was. However the majority of America's citizenz will never know this because we do not read; instead we listen to 'massa'-media's TV, radio and newspaperz. All it takes is a little desire to know thyself and the truth and you'll find ill shit like, Fouad Kamil, former diamond detective for Rhodes/ Oppenheimerz DeBeers Diamond Co. in the 1950s who said this of their operationz on enforcing Afrikanz quarry diamond mines in Afrika: *"We did everything...there were beatings, everything we could to extort the information from them. To put it bluntly, we were a Terrorist Group."* These wicked men rely on our desire to remain in the realm of ignorance to further their missionz as the soul controllerz of the world.

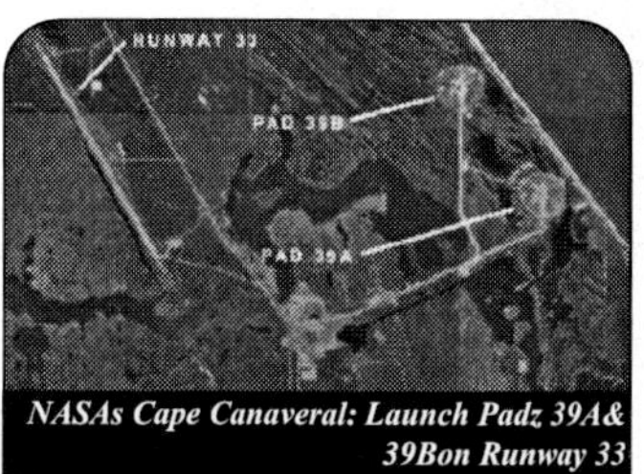

NASAs Cape Canaveral: Launch Padz 39A& 39Bon Runway 33

AS SEEN FROM THE STARZ

When we go back to 9/11, the 4 planes involved were 'American Airlines 11', 'United Airlines Flight 175', 'American Airlines Flight 77' and 'United Airlines Flight 93'. Besides all the 9s and 11s, we noticed that the flight that crashed into the Pentagon was Flight 77 at 9:39am, according to NBCs Dateline. At 39° the 3 belts starz of Orion was seen. Orion represents the god Osiris (Ausar), overseer of the dead, judge of the underworld and resurrection, also known as the "god of the dead." To find Osiris at such a point overlooking this scene of death and destruction was deep.

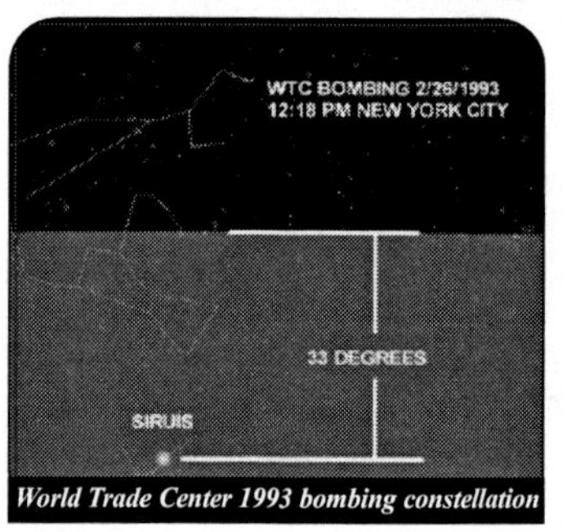

World Trade Center 1993 bombing constellation

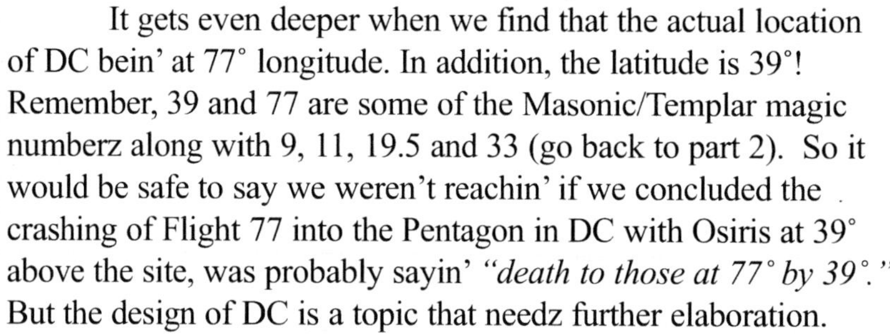

It gets even deeper when we find that the actual location of DC bein' at 77° longitude. In addition, the latitude is 39°! Remember, 39 and 77 are some of the Masonic/Templar magic numberz along with 9, 11, 19.5 and 33 (go back to part 2). So it would be safe to say we weren't reachin' if we concluded the crashing of Flight 77 into the Pentagon in DC with Osiris at 39° above the site, was probably sayin' *"death to those at 77° by 39°."* But the design of DC is a topic that needz further elaboration.

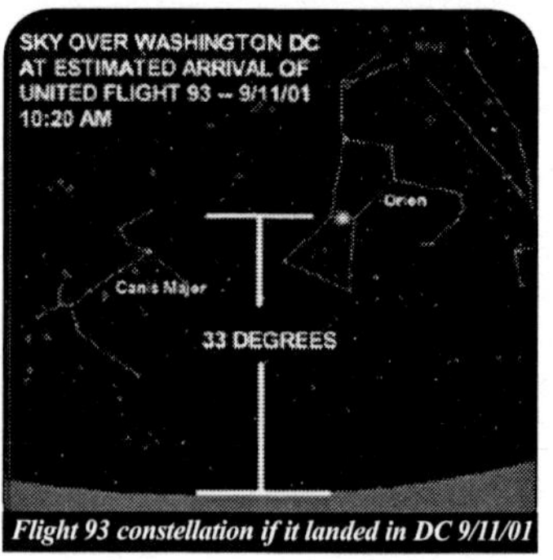

Flight 93 constellation if it landed in DC 9/11/01

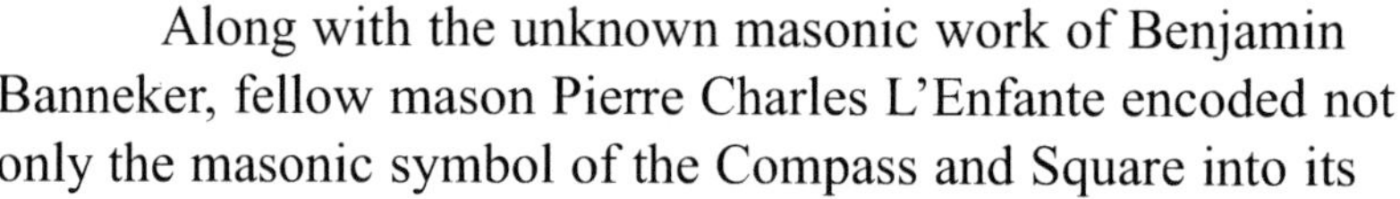

Along with the unknown masonic work of Benjamin Banneker, fellow mason Pierre Charles L'Enfante encoded not only the masonic symbol of the Compass and Square into its design, he also created an inverted pentagram, commonly known as the Goat of Mendez, the satanic symbol.

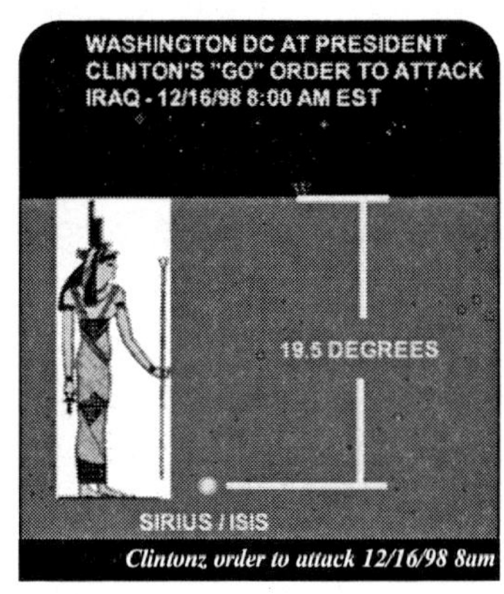

Clintonz order to attack 12/16/98 8am

In masonry, the pentagram is found commonly in the inner chamberz of the lodges. Before bein' adopted by satanic cult worshipperz, it was a symbol for the star Sirius, which is a character representation of Isis (Auset, wife of Ausar), later adopted by the Order of the Eastern Star, the female version of masonz.

The most obvious way to encode a masonic message in the creation of a city would be to place the city on an obvious tetrahedral latitude. However, 19.5° N by 77°W would have place DC off land and into the ocean off Mexico, an area the English pirates didn't steal as of yet. As well, placing it at 33°N would have left them trying to build their city in the Atlantic off the coast of Georgia. So the only logical place George Washington could choose in North America was 39°N, which at the tyme was literally a swamp (remember, 39 divided in half is 19.5). But the coding didn't stop there…

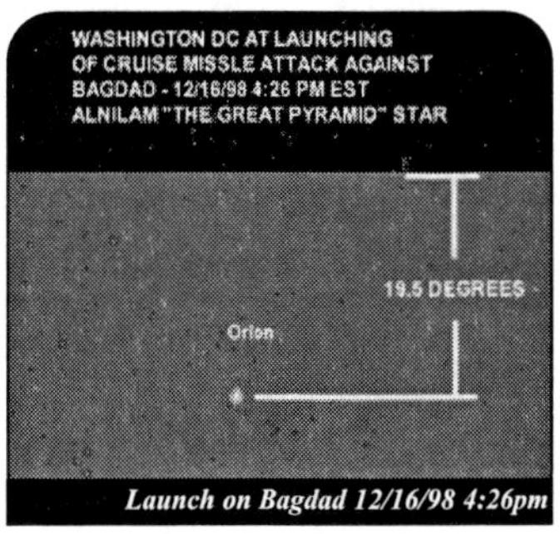

Launch on Bagdad 12/16/98 4:26pm

The 2 main streets in DC, Pennsylvania and Maryland Avenues, which connect the Capitol Building to the White House and the Jefferson Memorial, depart at the exact masonic angle of 19.5°.

One other popular, yet unknown place this can be seen at is Cape Canaveral, Florida. NASA (National Aeronautics and Space Administration, which have consistently chosen astronaut's who are masonz) launches the Space Shuttle from the Kennedy Space Center that has 2 launch padz numbered 39a and 39b.

Now ask yourself, Afrikan, Y would they start the number of 2 padz at 39 and not at 1?! Plus, if they're gonna start with 39, Y isn't the second one numbered 40?! On top of that, the runway down to the launch padz is numbered Runway 33!

United States "retaliates" 10/07/01

The name 'Cape Canaveral' is deep too, for it translates in English as the *"Cape of Reedz."* What ancient Kemetic deity was associated with reedz? None other than Auset (Osiris).

Lookin' at the Flights, number 93 the one that crashed in Pennsylvania, probably headed for DC as well, if you flip it you get 39. Back in 1993, the year of the first bombing of the Trade Center, we noticed some very deep thingz that were goin' on in the constellationz.

At 12:18pm, when the Trade Center was bombed, the star Sirius (again Auset, or Osiris), was at 33° at the horizon. When we look at Flight 93 of September 11th, it was expected to arrive in DC at 10:20am, had it reached DC, Orion was again at the masonic altitude of 33° on the horizon.

It must also be noted this is not the first tyme America

has had beef with Osama bin Laden. Just a few yearz ago, Bill Clinton responded to the attack on US embasseez in Tanzania and Kenya, August 7th, 1998. The deep shit was that the spot in Tanzania was at 39°E Longitude. In response, Clinton launched a cruise missile attack on bin Ladenz base camps in Afghanistan and Sudan on August 20th near the town of Khost and Khartoum.

Guess where his training camps were? 33.3°N. This spot was s'posed to be one of bin Ladenz nerve gas factoreez. But what they found was that this place was actually where they made aspirin, no way connected to bin-Laden. So Y did Clinton order the unauthorized attack? Because the location was at 33.3°E!! In addition, the tyme of the attacks was 1:30pm EST (Eastern Standard Tyme), or 13:30 (1+3+3=7) military tyme, but in Khartoum, the tyme was 19:30… or 19.5!! Oh, the shit don't stop there!!!

A few months later, Clinton launched a similar attack on Baghdad and Iraqi leader Saddam Hussein! The attack was done at 8am EST, December 16th, 1998 (16th: 1+6=7; 1998: 1+9+9+8=27 —> 2+7=9).

When we looked at the starz, we saw that at that tyme, Sirius (Auset/Isis) was at 19.5°W on the horizon. When they launched the first cruise missile at 4:26pm EST, the star of Orion was at 19.5°E!!

And what about Bush, Jr's response to the Trade Center bombingz on October 7th, 2001?! Bein' brought up in masonry, he himself, "retaliated" at 12:20pm EST where the start of Orion was at 19.5°.

So it should be clear that there's more to it than the United Snakes government wants us to know when they decide to go to war. They'll have you think these thingz happened at random, when in fact they make premeditated calculationz claimin' the lives of countless victimz and ignorant servants (the military). All these are premeditated murderz! So who's the real serial killerz?!

In addition to all this, let's not forget that, according to Gary Allen's, *'The Rockefeller Files'*, there really isn't war, it's all a fraud to get hedz to pick sides. The real deal is these crackuhz go to war for the sole purpose of makin' money! Oftentymz financing both sides, they are able to literally make a territory they want to colonize become indebted to them by simply supplyin' weaponry and supplies to their opposition.

Ask the so-called Indian; YT sold him used, defective gunz in trade for gold, then came back and fought them. No how you gonna win when you use the weaponz your opposition gave you?!

Still don't think these wicked men didn't premeditate this "War on Terrorizm?" Think. How long does it take to make a movie? The movies we see on the silver screen usually were in production more than a year ago. So how is it all of the sudden we got this string of war movies?! Think, Afrikan, with your 3rd critical-eye!

Within the last year, BEFORE this "War on Terrorizm", 'Behind Enemy Lines', 'Black Hawk Down', 'Hart's War', 'We Were Soldiers' and HBOs, 'Band of Brothers' were in production, with several airing before, around or just after September 11th. Could it be that Hell-y-wood was instructed by it's overseer, the Illuminati, to get the ignorant citizenz of this country to be a lil' more Patriotic, by getting in a war-type mood??

You'd be a fool to think not! See, while the majority of hedz started dawnin' the american flag on their carz, this country is puttin' into action possibly the final stages of a One World Government, where everyone will have to have a National (and eventual International) ID Card, so that your whereabouts, financial transactionz and god knowz what else for their surveillance files.

All this makes even more sense when you look at some of these silver screen companeez. As mentioned before, NASA is a co-conspirator to all this madness. Approximately a decade ago, they allegedly closed a program down called SETI (Search for Extraterrestrial Intelligence) allegedly for budget cuts among other thingz. This program was used shoot out signalz in space in hopes of the signal bounce off anything that may be out there, sendin' back info to confirm that there is intelligent life beyond the planet we call Earth.

The winged horse for death. It shouldn't be a surprise that the Rockefeller's MobilOil and Tristar Pictures, among other masonic owned/influenced businesses have adopted this emblem with 'pride'.

A little digging led us to September 1998, where SETI detected a signal in the direction of the star called 'EQ Pegasi' of the Pegasus Constellation. Hoagland, a symbol decoder, revealed that the name Pegasus meanz "death", emblematic as a horse with wingz.

Knowin' how romantically involved the Illuminati is with death (their 2nd chapter, Skull & Bones, goes by the alias, Brotherhood of Death), we find that many of their corporationz, that serve to establish legitimacy to their behind-the-scene demonic acts, have this horse with wingz as their insignia, one in particular that ringz out is Mobil Oil, owned by Rockefeller.

In Hell-y-wood, one of the top grossin' movies was Arnold Schwarzenegger in Terminator2: Judgement Day. Guess who distributed the film? Tri-Star Pictures. Ever seen their logo?? A white horse with wingz!

Part 4, We'll get more into Hell-y-woodz role in all this in a later piece, as well as Y YT is so interested in Space. Is there somethin' out there they know about that we don't?? Stay tuned!

MORE FIE-YAH!

For the past 3 issues, we've uncovered some heavy '–ish' dealin' with alternative perspectives behind this what YT proclaimz a 'War on Terrorizm'. I do not profess to be a guru on this, nor an expert investigator, I just know that when my flight was rerouted to Atlanta on that Tuesday morning, September 11th, thingz were not what the media professed to be. Simply mergin' myself with the vybration of questionz, I was blessed with an enormous amount of leadz, openin' the door to logistical reasonin' I know I'd never learn from YTs massa-media.

Pickin' up from where we left off in part 3, I found additional info on the Masonz, Hell-y-wood and YTs continued fixation on space. Plain and simple yaw, YT wants to leave this planet! I really don't blame them. I have longed wanted to overstand the physics of space outside of this space we call Earth.

Our Ancestorz explored this as well, and although we have no recorded evidence of them ever leavin', I have a strong feelin' they did FREQUENTLY! And because of all the plagiarizmz of *Our*story, temple break-inz and book burningz, I do believe YT has gotten *some* of that info. But the way they're usin' it, as usual, violates the pure and sane nature our Ancestorz used in comprehending one of Djhuiti's most profound principles, Correspondence (as above, so below; in order to understand the unknown, study the known).

PART OF THE WHOLE

We are the microcozm of the macrocozm, if you can recall the movie, *'Contact'* that came out in 1997 with Jodi Foster, the openin' act exemplified that. Briefly, the movie starts from the planet Earth and the view starts to pan-out passing Mars and then the Asteroid Belt [NOTE: Between Earth and Mars is what's called the Asteroid Belt. What YT refuses to tell us is that these asteroidz were once a planet called 'Fenex', the ancient name for 'Phoenix'. It is said they were responsible for finding the pre-Nile Valley civilization known as "Mu" in the American southwest (more on the significance of NASA and Phoenix, Arizona in part 5)].

The scene continues panning-out passing Jupiter, Saturn and all the rest of the planets in our solar system. Next comes the Nebula we're an immediate part of; then we see an image of the Milky Way galaxy. Joined at the hip of the Milky Way resides the Andromeda Galaxy. The scene continues to pan-out now showin' thousandz if not millionz of galaxies and star clusterz. Right when there seemz to be too many to count, we see all these galaxies comin' out of the left eye (which you know YT *had* to make blue) of a little white girl (Jodi Foster's character as a child) showin' that there is a connection micro- to macrocozmically.

Afrikanz, our Ancestorz knew we were part of the whole. You are a walkin' universe. If you break yourself down, you have many galaxeez inside you each with the same elements that are out there outside the Earth's thermosphere (the outermost region of Earth's surface about 53 miles up).

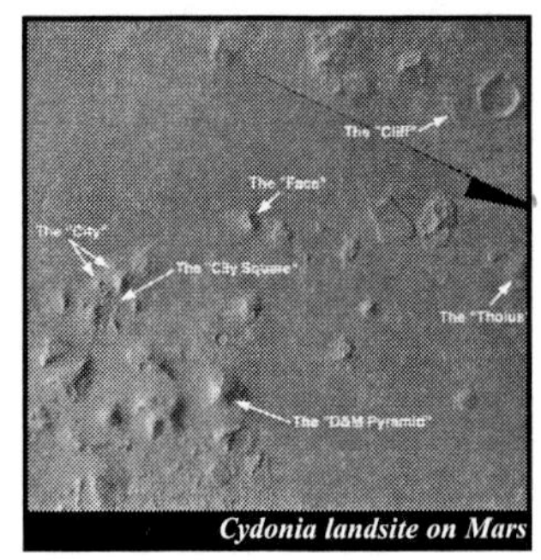

Cydonia landsite on Mars

By studyin' Correspondence we are able to get a better overstanding of what is actually out there and believe me Star, it ain't no green or grey skinned, bug eyed ETs out there! That's right! Afrikanz, we have every reason to believe that whateverz out there looks just like you and I, melanated, darkskinned people that may not go by the name Afrikan, but certainly looks like one in definition!

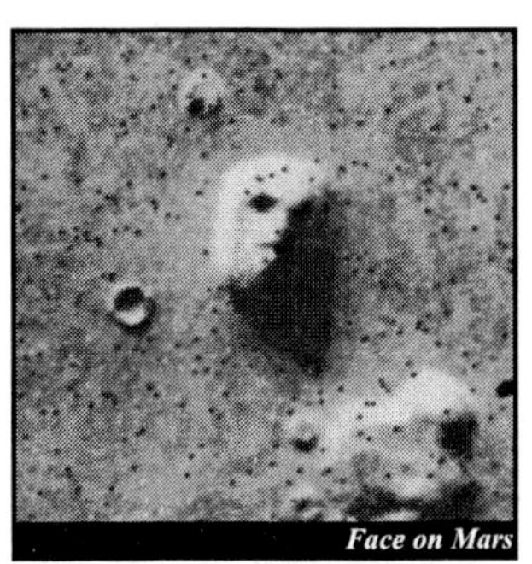
Face on Mars

Find it hard to believe? Hell-y-woodz done a number on our perception of what's out there with all these 'Independence Day,' and 'Invasion from Mars' fliks. Travel with me for a sec.

See, space is made up of primarily the same elements that exist on the Periodic Table (Chemistry chart), or should I say, the Periodic Table holdz the *known* elements of the polyverse (because there's many more we do not know of).

Note, that breakin' down the word 'Chemistry' is profound. The word 'Chem' comes from 'Khem' or 'Kemet' which meanz 'black'. Now '-istry' defines as 'the study of'. So what does chemistry actually mean? It meanz the 'study of Black' or better yet, Black which includes Afrikan people as well as melanin and carbon!

Large bushes or trees on Mars surface

Now how long has YT been studyin' us (they studied our endurance during enslavement, they injected us with death during the Tuskegee Experiment and continue to use us as guinea pigz with their Global2000 project)??

The major element in space is carbon, y'kno one of the elements that produces the gas our temples create when we exhale; the ones vegetation needz to survive that, in exchange, gives us oxygen. Carbon is also out in space. If we were to see it as a hard substance, its color is black.

Pyramidz on Mars

Space is said to be at least -1440°. That's below zero, yo! Meanin' if you were to step out in space with only a bubble goose, you'd turn to fragile glass immediately! It is said that space is infinite, so the sayin' that space continues to grow is oxymoronic, and if space *is* infinite, as we will see, there HAS TO BE other 'Afrikanz' or melanated dark-skinned beingz out there!

Now travel with me Afrikanz, let's go out in space and witness a star explode. What usually happenz is a very white, hot star growz in size to the point where it explodes. Before this star explodes, there's a

Mars

great possibility it was a solar system like ourz with rotating planets and — that's right — AND life on these planets. Unfortunately (but not really because if it's natural, it is not unfortunate, it's part of life), those planets and inhabitants of those planets probably expire due to either the explosion or the sudden elimination of heat and possibly either get blown out of the gravitational pull or freeze solid.

After the explosion, a new star is created, the core of the exploded star. This new star is able to grab the debris floating around and captures it in its gravitational pull, makin' these pieces of rock rotate around the new star which can now be called a Sun.

Sphinx in front of eroded Pyramid

Over tyme (probably thousandz and maybe even millionz of Earth yearz), what do you get when the coldness of space and combats with the heat of the sun beamin' on these rocks (planets in the making)? Yes, you get water! Now what is water but 2 parts hydrogen and 1 part oxygen which are 2 other key elements that support life as we know it here on Earth.

Followin' me Afrikanz?? –ight! Now, what happenz along with this water flooding the land? All kindz of elements are created, from algae to all other sorts of microorganizmz that create/support life. What do you think followz? Vegetation!

Blowup of Sphinx

Now of all the UFO movies we've seen, every plant that was shown was green. Melanin makes plants that color, so Y is it the same concept doesn't hold weight when it comes to the complexion of people? Because Global White Supremacy couldn't let you know of the dominance of the color Black; which is, by the way, the consumption of all colorz.

Along with plant life, you will have aquatic life (fish). Eventually, some of these fish may become land dwellerz, and so on. I'm not actually sayin' we stem from fish, but we do come from water!

3D-Rendered picture of Sphinx (front view)

Where are we first conceived? In liquid (semen that merges with an egg). We then spend the next 9 months (there's that number '9' again) developing in liquid. So by studyin' the known, logic points to us possibly evolving this way and not from an ape!

Now remember, this is likely happenin' throughout the universe as we speak and the rise and fall of galaxies are as common as we rise and fall each at the beginning and end of each day.

Eventually, this will happen to our star, the Sun, in what scientists say (but can't prove) will burn another 93 million yearz. As each million or so yearz, pass, the Sun will enlarge and eventually turn from orange to an oversized white star, possibly engulfing Mercury, Venus and possibly Earth!

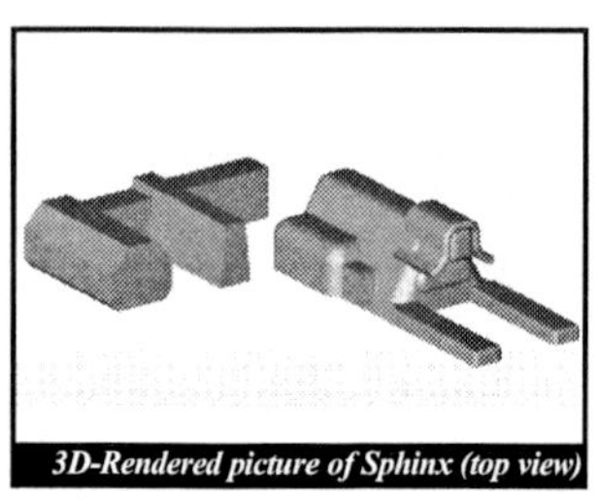
3D-Rendered picture of Sphinx (top view)

This points to a possible reason we're havin' this so-called 'Global' Warming, when in actuality it should be called solar system warming. Our solar system will then reform and the planets as we know it may be replaced by other pieces of debris.

So if this makes any sense to you Afrikan, if the plants are green, the soil is dark and the water is clear on these planets, Y wouldn't the FIRST inhabitants of these planets have naturally kinky hair, thick lips and nose's?!!? Deprogram your mind of all the movies and showz tell-a lie-vision told you about life. There is a reason YT will never tell you who you are! That is the reason they've established white secret societeez like the Masonz and the Illuminati! But we don't need YT to tell us for we already know. We just need to focus and transmit the right, HUMBLE, energy towardz our inner-selves where the true blueprint of life is imbedded in our DNA.

But the only way to fine tune this frequency is to live clean (or as clean as you can in this day and age) and keep as many impuriteez from our temple as possible, mentally and physically. However, admittedly, tryin' to tune in has its share of 'channel blocks'.

See, I believe YT knowz this and it also explainz their fascination with space and Y there's such a close relationship with NASA and Masonry.

YTs OBSESSION WITH MARS

Back in 1976, NASA had a probe land on Mars called the Viking 1 spacecraft (and Vikingz were known to be some of the biggest murdererz and thieves of all colonializm tymz!). Forward 21 yearz to July 4th, 1997 they revisited Mars landing in a region called Cydonia with the Pathfinder.

Now, as I've alwayz stated, when studyin' YT and global white supremacy, there is no such thing as coincidence! So the landing bein' on the day of America's independence, should not shock you. However, according to Astrologist's and conspiracy theorist's alike, this date had no numerical symbolz like all their other missionz.

The key ritual star, Sirius and the Belt starz of Orion did not line up at the expected 19.5° x 33° above or below the horizon or on the horizon (for mo' info on the Masonic numberz, read part 3 of this series). But somethin' did fit in Cydonia, but not for July 4th but July 20th.

Further research showed the point of Masonic reference was not in the sky but on the surface of Mars itself. Again, it was not a coincidence that NASA decided to land the Pathfinder where they did. As big as Mars is, they chose to land at Cydonia for a reason. One reason was that the landing site was 19.5°N x 33°W.

The landing was aired live on CNN that day and some tricky shit happened soon after. Pathfinder began transmitting image after image of the scene around the landing. These shots varied from right in front of the vessel to as far as the horizon could see.

Viewerz watchin' it live began calling in about the *"strange geometric rocks"* they were seeing. There were so many callz that CNNs science anchor, John Holliman asked the Pathfinder scientists about it on air. What hedz were seein' was somethin' NASA and the secret hedz behind them were not ready to explain to the masses.

What was seen was corroded metal objects, cannisterz with handles, shimmering glass-like geometric structures and even a couple of recognizable vehicle tracks! The ill shit is in that first hour of broadcast everything was seen. Soon after all the sharp images *suddenly* became blurred. The images NASA made available for download out of the blue, were no longer easily visible. What was YT tryin to hide? This is where it gets serious…

THE SPHINX

There was somethin' more to see than the metal object and cannisterz. About a kilometer away, the Pathfinder took some images of 2 mountainous regionz on the horizon of the landing site, again at 19.5°N x 33°W. In front of the highly eroded, pyramid-like mountainz was somethin' even more heavy, but because of NASAs blatant attempt to coverup somethin', hedz were unable to sharpen the images until a technique called Super Resolution Surface Modeling was invented a couple yearz after Pathfinder.

Because of this technique, the images that were initially downloaded of the Cydonian region, they were able to make out a Sphinx on Mars! That's right, just like Her-Em-Akhet that sits in front of the Pyramidz of Giza in Kemet!! In addition, the images on Mars turned out to be the exact replica of the Pyramidz of Giza!!!

There is no way other than that our Ancestorz in Kemet had some kind of relationship/influence/or they were influenced with the melanated lifeformz on Mars, for there is no other way to explain how there can be 2 identical settingz at specific points on each planet. Like on Earth, the Sphinx faces east directly toward the Martian equinoctial sunrise sitting in its ready-to-attack position guarding the temples behind it (just as Webster defines it, "to guard or protect").

This "Sphinx" has a triangular body, rectangular forepawz, a square face and a symmetrical style headdress. Behind the Sphinx is a flat, vertical wall, with a wedge shaped protrusion and a hexagonal protrusion to the left.

Regardless of whether the Sphinx is one object or two, it clearly has distinctive block-like features that are not produced commonly in naturally occurring rocks, especially rocks that sit at the base of layered, structured pyramidz that just happen to be at 19.5°N x 33°W.

THE CYDONIA/KEMET CONNECTION

If you remember the movie, 'Mission to Mars; that came out in 2000, the crew found what later was seen as a huge face in the ground that, on ground level, comes across as a mountainous region, but from atop looks like the now infamous, 'Face on Mars'. This face turned out to be a spacecraft.

Towardz the end of the movie, they were able to crack the frequency code, get inside the face and was approached by a "Martian" that showed how the planets were shaped and how life evolved on earth. The only thing that disappointed me was how the Martian looked. As I said, to me, logic would support this being — if it was an oxygen breathin' land dweller, to be dark skinned and kinky-haired.

MORE FIE-YAH!

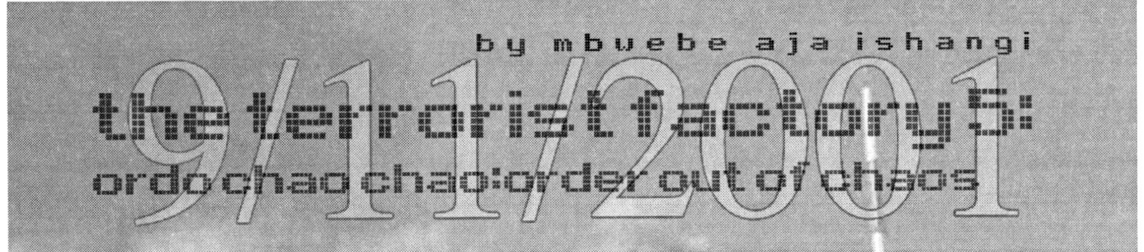

After takin' a couple months to gather more info, I've found that as the date September 11th (9/11) becomes etched in everyone's mind, there's so much hedz haven't a clue about concerning the events that lead up to this strategically chosen date. For those not up on the Terrorist Factory series, I urge you to refresh yourselves with parts 1-4 because it may prove to be a lil' difficult to follow part 5.

Before puttin' on our wetsuits and diving deeper into the abyss of secrets, it must be pointed out that the imbalance non-Afrikanz have — due to lack of mid- to high levelz of melanin (read texts about Melanin by Llaila O. Afrika and Carol Barnes) — may be the sole reason we find that of all these conspiraceez we find Afrikan culture as the foundation.

Europeanz have a history of distorting the truth, flippin' it from positive to negative and using it to their benefit. I say this so that no one will think, *"well if all this numerology and metaphysics is rooted in Afrika, it ain't YT to blame, it's Afrika."* Not true. Our mistake is that we shared our information with them, a species that used tricknology to have us believe they were sincere, yet proved different through plagiarizm and manipulation of a philosophy that was composed to have an inner-standing of Nature not to exploit it.

Aristotle and Pythagoras serve as 2 early pirates who literally stole our Ancestorz knowledge by writing it down and claiming to have created it themselves. It is well documented that they visited Kemet (Egypt) and was schooled there. Soon after they left Kemet, Aristotle began plagiarizing over 1000 texts on topics he claimed he originated. But in the end, both later confessed on their deathbedz the origin of their knowledge base… the Nile Valley in Afrika!

Let's be clear! The 9/11 scam is but the latest physical manifestation of a scripted war the illuminated ones want you to believe is goin' on. It is through 'Ordo Ab Chao', the order out of chaos, that they are able to achieve maximum control through havin' the masses bumpin' hedz running frantically like roaches pointing fingerz at each other not realizing the actual perpetrator is the one you never hear of… the Rothschilds/Rhodes secret society.

Let's be clear!! These faggots are using Afrikan philosophy, flipped, to control the masses! It is long overdue that we arm ourselves mentally and physically, in honor of our Ancestorz, to devise a strategic plan to cut the stringz the puppeteer has had on us for far too long.

One last thing, eliminate the term 'coincidence' from your mind, because when studyin' secret societeez, there is no such thing. These thingz are carefully planned…

NUMERICAL MYSTEREEZ

As mentioned in the previous joints, it's not just about 2 planes crashing into the World Trade Center and 1 into the Pentagon; nor is it about Bush representing the U.S. versus Osama Bin Laden reppin' the Arab Muslimz. Through just a lil' research, one can find connectionz to Freemasonry, the Illuminati, Metaphysics and Numerology.

To quickly refresh you, note that there are significant numberz that have been seen throughout this farce of a terrorist attack. The numberz 9, 11 and 77 stand prominent as, in addition, we found the numberz 3, 7, 13, 18, 28, 33, 39 and 666 or any multiple of these have connectionz to secret societeez.

• #3 — said to be the first perfect number which represents the Trinity. No, not the one you've been told through Christianity (God, Son & Holy Ghost). The original Trinity standz for the Afrikan deity, Ausar, Auset & Heru — erroneously called Osirus, Isis & Horus. It's been said that greater power is achieved when a sacred number is grouped in two's and three's, like #33 and 333.

• #6 — represents the soul of man showing the omnipotent power of God. Not to get biblically on you (I choose to also use my enemies toolz against them, proving they are not flawless), this can be seen in Revelation 13:18 where the biblical God assignz the number 666 to man and the beast. Remember, numberz have greater power when doubled or tripled: 6 —> 6+6+6 = 666.

• #7 — also known as the 'Invisible Center' and spirit of everything. Multiplyin' by this number creates an even more powerful sacred number. For example, 7x3=21. Because numberz are broken down to a single digit, 21 now becomes 3 (2+1=3).

• #9 — if you're familiar with the series I've written on the Boule' and Skull&Bones, you are aware of how often this number is seen. Nine is sacred because it is the first cube of an odd number. In Masonry, as told by author of *'Masonic Assassination'*, Michael Anthony Hoffman, we find the 9th degree is a ritual where one is decapitated.

• #11 — in Astrology and Numerology, 11 is considered to be a master number. It is also considered to symbolize sin, transgression and danger. 10 bein' the perfect number, 11 signifies the exceeding of both. See, 11, or 1+1=2, containz duality. And we find that YT has alwayz wanted to be equal to Afrikanz (mentally, spiritually and physically); just like how, biblically speakin, the devil wanted to be equal to God. This number is a master vybration and Numerologists choose not to reduce this number to a single digit. When 11 is multiplied by 3, we get 33. This number, as we'll soon see has a heavy significance to secret societeez.

• #13 — this number has been tagged a negative number because of Occultist's who believe because of its use in Genesis of the bible, the 13th year is said to be the year a rebellion was started against Chedorlaomer. From that, apostasy, defection, corruption, disintegration and revolution have become synonymous. Note the Masonic influence in the bible where the original testament has 33 titles and the new has 13. One of Rothschilds own, Adolf Hitler, was ordered to start World War 2 in 1939 not by accident. 39 is a multiple of 13 (13x3). Also, remember what the number was of the United Snakes original colonies…13!

• #33 — is a magical number. Most notably it's use in Freemasonry, this can be attributed to Albert Pike. Pike, a General of the Confederate Army, 33rd degree Scottish Rite Mason, author of the book that exposed the Masonz, *'Morals and Dogma',* a confessed believer in Lucifer and main founder of the Ku Klux Klan. It is not a coincidence he chose the acronym KKK because the letter K is the 11th letter and K, or 11x3 = 33! Now you won't get many Masonz, particularly Prince Hall, or Black Masonz to confess to this simply because (1)they are not taught this and simply don't know; (2)York and Scottish Rite Masonz aren't too welcoming to Prince Hall's; and (3)Most are not 33 degree Masonz and of those that are Prince Hall 33 degree Masonz, their 33rd degree is not the same and York and Scottish Rite.

But as I stated in previous pieces about the Prince Hall's, they don't realize they are some negroes who are tryin' to be like good 'ol massa, who won't allow you to join their organization but you're welcome to make a black-version that they'll acknowledge as long as they have subliminally, the same loyalty to white supremacy. Oh, and are you aware that this country honorz this faggot by puttin' a larger-than-life statue of him in, of all cities, Washington, DC, where the majority population is Afrikan people! To top that, Pikes statue was dedicated 39 dayz after fellow Mason, Teddy Roosevelt's Presidential inauguration in 1901 (—> 1+9+0+1=11)!! Proof we don't read, nor know our culture as well as our enemy!!!

Additionally, in the book, *'In God's Name'*, written by David Yallop, which exposes the murder of the Pope John Paul I, aka Albino Luciani, who was in power for only 33 dayz, points out the masonz as the key role in his death because of his threat to make drastic changes in the Vatican.

• #39 — this number can be seen in use with the Bilderberg Group, who maintainz a core membership of 39, who are broken into 3 groups of 13. According to researcher, Robert Howard, these 39 answer to the 13 who make up the Policy Committee who answer to the Round Table of 9. The United States *CON*-stitution has 7 articles that were signed by 39 memberz of the Constitutional Convention.

• #77 — along with being one of the flight numberz that crashed into the WTC, 77 represents the revenge of Lamech. Again, gettin' biblical on you, Lamech was a descendant of Cain, the first murderer and father of Tubal-Cain, who's an ancestor of Hiram Abiff. The bible sayz the following about the mark of the revenge of Lamech: *"And Lamech said unto his wives, Adah and Zillah, 'Hear my voice: ye wives of Lamech, hearken unto my speech: for I have slain a man to my wounding, and a young man to my hurt. If Cain shall be avenged sevenfold, truly Lamech seventy and sevenfold (77).'"* (Gen.4:23-24).

With the previous numberz as a reference, let's do the math. Get out your calculative mindz…

THE EQUATION PUT INTO EFFECT

In Revelationz 9:11, we read, *"And they had a king over them, which is the angel of the bottomless pit, whose name in the Hebrew tongue is Abaddon, but in the Greek tongue hath his name Apollyon."* Both Abaddon and Apollyon mean destroyer. So who's the destroyer??

Remember in parts 2 and 3, we revealed how all this stemmed from the Knights Templar. They were recognized in 1118 (1+1+1+8=11) although the original 9 founding memberz first mutually assembled in 1111 (11 & 11), takin' no new memberz for a period of 9 yearz.

The known Masonic puppets and unknown, behind-the-scene forefatherz of this country carried on the secret tradition of the Knights Templarz when they met many centureez later at one of the first Masonic Lodges, the Green Dragon Tavern, at *11 Marshall Street, Boston, Massachussetts* to decide America's future. Outside the Tavern, the building has 11 windowz while inside is the description of the Scottish Rite 33rd degree motto, 33 Sovereign Grand Inspector-General.

This degree Howard states, *"is conferred as an honorarium on those who for great merit and long and arduous services have deserved well of the Order."* The mottos of this degree are *'Deus Meumque Jus', 'Unio. Toleratio. Robur.', 'Ordo ab Chao', 'S.A.P.I.E.N.T.I.A.'* and *'Ad Universi Terrarum Orbis Summi Architecti Gloriam'*. The Lodge is draped in purple with skeletonz and skull and cross-bones. The Lodge is lit by 11 lights.

One of their most prominent memberz, Adam Weishaupt, formed the Masterz of the Illuminati, tyming it in a manner equivalent to power numberz. He chose May 1st as the day because May is the 5th month with the 1st day which equalz 6. He also chose 1776 because the numberz add up to 21 — so when you add the two up, 6+21, we get 27, which is 9. In addition, it is a power number because 27 is a multiple of 3, which in their eyes makes 9 three tymz more powerful!

The Grand Lodge of the District of Columbia, home to the Masonz, laid the cornerstone in 1911 (1+9+1+1=12 —> 1+2=3, the trinity). The *Cock*afellaz, oops, Rockefellerz that same year hired a high-level British Intelligence operative named Claude Dansey. Dansey is responsible for converting the US. Army Intelligence Service into a sub-division of the British Secret Service.

If we are to believe thingz that has happened on these dates are not a coincidence, we must realize in order for these dates to happen there had to be some serious planning; planning that was not 'on-the-fly'.

Weishaupt's creation of the Illuminati took massive planning, month's, yearz, probably even decades before it was put into play May 1, 1776. Sayin' this meanz we must also realize these families are most likely plannin' thingz yearz in advance. For example, they could already be planning for thingz to happen in 2050!!

The Marine Corps Green Dragon logo

First meeting place of Freemasonz
The Green Tavern, Boston, MA

9/11 HAS HISTORY

Along with all the bizarre "coincidence's" 9/11 has, we find this date has history! On September 11th, 1941, the groundbreaking ceremony for the U.S. Pentagon took place!!

On April 25th, 1945 (4/25 —> 4+2+5=11), Delegates from 50 nationz met in San Francisco to officially form the United Nationz. During this 2 month period, they completed a charter containing 111 articles which was approved on June 25th (6/25 —> 6+2+5=13) and came into effect October 24th, 1945 (10/24 —> 1+0+2+4=7).

2 months later, in December, the U.S. moved to establish the UN'z headquarterz and in August of the following year it was temporarily moved to Lake Success, New York, later moving to it's present place bordering the East River in New York City (<— 11 letterz).

THE NUMBER 28

I mentioned 28 earlier but didn't elaborate. The number 28, according to Howard is, *"one of the correspondences of Solomon in kabbalistic numerology"*. The Solomonic name assigned to 28 is 'Beale'. We find that the 28th degree of Templarizm is the *"King of the Sun"* degree. So when we look at November 22nd, 1963 [11/22 (2x11)], then president, Kennedy and his wife flew into Gate 28 at Love Field, Dallas, Texas (NOTE: Dallas, Texas is located 10 miles north of the 33rd degree of latitude). They then arrived in Air Force One, code-named *"Angel"*. The motorcade left Love Field to Dealey Plaza, a Masonic temple. We obviously know pretty much what happened next, *"Back and to the left, back and to the left"* (from the 1991 movie, JFK).

Jump up to George H.W. His reign of terror starting in 1989 [really as Vice President in '81 (1+8=9)], we come to a speech he made to Congress, September 11th, 1990 (11 yearz before 9/11/2001) referring to the war on Iraq is a *"rare opportunity to move toward a historic period of cooperation. Out of these troubled times a NEW WORLD ORDER can emerge."* And exactly 11 yearz later to the day, the attack here proves this New World Order regime is emerging.

Shortly after the attacks, Bush's son, got immediate assistance from Tony Blair, Prime Minister of Great Britain pretty much puttin' pressure on all other nationz to either join them on their alleged crusade *on* terrorizm (when it is they who in fact are the real terrorists) or be considered an enemy.

IF I'M LYIN' IM STILL NOT FLYIN'!

I'm not the supersticous type, but I will say that the followin' info I read from researcher, Robert Howard blew my mind!

On Wednesday, July 17th, 1996, TWA 800 took off from JFK Airport that night and exploded several minutes later over the Atlantic Ocean, near Long Island. Swiss Air 111 took off from the same airport, Wednesday, September 2nd, 1998 (9/2 —> 11) and went down in flames into the Atlantic near Nova Scotia, Canada.

The ill shit is that the number of weeks between these 2 mysterious crashes is exactly 111 weeks, the same as the Swiss Air flight. 111 weeks also converts to 777 dayz. Now remember what was said about 77? It is symbolic for revenge.

Contrary to what the white-owned 'massa'-media wants you to know, TWA Flight 800 didn't explode from a fuel tank but from a missile that was fired from a boat which then sped away, seen by satellite surveillance and hundredz of eyewitnesses in Long Island, whom the FBI never bothered to interview.

Back on December 21st, 1988, Pan Am Flight 103 was brought down over Scotland. Notice a connection between this flight and Swiss Air 111? PanAm 103 went down over Scotland and Swiss Air 111 went down over Nova Scotia, Canada, which is also called New Scotland. Scotland has a connection to masonry because there's the Scottish-Rite Masonz.

Even more bizarre is that the tyme between Pan Am 103 in December 88 and TWA 800 in July'96 is 7 yearz, 7 months! Again we see 77, the mark of revenge of Lamech.

Are you starting to see how this all dates back to the millennium-long battle of the Knights Templar versus the Arab Muslimz, I spoke of in part 3?

I'm gonna leave you to marinate on that until I reveal some even deeper subliminalz in part 6!

As I've stated before, we are diligently at work tryin' to get to the root of this fiasco. And we pledge whatever we find, you will know! Each one, teach one!

LIK SHOT!

On September 11th, 2001, the World Trade Center was hit in the heart of New York City's financial district; but so was the Pentagon out in Washington, DC. But have you noticed, with everything that happened on that day and since, there hasn't been much talk of what actually happened at the Pentagon?? Somethin' did happen at the Pentagon, exactly *what* is the question.

After readin' this, you'll see it certainly was not the Boeing 757 they claim! But before that, let's think about a historical link 9/11 and the Pentagon has. Throughout this series, we've dealt with numberz and dates, showin' these thingz are not randomly selected and have subliminal meaningz. Well, what happened in DC is no different.

Did you know on that same day, September 11, 1941 during the presidency of Franklin Roosevelt, was the ground breaking ceremony of the Pentagon? Is it possible the alleged terrorists' were tryin' to draw attention to the year 1941(1+9+4+1=15 —> 1+5=6 – read part 5 for the definition of the #6) as well as a connection with Roosevelt. Before you say *'no,'* consider this…

THE HISTORICAL SIGNIFICANCE OF 1941

Could what happened in DC be a subliminal call out for World War III? In part 2 and 3 of this series, we spoke of the millennium-old beef this whole thingz really about. It's an old grudge between the arab muslimz and descendants of the Knights Templar (the Illuminati). Now when we look at the year 1941, it was also the year World War II started.

Now, I could be reachin' but again, when studyin' global white supremacy, there's no such thing as a coincidence. So, 1941 comes out to equal 6 (1+9+4+1=15 —> 1+5=6); there are 60 (6+0=6) yearz between 1941 and 2001; and World War III (or 3) equalz 1050 (World=138+90+118+72+24=442; War=138+6+118=262; Three=120+48+118+30+30=346 —> 442+262+346=1050 —> 1+0+5+0=6 *(See DGT Numerical Mystereez, 50th issue, Jun/Jul 1997)*. See 666??

But there's more, it appearz Roosevelt has somethin' to do with this also. He was sworn in on the March 4th, 1933 as the 32nd President of the United Snakes. Hedz may not know he was also a 32nd Degree Scottish Rite mason.

In addition, the Vice-President, Harry Truman was a 33rd Degree Freemason! In 1945 Truman became America's 33rd President. Now, to commonfolk, they won't see a link, but to a deeply religious sect like the arab muslimz or someone who's anti-masonz, they might see them as grave enemies.

Geographically, the 32nd degree parallel passes just a little south of the city of Jerusalem. It has often been said the 'Mother Lodge' of the Scottish Rite Supreme Council of the 33rd Degree was fixed at the city of Charleston, South Carolina because the 33rd

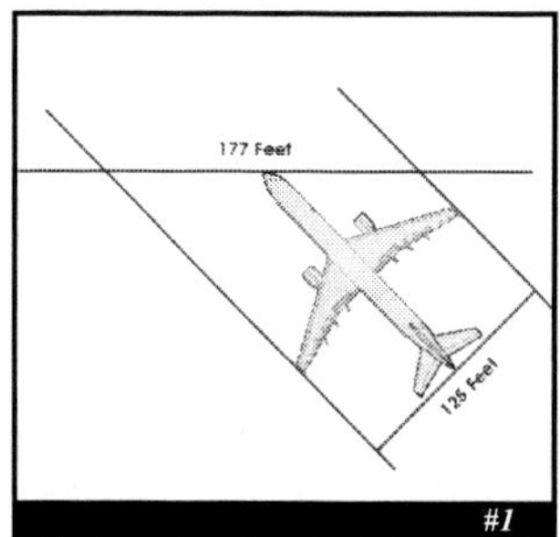

#1

#2

#3

#4

degree parallel passes almost right through it. Is this a coincidence?

In addition, in some certificates of the Scottish Rite 33rd Degree, the actual geographical latitude given in degreez is shown next to the name and location of the issuing lodge. This showz there's sort of a mystical connection between the "Degree" ritualz and the geographical latitude "degree" of the lodge. This can easily show how the arab muslimz might see the creation of the State of Israel — who created the Zionist Organization during the Roosevelt/Truman administration — which happenz to be stolen land that just so happenz to have a wealth of natural resources under it's soil.

We must have an innerstanding that all this has nothin' to do with terrorizm, because the western world [dominated mainly by the United States and (not so) Great Britain] are the biggest terrorists of all tyme. This is all about natural resources. It's about oil, gold, silver, uranium, copper, etc.

The thing is that the arab muslimz are no better! They both are fightin' over land that is not there's, it is on Afrikan soil! But we are the Black Zombies, Nas speaks of, unaware of what really a'gwan.

All that bein' said, let's focus on what YT continuously does… make mistakes. The unfortunate thing is because they control the media and they've got us all convinced what they tell us is the truth, they are able to make these mistakes with little to no chastisement.

AMERICAN AIRLINES FLIGHT 77 TYMELINE

Let's first look over the tymeline of American Airlines Flight 77 (AA77), Boeing 757 that allegedly crashed into the Pentagon:

- 8:20am: Flight 77 departs from Dulles Airport, about 20 miles from the Pentagon.
- 8:50am: Last radio communication with flight 77 recorded. The plane is now some 280 miles from the Pentagon.
- 8:56am: Radar receiver contact lost. Plane's now approximately 335 miles from the Pentagon.
- 9:00am: Flight 77 turnz and headz for the Pentagon. Now some 370 miles away from the Pentagon. The hijackerz finally make their move after waisting all this tyme and fuel flyin' away from a target they already were at.
- 9:37am: AA77 crashes into the southwest side of the Pentagon. Now, precisely 0 miles from the Pentagon. See this shit don't make sense! To give the Air National Guard/US. Air Force (USAF) a fighting chance the fearless hijackerz wait till they dam near 400 miles away from their target before turning back. Y IZ dat?! This "delay" gave the USAF more than 40

minutes to send up reinforcements to investigate and shoot down if need be. Oh, it get's more deep!

#5

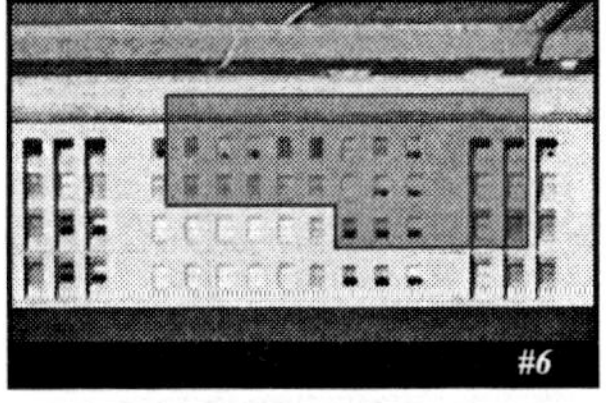
#6

#7

#8

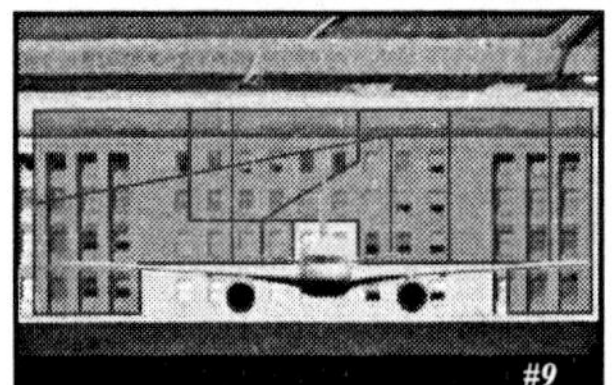
#9

When AA77 left the airport at 8:20am, the radio to track the plane wasn't turned on until 8:56a… that's over a half-hour later, yet it was still visible by radar!! This alone is proof positive this was an inside job, because planes are tracked using radio and radar. I would think proper rules would regulate one fully investigate any flying object that is on radar yet has no radio contact, afterall, it could be alienz (a lil' joke)!

Then, a couple minutes later, AA77 disappearz from all radar screenz near the Ohio border. Suddenly minutes later, a plane appearz on radar just south of Washington, DC. Then it crashes into the Pentagon. Notice I said "A PLANE appearz on radar," not Flight 77.

Now, mathematically, if it took AA77 40 minutes to fly 370 miles, how could it return to hit the Pentagon in a matter of minutes?!!? In addition, had it flown from the Ohio border back to DC it would be able to be seen on the radar, which there's no report of. So Y do we believe the large Boeing 757 hit the Pentagon? Simple… we were told by 'massa'-media. We've become so dependent on what YT wants us to know, we refuse to look into thingz ourselves! We accept what they want us to know with no question and certainly no investigation of our own. So, if this is so, where's the evidence?!

DID A BOEING 757 REALLY HIT THE PENTAGON??

Officially, YTs sayin' that AA77 was jacked by terrorists who flew it approximately 40 minutes unnoticed and then slammed into the Pentagon leavin' *no debris*. If you're familiar with the DC area, there's madd military bases around it, as far out as Virginia. So you got these cats who allegedly steal a plane and fly around a high military area with not one, NOT ONE fighter jet encounter! This shit is comical!! YT actually expects us to believe this!! The jokes really on us, because many did believe them.

Was there ever really a flight AA77? There are some skeptics who believe there wasn't and whatever happened at the Pentagon served some other purpose. When lookin' at the crash site, logic would tell you it was impossible for a plane that big, do so little damage as well as magically disappearing, leavin' practically no debris, as if the plane dissolved after the crash.

On top of that, there's photos THEY released that contradict what they're sayin'! Peep the photos, the damage to the Pentagon was not as bad as they led us to believe.

For one, look at how small the hole is in the Pentagon that was said to be created by the plane. What makes this more of a mystery is that the Bush administration has refused since day one, to release the black boxes, voice recorderz and any pictures of any

#10

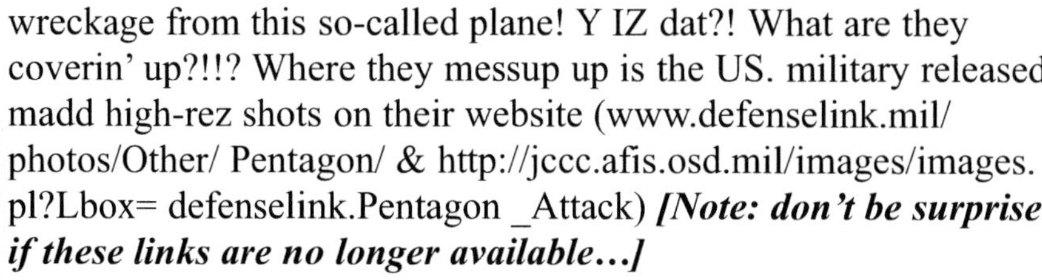
wreckage from this so-called plane! Y IZ dat?! What are they coverin' up?!!? Where they messup up is the US. military released madd high-rez shots on their website (www.defenselink.mil/ photos/Other/ Pentagon/ & http://jccc.afis.osd.mil/images/images.pl?Lbox= defenselink.Pentagon _Attack) ***[Note: don't be surprise if these links are no longer available…]***

HOW BIG WAS THE HOLE?

Research done by an unknown author on www.nerdcities.com, he was able to prove the contradiction in what was reported. If you look at the pictures, you will see 3 shots before the part of the Pentagon collapsed. You will also notice the outline showin' you the part that wasn't demolished. The 4th and 5th shot are the 3 images together, so that you can see how a Boeing 757 cannot possibly fit into the picture.

#11

Notice that the wingz do not fit. A plane that big traveling at a high rate would definitely do more damage. But what was found was if this plane did hit, it hit at about 45° angle. What does this do? It increases the wingspan!! Hittin' head-on, the wingspan woulda made a hole about 125ft. But since we know it hit at a 45° angle, this increased the wingspan to 177ft!

So, if you look at these pictures, you can resolve that the hole in the Pentagon wall is too small to have been made by a Boeing 757. In addition, you can see that the damage to the Pentagon is not all that extensive as 'massa'-media had us believe. We've seen the entry wound, what about the exit wound?

#12

YT tellz us a plane as wide as flight AA77, weighing about 100 tonz and traveling over 300 miles an hour, was only able to damage the outer ring – called the E-ring (of a total of 5 ringz) of the Pentagon. Now that's complete bullshit! C'mon yo, over 100 tonz? Travelling over 300 mph?? What, was the Pentagon made out of Kevlar?! Sure enuff, they want us to believe so.

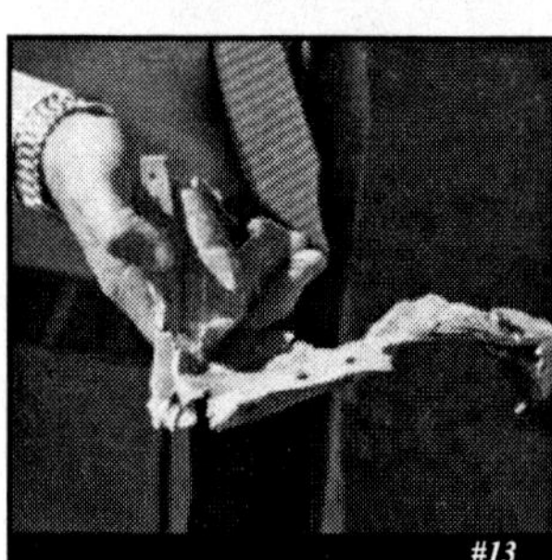
#13

The media reported that the Pentagon wallz and windowz were specially hardened to resist a crash. They also claim the aircraft hit the ground before and slid into the Pentagon. They said the wallz were specially reinforced. However, the outer Pentagon wall containz a framework of 10-inch reinforced concrete with the adjacent space filed with 8 inch thick brickwork. Over this was placed about 6 inches of limestone. So the outer wall is about 16 inches thick. That's like takin' a ruler and adding 4 more inches. Does that seem sturdy enuff to take a hit from a 100-ton 757?! Even if it was 16 feet, some serious damage would've been done!

Now, after this fact, the media will claim they said the wallz are blast-resistant. Maybe so, but that does not translate to crash resistant! A photo was released of the whole inside of the 3rd or 'C-ring'. The whole is about 12 feet wide and was later said to have been caused by one of the jet engines. This meanz in order to exit out the C-ring, whatever it was that did it, had to also enter then exit first through the E-ring, the D-ring, then the C-ring. But when we look at the photos, there is no sign of anything "exiting" through the 5th, 4th and 3rd ringz.

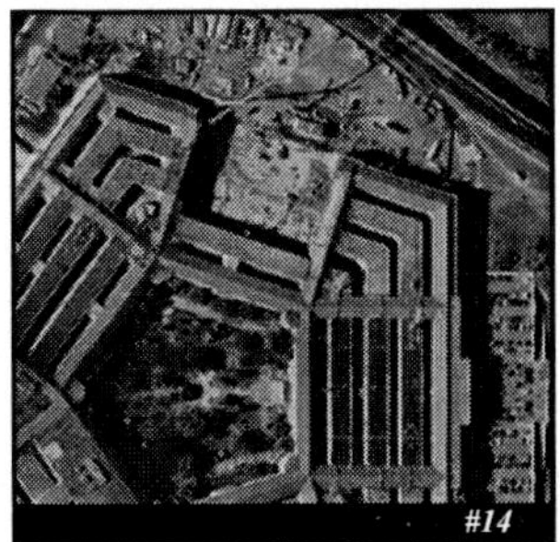
#14

The Pentagon has 5 floorz, and reports say the plane hit the ground and skid into the Pentagon — which would make the impact at ground level. But the photos ***(#5-9)*** show the damage was not at ground level. They say 3-ringz were damaged, yet we see damage in only 2 (the outer E-ring and inner C-ring), with *no* damage in between. To cover up this lie they could not explain, they chose to demolish the first 3 ringz ***(photo #14)***. So what about the crash site?

#15

THE CRASH SITE

As stated, the Bush administration still refuses to release the black boxes, voice recorderz or photographs of the crash site. This probably woulda been swept under the rug of mysteries had the military not release pictures of the crash site. From these photos ***(#10-13 and 16)***, we can see the remnants from the crash. Photo #10 showz the entire wreckage. #11 showz a blown up picture. Does any of this look like pieces from a Boeing 757?? All that can be seen are small metal scraps. Where are the large parts?! There's no way a plane can slide into a building and dissolve entirely into small pieces. The only big piece that was found was a part of a helicopter ***(photo #16)*** eye-witness, Lincoln Liebner, reported was struck by the aircraft before it hit the Pentagon. Now how many heard of this??

#16

#17

Speakin' of "slide" (as the media put it), if it did slide into the Pentagon, take a look at ***photos #12*** and ***17***, seemz to me the grass in front of the Pentagon is in tact. I don't see ANY signz of somethin' sliding into it. There's absolutely no evidence that showz wreckage from a Boeing 757 was at the Pentagon. Bush could clear all speculation just by releasing the wreckage, black box and recorderz of AA77, but again, he has not, and I'm sure will not.

Now I'm not sayin' an aircraft didn't hit the Pentagon. But it certainly wasn't the plane they said it was. The question that's also not been asked is if Flight AA77 didn't hit the Pentagon, where is it and where are the passengerz?! On the website www.Public-Action.com/911/bumble.html, *"the first report on NBC said there had been an explosion near the Pentagon heliport. There was no mention of a plane. If you were watching ABC, the first reports cited eyewitnesses who said a business jet had crashed into the Pentagon. Notice that this description is similar to the first report about the WTC (there was a New York woman who was the first eyewitness on NBC. She had no question about what she saw. She said she heard an airplane coming in low and looked up. She saw a small private jet, and watched it fly into the first WTC tower, the North tower. She was certain in her*

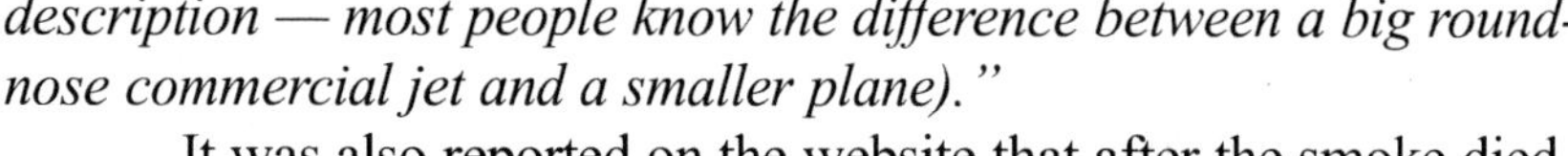

description — most people know the difference between a big round-nose commercial jet and a smaller plane)."

#18

It was also reported on the website that after the smoke died down, everyone could see the Pentagon but no one could see the plane. The Pentagon is made of masonry — limestone — not steel and glass. The aluminum wingz of the plane should have been ripped off and left outside the building. We should have been able to see wing wreckage. But there was none. Regarding the explosion that happened, somethin' even more fake appeared to happen. This leadz to more questionz as to what exactly happened…

EXPLOSION AT THE PENTAGON

#19

The government released a series of photos ***(photos #18-22)*** they claim were at the exact moment of impact. The photographs were not officially released by the Pentagon, but officialz say the images were authentic and had been provided to law enforcement officialz investigating the attack. Yeah right. Y didn't they include the black box and voice recorder?

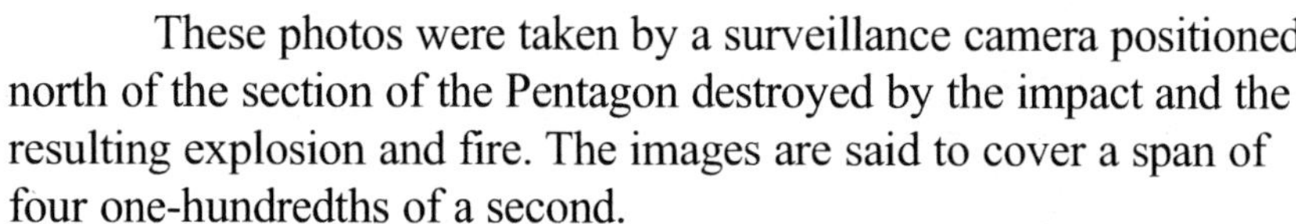

These photos were taken by a surveillance camera positioned north of the section of the Pentagon destroyed by the impact and the resulting explosion and fire. The images are said to cover a span of four one-hundredths of a second.

#20

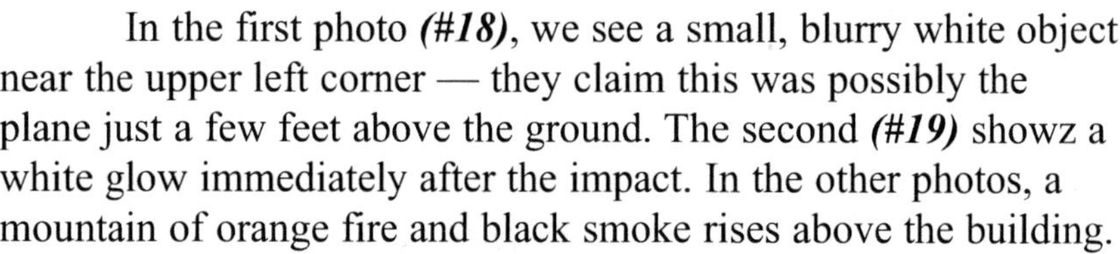

In the first photo ***(#18)***, we see a small, blurry white object near the upper left corner — they claim this was possibly the plane just a few feet above the ground. The second ***(#19)*** showz a white glow immediately after the impact. In the other photos, a mountain of orange fire and black smoke rises above the building.

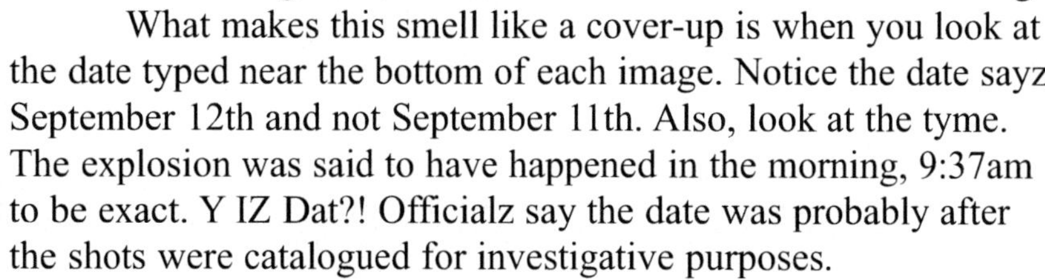

What makes this smell like a cover-up is when you look at the date typed near the bottom of each image. Notice the date sayz September 12th and not September 11th. Also, look at the tyme. The explosion was said to have happened in the morning, 9:37am to be exact. Y IZ Dat?! Officialz say the date was probably after the shots were catalogued for investigative purposes.

Sep. 12, 2001, 17:37:22 #3 impact
#21

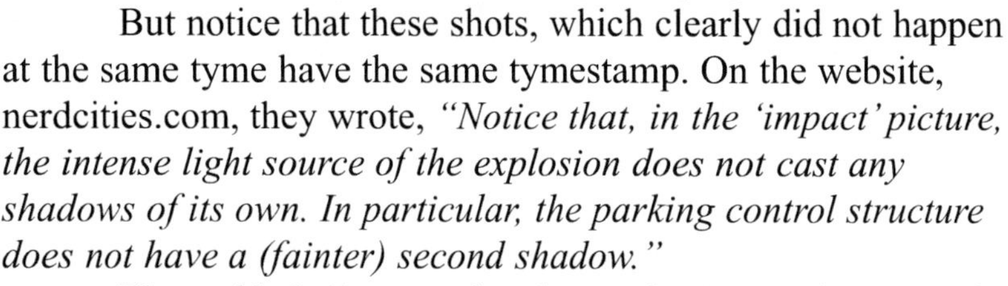

But notice that these shots, which clearly did not happen at the same tyme have the same tymestamp. On the website, nerdcities.com, they wrote, *"Notice that, in the 'impact' picture, the intense light source of the explosion does not cast any shadows of its own. In particular, the parking control structure does not have a (fainter) second shadow."*

#22

They added, *"notice also that in the 'impact' picture, the Pentagon wall is much brighter than in the other photos. The forger seems to have realized that the explosion would light up the entire Pentagon wall (but overlooked the fact that it would cast shadows of its own). He has tried to imitate the flash of the blast by increasing the brightness of the entire picture, unfortunately for him, this also increased the brightness of the areas that should still be in shadow (and thus darker). For example, the sides of the parking control structures facing the camera have also increased in brightness."*

In photo labeled 'plane' ***(#18)***, we are s'posed to be lookin' at the shadow of the tail of the alleged Boeing 757 just above the parking control structure. Real shadowz just don't come with their own outline, pointing out more evidence that the pictures have been touched up.

Also peep how the heliport control tower ***(#19-21)*** is engulfed in the fireball. The cat who touched up these photos seemz to have forgotten that the close (to the camera) end of the heliport control tower is a long way from the impact site. The remaining photos show the fireball has increased in size, but somehow it has managed to shrink back behind the heliport control tower, and leave it in shadow.

The camera took shots at 4 one-hundreths of a second, that's one picture a second. Oh, I see, the government has a high-powered camera that takes low-quality pictures. Still not convinced? Before I end this piece, peep this bit of info.

The crash, is not like the usual air crash. In a usual crash, when a plane hits the ground, the fuel tanks rupture and the fuel spill along the ground at high speed, mixing thoroughly with the air and exploding outward and upward. Well here, most of the fuel spillz into a confined space with little opportunity to mix thoroughly with air. With that bein' the case, the explosion should be much smaller than normal and since most of the fuel enterz the building, the direction of the visible blast would be parallel to the ground, as it explodes back through the entry wound.

In the faked explosionz here, we have a huge explosion, with the main direction of the blast being upward. Just before the plane impacts the wall, 100% of the fuel is still in the wingz and body of the aircraft. So this fuel cannot explode because it has not been mixed with air. It can't even burn until it is exposed to the air! Most of this fuel should've entered the Pentagon. The type of phony explosion in this series of photos, looks more like a Hollywood explosion.

Further, it was reported the fuel that did not enter the building, spilt for some distance down the wall, where a little of it exploded, but most of it just ignited and burnt. So explain to me how the fuel mixed with air before hitting the Pentagon wall?? Witnesses claimed the plane hit the ground some distance in front of the wall, spilling much fuel then sliding into the wall miraculously exiting in the inner side of the 3rd ring without leavin' an exit wound from the 1st ring, an entry into the 2nd, an exit from the 2nd and an entry into the 3rd.

It is clearly obvious there's some kind of cover-up. The question is Y? Y would our government conspire to mislead the world, claimin' to have this illusionary enemy, convincing us we could be attacked again at any tyme. Should we believe this, when the facts they have released make no sense? Are they doin' exactly what the Illuminati say they do, playin' both sides of field (victim and antagonizer)? Mi tink so!!

KRS-One (before he did a 180° turn from Afrikan philosopher to current christian evangelist) had a joint, "You Must Learn!" But when I look at the state of Hiphop today, have we NOT learned?!!? After attending numerous Hiphop Summit's over the past few yearz, it seemz the alleged vanguardz of this art (mceez, djayz, producerz etc.) mindset have been bamboozled again!

I've heard just about every artist from Ja Rule to the Zulu Nation speak, in so many wordz, about Hiphop bein' for EVERYONE! Since when did Hiphop encompass all people?!!? Since hedz got greedy and felt they could make more money by caterin' to whites, after all, they're the one's who buy the CDs, while we Afrikanz who claim we're broke (even though we have a nearly $300billion annual purchasing power) buy the 3 for $5 bootleg version.

If you look at Hiphop as a business, profit-wise, it makes sense to cater to YT, but at what expense? If Hiphop is a way of life, as KRS sayz, money should not override the culture. This is what happenz when you either work with YT or have a white-mindset. All they think of is exploitation for profit! Because some of our premiere mogulz have chosen to lie in bed with these pirates, we are once again losin' one of our greatest creationz ever!

HAVE WE NOT LEARNED?

Y do we feel the consistent need to give our gifts away? Have we not learned?! As long as we continue the relationship we currently have with YT (as an overseer of descendants of enslaved Afrikan), we will continue to give away our gifts to the world while YT inherits the (financial) benefits.

Look at history, our Ancestorz in Kemet shared the mystereez with the Greeks and what did they do? They overthrew them and then plagiarized all the knowledge sayin' they created it (Aristotle, Pythagoras, Plato, etc)!

Same thing happened in technology. General Electric (GE) would not be if it hadn't cleverly swindled countless inventionz — like the vacuum, refrigerator and stove — made by Afrikanz to sell it to them for literally pennies on the dollar (it is said GE bought the rights and patented these inventionz by givin' Afrikan inventorz a mere $30,000. Today, these inventionz are in practically every household translating into billionz of dollarz!!)!

In music, we've also duplicated this mistake at least a couple tymz. We shared with YT Jazz & Bebop. Today, how much press does Joe Sample get compared to Kenny G??

When you think of Rock'n'Roll, who pops in your mind Elvis or Little Richard? Have you taken a look at how many Afrikanz are in the Rock'n'Roll Hall of Fame compared to whites??

After creatin' and eventually loosin' these industrial and musical inventionz, we basically said, *"Ya'll can have it! We'll just create somethin' else!"* Realize we wouldn't have to invent anything else if we didn't let it go in the first place! I'm not sayin' we can't share the music with the world. What I *am* sayin' is when you start to see Eminemz, Bubba Sparxx, Kain (bitin' the legendary Big Daddy Kane's name), Dream, N'Sync, BackStreet Boyz, Remy Shand and Necro, among other up and comin' white artist's imitating Black life as their recordz go Gold and Platinum, doin' it, the only ones that profit are the Labelz and Producerz (some of which, but few are, black – P.Diddy, Timbaland, Dr. Dre'). But does the culture and community that birthed the art benefit?? No.

Hedz in the industry might not feel me now, but keep on with that *"Hiphop-we-are-the-world"* shit. Soon there'll be just as many white perpetratorz, I mean, 'acts' as there are Blacks. What ya'll gonna say *then* when the whole Hiphop section at Virgin Record store is filled with cracka mceez and when HOT97 blaze mainly white artists (some are even redoin' Eric B & Rakim classics) on the radio all day??

I wonder how Nas, Busta, Mystical and Nelly will feel when MTV gives Hiphop album of the year to a white artist. Better yet, how will they feel when their royalty checks dwindle down to nothin' because the market is swamped with white mceez who have now become the voice of "Real" Hiphop!

See, it's ok if there's a couple white mceez gettin' play, but what about when there's half of them gettin' more rotation than DMX, JayZ and Ja Rule?? How will they act when a white version of Wu-Tang is created?! Oh, it WILL happen, just like it did with Rock'n'Roll — ask Little Richard!

Ya'll gonna be beefin' then, right? But I guess the best thing you'll be able to come up with is goin' back to the drawin' board and creatin' yet anutha music form to literally give to the world again, free of charge!

HIPHOP IS AFRIKAN

Can we have ONE thing created and still controlled by Afrikan people?!!? Hiphop emerged as our voice to the injustices on Afrikanz-in-America. Stemmin' from Ancient Wordsmith's, commonly called Griot's, in Afrika, today, it has become a stage deifyin' the lifestyles of money, drugz, pimpin' and hoes.

The Meaning of Thug Life

These dayz everybody a thug. If you ain't thuggin' then you prone to get blasted for bein' the opposite... which is bein' righteous. It's been said power is in the verb and the verb dictates one's actionz, which are based on a thought. Whether one is aware (conscious) or not (unconscious) they are thinking. What's proven to be deadly is the thinkerz decision to be responsible or not of his/her thought process.

So, with that in mind, in relation to all this thug shit, here's a true testament of pure ignorance — because even in ignorance, there's the choice not to think clearly or, in this case, thoroughly.

Even though the standard definition of a thug is *"one who is a cutthroat or ruffian; a hoodlum,"* or even more precise, *"one of a band of professional assassins formerly active in northern India who worshipped Kali and offered their victims to her,"* Tupac Shakur was able to personify this word into one of the most dominate images that's still on the scene yearz after his death.

Not that I was ever a Pac fan (nor a Biggie for that matter), he is considered by most, the first to coin the phrase, *"Thug Life."* Today this has become the "lifestyle of choice" among ghetto youth, male AND female, alike!

With all the rapperz who claim this lifestyle as their own, it showz just how quick we are

Just like with everything else Afrikan people inhabit, we're the playerz and not the ownerz. Think of all the Hiphop artists out there, how many are signed to record labelz that are Black-owned? Better yet, how many Black-owned record labelz are there? 2! Cathy Liggins-Hughes, Radio One and Rap-A-Lot Records, owned by James Prince.

Hiphop is and alwayz will be Afrikan, it's just unfortunate Afrikan people are not aware of it and therefore cease to use this power to maintain control of Hiphop's destiny. As with everything else, the world leaches off the breast of Afrikan culture and we Afrikanz, are continuously duped into bein' afraid to be called reverse discriminatorz, allowing our culture to be passed to everyone else as they take turnz — with no vaseline — raping our creative vybrationz as if she's a blunt in a cypher.

Today, everybody claimin' they Hiphop. Even mceez and DJs from the Orient (Japan, China, etc), who never been poor and hungry the way Afrikan people have, growin' up in violent and underdeveloped housing projects; tryin' to avoid frequent acts of police brutality) are claimin' they're Hiphop! But they're not!

If you are not of immediate Afrikan descent, you are merely a guest of this culture, yet the nature of the people of this world is to become the landlord of any and everything Afrikan!

Some who read this may feel my viewz to be that of a separatist, and they're right! Hiphop is but an offspring extension of Afrikan music that lived within' the Afrikan community at birth until early adolescence. Then, at the tender age of 10-11, she was taken away from her natural parents and co-opted into a surrogate parents environment...YT's environment, strictly to be pimped, eventually turnin' tricks bein' someone she isn't (a gangsta, thug) now livin' within a world that only takes from her, offerin' nothin' in return but material wealth minus the cultural nurturing she so desperately needz.

We need to rescue Hiphop and bring her back home to our village, where bangin' beats swooned beautifully to stimulating conscious lyrics, inspirin' self-reliance, self-love and protection and production of self. We are hereby callin' for the D.R.O.P Squad [Deprogramming and the Restoration of Oppressed (Afrikan) People] to carry out this mission.

This is one of the only wayz we can save Hiphop and you, the reader, are the only one's who can do it. Do you really think Russell, Puffy and Master P gonna do it?!

As imbredded playerz to this game called racizm and exploitation, we should be well aware of the rules by now. It is tyme to stop PLAYIN' and start OWNING!

to adopt a trend without investigatin' the nature of it, even a little bit.

Afrikanz are notorious for breakin' shit down by usin' acronymz. Would it faze you if you were told what Thug Life meant to Tupac? To him it meant, *"The Hate U Gave Lil' Infants Fuck Everybody"*. Or in other wordz, if you don't invest moralz, luv and respect in di youth, they will grow up not givin' a shit and hence will pass this mind state on to the generationz that follow!

Now true, based on the Tupac's lifestyle, it'd be hard to see the consistency of this acronym, for he himself contradicted it on the regular — which is probably the main reason he was physically annihilated. However, this image has not died.

Now if these "thugz" today that tote revolverz, bake bricks and move commerce in di ghetto, were informed of this subliminal acronym, would they see that they are the hate they're givin' lil' infants that hurts everybody in the Afrikan community??

Will they see they are actually playin' out the role they claim their fatherz were, whom many despised?? I think not. All we got is a line of contradicting and confused young Afrikanz who just wanna spit rhymz on the mic but, in order to fit in, are somewhat "forced" to claim a ruthless lifestyle *"just to get a rep."*

Too bad they don't realize they on the wrong side of the war... Thug on, cutthroat assassinz worshippin' money and offering the lives of the Diaspora in exchange for material fortune!

2001

BY M'BWEBE AJA ISHANGI

WHAT IS MILK GOOD 4?

As we continue to quest for the God Complex, we find that the knowledge we learn serves as fuel for our mindz. However, there's one dimension of the conscious realm many front on. This dimension is the topic of health. I find it hard for one to be "conscious", "deep", "spiritual", etc. when they poison their temple with decayed flesh and liquid meat.

The scenario goes, *"How could you be so into God, but not into yourself?!"* To all you religious peeps, how could you be about being "good christianz" or muslimz, when you eat — and drink from — decayed flesh?! It's not so much that these animalz were murdered, it's the fact that's what they consist of is nothing but poison to your body!

Even those I meet on the path of righteousness that say, *"Oh, I don't eat pork, I only eat chicken!"* Some may even say they don't eat beef, but I seriously beg to differ! If you don't eat chicken, then you shouldn't be eating sunny-side up eggs! If you don't eat beef, then you shouldn't be drinking milk! These products are derived from these same animalz! C'mon yaw, let's get with the facts and stop ridin' the fence!

The greatest concern for Afrikanz should be our dairy intake. As Dr. Frank A. Oski, director of pediatrics at John Hopkins University said, *"Humans are the only species to drink from another species; as well as being the only to drink milk beyond infancy."* We've all seen the commercialz and adz displaying the subliminal command, *"Milk Does a Body Good"*. We've all been brainwashed to believe you can only receive calcium from milk. But as with everything else, we've never completely investigated our optionz. Just what iz milk good for?! If anything, it's good for business! In 1990, the Dairy Industry raked in $7.2 billion!

WHAT IZ MILK??

There are several reasonz dairy products — milk in particular — are very unhealthy and unsanitary for humanz. It's unsanitary because the production process is a very dirty procedure. It's unhealthy because of the way the cowz are raised and cared for.

Milk advertiserz still use the analogy that white is clean and pure; hence we get the lie that milk is good for you. Everything the cow ingests endz up in the milk. That would be cool if cowz were ingesting natural thingz like grass and water, but we find that is not the case. The farmerz need cowz to produce maximum milk so they can make maximum profit. To get more milk, they need more cowz. To get more cowz, they must come up with a chemical that will make them produce and grow at a faster rate. The chemical is recombinant Bovine Growth Hormone (rBGH). This increases the cowz production about 20%. With technology thrown into the milk industry, cowz are already producing 10 tymz more milk than they would naturally.

Not only is it unhealthy for us, the cowz, already stressed from the extensive production, get sick as well. Like anything that gets sick, puss and mucous formz inside of it. Remember, everything the cow ingests endz up in the milk. Puss and mucous is white or light in color and therefore hidden by the intoxicating, camouflaged white color of milk. Farmerz can't have sick cowz because they are of no use, right? So they pump them with up with antibiotics and as a result, the drugz are in the milk we buy; yet another chemical added to the already disgusting recipe.

You're probably thinking all these things are cleaned up in the pasteurization process, when in fact, pasteurization makes it worse! In order to maintain a consistent taste, milk must be combined. This dealz with the merging of milk from various farmz. Billy Joe Bob's milk is combined with Cecil's, Bubba's, AND Jetthro's farmz! And I'm sure there aren't many farmz that are run exactly alike!

This consumption of milk is then taken to the production lab for pasteurization. Technology cleanz, or *claimz* to clean, the milk with heat. Heat is called radioactive isotopes by lab technicianz. These isotopes are supposed to heat the milk to a certain level and boil out its impurities, but because there is such a strong demand for the product, the machines must move at a rapid pace. The heat barely reaches the level it should so the impurities remain in the milk and the radio isotopes are added; anutha ingredient to gumbo milk! Quiet as kept, radioactive isotopes are cancerous. One other secret ingredient: traces of the cowz urine also is part of the final product.

THE WHOLE MILK SHAM

When it comes to marketing this toxic-waste the FDA, government, USDA, "massa"-media, and a host of otherz partake in commercializing liquid meat, trying to convince you milk is good for the body.

John A. McDougall, M.D. callz dairy foodz "liquid meat" because of their nutritional contents are so similar. Eating foodz high in fat contributes to the development of heart disease, certain cancerz and stroke — the USA's three deadliest killerz.

Some say, *"well then I won't drink whole milk, I'll drink 2%"*. Cow milk and other dairy products are high in fat and cholesterol. The dairy industry has cleverly expressed fat content as a percentage of weight. Using this system, 2% milk, which is 87% water by weight, soundz like a low-fat product. Expressed as a percentage of total calories, 2% milk is in fact *31% fat*. Whole milk is *49% fat*. There isn't much of a difference between the two. Yogurt is 49% fat, cheese is 60-70%, and butter is 100% fat! But, as a consumer, we wouldn't know this because we are misled to believe we're drinking 2% of what whole milk is, when in fact, there's barely a difference. Even if I was drinking something that is 2%, or even 31%, of what is said on the carton, what is the other 98%, or 69%?! Probably more toxic shit!

WHAT ARE WE DOING?!!?

I touched on the medical fact that people are the only species to drink the milk of another species, and the only to drink milk beyond infancy. Whole cowz milk is suited to the nutritional needz of calves who double their weight in 47 dayz and grow to 300 poundz within a year!

After 4 yearz of age, most children develop the inability to digest milk sugar lactose. If they consume dairy products after early childhood it can cause diarrhea, gas and cramps. According to Dr. Milos Krajny, secretary of the Ontario Allergy Society, virtually every major allergy study implicates milk and dairy products as the leading food allergen. Not only does milk develop allergies, it also develops diabetes, cataracts and osteoporosis!

Although the thought of breast-feeding may turn a stomach or two, it is only because we've been reprogrammed. Milk is only essential in an infant's life in the first 3 yearz. Look at nature, Afrikan! Do you see grown dogz running up under his momz to get some milk?! Do you see any adult animalz drinking milk from their motherz?! Milk is not a necessary part of our diet like they have you thinking. The industry tellz you to drink milk so it will make your bones strong. But what they won't tell you is that, in fact, it does the opposite! Heard of osteoporosis?

Osteoporosis is bone loss due to calcium resorption, which the industry will not reveal that it is not halted or prevented by an increase in the intake of calcium. High protein foodz like meat, eggz and dairy products suck calcium from the body by causing excessive calcium loss through the kidneyz, making the kidneyz work harder and causing loss of mineralz such as calcium.

THE SYSTEM COVERING THEIR TRACKS

Western medicine has discovered the hazardz of drinking cowz milk, but the money-hungry beast does not want to do away with this $7 billion business. So what do they do for the environmentally and health conscious? They create a plan to market human milk! But they don't want the average consumer to be disgusted by this revolutionary product so they plan to have the human milk come out of a cow! They will combine human genes with cow genes to produce a mutant-like, fast growing species of cow that will produce humanized milk?!

This will not be your average farm cow. It will grow in a laboratory. Imagine what the cow will look like having half human genes! They believe this milk will be more healthier for babies, if motherz cannot breast feed, and they plan to make all dairy products with it, again, not warning the consumer.

WHAT CAN I DO?

Now that you know what milk is, it is now tyme to decide wha'chu gonna do. You may disregard the info and continue to persecute your body and soul, or you can look for calcium in other foodz and drinks like rice and almond milk, non-dairy ice-creams, sesame seedz, collard greenz, broccoli, orange juice, figz, nuts, navy and pinto beanz, and onionz. Eliminating dairy products and eating natural foodz will preserve yearz of your life, and aid you in being more spiritual. It's virtually impossible to be spiritual when you have violently-murdered, toxic substances inside you.

And lastly, do not let YT tell you what is healthy and what does your body good. Their body structure and ourz are totally different. What they lack, doesn't mean we do. Take caution about what you are eating, drinking and feeding to your youth, you may be doing more harm than good.

LIK SHOT!

Many are givin' up cigarettes, beef, chicken and pork due to research being released to the public. However, many of those still consume products of these animalz. Dairy (milk, butter & cheese) and eggz are 2 of the most popular products created from these toxic animalz. These products are often called 'Liquid meat'. At the same tyme, we've noticed a dramatic increase in breast cancer, particularly in Afrikan women.

If you're really interested in significantly reducing breast cancer (men can get it too!) and other diseases, you should seriously consider eliminating all dairy products from your diet. Here are some startling points found in the study of human milk consumption:

- According to the USDA, nearly 40% of the food the average American eats consists of milk or dairy.
- Milk is the foundation of heart disease and the explanation for America's number one killer.
- Milk contributes to heart disease.
- Milk is a poor source of calcium.
- Pasteurization does not work.
- Milk has a direct link to asthma.
- Milk causes diabetes, cataracts and osteoporosis (bone loss).
- The dairy industry spendz hundredz of millionz of dollarz to brainwash consumerz.
- Milk is the reason that one out of six American women will develop cancer of the breast.
- 25 million American women over the age of forty have been diagnosed with bone crippling arthritis and osteoporosis. These females have been drinking in excess of two poundz of milk per day for their entire adult lives.

Y are their doctorz blind to the fact that drinking milk does not prevent osteoporosis? Calcium in milk is not adequately absorbed and milk consumption is the probable cause of osteoporosis. Milk is responsible for allergies, colic, colitis, earaches, coldz and congestion in our youth. Research indicates that one bovine protein in milk destroyz the insulin-producing beta cellz of the pancreas, causing diabetes.

60% of America's dairy cowz have the leukemia virus. Ask yourself Afrikanz, is it wise to eat the flesh or drink body fluidz from diseased animalz? The Food *AND* Drug Administration (FDA) used to allow a small amount of antibiotics in milk. FDA scientists recognized that consumerz should not be drinking a fluid containing antibiotics.

In 1990, the one part per hundred-million antibiotic residue in milk standard was increased by 100 tymz to one part per million. As a result, new strainz of bacteria developed, immune to the 52 different antibiotics found in milk. Antibiotics no longer work because we have been drinking milk and eating dairy products containing increased amounts of these powerful drugz and, in addition, new strainz of emerging diseases.

Beer bellies are indeed making a comeback in America. According to the *'Food Consumption, Prices and Expenditures, 1996, Statistical Bulletin Number 928'*, published by the USDA. The average American consumed 24 gallonz of beer in 1994. That works out to less than 8.5 ounces of beer per day. Total milk and dairy products consumed per capita in 1994 equaled 26 ounces per day, more than triple the amount of beer. One 12 ounce glass of beer containz 144 calories and no fat. On the other hand, a 12 ounce glass of milk containz 300 calories and 16 gramz of fat. It seemz that beer is taking a bad rap. Protruding stomachs on overweight people should be called milk bellies, not beer bellies.

If you are the average American, today, from the combined total of milk, butter, cheese and other dairy products, you will eat 161mg of cholesterol, the same amount contained in 53 slices of bacon! If you add this up, by the end of the year you will have consumed the equivalent of 19,345 slices, and by age 52, your cholesterol level would be on the same level as if you've eaten 1million pieces of bacon!!

Milk is loaded with protein! 80% of that protein is 'casein', found in the same super glue that hold your furniture together and adhesive used to hold the paper label to a beer bottle! Casein is the primary cause of mucus, congestion and childhood earaches.

WAR VERSUS YOUR IMMUNE SYSTEM

If you've read the piece, *'War vs. Your Immune System'*, you are familiar with the notion that we live in a system that does not specialize in curing people, but steering them into the road of slow-death! Think, hospitalz are not in the business of makin' people healthy. Do you know how much money they make from hedz bein' sick?? If doctorz healed and cured everyone, they would inevitably become obsolete; there'd be no need for hospitalz, insurance, pharmacies, etc. Overstanding this, will allow you to believe that there are thingz they do not want you to know about your health. For one, dairy most definitely causes cancer!

There are studies that the dairy industry refuses to releases; evidence that there are bigger secrets than any revealed by the cigarette industry. There are thousandz of thingz out here that cause cancer, but there is only 1 hormone that you naturally produce that serves as the key factor in the growth of each cancer, in particular breast cancer.

There is only 1 out of millionz of hormones of all species that links us. When one drinks milk they are taking in the most powerful growth hormone naturally produced in our own bodies. However, this growth hormone is safeguarded by naturally occurring mechanismz unique to milk. That hormone is called Insulin-like growth factor-1 (IGF-1) and it is identical (70 amino acidz, same gene sequence) in cowz and humanz. When you drink a 12oz. glass of milk, you double the amount of that hormone in your body. This leadz to an imbalance and eventual dis-*ease* in the form of numerous cancerz.

There are several reasonz dairy products – milk in particular – are very unhealthy and unsanitary for huemanz. It's unsanitary because the production process is a very dirty procedure and it's unhealthy because of the way the cowz are raised and cared for.

To get the masses to drink it, milk advertiserz still use the racist analogy that white is clean and pure; hence we get the lie that milk is good for you. Take some tyme and analyze the countless milk adz and commercialz and who their geared toward...the youth! They have us ingesting this poison at an early age! This is also Y it's hard to convince someone of the effects of milk, because their logic is *"I've been drinkin' it all my life, Y stop now? I see my 80 year old grandmother still drinks it, Y can't I??"*

Everything the cow ingests ends up in the milk. That would be cool if cowz were ingesting natural thingz like grass and water, but we find that is not the case. The farmerz need cowz to produce maximum milk so they can make maximum profit. To get more milk, they need more cowz. To get more cowz, they must come up with a chemi(kill) that will make them produce and grow at a faster rate. The chemical is recombinant Bovine Growth Hormone (rBGH). This increases the cowz production about 20%. With technology thrown into the milk industry, cowz are already producing 10 tymz more milk than they would naturally.

Like anything that gets sick, puss and mucous form inside of it. Everything the cow ingests endz up in the milk. Puss and mucus is white or light in color and therefore hidden by the intoxicating, camouflaged white color of milk. Puss and mucus is white or light in color and therefore hidden by the intoxicating, camouflaged white color of milk. Stay tune...the war continues.

2000

No tyme for an intro, I need to go straight to the ingredients of this piece...
MATHEMATICS: For those that are caught under the biblical spell, you can recall a passage that talks about the enslavement of a people for 400 yearz in a land unknown to them. For those avid readerz of my writingz have heard me, numerous tymz talk historically of there being no race of people – other than Afrikanz – that not only went 400 yearz of enslavement, but whose number is fast approaching 6000 yearz (for those lost read, *"IZ YT Hueman? or Mutant!"* series)! But let's deal with the 400.

In 1444AD, the first Afrikanz were stolen from Afrika by the Persianz. The bible sayz we would be enslaved for 400 yearz, which comes to the year 1844. The so-called Emancipation Proclamation didn't happen until 1863 (19 years later). Now what did the bible *"promise"* after the 400 yearz? That *"...they would inherit the earth and everything that's in it."*

As we enter the new millennium – some 135 yearz later – we haven't even collected on the 40 acres and 2 mules we were promised! Suffice it to say the "reporterz" of the bible ('cause they weren't alive when these 'stories' allegedly happened in the bible) prophesies are inaccurate...in fact, I'll even venture on to say they lied (the history of the bible and the hundredz-of-thousandz of revisionz is anutha story)!

If the bible is truth, Y has our liberation been delayed so long?! Probably because we have stopped looking for truth and instead, settled for following man.

TRUTH OR MAN

Who do you follow, Truth or Man? For one, any "leader" that uses toolz of enslavement (ie. Bible/Quraan) as their primary toolz is not a messenger of truth! When we analyze todayz "negro" leaderz, most have some sort of (man-made) religion as their foundation. There is a difference between *"the Gospel"* and *"the Spoken Word"*. Most Afrikanz have been duped to be receptive to listening to the gospel, alias *"Feel Good Sessionz"*, where there is no need to worry about responsibility of living what you believe, there are no blunt instructionz to defeating the beast; just *"let the wrath of God take care of it"*. You know, that preacher or reverend you *revere* as the man with the golden tongue, who tellz you a bunch of confusing romanticismz of God and how he defeats satan but never tells you any names, nor points you in the direction of the physical oppressor who just claimed anutha Afrikan mind through white supremist tactics (through his eurocentric-valued schoolz, churches, etc.). When have you ever heard of your pastor tellin' you we need to make a move on Rockefeller?? Truth existed before it was written because truth is a way of life!

Negroes sprint from the Spoken Word because it deemz responsible reaction.

The Spoken Word comes from within – you don't need to read a book to realize shit ain't right. We have been drained of self redemption through assimilating YTs value system. YTs system benefits only those of pale skin. So if you tryin' to exist equally in a system specifically designed to benefit white people, what type of menticide (mental suicide) are you suffering from?!!? But it isn't entirely our fault. So far in this analogy we have talked about the puppet, what about the puppeteer?

TODAYZ LEADERZ VS. ANCIENT FREEDOM FIGHTERZ

Back in the day leadership was won through initiative and proof-positive action. Todayz negro leaderz merely shame freedom fighterz of the past because they have consciously chosen not to live up to the legacy of "do or die". I'm talkin' 'bout the so-called leadership of Jesse Jackson, the Congressional Black Caucus (Caucasian), the Boule', NAACP, the Black church and yes, even Louis Farrakhan. People come out in droves to see Jesse or Farrakhan speak whereas we couldn't pay you to come and see modern freedom fighterz like Dr. Yosef ben-Jochannan, the recently passed Dr. John Henrik Clarke, Ashra Kwesi, and Eraka Rouzarondu, to name a few. Y? Mainly because they have a man-made religion as their foundation and white supremacy has made it so we look outside of ourselves for spiritual enlightenment (like in books and churches/mosques) opposed to 'knowing thyself' and that all the answerz are within. White supremacy chooses our leaderz by utilizing their, already globally effective, massa-media outlets. They also place these negroes as diversionz to any "black messiahz" (as Gay Edgar Hoover put it) that may awake our people from our hibernation.

Each of our leaderz, self-appointed and/or endorsed by YT, have rapsheets that detail strong alliances with YT. The heavy hitterz, Jesse and Farrakhan are the two examples I shall dissect.

Jesse, a member of the Boule', Prince Hall Mason and Trilateral Commission (TLC) was groomed since his collegiate yearz. It is known by many Africentric scholarz that he spied on Martin Luther King and was strategically placed to replace him before and after they killed him.

If you can recall, Farrakhan, 10-15 yearz ago received NO PRESS! Shortly thereafter, the only coverage he would get is about his anti-semitic bashing. Now, he graces the cover of TIME magazine, newspaperz across the country and appearz on 60 minutes. Y? How could a man, once revered as a possible igniter of the resurrecting Black consciousness, now get all this positive publicity? Y is he now meeting with so-called "jewish" memberz of the Illuminati like Edgar Bronfman and Mike Wallace?? Because he claimz to no longer be anti-semitic and is on this atonement shit.

See, Jesse and Farrakahn ain't the first – and probably not the last. In the past, the white media gave us WEB DuBois [Council on Foreign Relations (CFR), Boule'] and Alaine Locke (Cecil Rhodes Scholar) to kill off the Marcus Garvey movement; Martin King to water down Malcolm X and the OAAU (Organization for African American Unity); Jesse and Maulana Karenga for the Black Panther Movement; and now Farrakhan.

But Farrakhan has been a more devastating blow because he is the first pawn that has(had) a blatant militant philosophy (Black muslimz used to call themselves separatists). But look at him today. Whenz the last tyme you heard him say, *"Blue-eyed devil"?* What has happened to his pro-black philosophy?? It got diluted with the 1990s version of the 1960s *"luv movement"...* ATONEMENT!

Y should I atone for unknowingly being miseducated, deprogrammed, despiritualized and severed from the umbilical cord of ancient Akebulan (Afrika)?! Atonement detainz action! While we're sittin' here bein' sorry and shit, YT is instituting FEMA, NAFTA, Global 2000, Biochip Technology, Cloning and an all-out preparation of war on people of color from health to education and everything in the 9 areas of people activity spoken in detail by Dr. Francess Cress Welsing and Neilly Fuller.

Atonement has had a docile effect on the progression of Afrikan liberation and Farrakhan, with his fortress in Chicago with his solid gold ceilingz – the money it took to buy that gold could be used to house, feed, clothe and educate countless Afrikanz – is singing lead as YT serves as the maestro to the acapelo number, *"Afrikan Menticide 666"!*

Be careful who YT sayz our leaderz are. The people YT has "told" us to accept have financial power but refuse to use it! All todayz leaderz want to do is be on tv, pack lecture hallz and make numerous unfulfilled economic pacts.

I'm on Farrakhan because he is (currently) the only man that has the clout to call for a million-plus Afrikan men to meet in DC. So much could have been achieved there other than talkin' this atonement shit! He could be the messiah Gay Edgar Hoover was talkin' about, or maybe not. Maybe he's...the "anti-christ" (you decide, look at the facts!).

I begin to wonder when I hear he met with the head of the Anti-Defamation League (ADL), Edgar Bronfman and Mike Wallace (the one who set up Malcolm for his death on 60 minutes by singling out the Black muslimz as the one's he thought were tryin' to kill him. Singling the NOI (Nation of Islam) allowed anyone else to do the job because the NOI would get the blame. *NOTE: This is not to clear the NOI. Clearly they were involved. To what capacity is the question.*), and talked about opening up some hotelz OWNED by YT (Illuminati) but ran by blacks. What kinda mind-fuck is that?! Just because you see Afrikanz working and the manager is black, doesn't mean it's black OWNED! In the book, *The Rockefeller Files,* by Gary Allen, he talks about how the Rockefellerz stressed the necessity to OWN (through financial investments) not RUN a company because it allowz you to remain anonymous.

Did you ever wonder Y you never heard of the KKK (Ku Klux Klan) having met with the NOI *during* the civil rights era? In Malcolm's autobiography, he talks about how they had a peace pact with the klan. I admire that they were able to basically tell the klan not to even think about comin' over here and lynchin' one of them, but Y did the pact only include memberz of the nation? Afterall, this was black versus white! So Y would they desegregate themselves and not speak for the whole black race??

In 1995, Afrikanz-in-america were told of the current chattel slavery (the same our great-great's experienced here) our people were suffering in Sudan, Afrika. In an October 23, 1995 edition of *National Review*, the NOI spoke in defense of slavery in Sudan and its muslim oppressorz. Augustine A. Lado, president of the Human Rights group Pax Sudani Network, said, *"the Congressional Black Caucus, Trans-Africa, the Rainbow Coalition, the Nation of Islam and the NAACP have forsaken us."*

AASGs (American Anti-Slavery Group) research director, Charles Jacobs, noted, *"for 2 years we tried to get Rev. Jesse Jackson on the record against slavery, but he returned our document packages unopened, saying this issue seemed anti-Arab."*

One of Jesse's aides further noted, *"Right now, slavery is not on his agenda."* WHAT?!!? You mean he'd rather boycott some japanese car dealer rather than save the already half-a-million (and counting) Afrikanz that have been murdered in concentration camps in Zaire, Rwanda, Burundia and Sudan by the Committee of 300 (the Resurrected Illuminati)?!

Y didn't Farrakhan allow the numerous anti-slavery organizationz speak at the Million Man March?! Y, instead, did we have to settle for Maya Angelou's '4-white-husband' luvin' ass?! This shedz new light as to Y nothing has really been accomplished since October 16th, 1995 (besides Farrakhan blowin' up!).

The CBC (Congressional Black Caucus – should be Black 'who wannabe' *Caucasian* Caucus) is anutha house negro organization. Any organization that claimz to be for Afrikanz but got the word Caucus, where the Caucasian came from (Caucus mountains in europe), should be taken as a front organization for white supremacy. The CBC has never expressed an interest in stopping the recolonization of Afrika by the NWO.

Former head of CBC and New Jersey Democrat, Donald Payne has fully supported the actionz of Laurent Kabila (responsible for troops who've killed more than 2.2 million Afrikanz since the invasion on Rwanda in 1994) and Yoweri Musevini (who issued, from direction of the Illuminati, to brutally takeover Rwanda, Burundi and Zaire). Payne was also against Million Man March. Y do we allow negroes like these to remain in "power"? Probably because we too, need a lesson in the history of the freedom fighter.

BACK WHEN REVOLUTIONAREEZ WERE REAL

Truth was the motivation for Afrikan freedom fighterz, not glory, money or power, but freedom. White supremacy is the reason the white american school system will not teach us of these wo/men, because they know it would be like equipping a starving man with seedz, water and a shovel. If we "knew thyself" we would "know our enemy" and take liberation into our own handz doing away with the front negro organization's (NAACP, Urban League, UNCF, Black colleges, Boule', Masonz, Religious sects, college frats/sororities, etc.). I will concentrate on the deedz of 4 men of antiquity of the 1800s: Toussaint L'Ouverture, Gabriel Prosser, Denmark Vesey and Nat Turner.

FRANCOIS DOMINQUE TOUSSAINT L'OUVERTURE

In Lerone Bennet's, *'Before The Mayflower'*, we find L'Ouverture, a Haitian, was one of the first anti-slavery freedom fighterz during the tyme of slaveholderz thomas jefferson and patrick henry. Once a slave, it wasn't until the Haitian Revolution (he was almost 50) gave birth to a man that literally sent shiverz down the backs of YT. He defeated the english and spanish armies, unified Haiti and rocked Napoleon. Toussaint joined the rebel army, *"serving as an ally of spain against france then as an ally of france against england and spain. Playing off the spanish against the french and the french against the english, he outmaneuvered the best diplomats of his day and gained freedom for the slaves."* (Bennet)

After the Revolution, he administered the contruction of roadz, buildingz and bridges. He made every citizen a soldier and spurred advancement in agriculture; clearly strategic tactics of self independence. Toussaint was a devout roman catholic, but gave up the oppressive faith in his later yearz. His nephew stated that he dissed the religion in a village church, *"You! You are the God of the white man, not the God of the Negroes! You have betrayed man, and deserted me! You have no pity for my race!"* He then hurled a marble crucifix to the floor. He died in a cell in a fortress on the french-swiss borderz after being captured by Napoleon.

GABRIEL PROSSER

Bursting onto the scene at the age of 24, Gabriel meditated on dreamz of a black state in the land of Virginia. In the summer of 1800 he held meetingz at fish fries and barbecues. Every Sunday he dipped into Richmond and studied the town, making a mental note of strategic points and the location of armz and ammunition. His plan was simple, the right wing would grab arsenal and seize the gunz; the left would take the gun powder house; the key central wing would enter the town at both endz simultaneously and would cut down basically every white person. After Richmond, he planned attacks like that of a virus on neighboring cities. Unfortunately, on Saturday, August 30th, 2 house negroes sold the rebelz out telling their master. Unaware of the betrayal, Gabriel and some 1000 slaves were unable to enter Richmond because a thunderstorm washed out the bridges and roadz making it impossible to enter. Before he could reassemble, the state attacked, arresting Gabriel and 34 of his men. They were all convicted and hanged in 1800.

DENMARK VESEY

An ex-slave of a slave trader, he knew the wickedness of slavery and that man was not meant to slave for man. It got to the point where Vesey couldn't bear to have a white person in his presence. He was very outspoken with his hatred for YT. When slaves bowed to YT in the street, he would rebuke them. When the slaves replied, *"But we're slaves,"* Vesey would reply, *"You deserve to be slaves."* An infamous quote you'll probably never hear of Vesey – even during Black History Month was when he said, *"We are free, but the white people here won't let us be so; and the only way is to rise up and fight the whites."* One of his planz was the takeover of arsenalz, guardhouses, powder magazines and naval stores in Charleston, South Carolina, but, he too, was betrayed by a house negro. Vesey and 5 of his aides were hanged on July 2, 1822.

NAT TURNER

Born the year Gabriel died, his mother had to be tied to prevent her from murdering him because she couldn't bear to bring anutha child into slavery. Madd humble and spiritual, he renounced tobacco, liquor and money. Turner explained Y he was what he was, *"...[H]aving soon discovered that to be great, I must appear so, I studiously avoided mixing in society and wrapped myself in mystery, devoting my time to fasting and prayer."*

He was clearly not the average enslaved Afrikan. He saw visionz and heard voices. One day he had an unusual vision: he saw black and white spirits wrestling in the sky. The sun grew dark and blood gushed forth in streamz; while walking in the woodz, he found Medu Neter (hieroglyphic) characterz and blood on the leaves. He concluded the day of reckoning on YT was near. Another vision validated this theory. The "spirit", he said, told him that on the appearance of a sign, *"I should arise and prepare myself and slay my enemies with their own weapons."* The sign appeared in the form of a solar eclipse in February 1831.

There was a Jerusalem in Southampton, Virginia in that year. Turner decided to attack it on Sunday, August 21st. They would strike that night, beginning at the home of his master, and proceed from house to house, killing every white man, woman and child. His first hit happened to be the home of Joseph Travis, Nat's slaveownerz. They killed him, his wife, 2 teenagerz and an infant. They continued to kill some 60 whites, with additional slaves joining them as they leveled each plantation. While he was at large, from North Carolina to Maryland, not a single white family could relax for fear the antidote to ending white supremacy would catch on.

When he was finally captured, he was taken to trial where he pleaded not guilty, saying he did not feel guilty. On November 11 he was hanged. Some may feel his acts were violent. The violence was already there. Slavery is violent, and Nat's acts were responses to that violence. He should not be condemned; he should be heralded as a hero, someone who was willing to fight back knowing the consequence would be his life..

It seemz our greatest foe isn't really YT, but noodle-back need-to-growz (negroez) who are afraid to cause a ripple in the pond. We need to cast out the spell of reactionary-izm that has been inherited by our people for generationz. We systematically will wait until one person decides to do what needz to be done, then we get involved and in most cases, only if it's "safe". This is where we lose. Most likely, the individual will be caught and made an example of, but what if we all struck at the same tyme? Think of how dope Nat's movement, although short-lived, was!!

Prosser and Vesey plotted revolts and were betrayed. Nat plotted and executed. The deedz of these bruthaz are but a few in the history of freedom fighterz. They were not afraid to neither shed blood nor lose their life for they were not bonded to physical life. They believed life was everlasting and if you remain a part of the problem, there will never be a solution.

Ask yourselves Afrikanz, are you a Farrakhan or a Turner? The so-called ending you may hear about is not the end of wo/man but the end of YTs 6000 year reign. There will be many that will perish (many of whom are waiting for that mystery god to come out of the sky), but the strong will survive. Those that use truth as their motivation realize the alleged "2nd coming" is not coming from a man, but from a movement. Just as YTs New World Order cannot be linked to one man, it is a movement – and so is the 2nd coming. It's not going to be Jesus – which is a movement outside of you – it's a movement (of the people) from within! Stop lookin' for leadership and be one!

Each and every one of us are faced with the same choice, do we learn about our story and the atrocities of our experience at the handz of YT and choose to live as if there is nothin' we can do about it; or do we become proactive, instigating the implementation of change. To know and not do anything is worse than not knowing at all. Now you know...our future is waiting...LIK SHOT!!

"Never give up until you either win or you die." – The Spook Who Sat Beside The Door

How many tymz have you heard a black person say, *"Yo, I got's to get in the shade 'cause I don't want to get black!"* When I heard this while I was coming into my reawakening, it made me vexed, yo! Y would a black person not want to be black?! This was self-hatred at its finest! But as my aggression has progressed from the unknown victim to the conscious culprit, my perspective has changed.

You can't blame black folk for saying some of the thingz we say; afterall, most are merely expressing ourselves through verbalz we heard from someone else. Truly if we took the tyme to reanalyze just what it is we're saying, we may, indeed, take back such a degrading statement. This piece is to heal, not to point fingerz at our people calling them "primitive thinkerz". As I've alwayz said, we are victimz of the puppeteer/puppet theory and from the proof of the way we carry and express ourselves, I can see the stringz that bind are not made of yarn but rather steel. So how do you "heal" a people that doesn't know they need healing? Let's play People's Court where I'll present the case and you be the jury.

The defendant, of course, is YT. Historically (on up to the here and now), it is this European who is responsible for the amnesia our people suffer of our illustrious ancient culture where knowledge of the power of Nature reigned supreme! My proof? If the familiar statement I spoke of isn't enuff — how the majority of Afrikan refugeez, stationed here in america, ignorance of the power of the Afrikan drum (vybration); our relinquished Afrikan wholistic diet (which didn't deal with decayed flesh, what many call meat), nor preservative toxinz making the food eaten today almost impossible to refrain from because it's *everywhere!*); the force used behind "making" us forget our native tongue and culture force-feeding us this imbalanced, western culture we have become accustomed to (how many Afrikanz can only speak one language and that being the language of our oppressorz... english!); and what about our denial of Afrikan (Natural) beauty and not blond hair, blue contacts and fake tits (ala, Lil' Kim)?! These are but a few of the symptomz Afrikanz suffer as we enter a new millennium. And to prove its effectiveness, note that we were enslaved some 500 yearz ago!

A lot of the mentacide has been done through YTs educational (brainwashing) institutionz and use of 'massa'-media. Afrikanz watch the most tell-a lie-vision of any race. There are so many charges to file against YT but one of the most important, and untampered, of accusationz is YTs quest to block the power (knowledge) of RA (the Sun)!

In our galaxy, the Sun is the key element to life. Without it, there would be no you, me, birdz, treez, water, etc. If you look at it astrologically, it is the Sun's heat that melts the cold ice caps (from the frigid temperatures of space) that enable Hydrogen and Oxygen to be released into the air enabling life to breathe. If the Sun stopped rising (really, if the earth stopped rotating), one side of the planet would not receive any light (heat) and would freeze in a matter of hourz; life as we know it would change [makes you see just how 'powerless' hue(black)man and mankind (kind of man: YT) really is when comparing the forces of Nature].

But we knew this and were one with this law in Ethiopia and Kemet (before there was a whiteman!). But we have been stripped of this knowledge and for the past 50 or so yearz, we have been re-tapping our ancestral data banks, relearning the power of the Sun coupled with Melanin.

If you understand global white supremacy, you understand just Y YT doesn't want you to recall this sacred knowledge. As the Sun works as our aide, it wouldn't be hard to see that is serves as the key annihilator to the entire white race. Y? Because of their pale skin, lacking ability to produce adequate amounts of melanin and their inability to escape the fact of recessive genetics. YT knowz their skin has the inability to take the tenacious rayz of ultraviolet light that comes from RA (the Sun, which is the term our Kemetic Ancestors used). Metaphysically speaking, we must realize that along with the rayz RA showerz planet E with, it is also giving us spiritual nurturing. But before we get into that, let's investigate what YT knowz.

For one, RA spellz A-N-N-I-H-I-L-A-T-I-O-N for YT. This is one force they cannot colonize or oppress. Even the "mightiest" of white supremist secret societies cannot step into the ring with the Undisputed Champ of Nature/Righteousness. This planet was made for melanated life, or life that has color, and they have the least (along with white lab mice) because their pale white skin is the absence (repelz light/knowledge) of color. [Note: Ever wonder Y they experiment with "white" genetically-grafted mice instead of the natural color mice, which is brown?? Makes you wonder who they're creating cures for!]

It is they who have an increase of skin cancer; it is they who are developing artificial melanin (melatonin) hoping this will make them 'darker' so that they may not have to eventually be locked in their homes unable to come outside; and it is they who are having numerous forumz talking about their recessive genes that will make them less and less of the population resulting in their eventual extinction. Understanding this formula, we have the motive for racizm! See racizm, as Francess Cress Welsing of *'The Isis Papers'* will tell you, is nothing but anutha name for white genetic survival!

The deep thing is when we loop all the pieces we've published dealing with YTs 6000 reign of the earth and it's tyme runnin' short, monitoring their behavior is enuff validation, for even they believe their tyme is short and they've basically sealed their own fate with the many inventionz that go against Nature, depleting the ozone layer — the "protective" layer (for them) from skin cancer — ranging from aerosol canz to numerous space shuttle missionz that cut holes in the layer.

However, their instincts leadz them to bring as many people of color (Afrikanz in particular because we have the most dominant genes of all races) down with them as they poison our mindz and bodies with misinformation and using toxinz like sun block (blocking the power and knowledge of RA) to seep into the thousandz of hair follicles in our temple (body), furthering the genocide through biochemical war tactics along with menticide. This upsurge in global control is greatly attributed to the scientific findingz of melanin.

WHAT IZ MELANIN?

Melanin is derived from the greek word *"Melano"* which meanz *"Black"*. *"Anin"* is derived from the word *"Amine"*, a nitrogen-based functional group derived from ammonia. When we look at the breakdown of *"Chemistry"*, which this is *"Chem"*, comes from the word *"Khem"* which is a derivative of *"Kemet"*, or *"KMT"* (our ancients didn't use vowelz), a term meaning *"Black"* which described the people of the land.

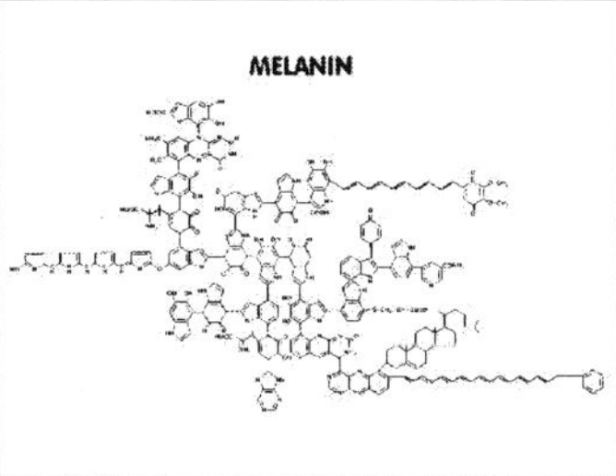

MELANIN

The Melanin Molecule

"-istry" is the study of a particular subject; so we find that Chemistry is actually the study of Blackness or Blacks; which is caused by a *"khem"*ical (chemical) called melanin. According to author, Carol Barnes, melanin can be found in our environment in places such as soil, plants, animalz and in the waterz of creeks, lakes, springs, seas and river. Most recognize melanin visually as the black chemical in our skin, eyes and hair. Otherz know that it is what makes Afrikanz "different" from every other ethnic background and it is most evident in the field of athletics, intellectualizm and creative arts. But melanin has other properties. *"It has chemical and physical properties personality traits which distinguish it from other chemicals and is so fantastic is may be considered "DIVINE"*, states Barnes.

Melanin has other physical properties such as a pleasant smell; thermal resistance of up to 1225°F, retaining 50% of its original properties; and flexibility and toughness like rubber or plastic (probably Y our skin is tough and hard to penetrate with a needle).

Melanin is black because its chemical structure will not allow any type of energy to escape once that energy has come into contact with its structure. No energy is reflected away from the surface of the melanin structure. In other wordz energy (such as sunlight) is not reflected off anything dark including dark skin. Metaphysically, our dark, melanated skin takes in RA's rayz (knowledge/spiritual insight) and is the key component for our maintaining our luvable, spiritual selves.

YT, or pale skinned people, on the other hand, repelz the knowledge RA offerz because white cannot entrap light, it spits it back out for their species have no tolerance for this light (wisdom). On the physical plane this is evident when people choose to wear white T-shirts over black in the summer. Black teez engulf the sun and make you hotter, whereas white teez repel the rayz allowing you to remain cooler. Although you may see a lot of 'em laying on the beach, too much of this light (wisdom) will kill in the form of cancer! So their ability to acquire this Natural divinity is limited. This is intended only for the Original wo/man whom, if you didn't know by now, is the Afrikan!

Afrikan people, again, the race that has the most melanin, can charge up our melanin by just being in RA or the right type of musical soundz. Melanin respondz to and absorbz light, sound (music) and electrical energy and uses this in the body as food. When sunlight hits your skin or when you play a phat mix tape, it comes in contact with the lifeforce in you and revives you. This is Y we excel in outdoor athletics; Y we yearn for the summer month's while dreading the winter; and this is the guiding force to our spirituality and creativity we express in our persona, art and intellect. Music, in particular the drum, is and alwayz have been a vital component to our spiritual culture. The white kidnapperz who took us to the America's knew this was a form we used as communication, that's Y they discarded it.

I don't want everyone to believe that ALL melanated people are "positive". There are many negroes ['necro' in greek, meaning "dead". I'll go further and call 'em 'brain' dead] who have acted on the devilish side instead of being righteous (ie, the Boule'). Melanin can become toxic. We exhibit this dis-ease in the form of supporting people like OJ, who, even though he went back to his new white girlfriend after a majority Afrikan jury got him off, we still got his back!

This is Y I believe a black man (such as memberz of the Boule') can be a devil, whereas YT can only be a demon. Only highly melanated people have the ability to be good or bad. On the contrast, collectively, YT only has the ability to be what s/he have alwayz been, evil, or anti-'live' or life. Historically you can see the pattern of their behavior has never changed. They are the *only* race who has historically oppressed a people using the drastic genocidal methodz they've parlayed on the entire planet, even on their own!

A devil will alwayz have the potential to be good, and vice-versa, but a demon is a demon inside-out! We have been led to believe that the devil is a red man with a pitch fork; no, the devil comes in the form of Moses, Jacob, the Boule', NAACP, Urban League, UNCF, black Masonz, etc. All of them had/has the "ability" to do right by our people, yet they choose to assist a monster they've created!

6 TYPES OF MELANATED PEOPLE

According to Barnes, there are 6 categories people fall into. I felt it was necessary to publish this because it may enhance your overstanding of the genetical makeup of people who inhabit planet E:

TYPE 1 — These individualz are white and cannot produce melanin.
- They have blue eyes, blond or red hair, white skin and often have freckles
- They have a Celtic (Irish, Scottish, Welsh) background
- They are most prone to develop melanoma and other types of skin and organ cancer
- They show aging early in life between the ages of 25-30 yearz.

TYPE 2 — These individualz are white and produce very low levelz of melanin.
- They have hazel or blue eyes
- They have red or blond hair
- They often have freckled skin
- They are very prone to developing skin cancer
- They show skin aging early in life between 25-30 yearz

TYPE 3 — These individualz are white and produce moderate to low levelz of melanin.
- They have blond, brunette or lightly pigmented hair

- They show a moderate to high risk of developing skin or other organ cancer
- They show skin aging by the age of 30-40 yearz

TYPE 4 — These individualz are whites who are lightly tan and include Japanese, Chinese, Italian, Greeks, Spanish and Red Indians. They produce moderate levelz of melanin.

- They show a moderate risk of developing skin or other organ cancer.

TYPE 5 — These individualz are brown-skinned and include Mexicanz, Indianz, Malaysianz, Puerto Ricanz and other Spanish speaking people. They produce moderate to high levelz of melanin.

- Their eyes and hair are deep brown or black
- They show aging after the age of 50
- They seldom develop skin or other organ cancerz.

TYPE 6 — These individualz are BLACK in color and include Afrikanz (Kemetianz, Ethiopianz, Nigerianz, American Blacks and Australian Aborigines).

- Their eyes and hair are deep brown or black!
- They virtually have no incidence of skin cancer
- They show skin aging after the age of 50-60 yearz.

You may ask, *"if we possess so much melanin, Y do we still exist in our oppressive state?!"* It is obvious that once you program a cat to act like a dog its madd difficult for the cat to go back to its natural self. For one, the cat must get away (be it physically and/or mentally) from the lifestyle that makes it act like a dog. We are no exception. There are so many tactics YTs using to keep us from understanding the "riddle of life", but what is most significant is their endeavor to keep the melanated people docile.

With the creation of "designer drugz" this return has met great resistance. Drugz like fluoride, cocaine, LSD, Heroine, Crack, amphetamines, marijuana and other hallucinogenz have been chemically structured to bind with and alter them melanin molecule, causing it to become toxic and even fatal. The molecular form of drugz have been designed to resemble melanin. When induced (dictated by oppression, depression, and lack of jobz and money), the body is fooled and its balance is thrown off as it relies on its drug-wrecked melanin in order to function. Even "legal" drugz such as tetracyclines and neuroleptic's (tranquilizerz) have a strong affinity for binding to melanin. With this mischievous plan in order, it is no coincidence when we find that, statistically, people with high melanin are addicted quicker, harder and longer than whites; therefore, this furtherz the notion of drugz being a form of genocide!

To rid ourselves of this plague, we must relinquish biochemical (toxic sun block lotionz) and menticide (self-hatred) and embrace the rayz of intuitive knowledge RA gives. Go out and get some sun, Sun. In fact, don't be afraid to get a little darker, afterall, *"the darker the berry, the sweeter the juice"*, or mathematically translated, the darker you are on the inside, the (potentially) more righteous and spiritual you are inside. I rest my case.

LIK SHOT!

224 yearz! 224 yearz of independence! 224 yearz europeanz have lived in dominance in america. It was also some 224 yearz ago that the implementation of the One World Government, aka the New World Order started!

137 out of the 224 yearz Afrikanz have lived emancipated from physical slavery. The rest have been the nice promotion YT gave us...mental slavery! Approximately 91 of those 224 yearz allowed the beast to set its governmental structure. This was enuff tyme to write the Declaration of Independence, the Constitution and the Emancipation Proclamation. These three documents mark the most profound conspiracies america has ever known. By turning this deadly reprogramming operation into a day of celebration (July 4th), YT has been able to turn something wicked into something "patriotic" or something worth to honor and rejoice about. Look at Mel Gibson's latest movie, *'The Patriot'*.

What Afrikanz-in-america have to realize is that either we believe, support and honor this system — that was founded *without* people of color and *for* pale-skinned people against all other ethnic persuasionz — or we don't. This points to mass confusion. I mean, we do get a day off and whatnot, so it's kinda hard not to support it because I can't see too many people opting to work July 4th. This is Y the cloud of confusion gloomz most effectively in Afrikan people.

Author, Tony Browder, spoke of one major dilemma Afrikanz face today. It's 2000 and we still don't know what to call ourselves! He wrote, *"As a child of the 60s, I was fortunate to live in an era where the racial epithets hurled in my direction were minimized because of the white response to our newfound identity with blackness and Africa."* We've gone from nigger, to negro, to colored, to black, and now to a closer, but still not close enuff, name. In December of 1988, we were asked to accept another name change. However, this one reflected a more direct, geographical and historical title; one which created a more constructed link to our people's past. That name was African-American.

The media interviewed several Afrikanz and asked them what name they preferred. To our dismay, some results were somewhat interesting. The first group felt

'African-American' was appropriate, because it correctly describes us as people of Afrikan descent who currently reside in america. A second group responded disturbingly, *"I just got used to calling myself 'Black' after all these years, and now I'm being told I should call myself an African-American."*

The final group replied, *"I'm not an African anything, I didn't come from Africa and I don't have anything to do with African people."* You can't blame the 3rd group, after all, they represent the majority of our Afrikan elderz in america. The 2nd group closely followed. There is a sickness that makes our people respond in this manner. That is because we have been psychologically and spiritually programmed to be dependent on YT's independence.

When our Ancetorz were kidnapped and brought over to the americas — more specifically, North America — via the Atlantic Slave Trade, we had to leave our culture, our beliefs, AND our names. The very first Afrikanz taken as slaves were named Adam and Eve in a european slave log. When we landed, those of us that survived, weren't given a tour of this new land. We were stripped and lined up in groups on slave auction docks and awaited our new "home". Many families were separated, never to be seen, nor heard from again.

The founding pirates of this country followed the steps of their forefatherz and agreed that they needed to implement a false documentation of lies that would work on their behalf. The wicked, Napoleon Bonaparte once asked, *"What is history, but a fiction agreed upon?"* Former prime minister beast of Great Britain, Winston Churchill, was quoted as saying, *"History is going to be kind to Britain, because I'm going to write it."*

The american pirates knew not to allow us to be rekindled with our ancestry so they gave us european names like Tom, Toby and Cecil. We didn't have last names, so they named us after our slavemasterz. We were given names like Johnson, which told you who you belonged to. You were *John's* son. Names such as Thompson, Jackson, Stevenson and Robinson accompanied the first name of many of our Ancestorz. Names mean something in Afrikan culture, but by giving us meaningless names, we couldn't even find worth in our names let alone our situation.

By calling us niggerz and black, we found it very difficult to link ourselves with any land mass on the globe. There is no place called North Niggaland or Blacktown. So how could our Ancestorz, who were not allowed to read or write, construct any geological origin of our people?

This is what was being done to us while YT reaped the benefits of their reprogramming operation, secretly run by the masonic societies of the New World Order. But the lessonz didn't stop there. Along with the physical abuse, mental abuse needed to be implemented. The 'William Lynch program' was proving a success to the plantation ownerz. Now they needed to condition their people to feel and operate in a way that would enhance, accelerate, and preserve the notion of white over black dominance. They began publishing books and writing articles to creating stereotypes about Afrikan people. There were cartoonz depicting us as gorillaz and other supreme physical, yet mentally deficient, characteristics that would not only make whites think we're mentally incapable, ie, the Bellcurve theory, but to convince Afrikanz to believe this lie as well!

In an 1884 edition of the Encyclopedia Britannica (written, influenced, and FOR Britain) YT went to great lengths to document the inherent inferiority of Afrikanz by stating that he occupies at the same tyme the lowest position in the evolutionary scale, thus affording the best material for the comparative study of the highest anthropoidz and the human species. They described the Afrikan skull as an *"...exceedingly thick cranium, enabling the Negro to butt with the head and resist blows which would inevitably break any ordinary European's skull."* Our skin was said to be a *"...thick epidermis, cool, soft and velvety to the touch, mostly hairless, and emitting a peculiar rancid odor, compared by Pruner Bey to that of the buck goat."*

These obscenities, of course, were to ensure dependency of their people for instructionz as well as Afrikan people. One of the most profound wordz ever relevant to this demonic scheme was revealed by le Baron Armel de Wismes of France. He is the author of *'Nantes Et Le Temps Des Negriers'*, a publication which documents the history of the slave trade in Nantes, France. He said, *"Wherever one finds African people outside of the continent, one is witnessing the visible expression of an economic and political reality as important in its day as Japanese car exports or OPEC oil are today."* He goes on to say, *"Whether we care to admit it or not, it (slavery) formed the bedrock on which our current world economy is built and...it surely explains in part the social and political frictions and misunderstandings between the world's whites and colored people to this day."*

This philosophy of white dominance bleedz in the veinz of many Afrikanz for many still believe history started in Europe. As well, most believe Afrikanz didn't come into play until we landed in Jamestown, Virginia as slaves in 1619. Although the New World Order was still a thought at that tyme, it was definitely part of the plan. It wasn't until 1776 that the order was put into effect.

The inception of the Declaration of Independence proves just who this country was founded for. This document was signed by nearly 90% memberz who were of the masonic cult (50 out of 56). This was purely a masonic document. According to former curator and overseer of the library of archives of the George Washington Masonic Memorial in Alexandria,Virginia, William Brown, *"the sentence structure of The Declaration is unmistakable proof of its Masonic nature."* (Please note that, again, it wasn't until 1863 that we were freed from slavery).

So we have YT declaring their independence from England and their right to live "free", yet they had enslaved people!! Thomas Jefferson, the writer of the declaration is known to have many children from an Afrikan slave he had an affair with. It should also be noted that on the date of the document, July 4th there were only 2 signerz (Jefferson and Hancock). It wasn't until August 2nd that the rest signed! So if there's really gonna be a celebration, it should be August 2nd, not July 4th.

It also showz the connection with the greco-roman period because July was named after Julius Ceasar, as was August named after Augustus Ceasar. This points out the origin of masonry (to greece and rome), which points its true derivation from ancient Ethiopia, KMT and possibly the lost city of Atlantis and Mu.

The constitution of the United States was signed on September 17, 1787 and we find yet again that at this tyme we were still enslaved. During all the celebration of this independence YT was celebrating, simultaneously creating dependence on its prisonerz that plague the mindz and streetz of americanz throughout. Although many are coming to light of this information, many accept/condone what was done, and feel compelled to continue the game plan because it has gone on for so long.

Even our bruthaz and sistaz feel this is a situation no one can rectify. Which proves how effective YT's reprogramming has been. Now that you know, what do you intend to do?! We can sit and talk about racial inequalities all day and can talk about racizm all night, but it comes down to this Afrikan, WHAT ARE YOU GONNA DO ABOUT IT??

It is clearly evident "asking" them to help us is dependence on independence. You cannot claim victorious from your adversary by asking. You cannot have respect for yourself and your people if you ask the very beast who decapitated your culture, to now help you. That's like inviting the Ku Klux Klan to attend service at your church because you're all christianz. No, respect is earned, first from self! Sometymz you have to do rash thingz to gain respect. Respect gives you confidence and vision. Until we make this structure atone for their misdeedz to people of color and nature, we will be just what we are today, dependent on their independence; celebrating *their* holydayz and admonishing *their* heroes!

Yes, this nation has bloody handz and the very soil we walk on was once flooded with our people's blood, sweat, and tearz. I think we should be more appreciative of that and do like the so-called jewz do, *"Never forget"* and never let the world forget. Maybe then we will not worry about whether YT respects us because we will develop our dependence on our Afrikan system, as we watch modern Babylon fall.

MORE FIE-YAH!!

A LETTER TO STEVE COKELY

BY M'BWEBE AJA ISHANGI

A letter to the Elderz, in particular, Brutha Steve Cokely

My Dearest Elderz/Brutha Cokely,

Respect Due, I greet you and all readerz of this piece in the spirit of MAAT. Although my attempts to correspond with you, Brutha Cokely, in the past have gone unsuccessful, I felt the only other avenue to travel was this way; for I believe the Afrikan diaspora, Pan-Afrikanists, those on the quest for truth, readerz of DGT, etc. need be informed about a situation I have been enduring for several yearz.

Word out, Brutha Cokely, is that you have labeled me as "an Agent" and "an Oathtaker". At first, I didn't dwell on it when you told a very dear friend of mine behind my back that I *"didn't come clean"* and that I need *"to confess"* what I know about bein' in a greek-letter fraternity (my bein' an ex-member of alpha phi alpha fraternity, inc.). It's just that this dilemma has not happened once or twice, but several tymz. In fact, this has been goin' on for approximately 4 yearz runnin' now.

So since I have not been able to speak with you and air this out, the best way I felt I could address this challenge was this way, in writing through DGT. For I believe I am not the first of the next generation of Afrikan Liberatorz who may have encountered this situation. If one were to read the series I did on the Boule', in particular part 2, they would see that I exposed thingz no one else has yet to reveal dealing with the black greek-lettered relationship.

Of the numerous lectures I've done on this topic, I've given ev'rything I know. At this moment and my research continues. To be called an oathtaker, I overstand your accusation. But an oathtaker never revealz what he knowz for that would be breakin' his word. Now look at my work. Did I not reveal thingz that you, yourself did not know?! Did I not have an in-depth conversation with you over dinner one night after a lecture and showed you my brand? So Y do I hear you say I'm concealing it?

I've never hidden my brand from anyone! Although it is something I wish I hadn't done, this mark will be on me as a reminder for life, but I look at it now as an advertising piece, because when greeks wanna greet me with secret handshakes and whatnot, I inform them of the Boule'. When the youth ask me about my brand, I tell them NOT to join a frat or sorority and give them the reasonz Y. Livin' with this mistake I've learned to use this to my advantage. Having been guided by the Ancestorz to your work, leading me to break my *unconscious* allegiance to greek life, has enabled me to dedicate portionz of my work to "freeing" other misinformed Afrikanz –

oblivious to the origin of black greeks.

There have been tymz that I wished I had not pledged a frat; but that thought immediately dies when I think of what I would not know had I not been "initiated". What if George GM. James – who would also be classified as an 'oathtaker' according to your definition – didn't write *'Stolen Legacy'* and kept the information to himself? Where would we be? I'm not equating my deedz to James, the brutha wrote it knowin' it would cost his life, but I most certainly did expose what I have revealed in his spirit!

I give massive respect for your dedication and courage to stand firm on your knowledge, and I give an even larger biggup to the Sister who was able to get the Boule' history book to you!! The length she was willing to go is commendable and greatly appreciated. We all make decisionz and rather than sit back, ponderin' on how "lost" I was to want to join what I thought was a "black" organization and finding out it is based on greek principles, I use the info to my advantage. Think of how many young Afrikanz you've saved from goin' down that road. I think of it all the tyme!

Now, I know you probably get vexed ev'rytyme you do a lecture and someone asks you about Da Ghetto Tymz and the info we put out on the Boule'. I am not sorry for that, Brutha. An ancient Adinkra symbol is the Nkonsonkonso, meaning *"We are linked in both life and death. Those who share common blood relations never break apart."* I wish that you could see that my work coincides with your work. Isn't the whole purpose of exposing info to promote awareness and eventual action to combat against it??

I've never claimed to be the griot on the Boule' nor would I ever. I am simply an Afrikan student who was blessed to be in your presence back in '94 and tried to do somethin' about it to make otherz aware.

My situation with you is not the first, for there have been and may be otherz in the future. That is Y I felt I should publish my thoughts. I find there are many tymz an Elder may find it difficult to share the "spotlight" as a messenger of Afrikan truth. Brutha, I seek no stardom (not to say you do). I have found that just as you have been effective in reachin' hedz, so have I and otherz like me, despite the age difference. Though our stylez may be different, we are still capable of reachin' our people, effectively. So Y am I being labeled *"not to be trusted"* by you? I was hopin' that you sorta see me as a student of your work, for I am also a pupil of Ashra Kwesi's – who's a student of Dr. Ben and Clarke; I'm also under the the wing of Tony Browder's works – who's also a student of Clarke, Dr. Ben and John G. Jackson. You are *one* of the shoulderz I stand on as I, in turn, prepare for a generation to stand on mine.

Back in 1991, I was blessed with a re-initiation into the realm of Afrikan consciousness by none other than Blast Master KRS-One. In addition to him I had been exposed to many enlightening historianz/writerz like Diop, Chancellor Williams, Sertima and even Boule' member, Asa Hilliard. But no one awakened me like KRS. Now this is no diss, for after KRS resuscitated the seed of Knowledge of Self, it was like I could now decypher Williams work on a deeper level. Diop's brilliant research on melanin appealed to me with much vigor. It was no diss to the works of those I was not yet ready to overstand...it simply was not my tyme. I was just like most of us are...

ignorant, rather, *ignoring* the constant vybration of our legacy. There was even a tyme when I could be quoted sayin' *"I don't wanna hear the 'Black' shit."* I now see it simply was not my tyme yet.

I'm sure everyone's heard of how someone can tell you somethin' a million tymz and you don't listen, then some new jack tellz you the same thing...AND IT CLICKS!

As many tymz as I heard and witnessed the atrocities of American-Afrikan people, I did not recognize the beckoning call of my *subconsciousness* to my *conscious* until I heard KRS speak. The message was the same, the delivery different; the tyming the same, for the vibration never ceases; yet it manifested to me at the right moment.

That is one of the main reasonz Y it doesn't bother me that most hedz may not feel me, or DGT. Because with continuity, coupled with tyme, some will be enlightened.

Brutha Cokely and my Elderz, I do not wish to stampede on the countless wo/man hourz of your study and research and dedication you have sacrificed. I stand on your shoulderz. But as I stand, you must overstand that we "co-exist". Your tyme is my tyme, as mine will be with the next flock of Liberatorz.

True, I am young and still a lil' damp behind the earz, yet I have the heart of a lion and stand with the wisdom of my Elderz who stand with our Ancestorz. There is no need to fret when you see my youthful presence preserve the work of you and otherz.

I hope you overstand my message and wish you continued success in your research. Although you may harbor the same feelingz even after reading this, I assure you, I will not have a problem sittin' in the front row at your next lecture. Because I know I'm there for the information, no matter *who* tellz it!

On the other hand, if you do feel me dear brutha, can you help a brutha get the post 1994 copy of the Boule' roster so I can include the new names on our website??

Reespek

**NOTE: To date, there's been no response from Cokely, nor have we been able to secure a copy of the most recent roster of the Boule'.*

1999

When it comes to Afrikanz changin' their english names the name of anutha oppressor, historian, Chancellor Williams couldn't have said it better: *"Blacks in the US seem to be more mixed up and confused over the search for racial identity than anywhere else. Hence, many are dropping their white western slavemasters' names and adopting, not Afrikan, but their Arab and Berber slavemasters' names!"*

Before I start, I'd like to note that this has been a very touchy subject for many of our people have been led to believe that only western christianity is something Afrikanz shouldn't convert to. I wouldn't be being true to the Creative Force, Ancestorz and myself if I make acceptionz on the origin of Islam. There are many American-Afrikanz who've left christianity to embrace Islam. In Black Islam, there are several denominationz: the Moorish Science Temple of America, Suni, Nation of Islam, 5% Nation and a few otherz; but they all are rooted in the same Islam that is practiced throughout the world.

For this, I will say once and one tyme only, *"DON'T TAKE THIS PERSONAL."* This is not a personal attack on you, the individual. This is a culture battling a vulture. As we will see, Islam was enforced on our people just as the other 2 western religionz (christianity and judaizm). We, at DGT, profess to free our mindz through the cleansing process called KNOWLEDGE OF SELF. This piece will first deal with the originz of Islam and end with a one-on-one session I had with a Minister (who wished to remain anonymous) in Harlem, 1997. Let the healing continue...

Historian, Chancellor Williams, put into perspective how effective it has been having lost a knowledge of ourselves taken: *"...as a direct result of this continued universal enslavement through education, Black youth are in revolt. That revolt will become increasingly dangerous as they begin to realize how completely they are blocked from self-realization in the very institutions that should further it; how difficult it is to find suitable textbooks in Black history or even "Negro" teachers who do not limit themselves to the viewpoints of the white masters who trained them. The frustrations become more intolerable as the young find themselves between 2 fires: The white racists who determine the very nature of their education and the Negro educators who also see the world through the blue eyes of the Saxons. In short, they are forced to turn to their own devices because they find so many of their own race, who should be working with them, in the camps of the "enemy". Insofar as periodization is concerned, no one should be so naive as to expect a proper division of African history while the field is almost completely preempted* [dominated] *by the enemies of the history. A proper division would tend to encourage a more all-inclusive research and a less biased interpretation of the results. Neither will happen until a new generation of Black research scholars and historians take to the field, becoming the foremost authorities in their own right – Black historians."*

Islam is one of the largest religionz Afrikan people in america convert to after leaving christianity. Most Afrikanz that come out of the American penal system are more likely to covert to some form of Black Islam than any other man-made religion. But because we have forgotten how to educate ourselves (outside of school), we gravitate to "whatever feelz right". Black Islam has given us one of our most inspiring role modelz, brutha Malcolm X. Elijah Muhammad and Louis Farrakhan have also dropped madd jewelz that would make you feel proud to be muslim; BUT, Islam is *not* Afrikan. It wasn't started by Afrikanz, nor voluntarily embraced by us.

Religion itself wouldn't be such a heated battle if the majority of the world wasn't out of touch with Spirituality. Because most have allowed themselvez to be taught "who God is" from someone outside their own self, many have fallen for this sham called religion, or to, as the dictionary sayz, *"reline you with the* (man-made) *belief's of God."* According to who? Which ethnic background is responsible for establishing the current belief system? They're certainly not of Afrikan descent!

Life is about lessonz and with lessonz must come elevation. Black Islam is responsible for freeing Afrikanz from western christianity, but guilty of shackling them to Islam. It must be noted that there is a great difference between Spirituality and religion. Religion is a man-made philosophy made to control one's ability to express their individual relationship with whomever they believe to be their maker. On the other hand, Spirituality (which is a system originated from our Ancestorz) was not a type of religion where there were rules. Each Afrikan had/has the freedom to practice their relationship with 'The Creative Force', 'God' or as I now call it 'Energy' on their own termz and are not penalized for being different. Many muslimz don't even realize what they practice is anti-Afrikan, Y? Because, just as with christianity, the power has been taught to be outside of you and not within. Islam, like any other religion has very little room for questionz and very seldom allowz a challenge.

For that last 50 yearz, amerikkka has seen its former enslaved victimz rise. For 500+ yearz, the criminalz exiled from england have tried to eliminate from its captives any affiliation with Mother Afrika. From taking away the drum to changing our names, these ailments still plague the psyche of Afrikanz worldwide. Analyzing this dis-*ease*, it has had detrimental effects on Afrikanz, collectively, since re-emerging in the "New World" as slaves.

The naming of a people has a direct link to a people's unity/disunity. We've seen our people search for ourselves through the mere definition of a name. A name of significance to a landmass is rehabilitating to the lifestyle and culture of any ethnicity. If that wasn't so, italy wouldn't have italianz, china wouldn't have chinese, and europe wouldn't have europeanz. Even more vital is how one's origin is carried with them as they venture to new regionz (ie. chinese-american, italian-american, etc.). So Y has it taken so long for Afrikanz to call themselves Afrikan-American?!

50 yearz ago we were called "negroes". This name links to the spanish term "black". However, the spanish version is interpreted from latin and they got theirz from the greeks. The greek word is "necro" which meanz "DEAD". Now think about that for a moment…

Next was "colored". Neither of the two ever influenced any racial pride; being the origin of 'negro' was played-out and colored was basically unclean (many Afrikanz, after the constant reminder that black was dirty, thought they could literally wash the black off them!).

Movin' on to the 1960s, we saw an emergence of attributing "black" with positivity and pride. COINTELPRO and other spy networks made sure the resurrection was halted by the bringing of the hippie age, where interracial relationships boomed, as well as the planting of addictve drugz in Afrikan communities like cocaine, weed, upperz, downerz and gunz.

The mid-80s saw the "politically-correct" Afrikan yearn for yet anutha change. "Afrikan-American" would be the first to link us to a landmass, reconnecting us to Afrika and broadening our spectrum to our victimized bruthaz and sistaz on the Mother continent and abroad.

This was good, but far from great. At a minimum, there remainz 3 stages of names we must go through before this "name-changing-thing" can rest. Next is, "American-Afrikan", "Afrikan" and finally "Alkebulan" or "Ta-Seti".

Looking at the difference between "*Afrikan*-American" and "American-*Afrikan*" needz serious reanalyzing. In "Afrikan-American", "American" serves as the noun or the essence and "Afrikan" becomes the adjective. This implies one who is, first and foremost, an American, and the kind of American they are is Afrikan. The fact that Afrikan or Alkebulan people were here *before* "America" was even a word is supported by the pyramid and Olmec Head findingz in Mexico and South America. And according to Websterz Dictionary, "America" was not a term used until around the late 1500s.

The Western world, including its educational system wants us to believe that the history of

When I was re-awakened in 1991, one of the first religious sects I gravitated to was the Ansar muslimz. No doubt, the knowledge that Black Islam parlayz is based with Kemetic philosophy, metaphysics and Masonry, is deep indeed. However, I see it as a religion but not the spiritual system we Afrikanz need. See, looking at history chronologically, Islam was not in existence when our Ancestorz built the pyramidz of Giza. In fact, Islam was *after* christianity (approx. 632AD). I was told by a brother that it was hypocritical to say I luv Afrika and at the same tyme, be a muslim, orthodox or not.

Regardless of the historianz I study, history is the best teacher and it teaches that Islam was millenniumz AFTER Afrikan people created the pyramidz of Giza; thousandz of yearz after they discovered electricity with the use of the Kemetic symbol, the Ankh; even more before we established our relationship with the starz and constellationz of the universe; realized the world was round; and established a oneness with Nature (Energy) and life.

There's one thing in particular that separates Spirituality from man-made religion, Spirituality encompasses the whole, whereas religion separates Nature with religion, law with agriculture, and so on.

INCONSISTENCIES: BLACK ISLAM & THE REST OF THE WORLD

Many Afrikanz in America may not be aware that Islam is practiced throughout the world. When Malcolm took his trip to Mecca, he was shocked to meet blue-eyed and pale-skinned muslimz. Afrikan people do not make up the majority of muslimz of the world. When we look at the obvious discrepanceez of Islam, we find that it is consistent with the other 2 western religionz... that being male chauvinistic. As with all religionz, Islam delegates male dominance over his counterpart. This is a code of the ancient Djhuitic principles that has been totally disrespected, which is GENDER.

Many may take (at least with Black muslimz) the offense and claim that they hold their woman high and acknowledge her as the mother of the earth. But they don't realize they're holdin' her up so high she's in the stratosphere; she can't breathe. They *over* protect her. I've been told by muslimz that the woman is too emotional and, therefore, needz the man to guide her. *"What da f___?!"* I think it is man who's too emotional 'cause we ready to "nuke" a country if we don't get our way or ready fi romp if someone steps on our Jordan's.

If that isn't enuff, observe how the setting is in a mosque. Most (if not all, admittedly I haven't been to every one) have their women draped in white clothing. Now, according to Webster, white is a good, pure and wholesome thing. But that's not what the Black muslimz teach. They teach that white is the exact opposite. So Y would they have their Queen draped in an evil color?!!? When they are havin' service in the mosque, Y are the women sitting on the left side with the bruthaz, usually wearin' the color of power, Black, sittin' on the *"right"*, or *correct* side?? Better yet, where are the Lady Farrakhan's?? Most, if not all the ministerz, heroes and role modelz are men. All these go against the principle of Gender; which is anti-Afrikan!

THE 5% NATIONZ VIEW OF THE PRINCIPLE OF GENDER

Founded by ex-Nation of Islam member, Clarence 13X, the 5% Nation findz its roots in the NOI. Therefore, much of the foundation of these two are one-in-the-same. The 5% Nation has a lesson that dealz with defining what a Queen is. In this doctrine/lesson (given to me by a member of the 5%), it speaks of how the woman is too emotional and cannot reach her potential without the influence of the Blackman.

You may have heard their version of the trinity, 'Sun, Moon and Starz'. They define the Blackman as the "Sun" and the Blackwoman as the "Moon", with the Starz being the children. I've also heard of the Blackman being "God" and the Blackwoman as the "Earth".

I got into a heated debate with a member some yearz back. I asked him to define what "Earth" meanz. He said the Blackwoman is earth because she produces, nourish, and sustainz life, like the planet. The Blackman, being "God", he said, is the *owner* of the Earth. He then summed it up as, *"the ruler/maker of all thingz."* I asked, *"including the Blackwoman, symbolically the 'Earth'??"* He responded by sayin' I wasn't undastandin' the mathematics. I told him I was, he was sayin' the Blackman was deemed to rule over the Blackwoman. Soundz chauvinistic to me. Besides, if the Blackman is solely the ruler and maker of all thingz, Y don't we carry the seed 9 months??

In regardz to the Sun, Moon & Starz trinity, we find additional male chauvinistic principles. Y does the Moon shine at nite? Because it has no light of its own. If we applied the chauvinistic theories of Islam, without the light (wisdom) of the Sun (Blackman), the Moon cannot be seen. Is that chauvinistic? I

Alkebulan people in America didn't begin until 1619. We all know many of our Ancestorz during that period were brought here against their will. In fact, according to the *CON*stitution, we were NEVER CITIZENZ (and *still* aren't), but classified as "chattel" or moveable property.

So we are not American... and definitely not "first and foremost". A more appropriate term (for those who must have "American" in their name) is "American-Afrikan", which is the complete opposite; therefore stating that I am, first and foremost, Afrikan and am a kind of one who resides in America.

This rehabilitating method allowz the link of Afrikanz worldwide to gel more cohesively. Instead of being just Jamaican (because most were brought to the Caribbean by the same europeanz, via the triangular Atlantic Slave Trade), they now become "Jamaican-Afrikan", "Brazilian-Afrikan", "Canadian-Afrikan" and so on. Think of how dope the annual Brooklyn West Indian Labor Day parade would be then; when everyone sees themselves as descendants of Afrika and not some British colonial pirate!

There are those however who feel as I and choose not to associate America's accomplishments — because most have been done by murder and theft. We insist on being called "Afrikan" alone.

And what deemz even more overstanding is that the Afrika, as we know it, is not called Afrika, but the land of Alkebulan, or what YT called Ethiopia — the land of burnt faces (however Afrika was a term given to us by YT as well, from the greek word, Aithiops).

The fact is, WE ALL COME FROM ALKEBULAN. The sooner we realize that, the sooner Alkebulan people will unite!

don't fault any ignorant follower of this unbalanced philosophy. Most likely, they were never given a chance to question because, like otherz, this is a man-made religion. The fault mainly lay on the originatorz of this mentality. Unfortunately, "power" leadz many astray from common sense and truth and we find so many defending something they themselves have not been given the tyme to entirely cipher. It's manipulatorz like Farrakhan and other black muslim leaderz that are responsible for crippling Afrikanz from distinguishing divine intervention from mental brainwash!

WHASSUP WIT' FARRAKHAN??

I hope Farrakhan has some tricks up his sleeve 'cause since before the Million Man March, he's had a brutha madd confused. Never was really a follower of him but respected his viewz in dealin' with the YT. Up until 1995 I felt he represented and defended Black folk, but I can't help but mention it's been a long tyme since I heard him utter the wordz made famous by his teacher, Elijah, "blue-eyed devil". In fact, I've heard him quote from the bible more than the qu'ran! Whassup Farrakhan?!

Y are you, as brutha Khallid Muhammad said, meeting and breakin' bread with the enemy? Y would you even think about workin' with fellow Illuminati member, Edgar Bronfmann (owner of Seagrams and sits on the Board of Directorz for Vivendi Universal, the global Illuminati-based 'massa'-media mogul, and ex-owner of Interscope Recordz — who created and financed gangsta rapperz from NWA to Death Row Recordz) on a Black(?) hotel chain??

Y do you live in, "Elijah's mansion", as you put it, with solid-gold ceilingz?! Y, when I come to see you speak, an hour of it is spent on ya'll beggin' us for loot, (when it was $15 to get in that piece) and you livin' luvly, flyin' first class, havin' already established businesses and shit like dat?! Damn, if you say you a prophet, you sure livin' like a king! If you woulda got that billion from Ghadafi, what would you have done wit' it? Did you even think about breakin' off each and every American Afrikan?

Yeah, it's easy to criticize. It's nuthin' but emotionalizmz airin' out. But the greatest beef comes with your suspicious connection to the ongoing enslavement of Afrikan people in Sudan.

In early 1996, you were approached by the media about the kidnap and enslavement of Afrikan people in Afrika. Your reply was, *"...where is the proof? If slavery exists, why don't you go as a member of the press, and look inside Sudan, and if you find it, then come back and tell the American people what you found?"* Well two journalist's from *The Baltimore Sun*, Gregory Kane and Gilbert Lewthwaite, took you up on the challenge and what they found was startling. Not only did they prove the accusation of the enslavement of Afrikanz was true by both Afrikanz that witnessed it and one's that escaped, they went a step further and "bought" several Afrikanz themselves!

Could this be Y you didn't let any antislavery organizationz speak at the Million Man March in 1995. Historian, John Henrik Clarke noted that there were various organizationz that wanted to use the march as an opportunity to relay to the world the atrociteez that were goin' on abroad!! Could it be you ignored their request because the very culprit's responsible for these barbaric acts are followererz of the same faith as yourz…ISLAM?!!?

In an article, *Genocide And Slavery In The Sudan: The Farrakhan Connection*, by Sabit Abbe Alley of *The City Sun* (June 6-11, 1996), Farrakhan had aggressively denied and defended the Islamic fundamentalist regime in Sudan against allegationz of them being the backbone to the whole enslavement industry.

He has publicly *"refuted all reports concerning the enslavement of the Sudanese Africans by their fellow Arab Sudanese"*, states Alley. Alley also states that Farrakhan is frontin' 'cause he got stakes in the slave trade, *"Farrakhan's defense of the Sudan government's war and slave machinery is predicated on some personal ulterior motives. [He] has a stake in the whole business. He is on Khartoum's payroll, pure and simple."* Alley has proof, *"the leader of the NOI is an agent of Sudan's Islamic fundamentalist regime has now been confirmed beyond any reasonable doubt by the unfolding of recent events in Khartoum. Reports emanating from the Presidential Palace in Khartoum indicate that, while Farrakhan was on his African tour, his Arab friends, President Bashir and the Cleric Turabi, asked him to travel to Zaire to persuade Mobutu to give the Islamists logistical support in the form of troops and arms and land access so that they could attack South Sudan from bases in Northern Zaire. In like manner, the two Sudanese leaders dispatched Farrakhan to Nigeria to secure for them some oil money from the ruthless dictator Abacha for the purchase of arms from China. As a result of Farrakhan's intervention on behalf of his Arab friends in the Sudan, money and arms have started flowing to the country."*

All this is being done because there is a war between the world powerz who are tryin' to recolonize Afrika. The muslimz are no exception, for every Afrikan they kidnap, they rename them with a muslim name and force them to practice Islam. This is the same method that was used by YT when he injected christianity into our Ancestorz pineal on the plantationz of the south. Even more suspicious is Farrakhan's perseption of our brutha and sistaz in the Sudan region.

During his Savior's Day address, February 25, 1996, in Chicago, he described the people of Sudan as *"very, very, very...very dark with kinky hair,"* as compared to the white to brown skinned Northern arabz, who he likened himself to. When he was describin' them as "very", he used the adverb 15 tymz emphasizing his color prejudice against the Souther Sudanese. Now Y would a lighter complexioned Black(?)man, feel justified in supporting the enslavement of his darker brutha?? Soundz like the 'house negro-field Afrikan' theory if you ask me.

But this ideology of light-skinned being better than dark-skinned isn't solely felt and expressed by just Farrakhan, for he is a product of Elijah Muhammad, who, himself claimz that Allah came to him in the body of a, get this… a *whiteman!* This shit is madd comical, yo! Look at this picture of Farrad Muhammad (next page). He is very light complexioned and has straight Black hair. Hmmm, come to think of it, I don't recall Farrakhan's hair being tightly coiled either. What seemz to be the most confusing question to me is Y don't the followerz see this?? Allah appearz to be white, just like Jesus does to the Christianz!

And in defense to those muslimz that say Allah is Black, Y don't the other billion-plus muslimz around the globe see Allah as a Blackman?? This is no different than a select percentage of christianz around the world sayin' Jesus is Black and the other sayin' he's

WD. Fard (Fraud) Muhammad. The alleged 'Allah in the flesh' to the Black muslimz of the Nation of Islam... who just so happenz to be a whiteman!

not (or color doesn't matter); YET THEY ALL STILL CLAIM TO BE OF THE SAME FAITH! Ya'll ain't no more organized than any other man-made religion who chose to pick what is convenient to their beliefs instead of the whole. That's Y today we have all these different sects of the same religion where hundredz of thousandz worship in the same God, yet they each pick only bits and pieces of the whole to suit their needz.

If these Godz left instruction on how to live your life with these "holy" texts (Bible/Koran, etc.), Y are so many finding it confusing to unite and practice their faith together?! I took these questionz with me to a reasonin' session I had with this anonymous Minister about Islam.

ONE-ON-ONE WITH AN ISLAMIC MINISTER

Although many of his points proved worthy to ponder, it was the origin of Islam I was after. Here's an excerpt:

***M'BWEBE**:* I've been told many tymz by muslimz that Islam is the true religion.
***ANONYMOUS MINISTER**:* Yes, that is true. It has alwayz existed; since the beginning of tyme, in Afrika and around the world. All other religionz are false. The Blackman is the original arab and we had Islam and were speaking Arabic long before any imposter came. Without Afrika, Islam, Judaism, Christianity, Hinduism, Buddism, etc., would not exist.

M: Do you believe in researching history from a chronological perspective?
AM: Without a doubt, sir.

M: Then let me ask you this… exactly *when* did Islam begin??
AM: As I previously stated, Islam has always been here. It is the Blackman's true religion ordained from Allah revealed in the holiest of texts, the Holy Qur'aan. To be a muslim meanz to be "one of peace"; we do not have blind faith but, rather, physical evidence that the Qur'aan is the infallible word of the Allah. We Muslimz sorta have bragging rights, we do not have blind faith, we have facts. In the Qur'aan 47:24, 6:79, 2:107 and 6:162, it reads, *"...[I]f you doubt that the Qur'aan is the Word of Allah, then produce another book..."*

M: Well, actually I was able to through anutha text. Not a religious text, mind you, for they oftentymz are biased towardz history. Now, since we talkin' about history, I got a book from a historian! According to Dr. Ben Jochannan's book, *African Origins of Major Western Religions,* he found that, *"A.H. 1; the year one after the Hegira, or 622 AD, Prophet Muhammad was already 52 years of age. It also marked the date of the birth of the Moslems' religion which is officially called 'ISLAM'".* Islam is not known to the world before this. Islam is not responsible for erecting pyramidz, conducting electricity from the ankh, traveling the galaxies, nor the writing of the Medu Neter. The philosophies and ideologies we practice today are rooted tenz-of-thousandz of yearz ago in Ancient Ethiopia and Kemet. The pyramidz of Giza is suspected to be anywhere from 5,000 to 20,000 yearz old. I don't recall ever reading about arabic writingz on the temples. That's because Islamz origin is arabic and just like how the portuguese, greeks and the romanz stole our culture, so did Islam (nearly 650 yearz later).

True, I will grant that Afrika gave birth to all religionz, but there was a tyme when religion wasn't even a word! Only spirituality existed. It is this philosophy that gave birth to the mathematics I hear muslimz parlay in the streetz and at the mosque's. The equationz are true, but the origin is not.

As well, if this religion is based upon one being "of peace", how do you explain the followerz of Islam in Sudan who've been kidnapping, raping, enslaving and murdering innocent Afrikanz and forcing Islam on the enslaved Afrikanz for the pat 20 yearz?? I know you cannot account for an individualz actionz, but right is right and there is obviously something wrong with how your fellow muslimz who practice Islam. Even if you do not advocate what's goin' on in Sudan, what are you, as a believer in Islam doin' to stop this?!

In addition, what is yall's perception of women? I've found that the first God of Islam was a woman. Her name was Al'lat. Can you tell me about that?

AM: No brother, I can't. This is not true. It looks like a Christian must've told you this. You can always tell the ones who read the Qur'aan from the ones who do not. Al'lat was never a God of Islam, Prophet Muhammad never taught Muslimz to worship Al'lat or any other false Godz!

He transformed a whole nation turning them away from worshipping false Godz and idolz to worshipping the One True God, the Father and his correct name is Allah!! Allah is not male or female, he was not created out of procreation. In the Holy Qur'aan, 112:3, it sayz that *"He be getteth not, Nor is He begotten",* meaning Allah does not have sex, setting him above all creation, also meaning he did not come into existence through the act of sexual procreation. He is not a human being, he is a Spiritual Being. He has alwayz existed and Allah is his proper name.

M: Guess I struck a nerve brutha. However in the true spirit of lyrical sparring — and I do *luv to spar* – I first noticed you said *"the One True God"* was *"the Father"* then you said in the same breath, he is not male or female…c'mon brutha! In regardz to Al'lat, or Allah, as you say the *"prophet"* TOLD you, based on no facts.

Dr. Yosef ben-Jochannan can assist my point again, *"Muhammad's family worshipped both El Ka'aba and Al'lat. Note that the name 'AL'LAT' was the origin of the LATER word 'AL'LAH,' or 'SUPREME GOD'."* Hold up, there's more, *"Between these 2 dates (622-29AD), however, the government in Mecca witnessed a mass conversion of its citizens from the worship of the Goddess Al'lat and El Ka'aba (the Black stone meteorite from Ethiopia, East Afrika)...They were also major sources of revenue for the treasury of the government in Mecca, as millions of the faithful of both religions come each year to pay homage and pilgrimage to the Goddess Al'lat and the El Ka'aba."*

Now this is going on even today! Which leadz me to believe that the Islam most Blacks in America practice is not based on historical facts. It showed when I posed the question of the first God of Islam being a woman; you went off! To not even fathom your God bein' a woman is a direct violation of the Ancient Djhuitic principle of Gender. You say Allah isn't male or female, but you use the masculine pronoun "he" and "his"; however to even conceive of Allah bein' a "she" would be undeniably ruled out.

If Allah is a Spiritual Being, Y is "he" referred to with male identities? You called Allah "He", "him" and the "Father", 'sup wit dat?! If it is such an abomination to call Allah a "she", shouldn't it be the same if Allah's implied to be a he??

This supports my whole argument of the chauvinizm and inequality that exists in ALL man-made religionz. I'm sure you could say more to "change what you said" but the action is what needdz to be changed. Islam has done a wonderful job in breakin' the Blackmanz gravitational hold on Christianity, but Islam has a hold of its own and it is equally detrimental to the spiritual liberation our people so desperately need. Towardz the end of the session, the tension was overflowin' and I obviously overstayed my welcome at the mosque, so I politely left, vexed because I felt he forfeit, yet charged because I had more arson I was ready to unleash. Guess it wasn't to be this day, so I went back to the lab, and a book I did grab, to find more elements of truth to combat this Arab.

I don't want to create enemies, I'm strivin' for truth and I believe on the path of righteousness you will make a few; but it is truth that I am after, not a crew. This will be an ongoin' topic, now that the debate has begun. Whatever you believe, never believe until you know, and you know only through study! In the immortal wordz of our Ancestorz, "Know Thyself"

MORE FIE-YAH!

1998

Niggers play football, baseball, and basketball while the white man is cutting off their balls...niggers tell you they're ready to be liberated, but when you say to him, "Let's take our liberation", niggers reply, "I was just playin'.

— The Last Poets, *"Niggers Are Scared Of Revolution"*

Most bruthaz, that are athletic have, at one tyme or anutha, thought of pursuing that dream of goin' pro. Mainly it's the games highest revenue sport's Basketball or Football. The game today is developing into more of a capitalist sport, where we find rich white (or blacks who have a white mentality) leeches who squeeze every nutrient and vitamin out of black athlete's as if they were Florida oranges!

You can't blame a brutha for staying at the courts into the wee hours of night, or lifting, running, and catching ballz day in and day out. Nobody want's to have a hard tyme paying bills, and everybody wants to be able to buy what they want, when they want. This eurocentric; dog-eat-dog; live-for-today, fuck tomorrow; mentality has made it so most bruthaz feel the only way "out" is through sports.

With the opportunity for jobs decreasing, minimum wage similar to what NIKE pays foreigner's to make his shoes, welfare next to elimination, and the cost of living rising, athletics seem the only "legit" way out. Most young Afrikanz think this. Most go to school because they want to receive a college scholarship, which will get them closer to turning pro — or as of late, do what Kevin Garnett has done and go pro from high school.

I believe the american amateur and professional athletic regime is a hoax. It is a "legal" pimping business that shatterz the mindz of many Afrikanz world-wide. I speak this from both the heart and experience. I received a 4-year Track & Field scholarship at a major university and I still suffer from the psychological spells they put on me.

Most kidz will tell you when they grow up they want to be some type of professional athlete. Not realizing the high risk of even making the high school team, most of these young beautiful, black shining faces will be crushed by the jawz of sports competition and most may never recover and become an asset to both our people and the community as a whole. You know some legendz in your burrough. *"Brutha Scoop, you know, the legend; he used to play at the park. He used to have a nice handle and crazee up's; he went to college, couldn't make it and ended up droppin' out. You may see him on the court still, but he ain't playin' he sippin' somethin' out of a brown paper bag and he's on crack!"*

Y is athletics so highly marketed? I say, it is a diversion to keep you from knowing yourself. To distract a people from what really needdz to be done, like, liberating our economic situation in this world through knowledge of self and setting up black business' that employ our people.

To understand how sports evolved, we must go back to a tyme when YT first realized he could use our melanated rhythm and garnish riches from it. True, after they raped KMT they had nobody else to kill, so they looked for other thingz to release their aggression. They had barbarous sports like fighting lionz inside an arena, but when they realized Afrikanz were, more agile, could jump higher, and was more spontaneous, creating sport was inevitable. Looking at the history of athletic competition, there really isn't much a difference in the mentality of YT. The caucasian has alwayz looked at the Afrikan in the eyes of profit. Therefore, we were never seen as men and women in their eyes. Our mental, physical, and spiritual development is what made them so infatuated with us, they felt the need to steal us all for themself, as if we were humanz with much tenacity, but no direction. That's like saying we're intelligent enuff to run the whole offense, but not intelligent enuff to be the quarterback. (In order to understand the nature of our relationship with YT, please refer to the piece, "IZ YT Human? or Mutant!")

We must also understand that athlete's are only good if they can produce (make money for YT). If you're injured, or in some cases like school, fulfill your 4 yearz of eligibility, you are no longer of use. In the process of the Atlantic Slave Trade, we were dispersed to the americas and the carribean. At the same tyme, over 100 million of us were either murdered, starved, or committed suicide in this nearly 25 year crime of kidnapping and led to nearly 500 yearz of hard, free labor. Think of how many of our Ancestorz bones lie on the bottom of the Atlantaic...deep! After reaching the docks, we were lined up and sold to the highest bidder for labor we have yet to be compensated for.

The modern pro sports auction bearz a close resemblance to the slave auction just over 100 yearz ago.

This is where the modern NFL and NBA drafts have similarities to the the Middle Passage draft. One of the most exciting tymes around the year is the draft (auction). Each draft (auction) is relatively the same, they hold training camps (plantationz) where athletes come and get clocked in the 40-yard dash, max-out bench press test's, speed and agility skillz. After these tests, the name of the athlete is passed on to ball club teamz, who try to get the player on their squad. What's mostly concentrated on is the height, weight, and strength of the athlete, because this is what attracts spectatorz, who'll pay to see them play. There's also "trading" Afrikanz, oops, athletes from one plantation, oops again, team as late as halfway into the season. This meanz the athlete must pack up and leave. So what he just bought a new home in New York, pack up, "ya ass is movin' ta Minnesota!"

What an athlete goes through to potentially become picked is somewhat sadistic. In athletics, they stress fitness. But Y IZ it dat their diets are so poor?! Most, if not nearly all athletes eat tonz of decayed flesh, or what you may call meat; carbonated acid (soda); and pop so many pillz they'd be considered a junky but because these are "prescription" drugsz and formula's, it's ok. In other wordz, you can be addicted to drugz as long as you continue to make loot for YT, but if you a junky on the street, you ain't shit! As these bruthaz build up their muscle strength, most have not exercised the biggest and most important muscle — the heart. With a poor diet, aritificial formula's, and other drugz ok'd by team physicianz, bruthaz don't even realize they are shortening their athletic career, possibly life! Most don't even think about "after athletics" until they are either too old, been benched, or injured. By then, most have made million's but got nothin' to show for it.

Back to the auction, everytyme I hear how much a particular Afrikan, being auctioned off, weighz or how fast and strong he is, I think about the slave auctionz (drafts) of the past. The only difference is that todayz Afrikanz are being paid for the work. But if you think about it, a $3-4 year million contract is but pennies to a franchise that racks up a couple hundred million annually and will be here far longer than the career of the brutha who just signed. In all actuality, we are in worse shape than when being auctioned for free labor a couple hundred yearz ago! Y you ask? Because we are given millionz of dollarz and we still ain't free!

Afrikanz in america ain't got shit! When we didn't have nothin' we had dreamz of what we would do if we had money. We said we'd open up our own businesses — which would create jobs for us and so on. Well, at present, Afrikanz, especially in america, are making the most money we ever had and the number is increasing. If we knew of our spending power, we could put any company out of business. In 1995, Afrikanz in america spent a total of $399 billion! All the other ethnic races — including YT — put together only totaled approximately $323 billion! If we all stopped purchasing NIKEs for a month, their stock would take a huge loss! If we did it to any business we patronize, they would feel our power! So y don't we have an Afrikan company that makes tv's, cars, or toothbrushes?! Because there is a catch!

Do you really think the white establishment (white supremacy) would give these amounts of money to Afrikanz, if he didn't think we'd just buy things for ourself and not think about using it to build Afrikan-centered schoolz?! Where is the modern source of such a way of thinking? The wack educational system and tell-a lie-vision, aka massa-media. It was also learned on the plantation. Heard of the crab theory?

There's a barrel full of crabz at a restaurant about to be cooked and they're trying to escape. To do so, crabz are climbing over each other. Instead of working together as a unit, climbing over each other until the last one's out, the crabz snatch the crab, who is nearest the top edge, back down with the rest of them as if to say, *"If I ain't got nothin'* (in this case, freedom)*, you ain't got nothin'! If I'm oppressed, you oppressed."* But the mentality changes when we get something. Our attitude is all about self. It is no longer "we,"it's now "me."

These athletes mostly have white agents (or white-thinking, Afrikan agents) who keep bruthaz away from the black burroughz, where most of our people live economically oppressed, and end up giving madd loot to charities like United Way (who's founderz and executives have alliances with the New World Order of white supremacy, therefore, they don't give 2 shits about Afrikanz being economically, socially, and spiritually oppressed globally) and other leech fundraiserz.

From the perspective of college athletics, these pimps have access to even more hoes. I'm not dissin' collegiate athlete's, I was pimped 4 yearz! Universities are making crazee lootchie! Football and basketball are considered the only revenue sports, is not. Think about it, Notre Dame would not be Notre Dame if it weren't for the athletes, right? They have a multi-million dollar contract with NBC. Who get's the money? It goes to coaches, the university president, and other leeches' salary. It keeps construction on campuses (which are jobz most Afrikanz construction companies don't get). It buyz the coaching staff their carz, their childrenz carz, their families vacation, their newly built home in the suburbz, their childrenz tuition, and so on. But what does the athlete get? A lil' tv coverage (4 yearz max) and a scholarship. As much loot as the college bowl games get, the NCAA (National Control against Afrikan Athletes) doesn't cut one check to the athlete. The athlete's family may get a couple crumbz, but their son, who just won the heisman trophy, has brought millionz of dollarz in university exposure ('cause he wearz their jersey, which is like saying who you "belong" to) and endorsements.

One year Notre Dame's "irish" mascot was black. How oxymorinic is that?! How can they be the Notre Dame "Fighting Irish" when there's mostly bruthaz on the team?! It made me think of all these white universities sports programz would not be contenderz without the black athlete. Ohio State, Florida State, North Carolina, Michigan, UCLA, this list goes on, none of 'em would be so popular if it wasn't for the black athlete!

Think about this. NIKE remakes athletes collegiate jerseyz who're in the NBA and sellz it. Do you think Chris Webber get's any percentage for making the #4 jersey for Michigan popular? If he does get paid, he is the last one in line. Just like we were on the plantation, the last to break from work, the last to eat, the last to drink, and the last to sleep. Michigan receives the largest profit because Chris was their property! Sound like the plantation theory now? When you are a college athlete on scholarship, you cannot play your sport for any money because it is a violation against NCAA rules. I was told if you play a pick-up game and receive money from it, it is a violation and you could lose your scholarship! Word. Control. The Afrikan cain't make no money unless the overseer gets a cut... a large cut!

I believe college athletes should be paid a salary. Did you see the movie *'Blue Chips,'* that starred Shaquille O'Neal? What was madd deep was how alumni took care of the recruits. Personally, I didn't see nothing wrong with that. After all, it is the playerz that go out and win the games, which bringz national attention to the universities, which breedz stand-out high school athletes around the country to sign letterz of intent with these universities (which is like signing yourself away to a specific plantation), which will ensure these universities will continue to make money in the yearz to come. This also attracts regular students to enroll at these universities, which is even more loot, knowhatI'msayin'?

In college football, the bowl games rack up so much loot, with the Rose Bowl leading the way. For universities that constantly produce national attention, they can count on that money being there for yearz to come. This is how coaches and other university officialz get over. Meanwhile, if I blow my knee out during a game and can't play any more, I'm no longer "the man" 'cause I can't score no more touchdownz for YT.

My college track & field coach was always suspect to fraud, in my eyes. For one, he had a son who was handicapped. His son, at one tyme, needed a couple major surgeries in one year. Also, that year, my freshman year, we won the outdoor Big East Track & Field championship and that following fall, he showed up in a new car. He also bought some expensive land out in the woodz, and had his home built there. I'm thinkin' to myself, where'd he get the money to do all this? Last tyme I checked, it was me and my fellow teammates that busted our ass and won the championship! And what did we get for winning? A funky polyester warm-up suit! Y IZ Dat?!

Athletes keep president's and ownerz of franchises families paid for generationz! Although professional athlete's get millionz for their work today, we are in worse shape! Think about it. We all wanna watch Championship Boxing matches, right? But we all don't have the loot to fly to Vegas for ringside seats. So we order the fight through Pay-Per-View, or watch on other cable systems like HBO and Showtime. Did you ever think about how much money these companies are making off the fight? Not to mention, the many undaground bets goin' on. If you add all that up, the fighter is making scraps! And he's the one that's out there "puttin' in work!" Who gets paid first after the fight is over? I don't know, but I bet the fighter is the last one!

Having millionz of dollarz is senseless if you just keepin' it for yaself! There ain't enuff nationally Afrikan-owned businesses in america, so what's up black athlete??!! Wha'chu waitin' on? There is a reason black athlete's don't know of Da Ghetto Tymz or of the self-empowerment philosophy. Professional sports don't facilitate their money management programz! Instead, athletes have white agents (or white-thinking, black-faced agents) who control athletes money and end up sucking them dry! If Shaq, Jordan, Magic, Foreman, Barry Bonds, and so on, thought of doing something nationally — or globally, for that matter — like supporting the construction of an Afrikan public school system, or a record label big enuff to contend with Sony and RCA, or purchasing an Afrikan-owned satellite that would air real Afrikan entertainment and not tell-a lie-vision's B-S station BET, we would have a stronger economic, and therefore, more unified race of people. We would have what Afrikan scholarz call balance. See, society doesn't want us to choose so they only show you one way and you, in turn, thinks it's the only way.

Some of you may ask, "Y IZ dis brutha talking about black stuff? Y does he want to have black business' and boycott others?" Because Afrikan-owned businesses produce jobs! Jobs for Afrikanz. This is how we can become self-reliant. Afrikanz in america have the highest buying power! Meaning, we spend the most money of any race! Y? Because we are 99% consumer and 1% producer! Everything we buy, someone from another culture made it. Whether it's buying a pair of NIKEs or some BBQ Ribz from the chinese restaurant 'round the cornah. White amerikkka knowz this and are starting to re-direct their marketing strategies so their products will appeal to us; which meanz we'll buy Nautica, or Tommy Hilfiger, because we saw Grand Puba wearin' it! And they're using our Afrikan athletes, as well as entertainerz, to endorse their product!

Look at how soulful the fast food commercialz be (McDonald's, KFC, Sprite etc.). Look at how their gear is lured to our headz by using bruthaz and sistaz to wear their gear. Even though Polo, Guess, Hilfiger, and so on, claimz 'when they make their clothes they ain't thinkin' bout black folk', they can say that because we still will buy their clothes. Or we'll drink St.Ides, because we saw Snoop and Wu-Tang rappin' about it even though we never saw them drinkin' it! Or we'll "obey" our thirst and drink Sprite because Grant Hill drinks it. Last tyme I checked, my thirst was sayin' get me some clean water, fuck carbonated acid, yo! I mean, think about it Sun, do you really think Jordan eats McDonald's every day the way they make it seem? Do you really think he wears Hanes underwear or eat Wheaties every morning?

I understand bruthaz wanna get paid. But you must look at who get's hurt at what cost. Athletes must be more responsible (and loving) and think about opening our own NIKE, our own McDonald's — BUT making sure we sell good, healthy food! Current and ex-athlete's, alike, must consider opening our own Afrikan professional league. It don't matter, all YT wanna see is Afrikanz dunking, rushing, or punching someone's lights out!

It doesn't make sense what Magic did. This lost nigga would rather give up is (I think) 5% of the LA Laker's he owned — which would've guaranteed him and his familiy millionz for as long as the league lasted; which is much, much more than he'll ever make being a player — and play for a couple more yearz. We need to stop limiting ourselves to just "playerz" and think about being "ownerz"! Think about it Magic, after they don't want you no more, they won't pay you! I know you're well off, but y can't you be like Tyson when he said you can never have enuff money, cause the more loot you have the more people you can help! If you kept your ownership you would still get "free" money from them and you could still play ball. Didn't you have a couple of teamz you were touring on before you came back? So don't tell me you came back for the game 'cause you never stopped playing!!

I propose that all you professional athlete's, or friendz and relatives of professional athlete's think about developing our own Afrikan league. Other's are/have done it (USFL, USBA, Arena Footbal, etc.), Y can't we have an Afrikan Football League and Afrikan Basketball Association?! Currently, there are 30 NFL teamz with a total of approximately 1410 playerz. We know that somewhere between 65-75% are Afrikan; the NBA has 30 teamz, totalling about 348 playerz, with over 70% being Afrikan playerz. If you bruthaz thought about droppin' those eurocentric agents and save 50% of your salary for the next 3 seasonz (until 2000), we could use that money to start a league, a national Afrikan-centered school system, and numerous Afrikan business' (automobiles, electronics, food, etc.) so that we'd be able to employ our own people, institute our own banks, armed defense, and import/export establishments so we will no longer have to sit at the table with YT "askin'" him to give us our 40 acres and 2 mules. That shit is dead! He ain't gonna give it to us, so fuck it! Let's cease from waiting for something that ain't comin'. We can make this cream ourselves, son, but we need you Afrikan athletes to leave them white women and white agents alone and come home!!

We need more conscious bruthaz in the league like Mahmoud Abdul-Rauf (even though he didn't hold out long enuff, I guess the lyrical lashing's he took from YT got to him. This brutha was one of the top shooter's in the league and doesn't have a shoe contract. That's Y he tapes his shoes so you don't see his logo. Y don't you use some of those millionz and pick up a creative Afrikan artist to design your shoe Mahmoud?! Afterall, NIKE, Adidas, Reebok, and FILA, got bruthaz designing their shoes!

It doesn't make sense that only 50 playerz from the NFL donated $10,000 to the United Negro College Fund (UNCF). Even though the UNCF ain't shit and it's founding was financed by beasts of the New World Order (ie, Rockefeller, Rothschild, Ford and other foundationz to keep an eye on us), the principle being that of all the money athlete's make, they could only raise $500,000 which was matched by the NFL. If every Afrikan player donated just $5000, they would have raised nearly $5 million! Y don't ya'll think of givin' Da Ghetto Tymz that kinda of cream?! We would institute an Afrikan educational institution where our people would be taught self-esteem and 360 degrees of knowledge, including self-reliance and abstraction from the one's who created all the mischief we see on mother earth!

We would also establish companies in all 9 areas of people activity, Francess Cress Welsing (author of *'Isis Papers'*), speaks of that maintainz white supremacy. Those areas are: 1)Economics; 2)Education; 3)Entertainment; 4)Labor; 5)Law; 6)Politics; 7)Sex; 8)Religion; and 9)War (I added Health as #10). By establishing an Afrikan centered gear/ shoe company (or supporting one's that already exist like Wu-Wear, Mecca, and Walker Wear), we could could break the financial arm of white supremacy by taking away NIKE, Reebok, Adidas, anything we wear, money and direct it toward purchasing OUR own gear. Same thing with carz, tv's, refrigeratorz, toothpaste, carpet, computerz, cassette tapes, pencilz, bread, hats, rope, steel, vegetables, gunz, fertilizer, napkinz, paper, towelz, staples, shoe stringz, crayonz, deordorant, toothpicks, jewelry, sunglasses, coats, broomz, toilets, ketchup, sandwich bagz, purses, weaves, powder, clipperz, soap, clocks, chairz, basketballz, dental floss, DAMN! Let me stop this flo'. I can go on for dayz. But you get the picture...anything YT makes, which is everything!!

We should also check the brutha and sistaz who s'posed to be representin'! Ewing, ya got's to pick it up baby. I'm tired of not be picked to run some ball 'cause I got on your boots! Kani, ya shit is too expensive! Jordan, ya got's to get on mr. knight and tell him to stop sellin' your sneeks for 140 beanz when we know it only took $7 to make the damn shoe! Bruthaz of the Negro Baseball League, ya needz to break your contract with those two white women who think their jewish and come back home and find a black clothing company that'll hook you up! BET, you just gotta go off air, cause you ain't black-owned! Brutha John Thompson, ya gots' to stop doin' those Taco Bell commercialz 'cause we know you don't recruit white boys! Also you shoulda stepped to bill packer for calling Allen Iverson a "tough little monkey" during the Big East Championship a couple yearz ago. You gettin' soft on us John?? KRS, ya got's to chill on televising the revolution and sayin' "it's about basketball" and wanting me to drink coca(cocaine)-cola products! It's too late in the day for house niggaz. You either for us or against us! 'Cause we know house niggaz is scared of revolution, but there will come a day when you won't have a choice — you will have to choose a side. I forewarn you to do it volutarily now, 'cause if you wait, Afrikanz ain't gonna take no "johnny come lately's", for real, Sun!!

LIK SHOT!!

As we come into knowledge of self, we must, as well, comc into knowledge of who doesn't want us to "know thyself". The average Afrikan who has some knowledge of white supremacy might feel it has – and only been – the "blue-eyed devil" that is responsible. True, but not truth. If you read my joint's, '*IZ YT Human? or Mutant!*' series, I spoke of the biblical bruthaz, abraham and moses, as one of the first sell-outs of the Afrikan Diaspora.

As you well know, this country was founded by criminalz who colonized this area just as they chalked up Afrika in the 1800s. As we had our plantationz in the south with house negroes (need-to-growz) and field Afrikanz, we find that this trend has never changed as the yearz have gone by. Thanks to research done by brutha Steve Cokely, we have found that there is a black secret society that has been closely associated with maintaining the grip of white supremacy on people of color. These same secret societies these house negroes answer to, have a long history rooted in the physical and mental enslavement of Afrikanz around the globe.

This black "secret society" is called the Boule' (pronounced, 'Boolay') aka. Sigma Pi Phi Fraternity, Incorporated, founded May 15, 1904 in Philadelphia, Pennsylvania. Said to be the 1st black fraternity in America and nearly 2 yearzs before the 1st black college frat, Alpha Phi Alpha Fraternity, Incorporated, founded December 4, 1906.

The Boule' is a black GREEK secret society whose foundation is that of another secret society founded at Yale University called Skull & Bones. The Boule's founderz consisted of Dr. Henry McKee Minton, along with Dr.'s Eugene T. Henson, Edwin Clarence Howard, Algernon Brashear Jackson, Robert Jones Abele and Richard John Warrick; all of Philadelphia. The founding member of the New York City chapter, the infamous(?) WEB DuBois, said the Boule' was created to *"keep the black professional away from the ranks of Marcus Garvey."*

One thing that needz to be pointed out is the tyme period, for tyme allowz us to put thingz in perspective. A short tyme after the founding of the Boule', was Marcus Garvey's "Back to Afrika" movement, which reached and potentially recruited a million plus people without using tv or radio.

DuBois emphasized, as Cokely stated, *"the importance to steal the black professional away from Garvey because an Afrocentric organization that articulated and captured the black professional would give whitey no safe haven in the black community, so the Boule' – the remaking of the house negro was necessary to build a group of negroes who had an investment in protecting the white system as produced by whitey having stolen this land ... This is post reconstruction. Taking away the articulate negro, now desiring to replace them with organized institutions to keep them away from self-improvement. So we find in the same period, as the founding of the Boule', the founding of the 4 black male (Alpha Phi Alpha, Kappa Alpha Psi, Omega Psi Phi and Phi Beta Sigma) and 4 black female (Alpha Kappa Alpha, Delta Sigma Theta, Zeta Phi Beta and Sigma Gamma Rho) college-based fraternities and sororities ... We also find the founding of the NAACP and Urban League."*

DuBois was one of the strongest opponents of Garvey and was an instrumental "pawn" in stopping one of the strongest grassroots movements of this century. What was Garveyz plan? His plan was to take as many Afrikanz from the America's and start a settlement in the nation of Liberia, Afrika and then help our new nation produce and control our own rubber crops and other industreez in natural resources. Garvey said, *"If the oil of Afrika is good for Rockefeller's interest; if iron is good for Carnegie trust; then these minerals are good for us. Why should we allow Wall Street and the capitalist group of America and other countries exploit our country when they refuse to give us a fair chance in the countries of our adoption? Why should not Afrika give to the world its black Rockefeller, Rothschild, and Henry Ford?" (*What's deep is that Garvey was aware of the Illuminati – aka New World Order – just by mentioning these 4 pirates)

This would've meant no Goodyear or US. Steel as we know it today because it would have set a precedent that would've made all Afrikanz aware of their land and mineral wealth, thus instilling a responsible sense of entrepreneurship. And it would've also inevitably smashed the financial arm of white supremacy!

DuBois, along with Alain Locke – the first black (Cecil) Rhodes scholar – publicly defiled Garvey by calling him a gorilla, dark, and anything else that referred to his radiant melanated natural appearance any chance they got. Again, lookin' at what point-in-tyme it was, there were many Afrikanz who had been so deprogrammed that they dreaded being dark with kinky hair and thick hips and lips and the fair-skinned DuBois and Locke knew this – because they were duped themselves – so they played on it, using it as leverage to keep Afrikanz from linking with Garvey and opting to be among the "talented tenth". Locke was quoted as saying, *"We hope the white man delivers cause we crushed a great black thing, but we know he'll deliver or our people will attack and plague us forever more."*

According to Cokely, these two house negroes made a bet that YT would come out on top and give a certain percentage to these greedy negroes, namely Boule' memberz, the wealth they stole from Afrika. What's even deepuh is they didn't believe in Kujichagulia (Afrikan self-determination and reliance) preferring YT to give them table scraps of the American pie instead of us making our own whole Afrikan pie!

Overstand, the Boule' represents the weakest element of Afrikan people. *"It took a type of nigger to form an organization like this. I mean, we just got our asses kicked during reconstruction, Afrika was divided before our very eyes (Berlin Conference), damn, this was 50 years before Rosa Parks!"*, sayz Cokely. The question is Y were these black devilz like this? The answer may lie in the fact that the Boule' is a GREEK organization.

The name Boule' is a greek term, meaning *"Advisorz to the King."* What your next question should be is, *"who is the king?!"* The king that they advise, or protect are the white secret societies responsible for white supremacy: the first white greek fraternity – Phi Beta Kappa, the Illuminati, Rhodes/Rothschild secret society, Skull & Bones, the Masonz, the Round Table Group, The New World Order aka One World Government, the Carnegie, Mellon, Rhodes, Rockefeller, Oppenheimer, Milner's Kindergarten, Bildebergers, The Rhodes Crown, Times Crown, All Souls Group, Clevedine Sect, Bohemian Club, Committee of 300 and numerous other wealthy family organizations (all are simply alias' who go by many names, but consist of mainly the same memberz if not the same ideology). These white beasts have raped, murdered and colonized our people for hundredz of yearz and their children continue the genocide against people of color (with a high, HIGH concentration on the Afrikan) around the globe.

One of the major problemz we should have with the Boule' (and the offspringz of the Boule'; the other 8 college frats and sororities) is that they falsely acknowledge the GREEKS as the founderz of civilization. We should know this to be a lie. Through the work of George GM James, we know that the greeks got their knowledge from the Nile Valley (ancient Ta-Seti, Kemet and Ethiopia, in Alkebulan or Afrika), and YT plagiarized 'our'story seeking to erase the Afrikan presence of Kemet by altering the complexion of the inhabitants. We should know Pythagoras did not create a theorem, but that he stole it from our ancient Afrikan mystery schoolz.

DuBois, famous for his talented 10th theory, and Locke, were bottyboyz (faggots); Locke definitely and DuBois was believed to have homosexual tendencies. I say this because this is somethin' that should be known, these memberz of secret societies point to Greece as the beginning. The society we live in today is loaded with Greek mythology, from the naming of July (Julius Caesar) to the way government is run. It has been written by memberz and non-memberz alike, the kind of homosexual ritualz and orgeez thattag'wan. If you study the hierarchy of Greece, men were classified as "upper-class", "prominent" and "important" by how many young boyz they sodomized!

Both Locke and DuBois worked closely together as pawnz of the Illuminati. Who is the Boule'? They are a mutation of a white man who seeks to represent something he is not ... GREEK! They are the "prominent" blacks white America chose for us without our asking. Collectively, the over 4000+ memberz (based on 1994 Roster) make up the wealthiest group of black men on the planet – and to think, none are working in the interest of Afrikan people; but instead, gets a kick out of holding YTs penis as he pisses on people of color (the house nigga/field Afrikan theory ain't dead)! As of 1994, there were 101 chapterz in the world; yes, as Cokely states, the Boule' is in your town! Anywhere there are professional blacks, the Boule' coagulates. The amount of their wealth (including strong political and economic connectionz – strong enuff to assist in killing Malcolm X and one of their own, fellow Boule' member Martin Luther King!) cannot be matched nor surpassed by any other 4000+ blacks anywhere in the world!

THE HISTORY OF THE BOULE'

Boule', again, meaning *"Advisorz to the King,"* is the lower house of greek parliament. Inside the Boule' history book, written by Boule' member, Charles H. Wesley – who also wrote the history books for Alpha Phi Alpha, the Elks, Prince Hall Masonz and founded Central State University in Ohio – wrote on page 28 Y one of it's founding memberz, Minton, who also owned the first black drugstore in the America, wanted to create such an organization, *"Minton wanted to create an organization which would partake in the tenants (basis, or root) of Skull & Bones at Yale."*

Now who is Skull & Bones?? Skull & Bones' – aka Brotherhood of Death, alias the 2nd chapter of the Illuminati, incorporated for business purposes as Russell Trust, was established in 1776 at Yale University in New Haven (Heaven), Connecticut. Ironically, President George Bush is a legacy (member because of his father and Grandfather) of this cult. Remember, this wicked cracka uses many different names to confuse you, but they are a part of the same global white supremist rule.

Most politicianz, black and white, are Masonz. But there is a difference. Non-whites can only attain 33° while whites can attain 33 and 1/3rd. It is believed the root of Masonry is of the knowledge (33 1/3°) sell-out moses gave YT when he came to 'civilize' them from living as beasts up in the caucus(where caucasian comes from) mountainz. They practiced homosexuality, killed and then ate people as ritualz they more than likely still perform today! They also pledged (through moses tricknology) never to let you, the true GOD, the Afrikan wo/man, know that Jacob (Yakub), who was black, made them and that we are the originatorz of the arts and sciences (360° of knowledge, not 33 1/3 which moses taught them).

If Henry Minton, who was a blackman, wanted to create a black secret society based on these beliefs and customz, what type of evil spirit is he? Page 38 of the Boule's history book, readz, *"In the building of the organizations plan, reliance was placed upon GREEK history and tradition. The reasons of this action are not difficult to discover, for it is well known that the study of greek civilization was basically an acquaintance with western civilization, although greek culture had relationships with the culture of the orient."* What they're not saying is that the greeks didn't have a relationship, they stole their information from our Ancestorz in Kemet! In addition, it's clever how they chose not to even mention Afrika settling for saying the "orient" which meanz east. In summation, every black and white greek fraternity and sorority manipulates the true history of where the Greeks learned what they know. This is Y it don't make sense to be called a black GREEK! I should know, I pledged one; and because of what Cokely exposed me to, in 1996 denounced my membership with them (a phi a).

If you are familiar with Masonry or secret societies in general, memberz take a pledge to never reveal the secrets of that organization, with the penalty for doin' so could possibly end in a serious beatdown or even death. This may be Y it is difficult to get any of the Boule' memberz to tell us what's up. Thanx, to an article written July

18th, 1990 of the *LA Times* and one published in the, *Washington Post*, November 23, 1991, this secret society was exposed at least, a second tyme, the first being around the Pittsburgh (Pennsylvania) Boule' convention in 1968, that was later changed to Philadelphia (word is, hedz were ready fi bun fire and expose the Boule', remember, this was during the Black Power Movement).

Because people are beginning to find out about the history of the Boule', in addition to their own children lacking interest in continuing the mental and spiritual rape of Afrikan people, the Boule' publicly claimz themselves as only a "social" organization. Fellow Boule' member – and so-called, Afrocentric scholar – whom I have the honor of exposing, Asa Hilliard, was confronted by DGT in Pittsburgh, PA about his affiliation with the Boule' in '95 and he shucked and jived and ended up sayin', *"we're just a group of people that throw banquets and picnics."* He was also confronted again this past January in Harlem, again, shuckin' and jivin' he claimed he only goes to *"certain meetings, so I don't know everything THEY do."* As if I'm to believe you can be a selective member of a wealthy organization, you participate in only "certain" functionz reducing your status to a selective member. Now this is comin' from a highly educated psychologist, yo! Knowin' he was lyin', he still felt it ok to put out an image of him bein' a member of an organization that is literally the anti-Heru (yaw say christ) to Afrikan people, and he don't know everything they about. That's like havin' a job interview knowin' nothin' about the company! But again, he's a psychologist, so he got psychological with me…

Even still, this, from a negro who has written many books, performed countless lectures and whose name has been mentioned in the same breath as Dr. John Henrik Clarke, Dr. Ben, and the like, should be exiled from the Afrikan Diaspora like we did to the paleman back in Kemet!

They hold regional conferences every year and a national conference every 2 yearz. Each May, as a *mandatory* ritual, each member must re-read the Boule' history book from cover to cover as a show of rededicating and revitalizing the mission of these Negroes... to continue bein' *"Advisorz to the King"* and never lettin' you know the names of who run the world, the Illuminati. So we know that each member has read at least pages 28 and 38 and know of the basis of their organization and it's false acceptance of the greeks being the founderz of civilization. What was interesting about the LA Times article was the association of the Boule' with Skull & Bones, *"...Like Yale's Skull & Bones secret society to which* (then president) *George Bush belongs, the Boule' has been criticized by some as a social anachronism, and has challenged members to change its image."*

The 1990 incoming Boule' president, Dr. Benjamin Major said he was aware of charges that the group is more interested in socializing and congratulating itself on its wealth and success, exclusively, rather than making a substantial contribution to the rest of black America. He said, *"We don't want to appear as if we were the remaining above the problems of most black people. We know we didn't get here solely by the dint of our own hard work. We owe a lot of people, AND we have to give back to our brothers and sisters."* The key thing he said is that he said they owe a lot of people and made this separate from them having to *"give back to our brothers and sisters."* Who do they owe for their success?? Their advisor...the King!

Boule' member Vernon Jordan, who is also on the Trilateral Commission and Board of Council of Foreign Relations (CFR) – started by Cecil Rhodes and Lord Rothschild, responsible for last phase of development of white supremacy – and Bill Clinton's current "boy" (replacing the mysteriously deceased Ron Brown), once said, *"We, the talented 10th, are the best able and the only ones suitable to save the black race."* This is the notably the egotistical mentality of all memberz of secret societies and can be traced back to its origin.

Overstand that mainly all black "leaderz" white America give us, actually had/has some connection with white supremacy, including Farrakhan! If you think about it, back in the early 1900s, we weren't even 40 yearz out of slavery. So the house negro/field Afrikan mentality was still in existence. Most Afrikanz, of that tyme, had gone through an enormous amount of self-denial. The old cliche', *"If you black, get back; if you brown, stick around; if you yellow, you're mellow; and if you white, you -ight!."* was rampant and most of our Ancestorz lost themselves through bleaching their skin, conking their hair, stayed miles from being seen eatin' watermelon and speaking 'proper' in order to be seen different than a field nigga. We must also realize that most of the co-founderz of black organizationz were mulattoz (very light-skinned). These house negroes had already felt they were better than dark-skinned blacks. And went out of their way to prove to YT they were different.

Because we were now physically "free", YT still needed to keep an eye on us. They needed an overseer. This is Y around during the same tyme as the founding of the Boule', we find the founding of the NAACP and the Urban League. These "black" organizationz were co-founded by jewish spies who used DuBois as their scapegoat! One must also note that NAACP co-founder, Joel Spingarn – a known jewish spy, established a surveillance operation on the Afrikan community – was also very influential in the founding of the Boule'. A lot of us don't know this.

These organizationz were really a front. They were s'posed to defend the countless atrocities against Afrikan people in america; and in contrast, found out the very whites we were complaining about, actually was the founding backbone of these organizationz! This makes a lot of sense now. I see Y the NAACP doesn't even own the building their national headquarterz is located at. Think about it. With all the loot the NAACP gets annually, and they still have to pay rent for their building?!!? That's because they have to answer to someone who is their major fundraiser. While we were being lynched, raped and murdered, we thought these organizationz would help us fight for justice; later to find out the person our "leaderz" answer to is the very culprits with blood on their handz!

Can you see Y we're in the shape we're in today Afrikanz?! It is very evident. In the wordz of Cokely, *"When we look at the Boule' closely, we find a confusion of values. Black men who felt that their advancement was edged upon a positive relationship with wealthy and influential white people. And I say that that may have an adverse impact on our revolution. Therefore, we give them (the Boule') today, this official warning ... Our goal is not to kill off the Boule'; but to warn them as an organization. To warn the individual that if they bring false values, or worship a false idol, into the community at a time the community attempts to self-determinate (liberate ourselves), if we gave the call, they will come and grab you, we have every one of your addresses and phone numbers, we can get you, if we choose to. But we only choose to ask you to step aside and the day we got to get "massa", you find some way to be on vacation...To kill off the Boule' would be like eating the peel off a banana and ignoring the actual banana."* In other wordz, in order to stop this maddness, you must stop the puppeteer, not the puppet.

We were able to get a copy of the 1994 Boule' membership book and found some very interesting names. It was also told to me by a source that the Boule' was aware of the names bein' exposed to the public and no longer prints the membership list, don't fret, with the Ancestorz guidance and one of their very own memberz slippin' up ('cause they always do…how do you think we got the first one?!).

Along with the name's and chapterz, we have their address' and phone numberz. Out of the list we found a lot of memberz we been givin' praises to every Black History Month such as, Dr. Daniel Hale Williams - performed 1st open heart surgery; Ralph Bunch - former UN Ambassador; Arthur Ashe; Urban League President, Whitney Young; Martin Luther King, Jr.; Benjamin Mays; Carter G. Woodson (all who died never speaking of the Boule' and therefore taking the secrets of white supremacy with them); Maynard Jackson - ex-mayor of Atlanta; Baseball great Hank Aaron; Tom Bradley - tv personality; Dennis Archor - mayor of Detroit; Elvin Big 'E' Hayes; Bill Cosby; Jesse Jackson; Earl Graves; John H. Johnson; Douglass Wilder; ex-Pittsburgh Steeler, Lynn Swann, and David Dinkins - ex-mayor of New York City, to name a few. Most Boule' members are of the "successful" group.

Yes the Boule' is in your town! Anywhere there are "prominent" professional blacks, chances are they're in the Boule'. We have the roster up to 1994, which includes 101 chapterz. Next piece, we will elaborate on the symbolism behind their logo, their colorz, the origin of college fraternities and sororities and the close relation to demonic masonry. Continue to seek knowledge and we shall find.

MORE FIE-YAH!

(to see the roster up to 1994, go to: daghettotymz.com/rkyvz/articles/boule'series/boule13roster/bouleroster list/bouleroster.html)

As we continue further inscissionz into these "advisorz to the king", I would like to go over a few thingz from part one to refresh your pineal glandz. Last piece, we laid the foundation of this wicked white-with-black-faced secret society called the Boule' or Sigma Pi Phi Fraternity, Inc. We unleashed our lyrical swordz and attempted to behead the beast of secrets exposing the organizationz founding 6 memberz, one being Dr. Henry McKee Minton of Philadelphia, Pennsylvania.

We also know, from reading the history book of the Boule' – written by charles h. wesley – we find that minton wanted to make this organization just like Skull and Bones, the 2nd chapter of a german-based white supremist organization (the Illuminati) which founded Skull and Bones at Yale University in 1776. We also found one of the basic premises for this wicked group was to steal the black professional from the ranks of Marcus Garvey, who, at that tyme was reaching over 1 million plus Afrikanz in america without tv or radio. We also realized that right after the Boule' was founded, the 4 black frats and 4 black sororities were founded, as well as the NAACP and Urban League. And we also found a close relation with masonry.

Our next incision we intend to go a level deeper. We will perform open heart surgery splitting open the aorta of so-called black greeks; we will define the meaning of the Boule's logo – the Sphinx; their colorz; and more of their connection with masonry. Let's start with their logo.

Most will say it is a sphinx. True, but not truth. Most will associate the sphinx with the tall, solid block statue our Ancestors built in ancient KMT (Kemet). Because we have been conditioned to accept without question, we never thought of looking up what sphinx actually meanz.

Look in any dictionary and it will tell you that a sphinx s a third part woman, one-third eagle and one-third lion (notice the breasts and wings). So when I think of the tall statue in KMT, does it look like a woman?? Where are the breasts?! What about the wingz?! The original, Afrikan name is Her-Em-Akhet, which meanz *'Heru of the Horizon'* and has the face of an Afrikan man. When we look up the definition of sphinx, it meanz *"to strangle, guard; gatekeeper or protect"*. This has nothing to do with KMT or Afrikan people.

The sphinx is a grecian myth and is a major part of masonry. We will see Y the black frat, alpha phi alpha, the frat I used to be a member of, adopted the sphinx and not Her-Em-Akhet. The history of the sphinx is wack, in fact, all greek myths is pure fantasty B-S!

According to the greeks, this beast was a guardian of the city of thebes. She sat on a cliff on the only path leading to the city. Anyone that wanted to enter thebes would first be confronted by the sphinx. The sphinx would ask one simple riddle and if you didn't know the answer, she would devour you, tearing you to pieces. The king, creon, was upset that many people were unable to enter his city. He consulted a homosexual named oedipus (NOTE: I call him a homo because he was. Homosexuality was the norm for the grecian culture. In fact, it is strongly believed Greece is where it originated).

The king offered his crown and his daughter if he could kill the sphinx. So he bounced to where the Sphinx was and he was the riddle, *"What has one voice, and goes on four feet on two feet and on three, but the more feet it goes on the weaker it be?"* oedipus responded, *"Man – who crawls on all fourz as a baby, then walks on two as an adult, and walks with a cane in old age."* After answering the riddle correctly, the sphinx committed suicide jumping off the cliff and oedipus was claimed king of thebes for outsmarting the beast.

When studying the history of black collegiate fraternities, it clearly makes sense Y alpha phi alpha, would choose to call it the Sphinx and not Her-Em-Akhet; because their knowledge base is greek oriented and not Afrikan!

Where do you see an Afrikan presence in this?! Nowhere. Remember, greek mythology is based on myths! It doesn't necessarily mean their stories actually happened. All pale-faced people's roots can be traced to the caucus mountainz and their intellect is based upon what abraham and moses gave them (33 1/3$^{rd\circ}$ of knowledge), therefore, they are incapable of being masterz of origination. They *are,* however, the masterz of plagiarism.

They could never understand what Her-Em-Akhet meanz. The statue faced the east because our Ancestorz knew the pineal gland is the seat of the Afrikan soul and when the sun rises, it hits the forehead (pineal gland), suppressing the beastly nature of man. As author Tony Browder puts it, *"Symbolically, the body represents the animal nature which exists in wo/man, and the lion exemplifies the royalty and power of the divine spirit that exists in its lower physical form. The head of a man symbolizes the intelligence of the mind which must be cultivated in order to elevate the consciousness into a higher spiritual state so that it may become divine. Metaphorically speaking, it is the suppression of the lower animal nature and the refinement of the thought process that leads to the spiritual evolution of man. Spiritually speaking, it is only by conquering the "beast" within that one is capable of truly knowing God."* It clearly makes sense Y the first black collegiate fraternity, alpha phi alpha, would choose to call it the sphinx and not Her-Em Akhet. The reason is because their knowledge base is greek oriented and not Afrikan!

The caucasian (including these people who think they're jewz) is incapable of an understanding this deep because of their calcified brain, lack of melanin, and long, stringy, lifeless hair (our 'kinky', coiled, curly hair – and is made up exactly like the curves in your DNA, the spiral look of the Milky Way galaxy we live in and so on – serves as antennas to ancestral data bank, or how we've been able to remain spiritual and aware of our Afrikan heritage despite, at one tyme not being able to read, being kidnapped from our homeland and

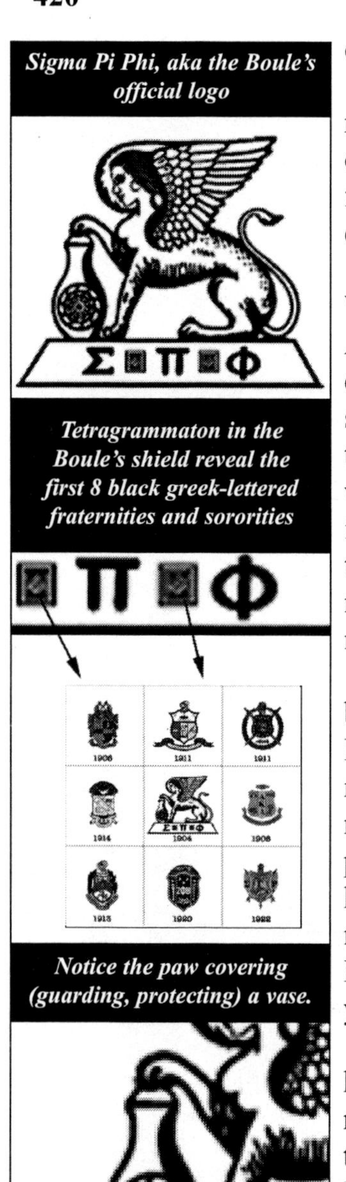

Sigma Pi Phi, aka the Boule's official logo

Tetragrammaton in the Boule's shield reveal the first 8 black greek-lettered fraternities and sororities

Notice the paw covering (guarding, protecting) a vase.

duped with white values).

Some who'll read this will think I'm makin' nothing but racist statements, which really isn't my concern. What *should* be of concern is that these statements can and have been proven from not only Afrikan historianz but european scientist's who still conduct studies and research today from melanin to anthropology!

WHAT DOES THE LOGO MEAN?

As stated before, Boule' meanz "advisor to the king", and we clarified last piece that the king is the Rhodes/Rothschild's secret society. If we were to bring some numerology into this, the sphinx's number is 9. Remember, the riddle was "what walks on 4, 2, then 3". That equals 9. '4' symbolized the ignorant man (baby); '2', the intellectual (young adult); and '3', the spiritual (old man with cane, which meanz wisdom). The masonic definition of the number 9 is the natural number of man AND in the lower worldz (or evil).

Looking at the logo, you will notice under the sphinx between the greek letterz, there are 2 sets of 3x3 squares. Historian, Steve Cokely pointed out after attending a Boule' national conference a couple yearz ago that each square represented each of the 4 black frats and 4 black sororities (alpha phi alpha, kappa alpha psi, omega psi phi, phi beta sigma, alpha kappa alpha, delta sigma theta, zeta phi beta and sigma gamma rho). The final square belongz to the one that headz it all, the Boule'! Understand, this ain't something I&I thought up to amuse you. We went to the lionz den to find what this beast is all about.

Remember what I told you about 9 being their number?! I know I don't have to think for you, weigh it yourself! You will also notice the sphinx with his right paw covering an earn (vase). Inside this earn we see a circle-within-a-circle with a dot in the middle. This has 2 meaningz: first, the circle-within-a-circle is the symbol of the Rhodes/ Rothschilds secret society. So what the sphinx is doing is clearly consistent with its definition, to *"protect, guard; or a gatekeeper"*. They are protecting the interests of white supremacy.

The second meaning is the circle-within-a-circle has a dot in the middle. The circle, including the dot is the symbol of Ra. Our ancient Sun God, or Heru of the original trinity, Ausar, Auset and Heru. The outer circle is like an enclosed layer, closing off the power of Ra, along with the paw to further conceal the truth of our ancient history the beast knowz is very vital to our upliftment! There are many symbolz out here that have racist definitionz. Remember the saying, *"a picture speaks a thousand wordz"?* This is a code of communication we originated on the wallz and temples back in KMT called the

#9

'Metu Neter' or as the greeks call it, hieroglyphics.

The Boule's colorz are light blue and white and is a gem within itself. Blue has a close relationship with masonry. In masonry, light blue resembled the lower protective lodges. These are also the code of silence lodges. They are the frontline of the protective layer.

The color white really needz no elaboration, but we will for those 'YT luverz'... it represents the race they respect the most!

THE BOULE'S NEED TO RECRUIT

The Boule' has taken a sworn oath to maintain the state of white supremacy and vow to never let you know the whites that rule the world. It's just like the house negro/field Afrikan theory. The white 'massa' needed a house negro to keep an eye on the rest of the Afrikanz to alert him if there would be any uprisingz.

The word 'negro' bearz clarification. Many have been taught that negro is spanish and meanz *'black'*. But the spanish got this word from the greeks, who called it *'necro'*. Necro in greek meanz *'DEAD'!* So what we are dealing with when dealing with 'negroes' are DEAD-thinking Afrikanz!.

The Boule' is no different. They are guaranteed table scraps as long as they keep the rest of us in check. They are allowed to get high paying salaries, luxurious carz, even their own businesses (although dictated by YT – look at Ebony, Jet, Essence, Black Enterprise, etc and notice the many white advertisements inside each issue. These are the one's who dictate what goes in and out of each issue of these so called "black magazines".) as long as they "advise the king" informing him of any resurrected Marcus Garvey's, Queen Tiye's, Malcolm X's and/or Queen Nzingha's.

As in the first piece, we knew the Boule' was founded to steal the black professional from Garvey. We know Garvey wanted to go back to Afrika because the Illuminati: Rockerfeller, Rothschild, Rhodes Carnegie, Mellon's and the Oppenheimerz, were conspiring colonializm in our motherland raping and stripping her natural resources of gold, silver, oil and diamondz and building mega-trillion-dollar industries. What we don't realize is Y and how white supremacy, using the Boule', got the newly pardoned young black professional.

Here's my theory. Think, around the early 1900s, the Boule' was founded in 1904; all black frats and sororities were within the first decade; the NAACP (National Association for the Advancement of *CERTAIN* People) and Urban League were also founded inside the first 10 yearz. We were barely 40 yearz out of physical slavery, B!.

The Civil War just passed. We were free (physically), but our mental was so damaged, there was so much self-denial going on. Many of our Ancestorz hated being dark, having nappy hair, thick lips, hips, the whole nine. A lot of this was enhanced with white amerikkka portraying us as monkeys, watermelon eaterz, shoe-tapping, broken english talkin', happy-go-lucky, turn the-other-cheek, passive negroes.

There were many products available to those blacks who no longer wanted to be their true selves. There were bleach creamz to make your skin lighter and the straightening comb (created by Madame CJ Walker, 1908). This made those who didn't want to be Afrikan, be something else, YET still not white! What was going here was separation. The people were divided. If you were dark-skinned, it wasn't much you could do. But if you were light-skinned (mulatto) you had a chance.

We still see this today, especially in our women having artificial hair, nailz, eyes, breasts, you name it! When given a deeper look, the "founderz" of these organizations, most found in the early 1900s, *"not only mimicked their prototype, white institutions, they attempted to 'out white' them"*, as writer Charles Grantham cited in his book "*Do 'We' Really Wanna Be Greeks?*" Most disagree, and you're probably wanna-be greeks, but ask yourself, if these organization are really for Afrikan people, why do you wear the greek letterz of the enemy?!!? You don't need ANY affiliation with the enemy to do well for your peeps!!

The first Afrikanz allowed to go to college were those that came from families that tried to be what they were not, white! These were the 'upper-class' negroes YT knew were busy trying to be like them. They knew these negroes didn't like being around their darker skinned brutha and sistaz. They knew these negroes tried to act and dress like them, eat, sleep, mate, speak, and worship the same demonic god like them! Now there *were* a couple of dark-skinned Afrikanz that got through. A couple of the founderz of the frat I'm no longer a part of had some. These were the one's most suitable to be the gatekeeperz of the concrete plantation the New World Order was beginning to physically manifest.

The 8 black frat and sororities are subordinates of the Boule'. The founders of alpha phi alpha, were affiliated, in some way with either the Boule' or masonry. Within the organization, they started segregation. In the history book of a phi a, there was a day called *'tap-day'*, where interested bruthaz were blindfolded and the memberz of the frat walked up and tapped on the shoulder the ones they wanted to become initiates. Those not chosen could not join the pledge process.

These bruthaz, envying the declined membership, chose to start their own frat, Kappa Alpha Psi, with the help of a "jewish" frat, Phi Nu Pi. Understand that all black organizations had black faces as scapegoats, but it was YT that used these negroes to further mentally enslave us, havin' us segregate ourselves.

The bruthaz of Kappa Alpha Psi, in turn, became just as selective. Along with the Alpha's not taking bruthaz solely because of our Afrikan link, two other frats emerged: Omega Psi Phi and Phi Beta Sigma. Today, there are even more frats, further dividing our people and enabling YT to slay us because we are not united.

The same goes for the sororities. It shouldn't come as a shock when learning what the AKAs initial requirements were for anyone to become considered a possible member when they first started in 1908, they had a system called "the brown bag test". This was a test that consisted of a brown paper bag (I also found in Thurgood Marshall's autobiography that the Alpha's also did this test in certain chapterz). They would line up the ones interested and put a brown paper bag next to their skin. If they were darker than the bag, they couldn't become a member.

Deep, DEEP hatred of our natural appearance and culture! Think of how many could not join simply because they were 'too dark'! Sistaz who were memberz of AKA, who didn't like what they were about, broke away and formed their own sorority, Delta Sigma Theta. Soon, two other's formed, Sigma Gamma Rho and Zeta Phi Beta. Today, we have more black sororities, even one's that claim they're a nursing sorority. As Cokely stated, *"You may be just an Alpha or AKA, but you are greek nevertheless!"*

The whole notion of becoming a black greek is wack! When pledged (and every initiate of every organization has to do this), one of the first things we had to learn was the greek alphabet. Y not the Metu Neter (erroneously called hieroglyphics)?! After all, that is our foundation, which preceded greeks! The reason? If you remember, in the Boule's history book, on page 38 it says, *"In the building of the organizational plan, reliance was placed upon Greek history and tradition. The reasons of this action are not difficult to discover, for it is well known that the study of Greek civilization as basically an acquaintance with western civilization."* So it makes sense Y they would carry on the legacy using greek letterz and reciting the greek alphabet. But it doesn't stop there. For all you black "greeks", I'ma 'bout to behead the whole 'crossing over' ritual.

If our Ancestorz of the Nile Valley could see us today! We have our people's "brightest" mindz (the Talented 10th) attend YTs institutionz of higher 'training' (not learning) and how do we honor our legacy?! Among the many erroneous thingz, we have a black sorority, Delta Sigma Theta who has a white woman, Minerva ***(pic1)***, who's the stolen story of the Afrikan Godess Neit; we have Alpha Phi Alpha Fraternity, Inc. who adopted Kemetic symbolz and dress ***(pic3)***, yet STILL associate themselves as black GREEKS! In addition, they associate themselves with Gorillaz!! ***(pic4)*** Y would they willingly equate ourselves to a primate?! What type of mentacide is that?! When will they realize there is no such thing as a black greek!!

CROSSIN' OVER... PAYZ HOMAGE TO WHO?!

Once an initiate has pledged a certain amount of tyme, there is a ritual that goes on before they arewelcomed into the organization. Most call it *"crossing the burning sandz"*. What many may not know is the history behind this ceremony.

I will need to use refer to the piece, *"IZ YT Human? Or Mutant!"* So go 'head and get your copy... Got it? Ai-ight! Remember the tribe of people who were ousted from KMT? It was Ad(h)am and Eve. If you recall, we ended our cypher knowing Adham and Eve were not literally man and woman, but that Adham was a tribe of people. We know Y they were exiled from KMT, because they were albino's who were grafted from Jacob (Yakub), causin' mischief. We know the pharaoh sentenced them to journey, by foot, across the Sahara Desert up to the caucus mountainz where they lived for 2000 yearz! While the beast struggled to make it across the "burning" (hot) sandz of KMT, our Afrikan ancestorz rode on camel back. We also know that, first Abraham, then Moses, went up to the caucus mountainz to "civilize" them with 33 1/3rd degreez of knowledge, which is also called "tricknology". They were instructed by these 2 sellout Afrikanz to come back to KMT (by this tyme they lost all their melanin and ability to understand nature) again and take over KMT. They came as the Persianz, Greeks and lastly the Romanz! Do I have to spell the connection?!

In one of masonry's ritualz (degreez), there is a riddle. A master mason asks an initiate, *"did you come by foot or camel back?"* If the initiate, unknowingly replies, *"by foot"*. This let's the master mason know he is talking to *"the beast"* who was exiled out of ancient egypt (Kemet) and he is not ready to earn that degree yet.

The masonz know about the story of Jacob and they know of their true origin. The underlying message is that we don't know! It is evident when black frats and sororities *"cross"*, by foot, over the burning sandz of egypt (KMT), they are mocking the travel of YT from KMT to the caucus mountainz!

This understanding is key, for if you are a member of something and do not know what it's really about, you have been misled; and if you are given this information and continue to misrepresent something that's s'posed to be Afrikan, you will be held responsible once we decide to liberate ourselves, and furthermore you will have to answer to the spirit of our Ancestorz!

As Cokely put it, *"I say to you black greeks, that if you control these organizations, to make them Afrocentric and change the name's and number's that you use to articulate them. They are letters and codes you can develop to be ancient Afrikan and the replacement would be supported by all of the black people; we would guarantee you that. But we serve notice to you that today it's the Boule', tomorrow, the other 8, you will have to stand into account for the wearing of the clown suit and impersonating a people of which you are not."*

So what's up black greek?! You can't be both. You can't ride the fence. You're either Afrikan or greek. Historically, our Ancestorz never had a positive relationship with the greeks. It is they who delivered one of the final blowz to our Kemetic mystery system by raping, killing, plagiarizing and defacing our people, along with the temples, to build what many today have been led to believe they created.

I have received madd heat from many black greeks because of my stance on greekdom. And most say they never joined with these intentionz and feel as long as they continue to do service projects (like taking blood from the black community and giving it to the blood-sucking Rockefeller owned, blood banks) then it's ok, 'cause they're *"active in the community"*. Yeah, but for who??

Of those black greeks who no longer associate with people like myself, we must realize these people only was down because we were trying to unknowingly be something we will never be....GREEK! It's unfortunate that once one does decide they want to be Afrikan and nothing else, they suddenly lose these so-called friendz.

And Even if some greek wan' romp because of this, I will simply ask before doing battle, *"are you steppin' to me as an Afrikan or greek?"* I need to know 'cause if you're greek, then I will attempt to slay you as a greek! The choice is yourz. I am merely doing what truth compelz me to do. I realize truth hurts. It took me several months before I realized what I had to do. Had I not canceled my membership to this demonic-based negro organization, I would be condoning the many killingz, rape and thefts these beasts' performed to our people; and still do in anutha form (mental) today.

I leave one last seed I want to plant in the mindz of every black greek readin' this series, *"Did you come by foot or camel back?"*

MORE FIE-YAH!

What has become, an ongoing scrics exposing one of the vital pawnz used in the Illuminati's global operation of caucasian dominance. Having obtained a copy of their history book, *'History of Sigma Pi Phi: First Of The Negro-American Greek-Letter Fraternities',* by Charles H. Wesley, we found the plan was for a fraternity *"conceived by one of them and partially perfected by two, to band together college degree men who were congenial (having the same nature or tastes)",* page 29.

We also found their insignia, the Grecian Sphinx, covering an urn (vase) with its right paw, the circle within a circle [representing both the Rhodes/Rothschilds Secret Society (which includes the Rockefeller Foundation) and the concealed history of Ra] also represents the container into which were placed the names of Greek citizenz who would be chosen by lot to lead the state. Sphinx can be best defined as *"to guard, protect or gatekeeper"* in Webster's Dictionary.

The Boule' is responsible for starting the 4 black fraternities and sororities, which started a couple yearz later. Their conspiratorial inception was to keep secret from Afrikanz who the real people in power is, therefore, "guarding/protecting" the secret establishment or "advising the King". This was during the early 1900s, a tyme where *certain* blacks were just being allowed to receive a higher education at colleges and university. The Boule' was very instrumental in stealing the educated Afrikanz from the infamous Marcus Garvey movement. This was done largely part, by one of the New World Orderz (NOW) best reprogrammed regimes, Henry McKee Minton.

HENRY MINTON: THE MIND OF A DEVIL

Henry Minton was a physician and the first black to have his own drugstore in the states. *"He was one of the growing groups of trained* (YT style*) community leaders, who were seeing clearly that a full life for themselves could not be assured without a sharing of their fellowship, camaraderie and idealism with others of like minds and hearts."* The ones responsible for training these negroes was, of course, YT.

Wesley goes on to say of Y Minton started the Boule', *"this organization should be a fraternity in the true sense of the word; one whose chief thought should not be to visit the sick and bury the dead but to bind men of like qualities, tastes and attainments into close sacred union* (exactly like Masonry and Skull & Bones...faggotitis!)*, that they might know the best of one another...In summary, Minton, wanted to create an organization which would partake, in his own words, of the "tenets* (like) *of Skull and Bones at Yale and Phi*

Beta Kappa..." If you read January '97s issue of DGT on Skull & Bones, you already know they are the second chapter of the German-based Illuminati (aka New World Order).

The Boule' protects the Round Table Group [it must also be noted that after an initiate becomes a member of Skull & Bones, they are called a 'Knight' (of the Round Table)]. Wesley was quoted once saying, *"The Round Table lives only in poetic life and history. They can live again in life. And we can make them live through us. It can continue as a dream – and it can continue through us."*

We know from our studies the Round Table Group still exists. The Round Table Group is a secret society started by Cecil Rhodes and Lord Rothschild in the late 1800s. They were responsible for the last phase of development for the global white supremacy we experience today. Rhodes and Rothschild, along with the Rockefellers and Oppenheimer – who inherited Rhodes trust-control the racizm we feel on all 4 cornerz of the earth and in between.

Rothschild is responsible for Europe; Rockefeller, North & South America, Canada and Mexico; and Oppenheimer, Australia, Afrika and the rest. The Round Table Group has connectionz with the CFR (Council on Foreign Relations), Committee of 300 aka the Olympianz, Imperial Brain Trust, Trilateralists and the Invisible Government, all white supremist organizations scheming demonic planz against people of color as we speak.

But not all negroes who were reprogrammed remained negroes. One Afrikan in particular, Geroge GM. James (the 'GM' standz for his middle name 'Granville Monah' as well as some referring it to mean 'Grand Master Mason'), who did what no other negro had the cahunaz to do! Yet, to this day he get's no respect 'cause literally no one referz to him or mentionz his works! Y? Hmmm, let's see...

CARTER G. WOODSON & WEB DuBOIS vs. GEORGE GM. JAMES

Carter G, the so-called "Father of Black History" and WEB, are two noodle-back negroes that couldn't find it in their soulz to do something as courageous and honorable as the late George GM. James. GM James, a mason, wrote the controversial book entitled, *'Stolen Legacy'*, that literally devoured YTs claim as the originatorz of the Arts & Sciences.

The book was published in 1954 and shortly after the release, legend has it, James died a masonic death (neck cut from ear to ear with tongue cut out). See back then, if you were a mason and you told secrets, you would pay with your life. His book clearly proved that Greek philosophy was stolen Afrikan history; demonstrated the Afrikan origin of the Mysteries Schools; and created a social reformation through relearned philosophy of Afrikan history. His work served as the foundation to Afrikanz finding themselves in Kemet before YT, thus giving our origin back to the Afrikan wo/man.

He was also able to prove several of the so called greek "scholarz" (who were confessed pirates) were known to have studied in Kemet, or were instructed by otherz who had studied there, and those who had not studied under the priests of Kemet had access to the texts stored in the Library of Alexandria which housed countless plagiarized texts of the Mysteries Schools, and upon those greek plagiarizerz returning to their native cities, many were exiled or condemned to death (ie. Socrates and Plato); and as young students, they disappeared from sight only to surface decades later as masterz of various schoolz of thought foreign to their native landz.

Carter G. became well known for his infamous quote, *"When you control a man's thinking, you do not have to worry about his actions. You do not have to tell him not to stand here or go yonder, he will find his proper place and stay in it. You do not need to send him to the back door. He will go without being told. In fact, if there is no back door, he will cut one for his special benefit."* Woodson became controversial and wrote his bestselling *'Miseducation Of The Negro'*, yearz after being exiled from the Boule' along with DuBois.

Woodson, a member of Omega Psi Phi, can be found receiving grant money from the Carnegie, Lord-Spellman and the Rockefeller Foundationz to assist in his education programz. He also lost most of the grant money because he refused to merge his operationz (under direct orderz of the foundationz) with Tuskegee spy, Robert Multon (also a member of Omega Psi Phi).

These revelationz made Woodson realize he had made a grave mistake and began telling our people we were being miseducated by white people, not just in schoolz, but in life itself... *YET,* he never gave any inkling to the black (nor white, for that matter) secret society he had once belonged to.

This showz that although he had been disgruntled with the learned conspiracies of Afrikan people facilitated by the Boule' (under orderz of the Round Table Group), he couldn't bring it to himself to relay this vital information to the people. Maybe he feared his death, like GM James experienced. Nevertheless, he chose to bury the secrets with him – which showz he still obliged the secretly sworn oath of maintaining the status of white supremacy and never letting any Afrikan know the whites who rule the world; who are responsible for our decreasing educational, economic and spiritual existence.

WEB emphasized the importance to steal the Afrikan professional away from Marcus Garvey because an Afrocentric organization that articulated and "captured" the black professional would give YT no safe haven in the Afrikan community, so the making of the Boule' was necessary to build a group of loyal negroes who had an investment in protecting the white system as produced by white supremacy.

DuBois was quoted once calling Garvey a gorilla and monkey attempting to "Tarzanize" his back to Afrika movement. However, yearz after his exile from the Boule' he, too became controversial. Most associate him with the start of the Pan-Afrikan Movement. This devil, who sold our people out by duplicating Woodson's sworn secrecy (protecting/guarding) the secrets of the Boule'. This negro, who hated Garvey and Afrika so much, actually ended up moving to and eventually dying in Ghana, West Afrika. Talk about a spineless hypocrite!!

DuBois was also the first negro to write for the Round Table Group's offspring, the Council on Foreign Relations, magazine *'Foreign Affairs'*. We know YT would never let a writer such as one from the DGT staff write for their white supremacist publication. So it should not be a shock to know YT would not have DuBois unless they felt DuBois was that kind of man who would write to their benefit.

THE NAACP CONNECTION

In 1919, a group organization protested against the Boule' in Washington, DC, exposing their allegiance to global white supremacy. The US. military investigated them and later adopted them as a spy network alliance. It must be noted that each member of the Boule' must take a lifetyme membership to the NAACP, so it serves as no coincidence that we also find during that same tyme, in the 1910s, the NAACP initiated the Anti-Lynch Bill with the US. government.

DuBois was one of the pawnz used as the poster-face in the finding of this so-called negro organization which is also started, owned and operated by the Round Table Group. The NAACPs major fund contributorz come from the Rockefeller Foundation who's given them as much as $3 million a couple yearz ago, and you *know* in order to stay in the foundationz good graces, they bes' carry out their ideas and aspirationz.

The government did not pass the Anti-Lynch Bill *until 1959!* This isn't even 40 yearz ago!! Y?? We found the government would comply with the "request" only if they (NAACP) would trade "Black intelligence". In other wordz, the government would not honor this bill unless the NAACP agreed to spy for them!

THE TUSKEGEE CATASTROPHE

Word out is the Boule' can also be linked to the Tuskegee Experiment in Alabama. Of the negro doctorz who injected Afrikanz with syphilis, they were Boule' hired on contract by the government. There was an incident with the local KKK because the clan did not believe the Boule' would not, could not, do such a thing as expressing loyalty to YT over their own people. So they showed up to make sure they would. Needless to say, they met no resistance, for the Boule' doctorz assured the clan the government hired to right group and that they would fulfill their assignment. These bootlickin' house negroes assured the illuminati there was a group of loyal negroes available to counteract any type of Afrikan the "king" did not like.

In 1917, one Lt. Col. Ralph VonDemon set up a negro spy network, under direct orders from then US Secretary of War, Newton D. Baker. Baker's special assistant, or negro laison, was Emmit Scott who was the Boule' grand archon in 1941 (Scott was also the one who was responsible for the emerge of Carter G.). Scott worked very closely with jewish spy, and one of the real co-founderz of the NAACP, Joel Spingarn. We also found that the spy, Robert Multon, Woodson refused to work with, was the one who got Emmit Scott his position with Baker. Multon was on duty during the Tuskegee experiment.

In fact, he was responsible for bringing the US Army to Tuskegee! Multon also was the one who stopped the KKK from having white doctor's in Tuskegee to instill the syphillis. VonDemon later hired "jewish" spy Joel Spingarn to "watch" (spy) the Afrikan community. This points out a direct link between the US government, the Boule' and the NAACP, all spying on the Afrikan community looking for, what "Gay" Edgar Hoover later called (in his COINTELPRO operation), the next "Black Messiah" who would emancipate the mentally enslaved Afrikan. All these organizationz were working under strict dictation from the Illuminati or Round Table Group.

The Illuminati's need to "control" the 9 areaz of people activity (economics, education, entertainment, labor, law, politics, sex, religion and war – and I'ma throw in a 10th: HEALTH!) as noted by Neilly Fuller and Francess Cress Welsing, had a significant impact in the realm of education.

There has also been the misconception that our HBCUs (Historically Black Colleges & Universities) were started by Afrikanz. This is not the case. The Illuminati used the Boule' when they started to build these so-called "Black" universities. Rockefeller and Julius Rosenwald joined forces in the financial backing of these breeding grounds mistakenly called institutionz of higher learning (should be called higher training).

Labeled the Push Foundation, Rosenwald joined the Rockefeller Foundation in 1922. Together they found Phipps, Atlanta, Dillard, Spellman, Howard and Clark Universities just to name a few. Most likely there is a Rosenwald Hall on each and every HBCU across the country. Stay tuned to future issues of DGT as we unearth more secrets of the original black dick ryderz!

LIK SHOT!!

NOTE: *We do not have all the shieldz broken down. It is our hope that any current or ex-memberz of these organizationz — or anyone who knowz for that matter — would be willing to step up and reveal the meaningz. If you'd like to shed some light, feel free to email us @ info@daghettotymz.com*

When names, symbolz and colorz are implemented, the finishing seal of any organization was authorized by conscious-thinking indivi(devilz). For instance, you will notice the shield of Alpha Phi Alpha (the first black collegiate fraternity, founded December 4th, 1906). It is not a coincidence they have (as well as Kappa Alpha Psi and Omega Psi Phi) a knight's helmet on the top of the shield.

Now what does a knight "in shining armor" remind you of? Camelot or King James and the Knights of the Round Table. Who were in search of the holygrail, which is subliminal for the 3rd eye or melanin! We know the Illuminati (Rhodes/Rothschild secret society) also goes by the name, the Round Table Group. The Rockefeller Foundation created the Boule', which created the 8 black fraternities and sororities. Rockefeller is a subdivision of the Rhodes/Rothschild or New World Order regime.

Now where in the history of Afrika (the Nile Vally in particular) did we have Afrikanz dressed up in armor?!!? Think about it Afrikan… to whom are these so-called black greek-lettered fraternities and sororities pointing their allegiance to? Afrika or Europe??

Lookin' at the shieldz on the next page, notice on their shield, the three sphinxes (not Her-Em-Akhet is facing westward and NOT east, which subliminally showz the preference of the western (white) philosophy and not the east (towardz Afrika).

Two of the three sphinxes are above what appearz to be two silhouettes of a fortress or castle from the dayz of Camelot (one black, the other old gold).

Practically in all the first eight shieldz we find a torch with a flame. In some you have two (the alpha's have two that cross each other and zeta phi beta has two on each side). This torch is a symbol of the Illuminati standing for enlightenment. My question is enlightenment of what?

In the shield of the Kappa Alpha Psi's, you will notice the greek wordz, 'Phi Nu Pi'. This was a "jewish" group that was the financial backing to their start. The sign "Pi" is also a coded symbol for the Illuminati.

Remember the movie, *'The Net'*? What was the symbol at the corner of the monitor that allowed Sandra Bullock to get into these 'secret' files?... Pi!

Also, what is Reebok's symbol? Steve Cokely noted first it was the British colonial flag, but now it's a Pi sign! This gives a deeper meaning to their slogan, *"this is my planet"*.

On the shield of Omega Psi Phi, you will see the knight with 2 crossed swordz behind him. This bearz close resemblance to Skull & Bones logo of a skull with 2 crossed bones behind it. In addition, we see reference to the Knights Templar with the helmet.

Phi Beta Sigma also goes by the name, the "Sigma's". Sigma is the 18th letter in the greek alphabet. For those that know numerology, Sigma breaks down to 1+8, which equalz 9. The number 9 is said to be used as an evil number in masonry – although in Kemet standz as a positive number, along with 13. It should also be noted that 9 is the number of the Boule' (8 frats/ sororities plus the Boule'). Also, the Sigma's go by anutha name, "Blue Devilz" and the signal they make with their hand is the devil sign (the index and pinky finger point up with the two-inside fingerz folded down).

As far as the sorority shieldz, the AKAs founding year, 1908, comes out to 18; which is also 9; along with their 9 founderz!

The Delta's have a deeper significance to white plagiarizm. At the top of their shield, you will notice a white woman on the top. Now Y is there a *white* woman on top of a *black* sorority's shield?!!?

The woman is Minerva, the roman goddess of wisdom (notice, even *she's* looking west). Minerva also went by the greek name Athena. The greeks (the first master plagiarizerz) copied Athena from the Afrikan Goddess Neit, which can be traced back to 4000BC!!

Just like the Alpha's choosing a grecian sphinx instead of the Afrikan Her-Em Akhet, the Delta's chose the grecian replica of the Afrikan Goddess Neit!

I haven't found much on the Zeta's yet (besides them being the sister to the Blue Devils), but there is one thing that drawz attention. The initiates of Zeta are called Archonianz. Archonz are what the memberz of the Boule' are called. As well, it isn't a coincidence that most, if not all, of the sororities call their annual

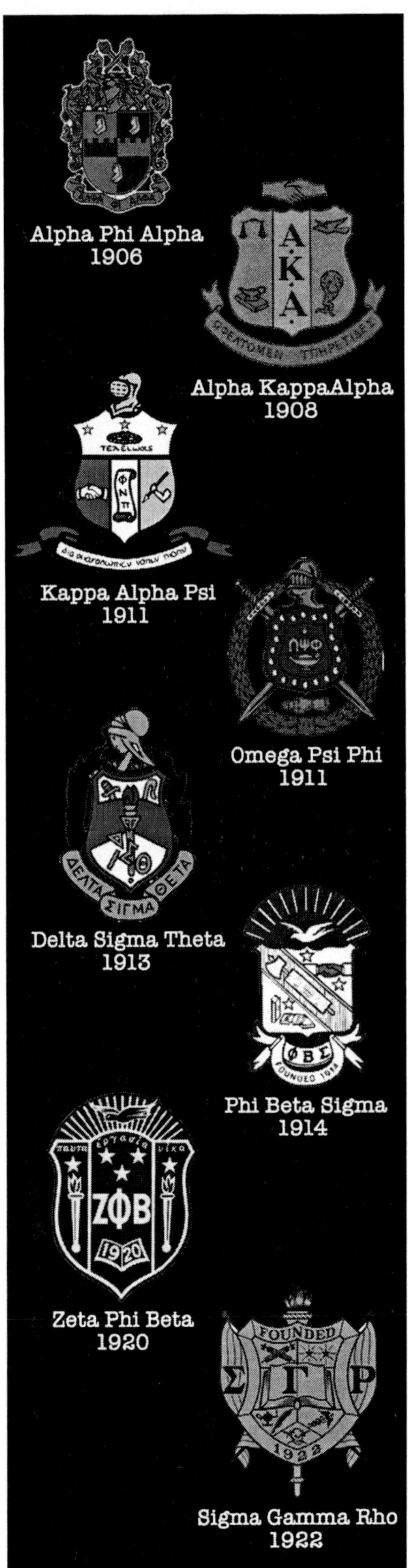

The original 8 surrounding the first black frat, Sigma Pi Phi, aka the Boule'

Notice the armored helmet, payin' homage to the dayz of Camelot and King Arthur?!!?

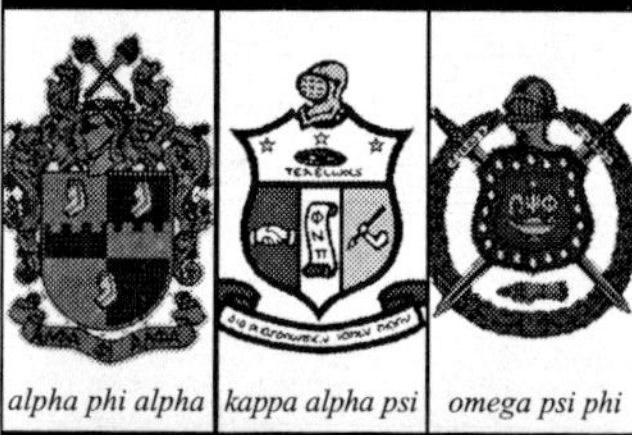
alpha phi alpha *kappa alpha psi* *omega psi phi*

The Delta's, a BLACK greek-lettered sorority, has a WHITE woman on the top of their shield, who's name is Minerva, a greek version of the original Afrikan Goddess, Neit, who has been traced back to the Nile Valley! Y do these "intelligent" women continue to refrain from putting the true Goddess on their shield and not some greek imposter?! Because their historical allegiance is to greece and not Afrika!

delta sigma theta

sigma gamma rho

If you take a look at Sigma Gamma Rho's shield (anutha Black sorority), you'll see it has an actual 'SKULL & BONES' logo on the bottom of their shield!! This greek system truly has Afrikanz wantin' to be more like greeks than our natural selves!

conference, yep you guessed it, *THE BOULE'!!*

If you look at the bottom part of Sigma Gamma Rho's shield, what do you see?...*A Skull with crossed bones!!* Just like the Illuminati's 2nd chapter, Skull & Bones!

None of this shit should be taken as mere coincidence. The choice of these symbolz on their logo's is not by coincidence. They are intelligent organizationz, so please believe a lot of thought was put into the choice of these symbolz.

If our fellow negro (brain-dead) founderz was about Afrika, they would've put Afrikan symbolz on their shieldz so there would be no room for doubt, but instead they were instructed by their overseer, the Boule'; who was instructed by Skull & Bones, which is the Illuminati, to put these subliminal characterz on these "guardian animalz" that keep watch over the Afrikan community for the YTs interests!

LIK SHOT!!

THE ROOT OF ALL WICKEDNESS

MASONRY

BY M'BWEBE AJA ISHANGI

It has been said if you want to study white supremacy, you need to start some 6000 yearz ago (when YT originated). Many noted scholarz (both Afrikan and europcan) have published many books and articles on the origin of white folks, Bobby Hemmit, Michael Bradley and Gerald Massey to name a few.

In the *'Iz YT Hueman? or Mutant!'* series, I parlayed how YT came on the scene. In this piece I spoke of Moses giving the beast in the caucus mountainz (hence, caucasian), 33 1/3rd° of knowledge, which is basically tricknology. We find that Masonry holdz the same degreez of knowledge (33 1/3rd). This bringz closure with the 5th Djhuitic principle – *'Rhythm'*. Everything works in cycles. Evil has reigned through white supremist organizationz for 6000 yearz, it is now tyme for truth to rule. This is Y hedz are talkin' this new world order shit, because the lies are unearthed and truth is shinin' through. YT has caused chaos in the physical dimension (earth) for far too long!

Activist, Khalid Muhammad said that the new world order isn't new, it's started with the first grafted people 6000 yearz ago. What is the new world order exactly? It can be best summed up by noting that it's mainly about colonializm, or the taking of land! Egypt (Kemet or KMT) is now inhabited by pirates. It was originally stolen by YT. The knowledge (termed secrets for outsiderz) of KMT were stolen, rearranged and plagiarized to falsely claim europeanz as founderz of civilization (namely the greeks). All secret societies, including masonry, view KMT as the birthplace of masonry. That iz Y they use numerous symbolz (ie, the all seeing eye) and numberz (altering the true meaning of #'s 9 and 13).

To study Masonry is to realize they had a deep affection with the ancient KMTic mystery school system. I was told by a 32nd° mason that in order to obtain the 33rd° you have to become black again! The 33rd° simply tellz you who God is...the blackman (even though I include the Afrikan woman)! Although they couldn't decipher the messages our ancients taught (probably due to lack of melanin), they adopted what they could and exchanged the messages and symbolz with negative ones.

Masonry's origination can be traced to the Knight Templarz, or Knights of the Temple of Solomon (who was an Afrikan). These Knights were christian warriorz involved in the war of Jerusalem in 1099AD. They served as guardianz protecting the Holy Land from Muslimz and the like. The Knights were only allowed to wear sheepskin under their armor. This served as a symbol of chastity for they were never allowed to bathe, nor engage in any kind of intimate activity with a woman, pending punishment up to death. Their banner resembled what we call a checkerboard, with the black block symbolizing sin and the white stood obviously for "purity". Now how "pure" is a stanky old white dude who *never* bathes and is dressed in sheepskin?? Even back then they saw black as evil and white as good; a reversed psychology our Ancestorz lived by.

Their initiationz were done in secrecy. The initiate was told just enuff info to permit him to take place at the bottom of the order. As he was promoted to higher levelz, he received further secrets [this practice is also done in masonry]. On Thursday, October 12, 1307, Jacques deMolay, the last Grand Master of the Knights Templar, was setup and on the 13th (Friday), King Phillip raided the headquarterz, putting 15,000 followerz in chainz. They were charged with rejecting christ (which was commissioned by law by Constantine in 1000AD), spitting on the cross, killing memberz who told secrets and *sodomy*. The chained Templarz were tortured to get a confession. They were put in dungeonz and chained to ringz in the wallz.

Some Templarz admitted, while being initiates, were required to deny god, jesus and the virgin mary and had to perform sexual acts like kissing the navel, penis and buttock of their initiates. For that, deMolay was burned alive.

At that tyme and age, we must realize it was forbidden to worship and believe in God other than what the "law" stated. Christianity, although rooted in Ethiopia, was used later as a tool of control by whites (and still is today). With the death of deMolay, masonry was born.

Jumping up to 1776, we find the new world order was 'reinstated' on May 1st with the resurrection of the Illuminati in Germany, by Adam Weishaupt. This was also the same day the Luciferian Conspiracy was signed in North American (months before there was a United States). Historian, Tony Browder states that, *"America's founding pirates were 18th century deists who were profoundly influenced by the philosophical ideologies of the secret societies in France, Germany and England."*

These men, who signed this pact with the devil, got together again 2 months later to sign the Declaration of Independence on July 4th. Well actually, only 2 signed – John Hancock and Thomas Jefferson – and the remaining 54 didn't sign until August 2nd (so should not this 'independence day' really be celebrated on August 2nd and not July 4th)!

Of the 56 signerz, 50 were masonz. They decided to use masonic (and stolen Afrikan) symbolz on its currency and became the only nation to print on its money, *"In God We Trust"*. It is clearly obvious that the God they're talkin' about isn't the spiritual God. These satanist's believed in the existence of God but also felt The Creator exercised no control over the lives of people after the creation of the world.

Observing the Declaration of Independence and the US Constitution (signed September 17, 1787 with 13 of the 40 signerz being masonz), we can clearly see the vital documents that make up America, are in fact, blatant followerz of satan. Albert Pike, a 33rd° mason and head of ku klux klan (kkk), is one of the many grand master devilz this country deifies. Think our accusation of masonz being devil worshipperz is all hype? This is what Pike had to say, *"To the crowd we must say: we worship a God, but it is the God one adores without superstition. To you, Sovereign Grand Inspector's*

General, we say this, that you may repeat it to the brethren of the 32nd, 31st and 30th degrees: all of us initiates of the high degrees should maintain the Masonic religion in the purity of the Luciferian doctrine. If Lucifer were not God, would Adonay...and his priests calumniate him? Yes, Lucifer is God."

A. Lantoine, a mason and historian who openly declared himself as an atheist, said in the excerpt, *'Lettre au Souverain Pontife', "So much the better, I say. Possessing critical and inquisitive minds, we are the servants of Satan. You, the guardians of truth, are the servants of God. These two complement one another. Each needs each other."* After this quote, Lantoine later said he didn't use the right term when describing the masonic sect. He said, *"I should have said servants of Lucifer."* All this is factual evidence linking them to the Luciferian pact signed by the pirates of this country in May of 1776.

See, masonry is just like the black fraternities and sororities. You won't know exactly what type of demonic shit you're involved in until the end. Young black college students join frats and sororities because all they see is service projects and stepshowz; never knowing they were founded by the Boule' (who was by the Illuminati). What we perceive on the undergraduate campus is merely what the Boule'/Illuminati wants us to see. By the tyme you graduate and if you're lucky(?) enuff to be recruited into the Boule', then is when you may find of certain alliances with white supremist organizationz, businesses and even individual white supremists who just so happen to wear suits and ties instead of white hoodz! At that point most, unfortunately, are so caught up in materializm after having been brainwashed with 'white success' for so long, they continue the degradation of righteousness and are rewarded with wealth both in the aspects of networking and finances.

George Washington wearing the Masonic Apron. Notice he's standing on a tetragrammaton

Any mason that tries to tell you they're not devil worshipperz are (1)lying to you (because, again, they learn this starting with the 30th°); or (2)they are just like the undergrad fratz: they haven't been told this secret yet. Masonry is rooted in knowing the true history of KMT; knowing the Afrikan wo/man is God and that they intend to not let you know this fact until you have been brainwashed for 32 degreez. Think about it. The average joe that goes through all 33 1/3° of masonry with the last degree telling them who God is; after they've been brainwashed for decades (because it takes about that long to obtain higher degreez in masonry), they now find out that they're God and not the whiteman...they probably think, *"what do I do? Afterall, I've been duped for so long, I figure they been good to me thus far, Y give it up? I got all these 'fraternal' conectionz...SHIIIIT! Ain't nobody gonna know, plus I don't wanna cause any ripples in the water."* They still remain loyal. That mentality is like taking an animal out of the wild, feeding him for 20 yearz, then letting him go. You think the animal is going to stay in the wild? He'll come running back just as fast as you let him go. Y? Because his master is all he knowz and he has been conditioned to only follow his master and

YT and the number 13
YT has a limited comprehension to many thingz and their usual reaction is to label it a mystery. One of them is YTs fixation with the fear of the number 13. This mystery can be traced to the life and death of Jacques deMolay.

This number, also a special KMTic number has been interpreted by them as bad luck, yet they contradict this belief when they have so many thingz they worship with the same number. Think, how many number of colonies they created when they came to america? 13. How many memberz were a part of King Arthur's clan of vigilanteez? 12 (+1, King Arthur, made it 13 — not to mention the secret societies of the world who base their secrecy on the virtues of King Arthur's Round Table Group and the Knights Templar); and how many memberz of the biblical Jesus made up his crew? 12(+Jesus =13).

But then they turn around and try to spook us out makin' movies like *'Friday the 13th'* and skipping the 13th floor in buildingz. How many elevatorz have you been on and there isn't a 13th floor? Y IZ Dat?!

I mean, technically there *is* a 13th floor. They think by not naming it as such, it doesn't exist, but the floor *does* exist! Just 'cause you label it the 14th floor, you still on the 13th! So Y create all the mystery? Probably 'cause they'd rather you not know the power of numberz.

not lead himself. This is what masonry does to black masonz who are mainly Prince Hall Masonz (we'll talk 'bout them in part 2).

One of the main objectives of masonry is in the field of political activity. Their object, similar to the Illuminati's, is to seize power and place masonz in positionz of command. It is evident with the Declaration of Independence (50 out of 56 signerz also had ties to other secret societies).

Candidates are carefully chosen (just like the Boule') and thoroughly screened long before even being approached. Once they are received into the lodge, they are sworn with an oath of secrecy, which is renewed each tyme they advance to a higher degree. Some examples of oaths are: *"I promise that I will not write, print, cut or engrave masonic secrets...binding myself under no less penalty than to have my throat cut across, my tongue torn out by the roots and my body burned."* [the Blue Lodge oath - 1st 3°]. The York Rites 9th° pledges, *"...to have my hands chopped off at the stumps, my eyes plucked out from the sockets, my body quartered, and then thrown among the rubbish of the Temple...so help me God."* What does God have to do with you pledging your life to satan?!!?

Again, initiates will not find out they been worshipping satan until the 30th°. In *'Freemason and the Vatican'*, by Vicomte Leon De Poncins, he states that after a mason is initiated into the first degree, *"a proces of doctrinal information* (or brainwashing) *begins, which will continue all his life...[A] neophyte learns that these terms* (degreez) *have a hidden meaning, which he will not understand until he has undergone further initiation...If the Mason is receptive, he climbs upward in the Masonic hierarchy, and yet he never at any time knows exactly where he stands in it, nor how many higher degrees or persons control the organization."*

"The Blue Degrees", writes Pike, in *'Morals and Dogma'*, *"are but the outer court or portico of the Temple. Part of the symbols are displayed to the Initiate, but he is misled by false interpretation. It is not intended that he shall understand them; but it is intended that he shall imagine he understands them."*

This is also Y each initiate is blindfolded (soundz familiar to all you black greeks, huh?... it happened to me when I pledged alpha phi alpha). This is symbolic for the initiate having an unconditional loyalty to the society despite what his eyez tell him.

In the early degreez of masonry when they have to enact the birth of Adam by coming out of a coffin, butt-naked and wrestle in the mud with a member of sect, then oral sex (an alleged ritual called 'riding the hump') is performed, he must have an unconditional blind faith to believe that the initiator knowz what is best for him. In masonic termz, the blindfold (or masonically called, hoodwink) is a reminder to the darkness and ignorance the initiate lived in before coming to the "light" of masonry.

I remember being told as a shorty that if you were a mason and you gave away secrets you would be killed. This blind allegiance with satan, coerced through the threat of losing your life, is Y we see so many blacks in fraternities and sororities not wanting to give away these so-called secrets. The deep thing is that all their silence is doing is continuing the level of ignorance this society has.

Case in point, THERE ARE NO SECRETS! THE SHIT'S BEEN OUT. THEY BEEN PUBLISHING WHO THE BLACK WO/MAN IS IN BOOKS FOR CENTURIES! But since we have been brainwashed to be afraid of knowledge and fear picking up a book, they can call this a secret! Well let's dig deepuh into these "secrets".

DEGREEZ OF MASONRY

There are 2 mainstream types of masonry being practiced. Both go through the same 1st 3 degreez. This takes place in what is called "the Blue Lodge." Blue is a masonic color which standz for *"the front line"*. It is no coincidence that the Boule's colorz are blue and white (white for who they protect); serving at the first line of defense to protecting the Cecil Rhodes/Lord Rothschilds secret society, the Illuminati. As well, you'll notice the police department's colorz are predominately blue, and they too, serve as the front line of protection to the system or '(as)syst(h)em' [assist-them...aka, YT].

All of the degreez in both the York and Scottish Rite are based on the life of King Solomon, a black man! The York Rite Mason's are only practiced in the US. and Canada. They added an additional 6° and embrace the Symbolic, Capitular, Cryptic and Templar Degrees. The Templar Degree is synonymous with the Knights of Templar during King Arthur's Court. It is also no coincidence that the Round Table Group (RTG), a Rhodes/Rothschilds secret society, also goes by the Knights of Templar.

The Round Table Group was started by Rhodes, who was a disciple of John Ruskin, a professor at Oxford University in England. The RTG was structured on the practices of masonry. Ruskin, along with Rhodes was also a member of the Adam Weishaupt's, Illuminati (founded the same day as the Luciferian Conspiracy). The RTG is responsible for the formation of numerous organizations like the League of Nations and the Council on Foreign Relations (CFR).

In the 4th°, the Mark Master, the symbol of the Illuminati is revealed (the double circle, the same worn on the logo of the US. Military Intelligence – a sphinx; as well as the double circle found inside the vase the Boule's sphinx is covering).

The Scottish Rite Masonz uses all the original degreez. The 6th degree callz for INTIMATE secrecy. Now remember when we did the piece on Skull & Bones and how their fellowship was based on men coming together, in secret...in intimacy? Again, no coink-e-dink!

The 13th° – the Perfect Elu or Grand, Elect, Perfect and Sublime Mason, revealed in the secret vault rests with a tetragrammaton (will explain in part 2) lies the four-letter unspoken name of God in hebrew, which is YHWH, or Yahweh who was indeed an Afrikan!

Although the secrets of who God is revealed start ing with the 30th°, there aren't many masonz who attain all 33°. For instance, in 1907 the total number of active 33° masonz didn't exceed 100. Therefore, there are hundredz of thousandz of masonz who *think* they know, but don't because they haven't reached the end where the truth is revealed. This goes for both white and black masonz.

GEORGE GM JAMES VS. WEB DuBOIS & CARTER G. WOODSON

Before we end part one of this series, you may recall my comparison of the Boule's WEB DuBois and Carter G. Woodson (both proclaimed by YT as our "heroes") versus George 'Grand Master (mason)' James. I feel this needz to be reiterated because fraternities and masonic sects share the same value of secrecy exclusively amongst memberz of the group. Along with the oath of maintaining secrets there are different distress callz and secret hand shakes to add mystical hype.

In the case of James versus DuBois/Woodson, it must be noted that James belonged to the York Rite Masonz and DuBois/Woodson to the Boule'. Both had to pledge oath's of secrecy presumably with the penalty resulting in death. DuBois and Woodson were later exiled from the Boule' for unknown reasonz. Not long after, DuBois became a PanAfrikanist; moving to Ghana, Afrika (a place he once strongly opposed during the reign of Marcus Garvey), and Woodson went on to publish the infamous text, *'Miseducation Of the Negro'*. Both basically made somewhat of a 170° turn once out of these white-based secret sects. Where they failed our people is they did not make the entire 180° turn. They remembered they took an oath to uphold the secrets of the fraternity – never letting you know who rulez the world (Rhodes/Rothschild); probably because they feared death. Yes, they did walk away from these white supremist organizationz, BUT they never let the people know who they were; therefore, not becoming part of the solution, but remaining part of the problem because they refused to tell you exactly what whites and blacks, organizationz and foundationz that are responsible for the hell our people have been enduring.

If it wasn't for the sacrifice of George GM James, on the other hand, we probably would never know about the greeks stealing Afrikan culture and claiming it as theirz. The book, *'Stolen Legacy'*, exposed the myths of greek philosophy and proved the ancient homo's actually stole our history from Kemet! After publishing his book in 1954, he mysteriously disappeared! It is said he died a masonic death (having his throat cut from ear to ear with his tongue cut out, then burning his body) for unveiling the secrets of the masonic sect. James knew his life was on the line but his luv for our people far outweighed the fear of death, and coincidentally, YT has never even mentioned his name as being a "hero" for black people! I think its well past-due!!

LIK SHOT!!

Last joint, we continued our open-heart surgery cutting into the aorta of white supremacy and exposing one of the western worldz oldest of secret societies, masonry. As The Creator continues to bless us with more element's this proves to become yet anutha series like the one's we done on the Boule' and the Illuminati/Skull & Bones. All of these are linked to the same wicked root of white supremacy and I've found that Masonry – the first secret society – has it's background in Kemet! YT has alwayz been astounded by the history of our past. Basically everything that exists in the world has a base in the history of Ethiopia and Kemet.

I can recall, during my "wanting to be a mason dayz", one of my partnerz was gettin' initiated into masonry. I wanted to be one because I was told my grandfather was one. As well, (at the tyme) I was in a frat and many go embrace masonry. My boy told me that I wasn't fit to be a mason (shit I already heard when I was tryin' to be an Alpha). So I knew the game. I thought he was just puttin' me through some pre-pledgin shit to see if I really wanted in. But my man was serious. He told me I wasn't fit because *"I couldn't keep secrets."*

Immediately, without thinkin', I replied, *"Yes I can!!"* But he was right. 5 yearz later I'm exposing fraternities and sororities, the Boule', the New World Order; all that 'em! And today, I'm uncovering secrets of masonry. Scalpel please...

This piece we'll get into some of the metaphysical sublimz that make up masonry. In particular, we will break down some numberz and basic geometrical figures, some of the ritualz both initiates and memberz experience, as well as their connection to other secret societies. For the foundation of masonry, you might want to peep part 1, otherwise, this piece will be difficult to follow.

We've learned that masonry is based on the 3 large pyramidz of Giza, in Kemet (erroneously called egypt). Each are positioned just like 3 starz of Orion. Historian, Ashra Kwesi spoke of our connection to the 3 starz and how they're the constellation from whence we came. The pyramidz also hold the key to extraterrestrial (spiritual) communication and entrance to and from our world. We will dwell in those in part 3. Masonry also has a connection to the life of King Solomon, the king of Israel (960BC), who was a black man.

One of the degreez practiced is the Templar degree. This degree has an origin with the Knights of Templar (KOT), a military and religious order established in the middle ages, around 1119AD in Jerusalem [quick note: the Rhodes/Rothschilds secret society also goes by that name, as well as calling the Round Table Group (RTG)]. The RTG and KOT have links to the history of King Arthur, who had 11 Knights, he also called the 'Knights of the Round Table'. As alwayz, when doing research, eliminate the word "coincidence". Things are for a logical reason.

King Arthur was in search of the holy grail; an alleged cup the historical Jesus drank out of. When I looked in the *'Dictionary of Symbols'*, by JE. Cirlot, the holy grail is not a cup, it is symbolic for the "Third Eye" or "Kiss of Ra"; which is melanin. He was not after a "cup" persay, he was after what YT has alwayz been after, melanin, or carbon, the key element to life which they have low to no count's of! It was revealed to me by a 32° mason that the 33rd° tells you who God is...the black wo/man (peep part 1)!

Masonry has been searching for the Holy Grail for centuries – which is symbolically Melanin found inside Afrikan people!

Because of YTs inability to possess melanin, their outer appearance is of a pale essence. Mentally and spiritually, the absence of melanin eliminates the ability to be "good". That is Y, historically, the white race has alwayz had the nature of a beast, stealing, lying, murdering, warring and plagiarizing! This isn't a racist comment, this is a historical fact! Of the 360° of knowledge we are capable of obtaining, they can only get 33 1/3rd°! That is Y their every move is so destructive towardz life.

That is also Y they went down to Kemet and blew off the nose of Her-Em Akhet, and had Aristotle change the colorz of skin from black to white on all the paintingz on the wallz of Kemetic structures. That is also Y 50 of the 56 signerz of the Luciferian Conspiracy made a pact with Lucifer, May 1, 1776

The 6th° calls for INTIMATE secrecy, and if you recall our series on Skull & Bones, intimacy went as far as homosexual activity. In the 14th°, the tetragrammaton is mentioned. The numerology of masonry is deep! Before I parlay on, it must be noted that the number system is based on 0-9. After 9, the numbering system is repeated. Each of the 10 prime numberz has a meaning. In Kemet, the #9, as well as #13 had positive energy. But, as alwayz, YT cannot process the true message behind our history so they alter the positive meaning with a negative one. It hasn't been revealed to me as to Y I keep seeing the #9 in masonry, but it must be there for a reason. You be the judge for yourself.

A tetragrammaton is 9 squares hidden inside 72 squares is hidden name of God, which is YHWH (Yahweh). I've come across the #666 when studying this geometrical figure as well. Its definition dates back to mean God in Hebrew now pronounced Adonai or Elohim. This name has been held sacred since 2-3rd century BC. In masonry, it has a numerical value of 9, for the 9 squares

The tetragrammaton also resembles a checkerboard with 72 black and white squares. As indicated earlier, numberz play a large role in masonry for it is known that numberz are the universal language. Our ancients sometymz spoke with numberz, as did the plagiarizing europeanz. 72 & 72 = 144. When we break it down we get 9 [1+4+4=9]. Also, when you break down 666, it also comes to 9: 6+6+6=18 —> 1+8=9. It is no coink-e-dink that the black version of the Illuminati, the Boule' also has the tetragrammaton on it's shield that, obviously, has a double meaning: 1)for it's ties to white secret societies and 2)for the original 8 black greek fraternities and sororities, with itself being the last one (peep back issues on Boule' series).

More history on the black (Prince Hall) masonz reveal the #9 as well! In 1775 (note: *before* there was a united states), Prince Hall and 14 otherz were initiated into the irish-based masonic lodge #441 (4+4+1=9; I'm not dreamin' this up, you do the math!). 12 yearz later, in 1787, Prince Hall opened the African Lodge #459 (4+5+9=18 —> 1+8=9).

What's also deep is the 15 hedz initiated into masonry is the same number of Skull & Bones initiates (15 at a tyme). As far as Skull & Bones, our series indicated their history starting in 1832 at Yale University in New Haven, Connecticut. Historian, Steve Cokely revealed in a lecture that another name for this city is New Heaven! The city also has another alias called the *"City of 9 Squares!!"* This shit is madd deep, Sun!!

The tetragrammaton is also linked with the Magic Square. This square has an origin in Alkebulan, present day Afrika (where all knowledge came from). Each combination of 3 boxes (up, down, across, diagonal) = 15. When you add all 6 sumz of 15, you get 90 (9+0=9). Again, #9 and 13 originally have positive meaningz, but YT changed it. The Magic Square is also the 9th chamber of the Cabala and has also been called the Square of Saturn.

If you look at the planet Saturn from atop the planet, you will see a circle-within-a-circle. This symbol also happenz to be one that white supremacist's Cecil Rhodes and Lord Rothschild's chose to be for their secret society, the Illuminati.

In Virginia, the department of military intelligence has a large sphinx (we distinguished the difference from Her-Em-Akhet in the Boule' series) in the front of the building. What's deep is, around the neck of this mythological beast, it wearz a medallion that has a circle-within-a-circle as the charm; clearly indicating the us government's military linked to the "new" world order.

As well, we revealed that the Boule' also has a sphinx as their logo. The sphinx has its right paw covering a vase and inside the vase is, drum roll please... a circle-within-a-circle!!

When you know what to look for, masonry isn't a mystery. Their secrets are based on the knowledge of our past. As mason, George Grand Master (Mason) James, stated in his book, *'Stolen Legacy'* (a volume that revealed the connection of masonry to Kemet; a daring sacrifice he knew would cost him his life), *"Greek mythology is stolen Egyptian History!"*

The evil one's of this world do not want us to know of our past, nor who they really worship. If Afrikanz found out this whole game of white supremacy is based on them not wanting you to know you come from a lineage of masterz who help shape the universe, white supremacy would fade away faster than the first host of the nightshow, VIBE (came and gone so

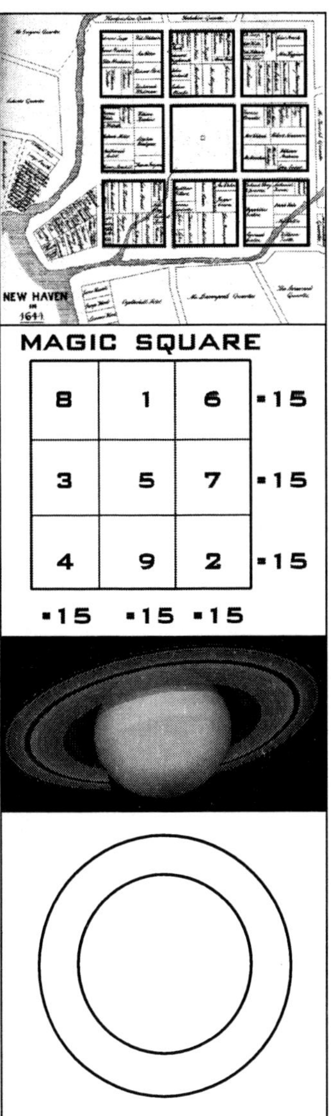

grafik 1: This is a 1644 map of the city of New Haven, CT, also called New Heaven. Notice the tetragrammaton!

grafik 2: The Magic Square

grafik 3 & 4: The Square of Saturn. Based off the planet Saturn. When you look at it from the top, the ringz around the planet looks like a circle-within-a-circle, which also happenz to be the symbol the Rhodes/Rothschilds Secret Society adopted.

fast I can't remember his name)!

Even one of western civilization's greatest(?) mindz, sir isaac newton, spoke of the relationship between Afrikanz and the greeks: *"The Egyptians were the earliest observer's of the heaven's...for from them it was, that the greeks, a people more addicted to the study of philosophy than of nature, derived the first as well as their soundest notions of philosophy; and in the Vestal ceremonies we can recognize the spirit of the Egyptians, who concealed mysteries that were above the capacity on the common heard under the veil of religious rites and hieroglyphic symbols."*

We assure that "we won't stop" diggin' in the crates for more elements. Until next tyme.

LIK SHOT!!

The belief that the National Association for the Advancement of Colored People (NAACP) is an organization to uplift Afrikan people, when looked at under the microscope of history on how they were formed and how they now operate, would bring one to the conclusion that it is false! The fact is, the NAACP is a european organization started by europeanz to control the movement of Afrikan people away from self-determination! Yes, this is a strong accusation, as you will learn Y we say this in this piece.

The cliche', *"if you want to hide a thing from a nigger, put it in a book",* never rang louder. The oldest civil-rights organization in the country has been selling us out for over 90 yearz and we just now finding this out!

As Afrikanz initiate our yearly Selective Buying Boycott during the last 3 hollow-daze of the year (Halloween, Thanks-taking and the Merry Christ-MESS), we find the initial goal of depriving white companeez from hundredz of thousandz of black dollarz are receiving stiff resistance from numerous parties.

With the NAACPs annual convention, it's kinda hard to see them being hurt by the boycott. For example, the 1997 annual conference for the NAACP was held July 12-17th in Pittsburgh, Pennsylvania. This convention brought an estimated $10-15 million to the city of Pittsburgh; more than enuff to recuperate from any losses during our boycott.

Focusing on the Pittsburgh branch of the NAACP, we find according to the Pittsburgh Courier, that neither president Tim Stevens, nor any staff could be reached for their position on the Selective Buying Boycott. In other wordz, these negroes evaded the public responding to whether they support the boycott or not. It is clearly evident they do not. That would jeopardize the conference. It should also be noted that the Urban League gave no comment as well.

The local branch acted as if they had no control in the conference coming to Pittsburgh, when, in fact, they had to bid to have it there just like Atlanta did for the Olympics! Once Pittsburgh was selected, the local branch had to pay a $150,000 (they say donation) to the national headquarterz in Maryland, in order to secure the bid. The payment went out December of 1996. What's ironic is sources from the Pittsburgh Post-Gazette wrote back in early November 1996 of Allegheny County donating $150,000 to the local branch in support for the conference. There is no coincidence this amount was the same exact amount that was needed to secure the bid. And Y wouldn't Allegheny county "donate" $150,000 when they know they're gonna make $10-15 million some 6 months later (who do you think is gettin' the better of the deal?)

So who is the NAACP really?? Y won't they support anything initiated by Afrikanz (ie, the Selective Purchasing Boycott and the Million Man March of 1995)?

THE ORIGIN OF THE NAACP

The NAACPs inception was during the first week of January, 1909. On February 12th (good ol' honest Abe Lincoln's 100th birthday), in New York City a group of (majority) whites and a few token negroes met. The whites who fronted like they "loved" black folk wanted to start an organization for us were: Jane Adams, Ray Baker, Haines Holmes, Mary White Ovington, Edward Russel, Joel Spingarn, Oswald Garrison Villard, Lillian Wald, English Walling and Steven Wise. All of these individualz were Liberal whites who wanted blacks to pursue the path of integration for racial upliftment despite the fact that none of them really approved of integration with blacks.

Two of the europeanz who formed the NAACP, Rabbi Steven Wise and Jane Adams, have two direct links to a secret society called the Round Table Group that was formed in 1881 at Oxford University in Ruskin College in England by Cecil Rhodes with the money gained from the colonization of Azania (South Afrika). If you're not familiar with Cecil Rhodes, he's the Afrikaknz version of what Adolf Hitler is to the so-called Jew.

He used, through free labor – resulting in millionz of deaths due to bein' overworked – millionz of our enslaved cousinz to dig up diamondz now sold and worn around the world, primarily distributed through his company, later heired to Oppenheimer DeBeers Mining Company.

Rabbi Steve Wise attended Oxford University for his postgraduate study in 1881 when the Round Table Group was formed by Cecil Rhodes, Arnold Toynbee and otherz. Wise then went on to partake in the finding of the NAACP and also the American Jewish Congress – a zionist organization that supported the european jewish colonization of what was called Palestine and is now the state of Is-it-real (Israel).

Jane Adams went to England to learn how to establish the first settlement houses in the US. from Toynbee. Settlement houses were founded so that educated rich people could live in the "slumz" in order to assist, instruct and guide the poor. Adams then went on to help find the NAACP.

The NAACP is not a secret organization; their information can be found in books. For nearly 100 yearz, they've acted as the illusionary voice and shield of minorities in America. However, researching their origin revealz they carry out the ideas and philosophy of the Round Table Group. They have the Afrikan population at large thinking its founderz were Afrikan (DuBois and Ida Wells-Barnett) when they were used as scapegoats, giving the false perception this organization was founded by Afrikanz, *for* Afrikanz.

The NAACP is most notably known for initiating the Anti-Lynch Bill during the 1910s. They called for the government to pass a bill prohibiting the lynching of Afrikanz. What many do not know is the bill did not pass congress until 1959!!! This is some 40+ yearz later! We also find, the government, in exchange for such a bill, would oblige only if they (NAACP) would trade "Black Intelligence". In other wordz, the government would not honor this request unless the NAACP agreed to spy for them! This is how the Boule' ties in, for each member of the Boule' must be a lifetyme member of the NAACP.

FIRST MEMBER WEB DuBOIS: "ADVIZOR TO THE KING"

WEB DuBois was the first negro to become involved with the NAACP being the only negro founder. This was a Wise choice for this organization due to the fact that DuBois was a member of the first black greek secret fraternity called Sigma Pi Phi, or the Boule', which was founded May 15, 1904 in Philadelphia, Pennsylvania, just a few yearz before the NAACP. In the Boule' history book, written by Charles H. Wesley, it states, *"...the Round Table can live through us!"* DuBois, being an Archon (name for member of Boule') made a coded pledge to help the very secret society — the round table group — whom the NAACP is an extension of.

DuBois' early career with the NAACP is a standing monument to their purpose. While editor of the NAACP newspaper, the *CRISIS*, he was a chief assistant to help whites destroy the largest organization for Afrikan self-determination Marcus Garvey and the United Negro Improvement Association (UNIA).

As mentioned in the Boule' articles, the Boule' started the 8 college black fraternities and sororities (Alpha's, Kappa's, Que's, Sigma's, AKA's, Delta's, Zeta's and Sigma Gamma Rho's).

Joel Spingarn, one of the founderz of the NAACP, and a jewish spy for the united states army, had the Spingarn medal started in 1914, and one of the founderz of Omega Psi Phi (Que's), Ernest Just was the first recipient of the award honoring the negro with the highest achievement (of selling out), and of course, we find Ernest Just was also a member of the Boule'!

THE NAACP TODAY

Kwesi Mfume has emerged as the NAACPs savior wiping out their alleged $3.2 million deficit in 9 months. The probable conspiratorz who bailed them out will probably not be known unless you obtain the 1996 annual audit... that's IF they release the foundationz true name. So far, we've had difficulty in getting it. It probably was a foundation like the Rockefeller's who, in the past, donated $3 million to the NAACP. Oh, yes, money does more than talk, it also controlz! Rockefeller has his clawz all up the NAACPs dress along with other families in the New World Order.

Mfume has written the Boule' in admiration of this black-with-white-faced organization, so we know he knowz what the Boule' is all about. I have a question for Mr. Mfume. It is said your name meanz, *'conquering son of kingz',* well, Kwesi, Y don't you try conquering the ADVIZORZ to the king, the Boule'?!

BEN CHAVIS MEETS WITH ANTI-DEFAMATION LEAGUE (ADL)

Several yearz ago before he merged with Farrakhan and the Nation of Islam, ex-CEO of the NAACP, Ben Chavis, spoke about an encounter he had with the ADL when he first took office. He was summoned for a meeting with the then president of the ADL, Abraham Foxman in New York City and his testimony was startling. Chavis claimed the ADL [the infamous "jewish" clan that basically makes any public figure that speaks with an anti-semitic tongue, repent publicly, ie, Jesse (Boule') Jackson with his remarks of hymie town back during the 1988 presidential electionz] relayed to him they had in their possession, numerous tapes of him using anti-semitic slurz.

Chavis asked them if that was their job, monitoring (spying) on people and collecting data. They replied yes. Along with that, Chavis said Foxman told him bluntly, *"the NAACP is my organization!"*

When you check the auditing recordz of the NAACP, you may find numerous european organizationz on the list as major contributorz. In *'The Rockefeller Files'*, by Gary Allen, Rockefeller speaks of the power of *"not owning a corporation but controlling it through money."* Money dictates power. And if the NAACP can't produce its own fundz (which it hasn't since it started), then who ever keeps them in existence, they owe their lives to. *(refer to the Anti-Lynching Bill fiasco in The Boule' pt.3)*

Like the settlement house movement, the NAACP both served the purpose of monitoring (spying) on Afrikan people and preventing true "advancement."

In summation, the NAACPs so-called purpose, primarily, was to cease the countless lynchingz of innocent Afrikanz. Studying the blueprints of this sham organization, we find the very people our Ancestorz were running to for help, had an allegiance with the very lyncherz. This points out they were devised to simply monitor, or spy, on any and all Afrikanz that try to take their liberation into their own handz.

The NAACP isn't an organization that represents the Afrikan community. In fact, its name should be changed to the *"National Association for the Advancement of CERTAIN People"*.

The NAACPs days are numbered for the truth is being revealed and the people want to know!! For those that wish to vent out questionz or frustrationz to the NAACP, their national number is 1800.NAACP.55. Heat needz to be applied to both national and your local branches.

MORE FIRE!!

"Skull and Bones is a chapter of a corps in a German University. It should properly be called not Skull & Bones Society but Skull & Bones chapter"
— Antony Sutton

"Wise statesman...established these great self-evident truths, that when in the distant future some man, some faction, some interest, should set up the doctrine that none but rich men, or none but white men, were entitled to life, liberty and the pursuit of happiness, their posterity should look up at the Declaration of Independence and take courage to renew the battle which their fathers began..."
— Abraham Lincoln

This series goes to the wannabe drug hustlaz and Colombian warlord fanz! WAKE UP!! We got negroes (dead-thinking Afrikanz) out tryin' to be what they ain't... a drug sellin' don-dodda. We got all these artists from both coasts and in between frontin' like they gangstaz. What's worse, we see the east coast [the Kemet (not Mecca) of Hiphop] wanting to be Colombianz all of a sudden! Hedz are adopting names like Noriega, Escabar, Junior Mafia and Cormega. I mean, what?! Do you *really* think they (Colombianz) like yo' Afrikan ass?! They'll call you a *'mooley', 'spade'* and *'egg-plant'* in a second; yet we glamorizin' these kidz.

What's even more dramatic is how these negroes think 'cause they say they from the streetz that they got some kind of juice. You got no juice, Sun, all you got is sugar water!!

Negroes don't study, plain and simple. Because if they did, they wouldn't be about gun totin', weed inhalin', and drug sellin', they would be about cleanin' up the Afrikan community by, first, cleaning up our mindz!

For all you heat carryin' pound sellin' fiendz, if you wanna know about the real drug smugglaz – the one's with the *real* juice, whose responsible for the exporting of drugz from foreign landz to our boroughz – you might wanna read this piece, for it is the Illuminati, coupled with the 2nd chapter, Skull & Bones, who are the Original Gangstaz!!

There hasn't been much written on Skull &Bones (heretofore known as "S&B"), due to contained secrets, but according to writer, Ron Rosenbaum, in an article, *"Last Secrets of Skull & Bones,"* written in the September 1977 edition of *Esquire magazine*, S&Bs purpose is *"to produce an alliance of good men...good men are rare of all societies, non is more glorious, nor greater strength, than when men of similar morals are joined IN INTIMACY."*

This is nothing but masonry, for one of their ritualz deal with each initiate coming out of the tomb, NAKED, and has to mud wrestle with a fellow initiate. It is said the ritual endz with anal intercourse performed on the initiates. This is s'posed to resemble the creation of Adam [and we *know* Afrikan people were before him right? (read *'IZ YT Human? or Mutant!'*)]

Under the skull and crossed bones of their logo we see a number. '322'. This number is in honor of Desmosthenes, who was a popular greek homosexual. During the greeks reign, homosexuality, or faggotitis was a norm. Back then, these homo's status was based on how many little boyz they fondled. If a man was not "bonin'" his fellow man, his status was demoted. Just as heterosexual relationships is what the majority population practices now (although its on the decline as we see this sick practice spillin' into the Afrikan community), men being with men was the norm back then.

Intimacy between males was accepted as natural, whereas, the woman was only used for procreation. This may also be the reason so many white men (and even black-faced, white-thinking men) prefer to "trust" and "bond" more with their fraternal bruthaz opposed to their natural opposite, the female.

I'm not implying every fraternity practices homosexual ritualz, afterall, I was once a member of one, BUT, adopting customz we have no clue of, does not make it an excuse to represent it! I'm sure many Afrikanz-converted-into-negro-greeks can attest that as initiates, we are not taught much of the greek culture. In fact, we are taught negro history and very little Afrikan history! So Y do we *still* adopt their (greek) letterz and not Kemetic (Medu Neter, aka hieroglyphic) letterz?! This is a pure example of the influence YT has had on our people. He is able to create white-rooted organizationz for black folk and we accept, honor and cherish them even though we don't have a full understanding of the history of Greece in relation to the Nile Valley of Kemet, AND the history of YT for that matter.

That's what they do! They instill confusion. They take alias' making it damn near impossible to link its origin. Not only do they confuse negroes, they strategically create havoc around the globe! S&B has alwayz had a history of playing both sides of the fence.

For instance, S&B, through President Taft and Theodore Marburg started *'The League to Enforce The Peace',* which fronted in promoting world peace; while at the same tyme, they were also very active in urging U.S. participation in WWI. Andrew Carnegie profited from war through his vast steel holdingz, but was also an enthusiastic president and financial backer of the American Peace Society. How could these beasts be for war and peace at the same tyme?! Scalpel please....

THE HISTORY OF SKULL AND BONES

S&B can be linked to Cecil Rhodes who is famous for robbing Afrika of her natural resources, as well as raping then murdering countless young Afrikan males for his pleasure. YT could not have built their trillion dollar diamond, gold, silver, copper and oil dynasties without dehumanizing Afrikan people by enslaving us and reteaching us to forget who we are, where we came from, and who the true heirz of the earth are.

Through study of the imbalanced greeks, thanks to our ongoing series on the

Boule', we found S&B and the Illuminati have a strong association to ancient greece... home of faggotitis! This led us to the greek homo Desmosthenes (384?-322BC), a spy for the city of Athenz. It's been said Alexander the (not so) great is in his bloodline. Alexander is said to be the culprit behind the shooting of the nose and lips off Her-Em-Akhet (sphinx) in Kemet somewhere between 1799-1801.

S&B is also known as Chapter 322, commemorating the death of this homo, Desmosthenes, on the date of his death. Chapter 322 is also synonymous to the year 1832 and the second '2' is symbolic for the 2nd chapter Russell belonged to in Germany. Their logo is a skull and two crossing bones like the pirates they are.

The background to S&B is a story of Opium and Empire, and a bitter struggle for political control over the new U.S. republic. Samuel Russell, 2nd cousin to Bones founder William Russell, who established Russell & Co. in 1823. Its business was to acquire opium from Turkey and smuggle it into China, where it was strictly prohibited, under armed protection of the Brithish Empire.

What's deep is the gang of thugz who did this prior to S&B was created by Thomas Handasyd Perkins of Newburyport, Massachusetts, and they went by the name "Blue Bloods". It's ironic and should not be seen as a coincidence that the negro version of gangz adopted both the color of "Blue" – for crips; and "Blood" for the other gang that wearz red.

Forced out of the lucrative Afrikan slave trade by U.S. law and Caribbean slave revolts, leaderz of the Cabot, Lowell, Higginson, Forbes, Cushing and Sturgis families had married Perkins' siblingz and children. The Perkins' opium business had made a fortune and established power over these families. By the 1830s, the Russell's bought out the Perkins and made Connecticut the primary center of the U.S. opium racket.

Massachusetts families (Coolidge, Sturgis, Forbes and Delano) joined Connecticut (Alsop) and New York (Low) smuggler-millionaires under Russell Trust. By 1856, Russell Trust Incorporated their open pirte emblem – the skull and cross bones.

As author of *'America's Secret Establishment: An Intro to the Order of Skull & Bones'*, Antony C. Sutton states, in order to bring in this new world order *"a planned order with heavily restricted individual freedom, without Constitutional protection, without national boundaries or cultural distinction," had to be devised. With the concentration on controlling society as a whole, they had to implement 12 areas of concern: 1)Education – dictating how the population of the future will behave; 2)Money – controlling wealth and exchange of goods; 3)Law – enforcing the will of the state, a world law and a world court; 4)Politics – directing each state; 5)Economy – creating additional wealth; 6)History – making the people believe what you want them to think; 7)Psychology – controlling how people think; 8)Philanthropy – so people think well of the controllers; 9)Medicine – power over health, life and death; 10)Religion – the people's beliefs, which is the spur to action for many (except Afrikans); 11)Media – power over what people know and learn of current events and; 12)Continuity – appointing follower's to ensure the longevity over generations. Judging by today's reality, we can see their plan has proven successful."* Damn yo! Can you not see all these cylinderz workin' cohesively maintainin' global white supremacy?!

Each year S&B chooses 15 memberz to be initiated. The 15th and last member notified is said to traditionally be the highest of the high and a mighty honor. One of S&Bs

most famous of initiates, former president George H.W. Bush, Sr. was the last one notified of his intitiate class into S&B in 1948. In the article I wrote, *'Who Iz the UNCF?'*, you'll recall the Bush family having significant positionz in this so-called institution for negroes.

Jonathan Bush (George's bruh), was chairman of the UNCF until 1994 and George, himself, is still the honorary chairperson!! Bush also served as director of the CIA before running for office (also run by the Illuminati). Y would the UNCF, if "founded" by negroes, have one of satanz followerz occupy a high administrative position such as honorary chair?! It doesn't make sense...that's because the UNCF wasn't founded by negroes, it was founded by memberz of the Illuminati & S&B!

In *'George Bush, The Unauthorized Biography'*, it talks of Bush's upbringing. His father, Prescott Bush (also S&B, Class of 1917) and several other relatives and partnerz, in particular, Roland & Averell Harriman (also S&B), who sponsored the Bush family, the ones responsible for "grooming" George since an infant, to be the political figure he is today.

By special act of the state legislature in 1943, trustees are exempted from the normal requirement of filing corporate reports with the Connecticut Secretary of State. As of 1978, all business of the Russell Trust was handled by its lone trustee, Brown Brothers Harriman partner John B. Madden, Jr. Madden started BB Harriman in 1946, under senior partner Prescott Bush.

SKULL & BONES AND THE GERONIMO CONSPIRACY

One of the traditional artifacts collected and maintained within the High Street Tomb (S&Bs frat house on Yale's campus) are human skeletal remainz showcased in see-through coffinz. One in particular are the remainz of the infamous Geronimo, an Apache faction leader and warrior, who led a party of warriorz to fight YT after the Apaches were moved to the San Carlos Reservation in Arizona.

He led other revolts against US and Mexican forces well into the 1880s, being captured, then escaping many tymz. He later died at the age of 79 in Fort Sill, Oklahoma. Some 75 yearz later, his tribesman demanded his remainz returned back to Arizona.

According to Tribal Chairman of the San Carlos Apache Tribe, Ned Anderson, around the fall of 1983, they tried to get his remainz returned. After conducting an Apache Summit in Fort Still, Anderson was written up in the newspaperz as an articulate Apache activist. Soon after, in early '84, an S&B member contacted Anderson and leaked evidence that Geronimo's remainz had long been stolen by Prescott Bush – again George's pops.

The informant said that in May 1918, Prescott and 5 other officerz desecrated the grave of Geronimo. They took turnz watching while they robbed the grave (sound familiar to what YT did to our ancient Kemetic graves?), taking itemz including his skull, some other bones, a horse bit and straps. These itemz were taken back to the Tomb (frat house) and put into a display case, which memberz and visitorz could easily view upon entry to the building.

The informant said the remainz are used in performing some of their Thursday and Sunday nite ritualz with Geronimo's skull sitting out on a table in front of them. The general attitude of YT has long been that oppressed people of color should be stuffed and mounted for display to the "Fashionable Set."

Anderson was provided S&B recordz of the actual account, written by alias *'The Little Devil'*, dated June 17, 1933: *"From the war days* (WWI) *also sprang the mad expedition from the School of Fire at Fort Sill, Oklahoma, that brought to the T(omb) its most spectacular "crook," the skull of Geronimo the terrible, the Indian Chief who had taken 49 white scalps. An expedition in late May, 1918...an axe pried open the iron door of the tomb, and Pat(riarch) Bush entered and started to dig. We dug in turn...finally Pat(riarch) Ellergy James turned up a bridle,...then, at the exact bottom of the small round hole, Pat(riarch) James dug deep and pried out the trophy itself....We quickly closed the grave, shut the door and sped home to Pat(riarch) Mallon's room, where we cleaned the Bones. Mallon sat on the floor liberally applying carbolic acid. The Skull was fairly clean, having only some flesh inside and a little hair. I showered and hit the hay...a happy man..."*

Ellery James was in Prescott's wedding 3 yearz later, Neil Mallon, who applied the acid to the stolen skull, was chosen by Prescott as chairman of Dresser Industries. Mallon hired Prescott's son, George, for his first job, and George, in return, named his son Neil Mallon Bush, after the flesh-picker.

So you can see there was obvious allegiance to this family of thugz. In 1988, the Washington Post ran an article entitled, *'Skull for Scandal: Did Bush's Father Rob Geronimo's Grave?'*, BUT the article neglected to mention the otherz, pointing out Bush as the lone assailant.

As mentioned, each year S&B selects 15 third-year Yale students. Graduating memberz are given a sizeable cash bonus to help get them started in life. Older graduate memberz, the so-called "Patriarchs", give special backing in business, politics, ESPIONAGE and legal careerz.

S&B excellz in espionage. In fact, they served as Hitler's secret financerz during WWII. NY-based Chase Manhatten Bank, along with Ford Motor Company, was selected by the Treasury Secretary (Morgenthau) for post-war investigationz of pro-Nazi activities. Many large American firmz operated in France during German occupation.

As well, S&B has roots in Ingolstadt (remember? the home of the Illuminati). Chase is owned by the Rockefeller's, as well as Standard (now Exxon) Oil of New Jersey. The Rockefeller's can be linked to 1941, when they had 6 oil tankerz under Panamanian registry, manned by Nazi officerz to carry the fuel from Standard Oil to the Canary Islandz, a refueling base of Nazi submarines..

Chase and Ford also has a history of exporting U.S. technology to the Soviet Union as far back as the 1920s. Again, they play both sides of the fence, and profit immensely from it.

SKULL & BONES: A SECRET SOCIETY

Secret Societies have existed for some 200+ yearz in this country. Those on the inside know it as 'The Order', or as we say, New World Order or One World Government. This is the same order that is written on the back of the dollar bill, *"Novus Ordo Seclorum"*. This order also has an alias known as 'Chapter 322', the 2nd chapter of the German-based Illuminati. The story beginz at Yale University, New Haven, Connecticut, where 3 threadz of global white supremacy combine: espionage, drug smuggling and secret societies.

Elihu Yale

Elihu Yale, whom the University was named after, was born near Boston and educated in London. He served with the British East India Company eventually becoming governor of Fort Saint George, Madras, in 1687. He amassed (through theft) a great fortune and returned to England in 1699. He became a philanthropist and gave a lot of money to the Collegiate School in Connecticut. After numerous donationz of money and books, Coton Mather suggested the school be name Yale College in 1718.

Note that Yale University was here *before* there was a United States, implying that the secret societies out of Yale, including George Washington (who was a mason), were not working in favor of the U.S., because there *was no* U.S.! In fact, most, if not all citizenz of the "new world" were criminalz sent here to spy for England and Germany!!

Nathan Hale

A statue of Nathan Hale standz on the campus of Yale. A copy of the statue standz in front of the CIAs headquarterz in Langley, Virginia. Another is in front of Phillips Academy in Andover, Massachusetts, where fellow Bonesmen including ex-president George Bush, Sr. attended prep school.

Nathan Hale, along with 3 other Yale graduates, was a member of the Culper Ring, one of Americaz first intelligence operationz (spy agencies), established by first U.S. president, George Washington. The Culper Ring proved successful throughout the revolutionary war, except for Nathan, whose cover was blown and was hanged in 1776.

The First Chapter

The Illuminati was publicly founded May 1st, 1776 at the University of Ingolstadt by Professor Adam Weishaupt (this same day was the day americaz forefatherz signed the Luciferian Conspiracy.) This was the beginning of the new world order, or *"Annuit Coeptis, Novus Ordo Seclorum"* printed on the back of the $1 bill around our stolen pyramid.

The earliest memberz of Weishaupt's new order were drawn from among his students. On December 5, 1776, students at William and Mary college founded the first American secret society chapter of the Illuminati, Phi Beta Kappa. Phi Beta Kappa is the parent of all fraternal systemz in American "higher" education. This includes ALL negro fraternities (from the Alpha's to the Sigma Gamma Rho's and everyone thereafter) as well as their father, Sigma Pi Phi aka the Boule'.

The anti-Masonic movement of the1820s held groups such as Phi Beta Kappa, in a bad light. Because of the pressure, the society went public and what may seem simultaneously, S&B (the 2nd chapter of the Illuminati) was formed at Yale.

S&B has had major influence in politics since its inception. To name a few, S&B controlz the Council on Foreign Relations (CFR), which was started in 1922; the Rockefeller owned, Trilateral Commission (started 1973); and countless other organizationz that are all in on the control of people around the globe.

S&B AND THE DRUG GAME

In 1823, Samuel Russell established Russell and Company for the purpose of acquiring opium in Turkey and smuggling it to China. Russell and Co. bought out the Perkins (of Boston) syndicate in 1830 and moved the primary center of American opium smuggling to Connecticut. Some of the great American and European fortunes were built on the "China" trade. Most was made off the rape and smuggling of Afrikan natural resources such as oil, copper, silver, gold and diamondz as well as Afrikanz!

But Y all this interest in China? Because China is the largest producer and user of opiates of the world. In the 1800s, the Yankee Clippers, out of Connecticut and Massachusetts, were the fastest ships on the ocean. Whomever made the trip from Turkey, India to Macao, Hong Kong and Shanghai first got the most of their goodz.

In an article, *'Konspiracy Korner'*, by Kris, he wrote, *"During the Opium Wars, the US chose to stand on the sidelines and cheer for the English and French; knowing because of treaty obligations, the US would share in the profit. Russell & Co. was sometimes the only trading house operating and advantageously used the opportunity to form strong commercial ties and handsome profits. By 1843, the port of Shanghai was opened and Russell & Co. was one of its earliest traders."*

S&B has played a vital role in the worldz largest trade on the planet...the narcotics trade. George Bush, who's been with the CIA since the early 50s, was responsible for consolidating and coordinating the worldwide trade. Before the Vietnam War – which was a front so that Bush & Co. (S&B, Illuminati) could put this into effect – the Golden Triangle was run by French Intelligence and Corsican mobsterz, during, and since the war, the triangle has been run by U.S. Intelligence, with aid from Sicilian mobsterz. This is Y there should be no question as to the role of the CIA and the nationwide crack-cocaine epidemic that has plagued our Afrikan communities for some 15 yearz.

The wholesale importation of cocaine into the US during the Iran/Contra scam is also well documented and Bush is shown to be inner-connected with many of the playerz. Narcotics such as cocaine and heroin cannot be made without the precursor chemicalz. The largest maker of these is the EJ Lilly Company of Indianapolis, Indiana. The (Dan) Quayle family is a large stockholder and Bush has been on the Board of Directorz. EJ Lilly is also the company that first synthesized LSD, so the CIA could have an unlimited supply for the countless demonic spellz they've cast over the Afrikan community.

Yale University's administration has long been controlled by S&B, even before S&B was started! During the 150 year interval since 1833, active membership has evolved into a core group of perhaps 20-30 families. These families fall into 2 major groups:

1) Old line American families who arrived on the east coast in the 1600s, ie, Whitney's, Lord's, Phelps', Wadsworth's, Allen's, Bundy's, and Adams'. These families are mainly called 'Born Men'.

2) Families who acquired wealth in last 100 yearz who sent their sonz to Yale and, in tyme, became almost old line families, ie. the Harriman's, Rockefeller's, Payne's and Davison's. These families are called 'Made Men'.

Most memberz are from the eastern seaboard of the U.S. As late as 1950, only 3 memberz resided in LA, whereas a large number lived in the New Haven, Connecticut area. The family weed (not tree) of S&B is truly from the history of wickedness.

Rev. Nodiah Russell was one of the first 10-12 men who founded Yale University in 1701 along with Rev. James Pierpont. Nodiah had a son, William, who married James daughter, Mary. James other daughter, Sarah then married Jonathan Edwards who was president of Princeton University (then called College of New Jersey). William and Mary had 2 sonz, Nodiah and Samuel who both had sonz, Matthew Talcott Russell and Captain John Russell. William Huntington Russell, founder of S&B was the son of Matthew; and Samuel Russell who founded Russell Manufacturing Company and president of Middlesex County Bank was the offspring of Capt. John.

Sarah and Jonathan had 3 children, Pierpont, Esther and Mary. Pierpont was made master of Connecticut Masons by the British Army then occupying New York in 1783. He had a son, Henry, who was governor of Connecticut (1833, 1835-38) and protector of Samuel Russell's opium-financed enterprises.

Esther married then president of Princeton, Aaron Burr, Sr. They had a son, Aaron Burr, Jr., who was vice president of the US (1801-05) and a Wall Street lawyer, who became known for killing Alexander Hamilton in a duel in 1804. He was acquitted of treason in 1807, but wanted for murder, so he fled to England until his return to the U.S. in 1812.

Mary married Major Timothy Dwight who had 2 sonz named Theodore and Timothy. Theodore protected Russell's opium enterprise along with his cousin Aaron Burr, Jr. Timothy became president of Yale from 1795-1817.

ENTER DA TOMB

S&Bs house, known as "The Tomb", was invaded by a student group calling itself *"The Order of File & Claw"*, on Friday, September 29, 1876 at 8pm. They entered by prying through iron barz then digging through wood and dirt. From this break-in, much of the history of S&B was made public.

In 1856, "the Tomb", a vine-covered, windowless, brown-stone hall was built. Meetingz were (are) held there each and every Thursday and Sunday. The invaderz of the tomb found in the infamous lodge-room 322, the 'sanctum sanctorium' (most important) of the temple, furnished in red velvet and on the wall a pentagram (like the devilz). There is also a life-size Bones pin inlaid in the black marble floor.

In the adjacent room, room 323, catalogues of S&B along with the constitution of Phi Beta Kappa (the first secret society in the U.S., later forced to go public because of a blown cover – most notably the 1st chapter of the Illuminati) and the catalogue of Scroll & Key Society, another secret establishment at Yale.

One of the Illuminati's ritualz (degreez) was leaked out and classified as the *"Regent Degree in Illuminism"*. In it, a skeleton is pointed out to the initiate and at the foot of the table laid a crown and a sword. He is asked whether that is the skeleton of a king, nobleman or a beggar. Obviously confused because all he see's are skullz, the initiate is unable to provide the correct answer. The initiator then explainz to to him that the character of being a man is the only one that is of importance. In other wordz, after you're dead, nothing else matterz, so you better live your life now, 'cause when you're dead, you're dead!

This is the philosphy of YT ever since they were led out of the caucus caves by Moses and Abraham (read *'Iz YT Human? or Mutant!'* series). They've never known the concept of life on other planes other than the one they know of right now. They don't

The Tomb

believe in other formz of life because they are soul-less.

This ritual is, essentially, the same as the writing in da tomb. Inside da tomb, a passage can be seen as saying, *"Wer war der Thor, wer Weiser, Bettler oder Kaiser? Ob Arm, ob Reich, im Tode gleich"*. This translates to, *"Who was the fool, who the wise man, beggar or king? Whether poor or rith, all's the same in death."*

Initiation rites are held on Russell Trust owned, Deer Island, believed to be somewhere off the coast of New York. The ritualz have been said to be strenuous and traumatic. The so-called highlight of the initiation is having the initiation immersed NAKED in mud and inside a coffin. This ritual is known to be almost identical to the ritualz Masonz perform. The naked initiate is then confronted with a physical confrontation which ends up with the initiate being a voluntary 'victim' (for lack of a better word) of anal sex. This dates back to the greeks, the originatorz of faggotitis, where older men sexed the younger initiates implying they were 'injecting' manhood into them(?!!?) This ritual is know the Masonz as "riding the hump".

After initiation, the initiate's name is changed to "Knight (of the Round Table Group – read Masonry series) so and so", whereas the old Knights (graduating class of seniorz), name is changed to "PatriARCH so and so".

One must note the link of S&B with the Boule': memberz are called ARCHon's. There is no coincidence, since they are both "advisorz to the king", that the word ARCH is used. The Patriarch's, long after college life, specialize in giving backing to business, politics, ESPIONAGE and legal careerz to graduate Bonesman who exhibit talent or usefulness.

FAMOUS MEMBERZ

Since its founding, Skull & Bones has only inducted about 2,500 memberz. At any given tyme, approximately 600 memberz are alive. Don't sleep, this small number doesn't point out the tremendous concentration of power in the handz of its memberz.

If the memberz of Skull & Bones were to select a Hall of Fame from among their own elite ranks, some of the people whose names would almost certainly appear at the top of the list would be:

* Alphonso Taft, a founding member of the Order who served as the Secretary of War under President Rutherford B. Hayes (1876-1880).

* William Howard Taft, the only man to ever serve as both the President of and Chief Justice of the United States Supreme Court.

* Henry Lewis Stimson, partner in the Wall Street law firm of Root and Stimson, Secretary of War under President Taft (1908-1912), Governor General of the Philippines (1926-1928), Secretary of State under President Herbert Hoover (1929-1933) and Secretary of War under Presidents Franklin Delano Roosevelt and Harry S. Truman (1940-1946).

* Averell Harriman, investment banker with Brown Brothers Harriman, director of the Lend-Lease program of the U.S. State Department (1941-1942), U.S. Ambassador to the Soviet Union (1943-1946), Governor of New York, Under Secretary of State for Asia (1961-1963), and presidential secret envoy to Soviet leaders Stalin, Krushchev, Brezhnev and Andropov.

* Robert Lovett, partner in Brown Brothers Harriman, Assistant Secretary of War for Air (1941-1945), Deputy Secretary of Defense, Secretary of Defense (1950), leading member of the New York Council on Foreign Relations.

* Harold Stanley, investment banker, founder of Morgan Stanley.

* Robert A. Taft, United States Senator (1938-1950).

* Prescott Bush, investment banker and partner in Brown Brothers Harriman, United States Senator from Connecticut, father of George Herbert Walker Bush

* George Herbert Walker Bush, (initiated in 1948) President of the United States. Comes from a complete Bones family. United States Congressman (1964-1970), Chairman of the Republican National Committee, United States Ambassador to the United Nations, first American Diplomatic Liaison to the Peoples Republic of China, Director of the Central Intelligence Ageney (1975-1977). Vice President of the United States (1980-1988), President of the United States (1988-1992). Father Prescott, a Bones initiate of the class of 1917. Uncle George Herbert Walker, Bones Class of 1927. US Federal District Court Judge John Walker is also a relative and a Bonesman.

* John Thomas Daniels, agro-industnalist, founder of Archer Daniels Midland.

* Hugh Wilson, foreign service officer, Counsellor to Japan (1911-1921), U.S. Minister to Switzerland (1924-1927), Assistant Secretary of State (1937-1938). Ambassador to Germany 1938), Special Assistant to the Secretary of State (1939-1941), Office of Strategic Services (1941-1945).

* William F. Buckley, Jr. (Bones Class of 1950) Founder of National Review, the leading conservative magazine in the United States. Brother James (Skull & Bones 1944) is now a member of the U.S. Court of Appeals. William F. Buckley, Jr., former CIA officer in Mexico, also built the political grassroots conservative movement in the U.S. in the 1960s. President Bush and Buckley have recently split over Buckley's strong pro-israelizm.

• McGeorge Bundy (Skull & Bones initiate of 1940) Scion of the Skull & Bones Bundy family. Father Harvey H. Bundy was Skull & Bones, as was brother William P. Bundy. McGeorge served in the War Department during World WarII as Henry Stimson's assistant and later became the Nalional Security Adviser to President

Kennedy. William Bundy became a CIA official and later served in key positionz at the Departments of State and Defense. McGeorge headed the Ford Foundation (1968-1980) and William chaired the Council on Foreign Relations (1972-1983).

• Alfred Cowles (Class of 1913): Built the Cowles Communication empire based on the Des Moines (lowa) Register and the Minneapolis (Minnesota) Star and Tribune. These two newspaperz play a significant role in shaping the early presidential primaries, especially in Iowa.

• Hugh Cunningham (Bones 1934); CIA man from 1947 to 1973. He served in top positionz in the Clandestine Services, the Board of National Estimates and later as Director of Training.

• Thomas Daniels (initiated in 1914) founder of the largest agro-business and grain cartel company in Minnesota-Archer-Daniels-Midland (ADM) Served in the Foreign Service and later during World War II as head of the Fats and Oils Section of the War Production Board. ADM Corporationz new head Dwayne Andreas is one of the most powerful figures in U.S.-Soviet trade relationz. Daniels'only son, John (Bones 1943), also works in ADM. The bank which underwrites ADM stock issues is the Morgan Stanley investment bank.

• Richard Ely Danielson (Skull & Bones 1907) Past publisher of the Atlantic Monthly magazine, one of the leading magazines for seeing which policy line on a variety of issues is coming out of the Eastern Establishment.

• Russell Wheeler Davenport (initiated in 1923); Fortune magazine writer and editor, made this magazine the leading authority on financial matters in the United States. Davenport created the Fortune 500 companies list.

• Henry P. Davison (Bones Class of l920): Key senior partner in the Morgan banking and financial trust networks. His fellow Bonesman Harold Stanley (1908) founded the investment bank Morgan Stanley. Davison and his family helped set up the Guaranty Trust Corporation which became Morgan Guaranty Thomas Cochran (1904 Bonesman) was one of the most powerful partners in the Morgan bank. The influence of the Mgrgan banking system can be seen in its relationship with the hierarchy of U.S. intelligence. The head of the Office of Strategic Services, Gen. William Donovan, worked as a Morgan intelligence operative in the 1920s and prepared the intelligence reports for the Morgan banking concerns on developments in Europe. F. Trubee Davison became CIA Director of Personnel in 1951 and placed key Bonesmen in the right positionz inside the CIA.

• Averell Harriman (1913 initiate). Scion of the Harriman railroad family. His brother Roland (Skull & Bones 1917) ran the investment bank Brown Brothers Harriman. Averell was one of the most powerful memberz of the Skull & Bones fraternity, His

Pillsbury Doughboy Linked 2 Illuminati!
You may be thinkin' what I got against the Pillsbury Dough Boy?? Behind this cute little cuddly WHITE piece of dough with a smile is one of the chief memberz of the Illuminati!

All thingz have a root and we did some research on Pillsbury. It was started by John Sargent Pillsbury (1828-1901), who was a Minnesota Industrialist who attended one of the Ivy League colleges.

He was also a politician who served as governor of Minnesota from 1876-82 and before as state senator (1863-75). With family memberz, Pillsbury established the Pillsbury Mills in 1872.

By the early 1900s, Pillsbury had become the worldz largest flour mill. What's deep they use the colorz of the Masonz (white and light blue)! More importantly these wicked beasts specialize in the selling of one of the 3 most lethal "food" substances on the market...WHITE FLOUR (the otherz bein' white sugar and white rice)!

In 1967 it became the first major U.S. food company to enter the restaurant business, acquiring Burger King. So we see they are also behind the Fast Food

government posts ranged from Ambassador to Russia during World WarII and various State Department positionz to chief negotiator on the Vietnam Talks. Confidential adviser to Presidents Roosevelt, Truman, Kennedy, Johnson and later Nixon and Carter. His investment banking firm is virtually a Skull & Bones bank (nine senior partnerz are from Skull & Bones). President Bush's father worked in Brown Brothers Harriman after helping to merge several companies in the United Rubber Corporation of America.

• Winston Lord (Bones Class of 1959): Chairmah of the Council on Foreign Relations (1983-1988). Former State Department official and CIA officer in Asia. China expert. Six memberz of the Lord family were Skull & Bones, including Charles Edwin Lord, former Comptroller of the Currency, Department of the Treasury. Oswald Bates Lord (Skull & Bones 1926) married Mary Pillsbury of the Minnesota based Pillsbury Flour Corporation. Winston Lord is their son.

• Robert A. Lovett (1918 initiate): Put together the Brown Brothers Harriman merger and later organized the aviation industry mobilization for World WarII. Became part of the most exclusive power group in World WarII under Henry Stimson. Lovett was one of the five or six most powerful men in the United States for nearly 40 yearz until his death in 1986.

• Henry Luce (initiated in 1920): Built the Time-Life publishing empire. Became the leading publicist of the "American century" doctrine.

• Dino Pionzio (Bones Class of 1950): CIA deputy chief of station in Chile during the overthrow of Chilean President Salvador Allende. Now works at the investment firm Dillion Read.

• Alphonso Taft (initiated in 1833): Secretary of War (1876), Attorney General (1876-1877) and later Minister to Austria and Russia. Co-founder of Skull & Bones.

• Robert A. Taft (1910 initiate); Speaker of the House of Representatives (1921-1926) and Senator (R-Ohio). Leader of the Isolationist movement in the 1930s. His son Robert A. Taft, Jr., also senator from Ohio, led the right-wing of the Republican Party in the 1950s and 1960s. Robert A. Taft, Jr., however, was the only member of the Taft family who was not Skull & Bones.

• William H. Taft (Skull & Bones 1878): President of the United States (1908-1912) and appointed Chief Justice of the Supreme Court (1921-1930). Secretary of War (1904-1908). Trustee, Carnegie Institution. Part of the long line of Tafts who served in the U.S. government.

• William Collins Whitney (initiated 1863): Secretary of the Navy (1885-1889). Promoter of the Naval Shipyards and financier. Part of the Whitney family which sent eight of its memberz to Yale to become Skull & Bonesmen. Family intermarried with the Payne, Harriman and Vanderbilt clanz. The Whitneys became some of Wall Street's most powerful financiers through the Guaranty and Knickerbocker Trust Companies.

S&B findz their greatest power in the control (through membership) of multi-billion dollar foundationz, ie: Carnegie, Ford, Peabody, Slater, Russell Sage, Rockefeller, Harriman (railroadz), Weyerhauser (lumber), Kellogg's (cereal), Dodge (carz), John Deer (tractorz), Pillsbury (flour, breadz), Dean Witter Investments, and so on.

When studying global white supremist's you'll find the beast isn't hiding anything from you. It's just that he has convinced you that you do not want to read, and therefore, cease to be interested in the true oppressorz of our ongoing daily mentacide (mental suicide) as we walk the streets of the concrete jungle not realizing that we are the originatorz of life, art and creativity. For those that look shall find, I'm a living example of it! Continue to elevate!

LIK SHOT!!

Conspiracy! Pillsbury entered the pizza business in 1975 when it acquired Totino's Finer Foods. Three yearz later, through Pillsbury technology and Totino experience, the company's new crisp crust pizza became the best-selling frozen pizza in the United States. By the mid-1980s, Pillsbury had acquired another leading brand of pizza and hot snacks, Jeno's, and was producing almost 300 million pizzas a year more than one million pizzas for every working day.

In 1979, Pillsbury acquired Green Giant and became one of the largest processorz of branded vegetables in the world a leader in canned, frozen, and fresh vegetables and in agricultural research, worldwide sourcing, and distribution. I say processed because all the nutrients are taken out of processed foodz and replaced with sugarz and preservatives high in salt, offering the body basically no nutritional value.

Plain and simple, you eat white flour, you will definitely develop health problemz from osteoporosis to eventual AIDS (when you entire immune system become deficient)! Eating white flour causes your body to turn on itself, eating its body organz alive, little-by-little.

White flour used in breadz, cakes and other baked "goodz" (notice how these bad substances are called "good") have proven to be one of the leading causes of ailing body parts causing millionz of deaths annually. In turn, with companeez like Pillsbury remaining in operation, they assure the hospital administration (most run by Rockefeller) a continuous flow of loot mainly because the people do not know what is and what isn't good for the body.

Yeah, the dough boy is cute and whatnot with his little laugh when you touch his belly, but did you ever think that maybe he isn't laughin' 'cause it tickles, maybe he's laughin' all the way to the bank!

Who's the Next Savior??

by m bwebe aja ishangi

BOOK OF COMING FORTH BY DAY (at least 4266 BC)
HOLY BIBLE (0 AD)
KORAN (622 AD)

Flashback! Countdown… December 31st, 1999, Y2K came and gone! The world awaits the beginning of a new era. While many are preparin' themselves for the party of a lifetyme, many await the *"2nd Coming"* of Jesus Christ. To no avail, Jesus is a no show! The faithful have been misled, though they refuse to believe it. Instead, they randomly try and choose anutha date to buy their fate some tyme.

What happened? Y didn't "he" show? Religious folk will say, you can't predict when "he'll" come, "he'll" come when "he" wants to, *"like a thief in the nite."* Think about the people back in, say, 4000BC, even further back, like 25,000BC (BC, being 'Before Christ'), do you think they were waiting for the infamous "2nd Coming"?!

It may be hard for you to realize this but the dayz of worshipping Jesus are numbered! Look through the eyez of tyme and history Afrikanz. You will find that each era had a God they prayed to, then as hundredz of yearz passed, anutha God was chosen. The worship of Jesus Christ as the savior will serve to be no different than any of the other Godz of our past. It may be hard for you to believe that we are, in fact, at the dawn of that new age! The worship of Jesus Christ as the worldz savior reign is comin' to an end. The question is who's the next savior?

ASTROLOGEEZ IMPACT ON RELIGION

Our Ancestorz knew an enlightened people could never be enslaved and an ignorant people could never be set free. I know, you thinkin' just because Jesus hasn't revealed himself when you wanted to does not mean he doesn't exist. I assure you, it's not about that.

Not is it only because of his reluctance to reveal himself at the turn of the century, more importantly, because our Ancestorz in Kemet wrote it in the starz over 6000 yearz ago! What was known as the "Great Year" determined by what is called the 'Precision of the Equinoxes', which operates on accord to the 23.5° tilt of the Earth's axis. Our Ancestorz, who were also Gnostics (who the Biblical Jesus allegedly studied with), studied the wobbling effect of the Earth's axis and carved a great circle in the heavenz According the Wayne Chandler, author of *Ancient Future*, the Kemetianz calculated the tyme it takes for the Earth to go through each house of the zodiac which takes 25,920 (2+5+9+2+0=18 —> 1+8=9) yearz. Chandler writes, they *"divided this astronomical event into 12 parts, each representing a constellation usually symbolized by an animal. From these…we derive the 12 signs of the zodiac originating from the greek word 'zoion', which means 'animal'."*

Each zodiac takes up 30°. When we multiply 30 tymz the 12 signz, it equalz 360 (degreez or whole). Each period lasts approximately 2160 (2+1+6+0=9) yearz.

Multiply that by the 12 zodiacs, we come to 25,920, the Great Year. Some scientist's estimate we've gone through thousandz of Great Yearz. With the Earth estimated to be as old as 4.6 billion yearz, we've had to have gone through almost 177,500 Great Yearz! Even though it is estimated by YT that the human species – as they'd like us to know it – have been on Earth for only 115 Great Yearz, or about 3 million yearz. As each age passed the zodiacs influence can be seen.

The age of Gemini (6000-4000BC) was a tyme when humanz were recorded to have developed writing. This is not to say of the Great Yearz before, there was no writing, this is just when it was first documented. The recording and storing of information was created. Note, this age bearz a coincidence that Gemini is also the sign of communication.

Next was Taurus (4000-2000BC) where the inhabitant's witnessed new technology in buildingz and art, with the age of Aries (2000-1BC) bein' known as the 'Iron Age', characterized by its militancy. Kemet was overthrown by the Persianz, Greeks and then the Romanz during this period.

With the age we just left, Pisces (around 1-2000AD) is the period where christianity was enforced on the land, with Pisces, as the symbol of the fish, being the sign of spiritual knowledge.

WHAT WE ARE TOLD ISN'T ALWAYZ THE TRUTH

The thought of there soon bein' anutha God to take the place of Jesus may be sacrilegious to many. After all, to make such a statement would perceive many to believe I am an atheist (to a large degree, they're right!). When questioning religion, we all realize this to be a very touchy topic to discuss oftentymz ending in argument while very seldom enhancing comprehension.

That is Y I chose to write this piece. Not to continue the argument, but to use history as the measuring stick and show that Jesus wasn't alwayz the 'God of choice', and by lookin' at the history of wo/man, we will show that just as each era had it's own form of worship, their tyme came and went and a new belief system followed.

Just as I was led to believe growin' up in a non-Afrikan environment (society) that Jesus and God were the only 2 holy people I really had to worry about. The Bible achieves this fabrication by starting out in Genesis with the infamous wordz, *"In the Beginning."* To most, if not all, 'In the Beginning' is all they need to know. Because of the way our educational system has instilled in us to accept without question, many perceive the beginning to be just that, 'the beginning' and nothing coming *before* that. Bein' an Afrikan devoting myself to reclaim *Our*story, I couldn't be satisfied with goin' along with the status quo. As a Being of intellect, we deserve to know…

So when one readz the Bible and it talks of the beginning, one is misled to believe the Bible has alwayz been here, since the beginning of man, and even more egotistical, the beginning of tyme!

Using the Nile Valley as my measuring stick, you'll find no presence whatsoever of a text called the Holy Bible. In fact, you won't find *any* story of Jesus either!. In fact, the proof that the written life of Jesus is an exact plagiarized copy of the recorded life of Heru (Horus) – son of Ausar (Osirus) and Auset (Isis) can be read in Anthony Browder's, '*Nile Valley Contributions to Civilization, Vol. I*'.

What you will find is a spiritual text entitled, '*The Book of the Dead*' aka, '*The Book of Coming Forth By Day*' discovered (meaning it was here well before that) around 4266BC, during the reign of Hesep-ti, the 5th pharaoh of the 1st Dynasty.

From this you will find numerous similarities that are found in the Holy Bible. Now, using intelligence Afrikanz, it would be a BIG coincidence for a book to surface, with practically the same storyline and not be related. With the Holy Bible as a text, nowhere near 2000 yearz old, plus with the religion Christianity barely just over a millennium, it's hard to believe it is authentic with all the plagiarizm and book burningz YT has done for what seemz to be eonz. In fact, it is well known throughout those who've studied this topic that the Holy Bible is equivalent to being a sort of "cliffnotes" to the Book of the Dead.

Ask yourself, from what you know of Kemet, have you ever read or seen any icon that depicted any image of Jesus? No, they had their own God. We must overstand that our Ancestorz used holistic knowledge to dictate tyme millenniumz after they've been long gone. They found immortality by preserving the knowledge we now use today, yet fail to overstand, due to the ignorance of YT.

SOME EXAMPLES OF EARLIER BELIEFS

Back in the Nile Valley, around 4000BC, a new age had dawned, the age of Taurus. The Kemetic government was suddenly changed in both political and religious matterz along with habits, customz and beliefs. For instance, the custom of tying up the bodies of the dead so they couldn't walk about at the nite was stopped, women were treated with more respect and dignity and human sacrifice was restrained.

With this sudden cultural shock, the people experience a new consciousness. The KMTic priests instructed the pharaoh to have his queen wear a new crown of 2 hornz, symbolizing the hornz of the bull Taurus, with a disc, which symbolized the moon, between them. Auset can be seen wearin' this crown.

This crown was to commemorate the dawning of the age of Taurus and to show that there is both a female and a male force. Read about the Ausarian Drama and you'll learn of Auset's tenacity. 2100 yearz into the age of Taurus, iconz and statues of the bull, called Apis (which turnz out to be the first letter of the English alphabet) could be seen among the people living around the Mediterranean. Following Taurus came the dawning of a new age of the zodiac, Aries, the sign of the ram. It was during this age Moses came up out of Kemet and said, *"I am the ram, the ram of God."*

When Moses came down from the mountain of Sinai in Exodus 32, he found the people erroneously lapsed back into worshipping the bull (Taurus) with the making of the golden calf. Exodus 32:20 readz, *"Then he took the calf which they had made, burned it in the fire, and ground it to powder; and he scattered it on the water and made the children of Israil drink it."* Y? Because Moses had learned from the Kemetic Priests that the age of Taurus had passed and that they were livin' in the age of *Aries,* therefore, his people were "worshipping" the wrong icon! Most have been misled to believe he didn't want the people worshipping idolz, but it wasn't that... he didn't want them worshipping the wrong one!

After the age of Aries came the next zodiac, Pisces, the age we are about to depart from. Although the transition took a while, this is the tyme where christianity came into dominance, with its followerz choosing the fish as their symbol. Again, this is the age we are now moving out of! If you've ever noticed, on millionz of carz, you may see the model of a fish in the rear. As stated before, our Ancestorz already had an outline for the priesthood to follow. In Matthew 4:19 of the New Testament, we find the announcement of Jesus who said to his crew he would *"make you to become fishers of men."* Many associate the lamb and even the black panther to him, but never the fish. This fish symbol standz as the symbol of christianity where drawingz of the fish back in the day were used as secret signz between early christianz. And just as the people established the current symbol for which they worship, the next age will bring yet anutha symbol and, dare I say, *anutha belief system!*

3200 B.C.E.	1500 B.C.E	1000 B.C.	600 B.C.E.	114 A.C.E.
Ox's Head	Aelph = Ox	Aelph = Ox	Alpha	A
House	Beth = House	Beth = House and Doorway	Beta	B
Boomerang	Gimel = Throwing Stick	Hook	Gamma	C
Door	Daleth = Door		Delta	D
Man Shouting	He = Shouting Man		Epsilon	E

grafik 1: The english alphabet we use today has its origin from the Age of Taurus

THE AGE OF AQUARIUS

Almost 60 centureez before our era, our Ancients watched the reflecting light of the moon, as it moved slowly across the Pyramidz of Giza. Based on the movement of the moon, they calculated the light as it shown directly on the center of the Pyramidz shadow.

These measurements were compared with the measurement's they got from the sunz shadowz and gave them a date 6000 yearz into the future, in the astronomical age of Aquarius, the water bearer.

There have been several dates said to be the start of Aquarius. According to author of '*5/5/2000*', Richard Noone, it started August 20, 1953; Astrologist, Joanna Martine Woolfolk believed it started January 2000; and then there's the Mayan calendar that posts the date of December 2012. Regardless, we are either in the age or it is upon us and it can be seen by its definition.

So what should we expect from the age of Aquarius, the water bearer? It is said this will be a tyme where the concept of individual nationz will fade and that humankind will join together as one people (yeah, *if* and *only if* white supremacy is annihilated, and I will admit, we can see *some* decay).

This is a tyme where society will experience a new awareness and scientific knowledge and invention throughout the airwaves. With the rate of inventionz like the internet and space travel behind us, no tellin' what the world will see the next 2000 yearz, maybe even travel outside our solar system! With these

grafik 2: A symbol used during the Age of Pisces was the fish. This age started around 60BC. During this tymespan, the biblical Jesus became the symbollic 'God' of choice.

We are currently exiting this age and entering the Age of Aquarius, set to begin around 2100BC.

Over the next 2160 yearz, tyme will witness the decline in the belief in Jesus — who's really a carbon-copy of Heru (erroneously called Horus) from the Nile Valley — and the birth of a new belief system.

The decline is already happenin'. With perverted priest's, numerous jihadz and reverendz livin' like pimps, it will also include the belief's of islam, judaizm and pretty much every other belief system. History has proven it...

possibilities, the concept of the God we know that walked this Earth seemz diminutive.

Aquarius is also a mental sign. This is an era where the information age will see heights we haven't attained since the dayz of the Nile Valley – and we may even surpass it! The question is will the information overpower us, ie. computerz becomin' so fast and intelligent that it surpasses the mental intellect of man, or will we be able to reach a height we haven't seen since Kemet. This can happen if, and only if, we use our Afrikan Ancestorz as our measuring stick. If we continue to use YTs western way, we may surely become part of a matrix that could end mankind.

I have yet to find out who or what will be the next savior. After all, we've still got over 2100 yearz to go in the age Aquarius. We may not be actual witnesses to this change but do know this, it will come. History has proved it!

The question really is, who you gonna listen to, your Afrikan Ancestorz who prophesized this millenniumz ago, or some cracka who wants to continue holding you down using one of the 3 major western religionz (christianity, judaizm, islam) to derail you from knowing thyself. The choice is yourz, but the forecast soon will come to light.

MORE FIE-YAH!!

1997

Ford Foundation

EXPOSING WHITE SUPREMACIST ORGANIZATIONZ

BY M'BWEBE AJA ISHANGI

I was informed recently that Columbia University (in New York City) is financially funded by the Ford Foundation. One may ask what is wrong with that? If this is true, the Afrikan students who attend this university need to know about the Ford Foundation and how Columbia University, as well as numerous other institutionz of higher training (not learning) are affiliated with global white supremacy.

The Ford Foundation is a white supremacist foundation having connectionz with other foundationz and organizationz who are the very beasts that have been bringing in the New World Order since this country's forefatherz signed the declaration of the Luciferian Conspiracy back on on May 1st, 1776.

The Ford Foundation is closely associated with the Rockefeller (family) Foundation, Cecil Rhodes, Lord Rothschild, the racist media, the United Nationz and a whole entourage of global white supremacists, too many to be mentioned.

The three primary connectionz Ford has is with the Council on Foreign Relations (CFR), the Trilateral Commission (TLC), and Skull and Bones (S&B), the second chapter of the Illuminati. Quick note: Bill Clinton is a member of the CFR and a Cecil Rhodes Scholar as well, not to mention that the majority of politicianz in office are a member of some secret society!

In the book, *'Ideology of Philanthropy'*, it states, *"The ties between the Carnegie, Ford, and Rockefeller foundations and the CFR, which has played a central if unrecognized role in the determination (of foreign policy) since the 1930s, suggest the form that this influence sometimes takes."* This obviously states the Ford Foundation is a major constituent to the CFR. Along with other foundationz mentioned, the book also states the CFR receives funding from these foundationz. In the book, *'The CIA and the Cult of Intelligence'*, pg 237 states, *"the influential but private CFR, composed of several hundred of the country's top political, military, business, and academic leaders, has long been the CIA's principal 'constituency' in the American public,"* meaning, whatever the CFR sayz, the CIA (Central Intelligence Agency) does.

The CIA has done damage to Third World countries and in particular, individualz of Afrikan descent, including spying on Malcolm X, murdering Patrice Lumumba and Steven Biko, and notoriously plaguing Afrikan communities across America with, cocaine during the 1970s, *"mainly done to disassemble the Black Panther movement"* then in the mid-80s with crack-cocaine. Starting in the ghetto's of the west coast, the epidemic took but secondz to reach the east, zombifying our people into petty-theft junkies and 5¢ hoes.

The CIA is also the organization that, if not actually bringing in drugz (which is hard to believe), has a part in the shipment and dispersing of drugz into this country.

In the Lumpen Times, vol 3 #22, the article entitled, *'Snow Job: The CIA, Cocaine,'* and Bill Clinton, indicates how the CIA was running cocaine smuggling operationz in Mena, Arkansas. The article also points out Clinton's role. A book entitled, *'Dope, Inc.',* pointed the CIA once again running drugz with the white house and Oliver *'I don't know nuffin'* North in order to covertly finance their secret missionz.

All of this indicates that the Ford Foundation supports the CFR and the CFR is the chief constituency to the drug running CIA! And it is also obvious that the Ford Foundation, as well as Columbia University condone these actionz. The Ford Foundation is also a major fund contributor to the TLC, another entity in on the covert plan to colonize Afrikan people and other people of color around the globe, into the one world order. The TLC is the brother organization to the CFR and both are responsible for the CIA's drug running actionz.

Some names of people who are/were on the TLC as well as being a trustee in the Ford Foundation are: Andrew Brimmer, Hedley W. Donovan, Edwin W. Spencer (once a director of the foundation), and Glen E. Watts. Henry Kissinger and Cyrus Vance, both trilateralists, made it possible for marijuana to enter America from Central America, Portugal and Spain.

If killing people of color with drugz wasn't enuff, the Ford Foundation also fundz the TLC's population plan in the third world. The Rockefeller Foundation, as well as Ford, started the funding of the Rockefeller family's 'Population Council', indicated in G. William Domhoff's book, *'Who Rules America New',* and A. Ralph Epperson's, *'The Unseen Hand'.*

In Holly Skiar's, *'Trilateralism',* she indicates that John D. Rockefeller III founded the Population Council to reduce the population explosion in the Third World. We can see this carried out in the Cairo Population meeting held a couple yearz ago. This is where YT and some other traitorz to Afrikan wo/men talked about how to destroy Afrikan families and babies. The evidence is the many plagues that have almost annihilated our people with diseases from the ebola virus to AIDS; man-made diseases probably engineered at the CDC (Center for Disease Control) in Atlanta, Georgia.

These foundationz are also the puppeteerz to our "black" organizationz and have hired soundbwoyz to trail our leaderz. The "house nigger, field Afrikan" theory is alive and well. Like enslavement, it has only taken a more 'undacuva-right-in-front-of-your-nose-but-you-don'-tknow' approach. Take for instance brutha Malcolm.

In *'The Autobiography of Malcolm X',* Alex (Boule' member) Haley describes how he informed on Malcolm to a very high *"government official."* He also provided a lead to the real killerz of Malcolm. Haley writes that he was asked to go to New York to meet with *"this government official and the president of a foundation in the office of the foundation."* Haley also writes that this foundation was very instrumental in donating money to the Civil Rights era. This could only be one of two foundationz... The Rockefeller Foundation or the Ford Foundation, or perhaps both.

It should also be noted that not only were they instrumental, both foundationz were the main financierz of the Civil Rights Movement! The indication is clear, for those who can cypher this ill subliminal; the order to kill Malcolm may not have come directly from Elijah Muhammad, but from the government through the Ford/Rockefeller Foundation!

How can global white supremist murdererz, like Ford and Rockefeller, fund a "legit" movement like the Civil Rights Movement unless this "legit" movement was working to their benefit?! Ask yourself Afrikan, what has the Civil Rights era done for us lately?!

'The Rockefeller Files', by Gary Allen, wrote the Rockefellerz were known as *"the family that preys together"*. He also noted that their motto was, *"the key to this system is giving up ownership but retaining control"* In other wordz, it is better to have your assets owned by a trust or foundation – which you control than to have them in your own name.

If you can make a company dependent on your financial contributionz, you can easily manipulate and even dictate that company's agenda. The Rockefellerz invented a scheme, used by the super-rich today, whereby the more money you appear to give away, the richer and more powerful you become. This allowz them to dictate to any organization to work to their benefit as well as evade paying taxes.

The deep thing is that most of the money they give away is to themselves!! For 3 generationz they've been "giving away" millionz – giving much of it to themselves. For example, they may give $1million of stock in the titanic oil corporation to the dogwood foundation – which the family controlz. They are not really out $1million; they just transferred title of securities to an alter ego.

This puppeteer (ie, Rockefeller/Ford) doesn't always have to do the work himself; he has puppets (the government, CIA, including the Boule', NAACP, Urban League, etc. – receive funding/instructionz from these and other unmentioned foundationz who make up the New World Order. It must be noted that the National Association for the Advancement of *CERTAIN* People's (NAACP) main financial contributor is... drum roll please... the Rockefeller Foundation!!

When we study America's institutionz of higher training, we will find that most, if not all, fall under the umbrella of the Illuminati. It is here where they begin to breed their poisonous virus into the mindz of soon-to-be pawnz (those who submit to their deedz and join the ranks), while those that resist will find it quite difficult to find work that'll keep food on the table.

Black colleges are no exception. If you research the founderz of these "historic" black colleges, you'll find they were white!! You'll find their major funding come from the bloody handz of the Illuminati, and you'll probably find the highest formz of surveillance/monitoring of possible future messiahz on these Black campuses (Martin Luther King was spied on as early as his collegiate yearz)!

LIK SHOT!!
(some influence from FRONTLINE magazine)

1996

For one to understand the relationship of any two subjects, you must alwayz, *alwayz* start at the beginning. Afrikanz, as the true heirz of civilization, must realize that this war, or struggle (as some call it), is not a physical one. It is more spiritual than physical. The physical *will* take a part, however it is but a small part of the cypher.

There's been a spiritual war going for nearly 6000 yearz and it's gettin' pipin' hot, Sun! As we strive for understanding and righteousness, we will get a clearer view of the beast that standz invisibly, yet very visible, before us. With that in mind, I now pose the following questionz: (1)Who was the first man and woman on the earth? And (2)how did we get all these different ethnic backgroundz from this one, or same man and woman? These questions have caused many to consistently attempt to sway away from gettin' to the real, hardcore truth of the matter. Often tymz, the seekerz have been told by our parents, teacherz, and preacherz that *"it doesn't matter, God made all of us."* Well that's open for debate. If this is so, my question is Y and how were all of us made?

I forewarn those sensitive, fragile mindz that might not be able to handle an in-depth perception I'm about to parlay over the next few pages, so for those, I suggest you go and pick up a copy of Reader's Digest or even contact your pimp, oops, I mean preacher to soothe (numb) your psyche so that you may run yet anutha 100 yardz from this topic. This piece is dedicated to those that strive to unrelish the many yearz of lies and lost information the devil hoped we would never ever find again...The true relationship between the Afrikan and the whiteman from the caucus mountainz.

I pose the next question, which happens to be the focal point of this piece, "IZ YT Hueman or Mutant?" Western science got people in a whirl. We don't know if man evolved from primitive apes or whether it just started with Adam and Eve. Western science is so quick to say we were once apes but cannot tell how and Y we evolved. The best theologianz can tell you about Adam and Eve is that they parented all the different colorz of people today. There is some truth to this Afrikanz, but you must separate it from the rest of the bullshit they want you to get entangled in.

Ask yourself, a far back as you can go, what group of people has a history of killing, raping, stealing, and suppressing other ethnic backgroundz? Everyone knowz what race is responsible for the deterioration of cultures (ie, the near total annihilation of native americanz) and the earth (the depletion of the ozone, oil spillz, toxic animalz used for food). The question is Y? Y are they like they are and Y do they have such a vendetta against the earth and people of color? Because they are not human. The root word of human is hue, which meanz black. So when we talk about humanity we talk about the black-faced people. But when we talk of mankind or kind of man, this is where YT fallz in.

BLACK PEOPLE WERE THE FIRST & WE MADE YT (THE WHITEMAN)

When studying the beginning you cannot start with Genesis. Before Adam was even thought of, Black people lived in a civilized manner. The bible sets the origin of Adam and Eve around 4000BC., or nearly 6000 yearz ago. Whereas, western science has contradicted its fellow theologianz of the bible by finding almost a full skeleton of a woman, in Afrika, and her bones dated at least to be some 200,000 yearz old, or nearly 180,000 yearz ago! The bugged shit is that they gave her a european name, Lucy!

Our history goes back farther than the bible. The original trinity came from ancient KMT (YT's call egypt). The Ausarian Drama talks about the origin of Ausar, Auset, Horus, and Seth – you may have been taught that their names were Osiris, Isis, Heru, and Set. Seth (anutha name of satan) was the brother of Ausar.

The first creation of Godz (I'll explain what God meanz later) brought forth a set of twinz. Each pair of Godz were only supposed to bear one offspring. Each offspring consisted of a set of male and female twinz. The first creation of Godz were the God Shu and Goddess Tefnut. Next came the God Geb and Goddess (of the sky) Nut. They beared Ausar and Auset. Geb and Nut unwillingly bore another set of twins, Seth and Nepthys. The forced manifestation of Seth disturbed the regular process of creation. From day one, Seth was not right. On the scribes inside the pyramidz can be read how Seth's own mother disowned him because of his wickedness.

WHO IS GOD AND WHAT IS THE GOD COMPLEX?

Many wonder, if we were so in touch with ourselves and our maker in ancient KMT, how did we lose everything? This is anutha story very seldom told. Most do not know that Seth was, at one tyme, elevated to a deity of God of state beside Amon, Ptah, and Re. First, it must be known, that our Ancestorz, initially, wasn't down with the concept of Seth (who, at that tyme, long after known as the lord of the desert people – will explain later). If you read Psalms 82:6-7, it sayz (in so many wordz), *"I have said ye are Gods and children of the most high, but you shall die like men."*

The term 'God' comes from the Hebrew, 'Elohim', which is the plural term for male and female. Elohim, or God, was never meant to be a name, it is a title. If you look metaphysically, God comes to 180 degreez, or half of 360 degreez. Which explainz Y wo/man has the "choice" to either be a God, or a doG (which spelled backwardz depicts a lower, beastly self).

This concept is synonymous with Her-Em-Akhet (incorrectly called the sphinx), because it represents the body of a lion, the king of the beasts; and the head of a hueman, which is the God in you taming the beast, or 180 degreez of negativity in you. This, of course, was our original mathematics before the concept of evil (again, which didn't evolve until around 4000BC). Before that tyme, our Ancestorz possessed 360 degreez positivity; which meanz they knew no degreez of negativity. So it was hard for them to not trust these devilz, who came back to KMT, claiming they were our 'lost cousins' and were victimz of being "grafted" into their current mutative state. So they took the desert people into their heart.

WHAT IS THE ORIGIN OF YT?

To get biblical on you again, if you read Genesis 1:26, it sayz, *"Let Us make man in Our image..."* Who is *'Us'*?!!? Is that not in plural form?! The bible never sayz that Adam was the first man and never sayz that he was good like everything else "he" created. In fact, Adam was the first who sinned. It was through Adam where sin entered the world. In the 14th century, Tomas Scoto, a spanish monk wrote a book talking of this. He wrote, *"There were men before Adam and Adam was made by those men."* It must also be noted that he was executed for displaying such truth to the people. If you read the Holy Qu'ran 2:28, it talks about the Angelz warning that the arrival of Adam would only *"cause mischief and cause the shedding of blood."*

We also were never told that Adam and Eve represented a group of people; they were not singular. The word, Adam, was originally written Adham, and is plural for male and female. This word stemz from the hebrew root 'dm', which meanz reddish or ruddy in color. When you look up the word ruddy, we get the definition, *"pink colored or reddish"*. Because Adham lacked melanin (skin color), his blood showed through his skin. Adham was the first albino. This is where we start building: Adham and Edom both mean red. Edom was another name for Esau, the twin brother of Jacob. Muslimz know him as Yakub.

WHO WAS JACOB (YAKUB)?

In Genesis 25:22, we read of Jacob and Esau struggling with each other in Rebecca's womb. We must note that the story of Jacob and that of Yakub is very similar, practically identical – just like the story of the mythical Jesus and Heru. When Jacob(Yakub) was 6, while playing with 2 pieces of a magnet, he discovered that opposite poles attract and the like poles repelled. He later drew the hypothesis that unalike attracted alike. He then swore that he would make a race of people, who would be unalike, and teach them how to rule the alike (Gen. 30:35).

At 18, he mastered many sciences and realized 30% of the Nile Valley people were dissatisfied. He put together a plan where the 30% would benefit. He became so influential, the pharaoh had him put in jail for potential disruption of what was the original (natural) way of life. But that didn't stop him.

In jail he took his theories and recruited more believerz. The pharaoh, getting word of this, met with Jacob and asked what he could do to appease him. The pharaoh ended up granting him the island of Pelan (aka Patmos) in the Aegan sea. The Aegan sea is above the Mediterranean sea between Greece and Turkey.

Jacob took, along with him, 59,999 followerz and settled on the island of Pelan. On the island, he became the ruler and set up birth control lawz. Marriage was based on how light the skin was. At the same tyme, he ordered all dark-skinned babies born to be killed at once. He lied to the motherz telling them the babies were angelz from heaven and needed to be sacrificed so that they may prepare a place in heaven for them. While, on the other hand, the motherz of the lighter-skinned babies were told to take good care for their children. They were instructed to educate them so that one day they would be a great people.

This process of elimination was referred to as “the grafting process”. Common sense would tell you that annihilating all black babies to where there are only light-skinned babies, and they grow up and have children of their own, that their child would not come out as a dark baby. That is because you cannot get a dark color unless you merge it with anutha dark color. If there are no dark colorz in existence, the color will, over tyme, turn lighter and lighter, generation after generation.

Jacob, or Yakub, lived to be 150 yearz old, but his grafting process lasted 600 (Gen. 31:41). At the end of 600 yearz, the once, melanated, dark complexioned Afrikan from the Nile Valley was a weak boned, reddish, pale-faced race. They then returned to the Nile Valley and cried unto the original black-faced people, claiming to be their descendants who had been badly mutated. The originalz, probably having at the tyme 360 degreez positivity and knowing no negative, took the them in giving them food, clothing, and shelter.

Some 6 months later, the visitorz started causing mischief. They started with tricknology. Spreading lies, pitting original against original, causing them to fight and murder each other. This is an ancient version of black-on-black crime; which was and still is, instigated by someone who ain’t black! It must also be noted that historianz can recall that around this same tyme, nearly 6 millenniumz ago, disruption began in ancient KMT. The originalz could not understand Y they could not reestablish peace so they consulted the pharaoh. The pharaoh indentified the culprit... it was the pale-faced abino’s.

The pharaoh instructed the originalz to round them up (Gen. 3:24), strip them of their clothes, put an apron on them to hide their nakedness, take all literature from them, and make them walk across the Sahara desert (2200 miles) to the caucus mountainz out of Eden. As they walked across the desert, the originalz rode on camelz. If anyone looked back, or tried to escape, they were killed instantly. If they were able to cross the desert alive, they were left to live in the *caucus* mountainz (is that not where the world *‘caucasian’* comes from? – think Afrikan, it ain’t that hard!).

They were sentenced to live there for 2000 yearz. This is also synonymous with Adham and Eve being exiled from the Garden of Eden, which is in ancient KMT. It wasn’t necessarily the apple that made them evil, they were from the beginning! They were instructed to watch the garden and never eat from the tree of life, the tree of life is symbolic for knowledge, not food for your stomach, but food for your spiritual development. So instead, they desecrated it because their lack of melanin made them incapable of doing!

To ensure they would not escape, or return to the Nile Valley, they were “roped” inside this area, which legend has it, is where we get ‘Europe’ and ‘European’ from. There was a great wall built, 666 miles in circumference, around the roped in area where they dwelled for the next 2000 yearz. Sentinelz (same name used for the huge robots on X-Men, but that’s anutha story), were placed along the wall to guard them and keep them from paradise.

By being cut off from civilization, and led into the cold, wild, and uncultivated mountainz of the northern hemisphere, they soon lost their knowledge of KMT. They went through a physical and psychological change. They lost the concept of God, they eventually lost their language and began grunting, the only life they could imitate was that of the beasts that roamed the land. They soon began to act like these beasts, lay with these beasts, and develop the psyche of an animal. That's where we get to terminology "survival of the fittest".

At the same tyme, the environment had a huge impact on them. They were already pale-skinned. They became even more pale because of the lack of light and heat from the sun. This is where their lips became thinner. This is where their hair began to change from kinky to long and straight. This is where their noses became longer so that the nostrilz could warm the air before it entered the lungz. The hair grew to cover up the body so that they could be warmer (ever see the amount of hair that growz on their backs?) This can also be linked to them practicing beastiality (sexin' it up with animalz). Could this be where we get doggy-style?

Anywayz, back to the disses; this is where their shapes went through a physical change; where their buttocks shrank and went inward because of them walking on all fourz. Some of this may seem raw, but think about it. We are physically different!

The survival tactics changed. Think about it. If you, and a whole bunch of otherz were starvin', plus you crazy cold, and you come upon some food you saw some wolves devouring, you'd probably end up fighting, and possibly killing each other before you would go for the food. Y? 'Cause that's how animalz act. They only share in the kill. But when its tyme to eat, they fight 'cause they don't know when the next meal is comin'!

This, now european, lived in caves, trees, and trenches. The trenches were holes they dug up and used as shelter. They would use their body waste (feces) to seal up the holes because the steam from the shit would warm the hole. But then again, they didn't wash – it was too cold to, plus they lost the knowledge of civilization.

They also started eating raw, unseasoned flesh, because they lost the knowledge of fire. You see, Afrikan when they talk about people coming from apes and living in caves, they're correct. Except we must know that it doesn't include us! This was the sentence the Godz (originalz) gave the them for being what he is... not original!

However, there came a tyme when a man by the name of Musa (or Moses) left KMT and came to this land to "civilize" these devilz. He taught them how to live respectful lives, how to build a home, and some forgotten tricknowledge their father, Jacob (Yakub), gave them. The forgotten tricknowledge consisted of 1)Devilishment; 2)Telling lies; 3)Stealing and; 4)How to master the original man. It was Moses who taught the devil to wage war against us! He is also greatly responsible for the demise of ancient KMT. Christianity wants you to believe Moses was good. But due to his "good" work, the children of these albino's, came back to KMT as the persianz, greeks and romanz, and now modern euro's/caucasianz and currently have been on a rampant move to destruct the original wo/man and the earth!

This bringz us to the here and now. We all know that YT despises us, yet wants to be us! We know this because you can go to any vitamin store and see the increasingly popular sale of a new product called "Melatonin"! What is the root of the word? Melanin. It is what gives us our skin complexion. It is also responsible for the rhythmic affiliation we have with The Supreme Being/Creator, The Universe, and Life itself. We must understand that this is a war based on good vs. evil, black vs. white, and melanin vs. melanin-less.

You can also see the infatuation with blackness that YT has. The need to get a tan bearz confirmation. They've taken rock-n-roll, blues, jazz, and are in the process of takin' Hiphop. The fact that a womanz ideal man is, *"tall, DARK, and handsome"* is even more truth. Racizm and white supremacy exists is anutha obvious fact. We must understand that dating back to the first tyme we dealt with YT they tried to take. We welcomed them back into KMT, feeling sorry for their being grafted, and what did they do? They alwayz will come to us as peaceful, loving people at first, but behind our backs they are the barbarous, unbalanced, and heathenish, just like how their foreparents were.

This beast knowz his tyme is up. He was given a chance to walk the earth for 6000 yearz and try to take the original people away from their God complex. He has done so by using white religion (many call christianity, catholicizm, and islam) to have us believe that we are all one, including YT. It is tyme we begin to seek the truth ourselves, AND YOU WILL NOT FIND IT IN A CHURCH!!

YT can never attain a God complex and he knowz it. YT knowz that we are "god". That is Y they tried to destroy everything in KMT and stolen our arts and sciences. That is Y they went through great lengths to bring us over here to build their nation. The leaderz of The New World Order know we are God. That is Y they are trying to genetically merge with melanated people (Biochip technology). Knowing that we are "God", they also know that they are not. Yet, still they want to be. They are trying to be, but their genetic makeup only allowz them to be the opposite of good. That is Y he tries to do it artificially. That does not mean we should have pity on them. Afterall, who's responsible for the world warz, famine, theft and corruption?? YT!!

We've been doing that for almost 6 millenniumz and, instead, we are the ones who die spiritually and physically from it. That is Y they are selling melatonin. That is Y they think they understand our music – that is also Y they are trying to take anutha music art form, reggae. Everything they do is artificial. They artificially think they got the holy ghost, they artificially think they are of The Creator, they artificially think they can dance, and artificially think they are going to bring the original wo/man physically and spiritually down to their level.

As we draw near the ended contract of wickedness, know that he is not going without a fight. He will try to kill everyone on the planet if he can. The revolution may happen within our lifetyme bruthaz and sistaz. Y sleep and do nothin'? This is the day of a new awakening where Afrikanz will no longer let otherz dictate to us what we should and should not know. The knowledge is out there, you just gotta dig for it. Remember, *"Knowledge of Self Can Only Be Found Undaground!"* Besides, who's side are you on, the Huemanz or Mutants?!

I know a lot of you may find it hard to believe what you just read. Since many of us have to hear it from someone else who's been published before we believe, part 2 will entail several sources written from both black *and* white authorz. Read on!

LIK SHOT!!

It seems that YT can't get enuff of this race-relationz talk. Y? Y is there sudden resurrected mass debate in schoolz across the country about race? Y has the jewish pirate, steven speilburg, put out a movie about the Afrikan uprising on a slaveship (Amistad)?

Could it be that the zodiac's prophecy is true? Could it be we are entering the age of Aquarius – where the need to know truth is ever-increasing?? Could YT be trying to set up a diversion so that the message will be confusing?? Since all the newspaperz and TV's are talkin' about race, I knew the Ancestorz were preparing me to come with a part 2 to the controversial piece, *"IZ YT Hueman? or Mutant!"*

YT has alwayz been anti-natural creation since *their* creation. Probably because they were not equipped with all the gifts that make up their parents, the Afrikan (originally called Akebulan). Historian, Llaila O. Afrika, analyzed the historical behavior of YT to the deficient amount of natural elements in the caucus mountainz, from whence they came. When the pineal gland is deficient of melanin producing elements (fruits and nutrients in the soil), it makes one think more with their left (destructive) side of the brain. It must be noted that the body is made up of pairz: 2 feet, armz, legz, handz, eyez, nostrilz and even brainz – the right and left brain.

How did YT get to the mountainous region in order to have such deficiency in the first place?? If you haven't read part 1, here's a summary. NOTE: As in part 1, I will be using several books as a reference including the bible. Y? Because, by showing you certain gemz within the very book many of our people have been programmed to revere, it still has some truth in it.

Between 6-7000 yearz ago, signz of disruption began to appear in the ancient civilization of the Nile Valley, in Afrika. Still Afrikan and not quite white yet, they first appeared on the island of Pelan, near the Aegean Sea; this is where the transformation began by a process of selective breeding called "grafting".

Yakub (biblically, Jacob), a black man, was the leader of Pelan. He placed a system of birth lawz by which marriage was based on skin color with only the lighter complexioned babies being allowed to survive. After 600 yearz of grafting, the people had become very pale and white. When these 'pale-skinned, but Afrikan featured' (aka Albino's) showed up again in the Nile Valley, they were soon driven out and exiled to the hillz of West Asia where they stayed for 2000 yearz. In West Asia (really Europe), over 2 millenniumz without the knowledge of Kemet along less sunlight, limited plantlife and the absence of melanin in the soil, they slowly slipped into a life of savagery imitating wild life. This is where we see the grunting and walking on all fourz of the caveman evolved. Even the great(?) Charles Darwin of the Darwin Theory spoke of some form of selective breeding had to have occurred in order for all the different ethnicity's to exist today.

History showz that the disruption that occurred in the Nile Valley I spoke of earlier happened just BEFORE the sudden appearance of YT in West Asia! I don't know Y Moses did it, but, according to the bible, he went to the caucus mountainz and gave YT 33 1/3 (which we know as tricknology) of the 360 degreez of knowledge of ancient Kemet. It is he who taught the beast to wage war against Kemet! They returned blazing temples, stealing and plagiarizing our history and murdering the people, and we have Moses to thank for this!!

Let me make this clear, the "hallow", I mean, "holy" bible never sayz Adam was the first man. Gen. 30:35, speaks of Jacob being able to produce unusually colored flocks of sheep and goat through a skillful technique called breeding (grafting). Biblically, it took him 6 yearz to change the flock (Gen. 31:41).

Tomas Scoto, a 14th century Spanish Monk, was put on trial and executed after he tried to reveal this information. He said that the 'Adam & Eve theory' was simply the making of one group of species by another. He was quoted in recordz – still held in the Church of Spain – saying, *"there were men before Adam and Adam was made by these men."*

Even in the Holy Qu'ran (2:28) the angelz give warning before the making of Adam, saying his arrival would *"only create mischief and cause the shedding of blood."* Has there not been more bloodshed since YT's arrival? Have not the number of warz more than quadrupled??

Early followerz of Jesus also believed people lived before Adam. The early church fatherz, St. Paul and St. Augustine wrote about it. In 1655, Isaac de la Peyrene, an orthodox priest, published a book entitled, *'Men Before Adam'*. He stated that Adam was the *"one man through whom sin entered the world."*

If you read Gen. 1:26, it states, *"...and God said, Let US make man in OUR image..."* The english word "God" is from the translated hebrew word, "Elohim", which is plural. 'El' meanz God, divinity, from which comes the second, a feminine form, 'Eloh', meaning Goddess; and 'im' is masculine plural. Elohim isn't a name, it is a title!

In Gen. 6:1-4, it talks about the rape of the Afrikan woman and the birth of a mutant kind-of-man (or mankind), birthed from a man not of a woman. What we have living with the Originalz (Afrikanz) is a mutated half-brutha. Those who govern the material power of the earth [the one world government (OWG), aka new world order] are those who have fallen from the higher heaven. The fallen are imperfect (lack melanin) that use their power to establish themselves as godz in the lower world.

The global genocide against natural creation, the Afrikan holocaust, is a planned event by the fallen ones, the OWG. In essence, there is no Afrikan-American, Haitian, Jamaican, nor european for that matter. There are nothing but neocolonial titles set up by the OWG who just so happenz to be our evil half-bruthaz – the descendants of the romanz, greeks, so-called jew and arab – who are nothing but a carbon-copy of the

The Book of Enoch was removed from the Bible probably because it spoke of Azazel being made to live in the caves for 2000 yearz.

original creation.

In Ethiopia, a group of 19th century explorerz uncovered an ancient document called *'The Book of Adam & Eve',* believed to be part of the Lost Books of Eden. It talks about a people's forced walk across a desert and eventually living inside a cave. *"And, indeed when Adam looked at his flesh, that was altered, he wept bitterly, he & Eve, over what they had done...And as they came to it, Adam wept over himself and said to Eve, 'Look at this cave that is to be our prison in this world, and a place of punishment.'"* Now what do they mean by Adam's flesh being "altered"... altered from what, to what?!!?

It must be noted that once a year, on the eve of the Jewish Day of Atonement, a ceremony is traditionally performed in which a goat (Azazel – anutha hebrew name for the white race and also the devil) is tied to a rope and led away from the people out into the desert and abandoned in a place of hillz and rocks. This ceremony can also be found in Leviticus 16:21-22: *"He shall put both hands on the goats head and confess over it all the evils, sins and rebellions of the people of Israel, and so transfer them to the goat's head. Then the goat is to be driven off into the desert by a man appointed to do it. The goat will carry all their sins away with him into some uninhabited land."*

Also if you read Leviticus 14:4-7, white birdz are used in the so-called "purification" of leperz. Goats, white birdz (doves) and leperz are all representatives of YT.

The Book of Enoch was removed from the Bible probably because it spoke of Azazel being made to live in the caves for 2000 yearz. The life of the caveman was a grotesque punishment indeed. Not only did he reside in caves, he also lived in man-made holes. The holes usually were 10-15 feet. In the winter, he would cover the hole with his manure (shit), which served as a blockade against the cold air. The steam from the shit also proved useful as a humidifier. No question, it was a *"good place for a Stick-Up!"* Through study of the history of Europe, I found staying beneath massive piles of human waste was commonplace throughout!!

The 'mind fuck' put on Afrikanz started with the bible. Historian, John Henrik Clarke stated, *"during the period of slavery, Africans in America estranged from their culture and their religion wanted to associate with a people who had escaped from bondage. Those who could read the Bible accepted the story of the Exodus literally. This story of Jews escaping from bondage in Egypt became more real to them than to others because they were slaves holding onto the thin hope of escape. Jewish joke, I mean, folklore became real to them. This is a part of Black America's sentimental attachment to the Jewish people, sometimes called friendship and an alliance...Today, a large number of Black Americans think of the Jews as people of The Book, and they look more favorably on them than on other Caucasians. These poorly informed Blacks do not know that the Jews of Europe played the same role in their enslavement, oppression and colonization as other Europeans."*

He further stated, *"This charge* (being labeled anti-semetic), *too often repeated, tends to inform the Jews are not to be judged by the same rules as are the rest of humanity."* It must be noted that the word 'Jew' is nothing but a European creation. Although YT created confusion with man-made translated religion, there are thingz in the bible that the youngest searcher for truth could find. Up until the last century or so, YT had not one care for people of color. Not once did they think the hundredz of thousandz of rapes, lynchingz and murderz were "non-christian". Psychologically speaking, they were being true to themselves, for that is exactly what they learned being in the caucus mountainz, away from the touch (knowledge) of Ra (the Sun). Their behavior has and alwayz will be correlated to the wild beasts of nature, the lower self or the lion part of Her-Em-Akhet we studied in Kemet.

Just recently YTs been "acting" like they're humanitarianz; tryin' to conserve energy, LiveAID concerts and 'Save the whales' and shit. Notice how they will raise millionz of dollarz to save whales instead of starving, homeless and/or uneducated people!

Now they want to reverse gearz and claim we are all the same! Y the sudden change?? Because the root of truth is breaking through the concrete pavement of white supremacy. As YT seez more and more Afrikanz re-transforming to their natural selves (growing locks, moving from 'negro', to 'colored', to 'black', to now 'African-American'), they shittin' they pants! So they try to drug us again with religion. But even the biblical Jesus showed he wasn't down with YT.

In Mark 7:24-29 and Matthew 15:21-28, he refused to help a woman because she was white (a Greek) and also called her a dog! Since she was so persistent, his crew of disciples persuaded him to help her before her cries attract the Roman soldierz (da police bwoy dem). Matthew 10:5-6, he commanded his crew to go NOT to the Gentiles (YT), *"But go rather to the lost sheep of the house of Israel,"* (Afrikanz).

IF WE *WERE* BACK IN THE DAY, HOW DID WE LOSE IT??

After the making of YT, Yakubz revelation was soon lived out. Yakub, through his birth control lawz, had each and every dark seed killed, leaving his lighter complexioned babies to survive until eventually there was a pale-skinned race of people. They were told that one day they would rule the world. The way YT colonized Afrika in the 1400s was somewhat complex, yet very simple in principle... simply divide and conquer!

There were many tribal warz at that tyme with the stronger Afrikanz pushing the weaker Afrikanz to the coastal areas. YT approached the weaker Afrikanz offering gunz and ammunition to help them ultimately conquer the stronger Afrikanz. The weaker Afrikanz now had superior weaponry and was able to attack the stronger Afrikanz effectively.

YT came in as the fight promoter, oops, peacemaker (aka, missionary) to allegedly calm the war amongst the two, but in all actuality, they were there serving as the 'middle-man' instigating tribal confrontationz, all-the-while knowing the weaker Afrikanz would protect them as they subliminally attacked the stronger Afrikanz from the inside.

THE PSYCHOLOGICAL BREAKDOWN OF YT

For yearz, science has been trying to understand the similarities and differences between the cornerstones of races: Blacks and whites. Author, Michael Bradley (a european) stated, *"Caucasian descendants are significantly more aggressive than other major genetic groups because of their unique glacial evolution... Neanderthal bones exhibit a much greater number of violence-inflicted injuries than any comparable number of bones from other groups of human ancestor's."* Think about it. Who invented Slam-dancing? Daredevil stunts and bungie jumping?? Not no brutha!

And their aggression hasn't stopped for one second! Knowing they are the real minority, they are tryin' to balance the scales unnaturally! One of the war tactics is eugenics' (anutha form of cloning).

Eugenics is the categorization for the manipulation of genes in order to bring about a more desirable kind of human. In the book, *'Skeletons In The Closet'*, by Adrian Woolridge, she writes, *"Eugenics, the pseudo-science that tries to improve the human species by controlling reproduction, remained fashionable long after Hitler committed suicide in his bunker."*

The cream behind the Eugenics project was funded by none other than the notorious Carnegie and Rockefeller families. Woolridge goes on to say, *"Swedes not only introduced eugenic laws at roughly the same time as the Nazis but also left them on the statue books until the mid-1970s. Between 1935-76, no fewer than 60,000 Swedes were sterilized, including children of racially mixed parents, unwed mothers with large broods of children, habitual criminalz and even a boy deemed 'sexually precocious'"*. Dam! Does this not sound just like what Yakub did almost 6000 yearz ago?!!?

The Swedes enforced eugenic lawz as early as 1929. About 11,000 were sterilized, more than half against their will! The Finns have confessed to sterilizing 11,000 people with 4000 involuntary abortionz performed between 1945-70, and the Norweiganz sterilized 2000. How many do you think the great 'ol U.S. has involuntarily killed?? The State of Virginia alone sterilized more than 7500 people up until the 70s, with a particular emphasis on unwed motherz, prostitutes, petty criminalz and juvenile delinquents.

All these countries introduced eugenics for similar reasonz, primarily to prevent the degeneration of the race. *"It was invented not in the Germany of the 1930s but in the Britain of the 1880s, and not by some deranged Nazi but by the respectable gentleman Francis Galton, a cousin of Charles Darwin and a leading member of the scientific establishment,"* Woolridge states.

Think there's not a governmental conspiracy? Francis Crick, the co-discoverer of DNA, suggested putting chemicalz in drinking water to sterilize the entire population, and then distributing an antidote to a eugenically desirable few.

Prenatal genetic screening has enabled parents to avoid having children with defects. Sperm banks specialize in providing women with greater opportunities (playing God) for breeding with "superior" men, allowing scientists to manipulate the basic hereditary process, eliminating defects as they go.

Woolridge was quick to point out that *"many anti-poverty campaigners happily have added contraceptive drugs such as Norplant to their armory."* What's deep is that sterilization is far more common among Afrikan and American Indian women than among white women. Of the 750,000 hysterectomies performed each year in the U.S., well over 90% of the patients are Afrikan!

Dr. Jewel Pookrum, an Afrikan doctor, is the first person to address this hidden agenda. If this number is combined with the other sterilizationz of Afrikan women around the world, experts predict that within the next 12 yearz, Afrikan people MAY BECOME EXTINCT! Hard to believe, but somebody's tryin' to make it happen! Believe dat!!

All Afrikan sistaz, Y IZ it Dat 1 out of every 3 Afrikan women living in a eurocentric society develops fibroid tumorz?! You can't have a seed without them!

WHAT THIS SHIT IS ALL ABOUT

This is about a mutants declaration of war on all natural creation! This is what global white supremacy is about – global genetic dominance! YT is well aware they are the real minority of the world, making only 10% of the population and dwindling. They buggin' over the concern of the low number of birthrates. They're the only ones with sperm banks, and the only ones wylin' over some white chick who gave birth to 7 babies – what they failed to mention to the media is that she received numerous birth enhancement injectionz 'cause she couldn't conceive a child naturally. In addition, according to writer, Suzar, their genes are recessive to the genes of all people of color, especially Afrikanz because we have the most dominant genes on the planet.

If a white person has a child with a black person, the child turnz out to be more black. *"The reason for their recessive genes,"* Suzar states, *"is because white skin is a form of albinism. If you understand this science, then you overstand why there's the creation, refinement, maintenance and brutal enforcement of the world's greatest system of mass injustice; white supremacy – which is the ONLY racism that exists..."*

In closing, there are some other significant points to consider. One being that our history can be seen in YTs religious system. Our slavemasterz still have us worshipping the Sun and we don't even know it. SUNday is the day for the Sun and on this day, we go to our slavemasterz church. Are we worshipping the Son of YT or the SUN which is the dominant light of our galaxy that gives life to all living thingz? As well, who do you think you're praying to when you end it with "Amen"?!!? Amen comes from the ancient Kemetic Afrikan pharaoh named AMENhotep.

YT has clearly shown through movies (like the last Aliens flik) what their intentionz are since cracking the DNA code. They intend to create a being just like they were created. They are merely doing what was done to them. And if our half-brutha has the intentionz of creating a child for himself, we've got double trouble!

LIK SHOT!!

1995

As more Afrikanz are becoming aware of the conspiraceez of global white supremacy, many are starting to realize where one of the most profound battles is being fought... your immune system!

Many Afrikanz are embracing the philosophy of vegan and vegetarianizm; it's just that most have been misinformed as to what it really is. Many think if you don't eat pork and red meat, you are a vegetarian. Although the absence of these two substances, mistaken for food, is admirable, it is but a small fragment of the whole scheme.

There are many Afrikanz that call themselves vegetarianz yet they still eat chicken, turkey, fish and dairy products. Vegan and Vegetarianizm dealz with the absence of all, once living and moveable animalz that are consumed as food.

There is no doubt that changing your eating habits entailz wisdom, understanding, perseverance and most of all, focus! But the benefits of cleaning your temple (body) revealz many profits. Most know of what red-meat and pork is about, but many have not been exposed to a substance much more lethal to the temple than the two mentioned.

The poultry processing industry has been listed, by the U.S. Bureau of Labor, as one of the most hazardous occupationz. They said the chicken we buy is *"grossly contaminated with both coliform, bacteria and salmonella"*. First, it must be known that there are two types of chickenz that are eaten. The first is the chicken we eat, which is called a "broiler". The second, is the hen who layz the eggz we eat, and they're called a "layer".

Chickenz have a life expectancy of 15-20 yearz; however, living on farmz like Purdue's, they will live no longer than 2 months! The chicks diet doesn't contain a natural food diet; instead of eating wormz like we see on cartoonz, they are fed antibiotics, steroidz and growth hormones. Antibiotics are used because they become so sick from this unnatural food diet, they must have the drug or they'll drop dead, if they drop dead too soon (as if 2 months isn't), they will not be profit making for the chicken biz. According to a 1970 government report, they found that 90% of all chickenz had leukosis or chicken cancer.

The food fed to chickenz are purely to accelerate their growth. This increases their weight gain since they are sold by the pound. Most are so overweight before they are killed that they cannot hold themselves up. That is Y you may find some bones already broken when you see chicken while you eat it.

Because of this unnatural food diet, the chickenz immune system weakenz and causes dis-*ease* (uneasiness) or disease to set in. Now if a chicken dies because of a weakened immune system (which is what AIDS is), Y don't you think once you consume this dis-eased, decayed flesh, that YOUR system won't be affected?! What's even more alarming is as of 1996, the USDA does not check chickenz for salmonella!

As far as dairy products, you can say you don't eat beef, but you eat the liquid emissionz from the same animal, the cow. People are the only beingz that drink the milk of another animal. You never see a cat sucking on the nipples of a dog! Most do not even know what milk is. Cow milk is nothing but urine and toxic emissionz that didn't cling or become a part of the muscle of the cow. On top of that, you may think the milk is pasteurized, but what is pasteurization?! RADIOACTIVITY! So in reality, you are drinking toxic-filled piss, with additional cancer-causing radioactivity, making it even more potent!

Milk is the main ingredient in cheese, ice cream, butter and most pastries! Yeah, you probably vexed by now. You're probably wondering, *"what do I eat now?!"* You may want to take a more in-depth look into vegan and vegetarianizm and start eating products that does your body good. Don't be a slave to your tastebudz and wallet (fast foodz $1 menu), eating something because it tastes good or fits your budget. Chances are you'll find it is destroying your physical and more importantly, your spiritual temple!

You are what you eat! Whatever your body consumes as nourishment becomes one with your body, your thoughts (psyche) and spirituality. If you are eating foodz that lived a violent, imprisoned and unnatural (psychotic) lifespan, you're also eating their poisonous adrenaline they gave off before they were murdered.

But the Food and Drug Administration (FDA) won't tell you that eating a once living organizmz adrenaline like an animal can be fatal— not to mention, being murdered before reaching its natural physical maturity — what makes you think those same qualities don't become a part of you?! WAKE UP!

1994

In Sickness and in Health? or Potential Wealth!

by m'bwebe aja ishangi

When present at a marriage, one can recall the vow, *"In sickness and in health",* but in the vow of life livin' within this Eurocentric society, the proper additional vow should be *"or potential wealth!"* Have you ever asked yourself *'Y IZ it dat'* Afrikan people have such an illustrious past, but can't seem to pick ourselves up today? I have numerous tymz. After meditation, I came to an epiphany. There are many reasonz, and one seldom discussed has somethin' to do with our health and the medical field!

I've often heard the saying, *"One should be proud to be an American."* Based upon the history of how this rich country came to be, I seriously beg to differ. *"Only in America"* is individualizm more important than community; *"Only in America"* do you read and hear of this bein' the *'Land of the free, home of the brave'* and at the same tyme the rich getting' richer and the po'…well you know! *"Only in America"* do you hear of this bein' the *'Land of Opportunity'*...if, and only if you have a conservative European mind-frame.

The very wordz America speaks are contradictory indeed. America doesn't stand for love of all mankind. The truth for what it standz for is all around you! Money is far more important than people. Y? Because people are expendable, especially an oppressed, miseducated flock like, say, Afrikanz who live in this country still tryin' to be included! For history's sake, let's look at one… just one of the many medicinal and technological holocaust's our people have endured from the handz of YT.

THE TUSKEGEE STUDY

Instead of vaccinating 600 Afrikan men, as first promised from a virus made by none other than YT themself, they were injected with syphilis. According to the July 26th, 1972 edition of the *Jew,* oops, *'New York Times'*, page 1 and 8, *"For 40 years the United States Public Health (PHS) had been conducting a study of the effects of untreated syphilis on blackmen in Macon County, Alabama, in and around the country seat of Tuskegee. The Tuskegee Study involved a substantial number of men: 399 who had syphilis and an additional 201 who were free of the disease chosen to serve as controls"* (anutha word for guinea pigz!).

The mad scientists behind this made a fortune in the data they got from these bruthaz who suffered unknowingly by the very personz they expected to help them. Let me make this clear Afrikanz, AMERICA IS A BUSINESS! America does not stand for the people, hasn't since the Revolutionary War when George Washington allowed Lord Mayer Amschel Rothschild finance his victory. Rothschild, when asked what he wanted in return, was quoted as sayin', *"I don't care who runs the country, I want to own the money!"* Hence, this is where we see 'Federal Reserve Note' on top, again, *on top* – or *before* – we see *'The United States of America'* on the dollar bill.

America, co-conspirator to global white supremacy, has set up a system that assist's them in creating a cycle that ensures economic prosperity as long as the people remain ignorant.

First I'd like to address the problemz with the Food and Drug Administration (FDA). Remember the old sayin' *"The best way to hide somethin' from someone is to put it right under one's nose"?* If we opened our eyes we could see the countless traps laid before us. For instance, the very wordz Food *AND* Drug Administration clearly states what they do to our food...they put drugz in it!

Gas is to car, as food is to human. Our digestive system is quite similar to an automobile's engine. What causes wear and tear leading to the eventual breakdown of a car? Excessive usage and tyme. The same thing applies to the human body, with the excessive usage being the uncalculated tymz your digestive system breaks down each meal you eat and liquidz you drink.

Where there's more quantity or need, there's less quality or tyme spent on the product. For instance, lookin' at the fast-food industry, these companies make maximum profit by selling the cheapest product. Ever notice Y McDonald's just launched its "Dollar Menu" to compete with Wendy's "99¢ Menu"? Trust me, in any business the name of the game is to "spend less" in order to create profit. You may find no fault in this, and actually there is none, unless you're in the food industry. See, this is where I draw the line because we need food to survive.

Food industries – those that specialize in meat, chicken and fish – have factories that process these live stock to be murdered, ending up on your dinner plate. Think of all the chickenz Kentucky Fried processed with other additives to make its processed chicken. We never ask where did these millionz of chickenz come from, how long ago did they die and how long they were allowed to live. [NOTE: In 1991, Kentucky Fried Chicken changed its name to KFC. Legend has it, they no longer use real chickenz but some kind of processed chicken]

We don't think about how these once living specimenz breathe in the same oxygen we do; have blood flowin' throughout the veinz of their body like we do; and have a functional brain (no matter how small) that can tell the difference between freedom and imprisonment, and can experience anxiety attacks when the smell of death is near.

We have been conditioned to only see the end result. We don't know what it's like to live in a dark, cold cage with injectionz of all kindz of rBGH (recombinant Bovine Growth Hormones) and steroidz to make the animal grow faster than natural, while never seein' daylight. We haven't seen pictures of what goes on in slaughter houses. We haven't envisioned trading places with a cow that is escorted to its death as its neck is cut leavin' left to watch its own blood trickle down before him while hanging upside-down. We don't think of these thingz because there are entities responsible for shielding you from seein' this.

Think, if the FDA and WHO (World Health Organization) – 2 major corporationz responsible for the quality(?) of food we eat – actually showed you the process of takin' a month-old calf, inject it with all these drugz, murder it well before maturation and then deliver it to your local foodmart color-dying it red so that you think it's fresh (as if bloody meat confirmz freshness). If they did these thingz in public, EVERYONE would be a vegetarian! There would be no FDA, WHO, ADA (American Dental Association), AMA (American Medical Association), the Pharmaceutical Industry, etc. because all would cease to exist! So they must hide this from you!

SUPPLY AND DEMAND

If a product is in demand and you gettin' paid, you would want to continue production for more profit, right? But how can you when a chicken has to grow in size and thickness, from bein' a baby chic? Naturally, this process would take several months, maybe even a couple yearz. But the way the industry is today, tryin' to supply a demanding need, they cannot wait that long or they would lose business! So what remedy do they opt to use? In comes anabolic steroidz, rBGH that causes the chicken, pig and cattle to double it's size in a matter of a couple weeks. With their increased size, they are seen as "mature" or "meaty" enuff to be slaughtered, processed and eventually wind up in the meat section of your favorite supermarket.

Speaking of slaughter, do you think the Slaughter houses are clean? If you ever wanted to enter a house of death, this is it! Throughout the building you can hear the moanz and screamz of animalz being murdered, cries of pain, as well as witnessing their own kind being butchered. Envision yourself as one of these animalz for a moment. If there's one thing Afrikan people and these animalz have in common is bein' imprisoned against their will, packed in a cage like our Ancestorz were on slaveships. Couple that with a poor diet, constant steroid injectionz, no daylight and no ability to move around, you begin to develop a sense of paranoia, anxiety and depression.

YOU ARE WHAT YOU EAT

Ever heard of the old cliché *"you are what you eat"*? The food industry wouldn't dare echo this. Far too often people talk of health, but not from where and how food gets to your plate. The miseducational system has neglected in teachin' us in health class where certain foodz come from and how they actually become food. To think what you eat does not become a part of you is the primary reason Afrikan people, in particular have the health problemz we do.

Take a look at yourself now. Your body is the result of all the breakfast, lunch, dinnerz *and* snacks you've eaten. Whether nutritious or not, everything you put in your body becomes processed and become a part of you…yeah even that piece of gum! This shedz a deeper insight to the cliché previously mentioned. So, with that fresh in your mind, let's look at the animalz some of us eat.

The blood and cellz that circulate through the muscles – strategically called meat, 'cause you probably wouldn't eat it if you were told meat is really muscles –

have now been swallowed by you, eventually (through digestion) becomin' a part of you. We must realize everything that you eat doesn't come right out when you take a shit, if that were the case you would never maintain a weight. Just like a car, when you fill the tank up with gas, it goes in as a liquid, but the part the car doesn't need comes out as fumes.) When you closely look at meat (muscle), we are not taught that our emotional state has also become a part of the muscle. Throughout the life of a breathing entity (human or animal) there's all kindz of intelligence. We take for granted that the heart beats automatically; that our bodies begin the process of healing automatically after we cut ourselves, and how our we recharge naturally after a night's sleep.

All this "intelligence" can be cultivated righteously or become defective. The emotionz the animal felt during its imprisoned life, all the way up to its death, including depression, anxiety, rage and horror, make up that piece of (dead) chicken on your plate. Before this animal was killed, it was quite aware of its death. When your life is in danger, or even if you 'bout to romp with someone, your heart starts to race and your body creates a defense mechanizm called adrenaline; that butterfly feeling you get in your stomach.

Adrenaline is used once you perform. However, the adrenaline produced in slaughtered animalz doesn't get used because they can't defend themselves. In the slaughter houses, they aren't given the chance to fight for their lives. They're chained up, and oftentymz hung upside-down. Case-in-point, once the animal is dead, the adrenaline that wasn't used now becomes toxic…that's right, POISON! This poison, along with all the steroidz and rBGH injectionz are still alive and kickin' in the now overcooked piece of decayed flesh sittin' in front of you on the dinner table. But it doesn't stop there.

Geraldo Rivera did a show back in 1993 where he had an episode on the selling of aged meat. They had an undercover camera placed in a deli at a supermarket. They found that major stores sell old meat to their consumerz! In one store, a worker was videotaped takin' bologna from an Oscar Mayer package and put it in the window to sell. The startling thing was that the package's 'sell by' date was **June 1988!!** What I found was that manufacturerz of meat kill so many animalz – to meet the demand – thanks to rBGH and steroidz. They produce so much meat they *have* to freeze it!

What happenz when you freeze meat? The frost you see on it isn't just ice, it's also bacteria! According to Geraldo's special, there is an allowance by the FDA to be no more than 7000 colonies of bacteria and other germz per slice of bologna. They sampled several from major food marts and found they had at least 1 million colonies of bacteria and germz…and this is per slice, Sun!! And you wonder Y we get sick and catch viruses!!

No, chances are you won't suddenly die after eating this meal. You might not directly feel the affects for yearz, because these are silent killerz. But your immune system – the human body's defense mechanizm against illness, will be attacked. This is how the AMA and FDA make their money! They feed you, get you sick and then supply you with "medicinal remedies" you think will make you better but wind up creating an additional dependence because they never tell you to stop eatin' which is what made you ill in the first place. Now you're still eatin' the same crap plus you're poppin' pillz. Common sense would tell you the root of your problem is what you've been eatin', but when you live in a society where ignorance is 'pon the mind of the masses, very few are able to fight through this ignorance and create a better eating lifestyle.

Who's to say the FDA is really concerned with our health? They say we should eat at least 3 tymz a day. They encourage us to eat from the 4 basic food groups, which are (1)Meat & Fish; (2)Dairy; (3)Wheat & Grainz; and (4)Fruits and Vegetables. We have been conditioned to live to eat rather than eat to live. We haven't been made aware that our Ancestorz who carved Her-Em-Akhet (erroneously called the Sphinx) and the Pyramidz of Giza were actually *herbivores,* or plant eaterz and did not eat meat.

It is no coincidence that a people with such a natural diet was able to erect a monument that has withstood the tests of tyme; a feat not even the modern worldz alleged most intellectually mindz couldn't duplicate. Japanese people are said to be the worldz most tehchnologically advanced race, and even they were unable to recreate a Pyramid structure, like those of Giza, in 1977.

An important note is that we haven't been educated on the vital relationship food has with the Afrikan body. We haven't been taught that the reason your stomach growlz, even a short period after you eat, is most likely because what you just ate may have filled you up, but it lacked the nutrients your body *needz,* so your body still craves for it. And overtyme, if you continue to just fill your belly with man-made, processed foodz but not the food your body needz, it will start to pull what it needz – in order to survive – from its ownself! Meaning, if you continue to eat white rice, white flour and white sugar – 3 known substances that *pullz* vital nutrients from your body instead of *puttin'* in, your body will pull these nutrients from itself, which, of course if counter-productive. How can a car pull gas from itself when it needz gas to run? The difference is that a human body has reserves, but these reserves have a limit. And once these reserves are empty – after yearz of an unbalanced diet, cancer sets in. Cancer isn't somethin' you catch, it's somethin' that's manifested from within.

Cancer is when your body turnz on itself and starts to eat itself alive! Actually, it already turned on itself when you didn't give your body what it needed after all those chicken dinnerz, ice-cream, candy and fast-food restaurants. This is where the conspiracy sets in, because the very people that tell you to eat this shit, *make you sick* and who do you run to once you are? The very people who have been poisoning us body and mind all along, the Medical/Hospital administration!

America has had a plan to control the population as well as ensuring a hefty profit. First, the Medical/Pharmaceutical Industry (a constituent of the FDA) supplies the FDA and farmerz with anabolic steroidz and other toxinz to be given to their livestock. Second, after they literally blown up 3-4 tymz their natural size, the farmerz slaughter the drug-infested animalz and the FDA approves the selling of them to the public for food to be "safely" eaten. Thirdly, after yearz of eatin' these sanctioned 'food' products, we develop problemz with our digestive and respiratory system, from heart attacks (really you attacking your heart) to colon cancer; and last, we come full circle where you, the ailing patient crawlz to your doctor in immense pain hoping for a miracle cure to your suffering. Your doctor, instead of tellin' you what you can do holistically to cure yourself – because he took the Hippocratic Oath (can you see the word, HYPOCRITE?) – instead opts to perform expensive surgeries on your temple, leaving you addicted to painkillerz from radiation treatments.

Think Afrikanz, if we all practice holistic health, there would be no need for doctorz, hospitalz, pharmaceez (notice how many chain Drug Stores are poppin' up in our communities??) and there'd be no Food and Drug Administration. Our health is the seat to our liberation and YT knowz it. That's Y they market all the soda, milk adz, malt liquor and fast-food joints largely to Afrikan communities. Take a look at our people. According to a 1994 Study by the CDC (Center for Disease Control), 66% of Afrikan women in america are overweight with 37% technically obese!

How are these food companies able to market to our people so effectively? They overstand that a people ignorant to the one thing they can control, your human body, will be a slave eternally! It painz me to see 40-50 year oldz on up to our Elderz forced to walk with canes and oxygen tanks because they're unable to walk up a flight of stairz for fear they may break their hip because of osteoporosis, diabetes, and cardio ailments.

What's worse, I see oversized youth — with their depleting interest in sports and increased attention to web-surfing, bad diet and little to no physical activity leading to obesity and a shortened lifespan! Our young women, who now reach puberty as early as 8-9 yearz old because of the high doses of rBGH given to cattle and chickenz. If it made the animalz large, if one eats them, Y wouldn't it make them fatter and shapely quicker as well?! This can be seen as our teenage sisterz have the physical appearance of 25 year oldz. What many are not aware of is this food promotes accelerated growth which also can be known as 'accelerated aging'! So yeah, a teenager will look like a 25 year old, but eventually at 40 year, their body may be actually 50 or 60!!

All of this equates to one thing and you have a choice Afrikan, you can either disregard this piece without further investigation, or you can take your health into your own handz. Many of us have chosen the re-Afrikanization Process of our mindz, but refuse to reanalyze how diet is just as vital. Until we take the burden of truly Knowing Thyself, we will be co-conspiratorz to the assassination of ourselves. See, YT don't have to lynch Afrikanz no more, we can't wait to do it with our next meal! When you're diagnosed with an ailment that needz medical attention, don't blame anyone but yourself, because it is you who broke the vow, *"In sickness and in health"* and opted for adding to their wealth. Oh, and as far your cut? Yourz will be escruciating pain which will lead to an eventual slow premature death!

LIK SHOT!

Sistaz Can Spark Da Revolution!

by m'bwebe aja ishangi

Several yearz ago, I published a piece that, I felt, may have gone overlooked by our people. Many mistook this article as a promotion piece for the male conscious crew to get props by biggin' up our sistaz, for we know the weight of our fate bearz primarily on your shoulderz. On the contrary, since this piece, I've dealt with more sistaz that felt a brutha was just tryin' to get physical, than my just wanting to mentally stimulate my counterpart with an idea that could evolve to be one of the greatest strategic moves on the board!

As I engulfed denial and sometymz laughter ('cause there's a lot of sistaz who don't care about bein' conscious, dem wan fi know how large you livin'), I at first grew frustrated, even to the point where I felt sistaz, in their present mindstate couldn't spark da revolution! But as I turned to the Ancestorz for guidance, I was blessed with a perspective that changed my once slighted view upon the sistaz of today.

This piece goes to the Supreme Goddess' who have the true spirit of, Queen Nzingha, Tiye, Assata, Yaa Asantewa, Auset and all other unmentioned sistaz who are the real divaz of Afrikan antiquity. This piece is also guided by the 7th Djhuitic principle, 'Gender' (everything has both masculine and feminine qualities), for the pendulum of white supremacy is coming to an end and beginning to swing to the positive side of Afrikan liberation and we bruthaz who claim consciousness must relinquish our male chauvinizmz and make way for the other half of the whole!

This is a principle violated by both male and female. That's Y it's difficult for even conscious folk to allow sistaz to take their rightful place, BESIDE the Afrikan man, not BEHIND. I've witnessed it numerous tymz where "conscious" bruthaz have a problem allowing sistaz to lead, much less share the frontline. Although their intensionz may be to "protect" her, because of both personz ignorance of the principle of Gender, even the sista willingly steps backward!

Wayne Chandler, author of *'Ancient Future'*, stated, *"[T]his principle is absent in Western culture, most probably due to the entrenched patriarchal customs and mores of a male-dominated culture and society. The Judeo-Christian tradition attributes the genesis of all creation to a lone male deity, God. [T]here is the Trinity of God – three persons in one God – the Father, the Son, and the Holy Spirit (or Ghost), all of whom are masculine. How can the concept of God be without the woman??"*

Even those sistaz that say God is a woman, Y do they continue to stand behind the man?! I am not professin' sistaz become independent, I'm merely statin' if he will not give you the mic, TAKE IT! It's clearly evident to me we men have not been successful as sole-leader without your commanding presence to compliment us!

Y do I still feel sistaz can still spark da revolution? Y do I feel sistaz haven't thus far? These will be answered, but first, I want the reader to overstand that I intend no harm to those who this info does not pertain to (unfortunately, I would not be publishing such a piece unless I felt the majority of sistaz needed to lend an ear to this). As well, this is not a piece to attack sistaz, while biggin' up the bruthaz. I hope this will inspire sistaz to send DGT a piece tellin' us how bruthaz can spark da revolution. It's about balance.

I want to first point out Y I feel sistaz can be the spark to Afrikan liberation. I'd like to use then president, Gay (Jay) Edgar Hoover's quest to stop the next "black messiah", as he called it, with his infamous COINTELPRO operation. He had a 3-point rating scale to Afrikan organizationz that posed a threat to white supremacy in the late 60s, early 70s. With 3 being the highest, any organization ran by bruthaz received 1 point on the scale of being a threat. Any organization managed by bruthaz and sistaz received 2 points. And lastly, any organization governed by Afrikan women received 3 points. Clearly even this wicked half-breed sees that if sistaz had they shit in check, Hoover and the rest of white supremacy would be in big trouble, so they had to devise a counter-attack which I will elaborate on in a sec.

If you were to look back in *our*story, you would find that some of the major battles fought were led by Afrikan women! But these Goddess' didn't sit in some office, behind the scenes, giving orderz thousandz of miles away via radio; these women fought, often-tymz, on the FRONTLINE! Sistaz of today carry that same spirit, it's just many have been severed from this knowledge by the countless ill subliminalz perpetuated by YT.

An example of this attack on our sistaz happened at the 1997 Million Woman March, in Philadelphia, PA. It was completely different than the Million Man March of '95. Although both did nothin' other than serve as a million-plus cookout, the deeper thing was that there were madd vendorz at the Woman March! Just who was responsible for okayin' an outside mall at the Million Woman March, 'cause you know you cain't get anything accomplished when there's all kindz of shit for sistaz to buy! Shoulda been called the Million Woman Flea Market!

In the Afrikan community, sistaz are the backbone of the family. Where we find many of our fatherz were absent leaving many of our motherz with several mouths to feed and little work available. It must be noted a large number of fatherz were initially ousted by the government who issued the welfare program that stipulated poor families would not receive welfare if a man was present in the house. So what did many of the motherz do? They kicked him out so they could receive the funding.

True indeed, we can see sistaz are here fightin', but do they know what they're fightin' about? or for? Do us bruthaz?! As just mentioned, the system could not risk having the Afrikan woman rise, so they needed to create a diversion and one of them is the cosmetic industry!

What does makeup have to do with detaining sistaz from liberation, you ask? Simple. Define beauty. What have you been taught as the pictgure of beauty? Take a look around you. How many pictures of Afrikan women do you see that has fake, long, straight hair? How many are wearin' every color in the rainbow [with blonde bein' the most popular (Lil'Kim, Mary J.Blige?, etc.)]Now ask yourself have you ever been taught what Afrikan beauty is? I've held this inside for a seriously long tyme, but this yearning led me to do more insight and research and what I thought seemz to be quite true: Afrikan women have been taught to be something other than what they are naturally!

Y the attack on makeup? Because our women are doing just that, *making themselves up* to be something they naturally are not! Our sistaz are constantly bein' told how to look, what's attractive to men and it's companies like Covergirl, Victoria's Secret, Avon, Cosmopolitan, Vogue and yes, even Essence (because they have these companies advertisements throughout the magazine). Now how does white supremacy fall into this? For one, the excessive amounts of chemical toxinz women induce not only causes eventual physical and health problemz, but it, most importantly, causes serious mental disorderz!

For instance, what is it you sistaz say you do to your hair, *"I'ma get my hair RELAXED!"* Well what does "relax" mean? The illusion is that until chemicalz reach your hair, you consider your hair unrelaxed, or better yet, wild. But isn't "wild" s'posed to be free and natural? When you go to animal prison (zoo) and you see a lion, is he "relaxed" or "free"? We have been miseducated by hellywood to think that wild meanz uncivilized and beastly, which is commonly called "The Tarzan syndrome". Although there are parts of Afrika where the wild run free, all of Afrika isn't like that, and we, descendants from Afrika, aren't like that. Let's go deeper...

What was your hair like before your first temporary (the real name, not a perm)? It was natural and free. Yeah, we were taught by YT that kinky, knotty hair was bad so we yearned for our hair to be "more manageable", just like theirz. It is a known fact, through studies of art and sciences in Kemet, everything in life is made in curves, spiralz and waves. The DNA chemical structure of your body is in a spiral; the curve of the Afrikan body is curved; sound moves in patternz in the form of waves; even the makeup of the Milky Way galaxy we live in is spiral; and yes, the molecular makeup of a strand of your natural hair is spiral. We see life in waves and spiralz, whereas we witness the absence of life, or energy, in flat lines (in the hospital, one can know your living by the pattern of waves on a respirator. If you expire, you see a flat line). So the same math must apply to hair as well.

THE TRUTH ABOUT HAIR

What is hair? What is the use for it? It has long been noted that Afrikan spiral hair can serve as "antennas" to our Ancestral data banks. You ever get vybz or say something and don't know where it came from? It does come from within, but it is also assisted by the upper most part of your body, where hair resides. Look at your hair as if you would a tv antenna on top of a house. One of the elements our temple (body) is made of are electronz, therefore, we have electric currents running throughout our body. That is also Y you can rub a balloon on top of your crown (head) and stick it on a wall. The unfortunate thing is that many of us ignore the telekinetic vybz we receive from the universe via our hair and hair follicles.

If you were to take a strand of natural Afrikan hair and compare to "permed" hair, you would see that the "permed" hair seemz almost lifeless, whereas the spiral, kinky hair has several curves and shapes. This has a lot to do with the different chemical and biological makeup of Afrikanz opposed to YT (Read *'IZ YT Human? or Mutant!'* series).

When one permz their hair, they are dulling their connection to our Ancestral data banks immensely! This is where the story of who we are, our spiritual connection to the Ancestorz, and our ability to enhance intuitive learning, resides. The hundredz of thousandz of hair follicles are drowned with toxic-killing chemicalz that have turned our Goddess' into the material "wannabe" eurocentric-looking image she is today.

Gone are the knotty Nubian locks, real braidz and naturalz, in comes Essence, Ebony, Black Hair and countless other heavily white-influenced black publicationz telling us what to do to our hair because they know, the uppermost part of our temple houses our Ancestral antennaz; the most important invention given by the Creative Force (I refer to by name as 'Energy'), YOUR AFRIKAN MIND.

When I look back to the late 60s, sistaz were wearing naturalz and braiding their hair. This was the re-evolution of our Afrikan heritage. This strategic move scared YT so much that they had to dupe it, creating a diluted message by making the movie '10', which starred the sick skeleton-looking Bo Derek, giving the official "Cracka pardon" for the braided look. After that movie came out, madd white women got their hair braided, B!

The cosmetic industry was ushered into the Afrikan community to alter the Afrikan meaning of beauty – which should be self-defined and come from within – to accommodate the western, eurocentric, unbalanced, sex-crazed society we live in today. Bruthaz have become more attracted to the body than the mind, and sistaz have relinquished their mental beauty for that moment they can "exhale" in the armz of a relationship that is primarily based on sex.

Now, I ain't gonna front, I suffer from the same addiction as most bruthaz. I have to literally re-train myself to not look at an Afrikan woman sexually first, but mentally. This must be on the record because I don't want to make it seem as though I am cured from admiring the beauty of our women, I am simply relaying the symptomz.

One question puzzles me the most when on the topic of perming. If surgeonz stress not to get permz when you are pregnant because it may cause fetal damage, what makes you think it doesn't cause any damage to you when you're not?!!? The (brain) damage is already done when you let a common assertion such as this pass you by.

This is Y I believe there has been a war declared on the Afrikan woman and she doesn't even know it! Something hellywood and the country's government also did to further detach the Afrikan from our culture is convince everyone, through tell-a lie-vision, that to be natural with cowrie shellz and drumz would be duped as "voodoo" or "black magic".

Remember the movie, *'Serpent and the Rainbow',* with Lisa Bonet that was staged in the south where they had our people killing chickenz and showerin' themselves with the blood while playing drumz, singing and dancin'? This is this ignorant cracka using the silver-screen to instill lies of us bein' savages and performerz of demonic ceremonies, when in fact if you research masonry and other secret societies like Skull & Bones and fraternities, you will find it is they who perform demonic ritualz like initiates having anal intercourse with each other... in the name of brotherhood!

So this is how they got bruthaz to fear the natural looking, shell wearing, spiritual sistaz and opt for the long straight and blond-haired, made up (wannabe) sista we see today. No doubt, some of ya'll look appealin', but when I think of how we have been brainwashed to think negative of our natural looking self, it's not enuff for you to feel you can show yourself in public, it makes I&I wonder just who you are trying to look like, Queen Tiye? or queen elizabeth?!!?

But even so, you have those sistaz that are now wearing the braided weaves. The beef is that it is still "fashion" if you are not doing it natural. Peep, not even 10 yearz ago, if you had a weave or extensionz, you were the punch line of every snap! Now, everybody wearing so-called "hair" because they say you don't have to worry about doing it, while at the same tyme, you makin' them Koreanz rich. Yo, that's madd lazy, yo. I can't tell you how many 5 and 6 year-oldz I've seen that gotta weave. On top of that, according to health historian, Dr. Imhotep Llaila Afrika, there is a chemical used to make weaves called *'Cacinologue'* that causes not only mood swingz, but breast and prostate cancer!

One should take pride in his or her appearance instead of looking for a short-cut. I get vexed when I see my Afrikan sistaz with extensionz, blue and blond extensionz because I have been locking my hair for a several yearz now and I've gone through madd shit gettin' to this point, and when I see a sista with the fake braidz, I think, yo, she does not have the overstanding of locks and is cheating the whole natural and spiritual process; therefore, skipping the whole meaning. Besides, with all the loot these weave and nail shops make off our sistaz, how many of these shops are Afrikan-owned?!!? Most are owned by them Korean muthafuckaz and you know they takin' all the loot and using for their next relative they bring to America. Think about it, they not only feedin' us (chinese restaurants), they also definin' our beauty.

Afrikan women have been reprogrammed to believe what beauty is by someone who ain't Afrikan. And this non-Afrikan tellz our sistaz what is and what isn't beautiful and won't hesitate to sell it to her! Our most precious jewel, the Afrikan woman, is being attacked on all fronts. If it's not makeup or permz, it's douches and sanitary napkinz (take a look at the ingredients and you'll find douche's and padz cause yeast infectionz, leading to numerous cancerz and tumorz of the vagina, the gate of life).

I know most sistaz may be vexed at we right now, but, aside from all my personal critiques, the most important is that these chemi(killz) cause major damage to you sista. They say a nation can only rise as high as its woman. Well, sistaz we know we have been cella dwellaz for a madd long tyme! I think it's about tyme you give up Maybelline, Avon, Victoria Secret, Cosmopolitan and Dark & Lovely and think about what you are not only doing to your Ancestral data banks, but your seedz. We bruthaz need you, we cannot rebuild without you, in fact, we need you to lead us!

That cracka is well aware that the Afrikan woman is the key to their demise and to combat this, has waged an all out subliminal war against your health (for if they can dictate your health habits like eating decayed flesh with high levelz of recombinant Bovine Growth Hormones (rBGH) and steroidz which is Y our young Afrikan girlz are reaching puberty earlier; 14 year oldz with the body of a sista in their mid-20s) and your mind [with toxic depleting chemi(kills) that dull your intuitive reasoning]. These 2 operationz have assisted in the ongoing delay of bruthaz and sistaz finally uniting and liberating us from the grips of white supremacy! When will you be ready Queenz?!!? WAKE UP! A large percentage of our fate is on your shoulderz!

MORE FIE-YAH!!

Other Notable Pieces on my website: DaGhettoTymz.com

Video Articles on DGTv: Conscious Webvision — *daghettotymz.com/dgtv/dgtv.html*
• The Truth About Cigarettes — *daghettotymz.com/dgtv/videoarticles.html*
• Secret In the City — *daghettotymz.com/dgtv/videoarticles2.html*
• The God Complex — *daghettotymz.com/dgtv/videoarticles3.html*
• The Mark of the Biochip — *daghettotymz.com/dgtv/videoarticles4.html*
• Canola Oil: A Drop of Death — *daghettotymz.com/dgtv/videoarticles5.html*
• The Making of DGTv — *daghettotymz.com/dgtv/videoarticles6.html*
• Numerical Mystereez — *daghettotymz.com/dgtv/videoarticles7.html*
• The Riddle of Her-Em-Akhet — *daghettotymz.com/dgtv/videoarticles8.html*
• White Sugar: The Mark of Cane — *daghettotymz.com/dgtv/videoarticles9.html*

Articles
• Afrikanz In the Olympics: *daghettotymz.com/rkyvz/articles/olympics/olympics.html*
• The Boule' Roster:
daghettotymz.com/rkyvz/articles/boule'series/boule13roster/boulerosterlist/bouleroster.html
• The Future: Wha'chu Know 'Bout It?: *daghettotymz.com/rkyvz/articles/thefuturepiece/future.html*
• The Future II: The Long Awaited Sequel: *daghettotymz.com/rkyvz/articles/futureII/future2.html*
• Last Dayz: *daghettotymz.com/rkyvz/articles/lastdayz/lastdayz.html*
• National Black Boycott Month: *daghettotymz.com/rkyvz/articles/boycott/boycott.html*
• N'Toxicatin' Secrets: *daghettotymz.com/rkyvz/articles/ntoxicatin/ntoxic.html*
• The Olean Conspiracy: *daghettotymz.com/rkyvz/rkyvz.html*
• Some Validity to the Serena Williams Rumor: *daghettotymz.com/current/serenarumor/serenarumor.html*
• Vaccines That Kill: *daghettotymz.com/rkyvz/articles/vaccines/Vaccines.html*
• Who's Taxin' Who?: *daghettotymz.com/rkyvz/articles/irs/irs.html*
• War vs. Your Immune System:*daghettotymz.com/rkyvz/articles/warvsimmune/war.html*
• Who's Liberty?: *daghettotymz.com/rkyvz/articles/whosliberty/whosliberty.html*
• Who IZ the UNCF?: *daghettotymz.com/rkyvz/articles/uncf/uncf.html*

Hallow Daze (Holidayz)
• The Beast is in Easter: *daghettotymz.com/rkyvz/articles/easter/easter.html*
• Trick? or Treat!: *daghettotymz.com/rkyvz/articles/halloween/halloween.html*
• Thanks(Taking): *daghettotymz.com/rkyvz/articles/thanks/thanks.html*
• The Merry Christ-MESS: *daghettotymz.com/rkyvz/articles/xmas/xmas.html*

Analitikul Website
• *daghettotymz.com/analitikul/analitikul.html*

For More Information

M'Bwebe Aja Ishangi enjoyz hearing from his readerz. We welcome your letterz and comments. You can reach him via e-mail at *analitikul@daghettotymz.com*, or at DGT NTR-Prizes, LLC, POBox 71, New York, NY 10159. Give thanx!!

Notes